The
Psychoanalytic
Study
of the Child

VOLUME THIRTY-THREE

The Psychoanalytic Study of the Child

VOLUME THIRTY-THREE

New Haven
Yale University Press
1978

Library of Congress catalog card number 45–11304
International standard book number: 0–300–02297–2

Designed by Sally Sullivan Harris
and set in Baskerville type.
Printed in the United States of America by
Vail-Ballou Press, Inc., Binghamton, N.Y.

Published in Canada, Europe, Africa, and
Asia (except Japan) by Yale University Press,
Ltd., London. Distributed in Australia and
New Zealand by Book & Film Services, Artarmon,
N.S.W., Australia; and in Japan by Harper & Row,
Publishers, Tokyo Office.

Contents

IN MEMORIAM

Rudolph M. Loewenstein
1898-1976

RICHARD NEWMAN, M.D.

RUDOLPH LOEWENSTEIN DIED ON APRIL 14, 1976. HE WAS A MEM-
ber of the Editorial Board of *The Psychoanalytic Study of the
Child* for 30 years, a close friend and collaborator of its
founders, and an esteemed teacher of psychoanalysts for half
a century.

Rudolph Loewenstein was born in Lodz, in Russian Poland,
in 1898, the youngest of eight children. There was discord in
the home because of religion and probably other matters; his
father was orthodox, while his mother came from an assimi-
lated baptized Jewish family. The French governess who
joined the family when Loewenstein was 3 seems to have provided stability and warmth. Later he often spoke of her with
affection.

Loewenstein was still in high school when World War I
broke out. In 1915, following a year of increasing difficulties
with his father, he left his parents' home, wanting to go to
France. He stopped in Zurich, where he remained and entered a technical school, planning to become an electrical engi-
neer. There he met Henry Nunberg, Herman Nunberg's
brother, and the Russian analyst Leo Kaplan, with whom he
began an analysis. This analysis lasted only a short time, but

Clinical Professor of Psychiatry, Emeritus, Yale School of Medicine; faculty, Western New England Psychoanalytic Institute.

I am indebted to Dr. Frank Hartman for many biographical details.

3

probably influenced his decision to become an analyst and with this goal in mind he changed his field to medicine. His father, who died in 1918, had, in fact, wanted him to become a doctor. With considerable difficulty, because he was now stateless, he went to Berlin. There in 1920 he simultaneously matriculated in the newly founded analytic institute and the medical school and began his analysis with Hanns Sachs.

Loewenstein graduated from the Berlin Institute in 1922 and with Hans Lampl and Otto Fenichel worked in the analytic polyclinic until he achieved his childhood wish and moved to Paris in 1925. There he earned another medical degree, in addition to his medical degree from Berlin.

With René Laforgue and Marie Bonaparte he helped found the Paris psychoanalytic society and from 1934–1939 was active in the Institute's program, training many of the French analysts.

He met his first wife in France, where she died leaving him with two young children. A daughter was born to his second marriage, which ended in divorce. Later he married the analyst Elisabeth Geleerd who predeceased him. Their son, Richard Loewenstein, adopted his parents' profession.

When World War II broke out Loewenstein joined the French army and served until the fall of France. In 1942 he had to leave a city and country he loved. In the introduction to *Christians and Jews* he writes how completely he identified himself with France. He retained his love of its language, foods, and wines, his memories of living and working in Paris, the association with Marie Bonaparte and other analysts, his summers and weekends in Brittany, near Concarneau, and sailing its rough off-shore waters.

Yet Rudolph Loewenstein soon adapted to life in the United States, where he joined the faculty of the New York Institute and quickly became a sought-after analyst and supervisor. The adaptation to a new language, however, must have involved a tremendous effort. In his course on technique he told of one of his first patients in New York who was distrustful of refugees and who contrasted Loewenstein's use of English with that of the referring American analyst. Loewenstein acknowledged his difficulties with the new language and only then was able to approach this patient's criticisms and resistances analytically. But Loewenstein himself remained keenly aware of his linguistic limitations. For some time he continued to think in French. He felt that he did not really resume analyzing until he had stopped translating. We all know that analysis in this country was enriched by the analysts who fled Europe, but we may be less aware of their achievement in learning to analyze in a new language. He remained concerned with problems involving language and speech—the tools of psychoanalysis.

Loewenstein continued his early interest in engineering in his hobbies. He was always curious about how things worked, was intrigued by tools and machinery, and especially liked woodworking. He was interested in art, loved the country and gardening, and read widely in the fields of anthropology and archaeology. But he devoted his professional life to psychoanalysis.

Rudolph Loewenstein's major scientific interest was the clarification of analytic theory and its application to clinical problems. Shunning oversimplifications, he invariably stressed the complexity and richness of psychoanalysis. He made no major discoveries, he did not introduce new terms that are connected with his name, yet in each of his papers he refined psychoanalytic theory and practice and described clinical phenomena in innovative ways. Perhaps he disproved Ernst Kris's statement that one did not become known by agreeing with Freud.

His publications[1] fall into four main groups and areas: (1) papers on instinctual drives and their vicissitudes: (2) anti-Semitism; (3) theoretical papers written jointly with Heinz Hartmann and Ernst Kris; and (4) the papers on technique.

1. Loewenstein's early papers are concerned with masochism, forms of self-punishment, phallic passivity in men, and genital impotence. His first major contribution was "The Vital and Somatic Instincts" (1940). After reviewing Freud's writ-

1. A complete bibliography of Loewenstein's writings was published in the *Psychoanalytic Quarterly*, 42 : 4–9, 1973.

ings on instincts—the development of the dual instinct theory from "the sexual instincts" and "ego instincts" to Eros and Thanatos—Loewenstein returns to, adopts, and develops Freud's older theory, but the duality now is between the sexual instincts and the instinct, or instincts, whose function is self-preservation, which may be subsumed under aggression. Loewenstein stresses the connection between aggression and man's "greatest interests and most vital needs." Moreover, the analytic concept of instinct "enables us to link up with other scientific disciplines which are concerned with man" (p. 379). He writes that the question of a death instinct may be decided by biology, not by analysis where it is not needed and where the idea departs from our concept of "instinct as a tension of energy, emanating from an organic source, which impinges upon the mind" (p. 384). The importance of aggression in understanding certain clinical conditions, in understanding man's development individually and as a species, is elaborated, and some of our difficulties in dealing with our aggression are described. While there is some biological and anthropological speculation, the paper is basically a clarification of theory, similar to what the three collaborators subsequently did jointly and individually.

One area in which Loewenstein individually pursued his early interests was that of masochism. In "A Contribution to the Psychoanalytic Theory of Masochism" (1957), Loewenstein asks how is it that human beings can act counter to their own welfare, counter to the reality and pleasure principles, and in a narrower sexual sphere gain pleasure from pain. In trying to answer these questions he examines the pertinent theories advanced by other writers. His own contribution consists in the attempt to understand the pathological phenomena seen in adults in terms of a prototype of normal behavior in early development—an approach to which he may have been alerted by serving as a consultant to the longitudinal and family studies at the Yale Child Study Center. He describes a game played by an 11-month-old child and her grandmother. The girl was "jokingly scolded by her grandmother for putting her thumb in her mouth. The baby would, with visible

fright, observe the stern face of her grandmother; but as soon
as she saw the grandmother smile, she would start to laugh
and put her thumb back into her mouth, with a naughty and
provoking expression. . . . When the prohibition became
serious, however, i.e., when the grandmother's face remained
serious, the child burst into tears. Needless to say that she
would try to transform every prohibition into a game of this
sort, to elicit the smile of the grownup, to create that affectionate complicity which undoes the prohibition and elimi-
nates the danger of not being loved" (p. 214). He called this
behavior "seduction of the aggressor" and stated that these
games come to resemble the patterns in masochistic perversions. Underneath "the self-destructive tendencies involved in
moral masochism, one can see at work in it the desperate attempt to seduce the aggressor, the harsh conscience, to ap-
pease the gods or fate by suffering; i.e., to revert to childhood,
to the state when threats and dangers could actually be
averted or minimized by using the method which was effective
then. . . . The mechanism appears at that early age to ensure
the existence of parental love, at a time when parental love is
as necessary for the development of sexuality as it is for survival" (p. 230f.).

2. A second area of interest was in the roots of anti-Semitism. In his paper "The Historical and Cultural Roots of Anti-
Semitism" (1947) and the book *Christians and Jews* (1951), Loewenstein traces the religious, economic, social, political, and
other reasons for and uses of anti-Semitism. From the ambivalence about Jews in his patients, and in history and legend,
he traces the duality of the relationship between Jews and
Christians, Judaism and Christianity. Christianity's ambivalent
feelings about its Jewish heritage are spelled out. Loewenstein
compares the two religions, which offer two different but related solutions of the same conflict: "Nineteen centuries have
passed since the first generation of Christians broke away
from Judaism and adopted the religion of God the Son
against the religion of God the Father" (p. 197). The pairing
was congenital because Jesus and his mother were Jews, as
were the disciples. A mixture of conscious rejection and un-

conscious veneration makes the Jew a tabooed object and binds the two religions and groups together. Loewenstein characterizes this phenomenon by the name of "cultural pair"—a formulation which in some respects resembles that of "the seduction of the aggressor" in that it stresses the mutual dependence in an ambivalent relationship.

3. The papers written in collaboration with Heinz Hartmann and Ernst Kris are the best known, especially to readers of *The Psychoanalytic Study of the Child,* where most of them were published between 1945 and 1962. Of this collaboration he wrote in 1970: "For me it was a period of great intellectual enjoyment, comparable only to the enthusiasm I had experienced at the time when I discovered and learned psychoanalysis." These papers represent a comprehensive and persistent effort to bring order into theoretical concepts. While Freud revised certain aspects of analytic theory, he only rarely spelled out the implications of such revisions in areas beyond his immediate focus of interest. The three authors attempted to fill this gap. I will not detail their specific clarifying formulations because in a joint authorship it is not possible to single out what each contributed. However, I would summarily say that these papers are the basis of what is called psychoanalytic ego psychology today.

4. In applying these basic revisions of psychoanalytic theory to technical problems, Loewenstein incisively shaped the thinking and technique of this generation of analysts. The combination of his many years of experience, his association with Heinz Hartmann and Ernst Kris and their mutual wish to clarify without simplifying, his curiosity about the analytic laboratory, resulted in over 30 papers on technique.

While there were earlier papers on technique—the first in 1928, "La Technique Psychoanalytique"—papers on technique fill the years from 1964 to 1972. They deal with every aspect of technique—autonomous ego functions and the defensive organization, free association, interpretation, transference, silence, the role of speech among others.

In his last years he worked, with Milton Horowitz, on what

he hoped would be his book on the subject. For students of analysis, all of us, it is unfortunate that this was not completed.

It is especially unfortunate because something of what gave Rudolph Loewenstein his uniqueness—and was known to his students, supervisees, and analysands—comes through when he writes about clinical material and the analytic situation, technique, and the problems in understanding a person and in conveying that understanding to him. Courtesy and tact—a term Loewenstein used to mean more than consideration for another person's feelings—are in every page of his papers. Part of his sensitive humanity as an analyst was his awareness of what was implicit in what he said, and this may have contributed to his ability to use language as he did, his ability to say just the right word or phrase. These qualities—the appreciation of the complexity of human beings and human behavior and the world we live in; the patient, intelligent, informed, sensitive thoughtfulness required to understand another person; and the tact and appreciation required for an acceptable interpretation—fill the papers regardless whether the topic is free association, transference, silence, the basic rule. His life as an analyst is perhaps best characterized by what he once wrote: "The basic rule is to understand the patient."

Edith B. Jackson
1895-1977

MORRIS A. WESSEL, M.D.

EDITH B. JACKSON, CLINICAL PROFESSOR EMERITUS OF PEDIATRICS
and Psychiatry, Yale University School of Medicine, psychoanalyst and pioneer in the efforts to introduce psychoanalytic
concepts into the mainstream of child care, died quietly in her
sleep on June 5, 1977, in Denver, Colorado, at the age of 82.
Her death ends a half century of dedicated clinical service and
teaching in pediatrics and psychiatry. Few individuals maintain as steadfast and important a professional role as she did.

Born January 2, 1895, in Colorado Springs, Edith Jackson
grew up in a Quaker family whose members were leaders in
community affairs. Her father, William Sharpless Jackson, a
railroad executive, actively supported the movement for improving the status of native American Indians. It is understandable that Edith Jackson became a strong advocate for the
causes she believed to be important.

She graduated from Vassar College in 1916. Her characteristic warmth and quality of caring were appreciated by her
classmates, who prophetically wrote in the yearbook: "Edith
won't need to use much medicine when she becomes a doctor,
for her own good spirits alone will effect many a cure."

Edith Jackson received her M.D. from Johns Hopkins in
1921, spent one year interning in medicine in Iowa City, and

Clinical Professor of Pediatrics, Yale University School of Medicine, New
Haven, Connecticut.

another year in pediatrics at Bellevue Hospital in New York.
In 1923, she joined the staff of the New Haven Rickets Project
at the Yale Department of Pediatrics. The group studied the
clinical and laboratory aspects of rickets and established that
exposure to sunshine or the oral administration of Vitamin D
could prevent this disease.

A number of women who rose to prominence in medicine
were associated with the Yale Department of Pediatrics during
this period. Among Edith Jackson's colleagues were Marion C.
Putnam, later director of the Roxbury Children's Center, Marjorie Murray Burtt, psychiatrist, now of Ithaca, New York,
Martha Eliot and Ethel Dunham who assumed leadership responsibilities at the United States Children's Bureau.

In 1928, Edith Jackson became assistant physician at St.
Elizabeth's Psychiatric Hospital in Washington, D.C. She left
Washington in 1930 to enroll in the Vienna Institute of Psychoanalysis and to undertake psychoanalytic training with Sigmund Freud. Anna Freud recalls that Edith Jackson's strong
interest in preventive pediatrics stimulated colleagues to focus
attention on observing and treating psychological disturbances
in young children. She was a founder of, and helped to maintain, the Jackson Day Nursery in Vienna, the forerunner of
the Hampstead Nursery in London.

Edie Jackson, as she was known to friends and colleagues,
returned to Yale in 1936 to accept one of the first joint appointments in pediatrics and psychiatry in the United States.
Grover Powers, chairman of pediatrics at Yale, was proud of
his world-famous department. He considered his three superb
senior clinicians—Daniel Darrow in biochemistry, James Trask
in infectious diseases, and Edith Jackson in behavioral pediatrics—to be of equal importance.

Edith Jackson developed a psychiatric consultation service,
maintaining close contact with students, pediatric house officers, colleagues, patients, and parents. She was readily available to help a student or colleague better understand a child's
behavior.

Over the years, Edith Jackson was drawn increasingly to the
lying-in and newborn service. She recognized that the institu-

tionalized, rigid baby care practices recommended by doctors and nurses and communicated as *musts* to mothers were incompatible with the individual needs of many infants whose physiological temperaments necessitated a flexible feeding pattern. In 1940, she and Herbert Miller, director of pediatric house officer training, instituted a program for interns to visit new mothers and babies at home shortly after discharge from the hospital. This program, which also provided for the rare occasion that a house officer visited a home, represented one of the initial collaborative psychiatric and pediatric supervisory programs in a university medical center in the United States.

In 1946, Edith Jackson withdrew completely from ward consultation and, until her retirement from Yale in 1959, concentrated her efforts in the lying-in and newborn sphere. With her unfailing persuasive insistence and aided immeasurably by the backing of Grover Powers, she convinced obstetricians, nurses, pediatricians, psychiatrists, hospital administrators, and public health officials to support the development of an experimental rooming-in unit where mothers might have their babies alongside of their beds and care for them uninterrupted by rules and regulations. The Yale Rooming-In Project served initially as a unit to improve the care of mothers and babies and as a setting where fathers could participate in the care of their infants. It served eventually as a model for architectural plans and for staffing patterns for a new obstetrical unit at Yale-New Haven Hospital and for countless lying-in services throughout the world. The degree to which Edith Jackson and her rooming-in unit stimulated institutional change toward improving the care of mothers and infants throughout the world is immeasurable and awe-inspiring.

Rooming-In in simple terms describes a spatial and administrative setting where mothers and baby, accommodated side by side, were considered as a unit and cared for by one nurse. At Yale, it also reflected a collaborative effort with the obstetrical staff and a center where psychiatrists, pediatricians, obstetricians, nurses, mothers and fathers could unite to give the oncoming generation the best possible start in life. The professional goals were to help parents establish confidence and understanding at the outset of their parental role. Nurses and doctors were far more able to offer support to mothers, particularly in the establishment of breast feeding, than in the usual setting where the baby spent most of the day in the nursery and the mother in her room down the hall.

The attitude of all professional staff working in the Rooming-In unit was set by Edith Jackson, who in her daily visits was always ready to listen to, try to understand, and help a new mother, rather than to impose authoritarian recommendations. The countless nurses, medical students, and house officers who worked in Rooming-In learned the importance of the supportive role they could play during the lying-in period. Grover Powers called this unit the "heart of pediatrics." Many physicians and nurses trace their current interest in, and the high priority they give to, this sphere of health care to their experiences in the Rooming-In unit.

What did Edith Jackson offer younger colleagues which causes so many to look back with appreciation many decades later? Her conviction that a physician's attentive readiness to help a mother, father, child was a powerful therapeutic force set an example for all who worked with her. Countless younger colleagues learned, often for the first time, that sitting at a bedside and actively listening to a mother, or examining a baby while a mother observes, were important ways of relieving concerns. Once having seen Edith Jackson in this role, one never forgot that this was a professional responsibility of importance.

Directness and determination to get to the basic issues were her characteristic manner of approaching clinical problems. Students, house officers, and colleagues who sought Edith Jackson's counsel were initially often taken aback by her forthright questioning which brought a problem immediately into focus. I recall in 1941 asking her for advice on what to read to gain a better understanding of a specific child's reaction to hospitalization. I was overwhelmed by her response: "How did you happen to come to me just now with this question?" I recall telling her within a few seconds of my distress about this child's behavior on the ward and how that reminded me of my own anxiety when I was hospitalized for T & A at the age of 8.

I was one of the many students who maintained an ongoing relationship with Edith Jackson. She shared with me the observations made at the Hampstead Nursery in London. She continually compared the children described by Anna Freud and Dorothy Burlingham with the children and what was happening to them on the ward around the corner. I recall that I became a bit impatient with the repetitiveness of her approach, thinking it was so obvious it was unnecessary to belabor the point. I now realize that my response indicated that in her quiet, unobtrusive, matter-of-fact manner, she had taught me to grasp the psychoanalytic concept that children under stress regress to earlier developmental patterns of immature behavior which they had previously abandoned. Today this conceptualization of the clinical phenomenon of regression seems obvious to pediatricians, child development workers, and psychiatrists. It is important to remember, however, that these discussions took place in the 1940s, the early days of psychoanalytic observational studies of young children. Edith Jackson's pioneering role in bringing this material to the forefront is exemplified not only by the fact that these discussions occurred, but that they took place with a medical student in a pediatrics department in a major medical center.

Fourteen pediatric house officers spent a year or more as Fellows in the Rooming-In unit. They learned about the developmental task which young couples experience as they assume parental roles. They became familiar with the fundamentals of infant development and its normal variability. They learned that a young child's growth is uneven and that thrusts of mature behavior alternate with temporary regression. Fellows learned not only to understand, but to respect and predict these healthy responses in a child's life.

Edith Jackson's unique contribution lay in her earnest conviction that people and feelings were important. No way of improving a mother or child's comfort ever escaped her eye. She never asked whether a telephone call or a bedside visit was necessary; rather she wanted to know whether making it would help parents or a child. As a teacher she never missed an opportunity for improving a junior colleague's perception of how to develop his or her helping skills. She was firmly convinced that nurses, pediatricians, and teachers were key professionals in helping parents and children to develop and have faith in themselves.

Her daily clinical activities; her participation in numerous boards of social agencies; her local, national, and international committee responsibilities—all represented her desire to improve the welfare of children. In 1964 she was awarded the Agnes McGavin award of the American Psychiatric Association for outstanding contributions to the prevention of emotional disorders in children, and in 1968 the American Academy of Pediatrics presented her with the C. Anderson Aldrich Award for outstanding contributions to child development. These awards, one in psychiatry and the other in pediatrics, demonstrate the respect she earned in both fields, an accomplishment few have ever attained. She was a founding member of the Western New England Psychoanalytic Society and served as member of the Editorial Board of *The Psychoanalytic Study of the Child* since its inception.

Edith Jackson's personal and professional life exemplifies a constant devotion to improving the physical and psychological well-being of children. Her unique ability to apply psychoanalytic principles as a basis for helping pediatricians, nurses, teachers, and parents understand and improve their capacity to care for children serves as an inspiring model for all who knew her. She has taught us the tremendous therapeutic psychological importance of maintaining constant attention to every detail which can make life better for parents and children.

THEORETICAL
CONTRIBUTIONS

Transitional Phenomena in the Analysis of Early Adolescent Males

T. WAYNE DOWNEY, M.D.

AMONG THE DEVELOPMENTAL PERIODS, EARLY ADOLESCENCE HAS, for many, the distinction of being the most difficult one in which to initiate and sustain a psychoanalysis. What Anna Freud (1958) has said about the analytic treatment of adolescents in general seems particularly relevant to the analytic work with early adolescents: "the analytic treatment of adolescents is a hazardous venture from beginning to end, a venture in which the analyst has to meet with resistances of unusual strength and variety" (p. 261). One of the predominant hazards in working with early adolescents is their seemingly infinite capacity to maintain a steadfast negative attitude of defiance and hyperindependence which seems destined to thwart even the most patient and forbearing of analysts and create an air of therapeutic pessimism and despair.

It is my thesis that a focus on the presence of transitional phenomena, in Winnicott's sense of the term (1953), can be useful as a measure of the often elusive and debated presence of a developing transference neurosis in an adolescent analysis. Attention to these transitional phenomena may yield important clues to unconscious hidden aspects of the positive transference and the analytic alliance which are embedded in

Clinical Director, Yale Psychiatric Institute; Associate Clinical Professor of Pediatrics and Psychiatry, Child Study Center, Yale University, New Haven, Conn.

transitional phenomena. Such monitoring may ultimately provide important balancing information about whether, beneath
the negative transference storm or the apparent apathy, the
early adolescent is engaging or is capable of engaging in an
analytic alliance. The transitional phenomena manifested by
the adolescent in his particular developmental mix of words
and action may then provide a window on the occult, silent,
positive transference, and shed light on the potential for a
full-bodied transference neurosis which the adolescent, particularly the early adolescent, is often vigorously attempting to
fend off, negate, or flee.

The Literature on Adolescent Analysis

There are many reports similar to Anna Freud's attesting the
difficult, arduous, uncertain, and often unproductive nature
of analysis in early adolescence (Blos, 1962; Harley, 1970;
Fraiberg, 1955). Maenchen (1970) has enumerated the per-
plexities and the problems which clutter the course of early
adolescent analysis. She aptly refers to early adolescence as the
developmental period least understood by analysts. Even in
apparently successful treatments, the whys, hows, and whats
of technique and treatment remain tentative, vague, and ill-
defined. The confusion and blurring around matters of technique for this period is further compounded by the fact that
many reports do not distinguish between psychoanalysis and
psychotherapy. The literature, rather than containing descriptions of successful cases, is full of ruminations about the causes
of treatment failures. The authors usually point quite correctly to the turbulence of the developmental period which
combines with the individual psychopathology to make analysis impossible. Children may be maintained in their analyses
through early adolescence if they have commenced treatment
in an earlier developmental phase, but even then, as Fraiberg
(1955) points out, there are many hazards to initiating treatment at this time. In adolescence, treatment often becomes
disrupted when transference events precede and to some extent stimulate the developmental advances associated with

breaking the incestuous ties to the parents. Then the analysis is interrupted prior to or concomitantly with the breaking of these parental ties (Fraiberg, 1955; A. Freud, 1958; Maenchen, 1970). This development in early adolescent analyses vividly highlights the risk that treatment as it progresses may get caught up in an uncontrolled manner with the ongoing issues and with the regressive and progressive changes of development. As a result, there is a replication of the conflict in the analysis before the conflicts can be analyzed and worked through to a solution in which the analyst and the parents are kept apart. The analyst in the adolescent's mind is thus often not sufficiently differentiated from parents, and treatment then may be disrupted as further acting out of the regressive conflict with the parents.

The analysis may on many important levels run counter to desirable psychological developments such as the attainment and maintenance of the capacity and need for secrecy, privacy, and autonomy. These developments are spurred by upsurges of sexuality, physicality, fantasy life, and greater conflicts around passive strivings. The literature does not make it clear when the adolescent's need for secrecy and privacy should be honored and the adolescent left to his or her own devices and when this developmental thrust should not be honored but replaced by the analytic requirement of openly sharing inner psychological life. Even in the most open and unfolding adolescent analyses, this movement toward privacy and separateness, which is in the very nature of adolescence, creates tension. We often see that the adolescent presents himself physically for analysis in a negativistic and balky manner, but paradoxically is neither mute nor withholding. He may come with a pressure to find a private place away from home, a private place where he can organize and articulate thoughts and where he may share his secrets *with himself* and with another person. Often he does this to some extent with peers. The developmental need for an adult with whom to share thoughts has often been minimized or confused in the work with adolescents. My presumption is that adolescents also need adults they can talk to and with.

Fraiberg (1955) emphasizes that ambiguous preparation of the child for analysis presents the greatest danger to the analysis in the critical early phase. To avoid early treatment disruption, the adolescent must quickly but patiently be brought to some agreement (implicitly or explicitly) about his or her need for analysis. This cannot be left to the analytic work proper, as it might be done in the case of a younger preoedipal or latency child who distresses the parents. If an explicit agreement or a sense of agreement cannot be reached with the adolescent, the analyst remains identified with the "outside" world of the parents and is never able to achieve anything approaching a therapeutic alliance with the adolescent patient. The analyst indeed then does not have a patient, or even an adversarial patient, but only an adversary. As Eissler (1958) has emphasized, analysts of adolescents must be flexible in their technical approach, changing it as necessary to resonate with the teen-ager's ambiance and pathology. Marianne Kris stressed the need to consider development as a continuum to which the analyst brings an adaptive approach with regard to any modifications of technique (see Casuso, 1965). The analyst should fit the technique to the adolescent patient rather than attempting to fit the analysand in this developmental phase to a preconceived idea of technique. Finally, Anna Freud (1958) concludes her paper with the somewhat gloomy prescription that the developmental thrust for privacy and autonomy should be respected and that the adolescent should be given time and scope to work out his own solution.

But what of the great number of disturbed adolescents who do feel in need of treatment, yet have a marked tendency to ward off a positive attachment to the analyst by negative transference reactions? The analyst is still left with perplexing questions of how to understand these troubled teen-agers, how to build an analytic alliance, and how to foster and facilitate healthier resolutions than these adolescents can achieve on their own. How can the analyst discern the latent yearnings and entreaties for help and assess their potential for developing into a therapeutic alliance in a person with the overdetermined, developmentally supported, manifest qualities of defiance, activity, and insular hyperindependence?

These questions are another way of asking how the analyst can, in a very particular way, participate in the loosening and reshaping of an adolescent's preoedipal and oedipal object ties. When positive transference manifestations are seen as so dangerous and threatening in relation to adults (and often to peers as well), how can the analyst intervene in a helpful way? Paradoxically, the management of the positive aspects of the transference, rather than that of the negative transference, becomes of paramount technical importance at this age. Implicit in this is the necessity to identify and conceptualize the existence of an actual ongoing full transference process (with positive and negative aspects) in early adolescents, another point of contention in this contentious developmental phase.

THE THEORY OF TRANSITIONAL PHENOMENA

Two early adolescent boys presented a similar puzzling picture. In the midst of angry tirades against me and the analysis, they would suddenly relax and assume a "reverent" subdued attitude toward some item or article of clothing which they would call to my attention. In thinking about the qualities of this markedly different mental state, I was struck by the apparent similarities between their behaviors and the way toddlers treat their treasured transitional objects.

THE CONCEPT OF THE TRANSITIONAL OBJECT

Winnicott (1953) has provided a vivid description of the blanket as transitional object: the "sedative which always worked," which decreased anxiety, and which both stood for the mother or her breast and yet was more important than the mother to the child. He emphasized the commonality of blankets, stuffed animals, etc., as transitional objects for infants and toddlers. They belong in an intermediate area. "This intermediate area of experience, unchallenged in respect of its belonging to inner or external (shared) reality, constitutes the greater part of the infant's experience and throughout life is retained in the intense experiencing that belongs to the arts and to religion and to imaginative living, and to creative scientific work" (1971, p. 14). In the course of development, the child leaves behind the original transitional object, but not its qualities. These become available for transfer to a number of other items and activities as transitional phenomena in this "third area" of "imaginative living." It seems to me that in adolescence there is a resurgence of and reemphasis on the importance of transitional phenomena for psychological growth and development.

Given the difficulties of working analytically during adolescence and following the premise that focusing on transitional phenomena in an analysis will provide reference points for the ongoing analytic work and the state of the transference, some integration and elaboration of pertinent theory is necessary. What I am attempting to clarify are psychological events and markers which are easily taken as trivial, superficial, or otherwise relegated to the category of general psychological resistance and "static." When looked at closely in a certain developmental framework, however, in the context of the analytic setting, they take on heightened meaning and importance as indicators of the presence or absence of an ongoing developing analytic process.

While Winnicott rarely referred back to Freud and treated his thoughts and discoveries as uniquely "Winnicottian," it seems to me that there are often direct conceptual connections between his work and Freud's in the areas of object relations and ego psychology. These connections have tended to be overlooked or undervalued. One of these is in the area which Winnicott has characterized as pertaining to transitional objects, phenomena, and experience—the "third area" between inner and outer experience. This is the area which is so important in the individual's mediation of the inner bodily drives and outer "reality." In 1925, Freud alluded to this intermediate area in psychological experience when he attempted a metapsychological definition of subject, object, internal and external:

> It is now no longer a question of whether what has been perceived (a thing) shall be taken into the ego or not, but of

whether something which is in the ego as a presentation can be rediscovered in perception (reality) as well. It is, we see, once more a question of *external* and *internal*. What is unreal, merely a presentation and subjective, is only internal; what is real is also there *outside*. In this stage of development regard for the pleasure principle has been set aside. Experience has shown the subject that it is not only important whether a thing (and object of satisfaction for him) possesses the 'good' attribute and so deserves to be taken into his ego, but also whether it is there in the external world, so that he can get hold of it whenever he needs it. . . . The antithesis between subjective and objective does not exist from the first. It only comes into being from the fact that thinking possesses the capacity to bring before the mind once more something that has once been perceived by reproducing it as a presentation without the external object having still to be there. . . . The reproduction of a perception as a presentation is not always a faithful one; it may be modified by omissions, or changed by the merging of various elements [p. 237f.].

While Freud is discussing reality testing, he comes very close in his description to enunciating the psychological state in which transitional objects initially come into being. In his 1953 paper, Winnicott specifies how the ego comes to do what Freud sketches out as "something which is in the ego as a presentation can be rediscovered in perception (reality)." I think Winnicott fills in an intermediate stage in the establishment of this reality testing when he focuses attention on the transitional object. He has described how the young child at an early age reproduces the essence of mother as caretaker in the transitional object which, in Freud's words, becomes a "reproduction of a perception . . . modified by omissions or changed by the merging of various elements." Winnicott's concept provides a step in the chain of psychological events by which the child masters "inner" and "outer" and comes to develop the object constancy which Freud's statement implies. This development of a constant group of ego functions for modulating inner and outer experience is, in my view, signaled by the establishment of the first transitional object. The appearance of the transitional object constitutes what Green-acre (1954) has described as the first creative experience. The transitional object could also be categorized as an essential precursor of what subsequently becomes established in language as metaphor. It is an initial attempt by the child's ego to fix meaning which transcends the actual object in the same manner that the metaphor transcends the actual words used to signify it. This mediation of internal and external as evidenced by the child's construction of a transitional object carries with it a necessary and essential ambiguity. It exists in the world. More importantly, it is an indication of a mental representation and evidence that a complex psychological process involving separation from mother physically and individuation from her psychologically is taking place, and to a certain extent has already taken place. Thus, the transitional object indicates the potential for a later capacity for symbol formation and symbol utilization. Along with this potential for symbol formation, the transitional object also points to a well-developed capacity for magical thinking and symptom formation which may have been only rudimentary or fleeting in the young child prior to the creation of a transitional object. In many ways, the child's attachment to a cherished object is also a prototypic and rudimentary expression of the dawn of the capacity for transference—the displacement of what was originally internalized, or partly so, from an important "other" in the outside world onto an item which is then endowed with the same qualities, conflicts, and experiences. In a general sense, then, the transitional object is a transference "object" as well, carrying with it important aspects of mother which have not yet been completely internalized but which are in the process of internalization into a constant mental representation.

When internalization of mother's mental representation is relatively complete and some degree of object constancy has been established, the transitional object is less necessary, but transitional phenomena generalized from the quality of the transitional object experience and transference phenomena will continue to share the same quality of being partially mobilized and externalized so that object relations can be maintained. As Freud described it (1914), "The transference thus creates an *intermediate* region between illness and real life through which the *transition* from one to the other is made" (p. 154; my italics). Indeed, what Winnicott describes as transitional phenomena seem on closer scrutiny to be activities of the ego, which initially are directed at mastering the experience of maternal absence and which occur at an interface between the drives and external reality. Transference phenomena are derivatives of the same process, constituting the resolution of this experience of absence *at a particular developmental phase;* e.g., the toddlers *use* toys, and the young adolescents *use* stereo equipment as actual and symbolic manifestations of particular mental operations having the aim of establishing a sense of mother at a "not mother" time.

TRANSITIONAL PHENOMENA IN CHILDHOOD AND ADOLESCENCE

For the infant beginning to ambulate, explore, and experience a strange but entrancing world apart from mother, there is one and only one transitional object which serves as a talisman for safe conduct on this journey of exploration. It protects the child from the point of psychological separation from mother until return and reunion. It is neither interchangeable with any other item in the child's world, nor is it dispensable. Toddlers consider their transitional objects absolutely necessary to their psychological well-being, at times more necessary than mother. With the adolescent, the transitional qualities are more diverse. They are spread over the psychological landscape of the teen-ager as transitional phenomena in the "third area" where the adolescent spends so much time experiencing, reorganizing, and re-creating his inner and outer worlds. Certain aspects of the teen-ager's life may be more likely to be invested with transitional qualities than others, for instance, clothing, living space, artistic media. However, within these areas there are often rapid shifts in the emotional investment and attachment to a pair of trousers, a record, or a film. Something which possesses intense transitional qualities one week is displaced by another item which is similarly treasured,

revered, and cherished the next. The adolescent's need for experiences with pronounced transitional components seems as
strong as the toddler's. The adolescent, though, imbues not
one part of his new and rapidly changing world but many
aspects with the transitional qualities which will allow him or
her a sense of safe conduct through it.

In part, the thesis of this paper rests on my ability to identify *elements* of the original transitional object in the ego phenomena of early adolescence. It also rests on a factor that
Freud (1905) pointed out: that adolescence is determined by
and repeats in diverse ways the early infantile fantasies and
conflicts. This factor makes it a prime developmental time for
working them through. Jones (1922) extended Freud's initial
statements in emphasizing the importance of repetition, recapitulation, and elaboration of the earlier conflicted developmental history in the "transitional stage of adolescence" (p.
502). He underlined a distinctive "correlation between adolescence and infancy," stating: "the individual *recapitulates and expands* in the second decennium of life the development he
passed through during the first five years" (p. 509). The psychological stages of infancy are passed through on a different
plane in adolescence, but often with discernible similarities between the earlier and the later stages in any individual. While
this kind of potential for repetition and recapitulation is
present throughout life, it seems to reach an apex of importance in adolescence. Blos (1976) reemphasized this quality in
what he calls "the psychoanalytic recapitulation theory of adolescence." He, too, emphasizes that it is the preoedipal material
which is recapitulated in adolescence. He feels the oedipal material is best viewed as a continuation of the earlier unresolved
complex, rather than as a repetition of previous states on
which some degree of developmental closure has been obtained.

Following the recapitulation premise, we might expect to
find disguised and buried to greater or lesser degree in the
transitional phenomena of adolescence the qualities that are
manifest in the transitional object of early childhood. As I indicated earlier, while the two may be quite close, they are not

identical. Other developmental phases have intervened with other conflicts and solutions. Sensory preferences, particularly tactile and auditory ones, persist across the phases. While the underlying quality and pattern may remain the same, it is a long way from the toddler's exclusive preference for a blanket to the adolescent's generalized insistence on a particular "uniform" or wardrobe. Clothing takes on other meanings of an obvious oedipal nature having to do with attracting or repelling the parents. Listening to music may at a depth be an echo of one auditory aspect of an early experience of using a squeaky or noisy toy as a transitional object in the mother's absence. At the same time, the stereo from which the music emanates may itself have important oedipal meanings having to do with power and competition with a father who is forever requesting that it be turned down. It may function to drown out stimuli which would lead to primal scene fantasizing as readily as it may provide cues for slightly disguised musing along the same lines.

The adolescent transitional phenomenon will have many of the same determinants as the blanket in terms of modulating inner and outer space, creating a more delineated body boundary, and making separation from important objects tolerable, but it will also show the imposition of later identifications with each parent or with developmental concerns of other phases. Sensory preferences, the resurgence of transitional phenomena, and the appearance of a pronounced emphasis on personal care as an issue seem for many early adolescents to be a direct response to an upsurge in drive activity. The increased appearance and heightened importance of transitional phenomena in the adolescent's emotional life mark an attempt by the teen-ager to reinstate what had been in the toddler period a relatively satisfying mode of stabilizing and maintaining the relationship to the object when the latter was absent (by virtue of mother's departure from the child or child's ambulation away from mother) or depriving. The reviewing process inherent in adolescence reevokes this mode as the adolescent appears to look back to the latency and oedipal periods. He has a more dependable capability for regulating and remembering, i.e., a more mature ego, and some experience that objects persist in the midst of emotional storms. These developmental accretions alter and differentiate the experience of the early adolescent from that of the infant. The original transitional object came into being as a means of helping the child to separate self from other and to allow a bridge from self to mother as a unique experience which the infant had previously been unable to achieve because of the ego's lack of maturity. It was something to soothe him in her absence, something to modulate his aggression, something indestructible and yet soft, something that altogether aided him in feeling intact and differentiated as an individual.

In a similar manner, but again at another level of complexity, the early adolescent is confronted with the task of reindividuation as he goes through a period which is similar to toddlerhood in that it is another phase of vast physical change. The toddler's motor development outstrips his psychological resources. He can absent himself from mother, which may make mother's absences all the more poignant. He has a greater sense of the distinction between a passive and active state. The toddler having rapidly left the mother's presence and experienced the exhilaration of that leaving may respond to mother's absence with a heightened sense of helplessness. The acquisition of speech also involves a physical equilibrium between mother and child. Similarly, the early adolescent goes through physical changes which estrange him from his body, which distort and stretch his body ego. As a result of the physiological vocal changes, the adolescent boy must learn, not to talk, but to speak with a new voice. The adolescent girl often experiences inner voices laden with the cracking intensity of the boy's outer voice. In an imperative manner, these changes thrust adolescents away from family and original objects in some ways and toward them in others. Still, the adolescent is often "out of phase" with his body and as anxious about it as the toddler learning to walk and talk.

This view opens another perspective on what Laufer (1976) has described in relation to the "central masturbation fantasy." There is a need to emphasize what is underemphasized, that physical growth per se may cause an increase in anxiety and aggression because it outstrips psychological preparedness, which necessarily must always be reactive and lag behind. In a sense, the "central masturbation fantasy" complements the employment of transitional phenomena as another mode of the ego for working through preoedipal issues, so that body ownership can be established as residing with the adolescent, not the parent, and with the body being the servant, not the tyrant, of the adolescent's self. In the same way, the transitional object emphasizes the infant's tenuous control of his own body, a circumstance that in the early adolescent revives old conflicts and old modes of conflict resolution. To the extent that the conflicts are preoedipal ones around self-object differentiation, transitional phenomena are called into play as practice toward solutions, just as the transitional object had been called into play under similar circumstances in toddlerhood. The central masturbation fantasy, deriving from similar needs in infancy, likewise becomes a focus for another aspect of the adolescent developmental crisis.

The point I am making here is not that oedipal issues and conflicts are unimportant at this stage of early adolescent development, they are critically important; but they may not be as accessible to interpretation and analytic work as they are with the adult patient. What could account for this? We would expect and do see that with an increase in sexuality previous conflicts become illuminated in preparation for developmental changes. Thus there frequently appear issues of rivalry. While the same-sexed parent is challenged, attraction to or drawing away from the opposite-sexed parent may occur. However, it seems that maturational factors may take over in determining whether the oedipal or preoedipal factors predominate in the early phases of analysis of these youngsters. One variable is the extent to which the parents or the environment emphasize one aspect or the other. Another variable would be the degree to which preoedipal conflicts have been reduced or partially resolved in other phases, allowing for a greater display of oedipal issues. In other situations, intense drive activity coupled with major oedipal and preoedipal conflicts would tend to lead to a predominant focus of the adolescent's distress around the earlier conflicts and fixation points. Again, this outcome is enhanced by the similar quality of the developmental stress experienced by early adolescents and toddlers; namely, the temporary outstripping of the psychological capacities of the child by a developmental thrust. This leaves the adolescent in the position of having to catch up in his or her psychological maturation with the rapid physical changes in the areas of sexuality, motility, and aggression. Once again the relatively undefended possibilities for expression of sexual and aggressive drives are present.

It seems to me that if the analyst is on the lookout for transitional phenomena as they occur in the often archaic, intangible, ambiguous, but nonetheless psychically overdetermined analytic process with early adolescents, this allows him to tap what is most available to be brought into the psychic sphere and verbalized. It permits the analyst to tap what can most easily be freed from the complex and continuing mixture of thought and action which the early adolescent usually presents in the session. Since the transitional phenomena discussed in this paper are particularly related to developmental issues of the preoedipal phase, the technical implication is that monitoring their presence, preponderance, or absence may assist the analyst in determining whether to interpret the oedipal or preoedipal dynamics. While the dictum in adult analysis has generally been to interpret the oedipal conflicts first and then the preoedipal, to interpret from superficial to deep, from preconscious to unconscious in structural terms, from proximal to distal in time and developmental terms, this may be disastrous with the early adolescent whose pressing need is for at least partial preoedipal resolution of self-other boundary issues and maternal transference issues before triadic oedipal issues in the intrapsychic and interpersonal spheres can be reviewed in a tolerable manner. Loewald (1977) made a similar point with regard to adult analyses when he emphasized that in the early phase of an adult analysis, attention to, and interpretation of, preoedipal transference dynamics may be quite effective in facilitating the analytic work. While some adolescents do bolt to avoid incestuous oedipal issues, for many the major focus of the transference is on preoedipal issues. The analyst's failure to respond in this area will lead to claims that the analyst is not understanding, that the analyst is indeed like the adolescent's parents who paradoxically flaunt the adolescent's immaturity while consistently pressing for behavior at a developmental level above that which the adolescent can maintain. So, technically, monitoring transitional phenomena gives the analyst greater scope in determining whether to make interpretations along oedipal or preoedipal lines.

CLINICAL OBSERVATIONS

The illustrations of these theoretical considerations are taken from the early phase in the analyses of two young male adolescents, Darius and Joseph. Both entered analysis at around age 13. Darius was brought to analysis by his parents when his previously precarious adjustment to school plummeted with the onset of puberty and he was faced with expulsion because of his severe disruptive behavior. This development was paralleled by increasing estrangement from peers. At home Darius alternated between withdrawn self-absorption and tormenting attacks on his younger siblings. Joseph also was experiencing a decline in his school performance, which was of great concern to his parents, particularly his father, who tended to measure his own worth as a parent by how well his son performed in school. However, Joseph's major area of difficulty was at home. As he was preparing for his Bar Mitzvah, he became explosively angry and demanding with his family, dominating them with his moods. He followed his mother around the home tormenting her with his presence. He, too, became estranged from the few friends he had made during latency. The parents of both Joseph and Darius became concerned with the ferocity of their verbal and occasionally physical attacks on siblings. In the evaluation phase both boys indicated that they were in psychological pain and were looking for relief, but shortly after the analysis started, each in his own way lapsed into a mixture of defensive defiance, silence, or

streams of apparently meaningless, inconsequential talk. Both
boys had transitional objects as infants. For both the treasured
object had been a blanket. Memories of the transitional object
came to the fore in both instances about the second year of
analysis. Darius's and Joseph's recollection of the fate of their
transitional objects seemed particularly interesting. Joseph,
who treated his mother as a transitional object, had a screen
memory of parting with his beloved blanket at his mother's insistence around age 5 by dropping it over his shoulder. His
mother then took it and disposed of it. Darius recalled that he
had passed his blanket on to his sister at age 3. At age 14 he
recalled its properties of safety and security as he described
cowering under a blanket in bed, listening fearfully to the
sound of his father sleepwalking.

During a highly defiant phase of his analysis, Joseph provided a particularly vivid example of the transitional qualities
which clothing had for him. Before his mother went to the
hospital for an operation, this early adolescent insisted that
she take him shopping to buy new, more "manly" clothes. The
clothes he purchased were all workman's overalls, which he
wore faithfully during her absence. They dramatized his intent to free himself from the white-collar professionalism of
his father. They were also too large and baggy, and as such
made this tall, awkward adolescent look like an oversized
toddler in infant's bulky overalls. This visual cue provided an
avenue to analytic work on his attachment to his mother and
its preoedipal aspects.

At this point, another illustration, this time from Darius's
analysis, may be helpful in highlighting what I am talking
about and providing a clinical example which must stand for
many which might be selected from his analysis or Joseph's.

It is winter, and it has been snowing. Darius, in the early
phase of his analysis, stomps into my office and immediately
shows me his down-filled ski gloves for the first time. He has
missed his previous appointment due to the snow. In the characteristic fashion of many his age, Darius has been consciously
defiant, angry, and negativistic about the analysis and the analyst since he started. In the evaluation phase he had appeared

receptive and had shown some perspective on his difficulties as well as pained and genuine interest in help. While protesting to his parents and me about having to come, he has appeared regularly and talked, but to all intents and purposes disclaimed any meaning to his words other than that contained in their manifest content. He has shunned interpretations.

This day he shows me his gloves, pointing out that they are "very old," a gift he received of a favorite aunt four years ago. "Notice the leather," he insists, "see how supple, wrinkled, well-used, and soft the leather is in spite of hard use." He pulls out the inner liner, turning the inside out. "See how warm they are." It is a trick to get the liners back inside the glove. "Sometimes the thumb sticks and then it may take ten minutes," he says patiently. "Notice the small tear at the base of the right thumb. It is from a rope tow. Not a bad tear, considering what rope tows are like. Any other pair of gloves would be all ripped up completely by now. And notice too this strip of red nylon tape across the knuckles. This means they are mine." It is an identifying mark along with a tiny white initial on the cuff, which he points out in concluding his minute inspection of his gloves. As he is finishing, he spies a tiny fleck of down in the air. Did I see where it came from? With some anxiety he searches his gloves for a leak. He is relieved to find none, but is worried that one day the liner will give way and his favorite gloves will be useless.

He goes on to other things in the hour, playing unconsciously with his gloves on his lap as he talks. While describing how famished he is, he squeezes and pulls at them. As he thinks of his grandmother and her feeding and disciplinary deprivations of him while his parents were away recently, he puts the gloves on and shows me how much padding they have when he makes a fist. "They can almost be a boxing glove." Then he smiles sadistically as he pounds his hands and says he hoped I'd have a heart attack shoveling snow on the day he was away. Immediately after this he becomes conciliatory and asks whether I saw his favorite TV show or bought his favorite record in his absence. As the hour comes to an end, he becomes angry at my mention of his description of the time away as one of deprivation and starvation. I comment on his struggling not to notice his feelings about the separation. He swears, throws the gloves down so they touch me but do not hit me, picks them up quietly, and concertedly elaborates on the absences. He couches his anxious, lonely, and depressive thoughts in negation. He *did not* miss anyone! He *did not* mind his parents being away, and so on.

Many of the qualities of an original experience with a transitional object were highlighted for me by this episode with Darius. This experience was not isolated but formed part of a consecutive number of manifestations of transitional phenomena which ultimately could be interpreted by me and heard by him. Along the way in the early months they provided markers. In the middle stages of the analysis, they lent themselves to the interpretation of separation conflicts. Darius's state as he talked about the gloves was important. It alternated from tender concern and microscopically focused attention to an angry outburst and an attempt to throw them at me. He also threw them instead of me. What he enumerated is important as a reflection of the transitional process present. They are old. They are a gift from a woman (identified in his analysis as a good mother figure). They are uniquely identified in multiple minuscule ways as his. They may be turned inside out (reflecting, I think, the inward-outward function of transitional objects). They have texture and provide a tactile experience; they are soft, supple, wrinkled, and warm. They are closely associated with oral issues. He squeezes them as he talks of feeding difficulties and hunger. This theme was a prominent part of his analysis. They are a prop which allows him to re-create the experience of losing and finding, throwing away and retrieving (and the other side, helplessness and being thrown away). Later in the analysis, we will be able to put these conflicts around separation and rejection into better words, but now the gloves help him tentatively to articulate his concerns. The concern about down escaping reverberates with my name and implicitly emphasizes the maternal preoedipal transference, positive but precarious and fraught with peril. As an infant he had experienced his mother as escaping from his destructive orality and punishing him by going to a younger sister after he had almost consumed her.

Darius's asking me about television and records emphasizes a connection with me and his curiosity about me through media which have a clear transitional aspect for many adolescents. The manner in which Darius used his gloves indicated that they were highly invested with preoedipal transference meaning and manifested multiple "third area" transitional phenomena. He uses them to modulate contact; to underline an old oral transference issue which he struggles angrily and ashamedly to hide; and in an attempt to establish covertly and tentatively a new object relationship with me. The gloves also have oedipal connections in relation to fighting fathers, beating older men, hitting them, attacking me (his father had nearly died recently), especially in his comments about my possibly dying from shoveling snow. Skiing, with its exhibitionistic appeal to his mother and his competency in a sport he enjoys with his father, also points toward oedipal dynamics. They pale, however, and do not carry the affective charge that is involved in his recitation of deprivation and loss with the attempted restitution through his gloves.

As Darius played, fretted, threw, retrieved, and examined his gloves minutely, it appeared to me that he was in a psychological state very reminiscent of, but far from identical with, that of a toddler fondling a transitional object. Toddlers fondling teddy bears, blankets, or dolls seem to be in a similar psychological state. The qualities may be the same in Darius's attitude and treatment of his gloves, but the exclusivity which was present with the original transitional object is absent and is replaced by a plasticity which allows many items to serve as soothing and comforting. In other sessions, it was a book, magazine, even athletic shoes that shared this soothing quality. For Darius, the gloves clearly are *his* gloves. This is an important distinction and difference. For the infant, the transitional object, a blanket, for instance, is never just a blanket or even partially that. It is always a transitional object, with a particular function in facilitating the establishment of self-other differentiation and in minimizing separation stress.

The early adolescents' use of transitional phenomena in

their struggle to adapt to rapid bodily change was dramatized
by Darius around his skiing. With growth, he had lost coordination, but he tried to compensate for this by emphasizing
his size and phallic potential—now his skis were longer than
his father's! At the same time, he spent months cataloguing ski
equipment, bringing into the analysis and looking at ski magazines before he again dared to leave the analysis for a week of
skiing. In this activity of looking and reading during analytic
sessions, he regressively transferred onto the analyst an ego-
syntonic (new) version of an old state of infancy in which he
was alone with his mother, being held, read to, and talked to
in an almost hypnoid transitional state. The new version is acceptable because the roles are reversed, with Darius in the role
of his mother engaged in a transitional activity.

With Darius, actions, activities, and objects such as his gloves
took on qualities of the original transitional object, although
with an updated specificity, intensity, and singularity of preference. At the early adolescent stage, developmental progres-
sions are analogous to those of the preoedipal period, helping
toward differentiating inner and outer reality and thereby
stabilizing object relations. However, the process is a widening
as well as a clarifying one. It facilitates the adolescent's making
an important shift from playing and acting to verbalization as
a predominant mode of conflict conceptualization, expression,
and resolution. Darius showed this mix of playing and talking
in his transitional use of his gloves. In an analogous manner,
the infantile transitional object allows the child a partial but essential or basic shift into a fuller mode of playing and action
while at the same time facilitating the integration of verbal
and incipient symbolic functioning. While the toddler is developing object constancy, he is also learning to talk and developing coherent dreams.

Harley (1970) has also made the point that while there is a
mix of material from other developmental phases and while
the oedipal issues are often quite apparent as they were in
Darius, the issues of autonomy and independence which are
closely related to psychological individuation and physical separation from mother are prototypically preoedipal. The early

adolescent usually does not have the necessary tolerances at the start of adolescence to deal with the blatant oedipal material stirred up by sexual development. Thus sexual issues become anal ones (sex as dirty) again, or oral ones (sex as devouring or all-consuming) as drive regression to antecedent libidinal phases occurs.

The analysis of Joseph provides another illustration. He entered analysis at age 13 shortly after his Bar Mitzvah. In their initial descriptions, his parents emphasized his constant presence with his mother in bedroom, car, and elsewhere, to the exclusion and exasperation of his father. What appeared to be, and was, full-fledged oedipal rivalry, as reported by Joseph's parents and to some extent by Joseph himself, gave way to paramount preoedipal issues in the early phase of his analysis. Joseph reported clinging and fusing behavior and fantasies about mother. He fought with her, or his sister in mother's place, around issues of independence, orderliness, and schedules. His shadowing of his mother had more the quality of a toddler's, who constantly tests and ascertains mother's presence.

Interpretations of preoedipal material were useful to Joseph as he brought them into the analysis through words and transitional phenomena. Often Joseph gave the signal that we were working in the preoedipal area by showing me a prized possession, usually a book or magazine. He would then proceed to puff the magazine out of all proportion as he described its pictures and stories, or rip and tear at it. He often stopped to roll and unroll it and then rolled it in the opposite direction, turning the inside outside and the outside inside in the mode which I suggest may accompany the transitional state. In later phases of the analysis it was possible to confirm the intrapsychic determinants of these props and actions.

Both Darius and Joseph were able later on in their analyses to acknowledge and clarify the preoedipal meanings which their use of books, magazines, and clothing seemed to broadcast. Inevitably, material having to do with differentiation and separation from the preoedipal mother in the transference was regularly signaled throughout the analysis by Joseph appearing with a book or magazine. The same sequence was present in Darius's treatment and, as the analysis progressed, could be interpreted in relation to conflicts of independence from mother.

At different times Darius brought in a steady supply of books which he had discovered but mostly rediscovered at home. Sometimes as he sat and talked, he merely held, dropped, retrieved, and fondled them, as he had done with his gloves. At other times, he withdrew into reading them when transference feelings, either positive or negative, became too strong. This observation would be consonant with another function associated with transitional phenomena—the protection of an affectively charged object from the drives by providing a safe target for drive discharge. With Darius, as mentioned earlier, this reading behavior could in part be traced to experiences of being read to by his mother in his second year of life. It involved an identification with his mother (who appeared to use reading to modulate her own drives), but also carried with it a more primary cathexis of the reading material itself as a transitional mode. This reconstruction from early adolescence suggests the way in which transitional object formation may be facilitated by adults in the surround, an aspect not emphasized but implied by Winnicott.

Joseph subsequently told me that bringing books to the analytic sessions was related to "having something with me to hide in, you know?" It was certainly that, but also much more. It was an indication of the advent (he did not always bring books to the analysis, only at a certain time) of his therapeutic alliance with me. In early adolescence the transference of an admixture of repressed erotic impulses and generally affectionate feelings (Freud, 1912) can appear in the cloak of negative feelings such as provocation and denunciation of the analyst and in apparent opposition to the analytic intent: "See, I don't have to talk, I can withdraw into reading or by reading to you." This rejoinder occurred when the reading was in fact an action metaphor for a developmentally confused positive attachment that borrowed important characteristics from the earlier transitional object experience.

Other important aspects of these situations should be mentioned. Often a defense against passive homosexual urges was prominent in the process. These were handled by reversals. At the same time that Darius read to me, the denied, feared, and yearned-for closeness would be played out in the transference in reverse—the patient as "parent," reading to the analyst "child." When looked at in a certain light, the tirades, angers, and actions of Darius and Joseph were often in reverse, subtly undoing, soothing, and obsessional.

With puberty, then, the adolescent's ego is presented with a challenge, the outcome of which will be heavily determined by the nature of previous adaptations to growth stress. With the pubescent upsurge of thinly veiled oedipal fantasies, there may be a rapid regression to preoedipal impulses and fantasies.

On the other side of the conflict, we may see the inclination to leap into adulthood. About a year after we commenced analysis, Joseph's mother had a birthday for which he bought her a birthday card. The message of the card indicated that she should not feel badly about aging because she was still "X-rated," which for Joseph meant sexually active and sexually attractive, something he feared in himself. As he became aware of the oedipal implications of his card, he became quite upset, angry, and denying. He entered the next session sucking on a vanilla milk shake and talking incessantly about when he would win his next athletic competition. He carried the belt from his Karate uniform. He finished his milk shake, and as he talked he rolled, unrolled, twisted, and pulled at this belt, marveling at its strength and indestructibility. (He had previously characterized the belt as something that could never be taken away.) It seemed clear that Joseph was partially immersing his oedipal feelings in toddler-based psychological activities of an oral and transitional type. The descriptions of the belt and the manner in which he used it seemed to provide plentiful indications of the transitional qualities with which it was imbued. In his fantasies, Karate and the various belts would (like analysis) provide an absorbing substitute for his parents (particularly his mother) while at the same time hold-

ing out the possibility of being rejoined with them through the
perfection he hoped to attain through Karate.

Another marker of the developing analytic alliance with the
rebellious early adolescent may sometimes be found in observing how he or she uses the analyst's office, the analytic "mi-
lieu." At certain points, both Darius and Joseph treated the
consulting room as an intermediate area between patient and
analyst, a space with transitional qualities. Winnicott (1958)
made the point that the "good enough" mother facilitates the
child's use of this intermediate area even when the child is
physically close, sitting on mother's lap. The experience with
adolescents suggests that they may use the analyst's room as a
parental lap. The adolescent often sits and playfully or teas-
ingly puts his feet on tables and walls, moves his chair around,
or leaps up in an attempt to jump and touch the ceiling. All
the while he talks to the wind, seemingly engaged in being
alone/together on the parent's lap. He treats the room as "not
me" one minute, and "me" the next. He dirties, despoils,
marks up, litters, and scuffs feet on walls. In the next instant,
he may be lovingly comparing the analyst's office to his own
room in size, shape, furnishings, and in fantasies about rede-
corating, cleaning, or repainting both of them. Early adolescents may become quite distressed if they feel they have actually marked up a wall with their feet. This seems to go beyond
obsessional concern. If they have torn a drape they habitually
twist, pick at, and periodically examine for wear and tear,
there often follows a series of guilty undoing statements which
are puzzling as they seem out of affective continuity and the
associational context. The analyst's thinking of the meeting
space as a possible transitional area for the early adolescent
may then provide further clues as to the development of a
transference alliance.

Adolescents are often in desperate conflict about wanting
and not wanting to make psychological contact with an adult
who in their eyes already has parental colorings, but who is
also attractive as a new nonparental object-in-the-making.
Both Joseph and Darius used to interrupt their tirades against
dishonest and enslaving adults to ask me whether I had seen a

certain TV program or movie. This question often appeared after I had been absent. While it could not be understood in the early phase of their analyses, later on it became possible to understand that this question carried with it a fantasy in which the patient, in reality apart from the analyst, was together with him by engaging in similar fantasy-oriented activities. By sharing something fantastic or artistic at a distance and through a transitional medium, the compelling loneliness and estrangement of this developmental phase would be decreased. The early tentative and guarded queries about TV shows which the analyst *might* have watched (although the patient thinks it is *highly* unlikely!), or about books he may have read or records he may have heard, have the function of fixing the analyst in the world as a new nonparental object and simultaneously incorporating him into the patient's fantasy world. Depending on the response, the teen-age patient may be able to say that the analyst is or is not like him, is or is not like his parents, thereby beginning to integrate a new object relationship.

In the beginning of an adolescent analysis, the analyst's tactful answer may facilitate the placing of the analyst in the world as a new object who has or has not seen certain TV shows, movies, etc. The analyst is then differentiated sufficiently from the parents to allow the later development of a transference focused around oedipal issues. This alliance also enables the adolescent to establish transitional processes which through illusion and fantasy buffer the thrust which in adolescence is away from both parents, not just mother. When Darius found out that I was interested in certain kinds of music, he interrupted his angry tirades to bring in tape cassettes with this music recorded on them and a cassette recorder. With great seriousness and ceremony he would then place the tape recorder between us and proceed to play it quietly as we talked over, above, through, and about the music. It became a filter with transitional qualities which made our contact less "parental" as well as more tolerable, because he had more control. It also replicated his use of music at home where it served to soothe and reassure him in his growing parental estrangement.

In the early phase of treatment, the younger adolescent tends to see the analyst as an agent of the parents, as a spying, intrusive, superego force. He is also seen as a stranger, a threatening representative of the foreign outside world of adults. Transitional phenomena (book or whatever) then become a protection from this stranger and strangeness which the boy sees in the analyst. But they also become, as I just indicated, a way of linking with the analyst (if he knows a particular book, magazine item) because the items brought in are usually viewed as parent alien. They allow the start on some level of a positive relationship which is new. In other words, the therapist has a chance of "being created" in the sense that transitional objects are created as a reassuring enduring presence—not yet a real person, but something of a part object, more illusory and yet more under the teen-ager's control. Now the young adolescent may begin to work out more safely the often incendiary intrapsychic conflicts which prompt analysis at this difficult age. In early adolescence we may be able to see on the surface some of what in the toddler period are silent unconscious processes related to the formation of transitional objects and phenomena. From the younger adolescent's perspective, transitional object formation is far from the neutralized ego activity, free of drive pressure and discharge as Winnicott described it, but much more laden with erotic and aggressive impulses. In times of stress and anger, both Darius and Joseph used gum in this way—as something soft yet indestructible to chew on furiously. Many other materials may be similarly enlisted and invested with transitional meaning.

SUMMARY

This paper attempts to identify some of the aspects of the analysis of early adolescents which may help the analyst to observe and respond to the emergence of erotic and nonerotic positive transference elements in the often bewildering welter of negativity and defiance which these patients bring to treatment. Winnicott's concept of a transitional process occurring in the "intermediate area" between inner and outer reality can be helpful in ascertaining the potential for, and the gradual development of, an analytic alliance. It follows that from the point of view of analytic technique with younger adolescents, the preponderance of affectively charged preoedipal material often must be dealt with before the patient can use interpretations of the more obvious but threatening oedipal elements. Paying attention to the presence or absence of these elements and gauging the feeling level associated with them may provide the analyst with important data by which to assess the strength of the analytic alliance and by which he can be guided in the choice of what to interpret.

BIBLIOGRAPHY

Blos, P. (1962), *On Adolescence*. New York: Free Press of Glencoe.
——— (1976), The Split Parental Imago in Adolescent Social Relations. *This Annual*, 31 : 7–33.
Casuso, G. (1965), Panel Report: The Relationship between Child Analysis and the Theory and Practice of Adult Psychoanalysis. *J. Amer. Psychoanal. Assn.*, 13 : 159–171.
Eissler, K. R. (1958), Notes on Problems of Technique in the Psychoanalytic Treatment of Adolescents. *This Annual*, 13 : 223–254.
Fraiberg, S. (1955), Some Considerations in the Introduction to Therapy in Puberty. *This Annual*, 10 : 264–286.
Freud, A. (1958), Adolescence. *This Annual*, 13 : 255–278.
Freud, S. (1905), Three Essays on the Theory of Sexuality. *S. E.*, 7 : 125–243.
——— (1912), The Dynamics of Transference. *S. E.*, 12 : 97–108.
——— (1914), Remembering, Repeating and Working Through. *S. E.*, 12 : 145–156.
——— (1924), Negation. *S. E.*, 19 : 235–239.
Greenacre, P. (1959), Play in Relation to Creative Imagination. *This Annual*, 14 : 61–80.
Harley, M. (1970), On Some Problems of Technique in the Analysis of Early Adolescents. *This Annual*, 25 : 99–121.
——— ed. (1974), *The Analyst and the Adolescent at Work*. New York: Quadrangle.
Jones, E. (1922), Some Problems of Adolescence. In: *Papers on Psycho-Analysis*. London: Ballière, Tindall, and Cox, 1938, pp. 500–518.
Laufer, M. (1976), The Central Masturbation Fantasy, the Final Sexual Organization, and Adolescence. *This Annual*, 31 : 297–316.

46 T. Wayne Downey

LOEWALD, H. W. (1977), In Panel: Conceptualizing the Nature of the Therapeutic Action of Psychoanalysis. Fall Meeting, American Psychoanalytic Association.
MAENCHEN, A. (1970), On the Technique of Child Analysis in Relation to Stages of Development. *This Annual,* 25 : 175–208.
WINNICOTT, D. W. (1953), Transitional Objects and Transitional Phenomena. In: *Collected Papers.* New York: Basic Books, 1958, pp. 229–242.
——— (1958), The Capacity to Be Alone. In: *The Maturational Processes and the Facilitating Environment.* New York: Int. Univ. Press, 1965, pp. 29–36.
——— (1971), *Playing and Reality.* New York: Basic Books, pp. 1–25.

The Transitional Phenomena

A Theoretical Integration

K. MICHAEL HONG, M.D.

"THE COMMONPLACE AND THE EVERDAY HAS ONCE AGAIN proved exciting in its implications. The diversity and richness of individual experience, which yet comes within the terms 'normality' can never fail to challenge the student of psychology" (Stevenson, 1954, p. 216). Ordinary, everyday events provide us with many subjects for research. The phenomenon popularly known as the "security blanket," or "Linus blanket," and as the "transitional object" in the scientific literature, represents one such opportunity.

Like many discoveries in the behavioral sciences, investigations of these rather common phenomena in the Western culture were initiated by psychoanalytic writers. Although Wulff (1946) first reported this phenomenon, conceiving of it as a fetish, it was Winnicott (1953) who systematically described it and coined the terms, "transitional object" and "transitional phenomena." His theoretical constructs were a landmark in understanding the developmental process of object differentiation. His article was so comprehensive and so profoundly insightful that subsequent psychoanalytic publications have

Assistant Professor at the Division of Child and Adolescent Psychiatry, Department of Psychiatry, University of Minnesota.

I wish to thank Dr. Gerald B. Olch and Dr. Nathaniel J. London for their invaluable advice and Dr. Lawrence M. Greenberg and Dr. William Hausman for their assistance.

been little more than expansions and refinements of his propositions, with the exception of Tolpin's (1971). By applying
Kohut's (1971) idea of "transmuting internalization," she proposed the hypothesis that transitional objects play an important role in the process of separation-individuation and in establishing a cohesive self.

The phenonemon of transitional objects has been discussed
from every conceivable angle, yet a critical examination of the
vast literature reveals that several crucial issues remain unresolved. First, there are diverse and often contradictory findings regarding the nature and the meaning of this phenomenon. Various functions and different significances in child
development were described and postulated, but no integration was attempted. Second, although psychoanalytic, experimental, and ethological writers seemingly study the same phenomenon, the extreme paucity of collaborative efforts and
cross-references is as striking as the lack of theoretical integration. Even the terms they use are different: "transitional objects" by psychoanalytic writers; "security blanket" by experimental researchers; "substitute objects" by ethologists. Third,
according to Winnicott, the transitional object always partakes
of mother and in part stands for her. However, there is a controversy among later investigators whether the blanket is simply a "mother substitute" or "transitional object." Fourth,
there is confusion in the use of the terms "transitional object"
and "transitional phenomena." The introduction of the term
"primary transitional object" by Busch et al. (1973) created
another debate over the necessity for categorizing the phenomena (Gaddini, 1975). Unclear definition of, and lack of
distinction between, the terms are partially responsible for the
confusion in the current literature. Fifth, recent cross-cultural
studies delineated the crucial role of tactile experience and
made it possible to reinterpret the meaning of the transitional
object in relation to attachment.

In this article I review the pertinent psychoanalytic, experimental, ethological, and cross-cultural investigations to
address the issues described above and to attempt a theoretical
integration as well as a classification of the transitional phe-

nomenon. While I recognize the difficulty and complexity of this endeavor as well as the differences among various theoretical positions, these are not the focus of this paper. I examine the similar and complementary aspects of different theoretical approaches in order to obtain a better understanding of this phenomenon.

REVIEW OF THE LITERATURE

PSYCHOANALYTIC LITERATURE

Winnicott's (1953) main contribution was the recognition of the transitional phenomena that occur during the transitional stage from nondifferentiation to differentiation of "me"-"not me," from a baby's inability to growing ability to recognize and accept reality. These phenomena are particularly noticeable during the transition from waking to sleep. He defined the transitional phenomenon as "an intermediate area of *experiencing,* to which inner reality and external life both contribute" (p. 90). The transitional object is "the first not-me possession" and "not part of the infant's body, yet [it is] not fully recognized as belonging to external reality." Winnicott's definition of transitional phenomena was quite broad and included many objects—possessions—such as blankets, stuffed animals, or other cuddly toys, as well as various songs and tunes while preparing to go to sleep. He stated that mother herself can be a transitional object. He regarded transitional phenomena as "universal and healthy."

Although Stevenson (1954) found no difficulty in obtaining many examples of the "first treasured possession," only a few studies of *the incidence* of the transitional object in the normal population have been made. According to the available reports (Gaddini, 1970; Busch et al., 1973; Hong and Townes, 1976), over 50 percent of the infants of primarily Anglo-Saxon culture have transitional objects.

In the opinion of different authors (Winnicott, 1953; Stevenson, 1954; Bowlby, 1969; Rudhe and Ekecrantz, 1974), the *onset* of the development of transitional object varies greatly from 1 month to 3 years. Using a rigorous definition, Busch et al. (1973) maintain that the attachment to a soft, malleable, cuddly object, such as a blanket, usually occurs between 6 to 9 months of age. This finding was supported by a cross-cultural study by Hong and Townes (1976). In contrast, the attachment to stuffed animals tends to occur in the second and third years (Stevenson, 1954; Busch et al., 1973; Hong and Townes, 1976).

Only two studies on the *length of attachment* to transitional objects have been available. Busch et al. (1973) reported that 10 percent of 2-year-olds were "weaned" from the blanket attachment at the time of their study, and Hong and Townes (1976) reported 3⅓ years as a mean duration of blanket attachment with frequent extension into the fifth year. Rudhe and Ekecrantz (1974) found that half of their subjects (6- to 7-year-olds) still displayed transitional phenomena.

The apparent differences in the reported incidence, onset, and duration of the child's attachment to a special object seem to be the result of different definitions of transitional objects, the selection of different objects for study, and unclear distinctions between transitional phenomenon and transitional object. (This will be discussed in detail in the section on classification of transitional phenomena.)

Transitional objects are *used* primarily at bedtime, at naptime, and periods of distress and tiredness, "inactivity," and on extended trips (Busch et al., 1973). When the transitional object is not available, the child becomes upset and is either inconsolable or shows extreme uneasiness and anxiety. Sometimes nothing can substitute for it, and even the mother cannot console the child (Busch et al., 1973). Most frequently children hold or embrace the object, and half of them suck their thumb or the blanket itself (Hong and Townes, 1976). Transitional objects are often used to stroke the face and are kept close to the face while sleeping. Thus, it seems that the transitional object is used mainly in a *tactile* fashion (Busch, 1974; Hong and Townes, 1976), the tactile quality of the object and the tactile gratification it provides being the most decisive factors (Busch et al., 1973; Gaddini, 1975). The importance of smell (Winnicott, 1953; Greenacre, 1969) was not supported by extensive observations (Busch et al., 1973; Busch, 1974). Finally, these objects are rarely handled in an aggressive manner and are rarely abused by the infant (Busch et al., 1973) but rather are treated as "treasured possessions" (Stevenson, 1954).

Various *functions* served by the transitional object have been observed and described. They include soothing and comforting and decrease and regulation of anxiety. It has also been postulated that the transitional object may be symbolic of part objects, such as the breast, mother, and reunion with the mother (Busch et al., 1973; Gaddini, 1970; Greenacre, 1969; Tolpin, 1971; Winnicott, 1953). The common element in all these speculations is that the transitional object either is equated with or symbolically represents the mother or certain functional properties of the mother.

Winnicott (1953) suggested that the transitional phenomenon plays an important role in the illusion-disillusionment process in *ego development.* Most mothers actively adapt to the infant's needs and provide the infant the opportunity for the "illusion" that her breast is part of the infant by placing the actual breast just there where the infant needs it. Thus, the infant creates the breast over and over again (illusion) out of his need. The mother's main task is disillusionment (reality acceptance). In this transitional period from illusion to disillusion, the infant feels the strain of the simultaneous impact of inner and outer reality. Relief from this strain is provided by an intermediate area of experience in which the transitional object represents continuity between the infant and the world. Many authors emphasize that the transitional object is the first step toward independence and ego autonomy in normal development. Coppolillo (1967, 1976) states that the transitional object and the transitional mode of experience are necessary elements in mediating the formation of ego structures and insuring the ego's optimal autonomy from id and environment. Greenacre (1969) postulated that the transitional object is a temporary construction to aid the infant in the development of a sense of reality and individual identity. Busch

(1974) views transitional objects as mediating "assistants" which lead to the development of psychic structure and self-soothing mechanisms.

The most innovative idea on the importance of the transitional object in ego development was proposed by Tolpin (1971). She described the infant's perception of his mother as the chief instrument of his sense of well-being and relief from distress during the symbiotic state. By creating transitional objects during this stage, the infant "has endowed his blanket with her soothing and tension-relieving functions. The formation of the transitional object thus enables the infant at an early age to begin to achieve a certain degree of independence from the mother by virtue of his own mental activities" (p. 321) and begin to form intrapsychic "soothing and anxiety-regulating structure." Contrary to Winnicott's statement (1953) that transitional objects simply lose their meaning when the child develops interest in other social activities and that they do not "go inside," Tolpin states that the soothing and anxiety-regulating functions of the blanket "go inside"—are *internalized*—as a mental structure and become part of the matrix of the ego. She says:

> When the infantile psyche "transfers" the mother's narcissistically cathected soothing functions to the blanket, this inanimate object becomes the treasured "not-me" possession that preserves the soothing effect of the lost symbiotic merger. With the blanket formed by this transferencelike process the child can dose himself with more soothing than even the "good enough" mother can provide. By re-creating the merger and the maternal functions on which it depends the psyche establishes an auxiliary pathway for the acquisition of tension-reducing mental structure [p. 347].

Thus, she argued that the transitional object becomes an "auxiliary soother" by innumerable minute internalizations and evolves into a self-soothing psychic structure. She concludes that through this process, transitional objects assist the infant in the work of separation-individuation toward establishing a cohesive self.

Little is known about the *etiological factors* in the development of the transitional object. What makes certain children and not others develop an attachment to blankets? Is it truly universal, as Winnicott suggested? The psychoanalytic literature gives only indirect clues to certain factors related to the development of the transitional object. Provence and Lipton (1962) report that deprived institutionalized infants do not develop any attachment to cuddly toys or blankets. A few such babies who were favorites of particular nurses and developed a personal relationship with the nurses, however, did show more interest in toys. The authors conclude that the interest of infants in toys is built upon the relationship to the mothering person.[1] Similarly, Winnicott suggests that "the intermediate transitional mode of experience" is necessary for the initiation of a relationship between the infant and the world and is made possible by "good enough" mothering. Stevenson (1954) speculates further that "conspicuous lack of any transitional object may be an indication of a deviation away from the normal" (p. 207). Thus, many authors seem to agree that physical or tactile contact is very important in the development of the transitional object and that this development is contingent upon the infant's "good enough" relationship with the mother. Both Winnicott and Bowlby (1969) state that the transitional object is an indication of a healthy mother-child relationship. In support of the healthy aspect of transitional phenomena, Horton et al. (1973) reported that the majority (17 of 19) of study subjects with severe personality disorders gave no evidence of childhood use of transitional objects and all of them were lacking "transitional relatedness."

While most authors agree that the transitional phenomenon is normal and part of ego development, several investigators have commented on the possible *pathological implications.* Wulff

1. Schaffer and Emerson (1964) reported that among 37 infants (19 cuddlers, 9 noncuddlers, and 9 intermediates), 10 of the cuddlers, in contrast to only 1 of noncuddlers, developed attachments to cuddly toys. They conclude that the more contact a child receives, the more he is likely to show other sensual responses. Rudhe and Ekecrantz (1974) also report that the more physical contact between the child and the mother during the first year, the more probable is the occurrence of transitional phenomena.

conceived of it as an infantile fetish. Winnicott also alluded that this phenomenon would help in the understanding of addiction, fetish phenomena, pseudologia, and thieving. Dickes (1963) and Sperling (1963) consider the transitional object to be definitely pathological and related to fetishism. Greenacre (1969) discussed the similarity and difference between the fetish and transitional object. Bak (1974) clarifies much of the confusion of terms and concludes that "infantile fetish" is a misnomer for transitional object, although the latter may acquire different meanings and functions, such as fetishistic element, in later developmental phase. Modell (1963) speculated that the borderline patient's object relations are arrested at the stage of the transitional object. Fintzy (1971) described the vicissitudes of transitional objects in borderline children and suggested that a history of prolonged attachment to a transitional object should make one consider this diagnosis.[2] He also believes that in borderline patients the transitional object does not disappear but merely becomes disguised in the form of shifting transitional objects. Obviously persistence of the transitional object beyond its "normal" age- and phase-inappropriate use would indicate the possibility of psychopathology. However, more empirical investigations are needed before the concept of transitional object is applied to psychopathology.

EXPERIMENTAL STUDIES

Although attachments to special objects are rather common, experimental studies did not appear until the 1970s. Castell (1970) reported that nonsocial objects alone did not reduce arousal of children. Gershaw and Schwartz (1971) studied the effect of familiar toys and the mother's presence on the exploratory and attachment behaviors of young children. They found that when the mother was absent, the infant had

2. A caution is required to interpret what is "prolonged" attachment. Fintzy's patient was 5½ years old, which is not an unusual age for retaining the transitional object. According to Busch et al. (1973), Rudhe and Ekecrantz (1974), and Hong and Townes (1976), significant proportions of normal children of 5 and 6 maintain their attachments to the blanket.

greater distress, which was not reduced by the presence of familiar or novel toys. However, neither one of these studies used blankets or cuddly objects in the experiments and did not distinguish between preferred and attachment toys. Weisberg and Russell (1971) were the first investigators to study blanket attachment in an experimental setting. They studied proximity-seeking behaviors and interactional responses when a group of young children were exposed to their own blankets, novel foam cushions, unfamiliar blankets, and familiar toys. The proximity-seeking and interactional behaviors were highest toward their own blankets when both mother and blanket were available. In 1975, Passman and Weisberg carried out a well-designed experimental study with 64 children, half of whom were attached to a blanket. They studied the effects of the presence of the mother, the blanket, a favorite toy, and no object, in a novel play setting. Throughout the study, the presence of the blanket had a similar effect on the performance of the blanket-attached children as that of the presence of the mother. The blanket-attached children explored and played without distress when the blanket or mother was available, whereas children who had a favorite toy or no object played significantly less. The presence of the mother and the blanket postponed the distress behavior more effectively than did the other conditions. Passman and Weisberg conclude that the mother and the blanket shared similar functional properties in reducing fearfulness and generating exploration and play. Moreover, the important factor in promoting security or reducing arousal was not familiarity with the object but rather that the blanket and mother acted as *attachment objects*. In summary, experimental studies indicate that there are differences between an attachment object and preferred toy and that the blanket and the mother serve similar functions such as decreasing anxiety and facilitating exploratory and play behaviors.

ETHOLOGICAL AND CROSS-CULTURAL STUDIES

I believe that the findings of Harlow and his associates (1958, 1970), on the attachment of monkeys to terrycloth surrogate mothers, provide some understanding of the attachment of the human infant to inanimate objects. Monkeys, reared in isolated cages, developed an attachment to terrycloth mother surrogates, and it was found that body contact was of overriding importance in the development of affectional responsiveness. Other variables such as lactation, different faces, motion, and temperature were less important than "contact comfort." Surrogate terrycloth mothers apparently provided enough emotional security to enable infant monkeys to explore strange situations and manipulate physical and animate objects. Similarly, Ainsworth and Bell (1970) report that human infants explore more and play more in the presence of mother.

Bowlby (1969) states that attachment behavior is a biologically and evolutionally based behavior system and defines it as proximity-seeking and contact-maintaining behaviors directed toward the mother or her substitute. He describes five main components of attachment behavior: clinging, sucking, crying, smiling, and following. Since these behaviors are biologically based, they are instinctively directed toward a substitute if the natural object is not available. For example, nonnutritive sucking is sometimes directed toward a pacifier or bottle, and clinging can be directed toward soft objects like blankets or cuddly toys. Thus, in societies in which the infant spends most of his time in close contact with the mother, attachment behavior to an inanimate object would be less likely to occur. Bowlby claims that this phenomenon is infant attachment to "objects towards which certain components of attachment behaviour come to be directed or redirected because the 'natural' object is unavailable" (p. 312). He suggested the term "substitute object" rather than "transitional object" to clarify the situation.

Despite Bowlby's suggestion that the incidence of attachment to inanimate objects would be lower in a simpler society where the infant has a greater amount of physical contact with the mother, studies of the blanket attachment have been limited to the Western culture, more specifically, to the United States and England. Only two cross-cultural studies have been reported in the literature.

Gaddini's work (1970) was a psychoanalytic study by intention and by interpretation, but it was an excellent cross-cultural study by design. She studied 1,184 children of three social groups in Italy: rural Italian children; Italian children in Rome; and foreign children mostly of Anglo-Saxon origin, in Rome. She found that 4.9 percent of the rural group, 31.1 percent of the Rome group, and 61.5 percent of the foreign children developed an attachment to a transitional object.

Similar results were obtained in our study (Hong and Townes, 1976) of 279 children of three different cultural groups: Korean children in Korea, Korean children who were born and reared in the United States, and American children. We found that 54 percent of American children developed an attachment to the blanket, in comparison to 18 percent of Korean children in Korea and 34 percent of Korean children reared in the United States.

The results of these two cross-cultural studies can be accounted for by the major differences in child-rearing practices in the following areas: (1) *Sleeping arrangements.* Most of the American and Anglo-Saxon infants sleep alone in separate rooms, whereas most of the Italian and Korean infants sleep in the same room with the mother who is available throughout the night. (2) *Going to sleep pattern.* While most American and Anglo infants go to sleep alone, the Italian mothers did more rocking and lulling of the infants at bedtime than the Anglo-Saxon group. Similarly, the Korean mothers patted, rocked, caressed, and even nursed the infants to sleep, and stayed with the infants until they were completely asleep. (3) *Breast feeding.* The Italian groups had higher rates of breast feeding than the Anglo group, and the Korean infants were breast-fed longer than American infants. (4) *Physical contact.* The number of hours of direct baby care was significantly higher in the Korean group than in the American group, and the Korean mothers seemed to provide more intense and frequent physical contact to infants than American mothers. We therefore concluded that attachment phenomena toward an inanimate object appear to be closely associated with child-rearing practices, and that the incidence of infant's attachment to inanimate objects is inversely related to the amount of physical contact.

Discussion

Since the blanket attachment appears to be a prototype of all transitional phenomena as well as the focus of most studies, this discussion first examines the characteristics of this particular transitional object and then transitional phenomena in general. In my use of the blanket, I also include its equivalents such as a bit of cloth, sheet, or diaper. *Blanket attachment* is used interchangeably with the primary transitional object as defined by Busch et al. (1973) and does *not* include teddy bears or other soft toys.

THE IMPORTANCE OF PHYSICAL CONTACT IN DEVELOPMENT

Increasingly, knowledge gained from animal experiments and observations is used to understand the nature of the human mother-infant tie. Moreover, the cross-cultural and ethological approaches have emerged as a bridge between animal and human psychology by demonstrating a continuum in many behavioral systems from animals, particularly the primate, to "primitive" and finally to "civilized" men. Bowlby's (1969) extensive review of primate studies, including Goodall's work (1965), indicates that clinging and physical contact are the integral parts of attachment behavior in subhuman primates in natural environments. Similarly, in experimental settings, Harlow and his associates (1958, 1970) repeatedly found "contact comfort" to be very important in the development of attachment behavior. Cairns (1966) also indicated the importance of tactile stimulation in the development of attachment in his subprimate animal study.

Most ethologists agree that the mother-infant tie in humans should also be understood as an attachment bond based on biological and instinctual behavior systems. Ainsworth (1963) studied the maternal behaviors contributing to the development of "secure attachment" in Uganda children and empha-

sized "frequent and sustained physical contact" as most important in the development of attachment. Bowlby (1969)
described clinging as a biological need and an essential component of attachment behavior in human infants.

The importance of physical contact in infant development
was recognized by a number of psychoanalytic writers, including Escalona (1953), Greenacre (1960), Provence and Ritvo
(1961), Shevrin and Toussieng (1965). Other authors (Winnicott, 1960; Call, 1968; Mahler, 1967) also pointed to the important role of "holding" in establishing a sense of love and security. These views were supported by a number of
experimental and learning theorists. Murphy (1962) found
that physical contact with mother reduced the tension and
fear produced by strange situations and permitted exploration
and other coping behavior to occur. Similarly, Mason (1967)
reported that clinging reduced the arousal of young chimpanzees. Gewirtz (1961) and Bijou and Baer (1965) agree that tactile stimulation is an unlearned behavior (primary reinforcer)
rather than a secondarily acquired learned behavior.

Thus, regardless of theoretical positions, physical contact
and tactile stimulation appear to be primary needs of the infant and play a crucial role in the infant's development (Hong,
1975).

IS THE BLANKET A SUBSTITUTE FOR THE MOTHER OR A TRANSITIONAL OBJECT?

Bowlby's (1969) substitute model seems to be supported by the
cross-cultural findings. Previously, Provence et al. (1961, 1962)
considered the attachment object as a specific substitute for
the mother in that it reproduces the sensation of contact with
the mother. In contrast, Tolpin (1971) and Rudhe and Ekecrantz (1974) opposed the Bowlby view. However, the substance of the argument is more apparent than real since the
conflicts stem from the lack of recognition that different
aspects of the same phenomenon are being studied (Hong,
1975). Ethological and cross-cultural investigators focus on the
origin of the blanket attachment in relation to the infant's con-

tact need; most of the psychoanalytic writers are interested primarily in the *intrapsychic* significance of this phenomenon in the process of ego development; and experimental investigators study the demonstrable *functional properties* of the blanket. Thus, the blanket attachment can be interpreted as both a substitute for the mother and as a transitional object. Both interpretations are valid ways of considering the same behavior and the different theoretical positions enrich the understanding of this phenomenon.

ETIOLOGICAL FACTORS IN THE DEVELOPMENT OF BLANKET ATTACHMENT

It appears, then, that blanket attachment is based on the *contact need* of the infant and emerges out of the infant's need to cope with the stress during the transitional period when the mother is not available. However, we must examine other variables in the development of blanket attachment.

Whether blanket attachment represents a biologically based contact-seeking behavior released by the mother-infant relation (ethological view) or a transitional step in ego development (psychoanalytic view), it can be assumed that the infant's "good enough" relationship (attachment) with the mother is a prerequisite for the blanket attachment. Indeed, Provence et al. (1961, 1962) reported that deprived institutionalized infants did not develop attachment to cuddly objects, and that interest in toys was dependent upon the relationship with mother. Schaffer and Emerson (1964) note that contact need varies considerably and suggest that constitutional factors play a role in determining the occurrence of attachment to cuddly objects. Some infants seem to prefer other means of maintaining contact with mother, including verbal reassurance and visual contact. Rheingold (1969) also emphasizes the importance of vision and hearing in the child's maintenance of close contact with the mother.

It is not only the infant who needs and seeks out the "contact comfort," but the mother may also have such a need (Schaffer and Emerson, 1964). Like the infants', the mothers' need for and attitudes to physical contact vary considerably, reflecting individual as well as cultural differences. Bowlby (1969) states that the amount of physical contact between the infant and mother varies according to the culture, reflecting an "evolutionary continuum" in attachment. Ainsworth's (1963) work and the cross-cultural study by Caudill and Schooler (1973) substantiate Bowlby's observation. Ainsworth reports an intense and sustained physical contact between mother and infant in Uganda. Caudill and Schooler report that the American mother deemphasizes the importance of physical contact and uses more vocal communication, while the Japanese mother places more importance on physical contact and less on vocal communication. Hence, the intensity and amount of physical contact the infant receives seem to be a function of both constitutional factors and maternal responsiveness and attitude to physical contact, the latter being much more influenced by cultural variables.

Certainly, learning plays an important role in forming and maintaining attachment behavior to the blanket. The blanket has some advantages over mother. The blanket never scolds, spanks, or neglects, and is more controllable and manipulable than mother. It is available whenever it is needed (Passman and Weisberg, 1975). As Piaget (1936) emphasizes, infants are always trying to learn how to bring their environment under their control and to come out as winners. Control of the blanket gives a greater sense of accomplishment and competence (White, 1963); this reinforces the attachment to the blanket, which sometimes cannot be "substituted" for by mother (Busch, 1974; Rudhe and Ekecrantz, 1974).

A CLASSIFICATION OF TRANSITIONAL PHENOMENA

Thus far, I have discussed only the blanket and its equivalents in relation to physical contact need. How does it differ from the other transitional phenomena?

When Winnicott (1953) introduced the terms transitional phenomena and transitional object, he did not clearly differentiate them. Later investigators have used the terms sometimes interchangeably and without making clear distinctions. This resulted in confusion and misuse of the terms. The implication is that caution is required to compare any two studies since they might have studied different objects and different phenomena. Therefore, there is a need to categorize the transitional phenomena and at least to clarify the terminology and the relationship between different transitional phenomena.

Stevenson (1954) described several examples of progression from a "primary" object (the blanket) to "secondary" objects (toys) and postulated that in many instances the first transitional objects or "object equivalent" passed unrecognized by the parents. This distinction was neglected until Busch et al. restated the distinction between primary and secondary transitional objects. Busch et al. (1973) proposed a more rigid definition of "primary transitional objects" based on six criteria: (1) attachment should be manifested within the first year of life; (2) attachment should be of lasting duration, usually more than one year; (3) the object must be soothing and bring about a decrease in anxiety; (4) the primary transitional object should be distinguished from objects which directly meet an oral libidinal need, such as bottle or pacifier; (5) the object should be discovered and chosen by the infant; (6) the object should be distinct from parts of the infant's and the mother's body; and the object, usually soft or malleable, should have been closely associated with the infant since birth. The "secondary transitional objects" are qualitatively different; usually soft toys, they appear in the second year of life or later, and meet different developmental needs. This proposal met with strong objections from Gaddini (1975), who asserted that the distinction between the primary and secondary objects was quantitative rather than qualitative in character. Coppolillo (1976) also believed that these distinctions were too restrictive and unproductive. Busch himself, in a subsequent publication (1974), abandoned this terminology, emphasizing that "the psychologically important element is not the [first or second] object but the attachment" (p. 217).

However, consideration of cross-cultural studies, ethological views, and experimental findings has led to a reinterpretation of the transitional object as an attachment object and to the following classification of transitional phenomena in terms of differential characteristics (see table 1).

Transitional phenomena encompass all the phenomena occurring during various transitional periods and providing the transitional mode of experience (Coppolillo, 1967, 1976) and the intermediate area of experiencing inner and outer reality. They include all the terms which Winnicott originally described, such as sounds, movements, objects or thoughts, and even mother herself.

Transitional object equivalents comprise the majority of the transitional phenomena, except the transitional object proper; they include sounds such as babblings, "mummum"; lullaby, songs, and tunes; rocking and rhythmic movement; mother's patting and rubbing the baby; all the rituals and habits while preparing for sleep; and the mother herself (Winnicott, 1953; Coppolillo, 1967; McDonald, 1970; Gaddini, 1970; Rudhe and Ekecrantz, 1974). They differ from the transitional object proper by their earlier onset (early part of the first year), broader repertoire, universal incidence, nonmaterial entity, and involvement in the earliest stage of ego differentiation. Their major role appears to be assisting the developing infantile ego by serving as a bridge between the infant and the outside reality ("me"-"not me"). These are the most primitive forms of transitional phenomena; they are provided largely by external sources and are still beyond the infant's control compared to transitional objects.

Transitional object is, by definition, only one of the many transitional phenomena and should not be equated with them. Although originally all soft cuddly objects such as blanket or teddy bear were included (Winnicott, 1953; Stevenson, 1954; Gaddini, 1970), the rationale for dividing the transitional objects into two categories is apparent (Stevenson, 1954; Provence and Ritvo, 1961; Busch et al., 1973; Passman and Weisberg, 1975; Hong and Townes, 1976).

Primary transitional object includes only soft, malleable, more or less amorphous, cuddly objects such as a blanket, a sheet, a bit of cloth, and a diaper (Busch et al., 1973). The primary

Table 1
Transitional Phenomena

Characteristics	Transitional Object Equivalents	Transitional Objects	
		Primary	Secondary
Description	Lullabies, songs & tunes; babbling, other sounds; rocking and rhythmic movements; patting and rubbing the baby; other rituals and habits at bedtime (mother, pacifier, thumb)	Blanket a bit of sheet, a bit of cloth, diaper	Stuffed animals, soft dolls and toys, possibly hard toys
Materials	Nonmaterial	Amorphous, soft, malleable	Definite forms and shapes
Manipulability and control by infant	Least	Most	Intermediate
Onset	First 6 months	Second 6 months	2nd and 3rd year
Degree of attachment	None	Strong (attachment objects)	Some (preferred or play objects)
Incidence	Most common; universal in one form or other	Intermediate; differs according to the culture and child-rearing practice	Possibly least, differs according to culture (?)
Duration	Transitory (but persist throughout life in different forms)	Lasting (terminates at 3–6 years)	Lasting (terminate at 4–?)
Important role in relation to	Differentiation of self and object, and inner and outer reality; continuity between the self and world	Contact need separation anxiety separation-individuation creativity	Autonomy and independence; strong elements of companionship; cognitive sophistication and child's choice
Common role	Adaptational phenomena to assist the infant during various developmental transitions		

64

transitional object is intimately related to the infant's physical contact need. This object can appropriately be called the *attachment object* since the child shows strong attachment behavior and affectional responses to it, and the incidence varies greatly according to different cultural and child-rearing practices. The onset is usually in the second half of the first year and coincides with manifestations of separation anxiety and attachment to human objects. It appears to play an important role in the separation-individuation process as described by Tolpin (1971) and is the prototype of *creativity* of the infant in the transitional stage of ego differentiation.

Secondary transitional object includes soft cuddly toys, such as the teddy bear, soft dolls, and probably some hard toys. This category has been least adequately studied, and we need further investigations like those of the primary transitional object. Nonetheless, I suggest that it differs from the primary transitional object by its later onset, the elements of play object and companionship, and definite shapes and forms which meet different developmental needs of the child. Although this object provides "contact comfort," it appears to be closely related to the development of autonomy and independence and reflects a more mature ego and cognitive sophistication. The boundary between secondary transitional object and later-developing play object is somewhat unclear.

The *relationship between these three categories* of transitional phenomena is not clear at this time, and awaits more investigations. Most items belonging to the group of transitional object equivalents are considered to be "precursors" of the transitional object proper by Gaddini (1970), who speculates that rocking the baby is a frequent substitute for the transitional object in Italy. Stevenson's (1954) report of progression from the primary to the secondary transitional object in several of her subjects is in disagreement with Busch's (1974) opinion that the child attached to a primary transitional object rarely develops an attachment to a secondary transitional object. In fact, in replacing the terms, primary and secondary transitional object, by "first" and "second" transitional object, Busch (1974) also wanted to avoid the implication of such a genetic sequence. However, some children abandon the blanket only to become attached to the teddy bear or another soft toy, and many teddy-bear attachments also appear in the first year (Hong and Townes, 1976). The issue of a genetic sequence of transitional phenomena is yet to be determined. I also recognize that there are some overlaps between the categories and that all three categories of transitional phenomena share common functions and roles, particularly in their contributions to progressive differentiation and their adaptive value in infant development. I propose this classification to clarify current issues, to reduce confusion in the literature, and to stimulate more scientific investigation. Obviously, there is a need for more objective studies to confirm this hypothetical categorization. One parsimonious way of solving the issues would be to use descriptive terms such as blanket attachment or teddy-bear attachment, instead of terminologies derived from theoretical positions.

THE ROLE OF TRANSITIONAL PHENOMENA IN THE CHILD'S DEVELOPMENT

Waelder's principle of multiple function (1930) states that any significant behavior must be the consequence of the activity of all the psychic structures, id, ego, and superego. Therefore it is not surprising that various functions and multiple meanings of the child's blanket attachment have been described. The transitional phenomena are believed to make various contributions to the development of the following areas:

1. *Object relations.* During the transitional period from the objectless to the object-related stage, the infant can maintain his relationship with his need-fulfilling (A. Freud, 1965) or primary attachment object (mother) by using the transitional object when she is not available or when she is perceived as separate. This object assists the infant's unstable ego in the separation-individuation process and in the formation of true object relation (Winnicott, 1953; Coppolillo, 1967, 1976; Gaddini, 1970; Tolpin, 1971).

2. *Perception.* The transitional object, particularly the blan-

ket, represents the role of tactile perception as a transitional mode of perceptual development between interoceptive-visceral sensations and distance perceptions such as vision and hearing (Spitz, 1965). The newborn reacts primarily to internal visceral stimuli and then perceives the outer world mainly by skin contact and tactile stimulation. Contact perception is a more primitive mode of perception than vision and hearing (Spitz, 1965; Ainsworth, 1974) and plays a very important role in early ego development. Jacobson (1964) suggests that the first impression of self is based on tactile perception. The infant must rely on tactile perception to insure contact and perception of reality until the distance perceptions become mature.

3. *Cognition and reality testing.* At this time there is nothing more to add to Winnicott's (1953) profound insight into the role of transitional phenomena in the process of illusion-disillusionment, and differentiation of "me"—"not me," and inner-outer reality. This is a crucial step toward further development of cognition and reality testing.

4. *Symbolism.* The transitional object represents a big step toward the symbolism important to the development of memory and other cognitive processes. The transitional object can be described as being symbolic of a part object or the mother or reunion with the mother, but its actuality and the fact that it stands for the mother are as important as its symbolic value. This object is the root of symbol formation and represents both the concrete and the symbolic presence of the mother (Winnicott, 1953; Gaddini, 1970).

5. *Ego structure (internalization) and "cohesive self."* The newborn infant relies almost exclusively on his mother for the physical and mental regulations to meet his needs and to cope with reality demands. The infant gradually develops his own intrapsychic structure to control, protect, and regulate his needs and his anxiety. Just as the infant internalizes most of the mothering qualities, it is understandable that the infant will internalize the soothing and anxiety-regulating functions of the blanket attachment. As Tolpin (1971) indicates, the child can dose himself with this soothing attachment object as

he needs it. For example, by using the blanket, the child can substitute the attachment object for the "good enough" yet not enough mother, by providing "contact comfort" and "security" for himself, particularly during the transitional period when the infant strongly needs mother. Thus, the transitional object serves as a phase-appropriate and necessary transitional mental structure, and a mediating "assistant" in the formation of ego structure and a "cohesive self" (Coppolillo, 1967; Greenacre, 1969; Tolpin, 1971; Busch, 1974).

6. *Creativity.* Transitional phenomena occur in a creative space between the subjective and the objective and are creative responses to "good enough" mothering. Blanket attachment is a primitive creative act of the infant by which he endows the blanket with an idealized component of his mother's soothing function. It is the infant who discovers and creates the meaning of the transitional object. Therefore, the significance of the transitional object lies in the primary creativity of the infant. This first act of creativity may be the prototype of all kinds of creative acts in later life (Winnicott, 1953; Tolpin, 1971; Coppolillo, 1967, 1976).

7. *Defense.* Winnicott states that the transitional phenomenon is a defense against anxiety. During the transitional periods of the first year of life, the infant's still unstable ego cannot avoid experiencing the strains imposed by the different realities, the impact of the external environment, and the affect stimulated by separation-reunion with the mother. The transitional phenomena aid the infant in keeping these strains and affects under control until a strong ego and ego autonomy are established. The child can regulate the separation-reunion with mother at his own pace by using a transitional object. In this way the transitional object might be the most primitive form or the precursor of later developing true defense mechanisms.

8. *Ego Autonomy.* The role of the transitional object as a first step toward ego autonomy has been emphasized by a number of authors (Winnicott, 1953; Stevenson, 1954). Sander (1962) described the need and the capacity of an infant to find grati-

fication in the outside world, apart from the mother; and Coppolillo (1967, 1976), using Rapaport's concept (1954) of the ego's relative autonomy, states that the transitional mode of experience insures the ego optimal autonomy from id and from the environment. The transitional object is part of the infant's move away from total dependence upon mother and provides the external stimuli instead of mother to establish the internal-external stimuli equilibrium which is the basis of relative ego autonomy. This autonomy is crucial in the separation-individuation process. Thus, the transitional object has "the double function of retaining the closeness to the mother and facilitating the liberating from her, simultaneously giving greater security to explore the outer world" (Rudhe and Ekecrantz, 1974, p. 398f.) and helps the infant to develop his own autonomy and independence.

These areas do not by any means exhaust all the possible roles and functions of transitional phenomena in development. Instead, they are cited to stimulate further investigation. It should be mentioned that not all transitional phenomena are involved in all the developmental achievements listed above. Depending on the environment, a transitional phenomenon can play important roles in different developmental areas or multiple transitional phenomena can be involved in the same developmental line.

VICISSITUDES OF TRANSITIONAL PHENOMENA

Not much attention has been given to the fact that analogous behavior may have different functional significance in different developmental phases. The meanings of the blanket or stuffed animal may be entirely different at the time of first acquisition and in later phases of development. For example, it can be argued that a transitional object may aid the infant in self-object differentiation during the first year, but in the second year, it may aid the infant in different areas of development such as independence (ego autonomy). Later on, it may become a companion and may gain some sexual meanings

(Bak, 1974). (A number of parents reported that their children became somewhat secretive about stroking the teddy bear or blanket at the age of 4 or 5.)

What is the fate of the transitional object? Our findings (Hong and Townes, 1976) that the mean termination age of blanket attachment is 3 years and 3 months is an interesting parallel to Ainsworth's (1963) observation that Uganda children exhibit strong attachment behavior toward the mother until the end of the third year. Just as children need less physical contact with the mother as they grow older, they would have less need of the blanket with maturation. This can be explained by Tolpin's (1971) hypothesis that the soothing and anxiety-regulating quality of the blanket is internalized ("goes inside"). When this internalization is completed, the blanket is no longer needed. Murphy (1962) suggests that the decline in frequency and intensity of mother-contacting or being upset over separation from mother would be a function of cognitive growth and learning of a wide variety of skills. Thus, children become less and less dependent on the blanket as they establish ego autonomy and acquire other ways of insuring protection and self-control.

However, the fate of other transitional phenomena, i.e., transitional object equivalents, is different. Winnicott (1953) assumes that "the task of reality-acceptance is never completed, that no human being is free from the strain of relating inner and outer reality, and that relief from this strain is provided by an intermediate area of experience" (p. 96). Therefore, he suggests that the transitional mode of experience continues throughout life. It appears in various forms such as play, artistic creativity, mystical and religious experiences, and recreational activities. Certainly, most adults have some bedtime habits and rituals, and rely on particular ideas and thoughts which are soothing and comforting. They, too, are sometimes "lost" in hobbies or sports. Coppolillo (1967) and Kahne (1967) speculate on the persistence of transitional phenomena into adult life, and Coppolillo (1976) states that transitional modes of experience such as artistic expressions are a psychological necessity for individuals. Horton et al.

(1974) report almost total lack of "transitional relatedness" among patients with a severe personality disorder who were unable to adapt to the armed forces. This finding is consonant with the belief that the ability to play is of prognostic significance in psychotherapy with children.

TRANSITIONAL PHENOMENA AS DEVELOPMENTAL ADAPTIVE BEHAVIORS

In view of the complexity and diversity of findings and explanations described above, an interpretation in the form of an integrative conceptual framework is needed. Hartmann's concept of adaptation (1939) is useful in meeting this need. Adaptation is a process by which a living organism "fits together" with its environment and connotes a reciprocal relationship between them. The human infant is born with a given constitution and with instinctual and ego equipments which are meager at birth. In his prolonged state of helplessness, the infant can survive only if his needs are met by the "average expectable environment." Adaptation thus starts at the very first moment of life and continues throughout life.

In order to understand the adaptational process, we must consider two sets of variables. One is an individual's internal needs, and the other is his environment. The individual's needs vary according to constitution and developmental stage. Whenever there is a transition from one developmental stage to another, an individual experiences strain due to the change of equilibrium between himself and the environment, and he needs some means to reduce the strain. It is during these developmental transitions that various transitional phenomena occur and play an important role in aiding the young individual to cope with change. One of the significant oversights in the literature regarding transitional phenomena is the fact that there is not a single but *multiple* transitional stages in child development and that each transitional stage has somewhat different characteristics and different needs. Among the many transitions during infancy, three transitional periods in relation to transitional phenomena will be examined.

The first transition or a nodal point (Mahler, 1967) occurs around the third month of life. At this time the infant can distinguish between animate and inanimate objects and demonstrates social smiling. This period has been described as the transitional stage from primary narcissism to object love (Freud, 1914); from the undifferentiated or objectless stage to object relations (Hartmann, 1939; Spitz, 1965); and from the height of normal symbiosis to the beginning of separation-individuation (Mahler, 1967). This is also the stage which Winnicott described as a period of beginning differentiation between the self and the world, and as a transition from the baby's inability to growing ability to recognize and accept reality. During this transitional period, the infant is bound to experience strain (Winnicott, 1953) and "organismic distress" (Mahler, 1967), and he needs a means to reduce this tension. Because of lack of ego differentiation and ability, the infant must rely on external resources, mainly the mother. Thus, the mother herself and her various soothing activities emerge as transitional phenomena. This group of transitional phenomena, which I label transitional object equivalents, aid the infant in reducing the strain by providing the continuity between inner and outer reality and between the self and the world. Winnicott's and Coppolillo's descriptions pertain primarily to the transitional phenomena occurring during this period.

The second significant transition falls in the middle of the second half of the first year when the infant shows clear differential responses to his mother, stranger and separation anxieties. At this stage, the infant actively seeks out the specific mothering person, demonstrates full-blown attachment behaviors, and becomes afraid of losing her. This period is characterized by the shift from mother's taking all initiative to the infant's taking the initiative in keeping contact between mother and child, from passivity to increasing activity of the infant, and from the first subphase (differentiation) to the second subphase (practicing) of separation-individuation. During this transitional period from relative passivity to increasing activity and at the height of the mother-child bond, the infant is now able to "discover" or "create" the blanket as substitute for mother and for contact comfort, or as an attachment object at the time of separation from the mother and distress. Thus, the blanket serves as a way of maintaining the close contact with mother and at the same time meets the infant's developmental need to establish relative ego autonomy. Blanket attachment therefore represents both the child's fear of separation and the need to separate. The contributions of Tolpin, Busch et al., and Passman and Weisberg are especially relevant to the understanding of this category of transitional phenomena (primary transitional object).

The third transition occurs at the time of a distinct developmental shift in the early part of the second year in terms of asserting independence and ego autonomy. At this stage the child clearly establishes the sense of separateness of himself from the mother and other people, and begins to use the mother as a secure base for exploration and play. The toddler explores the world at large and plays with different toys of various shapes and forms and establishes object performance (Piaget, 1936). During this stage, the stuffed animals or other soft toys are more palatable to the child since they not only provide the contact need but also meet the different developmental need to play with, talk to, and share their new world.

The common denominator of all transitional phenomena, despite the different onsets and functions, is that they occur, are used in transitional stages, and represent functional properties of mothering which are necessary elements for further development. Although the individual infant's needs are rather constant and similar in various cultures, the means of meeting these needs vary widely according to the culture and the different child-rearing practices; and the infant must adapt to the different environment. Nonetheless, child-rearing practices during the first few months do not vary greatly from culture to culture and consequently some form of transitional object equivalent is present universally. Child-rearing practices do differ appreciably, however, in the second half of the first year, and there are significant cultural differences with regard to transitional objects (Hong and Townes, 1976). In most Asian and African cultures, infants remain in close contact or proximity with their mothers during the first three years of life. The needs of these infants are directly met by their mothers, without requiring a great adaptational effort on the part of the infants, and the mothers function as a major auxiliary ego to soothe and regulate the infants' tension.

In contrast, in Western cultures, particularly those of Anglo-Saxon origin, the infant frequently sleeps in a separate room, more frequently feeds by other means than breast, spends more time alone, and has less physical contact with the mother, who places more importance on vocal or other non-physical means of communication. These infants must "create" or "discover" some other means of gratifying their biologically based needs. One good example of this kind of "discovery" is the blanket attachment. Therefore, the blanket attachment can be a "detour" to meet the child's contact needs and to help him fit together with his environment. Blanket attachment is an adaptational process. As far as the infant is concerned, the blanket is neither a transitional nor a substitute object, but it is an adaptive device employed to meet his needs and to cope with his particular environment. The blanket attachment is only one of the numerous adaptational events and the result of nature's experiment, which enable us to glimpse at some of the crucial roles of mothering in child development and the complex process of the separation-individuation.

The value of the transitional object is not limited to the infant's ontogenetic development but also extends to social and cultural adaptation. Man must adapt to his "natural" environment as well as to family and social structures. In the Western culture, infants must establish rapid ego development in order to adapt to an environment demanding early independence and achievement. Thus, the process of "creating" and "discovering" the transitional object enables the infant to "comply" with social demands and is indicative of the great adaptational capacity of the human infant. This "social compliance" has significance in the course of evolution which has led the human organism to an increased independence from his environment.

SUMMARY AND CONCLUSION

Psychoanalytic, experimental, ethological, and cross-cultural studies of transitional phenomena are reviewed and a theoretical integration is attempted. These different approaches provide a multidimensional view of the significance of transitional phenomena, particularly blanket attachment. Seemingly different theoretical positions are not necessarily contradictory but actually are complementary, and can be integrated in the light of cross-cultural findings and by using the concept of adaptation. A reexamination of the literature led to the following conclusions:

1. Although the various transitional phenomena (transitional object equivalents, primary transitional object, and secondary transitional object) all share common features, clear distinctions between them can be discerned and defined. A classification is proposed according to the age of onset, the nature of the object, and the different functions it serves. This classification is desirable to clarify the current literature and to promote more scientific investigation of the subject matter in the future.

2. The occurrence of blanket attachment is influenced by child-rearing practices and sociocultural factors. The development of the blanket attachment is inversely correlated with the quantity and quality of physical contact with the mothering person. Therefore, the blanket attachment appears to be a substitute for, or an equivalent of, certain components of mothering, especially tactile contact, and provides "contact comfort" to the infants, in addition to its other important roles in ego development.

3. Biological, evolutionary-based needs for physical contact, low level of physical involvement of the mother, and the stress the infant experiences at bedtime are the most important etiological factors in the development of blanket attachment, although constitutional differences, maternal need and attitudes, and learning are recognized as contributing factors.

K. Michael Hong

4. The transitional phenomena play a number of important roles in various areas of child development. They take part in the development of object relations, perception, cognition, reality testing, symbolism, ego structure, defense mechanism, creativity, and ego autonomy. In short, transitional phenomena aid an infant in ego differentiation and separation-individuation toward establishing a cohesive self.

5. The transitional phenomenon is evidence of the infant's satisfactory relationship with mother and healthy ego development and appears to be contingent upon the infant's attachment to the mother. There is also suggestive evidence that the transitional mode of experience persists into adult life and may play a psychologically important role.

6. While blanket attachment is a normal phase-appropriate response, the object may in the course of development assume a variety of meanings and functions which then give rise to psychopathological manifestations in certain individuals.

7. The transitional phenomenon is one of the many adaptive behaviors by which the infant "fits together" with his environment in order to meet his needs and adapt to the social structure of his culture.

8. The need for and desirability of interdisciplinary collaborative efforts among behavioral scientists of different theoretical persuasions are paramount.

BIBLIOGRAPHY

AINSWORTH, M. D. (1963), The Development of Infant-Mother Interaction among the Ganda. In: *Determinants of Infant Behavior,* ed. B. M. Foss. New York: Wiley, 2 : 67–112.
——— (1969), Object Relations, Dependency, and Attachment. *Child Develpm.,* 40 : 969–1025.
——— & BELL, S. M. (1970), Attachment, Exploration and Separation. *Child Develpm.,* 41 : 49–67.
BAK, R. C. (1974), Distortions of the Concept of Fetishism. *This Annual,* 29 : 191–214.
BIJOU, S. W. & BAER, D. M. (1965), *Child Development,* vol. 2. New York: Appleton-Century-Crofts.
BOWLBY, J. (1969), *Attachment and Loss,* vol. 1. New York: Basic Books, pp. 309–313.

Busch, F. (1974), Dimensions of the First Transitional Object. *This Annual*, 29 : 215–229.

——— Nagera, H., McKnight, J., & Pezzarossi, G. (1973), Primary Transitional Objects. *J. Amer. Acad. Child Psychiat.*, 12 : 193–214.

Cairns, R. B. (1966), Attachment Behavior of Mammals. *Psychol. Rev.*, 73 : 409–426.

Call, J. D. (1968), Lap and Finger Play in Infancy. *Int. J. Psycho-Anal.*, 49 : 375–378.

Castell, R. (1970), Physical Distance and Visual Attention as Measures of Social Interaction between Child and Adult. In: *Behavior Studies in Psychiatry*, ed. S. Hutt & C. Hutt. Oxford, Pergamon Press, pp. 91–102.

Caudill, W. A. & Schooler, C. (1973), Child Behavior and Child Rearing in Japan and the United States. *J. Nerv. Ment. Dis.*, 157 : 323–338.

Coppolillo, H. P. (1967), Maturational Aspects of the Transitional Phenomenon. *Int. J. Psycho-Anal.*, 48 : 237–246.

——— (1976), The Transitional Phenomenon Revisited. *J. Amer. Acad. Child Psychiat.*, 15 : 36–48.

Dickes, R. (1963), Fetishistic Behavior. *J. Amer. Psychoanal. Assn.*, 11 : 303–330.

Escalona, S. K. (1953), Emotional Development in the First Year of Life. In: *Problems of Infancy and Childhood*, ed. M. J. E. Senn. New York: Josiah Macy Jr. Foundation, pp. 11–92.

Fintzy, R. T. (1971), Vicissitudes of the Transitional Object in the Borderline Child. *Int. J. Psycho-Anal.*, 52 : 107–114.

Freud, A. (1965), Normality and Pathology in Childhood. *Wr.*, 6.

Freud, S. (1914), On Narcissism. *S.E.*, 14 : 73–102.

Gaddini, R. (1970), Transitional Objects and the Process of Individuation. *J. Amer. Acad. Child Psychiat.*, 9 : 347–365.

——— (1975), The Concept of Transitional Object. *J. Amer. Acad. Child Psychiat.*, 14 : 731–736.

Gershaw, N. J. & Schwartz, J. C. (1971), The Effects of a Familiar Toy and Mother's Presence on Exploratory and Attachment Behavior in Young Children. *Child Develpm.*, 42 : 1662–1666.

Gewirtz, J. L. (1961), A Learning Analysis of the Effects of Normal Stimulation, Privation and Deprivation on the Acquisition of Social Motivation and Attachment. In: *Determinants of Infant Behavior*, ed. B. M. Foss. New York: Wiley, 1 : 213–290.

Goodall, J. (1965), Chimpanzees of the Gombe Stream Reserve. In: *Primate Behavior*, ed. I. DeVore. New York: Holt, Rinehart, & Winston, pp. 425–473.

Greenacre, P. (1960), Considerations Regarding the Parent-Infant Relationship. *Int. J. Psycho-Anal.*, 41 : 471–584.

——— (1969), The Fetish and the Transitional Object. *This Annual*, 24 : 144–164.

Harlow, H. E. (1958), The Nature of Love. *Amer. Psychologist*, 13 : 673–685.

‘——— & Suomi, S. J. (1970), Nature of Love-Simplified. *Amer. Psychologist,* 25 : 161–168.

Hartmann, H. (1939), *Ego Psychology and Problem of Adaptation.* New York: Int. Univ. Press, 1958.

Hong, K. M. (1975), Role of the "Security" Blanket. Read at the American Academy of Child Psychiatry.

——— & Townes, B. D. (1976), Infants' Attachment to Inanimate Objects. *J. Amer. Acad. Child Psychiat.,* 15 : 49–61.

Horton, P. C., Louy, J. W., & Coppolillo, H. P. (1974), Personality Disorder and Transitional Relatedness. *Arch. Gen. Psychiat.,* 30 : 618–622.

Jacobson, E. (1964), *The Self and the Object World.* New York: Int. Univ. Press.

Kahne, M. J. (1967), On the Persistence of Transitional Phenomena into Adult Life. *Int. J. Psycho-Anal.,* 48 : 24–258.

Kohut, H. (1971), *The Analysis of the Self.* New York: Int. Univ. Press.

McDonald, M. (1970), Transitional Tunes and Musical Development. *This Annual,* 25 : 503–520.

Mahler, M. S. (1967), On Human Symbiosis and the Vicissitudes of Individuation. *J. Amer. Psychoanal. Assn.,* 15 : 710–762.

Mason, W. A. (1967), Motivational Aspects of Social Responsiveness in Young Chimpanzees. In: *Early Behavior,* ed. H. Stevenson, E. Hess, & H. L. Rheingold. New York: Wiley, pp. 103–126.

Modell, A. H. (1963), Primitive Object Relationship and the Predisposition to Schizophrenia. *Int. J. Psycho-Anal.,* 44 : 282–292.

Murphy, L. B. (1962), *The Widening World of Childhood.* New York: Basic Books.

Passman, R. H. & Weisberg, P. (1975), Mothers and Blankets as Agents for Promoting Play and Exploration by Young Children in a Novel Environment. *Developm. Psychol.,* 11 : 170–177.

Piaget, J. (1936), *The Origins of Intelligence in Children.* New York: Int. Univ. Press, 1952.

Provence, S. & Lipton, R. C. (1962), *Infants in Institutions.* New York: Int. Univ. Press.

——— & Ritvo, S. (1961), Effects of Deprivation on Institutionalized Infants. *This Annual,* 16 : 189–205.

Rapaport, D. (1954), The Autonomy of the Ego. *Bull. Menninger Clin.,* 15 : 113–123.

Rheingold, H. L. (1969), The Effect of Environment on the Behavior of Infants. In: *Determinants of Infant Behavior,* ed. B. M. Foss. New York: Wiley, 4 : 137–166.

Rudhe, L. & Ekecrantz, L. (1974), Transitional Phenomena. *Acta. Psychiat. Scand.,* 50 : 381–400.

Sander, L. W. (1962), Issues in Early Mother-Child Interactions. *J. Amer. Acad. Child Psychiat.,* 1 : 141–166.

SCHAFFER, H. R. & EMERSON, P. E. (1964), Patterns of Response to Physical Contact in Early Human Development. *J. Child Psychol. Psychiat.,* 5 : 1–13.

SHEVRIN, H. & TOUSSIENG, P. W. (1965), Vicissitudes of the Need for Tactile Stimulation in Instinctual Development. *This Annual,* 20 : 310–339.

SPERLING, M. (1963), Fetishism in Children. *Psychoanal. Quart.,* 32 : 374–392.

SPITZ, R. A. (1965), *The First Year of Life.* New York: Int. Univ. Press.

STEVENSON, O. (1954), The First Treasured Possession. *This Annual,* 9 : 199–217.

TOLPIN, M. (1971), On the Beginnings of a Cohesive Self. *This Annual,* 26 : 316–352.

WAELDER, R. (1930), The Principle of Multiple Function. In: *Psychoanalysis.* New York: Int. Univ. Press, 1976, pp. 68–83.

WEISBERG, P. & RUSSELL, J. E. (1971), Proximity and Interactional Behavior of Young Children in Their "Security" Blankets. *Child Develpm.,* 42 : 1575–1579.

WHITE, R. W. (1960), Competence and the Psychosexual Stages of Development. In: *Nebraska Symposium on Motivation,* ed. M. Jones. Lincoln: Univ. Nebraska Press, pp. 97–140.

WINNICOTT, D. W. (1953), Transitional Objects and Transitional Phenomena. *Int. J. Psycho-Anal.,* 34 : 89–97.

——— (1960), The Theory of the Parent-Infant Relationship. *Int. J. Psycho-Anal.,* 40 : 585–595.

WULFF, M. (1946), Fetishism and Object Choice in Early Childhood. *Psychoanal. Quart.,* 14 : 450–471.

Trauma and Affects

HENRY KRYSTAL, M.D.

THERE ARE MANY REASONS WHY CONCEPTS OF TRAUMA SHOULD be reviewed. The present psychoanalytic uses of the term are so loose that it has become virtually useless. This looseness reflects the lack of a definition of trauma based on updated clinical experiences and providing a framework for therapeutic considerations. The economic conceptions of trauma and the stimulus barrier do not, in fact, help us to understand what the psychic reality of trauma is, nor how the aftereffects relate to its causes (Krystal, 1970). At present we have no way of conceptualizing the nature of infantile trauma and its relationship to the adult form.

In this paper, I will study the relationship between trauma and emotions. The working out of the genetic development of affects provides an opportunity to reexamine the nature and consequences of infantile trauma, and compare and contrast it to the dynamics, the psychic reality, and the sequelae of the "adult" form of trauma. The study of the affective experience in trauma yields information about aftereffects which tend to overlay manifestations with which we are familiar. Both infantile and adult trauma will be shown to have aftereffects in the area of affective and symbolic functions. In regard to adult trauma, the inquiry will be concerned with the consequences of the surrender to inevitable danger, which initiates the traumatic process.

Professor of Psychiatry, Michigan State University, East Lansing, Mich.

TRAUMA AND PATHOGENICITY

Freud's earliest and essential observation about psychic trauma, which remains the cornerstone of our understanding of it, goes back to something he had learned from Charcot (Freud, 1956), and which he confirmed in his own work (1940–41; Breuer and Freud, 1893–95), namely, that some hysterical attacks are the aftereffects of unbearable experiences in the past. The nature of the traumatic *situations* which Freud postulated in 1892 was rather nonspecific: "a single major fright (such as a railway accident, a fall, etc.) . . . [as well as] other events which are equally well calculated in their nature to operate as traumas (e.g., fright, mortifications, disappointments)" (1940–41, p. 152). While the question of sexual seduction provided a temporary distraction, in the renunciation of that theory Freud was able to focus on the fundamental area of psychoanalytic observations: *psychic reality.* The emphasis on the nature of the subjective experiences as well as on its unconscious aspects directed the main interest to the "final common path" in the traumatic *event*—the emotion involved. And so, in the *Studies on Hysteria,* Breuer and Freud (1893–95) give us the following definition: "In traumatic neuroses the operative cause of illness is not the trifling psychical injury but the effect of fright—the psychical trauma. In an analogous manner, our investigations reveal, for many, if not for most, hysterical symptoms, precipitating causes. . . . Any experience which calls up distressing affects—such as those of fright, anxiety, shame or physical pain—may operate as a trauma of this kind" (p. 5f.).

On the same page the authors reemphasize that when they discovered "to our great surprise" that the hysterical symptoms disappeared when the meanings were recovered from repression and brought into consciousness, they found that "Recollection without affect almost invariably produces no result." Here then is one paradigm of psychic trauma: an individual is confronted with *overwhelming* affects; in other words, his affective responses produce an unbearable psychic state which threatens to disorganize, perhaps even destroy, all psychic functions. Strachey (1961, p. 57) points out that "The notion of the ego being 'overwhelmed' . . . occurs very early in Freud's writings. See, for instance, a mention of it in Part II of his first paper on 'The Neuro-Psychoses of Defence' (1894a). But it plays a prominent part in his discussions of the mechanism of the neuroses in Draft K of January 1, 1896, in the Fliess correspondence." It should be noted, however, that Freud leaves open the question of what makes an affect unbearable or overwhelming. One's first impression of Freud's words is that *any* intensive and painful affect could be traumatic, but we know that most of the time this is not the case. This naïveté contributes greatly to the confusion which was multiplied as the concept of psychic trauma was expanded and built upon.

If we set these unanswered questions aside, however, we find in Freud's early writing a complete theory of the relationship of affects, trauma, and hysterical symptoms. When the emotions are unbearable, repression takes place, as a result of which the memory "retains the affect" and so *"hysterical patients suffer from incompletely abreacted psychical traumas"* (1893, p. 37f.). In this model then, the *unbearable affects* developed in the traumatic situation; and one of the consequences of the trauma was that, in order to terminate the unbearable state, the perceptions and associatively induced ideas were repressed, thus becoming unconscious and retaining their affective charge. The latter was envisioned as "strangulated" because repression prevented its normal working off, not just by "abreaction" but also because the cognitive aspects of the repressed "complex" could not be dealt with in "another manner which may be called normal" (Freud, 1939, p. 73).

Alongside the above model of psychic trauma, Breuer and Freud developed another one: that of the dynamics of unacceptable impulses.

It turns out to be a *sine qua non* for the acquisition of hysteria that an incompatibility should develop between the ego and some idea presented to it. . . .

> The actual traumatic moment, then, is the one at which the
> incompatibility forces itself upon the ego and at which the lat-
> ter decides on the repudiation of the incompatible idea. That
> idea is not annihilated by a repudiation of this kind, but
> merely repressed into the unconscious [1893–95, p. 122f.].

Freud was able to reconcile these two conceptions of trauma
only after he developed the second theory of anxiety (1926).
Having clarified the role of anxiety as the signal of (internal)
danger which motivates defenses, Freud explained that if the
defensive actions, notably repression, failed, anxiety mounted
and progressed to "automatic anxiety." There was an *automatic*
development of the situation of infantile trauma, the model
for which was the affective state at birth.

Thus, for many years, Freud had two separate models of
trauma in mind. One was the "unbearable situation" model,
emphasizing the affective states, and this view was reinforced
by the observations on war neuroses (1916–17, 1919, 1939).
The other point of view may be called the "dynamics of pathogenesis" model. Although Freud later explained that *in the
neuroses the development of the traumatic situation was actually prevented,* still the point was made that such neuroses were traumatic as opposed to those allegedly determined by hereditary
predispositions. In this view every mental illness which could
be demonstrated to have an understandable genetic history
could be considered traumatic, and its point of origin is thus,
by this definition, a traumatic moment.

Freud's emphasis that hysteria had a traumatic origin was
part of his struggle against the accepted opinion of his day
that the cause was degeneracy and/or some mysterious physical imbalance. Hence the matter of emphasis on the *traumatic*
origins of hysteria carries the burden of putting across such
ideas as psychic determinism and the influence of the unconscious part of the mind, as opposed to the then current descriptive and covertly condemning attitude of the medical and
psychiatric establishment and has to be appreciated in the
light of history. Freud (1937) finally made explicit his view
that the causes of mental illness were either "constitutional" or
traumatic (p. 224).

Freud maintained both models of psychic trauma throughout his life. He used the "unbearable situation" and the "unacceptable impulses" theories in a parallel fashion. It may be a key point in the understanding of the history of psychoanalysis to consider that the entire economic view of metapsychology represented an effort to reconcile these two views. (I will return to this point.)

Some of the confusing writing on this subject by other authors has resulted from their straddling the two views of psychic trauma. Ernst Kris (1956), for instance, talked about *"traumatic effects"* resulting from the "accumulation of frustrating tensions" (p. 73; my italics), but the "traumatic effects" are from pathogenesis, and not from the "unbearable state." When Khan (1963) elaborated and expanded upon Kris's concept, he made the point that the cumulative trauma "operates and builds up silently throughout childhood right up to adolescence" (p. 301). Why then, one may ask, is Khan talking about "cumulative *trauma*" rather than an accretion of pathogenic influences? Some circular thinking seems to be involved here, which illustrates the need for a better definition of the concepts of trauma. The entire thrust of Khan's paper is that the mother's function is to provide a temporary stimulus barrier for the child. He discusses the failures on the part of the mother to function as an effective stimulus barrier. Freud defined trauma as a breach in the stimulus barrier.

Khan (1963) clarifies the aftereffects of the mother's failure to protect the child from a variety of adverse circumstances. However, he does not consider what a trauma experience might be. In fact, he indicates that cumulative trauma is entirely silent, goes unnoticed by everyone concerned, and "becomes visible only in retrospect" (p. 296). Khan makes it clear that he is talking about "pathogenic effects," which he attributes to failure of the mother to function as a protective shield by definition, but this becomes so broad as to include any development or experience which is not conducive to the child's optimal development. Thus, the "breaches in the mother's role as a protective shield" (p. 290) may result in inadequate phase-appropriate frustrations, which can hardly be

imagined to produce trauma. Khan used the term trauma to
cover a multiplicity of sins; in fact, just about anything except
trauma itself. He quotes A. Freud to support his view of
trauma as "subtle harm . . . inflicted on this child, the consequence of . . . [which] will become manifest at some future
date" (p. 302). According to this view, childhood trauma consists of all unfavorable influences, anything and everything
leading to the development of psychopathology. In fact, Anna
Freud (1967) has expressed great concern about the confusion
and abuse of the term "trauma," which, like other concepts
that are used carelessly, would, "in the course of time, lead
inevitably to a blurring of meaning and finally to the abandonment and loss of a valuable concept" (p. 235). She reflected on
how she would proceed to limit her use of the term:

> Like everyone else, I have tended to use the term "trauma"
> rather loosely up to now, but I shall find it easier to avoid this
> in the future. Whenever I am tempted to call an event in a
> child's or adult's life "traumatic," I shall ask myself some fur-
> ther questions. Do I mean that the event was upsetting; that it
> was significant for altering the course of further develop-
> ment; that it was pathogenic? Or do I really mean traumatic
> in the strict sense of the word, i.e., shattering, devastating,
> causing internal disruption by putting ego functioning and
> ego mediation out of action [p. 242].

If, like Khan (1963), we accept the definition of trauma to
be every unfavorable influence in childhood, or, as many authors do, assume that every event and experience in the life of
an adult productive of psychopathology is also self-evidently
trauma, then the usefulness of the term is lost, and it may as
well be discarded. There is, however, a wealth of information
indicating that traumatic experiences do occur both in children and adults. The problem has been that we have tried to
account for too many kinds of adverse effects by this term,
and that within the conception itself there is a lack of distinction between two disparate models which became fused for
reasons of historical circumstances.

The tendency to mix the models of psychic trauma pervades

psychoanalytic writing. It reflects Freud's wish and lifelong efforts to create a unitary theory that would account for and unite the two models of trauma. This tendency can be observed through the years in Freud's shifting the use of terms from "affects" to "excitations" and finally to "stimuli." If the generalization can be made that stimuli can be overwhelming, then a unitary theory of trauma and pathogenesis would be secure.

I believe that the entire economic theory can be viewed as an effort to solve the problem of psychic trauma, abreaction, and "strangulated affects." The economic theory has provided us with metaphors which permitted us to advance our thinking in a number of directions, e.g., in the areas of attachment, mourning, and narcissism. In all of these areas, however, the economic view presented a limitation to the continued exploration as well. In regard to conceptions of trauma, many difficulties have resulted.

Since there is some appearance of similarity between Ernst Kris's concept of "strain trauma" and Khan's idea of "cumulative trauma" and Freud's original postulation of the existence of "partial trauma," I shall next examine whether the same critique applies.

PARTIAL TRAUMA AND EGO STRAIN

In the very same paragraph in which Breuer and Freud (1893–95) described the traumatic situation as an unbearable state they introduced the concept of "partial trauma": "In the case of common hysteria it not infrequently happens that, instead of a single, major trauma, we find a number of partial traumas forming a *group* of provoking causes. These have only been able to exercise a traumatic effect by summation and they belong together in so far as they are in part components of a single story of suffering" (p. 6).

The question left open is: When there is a "summation" of partial traumas, do they culminate in the development of the same unbearable state which was postulated for the acute traumatic event? If so, then partial traumas are simply preliminary events which sensitize the individual, and which add their influence in such a way that when their "suffering" is added up, a traumatic situation is produced.

If that is so, then we can consider Breuer and Freud's language regarding the "summation" of suffering as purely metaphoric. The handling of pain and painful affects involves a variety of resources and skills, which may become diminished by a variety of factors (Zetzel, 1949, 1965; Krystal and Raskin, 1970; Krystal, 1975). Every painful event is experienced both as a loss (of wished-for developments and magical powers) and as a punishment. Multiple misfortunes are especially likely to be experienced as a "doomsday signal." The occurrence of psychic trauma in a person's past may predispose him to respond excessively and maladaptively to intense affects: "this problem commonly is manifested by a feeling of being 'dead,' or by a variety of dissociative reactions, from depersonalization to psychosis" (Krystal, 1975, p. 209).

Murphy (1961) showed that in what might be considered an acute traumatic event, it is frequently possible to demonstrate a growing susceptibility resulting from a vicious circle of mounting depression and anxiety at the peak of which an otherwise manageable event will become traumatic. Like Murphy, Sandler (1967) started from the observations of mounting vulnerability that results from an "accumulation" of potentially traumatic factors. While it is possible for the traumatic event to be averted, the individual will nevertheless be significantly affected by the state of strain. He demonstrated that significant symptoms, behavior, and developmental modifications can occur in the absence of trauma. Sandler described how in the process of trauma prevention, serious emotional difficulties may still develop.

Ego strain not only leaves the individual with symptoms, but because of the ego changes and residual rigidities, it diminishes the freedom of choices for future protection from trauma and may thereby constitute a predisposition to traumatization. In addition, however, this view allows us to consider that certain psychic events, though not productive of the entire phenomenology of trauma, nevertheless may have extensive influences upon the various functions and adjustments of the individual. Some of the effects have been summarized by Solnit and Marianne Kris (1967): "Strain trauma not only promotes the development of rigid ego defenses, but such trauma also renders the individual more vulnerable to shock trauma. Thus an acute trauma is magnified because the individual does not have a repertoire of ego defenses necessary for a flexible adaptation to challenges from the environment or from the inner instinctual demands" (p. 205).

Keiser (1967) pointed out that because of the complexity and interrelatedness of ego function:

> . . . the loss of any one function must necessarily affect all the functions of the ego, since the ego must compensate or find other means of satisfaction for those drives or partial drives that can no longer be discharged or gratified via their accustomed pathways. Furthermore, energy must be expended on the alteration of the ego function. Hence it can be postulated that whenever the barrier surrounding a specific ego function is penetrated and that ego function is threatened with extinction, a feeling of psychic helplessness . . . may then be manifest primarily in the area of the damaged ego function [p. 790].

I return to the question posed by Freud's concept of "partial trauma." Each of the partial trauma events predisposes to a later overreaction to a certain psychic constellation. Probably only a minor part can be attributed to the "suffering" engendered; e.g., fear of the pain. The major aftereffects will lie in whatever changes have taken place in the available defensive operations and the fantasy explanations of the event. If the first misfortune has resulted in a feeling of guilt, the following ones may be experienced as the "doomsday signal" of dreaded punishment, the substance of which refers to infantile psychic trauma. *But none of the separate components of the "partial trauma" chain of events is productive of a trauma—save the last one.* In the end it is only the development of the psychic trauma that retrospectively makes those (subjective) experiences trauma-related.

THE PHENOMENOLOGY OF TRAUMA

Since the evidence of trauma is in its phenomenology, we need to keep the following picture in mind: a paralyzed, overwhelmed state, with immobilization, withdrawal, possible depersonalization, evidence of disorganization. There may be a regression in any and all spheres and aspects of mental function and affect expression. This regression is followed by characteristic recuperative attempts through repetition, typical dreams, and eventually by long-term neurotic, characterological, psychosomatic, or other syndromes. The so-called traumatic neurosis is *just one of many possible sequelae of traumatization.*

Although the aftereffects of the psychic trauma are many, there is a syndrome of affective disturbances which reflects *direct* sequelae of trauma[1] and is related to the nature of the traumatic state. In these individuals, we see a lifelong disturbance of affectivity. The patients have a history of multiple and/or even severe traumas. The events were clearly of the "overwhelming state" variety (Krystal, 1968, 1971, 1975; Krystal and Raskin, 1970). One cannot deny that in the lives of these individuals there was an accumulation of discrete traumatic experiences.

The experiences gathered in the 30-year follow-up on survivors of massive psychic traumatization in the German concentration camps showed that while virtually any symptoms or diagnosis may be found, there is a common element in the sequelae consisting of certain chronic disturbances of affec-

1. I am emphasizing the direct sequelae of trauma, i.e., those related to the trauma experience per se, because I hope that by paying attention to them we may learn about the nature of psychic reality in trauma. The development of, say, a neurosis would be a reaction not to the traumatic experience itself, but to the fantasies to which it becomes attached in terms of an attributed meaning, e.g., as a confirmation of the threat of castration, as evidence that dangerous wishes may come true or bring punishment. In the psychiatric and psychoanalytic literature virtually every diagnostic entity has been linked etiologically with trauma.

tivity (Krystal, 1971). The problem is most commonly referred to as "mixture of depression and anxiety" (Bensheim, 1960; Niederland, 1961; Krystal and Niederland, 1968). These observations led me to explore the other affective disturbances in the survivors. As a result of these studies I came to the conclusion (1974, 1975) that the "final common path" of traumatization was the development of overwhelming affects, as Freud indicated originally.

THE CHALLENGE OF THE AFFECT EXPERIENCE

All descriptions of the phenomenology of trauma include a disturbance in affectivity, but the precise role of affect in the genesis and prevention of trauma is not clear. The appreciation of the role of affect and the models used have varied considerably. In 1893, Breuer and Freud were quite straightforward about it: "Any experience which calls up distressing affects—such as those of fright, anxiety, shame or physical pain—may operate as a trauma of this kind" (p. 6). Under what circumstances do affects become a challenge to the ego and become potentially traumatic?

The affective experience can be studied in terms of its attributes, and we commonly (but arbitrarily) find it convenient to approach the cognitive aspects of an affect separately from the expressive ones. Although this artifice does create some problems (Krystal, 1977), it may help us to study the details of the threats posed by emotion. The cognitive aspect of an affect might be viewed as composed of its meaning as a signal and the "story" behind it. Each aspect of the affect may represent a challenge and a problem. The difficulty, for instance, with feelings of triumph which accompany every bereavement (i.e., survivorship) is that their cognitive aspect reveals competitive and aggressive strivings, including death wishes, which had been repressed or denied.

In regard to affective responses, two different types of psychoanalytic emergency can be observed. One is related to the cognitive aspects of the emotion as illustrated by the fear that aggressive wishes may get out of hand and magically cause great destruction. The other is an "affect storm," which represents quite a different problem. In this situation, the patient experiences himself as "flooded" by emotion and dreads that the emotion not only will be "endlessly" violent and unbearable and overwhelm all executive functions, but will go on to destroy him (Krystal, 1975). I do not equate the "affect storm" itself with trauma, because, as I will elaborate, the adult can tolerate intense (adult type) affects without becoming overwhelmed and disorganized by them. The fear of affects frequently represents the dread of the return of (the infantile type) trauma. Under certain circumstances, however, the affective responses may become overwhelming and initiate the traumatic state. Such a situation would ensue, Freud (1926) indicated, with the development of "automatic anxiety."

The key word in Freud's conception of trauma, however, was "helplessness." He asserted that "the essence and meaning" of the traumatic situation consists in "the subject's estimation of his own strength . . . and in his *admission* of helplessness in the face of it—physical helplessness if the danger is real and psychical helplessness if the danger is instinctual" (1926, p. 166; my italics). Freud reemphasized this point in the closing sentence of the paragraph, saying, in effect, that it is the subjective experience of helplessness ("erlebte Situation") which determines that a situation is traumatic as distinguished from one of danger. The point of the helplessness in this context is that it implies a "giving up," *a surrender.*

The essence of recognized and admitted helplessness is the *surrender* to the inevitable peril. With the helpless submission to the unavoidable danger, the affective state changes from anxiety to cataleptic passivity. Anxiety is the signal of the perception of *preventable* danger. Helplessly surrendering to the peril changes the affective state from the hyperalert and hyperactive response (anxiety) to one of the blocking of emotions and progressive inhibition. This surrender sequence has been referred to by Zetzel (1949) and described in great detail by Stern (1951a, 1951b, 1968a, 1968b; Meerloo, 1948, 1959; Krystal, 1975). Stern (1951a) has called the "freezing," immobile, inhibitory response the "catatonoid reaction" and pointed out that its cognitive and expressive form may be considered a "primal depression." Seligman (1975) reviewed the many studies of human and animal behavior which demonstrated that the catatonoid response is an affective reaction pattern ubiquitous in the animal kingdom.

When the emotions change from anxiety to surrender and the catatonoid reaction, the latter itself becomes a threat to the functioning, integrity, and even survival of the individual. In the catatonoid state we are dealing with the very moment of the self being overwhelmed with a phylogenetically determined surrender pattern which is also a potential psychological "self-destruct" mechanism. Jones (1929) was, of course, well aware of the lethal potential of such reactions which he called "aphanesis."

SURRENDER, PSYCHOGENIC DEATH, AND TRAUMA

My experiences with survivors of Nazi persecution indicate that a progression from the excited state to the passive surrender in the catatonoid reaction does take place in the face of unavoidable and overwhelming danger. In this state even military personnel such as the thousands of Polish officers in Katyn cooperated in their mass murder. Many European Jews obeyed orders in an automatonlike fashion, took off their clothes, and together with their children descended into a pit, lay down on top of the last layer of corpses, and awaited to be machine-gunned. In this state, a condemned person cooperates with his executioner. In fact, if this process continues to its full potential, the executioner become superfluous, as the individual will die of his own accord (Menninger, 1936; Burrell, 1963). Richter (1959) quoted the coroner of the City of Baltimore: "every year men die after suicide attempts when the skin has scarcely been scratched or only a few aspirin tablets have been ingested" (p. 311).

In concentration camps two forms of psychogenic death were observed. A large number of prisoners died soon after arrival (Bettelheim, 1943; Des Pres, 1976). Another form of lethal surrender reaction was called the "mussulman stage"

and generally took place when after some time in the concentration camp the prisoner's emotional and physical resources
were exhausted (Niederland, 1961; Krystal, 1968).

The phenomenon of psychological death is met with much
denial. We tend to think that it takes place in exotic situations—that "voodoo deaths" happen to savages. Or we imagine that one may die in circumstances of extraordinary physical peril. In fact, however, apart from Cannon's (1942) famous
paper, there have been many reports in the medical and psychiatric literature documenting that people die for reason of
their psychological reaction to "ordinary" events: in response
to the loss of a loved one, receiving bad news, losing self-esteem, being rescued from fires and other mishaps, at "happy
endings," and in anniversary reactions (Menninger, 1936;
Engel, 1971; Seligman, 1975). A few deaths of psychogenic origin have been recorded in the psychoanalytic literature as
well (Coolidge, 1969; Knapp et al., 1966). While the circumstances varied, the subjective state of all these patients was of
"unbearable situations of impass, of 'no exit' in which [they
could not] fight, and from which they [could not] escape"
(Saul, 1966, p. 88). The helpless and hopeless surrender was
documented in the studies of Engel (1968, 1971) and Meerloo
(1948, 1959). In addition to the situations in which the surrender pattern progresses to psychogenic death, there is an increasing awareness and documentation of the transient catatonoid reactions.

It has been found, for instance, that these surrender patterns are more common than panic in mass disasters (Dill,
1954). Allerton (1964) reports: "almost all available studies indicate that a stunned and bewildered response is a far more
likely group reaction than is panic" (p. 206). In four disasters
studied, Tyhurst (1951) found that 10 to 25 percent of the
people became stunned and immobile. In aircraft accidents, as
many as half the passengers in a crash develop what the air-
lines call "inaction due to negative panic" and therefore fail to
evacuate the burning or sinking craft (Johnson, 1970, p. 3).

As Freud stressed, the nature of the danger is of secondary
importance; it matters not whether it is "external" or purely

psychogenic. Neither does it matter whether an actual threat of peril exists. Lest anyone misconstrue that my considerations pertain only to extreme life-endangering situations, I reemphasize Freud's (1926) statement that the *sole* determinant of the psychological consequences is a person's subjective evaluation of the danger and "Whether he is wrong in his estimation or not is immaterial for the outcome" (p. 166).

I am emphasizing the lethal potential of the psychological surrender pattern because it makes us appreciate the magnitude of the forces involved in these reactions. The question is: what happens to people who surrender to what they experience as overwhelming danger and do not die? The survivors of the Nazi persecution, for example, spent long periods of time in a condition of robotization or automatization or, as Lifton (1967) called it, "psychic closing off." Such a state was often preceded by depersonalization, which represented an attempt to deny the reality and to "numb" one's emotional responses. In "closing off" there is a virtually complete suppression of all affect expression and perception. The physical immobilization observable in the catatonoid state is accompanied by a massive blocking of virtually all mental activity—not just affects, but all initiative, judgment, and others—to the point that a state of "walking death" may ensue. This may serve as the *model of an adult traumatic state.*

THE GENETIC VIEW OF AFFECTS AND PSYCHIC TRAUMA

The aftereffects of such trauma are many and complex. Among these there is a disturbance of affectivity consisting of a vagueness and loss of specificity of emotional responses, so that the patients cannot tell what feeling they are experiencing. Actually they are experiencing a mixed pattern of physiological responses—representing the "expressive" or physiological aspects of the affects. There is an accompanying impairment in verbalization of emotion and in the capacity for symbolic representation and fantasy formation. There is a very high rate of certain psychosomatic diseases, especially dermatosis, peptic ulcer, and arthritis (Krystal, 1971). These disturbances represent a regression in affective expression consisting of affect dedifferentiation, deverbalization, and re-somatization (Krystal, 1968, 1971, 1974; Krystal and Raskin, 1970). The presumptive developmental lines of affect, then, are differentiation, verbalization, and desomatization (Krystal, 1974, 1977).

The affective responses of the infant represent two basic patterns: a state of contentment and tranquillity and a state of distress. These two states represent affect precursors out of which evolve pleasurable and painful affects. In the normal course of maturation the mixed affect precursor pattern differentiates into specific entities.

The other developmental line of affect involves the gradual verbalization and desomatization of the emotional responses. This process makes possible the use of affects as signals, for affective responses which are primarily somatic are too dangerous and overwhelming and call attention to themselves rather than to the state which they signal. While some factors in the process of verbalization may have maturational aspects subject to hereditary influences, the maturational transformation of affects is intimately related to the early object relations. The mothering parent provides the first object for identification in regard to affective responses. Later the family as a whole influences the establishment of norms for affective expression. The mother's role in fostering harmonious and uninterrupted progress in affect verbalization and desomatization lies predominantly in protecting the child from psychic traumatization.

Possibly the most crucial and difficult aspect of mothering consists in permitting the child to bear increasingly intense affective tension, but stepping in and comforting the child before his emotions overwhelm him. Her empathy with the child is her only guide. If the mothering parent fails to prevent the infant's affect from reaching an unbearable intensity and overwhelming him, a state of psychic trauma may develop. Conceptions of the nature of the psychic experience in early childhood psychic trauma miss the point if they do not fully appreciate the nature of infantile affect precursors. To be overwhelmed with an adult type of affect, be it anxiety, rage, or guilt, may be most painful and even terrifying, but this is an inadequate model for the early childhood experience. It fails to convey the global distress occasioned by the total, unregulated flooding with the undifferentiated, somatic, pre-verbal, timeless, archaic affects of a young child.

What could be the psychic state of a child overwhelmed with the primitive affect precursors which involve a massive re-sponse mobilizing the entire autonomic system as well as the precursors of pain?[2] How can we imagine the child's *timeless* horror? Our clues from experience with adults who have suf-fered severe psychic trauma as children indicate that this kind of experience is the most terrible and indescribable hell known to man, literally a fate worse than death. Stern (1968a, 1968b), in struggling with the perceptions of this state, felt that Freud intimated that such a state referred to *Todesangst*— not a fear of death, but a *mortal terror*, an unbearable deadly state which Stern called the *biotraumatic situation*. Earlier Stern (1951a) had used pavor nocturnus as a model of childhood psychic trauma. There we can get the feeling of the inconsol-able state of a totally overwhelmed child.

The difficulties in imagining the dire cataclysmic nature of the infantile traumatic state are illustrated by our tendency to speak of the child's experience in an anthropomorphic way as "anxiety." In his references to birth, Freud indicates that it is the precursor of anxiety, and thus "the source and prototype of the affect of anxiety" (1900, p. 400f.). He calls birth "our model for an anxiety state" (1933, p. 93). He talks about "the earliest anxiety of all—the 'primal anxiety' of birth" (1926, p. 137), and so on, in many places.

In order to appreciate the quality of the infantile traumatic state, one must consider not only the immaturity of the psyche in general, e.g., its timelessness, and objectlessness, and other primitive characteristics, but that the affect precursors cannot be understood by reference to the psychic reality of the adult

---

2. Pain (or its precursors) is part of the undifferentiated distress pattern which is precipitated under these circumstances (Krystal, 1974, 1975, 1977).

type of affects. *Anxiety as we know it in adults does not exist in the neonate and infant but develops only through a gradual and complex process.*

What we observe in the *direct* aftereffects of severe childhood trauma in adults is a lifelong *dread* of the return of the traumatic state and an *expectation* of it. Emotions are frequently experienced as trauma screens; hence there is a fear of one's emotions and an impairment of affect tolerance (Krystal, 1975). Along with these disturbances there is a general and lifelong *anhedonia,* an impairment of the ability to experience gratification, which becomes interwoven into a variety of masochistic problems.

In the context of the prevention of severe childhood traumatization the mother can be properly described as functioning as a temporary stimulus barrier or protective shield. The mother's ability to prevent childhood psychic trauma is much less than we would wish, and this was the point of Stern's (1968a, 1968b) emphasis on the occurrence of "biotrauma" as an inevitable development. Our need to deny this helplessness in preventing the traumatic experiences in our children inclines us to disavow their occurrence and to talk, like Khan (1963), about the "silent" nature of childhood trauma.

Lipson (1976) has posed a most germane question: "How is a traumatic state terminated?" It appears that in childhood trauma there is a secondary "safety valve" between the traumatic state and its continuation unto death. The wisdom of ages is that the child, left alone in a state of extreme distress, will most of the time neither die nor remain in the traumatic state forever, but will go off to sleep. This is how parents have always been able to get away with letting the child "cry himself to sleep." Thus, in a manner which is not understood by us, the child is able to terminate the traumatic state by going off to sleep. There are indications that endocrinological and neurophysiological reactions are involved here; studies indicating the relationship between sleep and affective states may eventually provide some clues (Hauri, 1974).

While the child seems to be protected from psychogenic death by his ability to go off to sleep in a state of total misery and exhaustion, a repetition of such episodes results in a failure to thrive, marasmus, or anaclitic depression. Thus the child's going off to sleep in a state of despair and total physical exhaustion must represent a different psychic experience than the blissful going off to sleep of the contented baby. It can be assumed that the memory traces of such events may contain sequelae of infantile psychic trauma that have not yet been explored. They may yield essential information about the anhedonia mentioned above. Such people spend their lives avoiding pain, and are hardly able to experience pleasure, happiness, or joy. They represent one of the greatest therapeutic challenges, with the result that we tend to give up and attribute their problems to "inborn" deficits (Meehl, 1975). Anhedonia is in fact the most reliable "tag" of serious post-traumatic states. It involves a modification of the hedonic regulation. The mutual regulatory function of the pleasure and distress centers of the brain is very likely modified in ways for which we lack the psychological understanding.

INFANTILE TRAUMA AND ADULT TRAUMA

If the concept of trauma is to be rescued from the dilution which threatens its usefulness at present, we must assert that trauma refers to an overwhelming, paralyzing psychic state which implies a loss of ego functions, regression, and obligatory psychopathology (Furst, 1967; Solnit and Kris, 1967). In attempting to clarify the question whether adult psychic trauma is the same phenomenon as childhood trauma, I must separate the aftereffect from the phenomenology because I have pointed out that *massive* psychic trauma in adults may have very similar sequelae as significant (i.e., frequent, severe) childhood traumatization.

Although many adults live with the fear of the return of their infantile trauma, it is not possible for an adult to have exactly the same kind of an experience. In some psychotic states or in severe delirium tremens, it is possible for adults to come close to the degree of horror and overwhelmed state as we can infer the child goes through. In states of prolonged

torture and other externally and internally caused panic states
which combine suffering with total helplessness and reach the
catatonoid states, the existence of a traumatic state frequently
cannot be questioned. Nevertheless, there are significant differences.

Here again we must remind ourselves that the essence of infantile psychic trauma consists in the nature of the affect precursors and their potential for creating an unbearable state in
an infant. Regression in regard to affects is not only a possibility in adults; it is an everyday phenomenon, but the regression
is spotty and incomplete. The adult has the capacity for blocking emotions and constricting cognition. It is therefore *not possible for an adult to have such a complete regression in the form and
nature of affects, and the rest of his psychic function, as to experience
the psychic state of infantile trauma.*

One of the factors that accounts for this difference is the
structure of the adult psyche. It contains all these resources
for trauma prevention which we refer to as the "stimulus barrier." In regard to the trauma *experience,* however, the most
important single difference has been pointed out by Petty
(1975). In the *adult* traumatic state, an "observing ego" is retained. This discovery implies that as self-observing functions
develop, traumatic experiences and "near-trauma" states can
be utilized for the development of "trauma signals" (Sandler,
1967), the ultimate emergency response mobilizing alarm,
which may serve later for trauma prevention. The "trauma
signals" may mobilize a person's defenses, or may be involved
in his obtaining help from others (Petty et al., 1974).

What then is the nature of the psychic reality, the subjective
experience in the adult traumatic state? In the psychoanalytic
literature there is an amazing paucity of subjective reports of
what it is like to live in a state of trauma. What is available is
generally in the realm of external, behavioral, and aftereffect-
related data. Furst (1967) reviewed and summarized the report by Solnit and Kris (1967), who put together a reconstruction of the "psychic content" of trauma as a "feeling of helplessness in the face of overwhelming danger" and described
the traumatic state as " 'paralyzing, immobilizing, or rendering

to a state of helplessness, ranging from numbness to an emotional storm in affects and behavior.' This includes the disorganization of feelings, thoughts and behavior, as well as physical symptoms reflecting automatic disfunction" (p. 37). Although Solnit and Kris reported on a traumatic incident in the life of a 3½-year-old child, the above description is a composite which fits the *adult type* of psychic trauma as distinguished from the infantile one.

A major difference between the infantile and adult form of psychic trauma is its relationship to affects. For the child, the affects themselves become overwhelming and traumatic because of their primitive nature and the primitive state of the mind. In the adult, intense affects *themselves* do not constitute trauma, and under certain circumstances may actually be desired. Even affect storms are distinguished from psychic trauma in that they *threaten* to, but do not, in fact, overwhelm the individual's integrative and executive functions. It is the overwhelming of the ego, the surrender in total helplessness and hopelessness, and the progression to the catatonoid state that makes a situation traumatic. The traumatic state can neither be equated with nor understood by the intense affects which may initiate it. This may be what Eissler (1966) was referring to when he said: "Anxiety cannot traumatize the psychic apparatus, any more than the defense mechanism can" (p. 26). That statement holds true only if we are dealing with the mature, adult type of affect.

Psychic Trauma as a Process

In the traumatic state there is a psychological paralysis which starts with a virtually complete blocking of the ability to feel emotions and pain as well as other physical sensations, and progresses to inhibition of other mental functions. The subjects themselves are able to observe and describe the blocking of affective responses—a circumstance that has led to such terms as psychic numbing, "psychological closing off" (Lifton, 1967), and "affective anesthesia" (Minkowski, 1946). The paradox in the traumatic state is that the numbing and closing

off are experienced with relief in relation to the previously
painful affects, e.g., anxiety; on the other hand, it is also experienced as the first part of dying. For, along with the affective
blocking, there is a blocking of initiative and all life-preserving
cognition. The severe constriction, desymbolization, and fragmentation of mental functioning are not as easily observed
through reflective self-awareness as is the "psychic numbing."
The accounts that are available have been obtained in situations which were not *completely* overwhelming. For instance,
Jaspers (1933) found a personal account of a soldier in World
War I: "We were reduced to having to 'wait and see,' although
we were in immediate danger. Our minds froze, grew numb,
empty and dead." His soldier further reports that "feeling is
frozen. . . . The threatened man becomes numb, cool, objective—the senses slowly grow enveloped with a merciful stupe-
faction, become clouded and conceal the worst from him"
(p. 367f.).

It appears that the cognitive constriction rather than the
"numbing" accounts for the scarcity of reports of the psychic
state in trauma. Those we were able to unearth show that at
the peak of distress, the descriptions shift from the subject's
feelings and experiences to an account of the events, as if described by a third person. Personal accounts of traumatic
states may make brief references to the early phase of the process as being painful or frightening. They may mention some
numbing or depersonalization, but the story invariably lapses
into a description of the *events*.[3] Spectacular examples of this
process are provided by Kosinski (1965). Schliemann gave several accounts of his shipwreck in his "exercise books," yet this
extraordinary verbal man describes his traumatic experience
as follows: "I fell, hitting my mouth against the deck and
broke all my front teeth. But my terror was such that I didn't
feel the pain. I pulled myself up and fastened myself with
ropes [to the mast]. . . . I expected to die with every new

3. I am indebted to Marlene Handler, M.S.L.S., who has been most helpful in searching for the psychiatric, autobiographical, and fictional accounts
of traumatic states.

wave" (Niederland, 1965, p. 382). In other versions, there are more details of the circumstances, but no description of his feelings, as Schliemann always skips from the above sentence to loss of consciousness and then the rescue.

The readers or audience of such accounts, in contrast, experience a mistaken anticipation that the event will cause a continuing increase in pain, suffering, and distress. They also dread that the description will become unbearable and that it will terminate their empathic ability. Freud (1930) touched on some of these points when he said:

> No matter how much we may shrink with horror from certain situations—of a galley-slave in antiquity, of a peasant during the Thirty Years' War, of a victim of the Holy Inquisition, of a Jew awaiting a pogrom—it is nevertheless impossible for us to feel our way into such people—to divine the changes which original obtuseness of mind, a gradual stupefying process, the cessation of expectations, and cruder or more refined methods of narcotization have produced upon their receptivity to sensations of pleasure and unpleasure. Moreover, in the case of the most extreme possibility of suffering, special mental protective devices are brought into operation [p. 89].

I suppose that the "special protective devices" refer to the above-mentioned derealization, depersonalization, and, perhaps, states of modified consciousness, all of which may derive from the child's going off to sleep in the traumatic state. This mechanism may also underlie what follows the affect blocking: a progressive surrender of self-preserving initiatives through the *constriction and progressive blocking of mental functions such as memory, imagination, associations, problem solving, and so on.* A person in this state may become aware of the hopelessness of his situation and have a thought such as "I am going to die," and this thought may be couched in sardonic humor and bitterness. Other thoughts may come to mind or break through: anticipation of unbearable suffering associated with the return of the horror of childhood psychic trauma; and these may break down the functional inhibition of action. Either a purposeful or random attempt at action may result. These are the spasms of activity amid the catatonoid state. Thus the memory of the infantile unbearable state may mobilize adaptive action in the last moment. Frequently, however, such outbursts of activity are devoid of planning and even of psychic contents, and are reflexive in nature and self-destructive in outcome.

As the state of psychic trauma develops further, there is an increasing envelopment, with the self-surrender to death progressing to a point of irreversibility on both the psychological and physiological planes. Many of the aftereffects of psychic trauma result from this immersion in the early stages of psychogenic death. In massive psychic trauma following survival of events that destroyed entire communities or peoples, the problems resulting from the confrontation with death and survivorship have been described repeatedly (this literature was reviewed by Hoppe, 1971).

There are remarkable similarities between the psychic state in trauma and some descriptions of mental state in suicidal patients (Shneidman, 1976a). This finding should not come as a surprise in view of the fact that the psychic trauma state can progress to psychogenic death. Indeed, some suicide attempts and repeated self-mutilations may represent a means of interrupting the traumatic state (Simpson, 1976). When the psychic numbing sets in and the individual becomes aware of a feeling of "deadness" and some of the accompanying reactions of constriction, depersonalization, etc., and especially when there is a sentience of the lethal potential of the traumatic state, the suicide attempt or self-mutilation may (paradoxically) be life-saving in that the individual asserts mastery, thereby interrupting the state of helplessness and surrender. Some of the sudden outbursts of activity in the catatonoid state represent the same type of last-minute protest. It is the process of psychological *surrender* which is the lethal one.

Another startling similarity between the descriptions of suicidal patients and the patients in the traumatic state results from the severe constriction of mental functions which includes a blocking of and dissociation from one's past. The inability to describe the mental state in psychic trauma even in retrospect is due to the severe inhibition of the mental functions which reduces self-observation and cognition to a minimum. Shneidman (1976b) has made the same point about suicidal patients, stressing that they cannot write a "full and explicative" note (p. 91). He even asserted that if they could do it, they would not have to kill themselves.

DIRECT AFTEREFFECTS OF THE TRAUMATIC STATE

Individuals who have survived severe psychic trauma—trauma which has progressed well into the catatonoid state—and were in the incipient stages of psychogenic death, and especially if they remained in such a condition for a long period of time, frequently show a residual picture of extreme damage, even devastation. Murray (1967) has described such individuals with sensitivity and poignancy; he has characterized them as "dead to the world" since they manifest a state of:

> . . . temporary or permanent cessation of a part of psychic life—cessation of affect (feeling almost dead), . . . or the cessation of an orientation of conscious life—the cessation of social life (dead to the outer world) or of spiritual life (dead to the inner world) . . . or, instead of restricting oneself to two concepts—cessation (to stand for no life at all) and continuation (to stand for ongoing living processes)—it might be well to take account of different degrees and of changes of degrees of life-near cessation (as good as dead) or a trend toward cessation (diminution) [p. 9].

In order to focus upon the aftereffects of the traumatic process, I want to highlight the *direct* aftereffects of the following elements of the traumatic process: (1) the confrontation with death; (2) the affective blocking and numbing; (3) the constriction of cognitive and executive function, and (4) the defeat and surrender sequel.

I have discussed the dire consequences of fear of "prolectic" (Spitz, 1963) (i.e., gratification expecting) affects for the chances of forming satisfactory object relations (Krystal, 1975). Murray (1967) stressed the tendency to "deanimate the animate":

> Here it is as if the person's primal springs of vitality had dried up, as if he were empty or hollow at the very core of his being. There is a striking absence of anything but the most

> perfunctory and superficial social interactions; output as well
> as intake is at a minimum. The person is a nonconductor, to
> him the human species is wholly uninviting and unlovable, a
> monotonous round of unnecessary duplicates [p. 9].

This tragic state can be seen as a giving up of all hope of satisfactory human contacts, resulting from the destruction of basic trust. Thus Murray summarizes his observations of a patient: "all empathy was dead in him; he was inert as a stone, unmoved by the events or confrontations which moved others" (p. 10).

This description fits exactly the aftereffects of severe psychic trauma as outlined above. A case in point is *The Pawnbroker,* a fictionalized portrait of a survivor of Nazi persecutions by Wallant (1962). Camus's character Meursault is another example, which Leites (1953) called "the syndrome of affectlessness." It illustrates that this condition can develop under traumatic circumstances which occur in everyday life. Murray (1967) felt that Herman Melville was the same kind of person, and that he portrayed his state in many of his characters, particularly Captain Ahab and Bartleby the Scrivener.

The next group of direct aftereffects of massive psychic trauma is a continuation of the psychic constriction in the trauma state. What makes the constriction persist is not clear. There certainly is a lack of motivation to reexpand one's mental function; there is an identification with death, and in survivors of a group disaster an identification with the dead (Niederland, 1961; Lifton, 1967); there also is a question of the possibility of lasting organic changes (Lipson, 1976; Weiss et al., 1975). At any rate, the posttraumatic psychic constriction is a widely occurring state, though it varies greatly in its intensity. Lifton (1976) has conceptualized this disturbance as "a form of desensitization; it refers to an incapacity to feel or to confront certain kinds of experience, due to blocking or absence of inner forms or imagery that can connect with such experience" (p. 27). The manifestations of the continued constriction of mental function take the following forms:

1. A general dullness, obtuseness, and a concomitant lowering of occupational and social functions which may last a life-

time. Some of the highly educated concentration camp survivors I studied have gone from responsible positions prior to the persecutions to the very lowest occupations after their liberation. In family life, the parents experience a blocking of their ability to evaluate individual acts of their children, and therefore cannot guide them or serve as models in anticipating dangers or problems.

2. Episodic "freezing." This response in situations of stress or danger is not consistent, but quite characteristic. In the Israeli Army, for instance, survivors of Nazi persecutions were found to be subject to such rare but disastrous occurrences (Krystal, 1971). These individuals appear to be "blunderers" because when they are under stress, some of the time they do precisely the wrong thing. The basic pattern is a paralysis, both physical and mental, resulting in inactivity or causing the person to be spasmodically ineffective or "dumb." Impairments in these and other functions become especially conspicuous in the presence of a dominant or threatening person, a phenomenon that represents a repetition of the *surrender* behavior. Among the lasting characterological changes following massive psychic traumatization are patterns of accepting a defeated inferior position and function for life. These patterns are easily observable in animals, for instance, in the lifelong reaction of submission of a "broken" horse or defeated male in the animal pack.

3. Pseudophobia, the continuing capacity of memory fragments to evolve intense affects. Some of these manifestations resemble phobias, but the object of the original fear is not forgotten. A person may be terrified, for instance, of anything referring to bombing, because he fears the emotions evoked by such explosions. Others become terrified of their own dreams, and may have to block them by the use of drugs (Krystal, 1971). Still others are especially fearful of certain stimuli which may bring back feelings of (survivor) guilt (Niederland, 1961) or depression. Thus, rather than dealing with the aftereffects of repression, the problem being anxiety, we are dealing with the aftereffects of the constriction of cognitive functions in the traumatic state, with the result that the cognitive and affective elements of the memories are, like the

rest of the trauma memory, unintegrated, and are therefore experienced as dangerous by virtue of their acting like a trauma screen. Thus, certain events mobilize the dread expectation of the return of the trauma. For example, a hospitalization for whatever reason may induce a panic of psychotic proportions in a concentration camp survivor.

As noted previously, the freezing of affects in the catatonoid state is followed by a virtually total paralysis of all psychic functions, in which just a minimum "observing ego" is preserved. When the traumatic state is over, the memory of it having occurred, its closeness to death, is terrifying. The traumatic situation, as contrasted to the traumatic state, is also frightening, and presents one with a variety of other affects such as shame, guilt, and triumph. That is one of the reasons why the aftereffects of trauma involve a great need to experience affects—like an enormous magnification of the delayed anxiety of the "near-miss" car accident. Another cause for the repetition of the intensive affects is the need to regain comfort in *having* these affects (Krystal and Raskin, 1971). The "affect-rebound" and the need for repetitious reliving of the traumatic or even near-traumatic state is, of course, the impressive part of the "traumatic neurosis" which is so inviting to economic metaphors.

Keiser's (1967) germinal contribution to the understanding of the effects of trauma has not yet been fully elaborated. He pointed out that many ego functions may become impaired with serious consequences for further vulnerability. This review of psychic trauma adds perspectives to these problematic sequelae. For instance, the occurrence of trauma breaks down the denial of death which is a prerequisite for normal functioning. This loss, in turn, impairs the function of hope and magnifies the reactions to the perception of danger, which is anxiety. This makes the averting of anxiety by symptom formation more urgent (Greenacre, 1949). A corollary to the impairment in the denial of death is the impairment of denial of psychogenic death, that is to say, the denial of the self-destructive potential of our affective reactions. With the breakdown of the denial of the lethal potential of emotions, the capacity to tolerate emotions becomes diminished (Krystal, 1975). In addition, there is a regression in the affects themselves, both their cognitive and expressive aspects (Krystal, 1974, 1977). This regression accounts for the high incidence of psychosomatic disorders (Krystal, 1971), and the disturbance in affectivity and capacity for verbalization which Sifneos (1967) called "alexithymia." Since their emotions are undifferentiated, the patients cannot identify them as feelings or use them as signals. There is a general impairment of the fantasy life and a preoccupation with mundane details of the external environment which Marty and de M'Uzan (1963) termed "penseé opératoire." This problem works synergistically, of course, with the aftereffects of the cognitive constriction and the blocking of fantasy and imagery.

THE TRANSITION FROM THE INFANTILE TO THE ADULT TRAUMATIC PATTERNS

At what age can we expect the psychic trauma to take its "adult" as opposed to its infantile form? Freud (1939) studied the traumas whose major aftereffects were the development of neuroses. He therefore stressed: "All these traumas occur in early childhood up to about the fifth year. The periods between the ages of two and four seem to be the most important" (p. 74). As we identify the multiplicity of factors in the form of psychic trauma, we have to make allowances for individual developmental sequences. The infantile form of trauma continues as long as the affects are undifferentiated, unverbalized, and mostly somatic. The adult form of psychic trauma comes into the foreground with the development of ego functions and the capacity for the utilization of such defenses as denial, depersonalization, and derealization.

Thus, while we must postulate a gradual development for a capacity to prevent the infantile trauma state, we can say that in the first two years of life it is the rule. The infantile form of trauma tends to coincide with preoedipal conflicts and lends them some of their characteristics, e.g., the nightmarish intensity of the fears. By the time when the elaboration of fantasies

of identification with the parents in regard to the "family romance" is noticeable, the child has identified with the parents
in regard to the handling of affects and made much progress
in affect verbalization, desomatization, and differentiation. To
the extent that this process has advanced, and to the extent
that affect tolerance has started to develop, we can expect a
gradual transition of trauma from the infantile to the "adult"
form.

Since the affective development in a child is subject to rapid
regression, the nature of the traumatic incident, its severity
and duration, may cause a shift in its form. A child may initially be able to respond with affect blocking and cognitive
constriction, but if the traumatic situation continues, there
may be a regression with a massive response of primitive affect precursors.

As an example, I return to the case of Solnit and Kris
(1967). This was a 3½-year-old girl who misbehaved in the
car, whining and making wild noises while they were driving
through a swampy, desolate area. The mother, enraged,
stopped the car and yelled, "Get out!" Whereupon the child
became frightened and promised to behave. At this point, the
child "demonstrated evidence of having been traumatized.
She immediately allowed herself to be strapped into the front
seat of the car and became a good, frozen child. She was
dramatically inhibited. Her overwhelming fears of abandonment and castration were from the time of the marshland incident repeatedly played out in thinly disguised ways in the
analytic treatment" (Solnit and Kris, 1967, p. 209).

I had earlier said that the child showed the adult type of
trauma response because she was able to respond with a blocking of her affective responses and, one may assume, cognition.
What would have happened if the mother had actually left the
child in the desolate area and driven away? The blocking of
affects may have continued for a while and become even more
severe. It is more likely, however, that the child would immediately have started to call desperately for her mother and
pleaded for forgiveness and rescue, and perhaps promised to
be good from now on. If she had not been rescued right away,
her emotional expression would have become more and more

violent, and in the process the affects would have become mostly somatic, mixed in kind, and overwhelmed her with sheer pain. After a while, she might have become exhausted, stuporous, or slept for a while, only to wake up startled to resume her frantic affective pattern till the next point of exhaustion. When the affective patterns assumed the state of overwhelmed, inconsolable infantile pattern, they would have become like those of an infant and we would obviously be dealing with the infantile form of psychic trauma. We can also imagine that the sequelae of such an event would be more in line with those outlined in this essay. The aftereffects described by Solnit and Kris would, of course, not have been canceled out, but they would probably have been buried under the more severe consequences of the traumatic event per se.

Thus in evaluating childhood psychic trauma, we have to consider the development of affects and their tolerance vis-à-vis the regressive potential of the event. The other functions related to trauma prevention—the "stimulus barrier" and the ability to accomplish "psychic closing off"—develop gradually, as a result of which transition in the form of psychic trauma is relatively slow. The establishment of executive functions of such reliability and autonomy that the self-observing ego is preserved in the midst of the traumatic situation is the hallmark of maturity. My review of the traumatic state shows that in order to survive a period in the catatonoid state of aphanesis and return to life, this observing ego must be able to continue to function in the face of imminent annihilation and despite the loss of virtually all of its usual supports. While in longer-lasting traumatic states it may be possible to recall benign object representations for fantasied protection, in the acute traumatic state one stands alone and abandoned by all sources of feelings of security. This requires an ability to face helplessness and death. The stability of the self representation must be such that it can be preserved through a period when all ego functions are surrendered to automatic, even vegetative responses. If the "observing ego" can be preserved under such circumstances, then it becomes possible to develop a utilizable "trauma signal," rather than continuing the usual dread of infantile childhood trauma, which is so great that it tends to sweep away all executive functions. Under these circumstances there is a further refinement of one's resources for the adaptive handling of affects, as signals, which prevents the affects from becoming the major threat themselves.

Trauma involves the overwhelming of the normal self-preserving functions in the face of inevitable danger. *The recognition of the existence of unavoidable danger and the surrender to it marks the onset of the traumatic state, and with it, the above-described traumatic process which, if uninterrupted, terminates in psychogenic death.* My consideration of psychic trauma indicates that the development of the full-blown adult traumatic state is relatively rare. For the most part, when the causes stem from intrapsychic conflicts, the process is aborted by the utilization of various defenses, which may, however, result in the development of symptoms or symptomatic behavior. This observation gives me the opportunity to reconcile the two theories of trauma I discovered in Freud's work, just as Freud himself had done in *Inhibition, Symptom, and Anxiety* (1926).

What is frequently referred to as psychic trauma actually refers to nearly traumatic situations which did not progress to a traumatic state, but which in the process of prevention precipitated neurotic or other syndromes. What we observe commonly corresponds to Sandler's (1967) description of "ego strain," but this kind of situation is referred to in the psychoanalytic literature as "trauma," and this usage is not likely to change. For this reason, I feel that it is best to denote the full traumatic process described here as *catastrophic trauma.* Its pathological consequences are superimposed upon all the various other problems that may develop if the process is stopped along the way (Furst, 1967).

In the prevention of trauma, a hierarchy of signals is utilized and thus various pathological reactions are spawned. In this, Freud's (1926) explication of the function of signal anxiety represents the first order of signals; Petty's (1975) emphasis on the trauma signal provides a second level alarm, specifically related to the danger of "catastrophic trauma." In the above discussions, and the exploration of psychoanalytic emergencies (Petty et al., 1974), other signals and defenses utilizable in the prevention of psychogenic death are suggested and need further exploration.

SUMMARY

Psychic trauma occurs in two basic patterns: (1) the infantile form, which is an unbearable state of distress involving affect precursors and mass stimulation; (2) the adult form which is initiated by surrender to inevitable danger and consists of a progression from anxiety to catatonoid state, aphanesis, and potentially to psychogenic death. The psychic *experience* of what I called "catastrophic trauma" consists of a numbing of self-reflective functions, followed by a paralysis of all cognitive and self-preserving mental functions. The full-blown picture of the adult traumatic state is a rare occurrence. For the most part, what we call trauma refers to near-trauma, in which the threat is handled by defenses and symptom formation.

The *direct* aftereffects of infantile and adult catastrophic trauma have certain features in common: a dread expectation of the return of the traumatic state, and an anhedonia; a disturbance in affectivity; an arrest in the genetic development of affect in the infantile form, compared to regression (dedifferentiation, deverbalization, and resomatization) after the adult trauma. There is also an impairment in affect tolerance. In addition, in the adult form, there is often a sporadic continuation of the constriction in cognitive function, which may become a part of a characterological pattern of submission.

BIBLIOGRAPHY

ALLERTON, W. S. (1964), Mass Casualty Care and Human Behavior. *Med. Ann. Distr. Col.*, 33 : 206–208.

BENSHEIM, H. (1960), Die K.Z. Neurose rassish Verfolgter. *Nervenarzt*, 31 : 462–471.

BETTELHEIM, B. (1943), Individual and Mass Behavior in Extreme Situations. *J. Abnorm. Psychol.*, 38 : 417–452.

BREUER, J. & FREUD, S. (1893–95), Studies on Hysteria. *S.E.*, 2.

BURRELL, R. J. W. (1963), The Possible Bearing of Curse Death and Other Factors in Bantu Culture on the Etiology of Myocardial Infarction. In: *The Etiology of Myocardial Infarction*, ed. T. W. James & J. W. Keys. Boston: Little, Brown, pp. 95–101.

CANNON, W. B. (1942), "Voodoo" Deaths. *Amer. Anthropologist,* 44 : 169–181.

COOLIDGE, J. C. (1969), Unexpected Death in a Patient Who Wished to Die. *J. Amer. Psychoanal. Assn.,* 17 : 413–420.

DES PRES, T. (1976), *The Survivor.* New York: Oxford Univ. Press.

DILL, D. B. (1954), Human Reactions in Disaster Situations. DN-18-108-CML-2275. National Opinion Research Center, Chicago Univ.

EISSLER, K. R. (1966), A Note on Trauma, Dream, Anxiety, and Schizophrenia. *This Annual,* 21 : 17–50.

ENGEL, G. L. (1968), A Life Setting Conducive to Illness. *Ann. Int. Med.,* 69 : 293–300.

—— (1971), Sudden and Rapid Death during Psychological Stress. *Ann. Int. Med.,* 74 : 771–782.

FREUD, A. (1967), Comments on Trauma. In: *Psychic Trauma,* ed. S. S. First. New York: Basic Books, pp. 235–245.

FREUD, S. (1893), On the Psychical Mechanisms of Hysterical Phenomena. *S.E.,* 3 : 25–39.

—— (1900), The Interpretation of Dreams. *S.E.,* 4.

—— (1919), Introduction to Psycho-Analysis and the War Neuroses. *S.E.,* 17 : 205–210.

—— (1926), Inhibitions, Symptoms and Anxiety. *S.E.,* 20 : 77–175.

—— (1930), Civilization and Its Discontents. *S.E.,* 21 : 57–145.

—— (1937), Analysis Terminable and Interminable. *S.E.,* 23 : 209–253.

—— (1939), Moses and Monotheism. *S.E.,* 23 : 3–137.

—— (1940–41), Sketches for the 'Preliminary Communication.' *S.E.,* 1 : 146–154.

—— (1956), Report on My Studies in Paris and Berlin. *S.E.,* 1 : 5–15.

FURST, S. S., ed. (1967), *Psychic Trauma.* New York: Basic Books.

GREENACRE, P. (1949), A Contribution to the Study of Screen Memories. *This Annual,* 3/4 : 73–84.

HAURI, P. (1974), Sleep in Depression. *Psychiat. Ann.,* 4 : 24–32.

HOPPE, K. D. (1971), The Aftermath of Nazi Persecutions Reflected in Recent Psychiatric Literature. In: *Psychic Traumatization,* ed. H. Krystal & W. G. Niederland. Boston: Little, Brown, 8 : 169–204.

JASPERS, K. (1963), *General Psychopathology.* Univ. Chicago Press, 1963.

JOHNSON, D. A. (1970), An Experimental Evaluation of Behavioral Inaction under Stress. IRAD Technical Report #D23-70-215, McDonnell Douglas Corp. Rep. #MDC j1008.

JONES, E. (1929), Fear, Guilt and Hate. In: *Papers on Psycho-Analysis.* London: Baillière, Tindall & Cox, 1950, pp. 304–319.

KEISER, S. (1967), Freud's Concept of Trauma and a Specific Ego Function. *J. Amer. Psychoanal. Assn.,* 15 : 781–794.

KHAN, M. M. R. (1963), The Concept of Cumulative Trauma. *This Annual,* 18 : 286–306.

KNAPP, P. H., MUSHATT, C., & NEMETZ, S. H. (1966), Asthma, Melancholia and Death. *Psychosom. Med.,* 28 : 114–133.

KOSINSKI, J. (1965), *The Painted Bird.* Boston: Houghton Mifflin.

KRIS, E. (1956), The Recovery of Childhood Memories in Psychoanalysis. *This Annual*, 11 : 54–88.

KRYSTAL, H., ed. (1968), *Massive Psychic Trauma*. New York: Int. Univ. Press.

—— (1970), Trauma and the Stimulus Barrier. Read at the Amer. Psychoanal. Assn.

—— (1971), Trauma. In: *Psychic Traumatization*, ed. H. Krystal & W. G. Niederland. Boston: Little, Brown, 8 : 11–28.

—— (1974), The Genetic Development of Affects and Affect Regression. In: *The Annual of Psychoanalysis*, 2 : 98–126. New York: Int. Univ. Press.

—— (1975), Affect Tolerance. In: *The Annual of Psychoanalysis*, 3 : 179–219. New York: Int. Univ. Press.

—— (1977), Aspects of Affect Theory. *Bull. Menninger Clin.*, 41 : 1–26.

—— & NIEDERLAND, W. G. (1968), Clinical Observations of the Survivor Syndrome. In: *Massive Psychic Trauma*, ed. H. Krystal. New York: Int. Univ. Press, pp. 327–348.

—— & RASKIN, H. (1970), *Drug Dependence*. Detroit: Wayne State Univ. Press.

LEITES, N. (1953), Trends in Affectlessness. In: *Personality in Nature, Society and Culture*, ed. C. Kluckhohn, H. A. Murphy, & D. M. Schneider. New York: Knopf, pp. 618–632.

LIFTON, R. J. (1967), *Death in Life: Survivors of Hiroshima*. New York: Random House.

—— (1976), *The Life of the Self*. New York: Simon & Schuster.

LIPSON, C. T. (1976), Personal communication.

MARTY, P. & M'UZAN, M. DE (1963), La "penseé opératoire." *Rev. Franç. Psychanal.*, S27 : 1345–1356.

MEEHL, P. E. (1975), Hedonic Capacity. *Bull. Menninger Clin.*, 49 : 295–307.

MEERLOO, J. A. M. (1948), *Patterns of Panic*. New York: Int. Univ. Press.

—— (1959), Shock, Catalepsy and Psychogenic Death. *Int. Rec. Med.*, 172 : 384–393.

MENNINGER VON LERCHENTHAL, E. (1936), Death from Psychic Causes. *Bull. Menninger Clin.*, 12 : 31–36, 1948.

MINKOWSKI, E. (1946), L'anesthesie affective. *Ann. Medico-psychol.*, 104 : 8–13.

MURPHY, W. F. (1961), A Note on Trauma and Loss. *J. Amer. Psychoanal. Assn.*, 9 : 519–532.

MURRAY, H. A. (1967), Dead to the World. In: *Essays in Self-Destruction*, ed. E. S. Shneidman. New York: Science House.

NIEDERLAND, W. G. (1961), The Problem of the Survivor. *J. Hillside Hosp.* 10 : 233–247.

—— (1965), An Analytic Inquiry into the Life and Work of Heinrich Schliemann. In: *Drives, Affects, Behavior*, ed. M. Schur. New York: Int. Univ. Press., 2 : 369–396.

PETTY, T. A. (1975), Personal communication.

—— KRYSTAL, H., LIPSON, C. T., RASKIN, H. A., & WARREN, M. (1974), The Emergency and the Psychoanalyst. Read at the Amer. Psychoanal. Assn.

RICHTER, C. P. (1959), The Phenomenon of Unexplained Sudden Death in Animal and Man. In: *The Meaning of Death,* ed. H. Feifel. New York: McGraw Hill, pp. 302–313.

ROSENBERG, E., *see* Zetzel, E. R.

SANDLER, J. (1967), Trauma, Strain, and Development. In: *Psychic Trauma,* ed. S. S. Furst. New York: Basic Books, pp. 154–174.

SAUL, L. J. (1966), Sudden Death at Impasse. *Psychoanal. Forum,* 1 : 88–93.

SELIGMAN, M. E. P. (1975), *Helplessness.* San Francisco: W. H. Freeman.

SHNEIDMAN, E. S. (1976a), A Psychologic Theory of Suicide. *Psychiat. Ann.,* 6 : 76–89.

———— (1976b), Suicide Notes Reconsidered. *Psychiat. Ann.,* 6 : 90–91.

SIFNEOS, P. (1967), Clinical Observations on Some Patients Suffering from a Variety of Psychosomatic Diseases. *Acta Med. Psychosom.* Proceedings of the Seventh European Conference on Psychosomatic Research. Rome, pp. 452–458.

SIMPSON, M. A. (1976), Self-Mutilation and Suicide. In: *Suicidology.* New York: Grunne & Stratton. Reviewed by E. S. Shneidman (1976), *Psychiat. Ann.,* 6 : 92–93.

SOLNIT, A. J. & KRIS, M. (1967), Trauma and Infantile Experiences. In: *Psychic Trauma,* ed. S. S. Furst. New York: Basic Books, pp. 175–220.

SPITZ, R. A. (1963), Ontogenesis. In: *Expression of the Emotions in Man,* ed. P. H. Knapp. New York: Int. Univ. Press, pp. 36–60.

STERN, M. M. (1951a), Pavor Nocturnus. *Int. J. Psycho-Anal.,* 32 : 302–309.

———— (1951b), Anxiety, Trauma, and Shock. *Psychoanal. Quart.,* 20 : 179–203.

———— (1953), Trauma and Symptom Formation. *Int. J. Psycho-Anal.,* 34 : 202–218.

———— (1968a), Fear of Death and Neurosis. *J. Amer. Psychoanal. Assn.,* 16 : 3–31.

———— (1968b), Fear of Death and Trauma. *Int. J. Psycho-Anal.,* 49 : 457–461.

STRACHEY, J. (1961), Editor's note [S. Freud, The Ego and the Id]. *S.E.,* 19 : 57, n. 3.

TYHURST, J. S. (1951), Individual Reactions to Community Disaster. *Amer. J. Psychiat.,* 107 : 764–769.

WALLANT, E. L. (1962), *The Pawnbroker.* New York: Macfadden.

WEISS, J. M., GLAZIER, H. I., POHORECKY, L. A., BRICK, J., & MILLER, N. E. (1975), Effect of Chronic Exposure to Stressors on Avoidance-Escape Behavior and on Brain Norepinephrine. *Psychosom. Med.,* 37 : 522–534.

ZETZEL, E. R. (1949), Anxiety and the Capacity to Bear It. *Int. J. Psycho-Anal.,* 30 : 1–12.

———— (1965), Depression and the Incapacity to Bear It. In: *Drives, Affects, Behavior,* ed. M. Schur. New York: Int. Univ. Press, pp. 243–274.

On Projection

A Study of Freud's Usage

DARIUS ORNSTON, M.D.

> . . . in ego psychology it will be difficult to escape
> what is universally known; it will rather be a question
> of new ways of looking at things and new ways of ar-
> ranging them than of new discoveries.
>
> FREUD (1933, p. 60).

ALTHOUGH PSYCHOANALYTIC USES OF THE TERM PROJECTION ARE
varied, there have been very few attempts to assemble a consistent way of thinking about projective mental activities.
Freud never published a systematic study of these ideas.
Therefore I have based this report on his writings. I will show
that Freud developed projection into a single and coherent
psychoanalytic concept. Modern usage is similar to Freud's,
except that his formulation of defensive projection is commonly misunderstood.

First, I will summarize Freud's development of this idea.
Then I will separate his usage into three parts: projection as a
constitutive mental activity, defensive projection, and projection as a mode of thinking and feeling in everyday life. Others
have tried to organize the psychoanalytic psychology of projection. I will review problems which these authors evidenced

Assistant Clinical Professor of Psychiatry, Yale School of Medicine, New
Haven, Conn.
In this paper, superior numbers refer to end notes.[1]

and summarize their suggestions for clarifying these ideas. Finally, I will list some of the important questions which remain.

As much as possible, I am going to defer discussion of terms which Freud did not use,[2] such as externalization[3] and projective identification,[4] although in modern writings these words sometimes clearly refer to Freud's concept. Also for now, I will set aside Kleinian usages of projection because they are so very different.

FREUD'S USAGE

Freud was writing about thinking when he said that the use of the same word for apparently different concepts "is no doubt accounted for by some identity in the psychical processes concerned which we have not yet grasped" (1913a, p. 85).[5] His deliberate strategy for the development of psychoanalysis as a science was to hold off comprehensive definitions of terms in order to allow unhindered observation and evolution of consistent conventions and conceptions. He was a fine writer: he disliked unnecessary technical terms.[6]

A major problem for a student of Freud's ideas and language is that he constantly experimented with terms, metaphors, models, and points of view. He used many different words for the same idea, and the same term to refer to several, somewhat different, ideas (I will give a few examples below). This may be one reason why the Index to the *Standard Edition* is quite incomplete; for example, it contains fewer than half of Freud's explicit uses of projection. Of course, it follows that the set of *ideas* which I am about to discuss is not indexed at all. Often, he eloquently detailed this concept without using any artificially specialized terms.[7] In this study all of my citations about projection refer to Freud's explicit use. There are two exceptions which are duly noted: they are his discussions of empathy and prejudice.

Freud's usage of projection (*Projektion*) was remarkably congruent throughout his work, both as a neurologist and in his psychoanalytic writings from 1895 until the end. (I will examine three apparent exceptions on p. 135.)

As a neurologist, he had used this term conventionally, to refer to a "point by point and element by element" (1893, p. 161) recomposition at a different level of neural organization. In his book on the aphasias (1891a), he had demonstrated that his teacher, Theodor Meynert, must be wrong about neuro-anatomical "projection, i.e., a point by point representation, of the body in the cerebral cortex" (p. 47) because cerebral projection of the body is anatomically impossible (1891b). Similarly, he had distinguished peripherospinal defects as due to a "projection paralysis," and contrasted them to the results of cortical injury. Representation in the cortex is the result of reorganization during transmission through several sets of neurons: therefore, "It is no longer a true projection" (1893, p. 161).

In one of his descriptions of the crucial concepts of condensation and displacement, he used point-for-point projection similarly (1900, p. 281). He said that he had formed his collective dream figure of Irma by passing over to her, point by point, everything that reminded him of the people involved in his dream thoughts. He described his composition of Dr. R., in his dream about his uncle with the yellow beard, somewhat differently;

> I did not combine the features of one person with those of another and in the process omit from the memory-picture certain features of each of them. What I did was to adopt the procedure by means of which Galton produced family portraits: namely by projecting two images onto a single plate, so that certain features common to both are emphasized, while those which fail to fit in with one another cancel one another out and are indistinct in the picture. In my dream about my uncle the fair beard emerged prominently from a face which belonged to two people and which was consequently blurred [p. 293].

Freud was developing projection as a *mental* activity. This was still implicit in Dora:

> A grown-up person who wanted to throw back abuse would look for some really exposed spot in his antagonist and would

not lay the chief stress upon the same content being repeated. In paranoia the projection of a reproach on to another person without any alteration in its content and therefore without any consideration for reality becomes manifest as the process of forming delusions [1905a, p. 35].

For Freud, projecting meant that a person experiences his own feeling, impulse, perception, fantasy, or whatever "peculiarities" (1912a, p. 117) as equally true of someone else, often quite consciously.[8] Such a person can think diffusely about some of the mental activities of self[9] and other as if they were the same. Then, and only then, he can withhold belief in his own mental activity and attend to or explain the other person's activity with "assimilatory delusions" (1950a, p. 227).

Freud suggested that normal ideas of reference may be both constant and unconscious:

> There thus runs through my thoughts a continuous current of 'personal reference', of which I generally have no inkling. . . . It is as if I were obliged to compare everything I hear about other people with myself; as if my personal complexes were put on the alert whenever another person is brought to my notice. This cannot possibly be an individual peculiarity of my own: it must rather contain an indication of the way in which we understand 'something other than ourself' in general [1901b, p. 24].

In ordinary and everyday life, that is, during what Freud called "normal delusions of observation and normal projection" (1950a, p. 209), we remain self-aware and can readily shift perspective.

He described hysterical attacks as "nothing else but phantasies translated into the motor sphere, *projected on to motility and portrayed in pantomime.* It is true that the phantasies are unconscious; but apart from this they are of the same nature as the phantasies which can be observed directly in day-dreams or which can be elicited by interpretation from dreams at night" (1909a, p. 229; my italics).

One can regard such projecting and portraying as relatively private and experimental, enactive cognition (Bruner, 1964).

This regressive activity is comparable to some kinds of play, to imitative learning, and to empathizing, which we do somewhat somatically. One of the differences between current usage and Freud's is that he rarely wrote about "the process which psychology calls 'empathy [*Einfühlung*]' and which plays the largest part in our understanding of what is inherently foreign to our ego in other people" (1921a, p. 108ff.). With *Einfühlung,* Freud denoted *only* a person's regressively thinking about, that is, diffusely experiencing or regarding, self and other as the same.[10] Thus, he began to heal an artificial rupture, traditional in the theories of academic psychology, where mental activity is broken up into cognition and affect. Freud never resolved this problem (1926a, p. 132f.).

When Freud suggested that the concept of a structural ego may "be regarded as a mental projection of the surface of the body" (1923, p. 26, n.), he offered a way in which his *colleagues* could *conceptualize* "a body ego" *psychoanalytically.* There is no question that he had established psychoanalytic projection as a distinct *mental* activity.

Throughout his psychoanalytic work, both clinical and metapsychological, *Freud described projection as one kind of thinking and feeling.* Despite his intent to develop a biologically based psychology, he made no other changes in his ways of using this term after 1895. I will now summarize the evidence for these judgments.

PROJECTION AS A CONSTITUTIVE MENTAL ACTIVITY

Ontogenetically, Freud used projection for two ideas about an infant's mental functioning (Rapaport, 1950). However, deferring definitions as premature (1915a, p. 117), he never compared: (1) projection, that is, an infant orienting himself by defining himself in relationship to surroundings (1915a, p. 134ff.),[11] an activity which Freud also called mental "differentiation" (1930, p. 67f.), with (2) the tendency of an infant or primitive person "to project his existence outwards into the world and to regard every event which he observes as the manifestation of beings who at bottom are like himself. It is

his only method of comprehension" (1927, p. 22).[12] He also
called this personification as well as animistic thinking.[13]

These two psychological activities are the early developmental bases for an adult to regress and think projectively
(1913a, p. 64ff.).[14] That is, after characterizing infant projection independently from adult projection, Freud linked these
activities with an ontogenetic formulation. A projecting adult
who mentally asserts that self and object representations are
enough alike for him to understand what another person is
thinking or saying, or, a person who unconsciously comprehends a present and puzzling situation by consciously or unconsciously remembering a past predicament, is using a kind
of thinking which a person outgrows but can never relinquish.

Freud did *not* conclude that an adult who thinks regressively
is thinking in the same way as an infant. In a part-for-the-whole manner, Freud often tended to call mental activities
which were transitorily, or somewhat, projective by that name.
In this way, he was able to demonstrate and emphasize ontogenetic and formal continuity. Yet, by using the same name
for primary or undifferentiated infant types of cognition and
for more integrated, regulated, and specialized secondary processes, among which regressive dedifferentiation may be but
one, constitutive activity or mode, Freud did obscure major
differences and foster some confusion (Rapaport, 1950, p.
347; 1951b, p. 338, n. 2).

From early on, Freud characterized adult projection as "a
psychical mechanism which is very commonly employed in
normal life," but which may be turned to *"abuse . . . for purposes of defense"* (1950a, p. 209).[15]

> . . . projection was not created for the purpose of defense; it
> also occurs where there is no conflict. The projection outwards of internal perceptions is a primitive mechanism, to
> which, for instance, our sense perceptions are subject, and
> which therefore normally plays a very large part in determining the form taken by our external world. Under conditions
> whose nature has not yet been sufficiently established, internal perceptions of emotional and thought processes can be
> projected outwards in the same way as sense perceptions;

they are thus employed for building up our mental representations of the external world [1913a, p. 64, p. 95ff.; see also: 1919; 1923, p. 20; 1925b, p. 237].

Freud's "Notes" on the Memoirs of Judge Schreber are generally regarded as a study of projection, although, in fact, he was writing about selected aspects of paranoia.

The most striking characteristic of symptom-formation in paranoia is the process which deserves the name of *projection*. An internal perception is suppressed [*sic*], and, instead, its content, after undergoing a certain kind of distortion, enters consciousness in the form of an external perception. In delusions of persecution the distortion consists in a transformation of affect; what should have been felt internally as love is perceived externally as hate. We should feel tempted to regard this remarkable process as the most important element in paranoia and as being absolutely pathognomonic for it, if we were not opportunely reminded of two things. In the first place, projection does not play the same part in all forms of paranoia; and, in the second place, it makes its appearance not only in paranoia but under other psychological conditions as well, and in fact it has a regular share assigned to it in our attitude towards the external world. For when we refer the causes of certain sensations to the external world, instead of looking for them (as we do in the case of others) inside ourselves, this normal proceeding, too, deserves to be called projection. Having thus been made aware that more general psychological problems are involved in the question of the nature of projection, let us make up our minds to postpone the investigation of it (and with it that of the mechanism of paranoic symptom-formation in general) until some other occasion; and let us now turn to consider what ideas we can collect on the subject of the mechanism of repression in paranoia [1911a, p. 66].

I think that in this passage Freud meant "suppressed" in the sense of consciously not thinking about a private perception. Previously, in 1895 or 1896, he had written that "in paranoia repression takes place after a complicated conscious process of thought" (1950a, p. 227), and that one who projects defensively "withdraws his acknowledgement of the self-reproach" (1896, p. 184). In chapter 7 of his book on dreams (1900), he had distinguished "*re*pressed" as meaning more unconscious (p. 606, n.).

Unfortunately, Freud always deferred a systematic consideration of projection. Strachey believed that he intended to publish a separate metapsychological study which never appeared.[16] Freud did discuss the metapsychology of paranoia, phobias, and jealousy, three pathological states in which a person uses projection (which is an ordinary activity) defensively. In the very few metapsychological discussions where he referred to projection explicitly, he said that a person behaves "as if" or "as though" he were projecting anxiety or excitation outward.[17] Projection was one way in which a severely disordered person could make bearable sense of his ideas and feelings by forming symptoms. *"The delusional formation, which we take to be the pathological product, is in reality an attempt at recovery, a process of reconstruction"* (1911a, p. 71).[18] In fact, the theoretical section of Freud's paper on Schreber's biography is mostly about repression (which at that time was still a rubric for all defensive activities), in the developmental history of a person who, later on, used projection to construct paranoid symptoms. In the last line of the passage I just quoted, Freud carefully drew this distinction. Projection was a formulation about adaptation. Defense was a motive. Freud's "Notes" are about the pathogenesis of paranoia and not primarily about projection.

Freud discussed projection similarly later on. After withdrawing attention from his own activity, a person can attend to real evidence of another person's "unconscious impulses of the same kind" (1922, p. 224).[19] Thus, for the most part, projecting was neither defensive nor pathological. These were merely two of the ways in which a person could use, or make evident, his projective thinking.

PROJECTION AS DEFENSIVE ACTIVITY

Dora complained to Freud, again and again, about her preoccupation with her father's sexual affair. She said, " 'I can think of nothing else.' " Freud likened this *"reactive* reinforcement" of her repression of her own sexual activities to a prejudice which is intensely asserted because it is a way of attenuatedly *gratifying,* while repressing, a contrary and unconscious thought about the same person or people (1905a, p. 54f.). Freud made similar observations about the symptomatic activities of the Rat Man (1909b). Thus, he showed, *"the patient's symptoms constitute his sexual activity* (whether wholly or in part)" (1906, p. 278).[20]

Dora was projectively fascinated in a homosexual as well as a heterosexual way (1905, p. 60). Later, Freud described feminine homosexual activities in paranoid disorders (1915b).[21] He thought that the link between homosexuality and paranoid thinking should be psychoanalytically refined: it might hold up only for certain *kinds* of paranoid thinking (1911a, p. 63f.) and *some* homosexual activities and relationships.[22] For example, when he wrote about Schreber, he added a line to his book on dreams, observing "how frequently reversal [of meaning] is employed precisely in dreams arising from repressed homosexual impulses" (1900, p. 327).

Defensive projection is always an assertion developed from ambivalence. In fact, Freud said that it is ambivalence which makes paranoid projection possible.[23] Ambivalence means that a person *simultaneously* experiences two or more aspects of a single, as yet undifferentiated, affect such as fascination and revulsion, or, pity and cruelty. Early developmental forms of loving and hating are hardly to be distinguished (Freud, 1915a, p. 139).[24] Infantile *ambivalence* precedes psychic *conflict* which requires more distinct affects and somewhat differentiated object relationships. A severely schizophrenic person is ambivalently unaware of emotional conflict because he regressively muddles feelings which we regard as contradictory (Bleuler, 1911, pp. 54f., 374ff.). Thus, ambivalence partially explains the sharp and sudden reversals of affect which are common when a person is functioning less integratedly and more passionately, more in accord with primary process.[25]

It follows that a person who projects defensively resolves ambivalence and yet tends to remain intensely conflicted. He may differentiate defensively, that is, he may mentally clarify and define himself by exaggeratedly contrasting another: *"He is effeminate,"* or, *"She is competitive."* At the same time, however, he asserts that he understands the other and sustains a mental relationship with the same individual. It matters to him. (Reality testing and judging are ontogenetically related but different [Freud, 1925b].) Such a person cares. By thinking projectively about his own mental activities as more true of another person, he can organize mentally in order to continue to care *consciously* (Freud, 1911a; Waelder, 1951). Freud reconsidered Little Hans as having projectively reorganized his ambivalent mental relationships into a phobic "system of thought" which was consciously manipulable (1926a, pp. 101–110, 126–131).[26] At about the same time, he wrote of negation as an analytic patient's way of both saying and rejecting an offensive idea, that is, *initially* bringing something to mind in the form of a projection: " 'Now you'll think that I mean to say something insulting, but really I've no such intention' " (1925b, p. 235).[27] And, remember Dora's riposte, " 'I knew you would say that' " (1905a, p. 69). Freud wrote of projection as a way of lessening guilt by justifying one's doing the same thing which one projected (1950a, p. 226),[28] or of shifting responsibility for one's thoughts (1910a, p. 221f.), or of regarding one's mentation or memory as credible (1918b, p. 37, n. 5). In everyday life, as in most analyses, a person can assess, modify, and even cancel a projection (Kovacs, 1912; Waelder, 1951; D. C. Smith, 1974).

Freud always recognized that paranoia posed very different problems. For example, he suggested four reasons why people are resolutely resistant about their paranoid ideas. (1) These ideas are usually historically, that is, developmentally, true. (2) A paranoid person secondarily revises his ideas to fit his present mental reality. (3) One always builds a delusion on at least a kernel of consensually valid truth in one's surroundings. (4) Paranoid people unconsciously induce or seduce corroborative activity from others.[29]

Freud steadily relied on pathology to make "discernible by isolation and exaggeration conditions which would remain concealed in a normal state" (1933, p. 121).[30] His theoretical asides about adult projection almost always came in the middle of a discussion of paranoia. This may be one reason why projection is often accorded an ominous taint, a paradoxical connotation of pathology. We have learned a great deal from the study of extreme and transparent uses of ordinary mental activities, but Freud was aware that the study of "abnormal mental life" distorts a writer's point of view (1928, p. 196).

He described one of his major contributions: "We perceived the close relations, the internal identity indeed, between pathological processes and what are known as normal ones" (1933, p. 145). He demonstrated common *processes* while distinguishing different *diagnoses*. This was one of the radical ideas in his books on dreams (1900) and sexuality (1905b). He was correcting a basic tenet and prevailing truth: most nineteenth-century psychiatrists were sure that all mental illnesses were brain diseases due to inherited degeneracy and altogether different from normal functioning (Decker, 1977). It is ironic that precisely Freud's careful demonstrations of the informative continuities between abnormal and normal have been misapprehended by those who regard projection as a primitive or pathological defense.

When Freud described projection as the most "striking" or *apparent* characteristic of symptom formation in paranoia (1911a, p. 66), he considered projection sequentially, wrested apart from other kinds of thinking. For the sake of descriptive clarity, he dissected this concept out from the complexly simultaneous ways in which any person actually thinks. He cautioned that this was a major distortion in his book on the aphasias (1891a, p. 57) and throughout his psychoanalytic work. While repression was still a general rubric for defense, he emphasized that "repression proper" must be constant and ongoing: it is never a definitive and permanent act (1915d). However, "we have no way of conveying knowledge of a complicated set of simultaneous events except by describing them successively; and thus it happens that all our accounts are at fault to begin with owing to one-sided simplification and must wait till they can be supplemented, built on to, and so set right" (1940, p. 205).[31] Thus, among other ways, he may appear to have construed projection as a momentary mechanism (Werner, 1948), something like a semiautomatic tool, which one either fires off in order to attribute one's own feeling or impulse altogether to another, or else one does not use it at all. After some vigorous editing, Freud can be quoted in support of this economic simplification.

Holt (1967a) pointed out that because of Freud's expository style, "No other writer is easier to misrepresent by quoting him out of context, for he characteristically states his points 'as it were, dogmatically—in the most concise form and in the most unequivocal terms' (1940, p. 144) and then later on puts in the reasonable qualifications that take the harsh edge of extremity off the original formulation" (p. 361).[32]

Freud experimented and dealt with evolving concepts which were very similar in two ways. Either he kept them apart until he could distinguish them: he always did this with transference and projection. Or he "began by exaggerating [a] distinction" (1905b, p. 212), setting up an artificially clear polarity which he could modify into a continuum. Mostly, he kept introjection apart from projection. In separate contexts he used both of these terms to refer to mentally asserting a common quality, to imitatively forming psychic structure, and in his basic formulation about loss and mental restitution.[33]

Thus far, I have found three passages in which Freud began with a bold assertion that introjection was opposite to projection. In each of these, he went on to demonstrate the commonality of these two ideas. For example, at the end of "Instincts and Their Vicissitudes" (1915a), he bolstered his case for two primary instincts with a set of irreducible polarities of psychic life. After quoting Ferenczi's (1909) idea of introjection as a vivid counterpart to projection, he immediately began to qualify. "For the pleasure-ego the external world is divided into a part that is pleasurable, which it has incorporated into itself, and a remainder that is extraneous to it. *It has separated off a part of its own self,* which it projects into the external world and *feels* as hostile" (p. 136; my italics).[34] Whenever he used projection he reasserted psychic continuity. Even for a putative pleasure ego, projecting was a way of continuing to think and feel about a disavowed or "extraneous" part of one-self (J. H. Smith, 1977). Rarely, Freud used graphic phrases like "expel" and "transpose outwards," but he always immediately qualified them, recognizing projection as a way of establishing what we loosely call psychological distance—that is, defining and mentally mastering in relationship to oneself.[35]

Until the end, Freud regarded acting destructively or aggressively on others as motivated by a death instinct and vital to self-preservation: "destroying some other thing . . . instead of its own self" (1930, p. 119). And he regarded affective or motor discharge as cathartic.[36] But he did not call this sort of thing projection. This common misunderstanding is very different from his way of conceptualizing projection as one, among several ongoing kinds of, mental activity; as one way of mentally approximating in order to perceive and then successively modifying. Projecting is the way in which a person characterizes a relationship by thinking about what at bottom can only be his own feelings, impulses, or other mental activities.

PROJECTION AS A MODE OF THINKING

While describing the ontogeny of thinking in economic terms, Freud (1911b) wrote that thinking requires delay[37] and "is essentially an experimental kind of acting. . . . It is probable that thinking was originally unconscious, in so far as it went beyond *mere ideational presentations* and was directed to the *relations between impressions of objects*" (p. 221, my italics; see also 1913a, p. 85). At first, an infant can only take for granted undifferentiated relationships. He does this by mentally representing self and object as very nearly the same (1923, p. 29), but these are "mere ideational presentations." When an individual begins to learn to orient himself by sorting out mental representations of self in surroundings, he has begun to think about "relations between impressions of objects," that is, to experiment with ways of mentally relating to objects by somewhat differentiating them (Rapaport, 1951b; Gill, 1967).

Thus, Freud developed a projective point of view. This is

one organized way of considering a person's mental activities, which is that most of the time one *thinks* more or less replicatively about relationships. Freud reasoned that *attention,* which "meets the sense-impressions half way, instead of awaiting their appearance"; *perception,* which "is not a purely passive process"; and *reality testing* are developed on the basis of the way one has learned to orient, define, and sort during infancy.[38] He asserted ontogenetic and formal *essential* continuity because "all [mental] presentations originate from perceptions and are repetitions of them" (1925b, p. 237; see also 1923, p. 20).

The following passage should be compared with Freud's characterization of condensation (cited on p. 119).

> When we, no less than primitive man, project something into external reality, what is happening must surely be this: we are recognizing the existence of two states—one in which something is directly given to the senses and to consciousness (that is, is *present* to them), and alongside it another, in which the same thing is *latent* but capable of re-appearing. In short, we are recognizing the co-existence of perception and memory, or, putting it more generally, the existence of *unconscious* mental processes alongside the *conscious* ones. It might be said that in the last analysis the 'spirit' of persons or things comes down to their capacity to be remembered and imagined after perception of them has ceased . . . immutability and indestructibility are qualities which we no longer attribute to conscious but rather to unconscious processes, and we regard the latter as the true vehicle of mental activity" [1913a, p. 93].[39]

Mental activity is mostly unconscious; and we know that *"the most complicated achievements of thought are possible without the assistance of consciousness"* (1900, p. 593).

Recurrently frustrated, baffled, or disenchanted; confronted with what Freud called "the bitter experience of life" (1900, p. 566), an infant learns to think. One does this grudgingly, and yearnfully remembers the good old days (Ferenczi, 1926). "The development of the ego consists in a departure from primary narcissism and gives rise to a vigorous attempt to recover that state" (Freud, 1914, p. 100). Thus, Freud proposed that during early infancy, and ever after, there is an "irresistible advance towards a unification of mental life" (1921a, p. 105).[40]

> Our waking (preconscious) thinking behaves towards any perceptual material with which it meets in just the same way in which the function we are considering [secondary revision] behaves towards the content of dreams. It is the nature of our waking thought to establish order in material of that kind, to set up relations in it and to make it conform to our expectations of an intelligible whole. In fact, we go too far in that direction. An adept in sleight of hand can trick us by relying upon this intellectual habit of ours. In our efforts at making an intelligible pattern of the sense-impressions that are offered to us, we often fall into the strangest errors or even falsify the truth about the material before us [1900, p. 499; 1901a, p. 666].

Precisely because of what he wryly called our intellectual habit, it is very difficult to get a human being to think about anything in an unaccustomed way (1905a, p. 11; 1916–17, pp. 214, 282).

If we cannot achieve mental "unification," at least we assert some consciously bearable "order." An adult remembers, perceives, and comprehends self in surroundings by unconsciously thinking in familiar terms.[41] We dream, and secondarily revise our dreams, by projecting.[42]

Neurotic people, most apparently phobic and obsessive patients, have developed a whole "system of thought" based on projection. We all think projectively in order to synthesize or sustain a delusion, or form a screen memory, or in order to organize a prejudice. Projection is our mode of creating a superstition, a myth, or a taboo.[43]

> There is an intellectual function in us which demands unity, connection and intelligibility from any material, whether of perception or thought, that comes within its grasp; and if, as a result of special circumstances, it is unable to establish a true connection, it does not hesitate to fabricate a false one [1913a, p. 95].

This passage is an exception in that Freud almost always distinguished between means and motives, unlike many modern writers on projection. In addition to the pleasure principle, he devised but did not develop another broad way of thinking about motivation. Although he did not explicitly consider mental projection in his "Project," he had drafted this idea:

> *Psychical attention* . . . has a prototype in the *experience of satisfaction,* which is so important for the whole course of development, and in its repetitions, states of *craving* which have developed into states of *wishing* and states of *expecting.* I have demonstrated that these states contain the *biological justification* of all thought [1950b, p. 361].[44]

Satisfaction, like "unification" or familiar "order," is a different concept from pleasure or constancy. From early on, an infant can mentally assert some semblance of a familiar relationship in which he feels safe or effective while further differentiating. Sandler (1960) pointed out that this problem has not been sufficiently explored. "The maintenance of this *central affective state* is perhaps the most powerful motive for ego development, and we must regard the young child (and later the adult) as seeking well-being as well as pleasure-seeking; the two are by no means the same, and in analysis we often observe a conflict between the two" (p. 149, n.).

The need for satisfaction, including self-esteem and safety, should also be compared to Piaget's theory of motivation, which he calls "desirability" (1936, p. 10ff.). This idea has been elaborated by the structuralists as "desire" (Leavy, 1977, p. 216). Furthermore, it is the basis for Rubenstein's (1967) alternative to the assumption of psychic energy, as well as the attempts of Loewald (1971b) and Kernberg (1976) to revise instinct theory.

SUMMARY

As a psychoanalyst, Freud reserved projection for an activity of mental life. He described infant projection in two ways and suggested that similar activities can be discerned in adult projective thinking. Usually, he distinguished these activities from the conflicting motives (such as pleasure, constancy, satisfaction, validation, order, mental unification, defense, safety, or reparation) which he was using to explain them.

Adult projection may refer to: (1) unconsciously and selectively organizing by regressively remembering; (2) consciously considering an initial version; (3) each successive review of one's latest mental approximation. Therefore, throughout life, projection is both a way of mentally clarifying and gaining perspective by reorganizing or revising (which, misleadingly, has been called "distancing") and, usually at the same time, a way of mentally mastering by continually asserting and modifying a mental relationship. A person who projects defensively may resolve an ambivalent feeling by attributing one aspect to another person, but he remains conflicted and very much involved. He cannot get rid of anything by projecting.

Prior Attempts to Organize Projection

Several analysts have tried to order the psychoanalytic psychology of projection (Ferenczi, Kovacs, Tausk, Jelgersma, Feigenbaum, Fuchs, Weiss, Knight, Waelder, Rapaport, Jaffe, Laplanche and Pontalis, Novick and Kelly). Each came up with a somewhat different set of formulations because none but the last reviewed Freud's usage. Although I have systematically compared these works (1977), for the following discussion I have selected a few examples of characteristic difficulties which highlight unsolved problems. These citations will be unfair because most of these writers recognized how complicated the problems are and they were willing to be inconsistent. When we describe and discuss matters which we do not yet understand, inconsistency is both inevitable and advantageous.

DEFENSIVE PROJECTION

In the first edition of their psychoanalytic dictionary, Laplanche and Pontalis (1967) concisely delineated most of the problematic uses of projection. For example, they remarked that Ferenczi had used "introjection" to denote projecting a common quality or regressively thinking about the activities of self and other as the same (pp. 230, 355).

Although their survey is quite useful, they made two major errors while trying to resolve these bewildering ambiguities. They asserted that Freud assigned to projection "a fairly strict meaning. It always appears as a defense, as the attribution to another (person or thing) of qualities, feelings or wishes that the subject repudiates or refuses to recognize in himself. . . . Freud holds that such assimilations [animistic beliefs and primitive personifications] have a *refusal to recognise something* as their basic principle and *raison d'être:* 'demons' and 'ghosts' are embodiments of bad unconscious desires" (p. 352). Here they broadly extended a common misunderstanding, the notion of projection proper (see below). Secondly, they wrongly based their mistake in Freud's writing.[45]

This error has a long tradition. For example, Feigenbaum (1936) divided projection into "exosomatic . . . upon the outer world," that is, "an eliminatory process . . . essentially a vital function" (p. 319); "and the more familiar endosomatic . . . evidenced most frequently in conversion symptoms, in which the projection naturally does not pass the bounds of the body, yet retains the essential characteristics of projection, namely, defensive purpose, expulsion from the danger zone, and libidinization (genitalization) of another organ remote from the locus of the alien excitation" (p. 313). He believed that he had explained why paranoid people tend to be hypochondriacal. Feigenbaum's endosomatic projection is consonant with Freud's concept of projection *if* we regard it as a description of the way a paranoid or hysterical person may unconsciously think and feel about his body (Tausk, 1919).

Exosomatic projection is a formulation about discharge of psychic energy from an open system. Freud never used projection in this way. In fact, "If energy is used for one purpose, less is available for another. . . . [This] is the essence of the economic point of view" (Holt, 1967b, p. 34, n. 1). Feigenbaum's second formulation is about such a closed system with a limited amount of energy. I think that there are serious difficulties with this second kind of economic formulation as well.

Feigenbaum could have cited Freud in support of his own view. Thus far, I have found three exceptional uses of projection by Freud which *appear* to fit Feigenbaum's scheme and to contradict my own. (1) Freud wrote of a sensation as "centrally conditioned and projected onto the peripheral erotogenic zone" (1905b, p. 184). This was consonant with current neurological usage; with Pavlov's work, of which Freud (1905c, p. 198) was quite aware; with nineteenth-century hydrodynamic neurophysiology; and with Freud's understanding of the reflex arc, which he used as the model for his economic theory.[46] It is important to note that Freud did not suggest that one could rid oneself of excitation by projecting it outside of one's body. (2) Somewhat ambiguously, Freud candidly observed that Schreber's delusional system was similar to his own economic formulations. However, I read him as referring to Schreber's regressive mode of conceptualization as "a concrete representation and projection outwards of libidinal cathexes" (1911a, p. 78f.). Again, Freud's formulation is about a closed system. He did not suggest that Schreber got rid of anything by projecting. In fact, earlier in the same paper Freud had argued that alcoholic delusions of jealousy do not involve projection because such people cast the whole process, including both subject and object, outside of themselves (p. 64). Here I think he overstated and simplified. (3) While grappling with the economic problem of masochism, Freud (1924) said that "if one is prepared to overlook a little inexactitude," one can regard the death instinct as "directed outwards, projected" in sadism and turned inwards or introjected in masochism (p. 164). I think that he clearly cautioned the reader about his metaphor. Later in the same paper he used introjection to describe a mental activity which is very much like projection (p. 168).

Ives Hendrick formulated defensive projection very differently. We know that as long as projection is unconscious, or at least private, it is more effective as a defense. Hendrick (1936) suggested that projection "is a successful defense so long as it is incomplete, and the hostility [or whatever] is experienced as though originating both in the ego and in the other person. This is supported by the fact that when projection is most complete, the intense anxiety of paranoid panic occurs" (p. 329).[47] Hendrick agreed with Freud about defensive projection as a way of mentally differentiating an ambivalent relationship by reconstituting a version which a person can consciously bear.

Knight (1940) tried to define projection by contrasting it with introjection.[48]

> *Projection* may be defined as a method of psychological economy whereby the subject attributes his own unacceptable unconscious tendencies to an object and then perceives them as tendencies possessed by the object. Thus while introjection is an Id process which alters the structure of the Ego of the subject, projection is an unconscious Ego (or Superego) process for dealing with Id tendencies which alters the perceived character of the outside *object*. Projection and introjection are therefore not the exact converse of each other [p. 334f.].

His analysis was incomplete (Schafer, 1968a, p. 141). He had only considered introjection structurally, as synonymous with incorporation. Other authors have used it in economic and dynamic formulations.[49] On the other hand, projection would be simply a method of psychological economy.

Knight's language is more consonant with Freud's usage than the formulation itself: he described projection as a kind of thinking whereby a person mentally attributes, perceives, deals with, and alters his unconscious tendencies. But Freud usually had described *how* a person thinks quite separately from *what* a person thinks about and *why*.

Knight went on to discuss both introjection and projection as constituent mechanisms of developmental identification, and he carefully described benevolent and organizing motives for adaptive projection.

Waelder (1930) developed Freud's discussion of homosexuality and defensive projection as an example of the principle of multiple function. "Every specific method of solving a conflict situation which a person experiences as coming from without, and in which he submits passively to these outer forces, is an attempt to solve certain tasks; it is a gratification of love and hate relationships and a defense reaction, and more besides" (p. 78). He understood that defense is one way of thinking about motivation in psychoanalysis. It is a point of view about mental activities. Therefore, it is always a serious "mistake . . . to regard mechanisms as pathogenic in themselves" (Glover, 1943, p. 9).[50]

Later, Waelder (1951) was writing about paranoid thinking when he tried to describe projection as "a biological concept" about "an elementary mechanism, one of the fundamental and irreducible responses to challenge," that is, "an attempt to treat an inner stimulus as though it came from outside so as to be able to apply to it the defenses which have proved useful in dealing with external stimuli" (p. 169).[51] Then he described as separate a psychological concept which he also reduced to a defense. He asserted that paranoid projection was qualitatively different from the passionate judgment of mothers and lovers, but he did not say what the difference was. He quoted Freud's observation that most cases of repression escape our notice precisely because they are successful and that we learn about repression only when it does not work. Although he recognized that defensive projection is quite common among neurotic and normal people, he did not apply Freud's idea about successful defense to projection. As many others have done while writing about paranoia, he asserted arbitrary differences and confusing discontinuities.

Schafer (1968b) developed a clinical suggestion of Freud's (1937b, p. 267f.). If one begins to analyze a paranoid patient's defensive use of projection, one should point out "that he is emphasizing something he believes to be true of the therapist and that he must be doing so for some reason. Around the question of emphasis there is some room for discussion; around the question of projection, so named, there is usually none" (p. 56). He was surely correct about how to take this up considerately and constructively, but he was not just writing about tact. Emphasizing is much more than a euphemism: it is an activity essential to the psychoanalytic concept of defensive projecting. A delusion is not only somewhat true. A person who projects temporarily dedifferentiates in order to shift emphasis and alter relatively diffuse mental representations. Redifferentiating, he continues "to enjoy his own excitement," or whatever, as if vicariously, and "thereby to keep in some kind of touch with himself" (p. 55f.).

In 1970, Novick and Kelly published the only review and classification of Freud's usage prior to this one. They traced the inconsistency of recent writers back to Freud's works, and demonstrated that he had used projection in formulations from each of the psychoanalytic points of view. Frequently within a single paper, Freud used this term in ways which Novick and Kelly separated as "mechanical descriptive" and "psychological explanatory" (p. 71).

By "mechanical" they meant that he continued the "pre-analytic, nonpsychological and mainly descriptive" meanings, which they called "surface reflections of inner processes" (p. 72f.). They suggested that all of these relatively nondefensive mental activities should be called "externalization." However, they did not attribute the term externalization to Freud.

They classified five "interrelated but distinguishable . . . psychological explanatory" uses which Freud had made of projection:

1. Projection which is an infant's earliest differentiation.
2. Presumptions of sameness which are made by an as yet undifferentiated infant, which Novick and Kelly called "generalization" or "animism."[52]
3. Attribution of motive or responsibility for one's thoughts or actions to another person, along the lines of "You made me think of such and such" (Freud, 1918b, p. 37, n. 5).[53]
4. They acknowledged that they were proposing two, very different, uses for the term externalization: (1) a synonym for all of what they had classified as "mechanical descriptive" uses of both projection and externalization, and (2) externalization would also be "a shorthand" (p. 82, n. 9) for externalization of an aspect of the self representation, which would include *interpersonal* manipulation. They listed several varieties of (2):

—as an adaptive way of gaining temporary perspective on one's own activity. They judged this to be normal for a toddler and usually pathological for an adult.

—as "a stepping stone on the way to identification" (p. 83).

—as a self-fulfilling prophecy when rearing a child (Loewald, 1960, 1962).

—as a defense against loss of self-esteem, or as mental reparation.[54]

5. "Projection proper," that is, projection as a defense in dealing with a drive derivative, motivated by fear of fantasied dangers consequent upon drive expression.

They suggested that an infant develops projection proper relatively late because this defense requires a differentiated object representation. As a defense, "projection proper . . . has little adaptive value," is "remarkably inefficient," and may leave one "a constant prey to anxiety" (p. 84f.).[55]

In contrast, they asserted that externalization of aspects of the self "can effectively do away with painful affect," because the subject "will perceive the object as unrelated to himself, as different from himself, and as something which may be ignored, derided, or treated with contempt" (p. 86). By externalizing, they said, one disavows meaning for, or importance to, oneself.

This is not so. For example, when we premonitorily guide a developing toddler, or when we empathically dedifferentiate in order to comprehend another person's experience, we attenuate our own experience by thinking of it as having more to do with the other person. However, we do not do away with painful affect. Novick and Kelly disregarded our conflicting reasons for thinking projectively about another person: we disavow and simultaneously affirm our interest. Fearfully, hatefully, or otherwise, one very much cares and continues to care about a mental relationship which one projectively asserts or mentally alters.[56] Their conceptual category "externalization of aspects of the self" included defensive projection which works adaptively in ordinary life. When defensive projection does not work, and therefore becomes evident to one-

self and others, Novick and Kelly would call this "projection
proper."

They missed the fact that what Freud called his "mechanical" or "pictorial descriptions" (1916–17, p. 427) were, quite
often, psychological formulations. Now and again, he judged a
theory as failing to explain or lacking "psychological significance" (1909b, p. 228), because he could not integrate it with
his "systematic or dynamic" (1920a, p. 20) and libidinal metapsychology. It is not clear what constitutes a psychoanalytic explanation. Certainly Freud's concept of projection extends our
ability to understand the way a person condenses various
meanings and motives. When Freud characterized a person's
fate as "only a later projection of the father" (1928, p. 185), I
think that he concisely summarized something of how and
why we stubbornly reconstitute our early mental relationships.
Rapaport's broad definition of projection, as a mode of organizing mentally (which Novick and Kelly reduced to externalization), is neither "a surface reflection of an inner process" nor "pre-analytic, nonpsychological and mainly
descriptive." Rapaport was beginning to develop testable hypotheses about how a person thinks and about a person's motives for thinking.

Novick and Kelly asserted that what they classified as "psy-
chological-explanatory use of projection . . . undergoes progressive modification [in Freud's writings] so that finally it
refers to mechanisms of defense" (p. 71). About this, they
were wrong. When Freud published his last revision of terms
for defensive activities, he made defense into "a general designation . . . which can cover all . . . processes that have the
same purpose [i.e., motive]—namely, the protection of the ego
against instinctual demands" (1926a, p. 163f.). He subsumed
repression as one, albeit special, kind of defense for two reasons. He supposed that (1) "there is an intimate connection between special forms of defense and particular illnesses"
(p. 164). He named repression and hysteria, isolation and obsessional neurosis, but he did *not* include projection and paranoia. (2) He thought it important to discriminate the defensive
activities of an infant from those of an adult with developed

psychic structure: he had tended to do this with projection all along.

As far as I know, Freud never used the term projection proper. In *Inhibitions, Symptoms and Anxiety* he used projection to refer to defensive, phobic thinking (pp. 126 and 128); and said: "The final transformation which the fear of the super-ego undergoes is, it seems to me, the fear of death (or fear for life) which is a fear of the super-ego projected on to the powers of destiny" (p. 140). The latter may be regarded as defensive projection. It may also be considered as orienting and organizing one's way of thinking about one's present situation by mentally re-creating a familiar and adaptive, *ontogenetically patterned,* distribution of roles (Hartmann, 1956; Weiss, 1957). That is, one unconsciously attenuates a problem by projectively recasting it, until one can bear to think about it consciously (D. C. Smith, 1974).

In 1927 Freud referred to projection as a "method of comprehension . . . following an infantile model . . . [in order] to establish a relation . . . it is in fact natural to man to personify everything that he wants to understand in order later to control it (psychical mastering as a preparation for physical mastering)" (p. 22).[57] Thereafter, Freud usually discussed activities like mental differentiation, delusion formation, and psychoanalytic interpretation and construction without using projection at all (1930, 1937b). In fact, when he made his case for every analyst periodically resuming a personal analysis, he wrote: "it seems that a number of analysts learn to make use of defensive mechanisms which allow them to divert the implications and demands of analysis from themselves (probably by directing them onto other people), so that they themselves remain as they are and are able to withdraw from the critical and corrective influence of analysis" (1937a, p. 249). Discussing this problem 25 years earlier, he had called it projection (1912a, p. 117).

PROJECTION IN GENERAL MENTAL LIFE

Although Heinz Hartmann wrote very little about projection, he and his co-workers used Waelder's principle of multiple function: "The term 'defense' should not suggest the misapprehension that the process . . . is either pathological or only of a negative importance. Rather it is correct to say that the human personality is formed by psychic mechanisms which serve, also, the purpose of defense" (1946, p. 28). Ten years later he wrote, "We know projection as a pathogenic mechanism, but it is, of course, also part of normal functioning. In the grownup, a workable equilibrium is normally established between what we . . . call 'our world' and the objective knowledge of reality" (1956, p. 48). In everyday life we do this constantly. He reconsidered autoplastic and alloplastic activities in the light of such developments as Loewald's (1951) gradient of ego-reality integration, and added a third kind of adaptive behavior, "in which the individual does not effect changes of himself or of the world outside; instead the relationship between him and the outside world is changed: I am thinking of the search for and finding of a more appropriate environment" (p. 40). He was writing about how ordinary people search for, find, and mentally organize both their relationships with others and environmental realities.[58]

Rapaport extended Freud's justification for the concept of unconscious mental activity (1915c, p. 167f.). He believed (1944, p. 211), as did Hartmann (1956), that our psychoanalytic postulates of psychic continuity and determinism require a concept like projection because the physical world is discontinuous. In fact, from this point of view, "any organizing of the external world according to a principle of organization of the subject's 'private world' is considered projection" (1950, p. 348). "Projective testing studies these organizing principles by inducing the subject to bring them to bear upon more or less unstructured material, incorporating [*sic*] it into his private world" (1952, p. 463). Mentally organizing by incorporating denotes consciously or unconsciously determining in what ways such material has to do with, or makes sense to, oneself—by projecting.[59]

Rapaport suggested a threefold approach to organizing the psychoanalytic psychology of projection. We could clarify (1) a hierarchy of kinds of projection (1950, 1952), all of which are overdetermined in accord with (2) an integrated hierarchy of *motivations* for selective perception and mental organization (1951a; 1952, p. 464f.); (3) we need to integrate this theory with the developmental work of Werner and Piaget, among others (1950). Just like Freud (1900, p. 602ff.) and Piaget (1962, p. 129), Rapaport emphasized that "thinking is never a purely 'cold' process" (1951b, p. 710). Probably, we always think more or less affectively (Schafer, 1976, especially pp. 267–357).

Another way to organize the various kinds of projection would be to characterize types of reflective awareness. Rapaport pointed out that this has not been done (1951b, p. 302). He identified this problem while discussing *kinds* of consciousness: self-awareness cannot be simplified into a quantitative or linear continuum of conscious-preconscious-unconscious, or otherwise. In everyday life, a person adapts to a situation by regressively regarding himself and others in an optimal variety of ways. He varies the ways in which he is aware of specific activities, perhaps by ambivalently personifying, or by setting conditions such as regarding himself as "passive" or "private"[60] or "typical." Two vivid variants are "pathologic generalizing . . . and pathologically distorted or exaggerated reflectiveness" (1951b, p. 707).

It may turn out that one cannot altogether refrain from some kind of reflective awareness, even during creative regression (Kovacs, 1912), and more automatic (so-called "passive") behaviors which are evident when a person is angry or in love or sexually excited.[61] Self-awareness is regressively altered, but not stopped, during psychotic "hallucinatory confusion" (Freud, 1940, p. 202); most, if not all, dreams (Rapaport, 1951b, p. 707); and ordinary daydreams (Schafer, 1968a, p. 88). In our work, we think regressively, but we probably cannot refrain from some kind of self-awareness and reality testing. Empathizing, we use "evenly suspended" (*not* "free-floating") attention (Freud, 1912a, p. 111; 1900, pp. 100–103). Therefore, when the work is going well enough, we enable ourselves to recognize and sort out the initial, conscious version of empathic experience *because*, as we make it conscious, we find we have imbued it with illusory mutuality and certainty. We can redifferentiate *because* we find ourselves thinking quite emotionally, somatically, eidetically, or bisexually (Weiss, 1947, 1957).

Psychoanalysis lacks a coherent and comprehensive theory of cognition, but many have agreed with Rapaport that projection could be ordered, and introjection sorted out, if we developed an ontogenetic-regressive hierarchy of various types of thinking.[62] More or less explicitly, this led to a consideration of Freud's much neglected concept of mental differentiation and dedifferentiation.[63] However, most writers have continued to try to put these concepts about mental activity into structural and economic terms.[64]

Freud wrote about mental "differentiation" throughout his work, although this term (like many others) was not indexed in the *Standard Edition*. Conversely, he said that all of the ways in which he had described regression came down to the same kind of basic activity, that is, "primitive methods of expression and representation take the place of the usual ones" (1900, p. 548).[65] If we called the latter kind of thinking dedifferentiated, we would have two common meanings.[66] Representational dedifferentiation would mean that one thinks about other persons and/or their activities as the same as one's own. Behavioral dedifferentiation would mean that one's activities are less specialized, integrated, regulated, and flexible; that is, one thinks more syncretically, diffusely (Jacobson, 1964), intuitively, and concretely (Werner, 1948). It follows that representational dedifferentiation is one kind of behavioral dedifferentiation. In a grownup, this kind of activity is usually transitory and unconscious, but always selective and necessarily incomplete.

The advantage in calling this kind of activity "regressive" is that we remind ourselves that an adult who is thinking dedifferentiatedly can never simply reverse prior developmental differentiation. Reflective awareness may be one clear difference between an infant's as yet undifferentiated experience and the diffuse or syncretic thinking of a psychotic adult. The advantage of referring to this kind of thinking as "dedifferentiated" is that, once again, we emphasize formal similarity, but we do so by obscuring important differences (Werner, 1948).

Fuchs (1937) proposed another way of distinguishing both infant and regressive, from adult projection: we could refer to primary and secondary projection. Primary process projection is relatively diffuse and unstable, timeless and prelogical. A person who mentally dedifferentiates thinks regressively, which is to say that he uses a less specialized and integrated, less verbal and more eidetic, or somatic and enactive, "mode of thought-activity" (Freud, 1921b, p. 271), while trying to order a dissonant percept, or to organize a consciously bearable sense of self in surroundings. Thus, a person can think syncretically of learning as suckling, or of seeing as assaultive, or of a pulsation in one's clitoris as the clicking of a camera, or think receptively about one's anus, and so forth.[67]

Projection is more of a secondary process to the degree that a person's mode of thought is more specialized and integrated, regulated and intricate, flexible and independent, temporally organized, logically unified and uncontradictory.[68] This kind of mental activity includes relatively differentiated (specialized) kinds of reality testing and self-awareness: a person sorts out and compares relationships and predicaments.

Freud had pointed out that a pure primary process is no more than "a theoretical fiction" (1900, pp. 598, 603). In fact, he described many different ways of learning to organize by developing gradients of primary process reasoning,[69] and "successive versions of the secondary process, each one more efficient and adaptive than its predecessor" (Holt, 1967a, p. 372). A pure secondary process is also a fiction about integrated kinds of mental activities which are *both* more and less organized.[70] Reality testing is an excellent example of such a complex continuum of intermingled, and varyingly regressive, activities (Schafer, 1968a, p. 90f.). Probably, reality testing, like reflective awareness, can neither be quantified nor altogether stopped.

SUMMARY

Although Freud experimented with several biological metaphors, he did not try to describe projection meta-psychologically. Other analysts, who have tried, have had great difficulty. They have had to disrupt Freud's intricate formulations about mental development and adaptive regression. Also, they have mistaken the psychoanalytic psychology of defense with a confusing simplification, and ironically named it projection "proper." On the other hand, they have brought out some of the difficulties which may be inherent in the assumptions of conventional metapsychology (Rapaport and Gill, 1959). Several others have suggested that we develop Freud's concept by studying the interaction of regressive with more differentiated kinds of mental activity.

OPEN PROBLEMS

We need to develop the concept of projection because it complements and connects with so many other psychoanalytic ideas. However, closure would be premature because we are still confronted with so many unsolved problems. Some of these are terminological. We will need a clear concept in consensual language before we can integrate a psychoanalytic line of development (A. Freud, 1965).

INTROJECTION AND IDENTIFICATION

When Loewald (1951) concisely outlined a continuum of motives for kinds and degrees of integration of ego and reality, he wrote that "In the beginning phases [of development], as in some psychotic disturbances, it is hardly possible to distinguish between introjection and projection, as the boundaries between 'inside' and 'outside' are still so rudimentary and fluid that the two terms signify different directions of the same process rather than two different processes" (p. 17). If regressing or dedifferentiating is a constitutive activity in all forms of projection (or introjection), then Loewald's point must be extended well beyond infant and psychotic thinking. Obviously, projection and introjection cannot be considered as "directions" of a process without implicitly switching over into a spatial and sequential metaphor. Freud (1940), of course, did this until the end. Loewald (1962) began to correct himself, and Freud, when he wrote that "structuralization obviously is not spatial" (p. 502). He pursued this problem, and superseded the criterion of inside or outside with the idea of "dedifferentiation":

> Identification as such leads to an identity of subject and object or of parts or aspects of them . . . Identification tends to erase a difference: subject becomes object and object becomes subject. While identification is a way-station to internalization, in internalization, if carried to completion, a redifferentiation has taken place by which both subject and object have been reconstituted, each on a new level of organization. . . . Internalization as a completed process implies an emancipation from the object [1973, p. 15].

Loewald's "internalization" nearly coincides with Freud's idea of *developmental* identification. However, Freud used identification for at least two, very different, kinds of activity.

> Thus identification is not [just] simple imitation, but [also] *assimilation* on the basis of a similar aetiological pretension; it expresses a resemblance and is derived from a common element which remains in the unconscious [1900, pp. 149f., 319–327; see also 1921a].

If structure is not spatial, then what does introjection mean? Is it really the informative counterpart to projection which Ferenczi (1909) intended?

Several years ago, Schafer reviewed these terms. Following Freud's usage, he added considerably to our understanding of benevolent projection, empathic projection, and organizing projection.[71] However, he had just begun to think about Freud's warnings of the severe distortions inherent in spatial models and directional metaphors. In his 1976 book (chapter 8), he showed why we get confused about developmental identification when we think about "inside" and "outside" of psychic representations or other structures. A theory about inside and outside is immensely appealing because it feels right. It fits both ordinary human experience and the psychoanalytic language of clinical description. However, judged as a theory, rather than as a way of paraphrasing a person's own fantasy about how he thinks, or develops, or mentally defends himself, it is a regressive mode of conceptualization. Incongruously, at the end of his critique of conventional psychodynamic formulation, Schafer suggested that projection was "simply synonymous with fantasied expulsion from the body" (p. 176). Here, he overstated his point. Freud developed projection into a complicated and essential psychoanalytic abstraction.

MENTAL ORGANIZATION AND THE THEORY OF MENTAL RELATIONSHIPS

If identification has nothing to do with inside or outside, and if structure is not spatial, then what do we mean? Another way of putting this problem is to ask: Why don't we have to start from scratch each time we begin to think about something (Rapaport, 1957a)? The most important or defining characteristics of mental structure may be specialization and integration, which is to say, organization. For example, it is generally accepted that the ego is an organization. Well differentiated and intricately coordinated, simultaneous activities are one way of preserving certain differences. These facilitate unconscious, and often pleasurable, regression in everyday life. Sustained differences also account for concurrent redifferentiation. We can sort out who feels what in a given interaction because we realize that certain ranges of activity are *not* common to both self and other. However, the idea of mental structure or organization remains ambiguous. Piaget confronts the same problem and we have much to learn from his work.

Sooner or later, psychoanalysts will have to settle a much broader question. Is psychoanalytic theory intended to extend our *understanding* of mental life? If so, then there may be a place for judicious use of somatic metaphors and biological models as temporary paraphrases and organizing abstractions. However, the terminological muddle which we are trying to resolve is the direct result of precisely such vivid metaphors

and preliminary models. Or, on the other hand, is psychoanalytic theory aiming for *explanation,* in the sense of a theory
which someday can be integrated with the more objective
sciences like neurophysiology? At the turn of the century, this
problem was not evident. In modern psychoanalytic writings
these two kinds of theory are increasingly divergent and contradictory.[72]

Depending on their assumptions, different psychoanalysts
formulate the same problem in very different ways. Some
write about projection as instinctual defusion and discharge
(open system economics). Some say that a person projects his
own feeling across boundaries onto an object representation
by cathecting it as an extension of the self (closed system).
Then, it is said that he can understand another person, or
identify with him, by introjecting his own, now modified, feeling (Malin and Grotstein, 1966). Some analytic writers put
both open and closed economic formulations into a single
paragraph (Jaffe, 1968, p. 674).

This is a very different kind of theory from saying that a
person thinks diffusely about self and other as if certain of
their activities were the same; or to say that a person regards
himself as empathizing with, or fearing, another person whom
he has cast in a role complementary to his own. Schafer's
(1976) proposals for the formal language of psychoanalysis
will be useful here, when they are integrated with his own
work on object relationships (1968a) and the broad revisions
of the theory of mental relationships on which Sandler (1960)
and Kernberg (1976) are working. Unfortunately, both
Sandler and Kernberg relegated the term projection to a putative, primitive defense whereby a person projects unwanted
qualities of his own onto others.

I think that a critical study will show that they are using
Freud's concept of projection at the very center of their creative theories, but that they both call this kind of mental activity introjection. Each structural unit of these theories consists
of (1) a version of self-awareness, (2) a mutual and/or complementary activity, and (3) a way of thinking about another person. In this kind of theory, the organizing connections are

classes of mental activities which are common to several relationships, rather than instinct derivatives, necessarily spatial
representations, or words as in structuralist formulation.

A brief example of a symptom may show what I mean.
Freud (1916–17) described a 53-year-old married woman who
was unconsciously in love with her son-in-law. She found relief
in a consuming delusion that her husband was having a sexual
affair with a young employee, a former schoolmate of her
maid. Freud explained that his patient had formed "a mirror-
reflection" of her own unconscious preoccupation in this "projection of her state onto her husband." This idea served as "a
cooling compress on her burning wound" (p. 252f.).

Using Freud's formulation that a patient's symptoms may
constitute her sexual activity, I would go further. What she
projectively re-created, and elaborated in a form which she
could bear to dwell on, was a revised version of her own unconscious sexual and affectionate yearnings for her son-in-law
and for her daughter, for her maid and the maid's schoolmate—as well as for her husband as a young and sexually active man and for herself as a frantically remembered young
woman. The organizing connection is tabooed sexual activity
across generational lines. This patient condensed many mental
relationships to achieve and sustain her fluctuating preoccupation, which then she could discuss with most of those involved.
Sandler, Kernberg, and Schafer are demonstrating that this
kind of theory can be used to understand developmental identification and mental organization, while emphasizing psychic
continuity. Loewald (1971b) is attempting the same.

DISPLACEMENT, CONDENSATION, AND TRANSFERENCE

In that last passage, Freud also described his patient as generating her delusion "by the mechanism of displacement" (p.
252). Earlier in this book he had characterized this term: "We
are in the habit of combining the concepts of modification and
rearrangement under the term 'displacement'" (p. 140). Displacement refers to "transferring" emphasis by reorganizing
in accord with overdetermination (1900, pp. 307, 562). It is

not a spatial concept (Gill, 1967). Piaget was reviewing Freud's work on dreams when he pointed out that " 'displacement' and 'condensation' are inseparable, since it is impossible to combine in a single image features borrowed from several objects, without displacing the affective stress" (1945, p. 192). As previously noted, condensation and projection are very similar psychoanalytic concepts. Finally, we know that "transference arises spontaneously in all human relationships" (Freud, 1910c, p. 51). Nunberg tried to settle this last problem by declaring that "transference is a projection" (1951, p. 1).

Loewenstein was writing about transference when he said "Once a usage has become established, it is difficult if not impossible to abolish it 'by legislation' or by appeal to authority. For scientific purposes, however, for mutual understanding among analysts, and for teaching, it would be important to specify in such cases the particular meaning in which a given term is being used" (1969, p. 586). Loewenstein's reform would be radical for many, although most major writers already comply. However, this practice merely enables—it does not accomplish—evolution of the consistent conventions and consensual definitions which Freud intended.

DEVELOPMENTAL DIFFERENTIATION AND REGRESSION, PARAVERBAL COGNITION

Infant mental development and individuation must be clearly distinguished from relatively adult regression and representational dedifferentiation. Obviously, this is an enormous problem and, as with the idea of psychic structure, no single characterizing criterion will suffice. We need comparative studies of the work of Piaget, Escalona, Mahler, Werner, and many others. For the study of projection, a catalogue of kinds of self-awareness would be one useful start.

Regression means to use developmentally surmounted modes of thought. In early infancy these may be more or less diffuse. They are always preverbal. Moreover, we assume that infant mental life includes undifferentiated cognition and affect. As mental activities are increasingly specialized and in-

tegrated during ordinary development, it is unlikely that affects are separated from ideas. Furthermore, throughout life
an adult may continue to differentiate and integrate—as well
as regressively to depend upon—other very intricate kinds of
*para*verbal cognition.[73]

It is not clear how projection as I have summarized it can be
integrated with structuralist ideas which are based on the assumption that verbal organization connects all mental activity.
Structuralist formulation constantly risks carving words away
from feelings. This kind of factitious bifurcation is a familiar
problem in metapsychology. Schafer (1976) showed that this
hazard can be mitigated, if not altogether avoided.

DEFENSE

Many kinds of defensive activity have been named, but often
the descriptions overlap or coincide. One reason is that writers
who discern and describe "mechanisms" often forget that defense is a *motive* in a theory which assumes ubiquitous overdetermination. Furthermore, the function of an activity changes
during development (Hartmann, 1950). Another reason for
this confusion may be that similar activities are differentiated
from common experiences. For example, Anna Freud (1936)
pointed out some of the ways in which defensive projection
"resembles most closely the process of repression" (p. 122). Although she suggested that projection and introjection "should
be assigned to the period after the ego has been differentiated
from the outside world,"[74] she cautioned that "the chronology
of psychic processes is still one of the most obscure fields of
analytic theory" (p. 53). In the light of my review, it is unclear
what is meant by a primitive defense. We need an organizing
study of the similarities between defensive activities which *appear* to be different.[75]

OTHER TERMINOLOGICAL PROBLEMS

One reason for the proliferation of technical terms[76] related
to projection may be that a writer who confines projection to

primitive or pathological defense needs Freud's concept and has to call it something else. Many of these terms are used as synonyms for projection.

Some psychoanalytic writers also use these same terms in formulations about the mental lives and interactions of two or more people, for example, "externalization" (Brodey, 1965) and "projective identification" (Malin and Grotstein, 1966). Psychoanalytic concepts were developed in order to understand the psychic life of one person at a time. It is a mistake to use them as if to explain sequential interactions of several people without considering inevitable differences (Kernberg, 1969; Ornston, 1978).

This distinction is important for theory and crucial in the clinical situation in which we are trying to discern the characteristic activities of a person in predicaments where he tends to think of himself as passive or helplessly reacting to others (Freud, 1926b; Loewald, 1971a). It is essentially psychoanalytic to try to distinguish between a person's *mental* attempts to adapt or relate and his interpersonal activities, let alone the psychic lives of other people.[77] Obviously this is equally important in the work of psychotherapists who try to sort out the concurrent interactions of several patients, such as in child analysis and work with families.

PARANOID PROJECTION AND HOMOSEXUALITY

We usually determine how pathological a person's projection is by finding out how he thinks about it. Yet it is not altogether clear how we distinguish between normal and paranoid projection. Often, creative people like Goethe, Mozart, Newton, Pasteur, and Freud stolidly regard themselves as mere "tools of a strange, usually superior, inspiration" (Kovacs, 1912, p. 263).[78] On the other hand, some forget the sources of what they come to regard as their own, original ideas; or they attribute their works to chance or fate. Are all of these variants of re-creative fantasy (Kris, 1934)? Occasionally in clinical work, ideas which may be developed into delusions are evident long before a person becomes paranoid (Freud, 1922,

1933). Are these ideas ubiquitous? Is this why we can em-
pathize with, and yet are so disturbed by, paranoid patients?
In what particulars is the impassioned thinking of scientists
and writers, patriots and fans, mothers and other lovers, different from that of paranoid people?

How can we account for the resolute, if not immutable,
resistance of people with paranoid ideas? Freud's observation
about the essential truths in their beliefs is only a beginning.
Tenacious resistance by people whom we tend to call paranoid
only begins to explain the taint of ominous psychopathology
which is inherent in the notion of projection "proper." How
did this distortion of Freud's concept come about? Why is it
sustained by some very systematic psychoanalytic writers?

Freud pointed out that obsessional, phobic, and paranoid
systems of thought have much in common (1913a, p. 95). Although some differences are obvious, this problem is far from
finished. Freud's question about some kinds of paranoid
thinking and certain kinds of homosexuality requires clarification. Diffuse thinking about self and other as somewhat the
same is characteristic of male and female homosexuals, as well
as more ordinary lovers (Kernberg, 1976). Furthermore, sucking and getting oneself penetrated are distinctly different activities. The idea of passive gratification in the structure of a
defensive activity does not settle this question. The place to
start may be with Freud's (1905b) distinctions of sexual activities from objects, and psychological activities from diagnoses.

SUMMARY

Freud proposed that from early infancy on, whenever we
mentally attend or tentatively classify, whenever we orient or
organize, whenever we anticipate or understand, we project.
We always regard a puzzling predicament as similar to a past
and familiar situation, or we think about our own mental activities as shared with, and complementary to, those of another person. Thus, unconsciously, we regress and can think
diffusely by using a developmentally surmounted mode of
thought. Simultaneously and sequentially, we sort past from

present and one immediate relationship from another. This is Freud's psychoanalytic concept of projection. At times he has been misunderstood.

Usually, Freud distinguished between mental activities and motives, one of which is to reassert some familiar kind of psychic unity, to understand if not explain. But projection is always overdetermined. When we transitorily deemphasize or disavow our own activities, and mentally attend to our own version of another person's activities as if these were the same; or when we mentally allocate a "passive" role to ourselves and an "active" role to another, a second important motive may be defense. However, Freud regarded projection as ubiquitous and "normal." It is merely more evident when it does not work very well, as in phobias and paranoid disorders. In ordinary life, we can regress comfortably and altogether unconsciously because at the same time we mentally maintain certain differences.

Freud congruently sustained projection from the beginning to the end of his work, always consistent with the principles of psychic continuity and overdetermination. He did this throughout and despite his constant attempts to design a biological psychology. His intricate concept is necessary to, and inherent in, psychoanalytic theory as it is currently being developed. The concept I have reviewed fits into some of the most useful work that is now under way.

NOTES

1. Five years ago, Roy Schafer and I completed a posthumously published paper by D. Clint Smith (1974). During that work, I compiled a catalogue of psychoanalytic meanings for projection and began to study Freud's usage. At that time, Dr. Schafer critically annotated a preliminary draft of this presentation. He has not read revisions during the last few years. More recently, Stanley Leavy, Richard Munich, Marc Schwartz, and Robert Arnstein read through various versions. Albert J. Solnit and Lottie M. Newman helped me to shape this report out of a larger work in progress. I am grateful to all of them for encouraging criticism as well as critical encouragement.

2. I have excluded many technical words which have to do with projective thinking or projection from this study. Examples are: appersonization

(Fuchs, 1937), exteriorization (Abraham, 1924; Fuchs, 1937), extrajection (Weiss, 1947), extraspection (Weiss, 1952), de-egotization (Federn, 1926), objectivization (Leavy, 1973), objectification (Feigenbaum, 1936), and objectivation (Hartmann, 1939; Laplanche and Pontalis, 1967; Loewald, 1951; Tausk, 1919; and Weiss, 1947).

3. Freud's translators inadvertently vitiated his language with "externalization" in a few places (1913a, p. 65, n. 2 [p. 22]; 1917a, p. 223 [p. 414]; 1916–17, p. 388 [p. 403]). It appears to be a modern term, but I have not found its origin. It is generally used quite vaguely, and customarily neither characterized nor indexed. See, for example, Hartmann et al. (1946), Jacobson (1967), Kernberg (1975), Kris (1939), Leavy (1973), Loewald (1962, 1973), Rapaport (1944, 1950, 1952), Sandler (1960), Sandler and Rosenblatt (1962), Schafer (1959, 1968a), and Laplanche and Pontalis (1967). It is used idiosyncratically by those who attempt to delineate a clear concept (Weiss, 1957; Brodey, 1965; A. Freud, 1965; Novick and Kelly, 1970; Schafer, 1976). It is not indexed in the *Standard Edition*.

4. Melanie Klein (1946) devised a complex and specific formulation which she called "projective identification." Most Kleinians, and Jacobson (1967) among others, have followed her usage. Rosenfeld (1949) broadened her meaning considerably. Kernberg (1975) bowdlerized her definition while bringing some Kleinian contributions into the mainstream.

5. See also Freud (1921a, p. 111).

6. See Holt (1967a, p. 361). See Freud (1914, p. 77; 1915a, p. 117; 1933, p. 81). On technical terms, see Freud (1891a, p. 55) and Strachey (1962, p. 63, n. 2).

7. For a few examples of Freud's implicit development of this concept, see: 1901b, p. 229; 1911b, p. 219, n. 4 and f.; 1912c, p. 99f.; 1913a, p. 94ff.; 1915c, p. 169ff.; 1916–17, pp. 39, 70f.; 1917c, pp. 141–144; 1921a, pp. 106–110, 129; 1923, p. 23; 1930, chapter I and pp. 125–143; 1937b, passim.

8. For example, see Freud's discussion of Dora's disgust at Herr. K.'s sexual excitement (1905a, p. 84). The chronology may look jumpy here, but Dora was written in January, 1901 (Strachey, 1953, p. 3).

9. Whenever I use the word "self" I intend to refer, abstractly and holistically, to one's own person. This connotes a variety of kinds of self-awareness, both of mental and somatic activity. I model this usage on Freud (1915a, 1930), Hartmann (1950), Jacobson (1964), Sandler (1960), and Schafer (1967, 1968a), but point out that I am setting aside some difficult problems, which will become more evident below.

10. Subsequently, Ferenczi described a therapist as oscillating continuously "between empathy, self observation, and making judgements" (1928, p. 96). Gradually, in a part for the whole way, this compound activity was accepted as the modern psychoanalytic concept of empathizing (Schafer, 1959; Greenson, 1960). See also Freud (1905c, pp. 151, 186, 192–198; 1907, p. 45; 1921a, pp. 84, 89, and especially p. 110, n. 2). In these passages, Freud used the concept of projection implicitly; he did not call it that.

11. See also: 1917a, p. 232ff.; 1920a, p. 29.

12. See also: 1905a, p. 35; 1912a, p. 117; 1913a, p. 91ff.; 1918a, p. 200; 1919, p. 234ff.; 1922, p. 224; 1931, p. 227.

13. See: 1913a, p. 65, n. 2 and pp. 64f., 91–99. See also: 1915c, p. 169ff.; 1918a, p. 200; 1919, passim.

14. See also: 1919; 1920a, p. 29; 1930, p. 68; 1931, p. 227.

15. See also: 1901b, p. 258f.; 1922, p. 227f.; 1930, p. 81.

16. See also: 1911a, pp. 66, 71; 1916–17, p. 427; 1917a, p. 224.

17. See also: 1895, p. 112; 1911a, p. 63, 78; 1915c, p. 183ff.; 1920a, p. 29.

18. Paranoia and jealousy: 1911a, pp. 59–79; 1922. Phobias: 1915c, p. 182ff.; 1916–17, p. 410; 1926a, p. 124ff.

19. See also: 1915b; 1916–17, p. 248ff.

20. See also: 1905a, p. 115; 1915c.

21. See also: 1916–17, pp. 248–254; 1920b.

22. Freud (1905b; 1910b, p. 101; 1922, p. 230ff.), Weiss (1947, 1957), Jacobson (1964, 1967).

23. See Tausk (1919, p. 540f., n.) See also Freud (1911a, p. 70f.; 1917a, p. 232f.; 1927, p. 22; 1928, p. 185).

24. I wonder if Freud recognized that Bleuler's concept, that is, ambivalence as a developmental precursor of mental conflict, is incompatible with a theory of two primary instincts. See also: Abraham (1924), Laplanche and Pontalis (1967, p. 28), and Loewald (1971b).

25. Freud (1911a, pp. 41, 66; 1913a, p. 63; 1921a, p. 105; 1922, p. 227; 1933, p. 124; 1941, p. 299).

26. See also: 1909c; 1913a, pp. 94–99; 1915c, pp. 182–185; 1916–17, p. 410.

27. See also: Lossy (1962), Leavy (1973).

28. See also: 1922, p. 224; 1936, p. 242f.

29. Freud (1901b, pp. 255–260; 1907, p. 80f.; 1911a, p. 41; 1916–17, p. 253; 1922, p. 226ff.; 1937b, p. 267), Kovacs (1912), Tausk (1919), Weiss (1947), Schafer (1968b).

30. See also: Freud (1950a, p. 209; 1901b, p. 255; 1913c, p. 318; 1914, p. 82; 1917a, p. 222; 1922, p. 228; 1930, p. 81; 1933, p. 59; 1937a, p. 235; 1940, p. 184) and Schafer (1968a, p. 198).

31. See also: 1900, p. 497; 1905b, p. 193, n. 2; 1905c, p. 164; 1913a, p. 85; 1915c, p. 206ff.; 1926a; and A. Freud (1936, p. 8).

32. See also: Holt (1973, pp. 42–47), Hartmann et al. (1946, p. 12), Loewald (1960, p. 17).

33. See Freud (1921a, p. 108; 1914, p. 94; 1926a, p. 139; 1916–17, p. 427; 1921a, p. 109).

34. The other two passages in which Freud counterposed these two terms are: 1924 (discussed below) and 1926a (compare pp. 128 and 139f.).

35. See: 1911a, passim, but especially p. 75; 1915a, p. 119 and 134ff.; 1915c, p. 184; 1917a, p. 232f.; 1920a, p. 28ff.; 1924, p. 164; 1925b, passim; 1926a, p. 128, 139–140; and chapter I of *Civilization and Its Discontents*.

36. See also: 1911b, p. 221; 1915a, p. 138f.; 1928, p. 181; 1933, p. 105; 1940, p. 150.
37. See also Freud (1923, p. 55; 1926a, p. 121; 1933, p. 89, n.), Gill (1963).
38. See: 1911b, p. 220; 1920a, p. 28; 1925b, p. 238; 1917a, p. 232f. See also: 1915b; 1915c; 1923, pp. 20–23; 1925a. Compare Hartmann (1956).
39. See also: 1900, pp. 565–568; 1905b, p. 222 and n.; 1925b, p. 237f.; 1926a, p. 98.
40. See also: 1920a; 1926b, p. 196.
41. Freud (1911b, p. 220f.; 1913a, pp. 64, 95–99; 1919; 1925b, p. 237ff.).
42. Freud (1917a, p. 223; 1913a, p. 64f.).
43. System of thought: Freud (1913a, p. 94f.; 1915c, pp. 182–185; 1916–17, p. 410; 1926a, pp. 101ff., 126ff.). Delusion: Freud (1909b, p. 243; 1911a, p. 66ff.; 1913a, p. 64f.; 1915b, p. 270f.). Screen memory: Freud (1899, p. 315; 1918b, pp. 40, n., 55f.). Prejudice (implicit projection): Freud (1900, p. 196f.; 1905a, p. 55; 1921a, p. 101f.; 1925c, p. 222; 1930, pp. 114f., 120; 1933, p. 32; 1939, p. 90ff.). Superstition: Freud (1901b, p. 257; 1909b, p. 232; 1928, p. 185). Myth: Freud (1897; 1901b, p. 258ff.; 1911b, p. 223; 1913a, p. 116; 1913b, p. 292). Taboo: Freud (1913a, passim; 1918a, p. 200).
44. See also: 1900, pp. 565f., 598–603; and compare: 1905b, p. 222; chapter I of *Civilization and Its Discontents;* Jacobson (1964, pp. 40–48, 96, 102–108).
45. Also, they uncritically accepted Strachey's insertion of "externalization" into the *Standard Edition,* but failed to supply a meaning for this word (p. 354). They omitted characterizations or definitions of several common psychoanalytic terms, for example: empathy, epigenesis, differentiating, de-differentiating, psychic continuity and determinism. They by-passed psychoanalytic ideas about thinking and learning. The structural point of view, and the very different idea of "structuralism," are buried under other headings.
46. Freud (1900, p. 538; 1905b, p. 170; 1916–17, pp. 310, 345), Apfelbaum (1965), Rubenstein (1967), Holt (1967b).
47. See also: Fenichel (1945, pp. 40, 110, 428f.), Lossy (1962), Leavy (1973), D. C. Smith (1974).
48. Ferenczi (1909) introduced introjection to psychoanalysis for this reason: he intended it to be an informative conceptual opposite.
49. For examples see: Kris (1939), Jacobson (1964), Kernberg (1976).
50. See also A. Freud (1936), Knight (1940).
51. Compare: Freud (1895, p. 112; 1915c, pp. 181–185; 1920a, pp. 26–33; 1930, pp. 64–68).
52. The disadvantage of calling this early kind of thinking "generalization" is that this word means "to deduce" as well as "to think inductively." It is more likely that a rather unindividuated infant presumes prelogically (Piaget, 1936; Holt, 1967a). Freud described "animism": "the first picture which man formed of the world . . . needed no scientific basis as yet, since science only begins after it has been realized that the world is unknown and that means must therefore be sought for getting to know it. . . . He knew what things were like in the world, namely just as he felt himself to be"

(1913a, p. 91). But "animism" implied that the thinking of primitive adults was the same as that of developing infants. Freud made this error (p. 64f.), and later corrected himself (1930, p. 71). Werner (1948) discussed the evidence for, and nature of, these differences.

53. See also Lossy (1962), Leavy (1973), D. C. Smith (1974).

54. See also Tausk (1919), M. Klein (1929), Riviere (1936), Fuchs (1937), Knight (1940), Weiss (1957).

55. For similar characterizations of defensive projection see: Ferenczi (1909, 1912, 1913, 1922), Feigenbaum (1936), Waelder (1951), Weiss (1957), Laplanche and Pontalis (1967), Sandler (1960), Kernberg (1966, 1975).

56. See Freud (1911a), Kovacs (1912), Knight (1940), Fenichel (1945), Hartmann (1956).

57. See also: Freud (1928, p. 185; 1931, p. 227; 1936, p. 242; and even 1941, p. 300).

58. See also: Hartmann (1939, p. 27), Ferenczi (1913), Freud (1925b), Weiss (1947, 1957), Waelder (1951), Winnicott (1948, 1953), Sandler (1960), Sutherland (1963), Schafer (1968a), Kernberg (1976).

59. See also: Knight (1940), Loewald (1960, 1973).

60. Schafer (1968a, p. 88).

61. See Hartmann (1939), Schafer (1968a, p. 94), Loewald (1971a, 1973), Kernberg (1975, 1976).

62. Rapaport (1950, 1951b, 1952, 1957a), Tausk (1919), Fuchs (1937), Hartmann and Kris (1945), Hartmann et al. (1946), Novick and Kelly (1970).

63. Kovacs (1912), Tausk (1919), Fuchs (1937), Weiss (1952), Loewald (1973), Schafer (1968b).

64. Kovacs (1912), Jelgersma (1926), Feigenbaum (1936), Fuchs (1937), Sandler (1960), Jaffe (1968), Kernberg (1976).

65. Freud (1916–17, pp. 210ff., 339–344; 1920a; 1921b; 1923; 1933, p. 19), Strachey (1966), Jackson (1969), Laplanche and Pontalis (1967).

66. Mahler (1968), Schafer (1968b, 1976), Loewald (1973).

67. Freud (1905a; 1905b, p. 222; 1909b, pp. 213–216; 1911b, p. 219, n. 4; 1915b, p. 270; 1915c; 1916–17, p. 266f.; 1918b, p. 101ff.; 1919; 1923, p. 21f.; 1925b), Kovacs (1912), Abraham (1924), Hartmann (1939), Kris (1939, 1950, 1956), Werner (1948), Waelder (1951), Bruner (1964), Schafer (1968a, esp. p. 117; 1968b).

68. Hartmann (1939), Rapaport (1951b, p. 512, n. 67), Mahler (1968), Loewald (1960, 1971a, 1972, 1973), Schafer (1968a).

69. Freud (1911b, p. 219, n. 4), Hartmann (1939), Rapaport (1960), Gill (1963, 1967).

70. Rapaport (1951b, pp. 512, n. 67, 705), Loewald (1951, 1972, 1978), Schafer (1968a, pp. 127, 142f.).

71. Schafer (1959; 1968a, pp. 14f., 36, 128ff., 175; 1968b, p. 57; 1976, pp. 90, 118ff., 182, 354).

72. Hartmann (1927), Hartmann et al. (1946), Apfelbaum (1965), Rubenstein (1967), Holt (1967b), Eissler (1968), Schafer (1968a, 1976), Grossman and Simon (1969), Loewald (1971b), Ornston (1978).

73. Affect is one example. An involved spectator who watches dancing, or other athletics, thinks enactively. Vicariously, he enjoys the result of elaborately organized remembering and re-creative planning by the performers. Some of the best athletes are bewilderingly inarticulate about what they do despite unending mental rehearsals, replays, and innovations. Other examples of paraverbal cognition are: tone, cadence, and rhythms; eidetic thinking about space, conformation, and color; taste and smell; and a wide variety of syncretic mental activities which we depend on probably much more than we will ever know.

74. In her first characterization of projection, she appeared to differ with Freud (pp. 43–53). Actually, she was distinguishing her views from the developmental theory of the Kleinians. Compare her chapter 10, which is quite compatible with Freud's usage.

75. For an exhausting list of defenses see the Appendix to Bibring et al. (1961).

76. See notes 2, 3, and 4.

77. Leavy's descriptions (1973) of transference interpretation as intersubjective activity make this point in a different way.

78. My translation. See also Kris (1939, 1950, 1956).

BIBLIOGRAPHY

ABRAHAM, K. (1924), A Short History of the Development of the Libido. In: *Selected Papers on Psycho-Analysis*. London: Hogarth Press, 1954, pp. 418–501.

APFELBAUM, B. (1965), Ego Psychology, Psychic Energy, and the Hazards of Quantitative Explanation in Psycho-Analytic Theory. *Int. J. Psycho-Anal.*, 46 : 168–182.

BIBRING, G. L., DWYER, T. F., HUNTINGTON, D. S., & VALENSTEIN, A. F. (1961), A Study of the Psychological Processes in Pregnancy and of the Earliest Mother-Child Relationship. *This Annual*, 16 : 9–72.

BLEULER, E. (1911), *Dementia Praecox*. New York: Int. Univ. Press, 1950.

BRODEY, W. M. (1965), On the Dynamics of Narcissism. *This Annual*, 20 : 165–193.

BRUNER, J. (1964), The Course of Cognitive Growth. *Amer. Psychologist*, 19 : 1–15.

DECKER, H. S. (1977), *Freud in Germany* [*Psychol. Issues*, Monogr. 41]. New York: Int. Univ. Press.

EISSLER, K. R. (1968), The Relation of Explaining and Understanding in Psychoanalysis. *This Annual*, 23 : 141–177.

ESCALONA, S. K. (1968), *The Roots of Individuality*. Chicago: Aldine Press.

FEDERN, P. (1926), Some Variations in Ego Feeling. In: *Ego Psychology and the Psychoses,* ed. E. Weiss. New York: Basic Books, 1952, pp. 25–37.

FEIGENBAUM, D. (1936), On Projection. *Psychoanal. Quart.*, 5 : 303–319.

FENICHEL, O. (1945), *The Psychoanalytic Theory of Neurosis*. New York: Norton.

FERENCZI, S. (1909), Introjection and Transference. In: *Sex in Psychoanalysis.* New York: Dover, 1956, pp. 30–79.

—— (1912), On the Definition of Introjection. In: *Final Contributions to the Problems and Methods of Psycho-Analysis.* London: Hogarth Press, 1955, pp. 316–318.

—— (1913), Stages in the Development of a Sense of Reality. In: *Sex in Psychoanalysis.* New York: Dover, 1956, pp. 181–203.

—— (1922), Freud's 'Group Psychology and the Analysis of the Ego.' In: *Final Contributions to the Problems and Methods of Psycho-Analysis.* London: Hogarth Press, 1955, pp. 371–376.

—— (1926), The Problem of Acceptance of Unpleasant Ideas. *Int. J. Psycho-Anal.,* 7 : 312–323.

—— (1928), The Elasticity of Psycho-Analytic Technique. In: *Final Contributions to the Problems and Methods of Psycho-Analysis.* London: Hogarth Press, 1955, pp. 87–101.

FREUD, A. (1936), The Ego and the Mechanisms of Defense. *W.,* 2.

—— (1965), Normality and Pathology in Childhood. *W.,* 6.

FREUD, S. (1891a), *On Aphasia.* London: Imago, 1953.

—— (1891b), On the Interpretation of the Aphasias [his own abstract of his book]. *S.E.,* 3 : 240–241.

—— (1893), Some Points for a Comparative Study of Organic and Hysterical Motor Paralyses. *S.E.,* 1 : 157–172.

—— (1895), On the Grounds for Detaching a Particular Syndrome from Neurasthenia under the Description 'Anxiety Neurosis.' *S.E.,* 3 : 87–139.

—— (1896), Further Remarks on the Neuro-Psychoses of Defence. *S.E.,* 3 : 159–185.

—— (1897), Letter #78 to Fliess. *S.E.,* 13 : x.

—— (1899), Screen Memories. *S.E.,* 3 : 301–322.

—— (1900), The Interpretation of Dreams. *S.E.,* 4 & 5.

—— (1901a), On Dreams. *S.E.,* 5 : 631–686.

—— (1901b), The Psychopathology of Everyday Life. *S.E.,* 6.

—— (1905a), Fragment of an Analysis of a Case of Hysteria. *S.E.,* 7 : 1–122.

—— (1905b), Three Essays on the Theory of Sexuality. *S.E.,* 7 : 125–243.

—— (1905c), Jokes and Their Relation to the Unconscious. *S.E.,* 8.

—— (1906), My Views on the Part Played by Sexuality in the Aetiology of the Neuroses. *S.E.,* 7 : 271–279.

—— (1907), Delusions and Dreams in Jensen's *Gradiva. S.E.,* 9 : 1–95.

—— (1909a), Some General Remarks on Hysterical Attacks. *S.E.,* 9 : 227–234.

—— (1909b), Notes upon a Case of Obsessional Neurosis. *S.E.,* 10 : 153–318.

—— (1909c), Analysis of a Phobia in a Five-Year-Old Boy, *S.E.,* 10 : 1–149.

—— (1910a), 'Wild' Psycho-Analysis. *S.E.,* 11 : 219–227.

—— (1910b), Leonardo da Vinci and a Memory of His Childhood. *S.E.,* 11 : 57–137.

—— (1910c), Five Lectures on Psycho-Analysis. *S.E.*, 11 : 3–55.

—— (1911a), Psycho-Analytic Notes on an Autobiographical Account of a Case of Paranoia. *S.E.*, 12 : 3–82.

—— (1911b), Formulations on the Two Principles of Mental Functioning. *S.E.*, 12 : 213–226.

—— (1912a), Recommendations to Physicians Practising Psycho-Analysis. *S.E.*, 12 : 109–120.

—— (1912b), A Note on the Unconscious in Psycho-Analysis. *S.E.*, 12 : 257–266.

—— (1912c), The Dynamics of Transference. *S.E.*, 12 : 98–108.

—— (1913a), Totem and Taboo. *S.E.*, 13 : 1–162 [*G.W.*, 9 : 1–205].

—— (1913b), The Theme of the Three Caskets. *S.E.*, 12 : 289–301.

—— (1913c), The Disposition to Obsessional Neurosis. *S.E.*, 12 : 313–326.

—— (1914), On Narcissism. *S.E.*, 14 : 69–102.

—— (1915a), Instincts and Their Vicissitudes. *S.E.*, 14 : 109–140.

—— (1915b), A Case of Paranoia Running Counter to the Psycho-Analytic Theory of the Disease. *S.E.*, 14 : 261–272.

—— (1915c), The Unconscious. *S.E.*, 14 : 159–215.

—— (1915d), Repression. *S.E.*, 14 : 141–158.

—— (1916–17), Introductory Lectures on Psycho-Analysis. *S.E.*, 15 & 16 [*G.W.*, 11].

—— (1917a), A Metapsychological Supplement to the Theory of Dreams. *S.E.*, 14 : 217–235 [*G.W.*, 10 : 412–426].

—— (1917b), Mourning and Melancholia, *S.E.*, 14 : 237–258.

—— (1917c), A Difficulty in the Path of Psycho-Analysis. *S.E.*, 17 : 135–144.

—— (1918a), The Taboo of Virginity. *S.E.*, 11 : 191–208.

—— (1918b), From the History of an Infantile Neurosis. *S.E.*, 17 : 1–122.

—— (1919), The 'Uncanny.' *S.E.*, 17 : 217–256.

—— (1920a), Beyond the Pleasure Principle. *S.E.*, 18 : 1–64.

—— (1920b), The Psychogenesis of a Case of Homosexuality in a Woman. *S.E.*, 18 : 145–172.

—— (1921a), Group Psychology and the Analysis of the Ego. *S.E.*, 18 : 67–143.

—— (1921b), Introduction to J. Varendonck's *The Psychology of Day-Dreams*. *S.E.*, 18 : 271–272.

—— (1922), Some Neurotic Mechanisms in Jealousy, Paranoia and Homosexuality. *S.E.*, 18 : 221–232.

—— (1923), The Ego and the Id. *S.E.*, 19 : 3–66.

—— (1924), The Economic Problem of Masochism. *S.E.*, 19 : 157–170.

—— (1925a), A Note upon the 'Mystic Writing-Pad.' *S.E.*, 19 : 227–232.

—— (1925b), Negation. *S.E.*, 19 : 235–239.

—— (1925c), The Resistances to Psycho-Analysis. *S.E.*, 19 : 213–224.

—— (1926a), Inhibitions, Symptoms and Anxiety. *S.E.*, 20 : 77–175.

—— (1926b), The Question of Lay Analysis. *S.E.*, 20 : 179–258.

—— (1927), The Future of an Illusion. *S.E.*, 21 : 3–56.

—— (1928), Doestoevsky and Parricide. *S.E.*, 21 : 175–196.

——— (1930), Civilization and Its Discontents. *S.E.,* 21 : 59–145.

——— (1931), Female Sexuality. *S.E.,* 21 : 225–243.

——— (1933), New Introductory Lectures on Psycho-Analysis. *S.E.,* 22 : 3–182.

——— (1936), A Disturbance of Memory on the Acropolis. *S.E.,* 22 : 239–248.

——— (1937a), Analysis Terminable and Interminable. *S.E.,* 23 : 209–253.

——— (1937b), Constructions in Analysis. *S.E.,* 23 : 255–269.

——— (1939), Moses and Monotheism. *S.E.,* 23 : 1–137.

——— (1940), An Outline of Psycho-Analysis. *S.E.,* 23 : 141–207.

——— (1941), Findings, Ideas, Problems. *S.E.,* 23 : 299–300.

——— (1950a), Extracts from the Fliess Papers. *S.E.,* 1 : 175–280.

——— (1950b), Project for a Scientific Psychology. *S.E.,* 1 : 283–397.

FUCHS, S. H. (1937), On Introjection. *Int. J. Psycho-Anal.,* 18 : 269–293.

GILL, M. M. (1963), *Topography and Systems in Psychoanalytic Theory* [*Psychol. Issues,* Monogr. 10]. New York: Int. Univ. Press.

——— (1967), The Primary Process. In: *Motives and Thought,* ed. R. R. Holt [*Psychol. Issues,* Monogr. 18/19]. New York: Int. Univ. Press, pp. 260–298.

GLOVER, E. (1943), The Concept of Dissociation. *Int. J. Psycho-Anal.,* 24 : 7–13.

GREENSON, R. R. (1960), Empathy and Its Vicissitudes. *Int. J. Psycho-Anal.,* 41 : 418–424.

GROSSMAN, W. I. & SIMON, B. (1969), Anthropomorphism. *This Annual,* 24 : 78–111.

HARTMANN, H. (1927), Understanding and Explanation. In: *Essays on Ego Psychology.* New York: Int. Univ. Press, 1964, pp. 369–403.

——— (1939), *Ego Psychology and the Problem of Adaptation.* New York: Int. Univ. Press, 1958.

——— (1950), Comments on the Psychoanalytic Theory of the Ego. *This Annual,* 5 : 74–96.

——— (1951), Technical Implications of Ego Psychology. *Psychoanal. Quart.,* 20 : 21–43.

——— (1956), Notes on the Reality Principle. *This Annual,* 11 : 31–53.

——— & KRIS, E. (1945), The Genetic Approach in Psychoanalysis. *This Annual,* 1 : 11–30.

——— ——— & LOEWENSTEIN, R. M. (1946), Comments on the Formation of Psychic Structure. *This Annual,* 2 : 11–38.

HENDRICK, I. (1936), Ego Development and Certain Character Problems. *Psychoanal. Quart.,* 5 : 320–346.

HOLT, R. R. (1967a), The Development of the Primary Process. In: *Motives and Thought,* ed. R. R. Holt [*Psychol. Issues,* Monogr. 18/19]. New York: Int. Univ. Press, pp. 345–383.

——— (1967b), Beyond Vitalism and Mechanism. In: *Science and Psychoanalysis,* ed. J. Masserman. New York: Grune & Stratton, 11 : 1–41.

——— (1973), On Reading Freud: Introduction to *Abstracts of the Standard Edition,* ed. C. L. Rothgeb. New York: Jason Aronson.

JACKSON, S. W. (1969), The History of Freud's Concepts of Regression. *J. Amer. Psychoanal. Assn.*, 17 : 734–784.

JACOBSON, E. (1964), *The Self and the Object World*. New York: Int. Univ. Press.

—— (1967), *Psychotic Conflict and Reality*. New York: Int. Univ. Press.

JAFFE, D. S. (1968), The Mechanism of Projection. *Int. J. Psycho-Anal.*, 49 : 662–677.

JELGERSMA, G. (1926), Projection. *Int. J. Psycho-Anal.*, 7 : 353–358.

KERNBERG, O. F. (1966), Structural Derivatives of Object Relationships. *Int. J. Psycho-Anal.*, 47 : 236–253.

—— (1969), A Contribution to the Ego-Psychological Critique of the Kleinian School. *Int. J. Psycho-Anal.*, 50 : 317–333.

—— (1975), *Borderline Conditions and Pathological Narcissism*. New York: Jason Aronson.

—— (1976), *Object Relations Theory and Clinical Psychoanalysis*. New York: Jason Aronson.

KLEIN, M. (1929), Infantile Anxiety Situations Reflected in a Work of Art and in the Creative Impulse. *Int. J. Psycho-Anal.*, 10 : 436–443.

—— (1946), Notes on Some Schizoid Mechanisms. *Int. J. Psycho-Anal.*, 27 : 99–110.

KNIGHT, R. P. (1940), Introjection, Projection and Identification. *Psychoanal. Quart.*, 9 : 334–341.

KOVACS, S. (1912), Introjektion, Projektion und Einfühlung. *Zbl. Psychoanal.*, 2 : 253–263, 316–327.

KRIS, E. (1939), On Inspiration. *Int. J. Psycho-Anal.*, 20 : 337–389.

—— (1950), On Preconscious Mental Processes. *Psychoanal. Quart.*, 19 : 540–560.

—— (1956), On Some Vicissitudes of Insight in the Therapeutic Process *Int. J. Psycho-Anal.*, 37 : 445–455.

LAPLANCHE, J. & PONTALIS, J.-B. (1967), *The Language of Psychoanalysis*. New York: Norton, 1973.

LEAVY, S. (1973), Psychoanalytic Interpretation. *This Annual*, 28 : 305–330.

—— (1977), The Significance of Jacques Lacan. *Psychoanal. Quart.*, 46 : 201–219.

LOEWALD, H. W. (1951), Ego and Reality. *Int. J. Psycho-Anal.*, 32 : 10–18.

—— (1960), On the Therapeutic Action of Psycho-Analysis. *Int. J. Psycho-Anal.*, 41 : 16–33.

—— (1962), Internalization, Separation, Mourning, and the Superego. *Psychoanal. Quart.*, 31 : 483–504.

—— (1971a), Some Considerations on Repetition and Repetition Compulsion. *Int. J. Psycho-Anal.*, 52 : 59–66.

—— (1971b). On Motivation and Instinct Theory. *This Annual*, 26 : 91–128.

—— (1972), The Experience of Time. *This Annual*, 27 : 401–410.

—— (1973), On Internalization. *Int. J. Psycho-Anal.*, 54 : 9–17.

—— (1978), *Psychoanalysis and the History of the Individual*. New Haven: Yale Univ. Press.

LOEWENSTEIN, R. M. (1969), Developments in the Theory of Transference in the Last Fifty Years. *Int. J. Psycho-Anal.,* 50 : 583–588.

Lossy, F. T. (1962), The Charge of Suggestion as a Resistance in Psycho-Analysis. *Int. J. Psycho-Anal.,* 43 : 448–467.

Mahler, M. S. (1968), *On Human Symbiosis and the Vicissitudes of Individuation.* New York: Int. Univ. Press.

Malin, A. & Grotstein, J. S. (1966), Projective Identification in the Therapeutic Process. *Int. J. Psycho-Anal.,* 47 : 26–31.

Novick, J. & Kelly, K. (1970), Projection and Externalization. *This Annual,* 25 : 69–95.

Nunberg, H. (1951), Transference and Reality. *Int. J. Psycho-Anal.,* 32 : 1–9.

Ornston, D. (1977), Unpublished manuscript.

—— (1978), Projective Identification and Impingement. *Int. J. Psychoanal. Psychother.* (in press).

Piaget, J. (1936), *The Origins of Intelligence in Children.* New York: Int. Univ. Press, 1952.

—— (1945), *Play, Dreams and Imitation in Childhood.* New York: Norton, 1962.

—— (1962), The Relation of Affectivity to Intelligence in the Mental Development of the Child. *Bull. Menninger Clin.,* 26 : 129–137.

Racker, H. (1957), The Meanings and Uses of Countertransference. *Psychoanal. Quart.,* 26 : 303–357.

Rapaport, D. (1942), Principles Underlying Projective Techniques. In: *The Collected Papers of David Rapaport,* ed. M. M. Gill. New York: Basic Books, 1967, pp. 91–97.

—— (1944), The Scientific Methodology of Psychoanalysis. *Ibid.,* pp. 165–220.

—— (1950), The Theoretical Implications of Diagnostic Testing Procedures. *Ibid.,* pp. 334–356.

—— (1951a), The Autonomy of the Ego. *Ibid.,* pp. 357–367.

—— ed. & tr. (1951b), *Organization and Pathology of Thought.* New York: Columbia Univ. Press.

—— (1952), Projective Techniques and the Theory of Thinking. In: *The Collected Papers of David Rapaport,* ed. M. M. Gill. New York: Basic Books, 1967, pp. 461–469.

—— (1957a), Cognitive Structures. *Ibid.,* pp. 631–664.

—— (1957b), A Theoretical Analysis of the Superego Concept. *Ibid.,* pp. 685–709.

—— (1960), Psychoanalysis as a Developmental Psychology. *Ibid.,* pp. 853–915.

—— & Gill, M. M. (1959), The Points of View and Assumptions of Metapsychology. *Ibid.,* pp. 795–811.

Riviere, J. (1936), On the Genesis of Psychical Conflict in Earliest Infancy. *Int. J. Psycho-Anal.,* 17 : 395–422.

Rosenfeld, H. (1949), Remarks on the Relation of Male Homosexuality to Paranoia, Paranoid Anxiety and Narcissism. *Int. J. Psycho-Anal.,* 30 : 36–47.

Rubenstein, B. B. (1967), Explanation and Mere Description. In: *Motives and Thought,* ed. R. R. Holt [*Psychol. Issues,* Monogr. 18/19]. New York: Int. Univ. Press, pp. 20–77.

SANDLER, J. (1960), On the Concept of the Superego. *This Annual,* 15 : 128–162.

—— & ROSENBLATT, B. (1962), The Concept of the Representational World. *This Annual,* 17 : 128–145.

SCHAFER, R. (1959), Generative Empathy in the Treatment Situation. *Psychoanal. Quart.,* 28 : 342–373.

—— (1967), Ideals, the Ideal Ego and the Ideal Self. In: *Motives and Thought,* ed. R. R. Holt, [*Psychol. Issues,* Monogr. 18/19]. New York: Int. Univ. Press, pp. 131–174.

—— (1968a), *Aspects of Internalization.* New York: Int. Univ. Press.

—— (1968b), The Mechanisms of Defence. *Int. J. Psycho-Anal.,* 49 : 49–62.

—— (1976), *A New Language for Psychoanalysis.* New Haven: Yale Univ. Press.

SMITH, D. C. (1974), Some Functions of Projection in the Analytic Situation. *Int. Rev. Psycho-Anal.,* 1 : 383–389.

SMITH, J. H. (1977), The Pleasure Principle. *Int. J. Psycho-Anal.,* 58 : 1–10.

STRACHEY, J. (1953), Editor's Note. *S.E.,* 7 : 3–6.

—— (1957), Editor's Introduction to Freud's Papers on Metapsychology. *S.E.,* 14 : 105–107.

—— (1962), Appendix: The Emergence of Freud's Fundamental Hypotheses. *S.E.,* 3 : 62–68.

—— (1966), Appendix A: Freud's Use of the Concept of Regression. *S.E.,* 1 : 344–346.

SUTHERLAND, J. D. (1963), Object-Relations Theory and the Conceptual Model of Psycho-Analysis. *Brit. J. Med. Psychol.,* 36 : 109–121.

TAUSK, V. (1919), On the Origin of the "Influencing Machine" in Schizophrenia. *Psychoanal. Quart.,* 2 : 519–556, 1933.

WAELDER, R. (1930), The Principle of Multiple Function. In: *Psychoanalysis.* New York: Int. Univ. Press, 1976, pp. 68–83.

—— (1951), On the Structure of Paranoid Ideas. *Int. J. Psycho-Anal.,* 32 : 167–177.

WEISS, E. (1947), Projection, Extrajection and Objectivation. *Psychoanal. Quart.,* 16 : 357–377.

—— (1952), Editor's Introduction. In: *Ego Psychology and the Psychoses* by Paul Federn. New York: Basic Books, pp. 1–21.

—— (1957), The Phenomenon of Ego Passage. *J. Amer. Psychoanal. Assn.,* 5 : 267–281.

WERNER, H. (1948), *Comparative Psychology of Mental Development.* New York: Int. Univ. Press, 1973.

WINNICOTT, D. W. (1948), Paediatrics and Psychiatry. In: *Through Paediatrics to Psycho-Analysis.* New York: Basic Books, 1975, pp. 157–173.

—— (1953), Transitional Objects and Transitional Phenomena. *Int. J. Psycho-Anal.,* 34 : 89–97.

Self-Objects and Oedipal Objects

A Crucial Developmental Distinction

MARIAN TOLPIN, M.D.

ANNA FREUD, PHYLLIS GREENACRE, AND HEINZ KOHUT DESCRIBE a frequently encountered disorder of structure formation which is regularly mistaken for the infantile neurosis in both child and adult analysis. I shall focus on the good psychological reasons for this "case of mistaken identity," on the crucial developmental distinction between the two disorders, and on the decisive differences in the therapeutic tasks and "psychic work" (Tolpin, 1971) that patient and analyst are called upon to perform and to accomplish, depending on whether the central psychopathology involves a nuclear (oedipus) complex or deficits in the psychic structure essential for cohesiveness of the self (Kohut, 1971; Tolpin, 1971).

It is important to continue to reevaluate the concept of the infantile neurosis, particularly when it is approached in the analytic "tradition to pay attention to and to learn from negative experience" with psychoanalytic treatment (A. Freud, 1969a, p. 135f.). Fortunately, the tradition started by Freud (1914, 1925) and exemplified by his hypothesis changes (Sadow et al., 1968) is continued in extensive writings by other analysts (Blos, 1972; A. Freud, 1968, 1969a, 1969b, 1970b;

Faculty, Chicago Institute for Psychoanalysis.
Revised version of a paper read at the panel on "The Infantile Neurosis in Child and Adult Analysis," American Psychoanalytic Association, Quebec City, April 29, 1977.

Kohut, 1977; Loewald, 1974; Rangell, 1975; Ritvo, 1974; Tolpin, 1970). These writings on patients with structural deficiencies, and Kohut's specific hypothesis change concerning the
minute (transmuting) internalizations, which go hand in hand
with the gradual formation of psychic structure and the development of a cohesive self, bear directly on "present-day difficulties in the path of psychoanalysis" (A. Freud, 1969a) and
the subject of this paper.

There is little doubt in the minds of analysts that Freud's
theory of the neuroses has stood the test of time. Since analysis can "succeed in doing what it is so superlatively able to do"
(Freud, 1937, p. 200) for disorders stemming from "inadequate decisions" made by the child's immature ego in regard
to the complex problems posed by the infantile neurosis, I
believe that negative experiences with analytic treatment are
relevant to the distinctions I am discussing.

The work of Anna Freud (e.g., 1968, 1970b, 1976), Greenacre (1971), and Kohut (1971, 1972, 1977) suggests almost
identical answers: serious consequences result from the analyst's mistaking the symptomatic manifestations and transferences of analytic patients with faulty structure formation for
the faulty conflict solutions, compromise formations, and
disguised derivatives of the repressed infantile neurosis which
return in a classical transference neurosis—the structural deficits, faults, and failures which stunt and impair the personality
from childhood on remain essentially unchanged by the treatment, and so do the deficits in self-esteem, self-reliance, autonomy, and object constancy which are their hallmarks. Despite the seeming similarities it is obviously imperative to learn
from the cumulative evidence of negative experiences with
treatment during "the era of the widening scope of psychoanalysis" (A. Freud, 1954, 1976); and it is imperative to distinguish between the central psychopathology of the infantile
neurosis—i.e., conflicts between the structures of the personality—and the central psychopathology which originates in
faulty formation of the very structure of the personality itself.
(In this connection see also Weil, 1970, 1973).

Anna Freud and Greenacre demarcate the deficit syndrome

from the infantile neurosis on the one hand, and from psychotic and borderline personality organization, on the other. They call attention to the same group of disturbances that Kohut (1971, 1972, 1977), differentiating them from the neuroses, psychoses, and borderline conditions, describes as disorders of the self, which are amenable to psychoanalytic treatment by the basic model technique (Eissler, 1953).

Anna Freud (1968) has consistently distinguished between the faulty solution of the infantile (oedipal) neurosis in which the child's immature ego plays the central pathogenic role and one type of "deficiency illness" in which the *parents' personalities* act as the primary pathogenic agents. Unlike the case in the infantile neurosis, the fantasied distortions of the parental objects which arise from the child's wishes and anxieties, and from the defenses he or she employs to deal with the pressures of the "nuclear complex" (including regression to pre-oedipal fixations) are not at issue. Instead, the primary psychopathology is a result of the fact that the parents actually "disregard and therefore frustrate important *developmental needs* of the child" (p. 115, my italics). The parents fail as the child's "expectable environment" (Hartmann, 1939) which normally almost automatically provides the "external agents" or "essential ingredients" necessary for normal growth: reliable emotional attachment, help with inevitable anxieties, stability, adequate stimulation, basic acceptance of drives, appropriate guidance, and pride and pleasure in achievements, including the positive achievement of oedipal impulses, desires, and goals. Thus one type of "deficiency illness" is due to psychological failings of the parents which prevent them from adequately fulfilling the child's ongoing, changing, and varying needs at every stage of development from infancy through adolescence. The fact that normal childhood development depends on the fulfillment of varying and ongoing developmental needs which go far beyond libidinal and aggressive drive wishes and drive satisfactions is well known to analysts, particularly to child analysts. Nevertheless, most theoretical propositions regarding the normality and pathology of development are based primarily on the vicissitudes of the drive

wishes and conflicts of the infantile neurosis and the preoedipal sexual organization. When these theories of development
are applied to psychoanalytic treatment and to the theory of
technique, they fail to take transferences of frustrated, intensified, and distorted developmental needs into account.

Thus Anna Freud, like Kohut, traces the genesis of a disorder for which many children and adults are now in analysis
to a psychological "environment" which is unable to respond
appropriately to legitimate childhood needs for firming, confirming, and guiding; and to the adverse effects that this specific type of lack of need fulfillment has on the process of internal structure formation. It is clear from their writings that
the functions of an expectable environment and the functions
of mirroring and idealized self-objects are one and the same
thing. (For a clinical example of the consequences of the failure of the expectable environment—i.e., of the child's self-objects—see A. Freud's 1975 discussion of the pathogenesis of
pseudobackwardness and severely impaired self-esteem in
children whose parents overlooked them and deprived them
of needed pleasure in their development and needed enthusiasm and encouragement.)

On the basis of her findings on a "basic transference" which
she repeatedly attempted to distinguish from the classical
transference neurosis, Greenacre (1971) also made a developmental distinction between patients with psychoneurotic conflicts and a delimited subgroup of patients with developmental
deficits which she attributed to parental psychopathology. In
her opinion, in spite of impairments in the individuation process and serious deficits in structures necessary for self-
reliance, autonomy, and object constancy—deficits that "go
beyond the borders of the metapsychology of the psychoneu-
roses" (p. 198)—the patients in this specific subgroup are not
borderline or psychotic and analysis seemed feasible and indicated for them. However, Greenacre was emphatic on this
score: their successful analytic treatment hinges on satisfactory
new theoretical formulations—that is, effective treatment
hinges on analytic work which succeeds in fathoming the basic
transference and bridging the wide gap between the extensive

new knowledge of development and the effective application of this knowledge to patients in the psychoanalytic situation (p. 173f.).

In short, both Anna Freud and Greenacre describe and discuss nonpsychotic and nonborderline individuals whose developmental deficits and deficiencies in structure formation go "beyond the infantile neurosis," the classical transference neurosis, and the explanatory limits of the theory of the neurosis and psychic conflicts. Both emphasize that failures to recognize the limits of this theory pose "the threat of sterility" to many analysts' clinical and theoretical endeavors (A. Freud, 1969a, p. 153; 1976) and that analysis may provide patients with insights that are no better than "an interesting encumbrance" (Greenacre, 1971, p. 196). Why, then, are deficit disorders still confused with an infantile neurosis? Paraphrasing Anna Freud (1968, 1970b), I suggest that a part of the answer is this: what she describes as "a neurotic superstructure" proliferates on structural faults, deficits, failures, and defects to the extent that *in the final diagnosis "neurotic problems" more or less obscure the critical psychopathology.* The finding that the critical psychopathology of many of his analytic patients was obscured by what he first took for the oedipal conflicts and regressions of an infantile neurosis was precisely the finding which led Kohut to go beyond the theory of the neuroses into the realm of the initial building up of psychic structure, the establishment of the cohesive nuclear self, and the normality and pathology of its ongoing development by way of a prestructural self-object tie.

Anna Freud considers the predominance of structural deficit disorders to be among the chief difficulties and challenges in the present-day path of psychoanalysis; and she repeatedly points out that analysis of conflicts is not effective when deficits are the major cause of the central psychopathology. I believe that Anna Freud is correct in maintaining that analytic patients with structural deficits outnumber patients with genuine oedipal and preoedipal conflicts. (She differentiates other types of preoedipal disturbances from the type of preoedipal conflicts which prepare "the way for regressions and . . .

which can be considered to be the true forerunners of the infantile neurosis" [1970b, p. 197].) Regardless of whether the
increase in patients who are not basically neurotic is more apparent than real (Loewald, 1974; Greenacre, 1971; Kohut,
1971, 1972, 1977), however, it is now vital to psychoanalysis
that we distinguish conflicts over infantile sexual drives and
inadequate conflict solutions undertaken by an immature ego,
from the insufficiencies, and their sequelae, which are due to
inadequate structure formation. Phase-specific drive conflicts
are not the main cause of inadequate structure formation. All
of the psychoanalytic work of the past decades on child development points to the fact that inadequate structure formation
in children who start out with average expectable endowment
and equipment is primarily the result of insufficiencies and
inadequacies in parental supplies and supports—the "essential
psychological ingredients" required for normal growth. As I
have put it earlier (1971), structural deficits occur when the
child's self-objects fail to meet normal endowment half-way
and do not provide the indispensable transitional precursors
of psychic structures which gradually undergo internalization
and effectively maintain the vitality, initiative, and self-esteem
of a cohesive self.

Yet, if a neurotic superstructure proliferates and eventually
overlays and actually obscures causative structural faults, two
crucial questions arise: (1) How are we to distinguish the one
disorder from the other? (2) How does the basic psychoanalytic method of understanding and interpreting transferences
in order to bring about structural alterations apply to analytic
treatment of structural deficits inasmuch as "the psychoanalytic technique, including the technique of child analysis, was
originally devised for, and has proved its worth in, the application to the neuroses proper" (A. Freud, 1970b, p. 202)? This
is another way of asking: can analysis succeed only with the
"fact of conflict" and the areas of psychopathology "irradiated
by the infantile neurosis," as Rangell (1975, pp. 90, 96) put it?
Or, as Ritvo (1974) suggests, are we limited to dealing analytically only with the "hyperacute psychosexual conflicts" of patients with structural deficits, in the hope that their rela-

tionship with the analyst as a "sought-for and needed new object" (p. 170) who values them and serves as an idealized figure will act as a progressive force in their development? In this connection, Berger and Kennedy (1975), following Anna Freud's (1965) discussion of a "corrective emotional experience with the analyst as a 'new' object" (pp. 228, 231), also assume that some children, for example, those with low self-esteem and a devalued self image, may benefit from a *"by-product of analysis"*—the experience of the analyst as a new object who values them and offers alternative identificatory ideals more beneficial than those of their own parents (p. 303, my italics).

These questions and the problems raised for psychoanalysis (as a unique treatment modality and a unique method of investigation) by the view that analysis can succeed only with conflict pathology, or that it must rely on a nonspecific *extra-analytic corrective emotional relationship* with the analyst, lead me to the main points I want to make.

PARENTS AS PRESTRUCTURAL SELF-OBJECTS

The conflicts of the infantile neurosis are not the precipitating cause of the protean symptoms which are often organized into a "neuroticlike superstructure" in patients with a "deficiency illness," impairment of individuation, or a disorder of the self. Symptom formation is not "explained by the classical formula of danger [from libidinal and aggressive oedipal impulses] →anxiety→permanent regression to fixation point→rejection of reactivated pregenital impulse→defense→compromise formation" (A. Freud, 1965, p. 219). (The classical explanation for hysteria and hysterical symptoms is based on rejection of reactivated infantile oedipal strivings.)

Intensive studies of the transference of patients for whom the analyst is, in fact, a "sought-for and needed" (Ritvo, 1974) new edition of the prestructural self-objects of childhood show that only the manifest content of (some of the) symptoms, fantasies, and dreams arising from structural deficits resembles the disguised derivatives of repressed conflicts (Goldberg et al., 1978). The latent content and meaning of the symptoms and their construction are fundamentally different. The underlying cause of the neuroticlike symptoms which are confused with drive fixations and compromise formations is invariably a threat to the cohesiveness of the self. Threats to self-cohesion—the danger of fragmentation and/or loss of vitality—occur as a direct consequence of traumatically frustrating empathic failures on the part of parents in their role as the mirroring and idealized self-objects which constitute the child's "average expectable psychological environment." In this case the parents are not experienced as objects of love and hate in the usual psychoanalytic sense. Instead, at one and the same time they are sought for and needed to fulfill developmental requirements and to act in place of self-sustaining and self-regulating psychic structure which is not yet formed. If the developmental needs Anna Freud describes are "unfulfilled to a traumatic degree" (Kohut, 1977, p. 81), structural deficits are incurred and the child's experience of being a whole self disintegrates. It is then that the child turns to (drive) fragments of the larger experiential unit which combines the self and the parents as self-objects—for example, to lonely stimulation of his erotogenic zones, with or without accompanying fantasies. Depressive oral, anal, or phallic zonal stimulation and associated fantasies and depressive voyeuristic and exhibitionistic enactments or fantasies are, in essence, distorted erotized replacements for the missing self-object functions which ordinarily provide mental structure by fulfilling normal developmental needs; these sexualized versions of missing structure and unfulfilled needs are psychological worlds apart from the normal looking and exhibiting to parents, and from oral, anal, and phallic drive activity, which is always an integral part of normal development and the child's cohesive self.

While a detailed discussion of the complex mental mechanisms involved in symptom formation in disorders of the self is beyond the scope of this paper. I wish to clarify the basic distinction I am making between neurotic and neuroticlike symptoms. Symptom formation begins when the cohesive self is threatened by the danger of psychological fragmentation and/or the danger of psychological depletion, enfeeblement, and loss of vitality. When vigorous demands and appeals directed to the self-object are to no avail, "disintegration anxiety" and/or "depletion anxiety" ensues, and sooner or later the child's healthy assertiveness is likely to break up into its disintegration products—narcissistic rage. The inner psychological states resulting from loss of cohesiveness—disintegration, depletion, rage—can be manifested directly, can be given any kind of symbolic expression or representation, and can be sexualized.

Disintegration anxiety (Kohut, 1977) is a broad term which refers to all of the anxieties experienced by a precariously established self in anticipation of the deterioration of its very structure. Thus the term refers not only to the fear of fragmentation of the self; it also refers to the fear of the impending loss of its vitality and to the fear of psychological depletion. In view of the frequency of this state in the child's original development, and its clinical importance from early childhood on, I suggest the special name of "depletion anxiety." Furthermore, in view of the frequent occurrence and importance of early and later childhood depressions when psychological depletion is unrelieved by parental recognition and responsiveness, I suggest the special name "depletion depression."

Kohut (1977) distinguishes between "guilt depressions" due to structural conflicts and "empty depressions"—what I call "depletion depressions"—in connection with his differentiation between two major classes of anxiety: (1) the anxieties experienced by a more or less firmly constituted self in anticipation of the various danger situations described by Freud (1926); and (2) the anxieties experienced by the precariously established self. He suggests that we refer to both anxieties *a potiori*—that is, to the first as castration anxiety and to the second as disintegration anxiety (personal communication). Thus, depletion anxiety, along with other specific anxieties evoked by the self's structural deterioration, is subsumed under the broad heading "disintegration anxiety."

MANIFESTATIONS OF DISTURBANCES OF COHESIVENESS

1. Disturbances of cohesiveness can be manifested directly in free-floating (disintegration) anxiety, and/or depletion (empty) depression (both of these states expectably give rise to the full gamut of separation problems); in a marked propensity for narcissistic rage, clinging, demanding, coercive, and manipulative behavior; in functional impairments or inhibitions in capacities of all kinds, such as those involved in taking new developmental steps, learning, motor and athletic abilities, socialization, sublimations; and in "impaired" synthetic and integrating functions (see Brenner, 1968; A. Freud, 1966, 1969a).

2. Disturbances of cohesiveness can be given *symbolic expression* in any mental representation and any mental content of any phase of development (see A. Freud's discussion [1970, pp. 172–178] of the manifest and latent content of fears and anxieties). That is to say, inner tensions associated with fragmentation, depletion, and narcissistic rage can be expressed symbolically as any of the anxieties associated with the genetic series Freud (1926) described—for example, as fears of darkness, noise, annihilation, starvation, helplessness, rejection, desertion, mutilation, illness, poverty, kidnappers, robbers, witches, monsters, animals, insects. (A. Freud [1970a] discusses the fact that while the fear and its symbolic representation can at times be correlated with, e.g., archaic fears, separation anxiety, fear of loss of love, castration anxiety, "On the whole . . . symbols are also interchangeable and, by themselves, an insufficient guide to diagnosis" [p. 176].) The inner tensions, furthermore, can find symbolic expression in more organized phobias, which are also apt to be confused with those associated with the infantile neurosis.

3. Disturbances of cohesiveness can be *sexualized.* By way of this mental mechanism the child who is not assisted to recover by the empathic responses of the (parental) self-objects which normally restore his intactness may attempt to regain cohesion (fill in for the deficits due to frustrated developmental needs) by reorganizing himself around his own body, especially the

erogenous zones and their functions and products, and around what he can do with his own mind. This is a way of saying that through resort to broken-apart fragments and remnants of normal infantile sexuality, normal assertion, and normal thinking and action, the child tries on his own to put himself back together.

In particular, the tendency to sexualize deficits and needs underlies a whole spectrum of symptomatic manifestations mistaken for the infantile neurosis in children and adults—habit disorders such as fecal retention and soiling, lonely masturbation, depression, addictive sucking and overeating, passivity, perverse fantasies and tendencies of all kinds, perverse behavior disorders (voyeurism, exhibitionism, homosexuality, sadomasochism), "Don Juanism," promiscuity in women. The attempts of the fragmented self to reorganize itself around the capacity to think is mistaken for obsessional neurosis; reorganization of the self around driven activity and actions (e.g., rituals) is mistaken for compulsion neurosis; and reorganization around chronic narcissistic rage and around retaliation and revenge is mistaken for a vicissitude of the aggressive drives in the neuroses proper.

That the danger to the cohesiveness of the self can be given symbolic expression in any mental content and any mental representation, and that the child (and later, the adult) frequently resorts to any autoplastic or alloplastic means available to stimulate himself in an attempt, albeit a pathological one, to regain cohesion and a lost sense of aliveness—these facts account for the finding that "in the final diagnosis" the manifest content of deficit symptoms may be indistinguishable from neurotic symptoms.[1] In other words, a *neuroticlike super-*

1. Many analytic writers (e.g., Kernberg, 1975; Modell, 1975, 1976) fail to make the essential distinction between pathological overt grandiosity and overidealization, and a still-remaining intact (split-off or repressed) nuclear grandiose self/idealized parent imago which enters into transferences. Pathological grandiosity and overidealization have to be understood and interpreted as the *distorted* outcome of childhood fixations and structural deficits and have to be distinguished from the infantile grandiose self and the genuine idealization of the parent imago which can "grow"—that is, undergo structural accretion and integration into the personality in the form of realistic ambitions and guiding ideals.

structure may well come to overlay and obscure the structural faults which stunt the child's personality, impair functioning, give rise to profound anxiety, depression, lack of initiative and zest, and to the pathological breakup of normal assertion which is manifest as narcissistic rage. (See Greenacre's [1960, 1969, 1971] cogent views on "normal aggression" in development and her attempt to distinguish between a progressive growth force and an aggressive drive.)

In the final diagnosis, however, it is the transferences of analyzable patients which make it possible to discern the latent content and meaning of symptoms and to distinguish between underlying structural deficits and an underlying infantile neurosis. Transferences to the analyst as a new edition of prestructural mirroring and idealized self-objects reveal that symptoms directly and symbolically express the threat of fragmentation and depletion, the need for missing or insufficient psychic structure, and the pathologically intensified, persisting needs for new versions of the self-objects which originally failed in their functions of adequately acting in place of inner firming, confirming, and guiding.

It should be mentioned again that patients with analyzable disorders of the self belong to the larger group of patients with deficits that Greenacre, Anna Freud, and Kohut describe. In general there are two major types of structural deficits—nonanalyzable and analyzable—although both lead to "alterations" of the personality in the sense that its development is "restricted" or "dislocated" (Freud, 1937). On the one hand, there are massive deficits in the child's prestructural self-object ties. These deficits lead either to a barely established self in constant danger of disruption and disintegration or to an irreparably damaged and injured self which resorts to delusional (psychotic) mechanisms to reconstitute itself. At this stage of our knowledge, patients with massive deficits who use schizoid mechanisms to protect themselves from falling apart, or delusional mechanisms to put themselves back together, can be treated psychotherapeutically, but they cannot be analyzed (Kohut, 1971, 1977). On the other hand, there are deficits in self-object ties of varying degrees of severity which do not preclude the irreversible establishment in the second to third years of a cohesive infantile self with nuclear phase-appropriate "ambitions" and idealized "goals" (Kohut, 1977). The irreversible establishment of the self, in spite of its deficits, makes analytic treatment possible. Given the chance in analysis, a sufficiently intact childhood self reestablishes a tie to the analyst as a reinstated mirroring or idealized prestructural self-object. Genetic reconstructions and interpretations of this type of transference tie, and of the reactivated childhood needs for appropriate response to missing capacities, to the renewed strivings to exhibit and achieve, and to "borrow" strengths to reach goals, lead to further structural development of infantile ambitions and goals, and the capacities to realize them. Gradual integration of all of these into the personality as a whole begins to occur, as though of its own accord, following the working through process.

Both the establishment and the working through of these transferences are "derailed" when the neuroticlike symptomatic manifestations of deficits are mistaken either for typical neurotic oedipal conflicts or for more archaic preoedipal psychosexual conflicts. Nevertheless, most analysts interpret the masked deficits as though they were such conflicts. For example, transference interpretations based on theories of conflicts and unconscious defensive struggles for and against "good" and "bad," "part," "split" introjected objects of libido and aggression *inadvertently* repeat the child's original rejections and rebuffs by parents who could neither understand nor respond to typical and expectable needs directed to them for admiration, enthusiasm, recognition, and help in self mastery. Specifically, analyzable patients begin tentatively and hopefully to look to the analyst, as to the parents or other important figures, for such responses. When they are told that they are defending themselves against their hostile and attacking impulses toward the analyst as a frustrating drive object who is withholding the drive satisfactions they seek, they feel psychologically injured. They then invariably become more anxious, depressed, or enraged; or they further retreat, or further sexualize frustrated, intensified, and often distorted needs for mirroring and for borrowed strengths from the reinstated self-objects who once again are psychologically unavailable.

In my opinion, Mahler et al.'s (1975) theory of a decisive, pathogenic "rapprochement conflict" with introjected "good" and "bad" objects of libido and aggression, and Kernberg's (1975) theory of pathological idealization, pathological grandiosity, and archaic conflicts misunderstand transference revivals of legitimate developmental needs toward their legitimate self-objects. (In this context, see Leo Stone's [1961] important discussion of analysts' inadvertent rebuff and rejection of these needs, and the "iatrogenic regressive transferences" which are "artifacts.") As far as patients with analyzable disorders of the self are concerned, there are transferences of childhood needs which are not drive needs to a reinstated childhood object, and this object is not a drive object.

Unfortunately, schools of analytic thought which postulate that archaic conflicts "split" the infantile mind and the developing structures have led some analysts to become wholly antagonistic to psychoanalytic developmental psychology and to consider it totally irrelevant to a theory of psychoanalytic treatment. For example, Brenner (1976) has abandoned his earlier interest (see Arlow and Brenner, 1964) in trying to understand "soft spots" in the child's structural development which compromise the later development of ego and superego; and he now attributes the normality and pathology of childhood development exclusively to the vicissitudes of normal and abnormal phallic-oedipal drive wishes. That is to say, he has returned to prestructural analytic theory in an attempt to clear up all the mistaken theories of early childhood development based on archaic conflicts. Yet, Brenner himself has simply added another untenable theory of conflict with phallic-oedipal objects to other untenable theories of structural conflicts before structures are actually established.

Greenacre (1971) also addressed this serious clinical and theoretical problem when she discussed the lack of assimilation of the findings of psychoanalytic developmental psychology into an effective theory of analytic treatment; and she made it clear that such an assimilation requires "a change of emphasis" (p. 174) and new theoretical principles and technical procedures. This "change of emphasis" and the shift in point of view from conflict to structural development have been made possible by the discovery of the missing piece of the childhood psychic reality of an expectable environment and its indispensable psychological functions—a prestructural self-object "environment" which for all practical purposes is indistinguishable from the child's own mental organization and his cohesiveness or lack thereof. The concept of the self-object as the precursor of psychic structure is the indispensable theoretical bridge which now links the most important contributions of psychoanalytic developmental psychology to a theory which is consistent with the child's need for structure, his normal and abnormal structural development, and to a theory of analytic treatment which actually fosters a needed process of further structural growth.

SUMMARY

In conclusion I particularly want to reemphasize some of the differences between the work of analyzing the conflicts of the infantile neurosis—the dangers arising from libidinal and aggressive oedipal drives, regressive defenses, and compromise formations—and the psychic work performed in the analysis of the self—the establishment, interpretation, and working through of self-object transferences and the transmuting internalization of the new psychic structure which eventually makes the transference "pass" (Tolpin, 1971):

1. For patients with structural deficits, genetic reconstructions and interpretations of conflicts are ineffectual because these interpretations bypass and obscure the central psychopathology; and they inadvertently repeat childhood psychological injuries which lead to artifacts and regressive transferences.

2. Patients who need analysis because of faulty self-esteem, a missing sense of direction, inadequately firmed ideals, fragmentation anxiety, or depletion anxiety and depression are

apt to manifest a neuroticlike superstructure which has to be differentiated from neurotic symptomatology; and they are likely to develop the various self-object transferences which have to be differentiated from a classical transference neurosis. The recognition of mirror and idealizing transferences and transference resistances and their specific interpretation are the necessary conditions for a systematic working through process, and the gradual replacement of the transference with new psychic structure, which then effectively maintains cohesion, self-esteem, a sense of direction, and the wherewithal to pursue ambitions and to follow inner ideals.

3. The discovery that the analyst is a new edition of the child's prestructural self-objects thus bears directly on the notion of the nonanalytic "corrective emotional experience with the analyst as a new object"; and on the notion that improved self-esteem and acquisition of purpose and ideals and a sense of direction are beneficial by-products of analysis (Ritvo, 1974; Berger and Kennedy, 1976). These are intrapsychic achievements which depend on the acquisition of new psychic structure—and these are precisely the acquisitions and improvements which are "expectable" when self-object transferences are explicitly recognized, interpreted, and worked through. In other words, these specific changes go hand in hand with the filling in of structural deficits. These changes are not merely hoped-for beneficial by-products of analysis—they are the goal and the outcome of the analytic work and the successful resolution of this species of transferences.

4. By the same token, the discovery of the transference reactivation of the psychological functions of the parents as the child's structure-providing self-objects now makes it possible for analysis to succeed with two broad facts of psychological life—the fact of intrapsychic conflict, and the fact of the disintegrating and depleting intrapsychic effects of structural deficits; and this discovery now also makes it possible for analysis to succeed with two areas of psychopathology—the one illuminated by the theory of oedipal and preoedipal objects and the theory of the infantile neurosis, and the other illuminated by the theory of the self and the theory of prestructural self-

objects and their role in the development and restoration of a cohesive self.

BIBLIOGRAPHY

ARLOW, J. A. & BRENNER, C. (1964), *Psychoanalytic Concepts and the Structural Theory*. New York: Int. Univ. Press.

BERGER, M. & KENNEDY, H. (1975), Pseudobackwardness in Children. *This Annual*, 30 : 279–306.

BLOS, P. (1972), The Epigenesis of the Adult Neurosis. *This Annual*, 27 : 106–135.

BRENNER, C. (1968), Archaic Features of Ego Functioning. *Int. J. Psycho-Anal.*, 49 : 426–429.

——— (1976), *Psychoanalytic Technique and Psychic Conflict*. New York: Int. Univ. Press.

EISSLER, K. R. (1953), The Effect of the Structure of the Ego on Psychoanalytic Technique. *J. Amer. Psychoanal. Assn.*, 1 : 104–143.

FREUD, A. (1954), The Widening Scope of Indications for Psychoanalysis. *W.*, 5 : 356–376.

——— (1965), Normality and Pathology in Childhood. *W.*, 6.

——— (1966), Obsessional Neurosis. *W.*, 5 : 242–261.

——— (1968), Indications and Contraindications for Child Analysis. *W.*, 7 : 110–123.

——— (1969a), Difficulties in the Path of Psychoanalysis. *W.*, 7 : 124–156.

——— (1969b), Foreword to *The Hampstead Clinic Psychoanalytic Library Series*. *W.*, 7 : 263–267.

——— (1970a), The Symptomatology of Childhood. *W.*, 7 : 157–188.

——— (1970b), The Infantile Neurosis. *W.*, 7 : 189–203.

——— (1975), Foreword to Berger & Kennedy (1975). *This Annual*, 30 : 279–282.

——— (1976), Changes in Psychoanalytic Practice and Experience. *Int. J. Psycho-Anal.*, 57 : 257–260.

FREUD, S. (1914), On the History of the Psycho-Analytic Movement. *S.E.*, 14 : 3–66.

——— (1925), An Autobiographical Study. *S.E.*, 20 : 3–74.

——— (1926), Inhibitions, Symptoms and Anxiety. *S.E.*, 20 : 77–175.

——— (1937), Analysis Terminable and Interminable. *S.E.*, 23 : 209–253.

GOLDBERG, A., BASCH, M. F., GUNTHER, M. S., KOHUT, H., MARCUS, D., ORNSTEIN, A., ORNSTEIN, P. H., TOLPIN, M., TOLPIN, P. H., & WOLF, E. S. (1978), *The Psychology of the Self: A Casebook*. New York: Int. Univ. Press.

GREENACRE, P. (1960), Considerations Regarding the Parent-Infant Relationship. *Int. J. Psycho-Anal.*, 41 : 571–584.

———— (1969), The Fetish and the Transitional Object. *This Annual,* 24 : 144–164.

———— (1971), Notes on the Influence and Contribution of Ego Psychology to the Practice of Psychoanalysis. In: *Separation-Individuation,* ed. J. B. McDevitt & C. F. Settlage. New York: Int. Univ. Press, pp. 171–200.

HARTMANN, H. (1939), *Ego Psychology and the Problem of Adaptation.* New York: Int. Univ. Press, 1958.

KERNBERG, O. F. (1975), *Borderline Conditions and Pathological Narcissism.* New York: Jason Aronson.

KOHUT, H. (1971), *The Analysis of the Self.* New York: Int. Univ. Press.

———— (1972), Thoughts on Narcissism and Narcissistic Rage. *This Annual,* 27 : 360–400.

———— (1977), *The Restoration of the Self.* New York: Int. Univ. Press.

LOEWALD, H. W. (1974), Current Status of the Concept of Infantile Neurosis. *This Annual,* 29 : 183–188.

MAHLER, M. S., PINE, F., & BERGMAN, A. (1975), *The Psychological Birth of the Human Infant.* New York: Basic Books.

MODELL, A. H. (1975), A Narcissistic Defence against Affects and the Illusion of Self-Sufficiency. *Int. J. Psycho-Anal.,* 56 : 275–282.

———— (1976), "The Holding Environment" and the Therapeutic Action of Psychoanalysis. *J. Amer. Psychoanal. Assn.,* 24 : 257–284.

RANGELL, L. (1975), Psychoanalysis and the Process of Change. *Int. J. Psycho-Anal.,* 56 : 87–98.

RITVO, S. (1974), Current Status of the Concept of Infantile Neurosis. *This Annual,* 29 : 159–182.

SADOW, L., GEDO, J. E., MILLER, J., POLLOCK, G. H., SABSHIN, M., & SCHLES-SINGER, N. (1968), The Process of Hypothesis Change in Three Early Psychoanalytic Concepts. *J. Amer. Psychoanal. Assn.,* 16 : 245–273.

STONE, L. (1961), *The Psychoanalytic Situation.* New York: Int. Univ. Press.

TOLPIN, M. (1970), The Infantile Neurosis. *This Annual,* 25 : 273–305.

———— (1971), On the Beginnings of a Cohesive Self. *This Annual,* 26 : 316–352.

WEIL, A. P. (1970), The Basic Core. *This Annual,* 25 : 442–460.

———— (1973), Ego Strengthening Prior to Analysis. *This Annual,* 28 : 287–301.

PROBLEMS OF DEVELOPMENT

Some Developmental Aspects
of the Verbalization of Affects

ROBERT A. FURMAN, M.D.

IN THIS PAPER VERBALIZATION REFERS TO COMMUNICATION BY words, not just to the use of words. This is in contrast both with the random, purposeless use of words which are not intended for communication as well as with the more familiar forms of nonverbal communication. Verbalization is often assumed to refer to verbalization of affects as evidenced by one dictionary definition: "to verbalize—to express in words; he couldn't express his feelings" (*Random House Dictionary of the English Language,* Unabridged Edition 1966). Specifically this paper is directed to that aspect of verbalization which, preceded by the naming of objects, deals with communication of feelings and needs.

In her classic paper "Some Thoughts about the Role of Verbalization in Early Childhood," Anny Katan (1961) presented three basic conclusions. The first stated that the verbalization

---

Faculty Member and Training Analyst at The Cleveland Psychoanalytic Institute; Director, Cleveland Center for Research in Child Development; and Assistant Clinical Professor of Child Psychiatry, Case Western Reserve University School of Medicine.

This paper served as the basis for the Keynote Address at the Annual Meeting of the New York State Council for Children on May 2, 1975 and was presented to the Cleveland Psychoanalytic Society on June 12, 1976. The author is indebted to Miss Elizabeth Daunton, Dr. Anny Katan, and Mrs. Erna Furman for their thoughtful and helpful reviews of various drafts of the paper.

of perceptions of the outside world precedes verbalization of feelings. In this regard she wrote of the child's learning that the verbalization of needs enhanced their fulfillment, a process facilitated by the parents' prideful encouragement. The second conclusion was that the verbalization of feelings leads to an increased mastery by the ego. Here she described how feelings expressed in words, in contrast to their expression in action, may diminish a child's conflicts both with his environment and his superego precursors. This gives the child greater opportunity for mastery without the interposition of interfering defensive activity. In this context she reported how verbalization, by allowing a delay in acting upon feelings so that the ego may evaluate its situation, is, in effect, trial acting, a part of the intellectual process. Her third conclusion described how verbalization, by helping a child distinguish his wishes and fantasies from reality, leads in turn to the integrative process, reality testing, and the establishment of secondary process. This was exemplified in regard to the child's magical thinking in his toddler phase and to the subsequent resolution of the oedipal conflicts.

This paper will examine some developmental aspects of the verbalization of affects, focusing in particular on the transition from action to words and later from words to thoughts, and emphasizing the role of the mother-child relationship. My purpose in focusing on this topic is to enhance our understanding of a process that is crucial for normal maturation and plays a basic role in psychoanalytic treatment. Further, understanding of the normal maturational sequence of the verbalization of affect as an example of the development of a function of the conflict-free sphere of the ego may contribute to understanding of what is now more commonly called deviational development.

In her 1965 paper on research on the symbiotic child psychosis, Mahler stated: "One of the cardinal hypotheses at the base of our research is that such (autonomous) ego functions as memory, reality testing, locomotor integration, cognition, etc., which, according to Hartmann (1939, 1952), are essential for the development of ego autonomy and belong to the conflict-free sphere of the ego, need the libidinal availability of the mother for their optimal unfolding and synthesis" (p. 163).

In *A Child's Parent Dies* Erna Furman (1974) wrote: "In patients who experienced the death of a parent as babies or toddlers, the stress appeared to affect basic aspects of their personality development. . . . Our interest focused on several patients whose difficulties centered especially on interferences with developing ego functions" (p. 173). She described three cases, illustrating interferences with speech, motility, perception, integration. After discussing pertinent papers from the literature, she advanced some tentative formulations, among them the following: "each developing ego function requires a certain amount of instinctual investment, both from the child and from his main love object, in order to follow its maturational course and to establish itself as an autonomous function integrated in the service of the ego. . . . [During a] critical period . . . withdrawal, imbalances and changes in the instinctual investment may lead to interferences with the function . . . we called this a primary emotional interference with an ego function" (p. 177).

Hartmann (1939) had earlier referred to the "enticing task to trace, in a concrete case, the interaction of those processes which assimilate the external and the internal stimuli and lead to average adaptiveness and normal adaptation, with those mechanisms which we know better and consider to be causes of developmental disturbances" (p. 10).

These statements of Mahler, E. Furman, and Hartmann pinpoint two of the difficulties inherent in the attempt to evolve developmental lines for functions of the conflict-free sphere of the ego. The first difficulty involves the role of the mother and stems from the common tendency to describe the developmental maturation of a process as it occurs in the child alone, omitting reference to its interaction with the mother. This interaction, even if it is not fully described, is assumed, though this assumption may become a progressively more silent one. Freud (1911), in a sense, spoke to this point when he wrote: "It will be rightly objected that an organization which was a slave to the pleasure principle and neglected the reality of the external world could not maintain itself. . . . The employment of a fiction like this is, however, justified when one considers that the infant—provided one includes with it the care it receives from its mother—does almost realize a psychical system of this kind" (p. 220n.).

The second difficulty is that the progressive development of a function of the conflict-free sphere of the ego is often hidden from view by conflicts which impinge upon it and distort its developmental patterns before it obtains full autonomy. This is particularly true with the cases of greatest clinical interest, those with the greatest skewing of the development of these functions.

I want to introduce my thoughts with two case examples. The first delineates some mechanisms of activity of the "mother's libidinal availability" in the maturation of an autonomous ego function. The second illustrates the interaction of the maturational process of this function with a developmental conflict, the oedipal conflict. One case was known through consultation at an inner city day care center, the other treated by way of the mother before and during a year at the Hanna Perkins Therapeutic Kindergarten.

CASE EXAMPLES

CASE 1

A word of introduction may be helpful. In studying the transition from action to words, the beginning of verbalization, we focus on a developmental phase which should normally start early in the second year. An arrest at the start of this maturational process either will preclude an analytic treatment that is based on verbal exchange or will be associated with ego defects which prevent a traditional analytic approach. As Anny Katan (1961) has indicated, we prefer to deal initially with such a difficulty educationally if the setting is available for doing so.

Timmie was 3½ years old, attending the Bingham Day Care

Center of the Center for Human Services. His case was brought to me for discussion at one of the consultation sessions I have with the Staff by the head teacher of the nursery school, Mrs. Ruth Harrison. She had many concerns about Timmie. Although he was physically well cared for, his speech was not clear. He used it randomly, naming a few objects as if for his own personal, private pleasure, not to make his needs known. When spoken to, he repeated back whatever was said to him. He called everyone in the school—teachers and children alike—by his name. He did not seem to understand directions. This lack of verbal communication was but one problem. His play was uncontrolled, purposeless, and aggressive; and he bit, kicked, hit, or slapped almost everyone with whom he came in contact. He seemed to enjoy this interaction and was puzzled when another child hit him back. He did dangerous things, often hurting himself, never learning from the experience not to repeat it, and never coming to a teacher for aid or comfort after hurting himself. He never accepted or offered affection. His attention span was short, his physical coordination was poor, and he was unable to participate in any of the usual nursery school activities.

Mrs. Harrison was equally concerned about Timmie's 18-year-old mother who had been directed to bring him to the day care center so that she might pursue a course of study. Although attractively dressed, she never smiled and evinced no apparent interest in the school or her son. She attended few of the regularly scheduled school conferences, walking out of those she did make. No accurate history could be elicited and she seemed constantly aloof and angry. She was most uncomfortable in all contacts with the staff. There seemed to be few healthy aspects to the mother-child relationship with no verbal communication or affection demonstrated between them.

Even before our first consultation, Mrs. Harrison had stopped any effort at regular conferences and history taking, limiting her contacts with the mother to brief, direct phone calls used only when absolutely necessary. These concerned concrete needs, such as for clothing for Tim at school or about preparing him for minor changes in school routine. Some-

times in brief conversations it was possible to tell her something Timmie had felt, such as a sadness when they were discussing how children missed mothers who were away at work
or school.

As our work began Mrs. Harrison instructed her teachers to
talk with Timmie as they would with a toddler just beginning
to talk, and to use brief simple sentences. When he was physically out of control, they held him, explaining they were protecting the other children from him as they would protect him
from the others. They gave him the correct words to use instead of the gestures he made toward things he wanted or
needed. They tried to identify his feelings in words as they became apparent. When he had to be excluded from the group,
he was with Mrs. Harrison, who reported, "Mostly I would just
sit and hold him on my lap, talking to him and naming objects
and children. He required constant supervision."

I did not hear much about Timmie for a year, a year of
painstaking and devoted work. A particularly poignant episode with the mother prompted the follow-up report. By this
time Timmie had made much progress: he was verbalizing
some of his own thoughts, needs, and feelings, no longer repeating back what was said to him. He knew all the names of
the staff and children; he could tell about home activities at
school and about school activities at home; he had begun to
paint, play with blocks, do all the school puzzles, ride a two-
wheeler, pump on a swing; when dirty, he would wash his
hands and attempt to clean his clothes a bit; he responded to
limits, though erratically. He now accepted and sought affection from the teachers, showed sympathy to the other children
with whom he talked, and he sought solace when hurt.

What prompted the report to me was the mother's response
when Timmie's progress had been shared with her; it was,
perhaps, we felt, the first good report about her child she had
ever received. She was pleased and explained she had been
applying at home what she had observed in school—talking to
him, explaining things to him, isolating him when he could
not manage. She wanted to help him do well in school. She
said, "I like him now and I kiss him good-bye when I leave
him at school and I wave back to him when I am leaving."

Timmie's story is not so very unusual and, with minor variants, could be duplicated many times over by consultants and educators who are familiar with this type of child. In our initial thinking about the case it was not possible to tell what potential existed for developing any significant improvement in the precarious mother-child relationship. Mrs. Harrison felt that the mother's response to her was not unusual for those mothers who experience any authority as a source of prying interference, especially when anything other than the mother's best interests is proposed. At Timmie's birth she was only 15 years old and had to divide the responsibility for him among many different caretakers, herself included. His well-cared-for physical appearance was initially the most obvious hopeful sign. It is significant for our purposes that Mrs. Harrison focused her communication with the mother about Timmie on the elucidation and fulfillment of his specific physical and emotional needs.

With Timmie we could only hope that he could learn to verbalize and develop some control of his actions through verbalization. We were struck by his inability spontaneously to seek help when hurt and could only conclude that he did not expect the fulfillment of any needs beyond those of being clothed and fed. His total lack of empathy was felt to relate to not having experienced from his mother an adequate understanding of his feelings and needs beyond the two mentioned above. It was striking that the words he knew were not at the service of his ego for communication, relating, or making his needs known. It was to these ends that all the educational efforts regarding verbalization were directed. Words were offered him in the context of a caring and protecting environment that wanted to meet his needs and help him acquire mastery and control.

In discussing the case of a slightly retarded, nonverbalizing child at Hanna Perkins recently, Erna Furman stressed that a child, if he is to aspire to verbalize, needs to experience some of the magic omnipotence of communicative speech. This experience is lacking when mothers cannot or do not respond with normal prideful encouragement, and specifically and concretely when they cannot respond to the child's attempt to verbalize his needs. Without this response verbalization does not proceed, does not continue its progressive development, with the grave risk it will not be available for use by the ego, as had been the case initially with Timmie.

Timmie's mother was able to observe the effects of verbalization at the Day Care Center and fortunately began to model her relationship to Timmie on what she observed. The process of verbalization initiated by Mrs. Harrison and her staff with Timmie, coupled with their sensitive approach to the mother, evoked a response that appeared to move the mother into the developmental phase of parenthood (E. Furman, 1969). We have often observed this, though more frequently in less dramatic situations, where the nursery school's demonstrated success in educating a child to verbalize can evoke such a response in the mother and establish the missing link in the development of the child's ability to verbalize: the mother's response to his communicated needs, be they physical or affective. For almost to the extent that Timmie saw words evoke response, his ability to verbalize developed, and with this step he began to acquire control over action by the use of words.

CASE 2

A word of introduction may again be helpful. In studying the transition from dominance by words to dominance by thought in the management of feeling, an analytic case might well have been used. It so happened that the clearest clinical material available was that of a treatment by way of the mother. This child was considered for an analysis at the start of the treatment and during the first year of work and this was discussed with the parents. Analysis did not become necessary, however, as the course of the child's treatment confirmed the initial diagnostic impression that he did not have a crystallized or rigidly entrenched neurosis, but rather had a combination of neurotic and developmental conflicts that could yield to treatment by way of the parents. I recognize that in many centers, lacking the facilities of a therapeutic kindergarten, analysis might well have been the treatment of choice. This case may, incidentally, illustrate once more the potential inherent in this treatment approach, both therapeutically and theoretically, as well as its closeness to the analytic process in its sequential unfolding and progress.

Work with Kent's parents started when he was 4 years, 4 months old, beginning his second year at a suburban half-day nursery school. The work continued for two years. During the second year he attended the Hanna Perkins Kindergarten. At the time of this writing, he has completed first grade, giving us some opportunity for a follow-up.

During Kent's first year of nursery school where he started at 3 years, 4 months, his difficulty had shown in daily unprovoked attacks on other children. This out-of-control aggressiveness had subsided somewhat during his first school year with the mother's admonitions and the teacher's ability to interest him in some learning aspects of school. But it had worsened at the start of his second year at the same school, and the parents feared that it would only increase in severity after some relatively minor elective surgery which was scheduled to be performed in about four months. At that point they contacted me. They described almost incidentally Kent's provocative seeking of punishment and his constant statements that no one liked him and no one would help him.

The parents were very reluctant to begin a treatment via the mother (E. Furman, 1957), apprehensive, I felt, that they had done something wrong or were doing something wrong, afraid its elucidation might make them too guilty. The mother focused her concerns in a fear that I would interfere with her life style, which meant a career for her and vacations with her husband away from the children. Ultimately this was understood as a manifestation of her difficulty with separations and, as these became more manageable through verbalization, the impetus for vacations away from the children vanished and her career planning was always well geared to meeting their needs.

With the parents' permission I contacted Kent's teacher who described his aggression as extreme; he actually knocked over other children on occasion. She knew that he was bright and had a good attention span. She was puzzled especially by his going around the room, bothering, provoking, hitting, or throwing things at the other children after he had done a job well.

I began weekly visits with the mother on the basis of helping her prepare Kent for the forthcoming surgery, while at the same time doing something of a long-term evaluation. I had to begin where they wanted to work, hopeful that during this time I could deal with her guilt so that this force could be mobilized to support the treatment. I felt I had a tenuous relationship as I thought their concern and skepticism about things psychiatric were as great as the concern I sensed about their guilt.

In my first working session with the mother she told me that Kent had a hard time going to bed at night because of bad dreams. She was unable to supply further details because she had never discussed it in depth with Kent. That night at bedtime she asked him to tell her about his trouble sleeping. He replied that he did not want to close his eyes because when he did, he had a nightmare about being locked in a box with the family pets, unable to get out, unable to reach his parents, with them unable to find him. Later he added that sometimes there was a monster in the box with him and he just could not get away.

It is significant that Kent then thanked his mother for talking to him about his worry and asked if they could please talk again about it another night. His deep appreciation of the opportunity to put his worry into words and to share it with his mother made a lasting impression on her, as did his evident relief the next day and evening when he went to bed. She knew at once from him that verbalization was right, that she needed help to continue it and made her initial commitment to the treatment.

We were able to piece the picture together over the course of the next two months. When Kent had just turned 3 the parents had gone away for a two-week holiday, leaving Kent and his sister with a rather kindly but ineffective baby-sitter. Kent's sister had responded to the parents' absence with out-of-control aggression. The sitter had not been able to prevent her sudden severe attacks on Kent. We saw that on the first level the monster was his sister with whom he was confined, totally unprotected, completely unable to reach his parents to bring him safety.

The mother's discussion of this event with Kent slowly brought an end to the sleep problem and effected a diminution of his aggressive behavior in school. First, she reviewed with him and sympathized with his helpless fear of being attacked when his parents were away during the vacation. Next she showed him how an out-of-control aggression entered the picture whenever he was away from his mother—at bedtime and at school. And finally she told him that he had taken his fears of being attacked to school—he was so afraid of assaults from the other children that he attacked them first.

Some beginning work was also possible on another level once the monster was recognized as Kent's own uncontrolled aggression. His mother helped him to put his fear into words and encouraged him to express his anger in words rather than action. It became clear to me that his anger was not just a response to his sister's attacks upon him during the parents' vacation when he was 3 years old; there was very suggestive evidence that he was also angry in response to being over-stimulated at home where bathroom and bedroom doors were left open and he was bathed together with his sister.

We could not get to this next aspect of the work because the pressure of preparing him for surgery intervened. He showed no apparent ill-effects after this relatively minor surgery and maintained the improvement in school where he continued to control his attacks. This improvement had been the result of a beginning verbalization of feelings as well as of a partial working through of the affects engendered by the traumatic summer vacation. But the improvement was not sustained and he soon fell completely apart in school, again attacking with such ferocity that his teacher excluded him. This forced the parents to face up to the extent of his troubles and they agreed to his attending our kindergarten the following year.

New symptoms had appeared. He was unable to separate

from his mother, the old interpretations about the summer
vacation trauma were no longer effective, and he had started
to wet his bed at night and his pants during the day. We understood the wetting as his attempt to show us his inability to
control his excitement which, when coupled with his inability
to control his aggression, made him afraid to be apart from
his mother and the external control she could supply. I
wanted to put the question of excitement into the work at the
first opportunity because there were so many clues that this
was a basic problem area. Among these were the fact that in
later versions the monster had cutting-up and cutting-off
characteristics.

The topic of excitement led at once to the question of privacy and modesty. The parents had been very conscientiously
immodest in the belief that this was the way to make sex acceptable and not taboo. It was hard for them at first to accept
the idea that they were reacting to their own parents' inability
to discuss sexual matters, not their parents' consciously remembered modesty about things sexual. Showing without telling, exhibiting without verbalizing, is of course a most common problem faced by child analysts in work with parents.
Successful alteration of parental behavior usually does not
occur until the parents are able to remember the sexual overstimulation that they themselves endured as children—an experience that is usually repressed behind the conscious memory of the parents' modesty. The best avenue to recall is
usually via pursuing their own parents' inability to discuss sexual matters. The open-door policy in Kent's home had been
accompanied by excited wrestling and had been punctuated
by one particularly sad and tragic episode a few months earlier. Kent, naked in his bedroom with his sister, had an erection which she had pointedly laughed at and ridiculed.

Once more Kent himself came to the support of the work,
this time joined by his sister. When the parents announced
one evening at the dinner table that they were instituting a
new policy of privacy in the home, both children were de-
lighted and openly said so. They religiously adhered at once
to the new program of closed bedroom and bathroom doors

which could be opened only after knocking and receiving permission. They also insisted from the start that everyone keep clothed in each other's presence. Here again the children's reaction greatly reassured the parents that they were on the right track.

What came next should surprise no one because it is inevitable that when the showing stops the talking starts. And did these children have questions that had never surfaced before! Kent went directly to the erections—what caused them, were they normal? And in conjunction with these questions came many about losing parts of his body; could his arm come off (his sister had once fractured her arm), could his finger come off (his surgery had been on his finger). The mother, to her own surprise, was up to her task. She picked up at once that Kent's worry about his erections was a worry that he could not control them, and that his wetting and uncontrolled behavior had been his way of telling them of his worry about controlling his erections. The mother told him that they were a most usual response to excited feelings and had been a concern to him because there had been just too much excitement at home for any boy to master. She assured him that as the excitement abated at home, he would be able to control his erections. Moreover, she feelingfully reviewed with him the dreadful time when his sister had made fun of his erection.

As these questions persisted over many weeks, the mother also dealt with Kent's worry about losing parts of his body. She connected this first with his surgery and then tactfully added that she knew some boys worried that their penises could be lost as well. To our surprise, he bluntly told her that he had feared she and Daddy would do that to him and had even figured out in fantasy what implements each would employ. He now wanted to have earlier talks about sex difference reviewed again and asked some very tentative questions about birth and conception.

As these difficult concerns were expressed in words and appropriately responded to, his behavior improved. The wetting stopped, he was able to separate better from his mother; and, after a school visit, his old teacher agreed to take him back three days a week when the mother could be in attendance close by in the building. After his return he adjusted well and the aggressive outbursts did not recur.

But then our work came to a standstill, a puzzling one that came strictly from Kent. His ability to separate from his mother had only partially improved and his very open and provocative playing with himself had not yielded to interpretation of his anxiety about his body integrity or to exhortation to tell his mother when he felt too excited so that they could seek the source of his overstimulation. He listened politely to the interpretations and did tell his mother when he was too excited, but this did not impede his open masturbation.

To make any sense of what was going on, a brief review is necessary. By putting his feelings into words, by being able to tell his mother about his worries, he had until now, with her help, achieved some rather impressive results. A severe sleep problem had been eradicated, day and night wetting had been brought under control, fears of body-part loss had been partially alleviated, aggressive outbursts had become manageable at school, and a dreaded surgery had been coped with very well. This must have seemed to him a rather miraculous response to putting feelings into words. It was, to be sure—and he was keenly aware of it.

Yet we were stymied in the work and remained stymied for a number of weeks. I knew some of the aspects of his problem that we had not approached, particularly his oedipal feelings, but he had offered no entry to these concerns. The crucial clue came one day when he was angry with his mother about her being away. He told her so when she returned, but then promptly tore up a picture which he had made for her earlier and which was hanging in the kitchen. It was a drawing of which she was particularly fond and he extremely proud. The mother was distressed and perplexed and angry and told him so, saying, "I just don't understand it. You told me you were angry. Why did you then have to go and do such an angry thing?" He explained that that was just the point: after he had told her he was angry, the anger did not go away and that made him even more angry. "Why didn't it go away when I told you?" he asked.

He thus made clear that for some very sound reasons he expected that putting things into words was some kind of magic end point in itself, that his job was done when he had told his mother what he was feeling. And this had in fact been the case on many previous occasions. His mother, knowing that this was wrong, blurted out that she felt his job was just beginning not ending when he put things into words. At first she could not explain this most insightful response of hers any further, but she told him that although she knew she was right, she did not know why and would think about it and tell him more later. She did add that she had been able to help him, not just because he put things into words, but because what he had told her had enabled her to understand his worries and explain them to him. She said that she had not done it alone, they had done it together.

When the mother discussed this incident with me, we could clarify what more she had wanted to tell him. Putting feelings into words was not meant to make the feelings go away; rather it was meant to help him know what he was feeling so that he could think about the feelings and then figure out what to do about them. Putting feelings into words was not meant to make the feeling disappear as if by magic; rather, it was meant to help him endure the feeling until he understood what it was all about and then knew what to do.

This was a lot to explain to a 5-year-old and, in talking with Kent, the mother divided it into two parts: first, putting feelings into words helped one endure feelings and that was what growing up was all about; and second, putting feelings into words helped him by helping him think about what he was feeling. He seemed to understand this at once; he made progress in handling his separation problem and played less with himself. On separating one day, Kent asked her apprehensively, "Will I be all right when you are gone?" She replied, "You'll be safe. What you feel will be your business and if you get afraid, know it, stay afraid but in control, and we will talk it over when I get home." About his out-of-control excitement, his masturbation, he said one evening to her, "I'm excited." She agreed, adding it was also clear that he was not managing it well, allowing it to be so public. "Why don't you think about it and see if you cannot understand yourself why you are so excited."

They had several similar exchanges in which she reiterated that the task now was to stay with his feelings, abide them, endure them, and bring his intellect to bear upon their management. I was particularly interested from an analytic point of view that within a matter of a week he asked specific questions about birth, conception, and death, and brought his oedipal feelings directly to the fore. One night he very thoughtfully told his father that he was angry with him. When his father asked why, Kent said he wasn't so sure, but he thought it was because Daddy could always be with Mommy whenever Daddy wanted to and sometimes that meant Kent couldn't be with her when he wanted to. Warming up to his task, he told his father that it made him very angry, that he wished he could be in Dad's place and it just wasn't fair. His father intuitively responded by saying that he was sorry it was so hard for Kent. There was a pause as they both were thinking, the father of what to say next. Kent finally broke the silence by declaring with much feeling, "But I love you very much, you know." The father said he knew and that he loved Kent very much too.

This exchange was followed by further changes in Kent, particularly by a desire to learn. The more Kent was in control of himself, the more he seemed to want to know—not just what things were but how they worked and why. His very keen intellect increasingly began to manifest itself.

The summer vacation interceded at this point. The following year at kindergarten was a year of review, consolidation, repetition, and amplification of the previous year's work. It was a year of integration as Kent moved into his latency. This nursery school dropout of the year before became a source of strength in his kindergarten class, a kind, thoughtful, considerate, and thoroughly bright boy "who was a pleasure to teach."

There is only a brief postscript to add. His first-grade teacher reported that she found him to be the fine student and citizen his kindergarten teachers had described, a boy who made a good adjustment to his new school. As prearranged, the mother paid me three visits during the following fall. In the first she reported that they all had had a rather successful and happy summer holiday and that Kent had made a reasonably good start in school. In her second visit a month later she was quite distressed. Kent had all sorts of difficulties—on his way to school he fought with other children who hit him; he was out of control on school trips to a museum and the fire station; many children did not like him; a sitter was unfair. She had been exhausting herself trying to manage these problems, watching him most of the way to school, exploring with the teacher and sitter what could be done to make life better for Kent. In just describing this to me, she recognized that she had been trapped by him into doing his work; she was dealing with the outside world and his feelings about it for him. In her third visit, a month later, she reported that she had told him in rather firm terms that he was trying to get her to do his work for him and that he would never grow up if he always had her intercede for him. His next complaint was met with, "And how did you think you would manage this?" Kent got the point and settled to solving his problems.

DISCUSSION

With the two children whose cases have been described it may be possible to get a better look in depth at verbalization. In considering the mother's role in the development of verbalization I have not referred to the more commonly understood initial acquisition of speech which is stimulated by the speech directed to the child. This is, of course, usually lovingly supplied by the mother. At its inception, in naming objects and in identifying his feelings and needs, the child in effect calls to his mother to alleviate them. Where feelings are concerned, if he is angry, his mother seeks to understand the reasons and tries to explain or alter the situation; if he is sad, she comforts; if he is excited, she calms; if he is out of control, she supplies control; if he is happy, she shares. At the beginning of verbalization, she responds by participating: on the one hand possibly lending a magical aura to the process of verbalization, but in a larger sense demonstrating that the verbalization of feelings leads to action or response and thus to mastery. The mother's response is essential if verbalization is to develop and mature, ultimately to become a part of the child's ego functioning.

This latter step occurs as the function of response slowly begins to be taken over by the child. At first his expressions of feeling will make clear the action he expects to follow his declaration. Still later, as he learns to endure larger quantities of feeling for longer periods of time, he increasingly brings his own thinking to bear upon them and seeks to alleviate them on his own. In effect he begins to internalize, to take over unto himself, his mother's part in the exchanges initiated by verbalization. As verbalization in this way replaces action, so thought begins to replace words. This internalization should start in the preoedipal years, achieve autonomy as a consequence of the introjective process that marks the resolution of the oedipal phase, and thus allow for greater control over feelings, including the choice of when to verbalize and when to keep feelings private.

The basic concepts of this paper, exemplified by the clinical vignettes, can be summed up as follows. As the mother's response to her child's verbalization of his needs is essential to sustain and continue his development of verbalization, so the child must internalize this process of response initiated by his mother so that thoughts eventually can have ascendancy over words. Timmie's difficulty lay in his mother's initial failure to respond to his verbalized needs. Kent's difficulty lay in his defensive or symptomatic inability to internalize the process of response which his mother perhaps found only a bit belatedly.

This understanding of the developmental aspects of verbalization may offer some clue to the proper approach to other complex problems of psychological development such as integration. An innate tendency to fit things together exists in all; but the degree to which this development continues and ultimately comes to be at the ego's service may well depend on a mother's response to her infant and young child's moments of distress. The mother's ability to restore harmony to her child, at first physical, later emotional, may be a forerunner of the synthetic function of the ego. Further, the internalization of the mother's comforting responses as part of the introjective aspect of the resolution of the oedipal phase may account for the increased strength of the synthetic function of the ego that characterizes the transition into latency.

A word can now be said about the interaction between the maturing capacity to verbalize affect and the resolution of the oedipal phase. Kent misused verbalization to keep his mother ensconced in the role of responding to his expressed needs. Thereby he kept her close to him as a source of oedipal gratification, but his reluctance to surrender this gratification precluded the full evolution of the function of verbalizing affect. But this interaction can also be viewed from another perspective: when the ascendancy of thought over words is delayed, the ensuing lack of privacy of feelings may delay the resolution of the oedipal conflict. We are familiar with the adolescent's and young adult's need in analysis to keep the feelings of his first love experience private (A. Katan, 1951). It appeared to me from Kent and from another boy of his age with whose mother I was working at the same time that the ability to confine oedipal wishes to the privacy of thought was necessary for their mastery. In the other boy, the delay in acquiring the ability to think rather than talk was much less pronounced than in Kent, but when he was able to take this forward step, he became fully involved in his final oedipal struggles that led into his latency phase.

Experience over the years with the treatment of under-fives by way of their mothers has impressed us with the importance of assisting a mother to recognize her child's first steps into latency so that she will not by her work interfere with this developmental step. Many conflicts and drives should become repressed at this point, a developmental step which could be interfered with by a mother's continued discussion of them. What is developmentally appropriate before the advent of latency—a mother working with her child on his drives and

defenses, and the conflicts and affects deriving from them—
may become developmentally inappropriate at the beginning
of latency. With some children the repressive force is so strong
that no mother could interfere even if she wished to and tried
to do so. With other children the transition to this phase seems
to evolve more slowly, and treatment via the mother then
poses the potential threat of at least temporarily jeopardizing
this step. As children vary in their mode of phase transition
(Silverman et al., 1975), so mothers vary in the pain they feel
when they lose access to their child's inner feelings and drives
and consequently vary in their facility in adapting to their
child's transition into latency.

It would seem that verbalization of affects, particularly
when this involves the direct expression of oedipal feelings to
the mother, can maintain a degree of cathectic investment in
the drives and their derivatives that can make repression difficult. Whether this is seen as operating in terms of interference with the drives and feelings becoming preconscious before they can become unconscious or with their immediate
repression will perhaps depend on one's theoretical orientation. But the phenomenon is well known to those who have
experience in treatment by way of the mother. It was one of
the factors that encouraged us to add a kindergarten year to
the Hanna Perkins Therapeutic Preschool facilities in Cleveland, to give us the opportunity to guide mothers in their
work with their children during this transition phase into latency.

In initially describing the purpose of this paper, I referred
to the basic role that verbalization of affects plays in analytic
treatment. For example, focus on the developmental aspects
of verbalization may help to clarify a difficult concept, that of
the analyst as a real person as opposed to his being an object
for transference or externalization.

In addressing this question Anna Freud (1965) directed her
remarks in part to those who might feel that all that transpires
in the relationship between analyst and analysand from the
very outset of an analysis is transference and who might tend
to ignore the child's reactions to the analyst as a new object.

She described the hunger in all for new experiences and relationships, a hunger stronger in the developing child than in the adult, a hunger that coexists with the urge to repeat. She stressed the difficulties in the task of the analyst who must constantly distinguish between the analysand's reactions that come from the transference and those that are a response to the analyst as a new or real object. Crucial here, it would seem, is her emphasis on new experience, not repeated ones, as the core of the analyst as a real person.

Bird (1972) basically agreed with Anna Freud in regard to the impact of the analyst as a real person at the outset of an analysis, the need sharply to set apart these responses from transference, and the difficult and continuous task the analyst faces in distinguishing between these responses. Bird focused on one aspect of the analyst as a real person when he stated that the very helpfulness of the analyst and his work may heighten his role as a real person and so interfere with the emergence and development of the transference. He stated succinctly, "One of the most serious problems of analysis is the very substantial help that the patient receives directly from the analyst and the analytic situation" (p. 285).

But an apparent paradox comes into focus when, referring to Fliess as Freud's object for transference in his self-analysis, Bird said, "As with any analyst, his 'real' impact on Freud was slight" (p. 270). If the impact of the analyst as a real person is as slight as was Fliess's impact on Freud, how could a serious problem emerge from the analyst as a real person, from an analyst's helpfulness enhancing his stature as a real person?

I believe it is clear from Bird's paper that he feels the impact of the analyst as a "real" person is slight in comparison with the impact the analyst may have through a well-conducted analysis, with ensuing structural or intrapsychic change. A brief vignette from the analysis of a 12-year-old boy may illustrate this point. In the second year of his analysis my patient was complaining bitterly of feeling "clobbered" every time he did anything that seemed just a bit wrong. This was particularly embarrassing because he was never able to stop himself from crying at these times wherever he might be. He knew that his conscience was "out of whack" somehow and he would contrast the response of his conscience to his minor transgressions with my response and that of his parents, teachers, and peers. But no matter how understanding and accepting I seemed to him, this of course had no effect on his trouble. One day as he reported a misdeed, he had the feeling that I might hit him. He was surprised at this, and it led to his recall that when he had been less than 5 years old his mother had hit him for misdeeds, sometimes figuratively with words, sometimes literally with her hand. He saw at once that the fury of his conscience came from his mother's fury in these earlier years, a response she had subsequently modified. With this recall, made possible through a transference reaction, change became possible and his conscience was modified, his new model not being just the analyst but also his parents as he now perceived them and the others in his environment to whom he had referred earlier.

As a real person I had had no impact in alleviating the harshness of his conscience regardless of how much he had wanted this to be the case. Only with the insight that came through the transference was there any significant impact, any intrapsychic change. It may also be important that the analyst's understanding and patience were not new to the patient and the analyst therefore did not emerge as a real person in this regard.

This leads to another aspect of the analyst as a helpful person and its effect on the analysis. Quite recently, in the seventh year of a reanalysis, I made a transference interpretation to a woman patient before an impending brief vacation. This patient has most difficult responses to separations that have been totally resistant to any psychoanalytic interventions. She is a woman who has used me and the analysis as very real helpers with her most difficult life and family. To my surprise, in this recent instance she felt that the interpretation was most helpful and responded with associations that seemed to confirm its accuracy. When I asked why the interpretation could now be helpful, she explained that previously what I had said had just seemed like words without meaning because she was so intent on just being able to manage, to get along. "Sometimes I felt you did not know just how sick I was, how much I was just trying to stay out of the hospital. I'm stronger now and guess I can begin to listen to what you are really trying to help me understand. I've never had anyone before to listen me out, to try to help me sort things out." It was fascinating that during this period of time when she was using me as a "real" person in the sense of a consistent, patient person to assist her, she did not see or notice anything personal about me. She explained that had she taken notice of things in my office, for example, she would have been flooded with thoughts and feelings that would have precluded her ability to function.

When I recently saw a patient of a deceased colleague, I was told, "He was so kind, so giving of himself, so supportive, I don't know what I would have done without him. I never had anyone like that help me before. I put myself together as a person with his help and then I was able to use his mind to begin to solve my problems."

In both these instances, it seems to me, the patients are describing a phase of development in which their needs for the analyst as a helping person, as a real person who offers a helpful experience previously unknown to them, precluded the possibility of their using the analyst as an object for transference. The first patient even struggled to avoid any awareness of common items in the office that might have stirred those transference reactions which would have interfered, she felt, with her utilization of me as a helping person.

It is difficult to distinguish those patients who to avoid the stresses of the transference defensively try to keep us ensconced as helpers from those who for developmental reasons must use us as helpers and are able to experience us only as "real" in the newness of the helpful relationship before they can develop a transference. Bird lists many factors which may contribute to the real value of the analytic situation for the patient: the stability, wisdom, reasonableness, understanding of the analyst; the honesty, openness, directness, regularity of the relationship; the opportunities for the patient to explore his past and clarify his goals. This list may, however, omit a most important component of the reality of the analytic situation, the most common one, which runs the least risk of interfering with the development of the transference, and which may most facilitate its emergence: verbalization of affect.

The analyst's responses to his patient's verbalizations occur well within the confines of the usual analytic technique and seem to me, in the newness of the experience for some, an example of the analyst being perceived as new or real. In initiating and facilitating the identification and verbalization of his analysand's feelings and in responding to these verbalizations with an attempt to understand the needs they express, the analyst may in effect be completing a task that a mother had only initiated or failed to manage satisfactorily. The analysand's response to these attempts of his analyst to understand is often covered over by transference, obscuring the significance of the real response of ultimate understanding that all experience to some degree. This analytic understanding can be a new or real experience and, as the process of verbalization and response begins to be internalized, something further that is new and hence real is experienced. How often in the course of an analysis do we hear our analysands say, "And I thought what you would have said to me and went ahead and managed the situation." Not so frequently, but often enough, we also hear an insightful patient comment that he no longer needs to go through this process, but is pleased to note that he is able to respond at once on his own, indicating that the sequence of verbalization and response has now become fully internalized. In these instances the analysts of adults have a firsthand opportunity to observe in action some developmental aspects of the verbalization of affects.

In concluding, I would like to be more explicit about two points that may have been left too implicit in the paper.

In describing some developmental aspects of the verbalization of affects I have focused on the role of the mother-child relationship. It seems to me that the mother plays a qualitatively different role in facilitating the maturation of such an ego function than she does in relation to the unfolding of instinctual development. We are all familiar with the necessity of her availability as an object for instinctual development, albeit even a seductive object at times. In facilitating the maximum development of an ego function, however, she may have to play a much more active part. Moreover, different mechanisms may be involved. Yet, many open questions remain: can generalizations be made from one autonomous function of the ego such as verbalization to others such as integration? What mechanisms are involved in the developmental unfolding of these functions?

Regarding verbalization itself I come to the conclusion that the development of this function should culminate in the individual's choice and a control over whether or not to verbalize. It is perhaps a paradox to say that full maturation of the function of verbalizing affects is reached in the ability not to verbalize, but this does indeed seem to be the case.

BIBLIOGRAPHY

BIRD, B. (1972), Notes on Transference. *J. Amer. Psychoanal. Assn.,* 20 : 267–301.
FREUD, A. (1965), Normality and Pathology in Childhood. *W.,* 6.
FREUD, S. (1911), Formulations on the Two Principles of Mental Functioning. *S.E.,* 12 : 213–226.
FURMAN, E. (1957), Treatment of Under-Fives by Way of the Parents. *This Annual,* 12 : 250–262.
———(1969), Treatment via the Mother. In: *The Therapeutic Nursery School,* ed. R. Furman & A. Katan. New York: Int. Univ. Press, pp. 231–273.
———(1974), *A Child's Parent Dies.* New Haven & London: Yale Univ. Press.
HARTMANN, H. (1939), *Ego Psychology and the Problem of Adaptation.* New York: Int. Univ. Press, 1958.
KATAN, A. (1951), The Role of Displacement in Agoraphobia. *Int. J. Psycho-Anal.,* 32 : 41–50.
———(1961), Some Thoughts about the Role of Verbalization in Early Childhood. *This Annual,* 16 : 184–188.
MAHLER, M. S. (1965), On the Significance of the Normal Separation-Individuation Phase. In: *Drives, Affects, Behavior,* ed. M. Schur. New York: Int. Univ. Press, 2 : 161–169.
SILVERMAN, M., REES, K., & NEUBAUER, P. L. (1975), On a Central Psychic Constellation. *This Annual,* 30 : 127–157.

Transference and Developmental Issues in the Analysis of a Prelatency Child

PHYLLIS TYSON

IN THE COURSE OF THERAPEUTIC WORK, THE CHILD'S RELATION-
ship with the analyst is often a complicated mixture of elements of a real relationship, an extension into the analysis of
current relationships, and a repetition or even a revival of the
past. The natural unfolding of the child's personality further
complicates the relationship, and it often becomes difficult to
determine whether the child is using the analyst in the expression of a new developmental step or whether he has cast the
analyst in a particular role in order to express neurotic conflicts from the past.

The clinical work on which this paper is based was done while the author
was at the Hampstead Child-Therapy Course and Clinic, London, which is
at present supported by the Field Foundation, Inc., New York; the Foundation for Research in Psychoanalysis, Beverly Hills, California; the Freud
Centenary Fund, London; the Anna Freud Foundation, New York; the National Institute of Mental Health, Bethesda, Maryland; the Grant Foundation, New York; the New-Land Foundation Inc., New York; and a number
of private supporters. An earlier version of this paper was presented to the
Wednesday meeting of the Hampstead Child-Therapy Clinic, London, in
1971. I wish to acknowledge my great indebtedness to the late Sarah Kut
Rosenfeld who supervised my conduct of this analysis and who was unfailing
in her insight, tact, and understanding.

Mrs. Tyson now is Guest Instructor, San Diego Psychoanalytic Institute,
San Diego, California.

The purpose of this presentation is to examine whether there are any circumstances in a child analysis in which the assignment of the roles by a child to the analyst may be said to form part of a transference neurosis. In doing so, I will also attempt to distinguish transference neurosis in children from other forms of transference and from developmental issues.

It is generally agreed that those aspects of the treatment relationship which are revived from the past as a consequence of analytic work can be subsumed under the heading of transference. In this view, the patient's past instinctual investments and internalized conflicts are expressed and reenacted in current perceptions, thoughts, fantasies, attitudes, and behavior in regard to the person of the analyst, thereby becoming accessible to further interpretation and modification. The role in which the patient casts the analyst therefore serves as a vehicle for the present expression of past investments. The transference neurosis—its appearance and subsequent interpretation—is a concept central to adult psychoanalysis, and it classically distinguishes psychoanalytic treatment from all other forms of psychotherapy. However, its place and applicability in the analysis of children have long been controversial issues. There is a general lack of consensus as to which of the particular attitudes displayed by the child, or to what extent any of the ways the child relates to the analyst, can be considered transference, and especially transference neurosis. The original, but subsequently modified, view was that as long as the child lived at home with his parents, he still had possession of his first love objects and therefore there was no need for him to repeat his conflict in relation to the analyst (A. Freud, 1927; Bornstein, 1945). Some analysts (e.g., Adatto, 1971) assert that the appearance of a transference neurosis is dependent on adequate developmental progress and therefore is possible only in a fully developed mature personality. Marianne Kris and Settlage (Panel, 1966) state that a transference neurosis, in whatever way we may define it, cannot take place in children until there has been sufficient structural development to allow for intersystemic conflicts. In this regard there is general agreement that a so-called full transference neurosis can not

develop until the superego is independent of parental influence, that is, around the age of puberty. Fraiberg (1966), however, discusses the case of a latency child with transference developments where it became clear that the factor of
independence from the original objects was not the only criterion. Both Harley (1971) and Rosenfeld (1971) make the point
that the dependence on the parent has to be weighed against
the degree to which processes of internaliz   n have taken
place. For once internalization occurs, th   a discrepancy in the child's mind between exter   psychic
reality, and the original objects are p   ed according to fluctuations in feeling   nd
structuralization. Furthermore, there
between the establishment of psychic inde
child's continuing need for actual physical and   e-
pendence, although the presence of the original o   he
child's current life may obscure the development of a   ier-
ence neurosis. Rosenfeld reported the case of an 11-ye .-old
girl in whom conflicts were first worked through in relation to
the original objects, but later were repeated with the analyst as
a central figure, and were resolved and finally given up only
when they were interpreted in relation to the analyst.

While there now seems to be some recognition that one or
another aspect of transference can appear in the course of
child analysis, most workers would agree with Anna Freud's
opinion (1974) that what is called transference neurosis in
children does not equal the adult variety in every respect; and
that when it does appear, it is quite circumscribed, is apparent
only for a short time, and is usually dissipated or somehow
disappears before all the constituent conflicts can be analyzed
primarily in relation to the analyst.

The difficulties in making distinctions between the various
forms of transference and other analytic roles and relationships are compounded by the frequently loose and uncritical use of the terms "transference" and "transference neurosis." An attempt to clarify the concepts involved has been
made by the Hampstead Clinic Index Group (Sandler et al.,
1975). They provide a useful (even if somewhat arbitrary)

framework in which to examine clinical material by distinguishing four subtypes:

1. Transference predominantly of *habitual modes* of *relating,*
   in which the child reveals various aspects of his character
   by relating to the analyst as he would to any person.
2. Transference predominantly of *current relationships,* in
   which the child's relationship to the therapist is an extension of, or defensive displacement from, his relationship
   to his primary objects. However, a current situation can
   reactivate an old situation, which may then be brought
   into treatment.
3. Transference predominantly of *past experiences* "refers to
   the way in which past experiences, wishes, fantasies, conflicts, and defenses are *revived* during the course of the
   analysis, as a consequence of the analytic work, and
   which now relate to the person of the therapist in manifest or latent preconscious content" (p. 423).
4. *Transference neurosis,* meaning "the concentration of the
   child's conflicts, repressed infantile wishes, fantasies, etc.,
   on the person of the therapist *with the relative diminution
   of their manifestations elsewhere*" (p. 427).

Sandler (1976) further suggests that the concept of transference be extended to include the "intrapsychic role relationship" whereby the patient unconsciously attempts to impose a special interaction between himself and the analyst as a
means of reexperiencing a gratification, instinctual or otherwise.

I will present some clinical material with special reference to
the roles my patient assigned to me at different times, how
these roles related to one another, and how they were used by
him to express a complicated intertwining of various kinds of
transference needs and developmental needs.

CASE PRESENTATION

REFERRAL AND HISTORY

Colin was referred for analysis at the age of 4 years because of
uncontrollable temper tantrums and outbursts of physical at-

tacks, death wishes toward parents and siblings, and suicidal fantasies. He was accident-prone and had had several emergency visits to the hospital. At nursery school his behavior alternated between antisocial, physical attacks on other children and adults, and being preoccupied and uninvolved. He also had a fear of ghosts, robbers, and monsters, and sleep difficulties. Colin was third in a family of five children, the two youngest being twins. By the end of treatment, there were seven children in the family. Colin's mother habitually had another baby every two to three years, as soon as the last one began to show independent strivings. The older children were mostly cared for by their father, an artist working at home.

It was the father who sought treatment for Colin and who participated in the initial and subsequent interviews. The mother successfully resisted all efforts to get her more than just superficially involved.

Colin was an unwanted and unplanned child, born during one of the many periods of extreme marital discord and temporary separation. The birth was normal and the baby was breast-fed for 9 months. The first year was reported to be satisfactory except for the fact that he was a clingy and a demanding baby. The mother, although depressed and withdrawn, appeared to be able to give him a "good enough" first year.

When he was 14 months old, Colin experienced a traumatic and sudden separation from his mother who had a miscarriage and was hospitalized for 10 days. Colin was cared for by a neighbor, but in unfamiliar surroundings he cried and screamed for his mother during the entire time she was away. On her return she was remote, distant, emotionally detached, and seemed unaware of how the experience had upset Colin. There were several more upsetting separations from the mother, who quickly became pregnant with twins, and many separations from the father before Colin came into treatment. Colin was sent to whole-day nursery school shortly after his second birthday, and just after his third birthday different-sexed twin siblings were born. While Colin had previously been aggressive and stubborn, after the twins' birth the aggressive symptoms intensified and were directed primarily to

the twins whom he said he hated and wished dead. He became
obsessed with the idea of killing and being killed and was quite
unmanageable at home and at nursery school.

Colin presented a curiously paradoxical picture at the beginning of treatment. He had a toddlerlike physical quality and
ungainly movements, and in spite of well-developed phallic interests, his behavior was immature, demanding, controlling,
obstinate, aggressively attacking, and hurtful. Yet he had a
precociously large vocabulary and conceptual ability which enabled him to express ideas, thoughts, and fantasies largely
through words, without depending on play material. He
seemed unusually mature in other respects as well, especially
in his attempts to deal with his aggression by turning it on
himself, and in taking care of himself which enabled him to
function in the absence of the mother. Colin also had a lovable
quality, for no matter how hurtful and aggressive he was, he
frequently demonstrated an affectionate empathetic concern
for the feelings of the other person, which usually evoked
some sympathetic response.

Very early in treatment, a central theme of the analysis took
shape in the form of problems around separation. The child
was hungry for a reliable and responsible real person to whom
he could attach himself, but he had had traumatic separations
in the past. Believing these would be repeated, he was afraid
of becoming emotionally attached to me. The problems
around separation were expressed on two levels—an early archaic anxiety around fears of object loss and abandonment;
and in a fear of loss of love and rejection, arising out of intense ambivalence conflicts from a later developmental level.

Colin freely verbalized the fear that he was so small and insignificant that he might be forgotten or abandoned. He identified with characters such as Bambi, who was abandoned in
the forest. He tried to defend himself against this anxiety by
identification with the aggressor, by becoming the one to attack. He claimed that even Bambi grew horns to kill the wolf.

An especially clear example of this defense was seen in the sixth month of treatment when I had to cancel a session. The father "forgot" the cancellation and dropped him off without checking to see if I was there. Waiting alone, Colin really felt abandoned and unloved. However, the next day he shouted profanities at me and tried to attack and physically hurt me. Analysis of his defensive use of anger led to the uncovering of a primitive anxiety, which mounted until the middle of the following week, when he panicked on seeing his father drive off. He helplessly screamed and cried that he just wanted his father to stay and wait for him, as a reassurance that he would not again be forgotten.

This was the first of a number of incidents that seemed to indicate the growth of transference. In feeling forgotten and neglected he repeated with me his current relationships with his parents. His aggressive behavior reflected his habitual mode of relating which served him as a defense against a profound anxiety. The analysis of this defense revived a past experience—the early abandonment—thereby making accessible the earlier panic anxiety, which was expressed in the treatment situation but primarily in relation to the original objects. As we worked through in the transference Colin's fear of abandonment and helplessness associated with the early trauma, he began to feel safer, but at the same time his libidinal attachment to me was intensified. With this step regressive preoedipal behavior patterns were brought into the analysis.

The second level of separation anxiety then became highlighted, that is, he also feared a loss of love, stemming from the ambivalent, preoedipal phase of development. The lack of a sufficient mothering response on the preoedipal and the oedipal levels had important consequences for Colin. One of these was the emergence of a self representation of a bad and angry boy. This self representation, however, was markedly different from his ideal self. This divergence further decreased his self-esteem, as a result of which he constantly looked to the external world for approval and narcissistic supplies. A separation, therefore, came to mean disapproval of him and a confirmation of his own feelings that he was unlovable. This complicated the technical handling of the case, because there was constant separations on weekends and holidays. Helping the child to maintain his self-esteem in the absence of an external object was one of the great tasks of the analysis.

After a long spring vacation, in the eighth month of treatment, the session time was changed, necessitating a change to a smaller room. At this new time, the clinic was crowded, which also interfered with Colin's growing oedipal fantasies of being my only patient and the loved one. Colin experienced his entire situation (long separation, smaller room, and other children) as a repetition first of the early separation(s) from his mother and then of being replaced not by only one but by two seemingly more important siblings.

The reactivation of this old situation in the transference brought a deterioration in Colin's behavior in the treatment sessions, where he abandoned all oedipal strivings. His play became messy and destructive; primary process functioning frequently broke through, with clang associations and rhyming taking precedence over secondary thought processes. He became very aggressive verbally and physically, and he alternated between attacking me and turning his aggression against himself. I took this as a repetition in the transference of his earlier and successful efforts to elicit his mother's concern when he was ill or badly hurt.

One particular episode illustrates part of the etiology of Colin's fear of loss of love. Colin verbalized his wish to "kill all the children in the world except those at home." He chewed a tiny plastic doll to bits, and in spite of the slip of the tongue where he used his brother's name, he denied any hostility toward his siblings. But then he ran to the window and shouted profanities and murderous threats to some children playing outside. When I interpreted the displacement, he replied, "Then I'd have my mummy all to myself, then I'd kill her too!" Immediately he became overwhelmed with anxiety and displaced the death wish onto me, lunging at me with a saw and threatening to kill me and calling me "monster." I had to restrain him physically and calm him down, whereupon he expressed a self-destructive fantasy of falling out the window. I used the remainder of the session to talk about his loving and hating feelings, and how he used aggression defensively, since what he really wanted was a loving response. Snuggling close, he solemnly replied, "I'm so bad inside, no one could ever love me," and he pleaded, *"Please* take away my horrible worries!"

This episode is another example of transference predominantly of current relationships, but it also contained significant elements of the transference of past experience. The special circumstances in the current treatment situation reactivated an old conflicted reaction to the birth of the twins. The old defenses and object relationships were revived in the context of the current treatment situation, and the transference was used to ward off sadness and hostile impulses directed toward members of the family—a defense that has sometimes been described as "splitting of ambivalence." Here one can also clearly see the motivation for doing so: the child protects the family from his revived hostile impulses by displacing them onto the person of the therapist in the treatment situation, allowing him to retain his positive investment in the primary objects.

This example also serves to illustrate the child's attempt to establish a particular interaction or "role relationship" between himself and the analyst (Sandler, 1976). The child may have had an unconscious need for an active response from the object, or a wish for physical contact. Past experience had led Colin to believe that he could arouse his emotionally withdrawn mother only through aggressive attacks; by lunging at me with a saw, he provoked me into physically restraining him to ensure his safety and mine. Snuggling close and expressing sorrow then elicited a show of affection from me which he needed to help replenish his pathetically low self-esteem. The furthering of the treatment alliance resulting from this episode was an important contribution to the development of transference manifestations and to their interpretation. Other significant aspects of the treatment alliance included Colin's awareness of psychic pain; moreover, as his treatment progressed, he developed an unusually sensitive self-observing capacity, while seeing me, among other things, as a helping agent.

In the course of the second year of treatment Colin became more tolerant of his instinctual wishes, no longer made such frequent use of regression as a defense, and his behavior outside treatment began to improve. As a result he received some positive responses from teachers and occasionally his parents, which also helped Colin to modify his self image of being wholly bad and worthless. Oedipal material now began to emerge with a much freer expression of masturbation fantasies and conflicts. The forward move, however, rendered the treatment relationship more complicated, and I was now called upon to perform various roles concurrently. As a consequence of his early maternal deprivation, Colin had experienced significant developmental interference, and he had entered the phallic phase actively looking for an object. When he experienced me as a warm and sympathetic person, an opportunity for gratifying unsatisfied developmental needs presented itself. He then invested me with all his passionate libidinal energies as well as ungratified longings from the past, attempting to use me as a real person in the fulfillment of his sexual fantasies. He developed an elaborate fantasied oedipal constellation in which I was a central figure. He would, for example, imagine fires in which everyone in the world was killed except us. He had day and night dreams about me, one being that I was being burned, but at the last minute he was able to save me. Even when he was angry with me and threatened to kill me, it would be to send me to heaven where, having killed himself in fantasy, he would join me and we would live together in eternal bliss.

As Colin began to seek gratification through such fantasies, he developed a form of transference resistance. Greenson (1967) described this as a "search for transference gratification," whereby the patient strives to satisfy urges rather than to do analytic work. Greenson also notes that the patient's wish or need to be loved, and a fear of loss of the analyst's love, are everpresent and underlying sources of resistance and lead to certain technical difficulties.

After some months of elaborating oedipal wishes, Colin could no longer deny the inevitable oedipal disappointment. With it came sadness, followed by the old defense of turning aggression against the self. He did this partly in an effort to preserve me, the ambivalently loved object, and partly because of the painfully increased gap between his self image and his ideal self, reinforced by the felt lack of gratification. Colin became depressed, saw himself as worthless, referred to himself as "Mr. Nobody," and threatened to kill himself. He became accident-prone in the sessions, though not outside. Using two little dolls, he told a story of how the "bad Colin" felt angry with his parents because they didn't love him, so he killed them. Then the "good Colin" pushed the "bad Colin" over the cliff. Clearly, he was struggling to get rid of a painful "bad aspect" of himself.

Helping Colin to sort out the difference between loss of love and lack of gratification led to the next significant transference development, which eventually brought about a resurgence of the first theme, fear of abandonment and object loss. However, this time the material was worked through primarily in relation to the analyst rather than Colin's original objects. Colin first turned to me for external confirmation that he could still be loved in spite of aggressive outbursts. He rapidly developed an insatiable demand for a new toy every day; when he did receive a toy, he saw it was a love token, as a proof that I had been thinking about him. He used the toys as a resistance against his hostile and negative feelings toward me; but as soon as he had the toy, he quickly became bored or broke it. After separations in treatment the wish for more toys increased, leading the way via the transference to reconstructions of early separations from his mother, when Colin had tried to replace her with toys. The insightful statement he made while pulling everything out of his cupboard, "Look, I have all these toys, but it still isn't enough," gives some indication that, in spite of maternal deprivation, Colin was able to reach a useful level of object constancy and to relate to his objects in more than simple, need-satisfying ways. He had essentially reached a stage where the object is experienced as gratifying and frustrating, but is less and less replaceable (Spruiell, 1975).

I wondered whether the insatiable demand for a new toy might usefully be included among the indications of the further development of transference, since it appeared only in the analytic sessions with me. Colin had been described as a demanding infant, but this behavior had not been apparent at home for some years. The intensity of emotion and the vicissitudes of conflict expressed in this "symptom" can be seen in the following example. Just before a very short break, near the end of the second year of treatment, Colin asked for yet another toy and I promised he could have it on his return. He became overwhelmed with an intense panicky anxiety, expressed at first through a temper tantrum, and screamed, "If you don't get it for me now, I'll never get it!" It emerged that the demand for the toy covered the anxiety that I would disappear and he would never see me again. Here the interpretation of the defense rather than its gratification exposed the well-defended panicky anxiety of abandonment. The panic was similar in degree and quality to that expressed in the first year of treatment when he was afraid he would be abandoned by his father. However, this time the anxiety was centered around me and confined to the analysis, illustrating Rosenfeld's point that, even in child analysis, the conflict must also be worked through in the transference in relation to the analyst. When the time came for the next separation, I referred back to this episode of panic and to Colin's fear that I would not return. He replied quite calmly, "But I know you will." The insatiable need for a new toy every day also dissipated.

The next significant development in the transference occurred a few weeks later and eventually contributed to Colin's more realistic and objective understanding of his parents and of the source of some of his narcissistic difficulties. For a while he had been enchanted with money, and he thought how important and valued he would be if he were rich. With every

good intention I gave him some play money, but this provoked another temper tantrum. He kicked, tried to strike and
bite me, and threw the money all over the room. "This is
worthless! How could you give me something absolutely
worthless!" He then claimed it was I who gave him worries
anyway. If I gave him something worthless, it must mean that
I thought *he* was worthless, and this made him feel worthless.
Through reconstruction we began to understand how Colin's
early misperception of his mother's withdrawal contributed to
his own devalued self representation. He had believed that she
ignored him because she was angry about his sexual and aggressive impulses. Her continued turning away confirmed to
him his idea that he was bad and worthless.

With the expression of these conflicts in the transference,
Colin began to complain about the growing intensity of emotion he felt only with me in the treatment situation. His behavior outside the sessions continued to be symptom-free. He
now reported more day and night dreams about me. Ostensibly I had become a central figure in the child's emotional life.
At this point I began to consider the possibility of the existence of a transference neurosis. To recapitulate briefly, the
first evidence for this was the panic episode over the toy when,
for a brief moment, it seemed that all the affect and anxiety of
his original traumatic separation returned and were relived
around me. It highlighted the nature of his early relationship
to his mother in which threats of loss of love, object loss, and
lack of safety were prominent features. Through the revival of
the traumatic separation experience in the transference, the
original anxiety around the object loss was repeated. This was
then followed by the second incident, the episode of the play
money, which aroused narcissistic difficulties expressed by
Colin in the feelings of being worthless. Working this through
in the transference with me, Colin was able to substitute a
more loving and understanding introject for a negative, critical, and hostile one, and this became increasingly apparent in
his greater ability to regulate his self-esteem.

More primitive conflicts then began to emerge in the transference. These were focused around problems of omnipo-

tence and oral sadism—conflicts that were phase-appropriate in regard to the original traumatic separation at 14 months, the experience around which his subsequent neurosis became organized. During the phase in which these conflicts were expressed, a new symptom arose: Colin began to stammer in the sessions, and his speech at times became very difficult to understand. The stammer was also confined to the treatment. He had not stammered as a child. Unfortunately at this point after two years of analysis, a long summer holiday intervened and two days before the break, Colin's mother announced that she was pregnant with her sixth child.

After the long holiday, Colin still complained of intense, conflicting feelings which he experienced only with me in the sessions. However, during the summer holidays he had begun to transfer back onto his mother good aspects of his relationship with me. Now the mother's pregnancy rearoused old feelings and Colin's attention increasingly began to waver between the home situation and the analysis. The mother was able to respond to this to some degree, because, being pregnant again, she felt better about herself.

This situation illustrates one of the great problems regarding transference manifestations in the treatment of children. Even if a transference neurosis does begin to appear, it is often broken off or interrupted before it can be fully elaborated and analyzed in all aspects in relation to the analyst. It also appears to be more vulnerable to disruption by reality events than is the case with adults.

The birth of a baby girl in the middle of the third year of treatment aroused Colin's early memories and old rivalries. He again felt left out and insignificant, which again evoked his defensive aggression. However, he was able to confine the expression of these feelings to the treatment situation; at home his parents felt he was cheerful and cooperative.

The next four months were a particularly lively period in Colin's treatment. In the transference I served as a displacement figure for his mother, who in turn became a transference figure for the mother of the past. However, in the sessions his behavior deceptively conveyed the impression that I was the center of his emotional life. He tried to cling to positive feelings toward me and again expressed vivid oedipal fantasies. He desperately wished I would give him a baby, as his mother had given daddy. Negative oedipal fantasies and conflicts for the first time became accessible and I became a father figure in the transference to whom Colin would present gifts, especially in the form of works of art, which he wanted me to admire. Identification with and envy and fear of the castrated woman came with Colin's intense passion for the color pink, his wish for my jewelry—once he exclaimed, "Look at all the riches you have and I have nothing"—and particularly with his sexual theories in which he expressed the wish to be a woman, since during intercourse the woman gets the penis and the baby, leaving the man with nothing.

Further revival and elaboration of these conflicts in the transference without gratification again aroused tremendous ambivalence toward me, which Colin could not yet deal with, and he again fell back on the defense of regression. Very primitive behavior patterns were revived. Colin became preoccupied with making messes as a way of reenacting anal conflicts. He found it increasingly difficult to contain his behavior in words, and the treatment situation deteriorated and became reminiscent of toilet-training battles. He kicked, spat, cried, and screamed whenever he did not get what he wanted. Death wishes toward me were freely expressed; for example, in anger he thought of gluing me to the wall and pounding me full of nails. Projected anger caused him to be afraid that I would turn into a beady-eyed billygoat who would gobble him up, and in terror he ran from the room to hide from me. Oral-sadistic incorporation fantasies, such as eating me and turning me into feces, brought the anxiety of loss of love, and further projection. He feared I would squash him like a spider and, not caring, flick him away, or that I would eat him and throw his bones into the dustbin. At the end of sessions he would try to make me drag him from the room. He threatened to urinate on the floor, saying he would kill me with his poison. He threw water and paint, making huge messes.

The stammering became increasingly obvious in the sessions

as he attempted to defend against early material around his narcissistic difficulties and oral-sadistic conflicts. It is very likely that Colin's somewhat precocious speech development was related to his efforts to contact his emotionally withdrawn mother. The revival of these early conflicts in the transference then disturbed his highly cathected speech functioning. This present behavior was entirely confined to the treatment setting; moreover, I had the impression that it was more extreme than at the beginning of the analysis. Various elements were evidently either completely new, or revived from a very long time ago. The extent of Colin's regression in treatment at this time aroused tremendous anxiety and confusion in him, and he ended up smearing black paint literally all over the room, declaring that black was his favorite color because it made the biggest mess. He decided he didn't want to talk anymore. Why did he have all these worries here, he never felt like this anywhere else. Besides, I was always talking of the past and that was boring!

I interrupt the clinical presentation at this point in the hope that these highly selected vignettes provide a sufficient number of examples to discuss issues relevant to the distinction between transference and developmental phenomena, and to a consideration of transference neurosis.

DISCUSSION

TRANSFERENCE AND DEVELOPMENTAL PHENOMENA

I have tried to highlight the various subtypes of transference seen in child analysis, namely, (1) habitual modes of relating; (2) the transference of current relationships; (3) the transference of past experiences; and (4) the transference neurosis. When various states of the transference are intertwined with the child's developmental progress, caution is needed in deciding whether the progress seen has resulted from the undoing of regression as a consequence of the analytic work, or whether a new developmental step has appeared. These are important issues in the assessment of the possible presence of a transference neurosis, because the energy required for the elaboration of this kind of relationship in treatment is unlikely to be available to the child who is trying to cope with the up-surging drives accompanying a new developmental phase. If a transference neurosis does attain some degree of expression, it is likely to be vulnerable to the forces of development and to disappear as these forward moves gain expression. The ana-lyst then often comes to serve as a "real" object rather than as a transference object.

One such instance in Colin's treatment appeared when he brought the positive oedipal material, with an enormous in-crease in his emotional involvement with me. This followed the working through of earlier oral and anal aggressive con-flicts which resulted in increased self-confidence and self-es-teem and a greater feeling of safety and trust in me. How should this be understood? Among the possible explanations I include the retracing of early oedipal experiences from which he had regressed prior to treatment, and the alternative view that Colin entered the oedipal phase for the first time by vir-tue of his using me as a "real" object, since his mother was unavailable to him.

A precise assessment of libidinal development at the time of referral is helpful in making the crucial but difficult distinc-tion between an arrest or a regression. Anna Freud (1965) suggests that one way of making this determination is by the level of libidinal development and degree of mental struc-turalization. The prephallic child, for example, shows symp-toms that are not interconnected, his conflicts mainly repre-senting clashes between an instinctual wish and a prohibiting influence in the external world. In the phallic phase, however, there are advances in mental structuralization:

> Unlike its forerunners, what is now the infantile neurosis is no longer the ego's answer to the frustration of single trends, but is an elaborate attempt to deal with the whole upheaval caused by the action of conflicting drive derivatives; conflict-ing, exciting, pleasurable or painful affects; mutually exclu-sive attitudes toward objects—i.e., with the whole range of the oedipus complex and castration complex, set against the back-

> ground of personal qualities and characteristics which have
> been established from infancy onward, and shaped by the fix-
> ation points which have been left behind during development
> [A. Freud, 1971, p. 87].

At the time Colin began treatment at the age of 4, I had the
feeling that he had developed to the point of an infantile neurosis. Evidence of mental structuralization was seen in his elaborate constellation of defenses and attitudes toward objects
and the self. His superego was harsh and primitive, and the
internal disapproval he suffered was a great threat. His attempts in treatment to externalize his superego onto me and
thereby make an internal problem appear as an external one
were largely unsuccessful. Precocious development of certain
ego and superego functions was also indicated by his marked
capacity for self-observation and self-criticism, the presence of
a highly developed ideal self, and some ability to view his
parents and me with a significant degree of objectivity.

In view of all this, it seems likely that Colin had achieved
some degree of the phallic-oedipal level of drive and ego development before treatment began. His overt appearance at
the time was due to a partial defensive regression of his object
relationships to an earlier level, with some drive regression as
well (Edgcumbe and Burgner, 1972). It would therefore seem
that the roots of the oedipal manifestations belonged to the
past and that their expression in treatment must be considered a part of the transference. The treatment situation, with
me as a transference object, then allowed Colin to consider the
possibility of a new oedipal solution. The transference issue
became complicated, however, because of Colin's great developmental need for a real object. Thus, to the newer aspects of
the oedipal relationship he brought all the passionate and unsatisfied longings from the past. Attempts to use me as a real
object often predominated, working against the establishment
of transference. It then became increasingly difficult for me to
determine what in the relationship was in fact a new development and what was transferred from the past. I heartily agree
with Rosenfeld's remark that in such instances, "The thera-

pist's skill is taxed to the utmost in negotiating a path between these two opposing trends" (1971, p. 12).

NARCISSISTIC EQUILIBRIUM
AS HIGHLIGHTED BY THE TRANSFERENCE

From the history and the treatment material, it seems safe to conclude that Colin had a "good enough" first year of life. Anna Freud (1971) stresses the crucial role of the early mother-child relationship in determining the capacity for object relatedness and in facilitating the development of internalizations and identifications which prepare the ground for inner conflict, i.e., neurosis. I am inclined to believe that if Colin's early relationship with his mother had been like the current one, and if he had not had the constant helpful presence of his father (Abelin, 1971), Colin would probably have shown a much more severe disturbance in object relations and would not have been able to develop the transference manifestations reported here. Yet, the type of anxiety Colin experienced over separation experiences in the transference, together with his view of himself as wholly bad and worthless, led me to feel that Colin's disturbance crystallized around the traumatic separation from his mother at 14 months and her subsequent emotional withdrawal. Colin's view of himself and of the world as divided into "good" and "bad" objects, his struggle to regain a more comfortable level of self-love and of self-esteem, and his efforts to reconstitute his shattered omnipotence in the transference, all pointed to the timing of the crucial event early in the rapprochement subphase, as described by Mahler et al. (1975). Some of the separation anxieties which Colin experienced in the transference might therefore be viewed as aspects of rapprochement and of the rapprochement crisis which were lived through again in the treatment setting. This quality of the transference may well have been in part responsible for my impression that at times Colin used me as a "real" object. On the other hand, the high degree of personality structuralization which Colin achieved before treatment started is remindful of Spruiell's contention

(1975) that we should not neglect the centrality of the oedipal
configuration in shaping narcissistic pathology.

According to Ferenczi (1909), Freud held that a patient
"always treats himself psychotherapeutically, that is to say,
with transferences" (p. 55; italics omitted). I have already referred earlier to the varieties of transference that are commonly seen in child analysis, and to the difficulties that interfere with the building up and persistence of a transference
neurosis in the analytic situation. I had the impression that
Colin was trying to treat himself with a transference neurosis,
and that particular episodes in his treatment provided evidence which strongly suggested the presence of the largely
unconscious structure we call by that name. For example, at
the end of the second year of treatment, his insatiable demand
for new toys was limited to the transference and revived and
repeated a much earlier mode of relating to his parents. It followed the appearance of oedipal themes, and became intertwined with issues of his vulnerable self-esteem and fears of
abandonment. It was given up only when the original conflicts
in relationship to his primary object were worked through in
relation to me in the transference. Another episode of
changed behavior in the form of a stammer, also limited to the
treatment situation, persisted into the third year of treatment
and was linked to earlier oral-sadistic conflicts and problems
around omnipotent feelings and wishes. This appeared after a
panic attack which had revived earlier anxieties of loss of love,
object loss, and lack of safety. The emergence of neurotic
symptom formation in the transference was emphasized by
Freud (1916–17), and in respect to child analysis by Harley
(1971), as a feature which aids in making the distinction between transference phenomena and transference neurosis.

Kepecs (1966) distinguished between transference and
transference neurosis by emphasizing that the term transference neurosis should be reserved for situations where the

original illness is recapitulated, i.e., the infantile conflicts are reactivated in their acute original terms, rather than their chronic aftermath. An example would be when a patient repeats his active struggle with his mother in the transference neurosis as opposed to a picture of chronic stubbornness, which could be found in any kind of transference reaction. Colin's later reenactment with me of his early oral and anal struggles would initially appear to be a convincing example of the existence of a transference neurosis, especially since the symptoms were concentrated around the analyst, were inappropriate, were different and more extreme than previously, and were confined to the sessions. However, there are alternative explanations. For example, one must consider the relative permissiveness of the analytic situation, which allows a decrease in pressure on the child so that he can limit regressed behavior to sessions and appear normal elsewhere. The mother's pregnancy and subsequent delivery also revived memories of an earlier situation when Colin had been at a different developmental level. Hence, what appeared to be regression in the expression of a transference neurosis in the latter part of treatment may also be understood as the revival of past conflicts as a consequence of current, external events. Once such conflicts are revived, the mother of the present may serve as a transference figure for the mother of the past. The analyst, being more available and also a "safer" object, is then used as a transference object by displacement from the mother.

The fate of the transference neurosis, to the extent that it appeared in this case, illustrates another important difference between child and adult analysis. The final year of Colin's analysis was used primarily to work through the various transference aspects as they appeared. The revival and resolution of his early conflicts enabled Colin to reapproach phallic-oedipal conflicts and to find more appropriate solutions. The analysis of his conflicts around aggression helped him to find and maintain a more adequate level of self-esteem. Furthermore, Colin was able to internalize the positive aspects of the treatment relationship and in turn to transfer these back onto his original objects and to establish more normal positive object relationships at home. Progressive trends in libidinal development became firmly established, a degree of calmness and maturity appeared, and Colin finally began to move toward latency. There were clear manifestations of repression, and appropriate sublimations began to evolve. Although not all aspects of the oedipal constellation had been worked through with me in the transference, in the service of ego development it seemed to me to be more appropriate to allow the unconscious to remain unconscious, rather than to attempt to reactivate conflicts that probably could not be fully resolved until adolescence gave him a second chance. Since Colin was approaching his eighth birthday and latency had already been significantly delayed, I had to conclude that his transference neurosis could not be fully resolved around the person of the analyst at this stage of his development. However, the goal of child analysis had been reached—the child was once again firmly set on the path of forward development.

CONCLUSION

This case illustrates how complicated the whole transference situation can become in the analysis of a small child, especially because of the ongoing and uneven personality development and the intrusion of environmental factors. In the end it may be impossible to determine what, where, and when transference neurosis did appear, at least in Colin's case, with our present conceptual tools. While this example may indicate some of the inadequacies of a concept taken from adult psychoanalytic theory and technique and applied to the treatment of children, I hope it will serve, as Ritvo suggested (Panel, 1977), to demonstrate how developmental concepts derived from work with children contribute to our understanding of adults.

BIBLIOGRAPHY

ABELIN, E. L. (1971), The Role of the Father in the Separation-Individuation Process. In: *Separation-Individuation,* ed. J. B. McDevitt & C. F. Settlage. New York: Int. Univ. Press, pp. 229–252.

ADATTO, C. P. (1971), Developmental Aspects of the Transference Neurosis. In: *Currents in Psychoanalysis,* ed. I. M. Marcus. New York: Int. Univ. Press, pp. 337–360.

BORNSTEIN, B. (1945), Clinical Notes on Child Analysis. *This Annual,* 1 : 151–166.

EDGCUMBE, R. & BURGNER, M. (1972), Some Problems in the Conceptualization of Early Object Relationships: Part I. *This Annual,* 27 : 283–314.

FERENCZI, S. (1909), Introjection and Transference. In: *Sex in Psychoanalysis.* New York: Basic Books, 1950, pp. 35–93.

FRAIBERG, S. (1951), Clinical Notes on the Nature of Transference in Child Analysis. *This Annual,* 6 : 286–306.

——— (1966), Further Considerations of the Role of Transference in Latency. *This Annual,* 21 : 213–236.

FREUD, A. (1927), Four Lectures on Child Analysis. *W.,* 1 : 3–69.

——— (1965), Normality and Pathology in Childhood. *W.,* 6.

——— (1971), The Infantile Neurosis. *This Annual,* 26 : 79–90.

——— (1974), Introduction. *W.,* 1 : vii–xiii.

FREUD, S. (1916–17), Introductory Lectures on Psycho-Analysis. *S.E.,* 15 & 16.

——— (1940), An Outline of Psycho-Analysis. *S.E.,* 23 : 141–207.

GREENSON, R. R. (1967), *The Techniques and Practice of Psychoanalysis.* New York: Int. Univ. Press, pp. 224–268.

HARLEY, M. (1967), Transference Developments in a Five-Year-Old Child. In: *The Child Analyst at Work,* ed. E. R. Geleerd. New York: Int. Univ. Press, pp. 115–142.

——— (1971), The Current Status of Transference Neurosis in Children. *J. Amer. Psychoanal. Assn.,* 19 : 26–40.

KEPECS, J. G. (1966), Theories of Transference Neurosis. *Psychoanal. Quart.,* 35 : 497–521.

KUT (ROSENFELD), S. (1953), The Changing Pattern of Transference in the Analysis of an Eleven-Year-Old Girl. *This Annual,* 8 : 355–378.

MAHLER, M. S., PINE, F., & BERGMAN, A. (1975), *The Psychological Birth of the Human Infant.* New York: Basic Books.

ROSENFELD, S. (1971), Some Comments on the State of Clinical Case Work Today. *J. Child Psychother.,* 3 : 7–21.

SANDLER, J. (1976), Countertransference and Role-Responsiveness. *Int. Rev. Psycho-Anal.,* 3 : 43–48.

——— KENNEDY, H., & TYSON, R. L. (1975), Discussions on Transference. *This Annual,* 30 : 409–442.

PANEL (1962), Transference in Children. *Bull. Phila. Assn. Psychoanal.*, 12 : 127–129.

——— (1966), Problems of Transference in Child Analysis, rep. H. Van Dam. *J. Amer. Psychoanal. Assn.*, 14 : 528–537.

——— (1977), The Contribution of Psychoanalytic Developmental Concepts to Adult Analysis, rep. P. J. Escoll. *J. Amer. Psychoanal. Assn.*, 25 : 219–234.

SPRUIELL, V. (1975), Three Strands of Narcissism. *Psychoanal. Quart.*, 44 : 577–595.

The Child's Understanding
of His Past

Cognitive Factors in Reconstruction with Children

KATHARINE REES, M.A.

SOME YEARS AGO, DURING THE TREATMENT OF A 4-YEAR-OLD
boy, I became interested in the cognitive problems of reconstruction with younger children. When this child was just over
2 years old, he suffered two separations: his father left the
household; and then a few weeks later, the boy was hospitalized with a viral stomach infection. He seemed to have recovered from the impact of these events. It was only a year later,
after his mother had a week's vacation away from him, that he
began to develop acute anxiety whenever he was separated
from her, and even refused to stay at his nursery school where
he had previously seemed well settled.

After a while in his treatment, he would end each session by
throwing toys all over the floor, and staging a silent and dramatic exit. His reason for dealing with the end of his sessions
in this way, his hurt feelings, anger, and attempt to be in control, were related to current oedipal feelings as well as to early
losses. I became aware that some of my attempts to relate
present to past experiences were not readily comprehensible

Faculty, New York Freudian Society. Clinical Assistant Professor of Psychology, New York University.

I wish to thank many colleagues for their helpful suggestions, especially
Dr. Charles Fisher and Dr. Louise Kaplan.

to him, and that I usually was more helpful to him if I dealt primarily with his current experience of separation and his ways of understanding and coping with this.

I subsequently realized that latency children also have certain difficulties in understanding connections between past and present, and that it is often not until adolescence that such connections become more comprehensible and meaningful.

Our increased understanding of developmental processes is invaluable for the work of reconstruction which goes on in the mind of the analyst. The child's past experiences are of course woven into his current ways of relating, affects, and fantasy activity which emerge in the treatment material. But such early experiences have changed in meaning in the course of development, and it becomes a more complex question how to use our reconstructive hypotheses with the child.

Kennedy (1971) and Furman (1971) have discussed many important issues involved in reconstructive work with children. In this paper I propose to explore the problems of cognitive maturation and conceptual ability which may be involved. Such questions form part of our more general interest in examining the processes by which children come to understand (or not understand) our various interventions.

I will briefly review some theoretical issues: (1) the aim of a reconstruction and the processes which make it effective; (2) some aspects of the theory of memory organization and functioning; and (3) how cognitive theory views the child's acquisition of concepts about his world and about himself as having a past, present, and future. I will then present clinical material from three patients: preschool, latency, and adolescent. The clinical material will be used to explore some of the problems raised, and their possible relevance for technique.

REVIEW OF THEORETICAL ISSUES

THE AIM OF RECONSTRUCTION

"The analyst is aiming to correlate, understand and then convey to the patient forgotten, repressed but psychologically important early experiences from the traces that they have left behind—traces which gradually emerge in the patient's free associations, behavior, dreams and transference reactions" (Moore and Fine, 1967, p. 85). He attempts to put into words what was previously not verbalizable, experiences which the ego could not at the time integrate because of the anxiety and defenses aroused, or for reasons of cognitive immaturity. He tries to unravel the kinds of connections made by the patient and offers new connections derived from his knowledge of child development and psychic transformations. It is expected that during the course of an analysis, the reconstructions can become more and more specific.

The therapeutic effectiveness of reconstruction concerns the manner in which this new understanding allows the patient to see both past and present in a different way, to appreciate the reasons for his former distortions, defenses, identifications, and so on. In this way the patient is freed to explore and integrate previously repressed or unverbalized material. The reconstruction may lead to the recovery of new memories, or to a "sense of conviction" that the new explanation "fits" his experience, and thus promotes further exploration of defended material.

In the Kris Study Group on *Recollection and Reconstruction* (Fine et al., 1971), David Rubinfine describes how the observing ego gradually becomes familiar with earlier ego states, and notes that such ego integration requires considerable synthetic capacity, conceptual skills, and self-awareness. The patient's "revised biography," his new understanding of his past, and an expanded self representation then secure him against the reestablishment of old repressions and defenses.

Analysts have differed as to which element of the process may be most important—and perhaps the emphasis would to some extent depend on the individual pathology involved. Some analysts have stressed the importance of recovering, via reconstruction, *actual traumatizing events,* since their impact is different from that of fantasy (Greenacre, 1956; Rosen, 1955). Others have suggested that we cannot recover the actual "event," since its meaning is constantly changing during development, and "subjected to the selective scrutiny of memory"

(Kris, 1956, p. 76). In the course of life certain episodes will be remembered or recovered that have become invested with greatest meaning and act as *nodal points.* Interpretations aim at the defenses attached to the memory image, rather than at the original events (Kris, 1956, p. 77). Other writers believe that the important element may be the analyst's provision of a *new conceptual framework,* making possible new connections through which the patient can see himself differently (Loewald, 1960; Novey, 1968). Kennedy (1971) suggested that "reconstruction in child analysis functions primarily as a means of providing a conceptual framework to the child whereby he can understand his present dilemmas" rather than being "aimed at giving him a complete and 'true' insight into everything that happened in the past" (p. 400f.)

MEMORY ORGANIZATION AND FUNCTIONING

The participants of the Kris Study Group regret that theories of reconstruction have not been incorporated into the theory of memory function (Fine et al., 1971), and it is clear that the whole issue inevitably leads one to many important questions concerning the ways in which memories are actually registered, organized, stored, and recalled. It may be useful to raise some of the questions involved, even though they cannot yet be answered.

One fundamental issue is that of the relationship between what can be called the trace theory versus the schema theory of memory conservation. Paul (1967) summarized the two viewpoints as follows: according to the trace theory, "an experience generates a replica of itself . . . so that recall can in principle be fully veridical with respect to the past event and to the way it was experienced" (as in the analogy of a tape recording). According to the schema theory, "an experience generates a conceptual rendition of itself, which is abstractive and skeletal with respect to the event. . . . Recall is the reconstruction of the past experience out of the ongoing process" (p. 221). Paul discusses at length the evidence for both theories, and then suggests a way in which the two may be integrated, namely, that "trace carry-overs (specific and general images, circumscribed and widespread networks) are constructed into an organization," which construction "is matched against a schema (the apperceptive mass, the conceptually organized setting). We can propose that a fundamental aim of the matching process is to preserve the schema (to 'justify' it). . . . Here, then, is the place not only for the operation of needs and defenses, but also for cognitive styles, for . . . interindividual differences in mode of remembering" (p. 257f.).

George Klein (1970) also points to the need for a psychoanalytic theory of remembering which would clarify clinical problems of forgetting and repression. He suggests that we could distinguish between several different memory functions, i.e., the process of trace-making and registration; the process of storage within short- or long-term memory; location within existing schemata of meaning, which is essential for continued use of stored experience; and the process of retrieval. For example, retained experiences may be expressed in such forms as acting out or somatic displacements, but may not be converted into a remembered experience, which involves "re-experiencing the awareness that occurred on the original occasion, but is felt to be past" (p. 302) (perhaps a particular problem for children).

COGNITIVE THEORY

Schimek (1975) reexamined reconstruction in the light of contemporary developmental and cognitive theories and placed it within the context of Piaget's work. Such theories emphasize the gradual evolution of the child's cognitive schemata which continually shape and change his perception, construction, and comprehension of his world. These theories suggest that "the concept of the unconscious as a storage container of specific images and memories may no longer be tenable or even necessary." We could rather consider "the ways in which originally unconscious [sensorimotor] action patterns become represented in consciousness at different levels of symbolic functioning (from concrete images to abstract relationships), the conditions which make the construction of such symbolic representations possible (beyond the negative view of merely lifting the veil of repression from an already pre-existing image or thought content), and their effect in modifying the very expression and structure of a motive or drive" (p. 171f.).

We will need to bear in mind that the earliest experiences can only later become organized into the developing self and object representations, which still later evolve into a more elaborated sense of self and others, and that the capacity for such representations affects the child's ability to organize and recall memories.

Developmental cognitive issues highlight still other facets of the general problem of reconstruction. What kind of phenomena are we able to reconstruct in children? How do cognitive issues influence the young child's ability to understand reconstructions?

Anna Freud (1965) has emphasized the need to adapt technique to the child's level of ego development. She has stressed such problems as the child's lack of introspection, inability to free-associate, concern with the present rather than the past, tendency to act rather than remember. She has also referred to the need to assist cognitive progression, e.g., by converting primary process into secondary process thinking.

Fraiberg (1966) and Blos (1972) have discussed the problems arising from the absence of a full transference neurosis in child analysis in which this pathway to the regaining of memories is not fully available. Although child analysts seek information from the parents, it is well known that such information can be misleading if one equates external events with the child's inner reality.

Since many authors have looked at how the work of Piaget can add to psychoanalytic understanding in general (Kaplan, 1972; Sandler, 1975), I shall concentrate on the possible relevance of this work to problems of reconstruction in particular.

There would seem to be two ways in which Piaget can be useful. First, he provides a guide to the *processes* and *sequences* by which the child gets to know about the world. Piaget's interest is in *how* the child is reasoning, how he makes connections, forms concepts, arrives at conclusions. For a full appreciation of a child's responses it is not sufficient merely to listen to his answers. When we present a child with a reconstruction, our main interest is to ascertain what he is making of this. For even though a child seems to be bringing corroborative material, he may not have converted our reconstruction into the inner reality we suppose. Second, Piaget has by now given us a detailed map of successive levels of cognitive organization, indicating what kinds of understanding can be expected from the child at different *levels,* in many fields of knowledge. We therefore begin to know the kind of reasoning possible for a child of 5 or 10 or 15 years. It is not necessary to repeat the characteristics of Piaget's three main stages, since these are by now widely known, but we could look particularly at his work on memory and time (1969, 1973).

Piaget (1973) discusses the integral relationship between memory conservation and the child's stage of cognitive development. He describes how individual memories are organized and reorganized according to the prevalent level of preoperational or operational schemata; that is, the same kinds of mental operations are used in understanding the past as in understanding the present. His ingenious experiments with children showed that their ability to recall and reproduce a design after a long time interval depends on the degree of their *understanding of the concepts* underlying the pattern or design, rather than on the conjuring up of a static photograph. Furthermore, the cognitive maturation that takes place during this time interval improves the child's ability to recall the original design, e.g., the reproduction was better eight months later than it had been one week after the test. (This could indicate how an experience might be absorbed cognitively at a later maturational stage.)

The child's concept of time is subject to a similar dependence on the structure of inner organization. A young child seems to give an impression of having a time index, for example, when he refers to his next birthday or to the last time he went to the zoo, but the child "simply seems to be placing one event in the context of another more outstanding event which is recollected without any clear reference to its location in a temporal order of events. It would appear that he is in much the same position regarding the days, weeks, and months as are most of us regarding the eras of prehistory" (Hunter, 1957, p. 54).

Piaget (1969) emphasizes that the young child has no innate sense of time. This has to be constructed and put together step by step through the formation of its constituent logical operations—the concepts of movement and velocity. At first a child cannot coordinate the times indigenous to several different events and movements. He has to grasp the concept of temporal intervals between succeeding temporal points and concepts of simultaneity, additivity, and associativity of temporal intervals. Piaget states that the concept of inner, psychological time involves the same operations as the concept of physical time.

Flavell (1977) further discusses the ways in which Piaget's ideas can be applied to what he calls "social cognition," that is, the child's understanding of other people, of himself, and the interactions between the two. How does the child come to know that percepts, thoughts, and motives *exist* in other people? When does he begin to see any *need* to understand these? How does he come to comprehend what evidence is necessary to make *inferences* about them?

For example, the child (from about 4 to 6 years) who is still in the intuitive, preoperational phase of thinking tends to see the world as an extension of his wishes and needs, finds it hard to take into account more than one aspect of an object, and is tied to his own immediate perceptions. In interaction with others, he therefore will tend to see only surface appearances, overt behavior, and global affects; he will "center" on only one striking feature, and find it hard to take into account two different aspects of another person or himself. He does not yet see things from another's point of view, and has little inclination to explain himself, to search for causes, reasons, or antecedents. He reasons by transduction, and does not see logical cause-and-effect connections. He tends to react to the immediate present state, and is not able to comprehend the transformations which lead from one event or state to another event or state. He cannot yet quite think of himself and others as stable beings who remain the same over time and circumstance. And he is not able to observe his own thought processes and retrace his lines of thought.

Flavell describes how the child's social cognition expands during the phases of concrete and formal operations. In the concrete operational stage (about 7 to 11 years of age) the child begins to understand self and others in a more complex way since he can now deal with more than one class of events at a time and can begin to see another point of view. He starts to see how parts relate to a whole, to see comparisons and differences between various experiences, to explore causal relationships, and begins to retrace his own lines of thinking. However, he is still quite tied to concrete, here-and-now data and experiences. Although actions become increasingly internalized, he has difficulty with problems that are purely verbal.

Steingart (1969) has discussed these concepts in relation to the evolution of self representation, pointing out, for example, that particular identifications can be integrated and experienced as reversible aspects of a basic sense of self only in mid-latency. Finally, it is only in adolescence that these operations take place fully in the realm of thought and rely on verbal elements alone, so that the adolescent can now deal with abstract problems, future possibilities, general laws, theories, inferences and hypotheses about his own and others' activities and thinking.

There are of course many controversies about exactly when and by which processes these concepts develop, and about the possible influence of the child's environment, anxieties, and motivational state on their acquisition. Vygotsky (1962), for example, lays stress on the crucial importance of language: "Thought development is determined by language, i.e., by the linguistic tools of thought and by the sociocultural experience of the child" (p. 51). Children who come into treatment from homes where interpersonal and self-feelings are often verbalized may possibly have more advanced concepts in this area, and our assumption might be that it is the child analyst's verbalization of these concepts which can assist the child's development. However, Piaget also has warned us that the child may acquire the vocabulary for these concepts without fully understanding them. While psychoanalytic insights and techniques remain essential for investigating the way in which impulses and defenses influence cognitive processes, Piaget can help us know more about the conceptual range available to children and the ways in which this may play into their psychopathology and influence their ability to understand themselves and their world.

CLINICAL MATERIAL

In presenting some case material, I cannot of course explore all the theoretical issues raised. Many issues require extensive investigation, especially questions pertaining to how memory functions. In particular, one would like to explore at length the ways in which Piaget's theories may have relevance to the technique of child analysis and child therapy, in addition to the particular problem of the use of reconstruction. I shall use the clinical material for a preliminary exploration of a few of the issues involved, concentrating on: (1) some ways in which technique might need to be adapted to the child's cognitive level; (2) how new cognitive structures evolve which influence the way in which the child or the adolescent comes to understand his present conflicts, and the way in which he begins to gain an understanding of his own past; (3) how the level of psychic structure and consequent capacity for transference may correlate with issues of reconstruction; and (4) the younger child's difficulty in fully conceptualizing his own past, although he can develop a deeper awareness of the varied aspects of himself and an expanded self representation.

A PRESCHOOL CHILD

Sara was in analysis between the ages of 4 and 6. Before I saw Sara, her mother had become increasingly depressed, was hos-

pitalized for three weeks, and thereafter continued in psychotherapy. Sara had a chronic sleep disturbance, with frequent
night waking since the age of 8 months, but this became much
more severe after her mother's hospitalization. She would
wake several times a night, come into her parents' bedroom
asking for a drink, and wanting to be reassured that she was a
good girl. The parents had done all they could to assure Sara
that she was loved, whatever she did, but to no avail. It was apparent that there was already a complex, internalized conflict
involved.

I shall briefly summarize the history, as given by the
parents. Sara was a welcomed child who received much cud-
dling and attention; the mother especially enjoyed the early
symbiotic phase. At 8 months Sara "weaned herself" off bot-
tles, but began to have wakeful nights, so her mother gave her
a pacifier, which she used until almost 3 years. When Sara was
15 months, her mother became more depressed. Sara still received quite a lot of attention and care from her mother, from
her father, whose free-lance job allowed him much time at
home, and also from close neighbors. When Sara was 2½
years old her brother was born; she was both jealous of and
affectionate with him. She had shown various minor fears of
the toilet, holes, and the dark, but otherwise she was a capable,
verbal child, liking to play with other children, with whom she
could well hold her own. The mother veered between manic,
hyperactive behavior and depression. The father was affectionate and playful with the children, but probably also somewhat depressed. Sara's disturbance seemed related both to the
current rather traumatic situation and to the accumulated
strain of her mother's depression. Yet her experiences were
extremely complex, as Kris (1956) suggests, and it was difficult, even when one knew the family well, to be quite sure
what the "real" situation had been or even was now. The
clearest indications came from Sara's own material.

The first sessions conveyed an impression of Sara's basically
good, but rather precocious, ego and superego development,
and her capacity for object relations, though she revealed her
difficulty in the direct communication of affects. She began to

introduce her inner experiences, via a dramatic play, in which I was to take the role of grandfather. In this play she and I went to her home, but found no one there, so we couldn't go to bed there. We went to another house (where her father's office was) and found a bed outside it. We also had "our baby" with us, and I had to say "Stop it, Sara" when she tucked him in his crib. We went to sleep and when we woke up, we found Mommy and Daddy there again. In this play one could already discern certain patterns—her fears of desertion and of her own aggression, and the retaliatory anxieties; attempts to turn passive into active, perhaps turn to her father; her fears of experiencing her feelings of sadness as well as her longing for reassurance, and need to regain contact. It also appeared that these patterns were now woven around the oedipal conflict.

More frightening themes then appeared in the next play, where I, again as the grandfather, left her, put her in a tiger's cage, and turned into a ghost who gave her pills for being naughty. These sent her to sleep, and she died, though the doctor woke her up again. This play introduced her particular concern with her mother's antidepressant pills, which put her mother in a drugged, sleepy state. The play further indicated the degree to which Sara was organizing her perceptions and experiences of her mother's depression and hospitalization around her own fears of retaliation and as punishment for her own aggressive and oral wishes. In later elaborations, the pills were seen as both poison and presents from doctor or father of whom she was deprived.

Sara then introduced another theme, apparently of primal scene observation, excitement, and guilt. Again, via symbolic play of giants who came at night to cut up their excited victims lying on the floor, she seemed to represent her sadomasochistic interpretation of intercourse and her own masturbation fantasies—her own excitement was quite marked when she played the role of victim.

Finally, in other play sequences, Sara revealed her intense jealousy, sadism, and death wishes toward her little brother, and the expectation of her mother's inevitable retaliation for this. This jealousy derived from both past and present, as her brother, now aged 2, was becoming more interesting to his parents.

The earlier, preoedipal and preverbal antecedents of Sara's conflicts emerged through their present derivatives and meaning. For example, her present oral neediness and sucking of candies undoubtedly had historical roots, but its symbolic meaning was also connected to the current levels of anxiety and guilt and to her wish for understanding from and emotional contact with her mother. Similarly, the penis envy she expressed in the analysis must have acquired meaning from the event of her brother's birth, but it was not clear exactly what this had been. Its meaning was now related to an intensification of her feelings of guilt over her aggression toward him, her sense of lacking worth and consequent feeling of deprivation. This material, viewed in terms of the preceding theoretical discussion, indicates the need to understand and take up with the child the current levels of meaning, which arise both out of past meanings and out of current cognitive ways of making connections.

From the material we began to understand the various ways in which Sara had experienced recent past events and was tending to perceive the present. In addition to understanding past connections, with so young a child, it was also necessary to help her move on from repetitive primary process associations and memories toward new and more reality-attuned understandings, as Anna Freud (1965, p. 31ff.) has emphasized. But it can be difficult to know just how to help a child to reach a different version of reality.

This little girl eventually became less anxious and guilty, more in touch with and able to communicate her affects, and to tolerate reasonably well her mother's illness. It may be of interest, however, to look over the material to see how the appreciation of her cognitive level might help one to assess which interventions were more meaningful to her than others, and how changes came about.

Using Flavell's (1977) criteria, we can see the "upper limits" of her cognitive capacities. It was obvious enough that she could not possibly comprehend the enormous complexities of her mother's personality, depression, her parents' relationship, and so on. Beyond this, many attempts at explanations (however simply phrased) of past causal relationships, e.g., between her mother's behavior and Sara's anxieties, probably were also difficult for her to follow. She did not yet have the inner structure to understand the relationship between her feelings and another's behavior, to seek for causes, put together temporal sequences, and so on, as Flavell has suggested.

What often seemed most effective was for us to explore the way in which her perceptions, fantasies, and conflicts were now coloring events and relationships, and for her slowly to become aware that she could have a different experience and way of understanding these. It seemed most meaningful when I verbalized *here-and-now interactions* with myself and her mother, in and around the treatment sessions. Here she could experience her conflicts, distortions, projections, guilt, and so on in such interactions and begin to observe different kinds of causal relationships. (We must bear in mind how much small children are tied to their immediate perceptions and activities.) For example, in a reenactment of the first fantasy she had communicated, she began "running away" first from her mother and then from me, until one day she fell over and began to cry. After I had sympathized with her, she looked up and said, "You really don't mind me crying?" and then could discover that her present thoughts and feelings and the sequence of her anxiety and guilt could be understood. Through repeated such experiences, she gradually became less anxious about her own impulses, more able to express herself and to elicit sympathy from her mother, so that her anxieties and defenses were slowly modified and her sense of self and self worth were strengthened. This process of learning, primarily through her own repeated activities and experiences, would correlate with Piaget's ideas about how the young child learns. He particularly stresses that the process of assimilation and accommodation can take place when each new experience is slightly different from the previous one. In treatment, this may mean enabling the child gradually to have differing experiences and to verbalize such emerging experiences so that they can slowly be built into new mental schemata. By the age of 6 years, when Sara ended treatment, one could already see a greater ability to understand new cause-and-effect relationships.

These considerations would also imply that the analyst avoid cognitive "leaps" which are too abstract or purely verbal. Even the events of yesterday may be too distant for the child to describe, and the linking, for example, of present anxieties over wanting to be messy with the original toilet training, can presuppose the understanding of quite complex psychoanalytic concepts.

When sometimes I did attempt reconstructions of the past, e.g., of the kinds of feelings Sara seemed to have experienced when her brother was born, it seemed to me that she mainly reacted to these as to *interesting stories,* rather than to her own history. Here one could see the relevance of Piaget's theories to a young child's difficulties with the concept of psychological time—and also of Klein's discussion of what constitutes a *remembered* experience.

Such reconstructions might have the effect of offering a new viewpoint and thereby assisting ego integration and modifying superego condemnation of certain *current* thoughts and feelings. One could therefore view them in terms of providing a new conceptual framework, as Kennedy (1971) has suggested; or, alternatively, as a form of defense or superego interpretation, which contributed to the gradual modification of these structures. However, in general, the treatment of such a young child suggested how much one needed to explore current levels of understanding and distortions and then help her progress to more reassuring, reality-oriented perceptions, experiences, and ways of understanding herself and her world. This kind of emphasis in the analytic interpretations enabled Sara to begin to experience and deal with her ongoing conflicts and relationships in a more reassuring way.

A LATENCY CHILD

Ben was in intensive treatment between 7 and 9 years of age. This child's conceptual capacities were expanding so that he began to understand simple cause-and-effect connections, for example, the workings of defense where one feeling can be understood as the reaction to another more painful one. He could see certain temporal connections and sequences and similarities between one situation and another, and he was able to solve some problems on a mental plane. However, he could not yet deal with more abstract or complex interconnections and hypotheses; he still worked best with concrete situations and examples, often those occurring within the session.

In latency the analyst is dealing with material under secondary repression and which therefore requires reconstruction; this material may emerge most clearly through transference reactions. Only as new ways of making connections about the present became established, often through the use of transference reactions, was Ben able to extend his understanding to the more complex problem of reintegrating repressed experiences from the past.

Ben's attempt to establish latency defenses and "realistic" concepts also made it difficult for him at the same time to integrate earlier irrational levels of thinking. Sarnoff (1976) states that a child in latency has achieved a "verbal conceptual memory organization. This interferes with more primitive forms of memory (eidetic and affecto-motor), resulting in an infantile amnesia and a requirement that memory and memory-based interpretations of the environment and new situations be patterned after socially dictated schemata" (p. 91). Again, it seemed preferable for the analyst to take very gradual cognitive steps, which Ben could himself follow and participate in, and to avoid interpretations involving implicit conceptualizations which inevitably were still mystifying to him.

When he started treatment, Ben was having learning problems, especially in mathematics and reading, where he kept forgetting each step he had learned. This was mortifying to him because he was also ambitious to succeed. His mother described him as having been an active, exploratory, rather wakeful baby, who became an alert, happy, determined toddler. But after his sister was born, when he was 2¼ years old, he became markedly stubborn, and increasingly envious of and rivalrous with her. He had had several minor falls, to which his mother tended to ascribe his fear of doctors and dentists; he also had bad dreams of skeletons and ghosts coming in through the window. The mother seemed affectionate and competent, the father was quite obsessional.

Ben was a small wiry boy, with a serious, determined expression. In his first session, he tended to avoid eye contact, and instead immersed himself in elaborately setting out two huge armies, in endless preparation for a battle that never began. He seemed locked in an internalized struggle over his sadistic impulses, relying primarily on such obsessional mechanisms as intellectualizing and alienating himself from his affects.

The treatment material disclosed his apparent fear of ego regression, and his reluctance to admit the kinds of fears and emotions that no self-respecting 7-year-old should have. Both his parents and he himself liked his "tough kid" appearance and behavior, but he also had a more defended infantile tie to his mother; for example, he wanted her to tell him what foods he liked. In addition, his passive attitudes to the father were strongly defended. He was afraid of rearousing earlier, less rational levels of thinking and feeling, either as regards the present or in contemplating the past. It seemed preferable very gradually to explore the variety of his present experiences.

The latency psychic structure promoted certain transference reactions, though, of course, not a full transference neurosis. It was through these that I could begin to reconstruct in my own mind Ben's enormous struggle with what he had evidently felt to be a very controlling mother. This struggle involved his sadistic conflicts, efforts to assert his autonomy, but also passive wishes to give in, and fears of submission. His perceptions and memories were now organized around these con-

flicts, which were in part causing his resistance to learning at
school. It was therefore through his transference reactions
that we could engage in detailed exploration of the current
derivatives of these conflicts and anxieties. This began to give
him greater understanding of the complexity of his feelings
and defenses, and of his less rational ways of thinking and his
more archaic fears. It also gave him more varied schemata and
new ways of making connections with which he could comprehend some of the influences on him from the past.

As Ben became better able to accept his varied emotions,
one day he suddenly asked me, "If you found a cat outside
your door, hungry and crying to get in, would you take it in
and keep it?" This led to a discussion of the cat's feelings and
his present feelings toward his own cats whom he alternately
liked to cuddle and to tease, and to some of his feelings toward myself. Ben then told me a memory of a cat who had
died when he was 3. It turned out that this memory was part
of the stock of family memories. When he asked his parents
about this event, we discovered that it had occurred just before they went away for a week's vacation (which had distressed him very much) and that soon thereafter his sister was
born (so he was in fact only 2 years old). (Here we would have
an example of the way in which knowledge of external events
might have been misleading in terms of the child's inner reality, and of the way in which a "nodal memory" had been
created.)

Ben now had an expanded schema through which we could
explore and reconstruct the sequence of events in his life and
his reactions to them. He became more aware of how he might
have thought about these, the continuity of certain patterns,
and how his sadomasochistic conflicts and passive wishes then
and now were related to his feeling about a partial loss of the
mother and to his underlying depressed feelings. The memories of the cat now included these feelings about the loss of a
loved object, though, as Kris (1956) suggested, these could
never be exactly the *same* feelings as the original ones. If reconstructions had been made early, before his acquisition of
new concepts, which in turn helped the working through of

present resistances and derivatives, they would not have had much conviction for him. Yet, I still had the impression that it was often difficuult for him to have a real sense of the "remembered" past, so that the exploration of current conflicts was frequently more concrete and meaningful to him.

In approaching his oedipal conflicts I of course also had to work back slowly through various layers of meanings and derivatives and within the framework of a new understanding of the complexity of emotions underlying these relationships. The conflicts had first been represented symbolically via the ghosts he feared at night. He then began to tell me about problems at school, where he was determined to become a member of a tough-boy threesome. He was in much conflict about this, though, because the other boys stole. We then discussed and explored his fears of giving in, and his anxieties over competing, being part of a threesome, and so on, which led back to these aspects of his relationship to his parents.

When treatment ended Ben had become able to integrate a sense of himself as a rational controlled person, who could also register rich and complex emotions. As Steingart (1969) suggests, there had been an advance in his cognitive capacity with respect to his self concept. Here we also see something that corresponds to Piaget's views of the development of concepts of inner psychological time in latency. Ben had been able to learn about and reconstruct different levels of understanding and thinking which coexisted within himself, and to tolerate their coexistence in a way which he could not do earlier.

AN ADOLESCENT

Daphne started analytic treatment at the age of 16. Her greater cognitive maturity gave her the capacity to consider abstract possibilities, formulate propositions, search out evidence and connections, scrutinize her own thoughts, and infer those of others—conceptual tools which are very relevant to reconstruction. However, her anxiety about exploring more regressed feelings also had to be taken into account, because of the usual adolescent struggle over moving away from her tie to her parents. Eventually she formed a transference neurosis through which more detailed reconstructive hypotheses could be made.

Daphne was the younger of two daughters who grew up in a midwestern family. Her mother was a kindergarten teacher, her father an advertising manager. When she came into treatment she was overweight, depressed, masochistic, and self-blaming. She hated her fatness, but was unable to curb her "food binges." She felt frightened of becoming friendly with boys, but had good friendships with girls. Her mother was gentle and overprotective, a great feeder. Her father was more volatile, but he too was overinvolved with her.

The first two years of treatment were taken up with the typical adolescent criticisms of her parents' personalities and her conflicts with their views as well as with her own efforts to gain greater independence, choose a line of study for herself, and meet boys. Daphne gradually began to see the patterns of defenses and identifications, which emerged through this exploration. Yet she could deal with the remaining intense tie to her parents only after she had found a boyfriend. As she moved away from her parents, she also began to form a real transference neurosis, as Blos (1972) would predict.

At one point in treatment, I had scheduled a vacation. At the same time, Daphne's boyfriend was planning to leave town, and her girl roommate, wanting to live alone, suggested that Daphne move out. As we examined the details of Daphne's anxiety over these separations, it became possible to reconstruct more of the details and general quality of her ties to her kind, feeding mother and her overinterested father, her anxiety over detaching herself, defensive clinging, and masochistic patterns. Her new heterosexual experience had enabled her to become much more aware of her tendency to be masochistically submissive both to her boyfriend and, to some extent, her girlfriends, and to appreciate the links to her relationship with her parents. In this context she brought some memories which, she said, "I guess I was not ready to think about until now." She recalled episodes of sexual play with a girlfriend when she was about 11; she also knew that her mother had been downstairs listening to them, yet rather than criticizing the girls, Daphne's mother had offered them more home-baked goodies. Recalling these events, she also reexperienced what might have been her excitement, guilt, and fear at that time. She also remembered, around the same age, seeing her father's Playboy-type magazines and looking at pictures of sadomasochistic sexual activities. She had a new memory from an earlier age, of a time when her father had been away in the hospital for two months. When he returned, she wanted to cling to him, and also recalled her particular wish for him to hit her. Similarly, in the transference, she was able to verbalize her wish to stay in the warm room, her need to eat before sessions, the clinging and masochistic trends, and finally more explicit oral sexual fantasies, both heterosexual and homosexual.

The heightening of her present conflicts and her expanded understanding of the interconnections between her present conflicts, anxieties, and symptoms gave her the capacity to acknowledge previously repressed material and then to integrate it, both in the present and in a reconstruction of the past. She now had available new schemata within which to organize her perceptions. This late adolescent also had sophisticated synthetic capacities with which she could recapture various past modes of experience and levels of meaning and at the same time integrate these within more mature modes, in the way Rubinfine described (see Fine et al. 1971). For example, she recaptured her childhood experience of her powerful parents and began to see both them and herself in a more realistic light. In this way she was able to conceptualize her own past and its intricate connections with the present, and to evolve a revised biography which helped her to see her present experiences in a new light, and to plan different solutions for her future.

CONCLUSION

Recent theorists tend to emphasize both perception and memory as ongoing, active, selective processes, determined as much by the current schema organization as by veridical imprints from the past. This view is relevant to our understanding of the process of reconstruction. It suggests that in the treatment of children we need to be informed about each developmental level of thinking and understand the child patient's current form of cognitive organization.

Such an approach can add to our psychoanalytic formulations of the ways in which anxieties and defenses also influence the child's cognitive development and his attitude to his past.

I have looked at clinical material from children in three different age groups to see how the level of psychic structure and cognitive maturity may relate to the need for, and possibilities of, reconstruction. I explored some of the ways in which these considerations might influence the material, the child's engagement in the therapeutic process, and our technical approaches.

The study of cognitive problems involved in reconstruction with children has led into the wider field of how such considerations may influence the technique of child analysis in general—problems that still require further examination.

BIBLIOGRAPHY

Blos, P. (1972), The Epigenesis of the Adult Neurosis. *This Annual,* 27 : 106–135.

Fine, B. D., Joseph, E. D., & Waldhorn, H. F., eds. (1971), *Recollection and Reconstruction* [Kris Study Group Monogr. 4]. New York: Int. Univ. Press.

Flavell, J. H. (1977), *Cognitive Development.* Englewood Cliffs, N.J.: Prentice-Hall.

Fraiberg, S. (1966), Further Considerations of the Role of Transference in Latency. *This Annual,* 21 : 213–236.

Freud, A. (1965), Normality and Pathology in Childhood. *W.,* 6.

Furman, E. (1971), Some Thoughts on Reconstruction in Child Analysis. *This Annual,* 26 : 372–385.

Greenacre, P. (1956), Re-evaluation of the Process of Working Through. *Int. J. Psycho-Anal.,* 37 : 439–444.

Hunter, I. M. L. (1957), *Memory.* London: Pelican Original, rev. ed., 1964.

Kaplan, L. J. (1972), Object Constancy in the Light of Piaget's Vertical Decalage. *Bull. Menninger Clin.* 36 : 322–334.

KENNEDY, H. (1971), Problems in Reconstruction in Child Analysis. *This Annual*, 26 : 386–402.

KLEIN, G. S. (1970), The Several Grades of Memory. In: *Perception, Motives, and Personality*. New York: Knopf, pp. 297–309.

KRIS, E. (1956), The Recovery of Childhood Memories in Psychoanalysis. *This Annual*, 11 : 54–88.

LOEWALD, H. W. (1960), On the Therapeutic Action of Psychoanalysis. *Int. J. Psycho-Anal.*, 41 : 16–33.

MOORE, B. E. & FINE, B. D. (1967), *A Glossary of Psychoanalytic Terms and Concepts*. New York: Amer. Psychoanal. Assn.

NOVEY, S. (1968), *The Second Look*. Baltimore: Johns Hopkins Univ. Press.

PIAGET, J. (1969), *The Child's Conception of Time*. London: Routledge & Kegan Paul.

——— (1973), *Memory and Intelligence*. New York: Basic Books.

PAUL, I. H. (1967), The Concept of Schema in Memory Theory. In: *Motives and Thought*, ed. R. R. Holt [*Psychol. Issues*, Monogr. 18/19]. New York: Int. Univ. Press, pp. 218–258.

ROSEN, V. H. (1955), The Reconstruction of a Traumatic Childhood Event in a Case of Derealization. *J. Amer. Psychoanal. Assn.*, 3 : 211–221.

SANDLER, A.-M. (1975), Comments on the Significance of Piaget's Work for Psychoanalysis. *Int. Rev. Psycho-Anal.*, 2 : 365–377.

SARNOFF, C. (1976), *Latency*. New York: Jason Aronson.

SCHIMEK, J. G. (1975), A Critical Re-examination of Freud's Concept of Unconscious Mental Representation. *Int. Rev. Psycho-Anal.*, 2 : 171–187.

STEINGART, I. (1969), On Self, Character, and the Development of a Psychic Apparatus. *This Annual*, 24 : 271–303.

VYGOTSKY, L. S. (1962), *Thought and Language*. Cambridge: M.I.T. Press.

Adolescent Suicide

Maternal Longing and Cognitive Development

H. SHMUEL ERLICH, Ph.D.

THE INCIDENCE OF SUICIDE PEAKS SHARPLY IN ADOLESCENCE. IT is extremely rare in children under 10. In the 10- to 20-year age group, however, suicidal ruminations, impulses, and action are a source of serious concern, and suicide assumes proportionately greater importance and ranks fourth as a cause of death (Jacobziner, 1965; Haim, 1974). Significant rises have been noted in suicide trends in persons under 20 years of age (Diggory, 1976). As much as a 100 percent increase in rates for white males aged 15 to 24 was reported for the periods between 1949–51 and 1969–71 (Linden and Breed, 1976; Schneer et al., 1975).

Clinicians, faced with the difficult task of correct assessment and management of suicidal risks in adolescence, often find themselves with little concrete evidence or sound ground on which to base their predictions. This may in part be due to the fact that most efforts to elucidate the underlying dynamics of the suicidal gesture are made with little or no differentiation

Chief Psychologist and Director of Adolescent Service, Eitanim Government Psychiatric Hospital, and Lecturer in Clinical Psychology, Hebrew University of Jerusalem. Visiting Lecturer in Psychology, Department of Psychiatry, Yale University Medical School (1977–78).

Earlier versions of this paper were presented at the Eighth International Congress of Suicide and Crisis Intervention, October 1975, and at the Fourth International Forum on Adolescence, July 1976, both in Jerusalem, Israel.

among developmental levels and therefore shed no particular light on the meaning of the suicidal act.

The contemporary student of psychopathology, in his effort to account for suicidal acts and impulses, utilizes mainly three groups of explanatory constructs: (1) suicide as the expression of aggression turned against the self, and especially against parental introjects; (2) suicide as vengeful, attention-getting, and supply-seeking manipulative behavior; and (3) the more openly psychotic striving for some otherworldly state. The first two categories are essentially cast in the depressive mold, and the third is familiar from work with schizophrenic patients. Neither deals in a special way with adolescent suicide.

In a paper written in 1929 Sullivan, who anticipated many in viewing adolescence as a developmental crisis, postulated suicide as one possible resolution of the crisis along with other choices such as hypochondriasis, schizophrenia, and health. He seems to limit its genesis and dynamics to the adolescent's struggle with emerging sexual drives, especially with masturbatory guilt. He thus describes suicide as "a revenge on the offending part of the somatic equipment" (1962, p. 338).

. Erikson (1968), on the other hand, ties the "wish to die" with the need for a delimited time perspective, in order to allow for the development of a real feeling of psychosocial moratorium. This wish becomes an actual suicidal wish only in "those rare cases where 'to be a suicide' becomes an inescapable identity choice in itself" (p. 170).

Toolan (1968) articulates the commonly held view that suicides in children and adolescents are expressions of disguised depressive feelings and constellations such as object loss, feelings of being bad and unloved, or unexpressed hostile feelings associated with these. Those familiar with adolescents can certainly verify that they undergo great swings in mood and affect (Jacobson, 1961). Mourning has been described as a normal aspect of adolescent maturation (Root, 1957; A. Freud, 1958). As clinicians and psychotherapists we may at times welcome a serious and "honest" bout of depression in an adolescent as a maturing experience which may facilitate the completion and final consolidation of psychic structure. On the other hand, Laufer (1975) has warned us of the ominous significance of suicidal attempts in adolescence which even retrospectively he always treats as an urgent crisis (p. 523).

THE PROBLEM OF SUICIDE IN ADOLESCENCE

The formulations described contain a good deal of valid and pertinent empirical and theoretical understanding. They fall short, however, of providing answers to some key questions. Why, for instance, does suicide make itself so ominously a part of human behavior precisely during adolescence? Furthermore, what is the particular and specific meaning of suicide in adolescence? Can adolescent suicide always be thought about and accounted for by the same constructs as are used in explaining suicide in the general population? Or are we, perhaps, dealing with a phenomenon different both existentially and theoretically? Lastly, could the answers to these questions help in developing more reliable means for the earlier identification of the high-risk group within the adolescent population?

In approaching these issues, I begin with a brief personal acccount. In an autobiographical note Martin Buber (1962) describes the awesome personal and most typically adolescent experience of grappling with the abstractions of space and time. He writes:

> I too, when I was 14, experienced this with a forcefulness that deeply affected the course of my entire life. Some inner compulsion, the meaning of which I did not know, seized me: to try again and again to imagine the outer edge of space, or the absence of such an edge; to imagine time with a beginning and an end, and time with no beginning or end. I could do neither, nor was there any hope that I would ever succeed. Nevertheless, it still appeared to me mandatory that one make a choice solely between two such senseless alternatives. I staggered and swayed, wavering back and forth under this insurmountable compulsion. At times I was terribly worried by the possibility that I shall lose my sanity, until suddenly the idea occurred to me to anticipate madness by committing sui-

> cide. . . . Redemption came to the 15-year-old boy in the
> form of a book, in this case Kant's *Introduction to Any Future
> Metaphysics* [my tr. from Hebrew; p. 328 in German ed.].

Buber's account of his adolescent suicidal impulse contains
at least two elements related to the topic at hand. First, it
describes a brand of thinking that is uniquely adolescent, and
not merely by virtue of first making its appearance at this
stage. It is characteristically and boldly, even brazenly, universal and expansive in scope, taking as it does nothing less than
the cosmos for its range. It is abstract while simultaneously
concrete in its treatment of abstractions, like the edge of the
universe or time. It stretches human thinking to some of its
loftiest possibilities, but does it in so cumbersome a way as to
immediately betray the facts of its youthful rawness, novelty,
and inexperience. It bears numerous earmarks of being a
newly found tool or toy, not yet fully mastered by its owner,
and while it flexes new muscles, it also leads to some embarrassing falls and losses of balance.

The second element barely hinted at in this short account,
yet pertinent to this discussion, is not so much cognitive as
emotional. The compulsive search that nearly drives its author
to the brink of suicide discloses some deeply felt longing or
yearning, which again has nothing less than something ultimate as its target. One may speculate about the kind of emotional solution that would have brought this particular 14-
year-old peace and tranquillity. We may sense between those
lines, written so much later, a kind of hunger, not unfamiliar
to us in more frankly expressed oral terms by other youngsters. We may even suggest that this hunger for knowledge of
things cosmic and universal, and frequently of questions of
roots and origins, is in some partial and circuitous manner a
manifestation of the longing to merge with a maternal object,
a return to the oceanic feeling of blissful symbiosis with
mother.

That the striving for blissful union with a maternal object
can be projected onto the grand screen of universal and cosmic questions we know well from other sources, including the

drug experience, analysis of borderline psychotic adolescents, and some schizophrenic patients. Some psychoanalytic accounts of suicide discuss the wish to die and the longing for union with the mother (Friedlander-Misch, 1940) and the return to the original paradise of oceanic omnipotence (Rado, 1927). The link between such deeply seated oral needs and suicide finds further corroboration in Bruch's (1973) statement that "obese people have a statistically higher morbidity and mortality rate for a whole string of diseases, with one exception: their suicide rate is significantly lower" (p. 127). She therefore regards obesity as a suicide equivalent.

In psychoanalytic writings the destructive and aggressive aspects of suicide generally receive more emphasis. In two accounts that pertain to adolescence, however, maternal issues seem prominent, yet are left relatively obscure. Helene Deutsch (1930) describes a young woman who makes a suicidal attempt on the eve of her marriage to an older lover. She writes: "At times during the analysis a painful yearning for the loved one returned to her, though she felt completely convinced that she would never meet him again" (p. 18). In my opinion, the material indicates that the "loved one" who remained unavailable in this case was the mother, not the lover.

Freud (1905) describes Dora's identification with her mother in her oedipal striving for her father. He relates the story of the suicide note in which the young girl leaves her parents because she can no longer endure her life. This letter, which essentially brought Dora to treatment, appears later in a dream which is analyzed in great detail. Freud regards this letter as a vengeful and manipulative act, which indeed it was, designed to frighten her parents, in particular her father. Interestingly, no mention is made of the longing for the mother that also appears in this connection. The dream in question starts with Dora's wandering through a town she does not know. She then comes to her own home and her room in which she finds a letter from her mother (traced in her own associations back to her suicidal letter). The dream ends with the sentence, "Mother and the others were already at the cemetery" (p. 94). The letter seems to appear as a gift or message from mother, shrouded with thoughts and images of death, longings and reunion in death.

Gaining insight into adolescent suicide may be greatly facilitated by psychoanalytic theoretical formulations relating specifically to adolescence. Following Anna Freud (1969) we may begin by viewing this phase as a developmental disturbance. This concept refers to a developmentally induced or incurred change in one or more aspects of the delicately interrelated areas of mental life and the internal and external environments, bringing about upheavals and alterations in the previously achieved equilibrium. Broadly regarded, the concept of a developmental disturbance implies that "every step forward in growth and maturation brings with it not only new gains but also new problems" (p. 41) or an ebb and flow of regression and progression.

The impact of the developmental disturbance in adolescence provides perhaps the clearest and most dramatic illustration of such disequilibration, involving widespread and far-reaching alterations and realignments in instinctual drives, the organization of the ego and its functions, the relation to objects, and the ideals and social relations of the adolescent. The marked rise in suicidal preoccupations and actions in adolescence seems to me to be closely related to these upheavals, and especially to the regressive and progressive moves in the areas of object relations and ego functions, their confluence and interaction.

Recent advances in charting adolescent development have much to do with the refined understanding of the changes that take place in his relation to the early objects. The reawakening and intensification of longing for maternal union in the adolescent, the prospect and necessity of separation and individuation are increasingly understood and focused upon (Blos, 1962, 1967). Greatly oversimplifying this highly complex, multifaceted developmental process, I would say that a pivotal component in it is the adolescent's resurging longings for the preoedipal mother, experienced and handled somewhat differently as a function of one's gender, and the successful transformation and resolution of these longings. The yearnings for the powerful, ministering preoedipal mother and for the blissful state of early symbiotic living with her (Mahler et al., 1975) are reawakened with a force and intensity unparalleled in later development (except for those instances of severe regression) before they are relinquished for what appears to be "forever."

The relationship between such longings and suicidal thoughts or an actual self-destructive act may be mediated through an intervening variable already alluded to, namely, the changes in ego functions of which the quality of structural-cognitive development characteristic of adolescence is one important element. Much support for this idea can be found in the developmental analysis of adolescent thinking by Piaget. He characterizes adolescent cognitive development as a shift from the preceding stage of concrete operations toward the final attainment of formal operations (Inhelder and Piaget, 1958). Stated differently, it is the capacity for reflective logical thought which takes as its object not merely the concrete facts but the operations of thought itself, which now become amenable to manipulation. This ability to engage in second-order propositional logic has many implications. It implies, for instance, a reversal of the relationship between what is real and what is possible so that the empirical fact is now regarded as a mere instance to be plugged into all the logically possible manipulations. This further implies a shift in relation to reality; the adolescent, unlike the child, lives in the domain of the future, of the hypothetical, and the spatially remote. This also makes the idea of death an abstraction to be dealt with either cognitively or experimentally.

Yet another phenomenon accompanies this shift. As in previous cognitive developmental stages, we also encounter an initial rise in egocentrism in adolescence. Thus at first there may be "a failure to distinguish between the ego's new and unpredicted capacities and the social or cosmic universe to which they are applied. . . . The adolescent goes through a phase in which he attributes an unlimited power to his own thoughts" (Inhelder and Piaget, 1958, p. 345f.).

I suggest that in the confluence of these powerful develop-

mental factors lie both the danger and at least a partial explanation of the adolescent's propensity for suicidal preoccupations and action. The intensification of longings for maternal
union at this stage is coupled with the tremendous ebb and
flow of egocentrism. The result of this egocentrism is a
uniquely peculiar admixture of abstract ideas and what appear
to be logical operations, which can be seen in the adolescent's
delving into realms of the fantastically possible with great and
driven forcefulness, while simultaneously treating such forays
quite concretely. Extremely abstract ideas and concepts may
be treated with equanimity, as if available for palpation and
manipulation, and not merely as examples of adventuresome
thinking. Under such circumstances, the longing for maternal
union can readily find its sublimated expression in symbolic
operations, or be displaced and projected onto universal and
cosmic concerns and issues, as in adolescent ideological and
philosophical productions.

Suicidal preoccupations and acts may result from the interaction of two necessary but in themselves not sufficient conditions; highly intensified longing for maternal union, and
specific proneness to vacillation between and mixing of structural-cognitive levels of formal and concrete operations. This
regressive-progressive interplay between the two areas may
lead to the concrete and actual treatment of death as the symbolic expression of union with the mother.

CLINICAL ILLUSTRATIONS

Two brief clinical vignettes are presented as an illustration of
the above propositions. In the main, they point up the heightened tendency to and preference for a cognitive style that
favors heavily abstract and symbolic ideas, yet treats these in
an egocentric and idiosyncratically concrete manner. They
also illustrate some of the possible ways in which the universal
yearnings for maternal union can find expression. They
should be regarded, not as proof, but as a partial demonstration of how the propositions developed here may be applied to clinical phenomena.

The first example comes from a suicide note written by a 17-year-old Israeli girl who came from a broken home. Her parents had divorced in her childhood and each had remarried. She had lived away from both parents for several years, and at the time of her suicide attempt shared an apartment with two other girls. She timed her attempt so as to make sure the other girls would be away for the weekend. By chance one of the girls returned, discovered her roommate unconscious from an overdose of sleeping pills, and found the following note:

> To Whom It May Concern
> Shalom
> I have a request perhaps a last one I don't know but in the event that I die I want to be buried in my mountain which is opposite the house not where the packing plant is but farther I do not want a headstone or something like that only a decoration of my red rose I do not agree that my body be played with as it is with no weeping and no tears because I am really not worth a tear
> I am merely a despicable creature like all of us in this crummy world sometimes I think that I have something to do something to fix and someone to help I would very much like to establish several small institutions for needy children good institutions with good people who will help all sorts of fate-stricken children but I know that this is only a wish that will never be realized actually I know I can be a good woman a good mother but I know it did not turn out this way because I have an evil past and I have a great deal of evil in me so much that I want to put an end to myself therefore I ask forgiveness if I hurt anyone I do not mean to I only want to sleep endlessly in the earth that receives everything money greed blood bodies and life so do not cry it's not worth it believe me I am worth nothing [my tr.].

Even a cursory reading points out some of the themes that form the dynamic background for this girl's suicidal impulse. One recognizes the deep sense of personal worthlessness and self-hate. Here we find support for the tenet that her suicide attempt is connected with aggression directed against the self, or with a cruel and punitive superego turning against a weak ego.

Her egocentricity is evident and pervasive. She speaks of "my mountain" and "my red rose." The view of the world here is both endless and boundless, with the mountain and the earth assuming universal and symbolic proportions, yet simultaneously remaining and being treated as concretely personal and childishly familiar objects. The imagery thus serves the dual role of a generally acknowledged symbol (i.e., flower, youth, beauty, femininity) and a personally and idiosyncratically possessed concrete object.

The identity issues are equally clear. The girl would like to become "a good woman, a good mother." Like all adolescents, she wishes to find some means of expressing these strivings through some undertaking or work—"something to do or fix." The "unfinished business" connected with maternal longings comes through in several ways. She translates her strivings toward some accomplishment and competence into the need to help someone, which is transformed into a thinly disguised fantasy of becoming the good mother herself and ministering to children who are needy, deprived, and "fate-stricken," like herself. These wishes thus represent her own longings for maternal supplies and warmth which she feels so deficient in and deprived of. The frustration and rage associated with her lack of fulfillment in this area, however, quickly spoil these altruistic fantasies, giving rise to feelings of hopelessness.

She demonstrates in the actual treatment of her death wishes the fantasy of returning to a state of maternal fusion and union, of being accepted fully and unconditionally, of losing herself in mother forevermore. She only wants "to sleep endlessly in the earth," a maternal symbol earlier treated by her as "my mountain." Her longing is for the same uncritical, personal and yet impersonal acceptance provided by the mother, much like the earth accepts, since the dawn of time, unquestioningly and faithfully, everything, "money greed blood bodies and life."

The second example comes from another 17-year-old girl, admitted to an intensive treatment program in a hospital in the United States. She was referred by her therapist, with whom she had worked for more than one year, because of escalating conflicts (temper tantrums and physical fights) with her family, particularly her mother; increased sexual acting out of her conflicts; and ruminative and progressive suicidal preoccupations heightened by her therapist's approaching vacation.

Shortly after her admission, she scratched her wrists, insisting that she had done this because of the staff's lack of concern. Her ward administrator wrote, "In her indirect manner, she did indicate she was frightened of losing control as much as she felt she needed to let feelings out; she seemed in particular to yearn to be held and contained. . . . It was the staff's job to take care of her." She talked about a depressed inner experience of emptiness, which appeared, at least in part, to be a defense against rage and unmet dependency needs. While "she had shown no manifest thought disorder, she presented a circuitous cognitive style which was vague and inexplicit."

This girl was the second child of her mother's first marriage to a man of different ethnic background, a marriage characterized by violence, beatings, and wild suspiciousness. The mother left her first husband when she was two-months pregnant with the patient, moved in with her parents, and subsequently had a significant depressive episode, requiring outpatient treatment. She remarried when the patient was 3 years old. After enjoying an initial period of loving attention from her new adoptive father, the patient experienced another loss when after one year a shift occurred in his affections with the birth of his own first daughter. Her early experiences of loss and deprivation, especially in quality of maternal readiness for love and engagement (implicit in the mother's depression following the breakup of her stormy first marriage) are briefly captured in these few highlights from the history. It should also be borne in mind that she was hospitalized as a result of her increased suicidal behavior in response to her therapist's anticipated vacation. Despite the therapist's great uneasiness that led her to hospitalize the patient, she was not able to focus this concern. Interestingly, the same vague feeling of uneasy concern continued to mark the informal communications of staff people involved in her care.

On her psychological tests, "an admixture of concrete and highly symbolic levels of thinking" was noted:

> She feels herself very much adrift, cut off, and banished from help and interpersonal closeness, and has traded her search after these in for ideational forays into the unknown and the mysteriously opaque. Although her overall thinking remains intact, there are moments in which it does not stand up to these internal pressures, becoming momentarily clouded through loss of distance, excessive literalness and even concreteness, and overly ideational, symbolic or abstract.

An illustration of this type of thinking is her definition of similarities of pairs on the WAIS which Rapaport et. al. (1968) regard as a measure of capacity for abstract thinking: *Coat and Dress:* "Neither one has legs [laughs]. Both cover the trunk of the body." *Dog and Lion:* "Both have four legs and a tail [laughs]. Both are mammals. . . . [Which one would you give as your answer?] Both are mammals. I suppose you could say 'tails,' because not all mammals have tails, and not all walk or have legs." *Table and Chair:* "Used to support things." It should be borne in mind that her intellectual endowment is clearly in the superior range and possibly even higher. She is also capable of giving correct, straightforward answers to more difficult items on the same subtest.

Her cognitive difficulty as well as her preoccupation with death along the lines of a fantasied other-state-of-being, of possible bliss and eventual rebirth, came across clearly in her verbalizations to a blank TAT card:

> Tell you what it makes me think about? Negative and positive. Just time and space. There is forever and ever. Makes me think of nothingness, like there is a consciousness but nothing else. [In response to questioning:] I don't know about death but think a lot about nothingness. . . . There will be consciousness but nothing physical. I don't know whether it's worth coping with all the craziness. . . . I guess it's all in my

head, I don't know. I can't stand the day-to-day living with nothing in the future, nothing I want now, or look forward to. I don't know what real happiness is, just wish it would go "snap"! I feel in limbo. . . . I have this crazy feeling inside of me—to get it to stop I have to stop. I'd do anything to get this feeling to go away. And there is only one thing that can do that at this moment: death. It follows me into my dreams. [How do you mean?] I dreamed that I drowned, died, and was reincarnated. Somebody carried me out of the sea in another time and place.

In these verbalizations this nonschizophrenic adolescent girl clearly employs her considerable cognitive ability in a way not unlike that of a much younger child as she grapples with the idea of ending her life. Death is treated by her as the admixture of an analgesic that would stop her pain, an abstract state of nothingness, and a very real possibility of rebirth and a fresh and better start in life. She can thus undo the very finality for which death stands by her various cognitive manipulations of the idea, "bending" the concept both abstractly and concretely, but always idiosyncratically and egocentrically. It is as though the adolescent paraphrases another question he grapples with, "What can life do for me?" to explore the possibility of what death may have to offer.

DISCUSSION

I have already cautioned that these clinical vignettes should be regarded not so much as proving the point advanced in this paper, but as demonstrating the sharpening of clinical and theoretical understanding of adolescent suicide. It is much more productive to view this as being brought about by the interaction of two factors—a developmentally incurred cognitive liability and the equally developmentally occasioned intensification of an early object relationship with its corresponding affects and drives. Although there is a good deal in the recent literature to support the independent operation of these factors, it is precisely the interactional view of their role that is never focused on. Thus Haim (1974), in what is probably the most comprehensive review of the field of adolescent suicide to date, discusses the cognitive development of the adolescent as reflected in his manipulation of the idea of death. Haim chooses, however, to cast this capacity in a strictly defensive mold: he treats cognitive development as the capacity for intellectualization, and reviews its helpful role in ego structuring, particularly as a defense against anxiety generated by ambivalence over the possibility of parental death. He fails to entertain the notion that cognitive developmental processes may generate their own levels of fluctuation and thereby become a source of dynamic pressure and a determinant in their own right. Furthermore, such cognitive fluctuations may also become a source of anxiety, rather than merely a damper on instinctual anxiety. The adolescent's forays into the unknown, his experience of instability attendant on such shaky attempts at comprehension, and the seductive pull of "half-baked" cognitive manipulations are much like the setbacks and negative feedback in the younger child's play.

Haim follows a similar line of reasoning to that advanced here in looking for factors specific to adolescent suicide and expecting to discover the answer within adolescence itself. Out of his partial appreciation of the complexities of this developmental stage, however, come some mysterious, tautological conceptual tools. He is tempted to elevate adolescence itself to the level of a suicidal cause, but because of the obvious difficulties with this idea he opts for an equally circuitous concept, namely, "movement," which I can only understand as a dimension of flexibility versus rigidity in moving between options presented in the developmental process. This may be valid phenomenologically, but will hardly do as an explanatory tool. Other concepts invoked are "thanatological tendencies," related to an archaic tendency to death and linked with primary masochism, and finally the "suicidal process" itself. Thus the suicidal process actually becomes the cause of suicide, begging the question under study.

A further and more important difference between Haim's approach and my own stems from the employment of different theoretical constructs. He selectively uses observations and constructs that are derived from later, essentially oedipal and postoedipal, periods (he refers, for instance, to the real present relationship with the mother as the substance of the adolescent's struggle for separation). I, on the other hand, have made use of a more cohesive developmental theory grounded in psychoanalytic ego psychology. This permits me to establish links between qualitative changes in object relations and similar alterations in cognitive functions. In particular, I emphasized the symbiotic phase and the vicissitudes of individuation-separation. Earlier, more archaic phases are more easily transformable into and understood at a symbolic level. And it is the symbolic treatment of and attempts at coping with death that provide the link between the emotional and the cognitive issues the adolescent is faced with.

Finally, the role of cognitive style and functioning in suicide has received increasing support in recent work. Neuringer, summarizing the evidence, states that "there is a difference in the cognitive structures and activities of suicidal individuals as compared to those of individuals who are considered normal and persons who are diagnosed as being psychiatrically disturbed but not self-destructive" (1976, p. 246). These differences can be seen along several cognitive dimensions: greater difficulty in utilizing and relying on internal imaginative resources (fantasy life); greater polarization of value systems; greater rigidity and constriction of thinking; and difficulties with time perception—a much more exclusive present orientation. More specifically related to the present discussion, Levenson and Neuringer (1971) found that suicidal adolescents showed greater cognitive rigidity, measured as capacity for problem solving, than a group of psychiatrically disturbed nonsuicidal adolescents.

The role of cognition in suicide has also been studied through the analysis of logical processes in suicide notes (Shneidman and Farberow, 1957). Their finding of a "catalogic error" describes a logical error of ambiguity regarding the self and leading to suicide: if anybody kills himself then he will get attention; I will kill myself: therefore I will get attention. It is interesting to note, in terms of the present line of argument, that aside from the cognitive error involved, the hint in this formulation of the catalogic error is that the suicide (as captured in the study of suicide notes) aims to regain love and attention rather than to express aggression.

In conclusion, it is clear that one cannot rule out a wide variety of pathogenic causes as contributing to suicide in adolescence, including some external events (such as actual experiences of loss of the object or the object's love). One may indeed find, with Haim, that a contributory cause exists in terms of the impact of adolescence itself as an experience of loss. In order to culminate in suicide, however, this contribution must be made specific and viewed in terms of the particular processes that mediate it. It is here that I propose, first, that adolescence, conceived of as a developmental disturbance, contributes to suicide by precipitating and exacerbating affects and wishes connected with the loss of the maternal object; and second, that in the adolescent in whom such stirred-up longings for maternal union are coupled with the operation of a specific cognitive factor, we encounter a heightened potential for suicide.

BIBLIOGRAPHY

BLOS, P. (1962), *On Adolescence.* New York: Free Press.
——— (1967), The Second Individuation Process of Adolescence. *This Annual,* 22 : 162–186.
BRUCH, H. (1973), *Eating Disorders.* New York: Basic Books.
BUBER, M. (1962), *P'ney Adam: Examinations in Anthropological Philosophy.* Jerusalem: Bialik Institute, 1965. [*Das Problem des Menschen. Werke,* 1. Munchen: Kösel Verlag.]
DEUTSCH, H. (1930), Hysterical Fate Neurosis. In: *Neuroses and Character Types.* New York: Int. Univ. Press, pp. 14–42.
DIGGORY, J. C. (1976), United States Suicide Rates, 1933–1968. In: *Suicidology,* ed. E. S. Shneidman. New York: Grune & Stratton, pp. 25–69.
ERIKSON, E. H. (1968), *Identity, Youth and Crisis.* New York: Norton.
FREUD, A. (1958), Adolescence. *This Annual,* 13 : 255–278.
——— (1969), Adolescence as a Developmental Disturbance. *W.,* 7 : 39–47.
FREUD, S. (1905), Fragments of an Analysis of a Case of Hysteria. *S.E.,* 7 : 7–122.

FRIEDLANDER-MISCH, K. (1940), On the 'Longing to Die.' *Int. J. Psycho-Anal.*, 21 : 416–426.

HAIM, A. (1974), *Adolescent Suicide*. New York: Int. Univ. Press.

INHELDER, B. & PIAGET, J. (1958), *The Growth of Logical Thinking from Childhood to Adolescence*. New York: Basic Books.

JACOBSON, E. (1961), Adolescent Moods and the Remodeling of Psychic Structures in Adolescence. *This Annual*, 16 : 164–183.

JACOBZINER, H. (1965), Attempted Suicides in Adolescence. *J. Amer. Med. Assn.*, 191 : 7–11.

LAUFER, M. (1975), Preventive Intervention in Adolescence. *This Annual*, 25 : 511–528.

LEVENSON, M. & NEURINGER, C. (1971), Problem Solving Behavior in Suicidal Adolescents. *J. Consult. Clin. Psychol.*, 37 : 433–436.

LINDEN, L. L. & BREED, W. (1976), The Demographic Epidemiology of Suicide. In: *Suicidology*, ed. E. S. Shneidman. New York: Grune & Stratton, pp. 71–98.

MAHLER, M. S., PINE, F., & BERGMAN, A. (1975), *The Psychological Birth of the Human Infant*. New York: Basic Books.

NEURINGER, C. (1976), Current Developments in the Study of Suicidal Thinking. In: *Suicidology*, ed. E. S. Shneidman. New York: Grune & Stratton, pp. 229–252.

RADO, S. (1927), The Problem of Melancholia. *Int. J. Psycho-Anal.* 9 : 420–438, 1928.

RAPAPORT, D., GILL, M. M., & SCHAFER, R. (1968), *Diagnostic Psychological Testing*. New York: Int. Univ. Press., rev. ed.

ROOT, N. N. (1957), A Neurosis in Adolescence. *This Annual*, 12 : 320–334.

SCHEER, H. I., PERLSTEIN, A., & BROZOVSKY, M. (1975), Hospitalized Suicidal Adolescents. *J. Child Psychiat.*, 14 : 268–280.

SHNEIDMAN, E. S. & FARBEROW, N. L. (1957), *Clues to Suicide*. New York: McGraw-Hill.

SULLIVAN, H. S. (1962), *Schizophrenia as a Human Process*. New York: Norton.

TOOLAN, J. M. (1968), Suicide in Childhood and Adolescence. In: *Suicidal Behaviors*, ed. H. L. P. Resnik. Boston: Little, Brown, pp. 220–227.

Narcissistic Transference and Countertransference in Adolescent Treatment

ISAAC TYLIM, Psy.D.

THE PART PLAYED BY TRANSFERENCE IN THE ANALYSIS OF ADO-
lescent patients remains a critical but as yet unsettled issue
(Harley, 1974; Scharfman, 1971). The contradictory and often
distinctive adolescent subphases yield complex transference
manifestations which call for refined techniques and therapeutic efforts (Aichhorn, 1925; Blos, 1954, 1968; Eissler, 1958;
Fraiberg, 1955; A. Freud, 1958; Geleerd, 1957, 1961; Gitelson, 1948; Lampl-de Groot, 1960).

The successive developmental stages in adolescence exert an
important influence on the therapeutic analyst-adolescent relationship. The maturational (or developmental) aspect of the
analyst-adolescent relationship makes it easier to distinguish
between those situations in which the analyst is a "new" object
and others in which the analyst represents an object from the
past (Silverman, 1971). These developmental considerations
enable us to clarify a critical distinction between the transference of neurotic adults and the transference of adolescents.
Unlike the former, which repeats earlier patterns of interac-

Staff psychologist, Elizabeth General Hospital, Community Mental Health
Center, Elizabeth, New Jersey.

I want to thank Drs. Stanley Moldawsky and Albert Shire as well as my
wife Resa for their helpful suggestions and encouragement.

tion, the latter stems mainly from maturational forces and phase-appropriate demands.

The needs of adolescents are multiple and diverse. Their ability to relate to many different figures having opposite characteristics may prevent even a well-experienced analyst from accomplishing the appropriate or desirable changes. Furthermore, an increased narcissism colors the youngster's analysis with idiosyncratic tones. Uncontrollable libidinal urges and the dangerous immediacy of the forbidden incestuous object drive the adolescent to withdraw cathexis from the object representations and to cathect the self representation (Jacobson, 1964). Therefore, narcissistic object choice predominates over attachment object choice (Eisnitz, 1969, 1974).

This cathexis of the self representation and the body self (narcissistic object choice) discourages the adolescent from involvement with external objects. Consequently, his capacity to develop a libidinal attachment to the analyst is impaired, and one cannot expect to analyze it as one would with the neurotic patient.

Freud expressly excluded narcissistic personalities and psychotics from analytic treatment. His exclusion could apply equally well to adolescent patients. Freud's approach to transference questions inadvertently assigned nonneurotic pathology and its treatment to a place outside of the psychoanalytic field.

FREUD'S CONCEPTUALIZATION OF TRANSFERENCE PHENOMENA

Freud conceptualized the transference: (1) as resistance and (2) as what is resisted.

Freud (1912a) considered the transference as a resistance, a resistance against analysis, in other words, against making the unconscious conscious. During the transference process there is a spontaneous concentration of libido which, according to Freud (1912b), is attached to prototypes or clichés (i.e., mother or father images in fantasy). This spontaneous concentration of libido arises from the libidinal need of the patient to find in the analyst a father or a mother who gives to him the satisfactions which the original parents did not give him. Thus, the affective relationship with the analyst which is created in this way is something which already exists in the patient; the patient repeats instead of remembering (Freud, 1913).

The transference relationship is not produced in its appropriate place, with the right object. It seems to be a repetition of what always happens to the patient who "transfers" infantile and internal conflicts to current situations and objects (the psychoanalytic session and the therapist) in ways that are out of place and inappropriate.

Although the analyst collaborates in the creation of the transference relationship, at the same time he never ceases to show to the patient the inadequate character, far from reality, of what happens in the session (for example, the analyst is perceived as a father by a submissive patient/son). As Freud (1912a) expressed it, the transference is created to be dissolved, because nobody (the infantile and internal conflicts) can be killed in absentia. The instrumental character of the transference is obvious.

Freud (1912a) also distinguished between two types of transference: positive and negative transference. The positive transference refers to the transference of affectionate feelings to the analyst. Those affectionate feelings (trust, sympathy, friendship) are connected with sexuality. The negative transference is the transference of hostile feelings (for example, doubts about the analyst).

It can be said that successful results in psychoanalysis depend upon the establishment of positive transference. The positive transference provides the necessary energy for collaborating with the analyst, the energy to face the unconscious and to overcome resistances. Where the capacity for transference is limited to a negative transference, the cure becomes almost impossible.

In 1920, Freud postulated that the transference is what is resisted. The reexperience of infantile sexual impulses with the person of the analyst is contrary to the pleasure principle and derives from what Freud called the repetition compulsion. Therefore, the transference works against the pleasure principle.

Freud understood that the impulse to repeat is an inherent characteristic of the instincts, that the ego opposes this repetition, and that it is the opposition of the ego which must be considered a resistance. Because the patient's ego represses the instincts and fights against them, during psychoanalysis the analyst must side with the instincts and struggle against the ego and its resistance which opposes repetition; that is, which opposes the transference of instinctual impulses.

Racker (1968) believes that the two aspects of the transference considered by Freud are responsible for two diverse techniques employed by two groups of analysts. For one group of analysts the transference is resistance. For them, the essential aspect of the analytic process is the recollection of the repressed infancy, and the transference is an instrument to attain this. For another group of analysts, the essential aspect of the psychoanalytic process is the transference itself; for these analysts, the transference is not an instrument to render childhood conscious, but the infancy is an instrument to render the transference conscious.

Whether the transference phenomenon is understood as a special form of resistance or as a renewed symbolic manifestation of unconscious wishes toward the analyst and related to the repetition compulsion mechanism, either form only provides a proper frame for the analysis of those cases in which the analyst is being perceived and cathected as a separate object by the patient. Thus, the analysis of patients who have not yet gained the ability to relate to others as separate "objects" and who establish a transference by relating to the analyst as a "nonseparate" object seemed an impossible endeavor to the discoverer of the transference.

NARCISSISM AND TRANSFERENCE

The historical link between transference and neurosis has until recently excluded narcissistic personalities and psychotics from analytic treatment. The deficiency of these patients in establishing sound object relations made Freud (1914) declare them incapable of developing a transference. Although Freud understood that that type of patient would prefer to be cured by love of a nonanaclitic type, it was not until the contributions of Kernberg (1970, 1974, 1975) and Kohut (1966, 1968, 1971) that a theoretical and clinical systematization of the transference phenomena of narcissistic personalities gained an eminent position in the realm of contemporary structural theory and confirmed the analyzability of narcissistic disturbances (Blanck and Blanck, 1974).

The confirmation of the analyzability of those narcissistic patients who, according to Freud, were not suitable for analysis can be generalized and applied to adolescents, who have similar narcissistic configurations. Narcissistic personalities, adolescents, and "nonneurotics" in general tend to develop a narcissistic transference which appears in different forms of expression according to the vicissitudes of the analytic treatment itself.

According to Kohut (1968, 1971), the two main manifestations of narcissistic transferences are the idealizing transference and the mirror transference. Both transferencelike positions appear in the treatment as a therapeutic reactivation of early narcissistic transformations of the original narcissism of the child: the idealization of the parental image on the one hand, and the all-embracing narcissism of the child on the other. While the idealizing transference revives the archaic projective identification with the omnipotent object via the analyst, the mirror transference reinstates in the transference field primitive stages in which self and object were not clearly differentiated and separated.

Narcissistic transferences in both idealizing and mirror forms appear as valuable tools in the analysis of adolescents. Both types of transference phenomena help the adolescent patient to fill in the gap left by the loss of the old omnipotent oedipal object. Actually the filling up of a gap in the patient's life was a procedure not alien to Freud (1937), who—although in a different context—used the term "construction" to refer

The analyst of adolescents thus fills in the voids of the adolescent self and models the security they lack and the sexual role they are looking for. Moreover, the analyst of adolescents is able to reflect back in the "image" of the mirror transference a whole body which under a projected form preserves the adolescent body image from total fragmentation. Thus, the adolescent with his analyst—as the child with his mother— starts experiencing a sense of identity, receiving from the mother (analyst) the reflection of projected libidinal cathexis (Lichtenstein, 1964).

An overall modification of internal figures will take place

when the analyst becomes a separate person with whom the adolescent can identify; thereby the internalization process with its subsequent "rearrangement" of internal figures is completed. Consolidation of internal structures and change in the quality of the introjects constitute final goals.

Kohut's (1971) statement regarding the healthy and necessary character of the narcissistic portions that are being reactivated during an idealizing transference and a mirror transference holds mainly true for the adolescent patient. The adolescent needs to learn to recognize and accept these forms of narcissism and the tensions elicited by their revival. The cathexis of an idealized object or a grandiose self in the treatment process will prevent the adolescent from suffering further regressions.

In the realm of the narcissistic transference, the idealized object or the grandiose self becomes part of a cohesive narcissistic configuration during a period when quantitative and qualitative changes of the drives threaten a weak ego with disintegration and psychosislike states.

The analyst, by understanding the narcissistic manifestations as neither ill nor evil but as necessary maturational steps, will serve the adolescent in the task of working out or transforming the original forms of narcissism into constructive and mature goals.

THE IDEALIZING TRANSFERENCE

In an idealizing transference the idealization of the analyst has a central position. Although as early as 1912 Freud understood that idealization is always a decisive component of a positive transference, he did not see how—in narcissistic disturbances—that component constitutes the essence of the treatment of "nonneurotic" patients. Unlike the auxiliary character of idealization in the positive neurotic transference, idealization appears as the cornerstone of the idealizing transference. In this context the idealizing aspect of the narcissistic transference serves not as a substitute for a loved or loving ob-

ject (as in the case of a neurotic patient with a positive transference), but as a replacement for a defect in the psychological
structure of the patient.

The analyst is then seen as though he were a missing part of
the patient's psyche, a part that under normal circumstances
should have been internalized, consolidating the normal idealization of the superego.

The main differences between the neurotic idealizations of
the analyst and the narcissistic ones lie in the fact that for the
former, the analyst possesses the status of an external object
with realistic traits and at times frustrating limitations, while
the latter perceive the analyst as a self-object or a partial object
that exists only as an extension of the patient's self. Thus, the
idealized analyst embodies projected omnipotent and godlike
narcissistic configurations of the patient, as the following vignettes illustrate.

Jim, a 16-year-old mourning youngster who came to therapy after he had been abandoned by a homosexual partner of
his own age, needed to perceive me as the possessor of all the
good and truth of his world. "I feel like you understand what
I am doing. I feel the truth and power coming out of your
presence."

Jim's idealization seemed to get stronger after brief separations or vacations. The latter were always an excuse for him to
write long letters to me in which he tried to revive, as he put
it, "the good feeling I got from you during the last visit." My
interventions were received as valuable gifts that Jim could
save forever after. A silent moment was regarded as a good
opportunity to figure out things alone, free from the usual
pressures imposed on him by parents and teachers.

Arnold, a 17-year-old high school graduate, extremely
preoccupied with his self image and struggling for control
over his impulses, projected onto me an ascetic idealized
image. "You are always in charge, on your feet; you never
seem to be bothered by problems. You are kind but diligent
like a bird. I can't imagine you eating or drinking."

Arnold was unable to imagine me engaged in "earthy" activities, like everybody else. He thought that a person should be

able to control desires and emotions, and that a way to achieve it was to become "silent and thoughtful as you seem to be all the time." I became a model to be imitated since being "cool," he believed, could help him to put up with the jokes and teasing of peers and older siblings.

THE MIRROR TRANSFERENCE

In a mirror transference, identification with the analyst prevails. As Spruiell (1974) interprets it, in a mirror transference, the analyst is seen only in terms of his responsiveness or similarity to, or his actual convergence with, a warded-off grandiose self. These identifications take three forms which correspond to three different degrees in the development of the grandiose self and which reflect the extent to which the self is separated from the object. They are: (1) the merger through the extension of the grandiose self; (2) the alter-ego transference or twinship; and (3) the mirror transference in the narrower sense (Kohut, 1971).

The merger through the extension of the grandiose self is experienced as a regressive diffusion of the self to a state of primary identity. In other words, the analyst is experienced as part of the self.

Jean, a 15-year-old overweight and depressed teen-ager, scapegoat of marital conflict, was reluctant to talk during the first two months of treatment. She did not answer any questions, sitting peacefully in front of me, usually deciding when the session was over and leaving the office without a word or greeting. Although most of the sessions were spent in silence, Jean seldom missed a session. Wondering about what she was getting out of the treatment, she said, "I like to come here because I don't *have* to talk. I like you just being there with me." Thus, through the silence, Jean merged with me without having to experience the pain of being separated from the object as well as being rejected by it.

My rapport with her silence cemented the base for a sound working alliance. If I could be quiet and calm at the same time, she could feel secure and protected. Jean thought that for the first time "to be silent wasn't suspicious" like it was to her mother.

The alter-ego transference or twinship is a less archaic form in which the analyst is experienced as possessing some attributes or characteristics of the grandiose self.

Sam, a bright 14-year-old junior high school student, could not accept what he regarded as "an order for submission and compliance" coming from authorities, especially school authorities. His assertiveness and rebellious acting out had omnipotent qualities to the extent that he seriously thought of starting a campaign to change the current administrative system. Since I was not related to the school authorities—as he was not—I was perceived as an "assistant" or appendix. In fact, the therapeutic alliance became consolidated through Sam's convictions that I was there to help him manage his "business," to mediate between school and home, to be a sort of older, wiser brother who, as he once stated, was as smart and courageous as only he could be.

Sam was convinced that I was anti-establishment, as he thought he was. He based his assumptions on my hair style and clothing. He praised my ability to talk to him since no one in his family was able to do it without scorn or disdain.

The mirror transference in the narrower sense is the most mature form of the grandiose self. In it the analyst is perceived as a separate object bound to reflect the patient's narcissistic demands for exhibitionism and recognition. As once the mother was, the analyst in the mirror transference becomes the eye that witnesses and also responds to the narcissistic exhibitionism of the narcissistic self.

Ronald, a sensitive and creative 18-year-old musician, self-referred to therapy, wanted to resolve his ambivalence about leaving home and going to an out-of-town college. The father, a successful lawyer, could not accept his son's wish to study art. Ronald literally loved to be on stage and admired by an audience. He felt that his life was destined to provide enjoyment to the masses of all ages. In treatment, Ronald was not interested in finding out any aspects of my private life. Ronald described me as "a good listener or reflector," a serene echo of his narcissistic displays.

Occasionally, Ronald brought his guitar to the sessions, stating that he could talk without words. He often spent almost the entire session in describing his fondness for clothing, expecting me to react to the fact that he was dressed differently each time he came to the office.[1]

ON COUNTERTRANSFERENCE

The analyst's countertransference to a narcissistic transference of either the idealized parent imago type (idealizing transference) or the mobilized grandiose self (mirror transference) has a peculiar character which can only be understood through the examination of the analyst's own unresolved narcissism and adolescent conflicts.

Adolescent patients stimulate repressed conflictual nuclei in the analyst. These nuclei might prevent him from exerting the necessary empathic capacity which constitutes the core of adolescent analysis. The adolescent's communications may impair the development, in the analyst, of a countertransference in the sense of counteridentification and empathy (Gitelson, 1948). Under the worst of circumstances, the analyst might become either the substitute for the old parental imperfect figures or the conspirator against them.

The adolescent has lost faith in the old parental imagos. He looks for new ones to replace, with their perfection, what was lacking in the former ones. Primitive defenses of a magical and omnipotent sort are remobilized. In other words, the adolescent wants to restore the lost narcissistic attachment to an idealized, powerful object. Therefore, a successful therapist should be able to allow and maintain an essential narcissistic contact by accepting, without interference, the adolescent's idealizations and admiration.

The analyst's narcissistic tensions manifest themselves in different ways: (1) as verbal or nonverbal rejections of the analysand's idealization; (2) as early drive interpretation (especially

1. *Editors' note:* In this context, see T. Wayne Downey's discussion of "Transitional Phenomena in the Analysis of Early Adolescent Males" in this volume.

of aggressive tendencies) due to the analyst's failure to differentiate "the shyly germinating tendrils of idealization . . . from the exaggerated praise of a patient which is accompanied by allusions to unconscious hostility" (Kohut, 1971, p. 266).

From another point of view, overt hostility toward the figure of the analyst can be regarded as a defense against the establishment of an idealizing transference. This defense might re-create, in the adolescent, an illusion of control or of omnipotent domination over the analyst, which serves as an important tool in overcoming the initial fears of passivity or castration anxiety. However, whatever the case may be, the analyst should be aware that he is dealing with the patient's defense and avoid misleading interventions and poorly timed interpretations.

The progress of the treatment seems to rely upon the systematic working-through process of the narcissistic bond which eventually will bring the figure of the analyst from the status of a self-object or partial object to the status of a separate one, with realities and shortcomings of his own. Alternative periods of admiration and contempt for the analyst appear as a regular part of the working through in the idealizing transferences. On the other hand, exposed to a mirror transference, the analyst, cast in the role of a passive reflector, might feel bored, aloof, or inattentive in the absence of the patient's object-instinctual cathexes. The analyst's ability to sustain the effects of affective oscillations while avoiding "counter-acting out" will aid in his treating adolescent patients.

The analyst's countertransference expectations which underlie his stress on conformity and "social adjustment" (neurotic "establishment conflict" of the analyst) may put an additional strain on his overcoming the numerous complications of working with adolescent patients.

BIBLIOGRAPHY

AICHHORN, A. (1925), *Wayward Youth*. New York: Meridian Books, 1960.
BLANCK, G. & BLANCK, R. (1974), *Ego Psychology*. New York: Columbia Univ. Press.

BLOS, P. (1954), Prolonged Adolescence. *Amer. J. Orthopsychiat.*, 24 : 733–742.
——— (1968), Character Formation in Adolescence. *This Annual*, 23 : 245–263.
EISNITZ, A. J. (1969), Narcissistic Object Choice, Self Representation. *Int. J. Psycho-Anal.*, 50 : 15–25.
——— (1974), On the Metapsychology of Narcissistic Pathology. *J. Amer. Psychoanal. Assn.*, 22 : 279–291.
EISSLER, K. R. (1958), Notes on Problems of Technique in the Psychoanalytic Treatment of Adolescents. *This Annual*, 13 : 223–254.
FRAIBERG, S. (1955), Some Considerations in the Introduction to Therapy in Puberty. *This Annual*, 10 : 264–286.
FREUD, A. (1958), Adolescence. *W.*, 5 : 136–166.
FREUD, S. (1912a), The Dynamics of Transference. *S.E.*, 12 : 97–108.
——— (1912b), Recommendations for Physicians Practising Psycho-Analysis. *S.E.*, 12 : 109–120.
——— (1913), On Beginning the Treatment. *S.E.*, 12 : 121–144.
——— (1914), On Narcissism. *S.E.*, 14 : 67–102.
——— (1920), Beyond the Pleasure Principle. *S.E.*, 18 : 3–64.
——— (1937), Constructions in Analysis. *S.E.*, 23 : 255–269.
GELEERD, E. R. (1957), Some Aspects of Psychoanalytic Technique in Adolescence. *This Annual*, 12 : 263–283.
——— (1961), Some Aspects of Ego Vicissitudes in Adolescence. *J. Amer. Psychoanal. Assn.*, 9 : 394–405.
GITELSON, M. (1948), Character Synthesis. In: *Psychoanalysis*. New York: Int. Univ. Press, 1973, pp. 99–114.
HARLEY, M., ed. (1974), *The Analyst and the Adolescent at Work*. New York: Quadrangle.
JACOBSON, E. (1964), *The Self and the Object World*. New York: Int. Univ. Press.
KERNBERG, O. F. (1970), Factors in the Psychoanalytic Treatment of Narcissistic Personalities. *J. Amer. Psychoanal. Assn.*, 18 : 51–85.
——— (1974), Contrasting Viewpoints regarding the Nature and Psychoanalytic Treatment of Narcissistic Personalities. *J. Amer. Psychoanal. Assn.*, 22 : 255–267.
——— (1975), *Borderline Conditions and Pathological Narcissism*. New York: Jason Aronson.
KOHUT, H. (1966), Forms and Transformations of Narcissism. *J. Amer. Psychoanal. Assn.*, 14 : 243–272.
——— (1968), The Psychoanalytic Treatment of Narcissistic Personality Disorders. *This Annual*, 23 : 86–113.
——— (1971), *The Analysis of the Self*. New York: Int. Univ. Press.
LAMPL-DE GROOT, J. (1960), On Adolescence. *This Annual*, 15 : 95–103.
LICHTENSTEIN, H. (1964), The Role of Narcissism in the Emergence and Maintenance of a Primary Identity. *Int. J. Psycho-Anal.*, 45 : 49–56.

RACKER, H. (1968), *Transference and Countertransference.* New York: Int. Univ. Press.

SCHARFMAN, M. A. (1971), Transference Phenomena in Adolescent Analysis. In: *The Unconscious Today,* ed. M. Kanzer. New York: Int. Univ. Press, pp. 422–435.

SILVERMAN, J. S. (1971), Transference and Development. In: *The Unconscious Today,* ed. M. Kanzer. New York: Int. Univ. Press, pp. 417–421.

SPRUIELL, V. (1974), Theories of the Treatment of Narcissistic Personalities. *J. Amer. Psychoanal. Assn.,* 22 : 268–278.

THE PSYCHOANALYTIC
PROCESS

The Psychoanalytic Process in Childhood

SAMUEL RITVO, M.D.

PSYCHOANALYTIC PROCESS IS A COMPOSITE OR CONGLOMERATE concept. It refers to the complex of psychic interactions between analyst and analysand which characterize and are essential to the establishment and maintenance of the psychoanalytic situation and endeavor, with the *mutual* aim of effecting a change in the psychic organization of the analysand. A change may occur in the psychic organization of the analyst as well since the psyche of the analyst is an essential instrument in the process. The close look into another human being's life-style and relationships, the self-observation and analysis of responses to the analysand's transferences, the analysis of one's own countertransferences, the analyst's reactions to being the target of love and hate—all these work changes in the psyche of the analyst. The fact that we use the term process indicates that we have in mind an endeavor which has a continued directional movement or shows continuous change in time. An examination of the question must consider what the elements are which bring this process into existence and make possible its maintenance over a period of time. When we speak of the

Clinical Professor of Psychiatry, Yale University, Child Study Center, New Haven, Connecticut.

Presented at a Panel on "The Psychoanalytic Process in Different Developmental Phase," Meeting of the Association for Child Psychoanalysis, Jerusalem, Israel, August 21, 1977.

psychoanalytic process in child analysis, we address the specific question: how are the establishment and maintenance of the process related to the psychic development of the child at different ages?

Analysts who have studied the psychoanalytic process in the fully developed adult have focused on different features. Kris (1956) describes psychoanalytic therapy as having the property of a process "with a notion. . . . of progressive development over time in a definite direction" (p. 445). Kris was chiefly concerned with the integrative forces at work in the patient and the change in alignment which begins to be felt when an interpretation clicks. Kris held the view that the preliminary work of the analysis loosens countercathectic energy and the energy attached to repressed material, and that some of this is then available to participate in the functions of the ego, promoting reorganization. For him, this was the essence of the analytic process. In the adult, the analysis of the transference contributes greatly to this process. Greenacre (1968) considered the analytic process not only in terms of the realignment of forces which occur, but also in terms of what sets them in motion, i.e., not only process but procedures as well. In her view, the main medium through which it works is the transference, the total relationship between analyst and analysand during the course of treatment. She divides this general transference relationship into two parts: first, the attitude of the analysand with which the analysis opens, usually, but not always, a sufficiently positive feeling to permit a fair degree of rapport; second, the transference neurosis. Greenacre has the conviction that "the psychoanalytic process, at its best, involves essentially a progression of growth . . . not so much stimulated as liberated to take its own course" (p. 212). She stresses the psychoanalytic process as "a re-creative growth process" (p. 213), which requires the analyst to be regularly on hand watching, listening, and explaining. The analyst's responsiveness resembles that of the ideal mother or teacher of a young child. Loewald (1970) stresses that the psychic structures of the individual are "formed . . . and maintained and, within limits, can change by intercourse with other persons"

(p. 50). In the psychoanalytic process, the vicissitudes of the genesis of psychic organization become perceptible again in the transference illness and its resolution. In Loewald's view, Freud (1933) had this growth potential in mind, especially in regard to the psychoanalytic process, when he said: "where id was, there shall ego become."

In regard to features of the analytic process which have closer bearing on the analysis of children, Loewald points out that the analyst and the analysand are both participants in the process and that the analyst must be capable of a measure of objectivity toward himself as well as toward the analysand. For the process to get underway, the analysand must have developed an observing ego. Loewald stresses that psychoanalyzing someone means to intervene in his psychic life. Such an investigation is undertaken only upon the request and with the active and informed consent of the analysand. Without the analysand's participation and capacity for active work, the psychoanalytic investigation does not get very far. These are some of the critical differences between the analysis of children and adults. With children the analysis is rarely undertaken upon the request of the child, especially in the case of children under the age of 9 or 10. The active and informed consent of the child analysand is likewise rarely obtainable at the outset of the analysis and at best is only gradually attained in the course of the analytic work. The attainment depends on the child's developmental progress in abstract thinking, language, cognition, the capacities for self-observation and self-evaluation, and the ability to project present conditions into the future. The child's active participation in the process is perforce more sporadic and less reliable than that of the adult.

Feigelson (1977) used an illustration from the analysis of a 6-year-old girl to demonstrate what he regards as a sine qua non of child or adult analysis—the existence of a discernible process that leads from defense and character analysis to repressed wishes, impulses, memories, and fantasies, with a goal of increasing self-awareness and problem solving, eventually leading to a higher level of psychic organization. Feigelson argues that the existence of this process makes short-range prediction possible in the course of an analysis. He seems to argue the converse as well—that predictability is evidence of the existence of an analytic process. Feigelson seems to view the process as existing almost *ab initio* in the analysand, with the analyst's function being to facilitate the process with his presence, understanding, and interventions.

Predictability in analysis need not always be a reflection of the presence of a process. Especially in the early phases of analysis some predictions may be possible because of the sign function of behavior (Hartmann, 1950). In my view, the psychoanalytic process exists only as the joint creation of analysand and analyst. It is possible only because the analyst uses his conceptualization of the analytic process and his understanding of the phenomena of transference, resistance, defense, and so forth, to initiate, guide, and intensify the process. With this initiation and guidance, the analysand at some point becomes an active partner in the process through his self-observation and his own understanding of the process which are derived from the joint undertaking with the analyst.

With the child a crucial question, quite apart from resistance and defense, is the degree to which the child's development makes it possible for him to have the self-awareness, objectivity, and intellectual comprehension to have a full partnership in the process. This capacity may grow extensively over the time span in which the preoedipal, oedipal, or latency child may be in analysis. I think this fact is frequently not taken sufficiently into account by analysts who describe changes in a child which take place toward the end of a long period of analysis. In such instances we should examine more carefully what part the advance in development plays in the changes that take place. One way this may become apparent is by examining the differences in the constructions and interpretations we offer the child at different ages in the course of a long treatment. If we do so, we will find that they reflect the maturational changes in psychic structure and organization, the shifts in relative strength of ego and drives, and the growth in the intellectual capacities of the child.

A recent panel discussion brought out differing views on

transference in the establishment and maintenance of the analytic process in childhood. In that discussion Weiss (1976) laid strong emphasis on the establishment and analysis of transference in child analysis, adapted, of course, to the cognitive development of the child. He advocated that in his behavior, comportment, and interventions, the child analyst follow a model of neutrality such that the patient's tendency to transference would be potentiated and maximized. Feigelson (1977) took the view that the analyst should concentrate on activating the psychoanalytic process by analyzing defense and resistance without special regard for transference, and the transference "will take care of itself," implying that the analyst need make no special effort to encourage the transference. This view relies on transference as a basic feature of human psychic life which will manifest itself in every significant relationship and especially in the psychoanalytic situation, which is planned so as to maximize it. Analysts have repeatedly emphasized that the child has less of a tendency or need to make transferences to the analyst because he still has his primary love objects in his daily life for instinctual drive gratification or for symptom formation, which lessens the involvement of the analyst in the transference or the transference neurosis.

What contributes so much to the importance of the transference in the analytic process is not only what it makes possible in terms of understanding, interpretation, and reconstruction: it also restores the feeling of immediacy, reality, and conviction to psychological phenomena arising out of the past. This is part of the process of ego becoming where id was. For this process to occur and progress requires the existence and functioning of an ego which can observe the self and set in motion the recognition of distinctions between past and present, between objective danger and neurotic anxiety, which arises out of the interplay of wish, fantasy, and inadequate understanding due to the immature thinking of the child. Certainly, there is a vast difference between the capacity of a child of 4, a child of 6, and a child of 11 to participate actively in this process. Despite great individual differences in the capacities of children at the same age, there are limitations which stem

from the maturational process itself. Though we can argue
that the analytic process and the therapeutic action of analysis
depend in children, as in adults, on the analysis of transference, defense, and resistance, the process in children not only
must be adapted to the development of the child, but is in
many instances limited by his developmental status as well.

Transference and resistance are basic human psychic interactional phenomena. As such they play an important part
in child as well as adult analysis. The child looks to the parents
for relief of discomfort and suffering, whether it is physical or
psychic. Just as the parent invests the toy for the young child
in the interest of the pleasure of play, so the adult invests the
analyst for the child in the interest of the relief of discomfort
or suffering. In this way the basic transference of the analytic
situation is initiated. In this sense Feigelson is correct that the
analytic process is present from the beginning. This was implicit in the early technique of child analysts when they focused on making themselves psychically useful to or needed
by the child as a preparatory step for analysis. The same recognition of the need for the establishment of a basic transference is apparent in Berta Bornstein's (1949) analysis of Frankie. Although that case report is a milestone marking the
influence of ego psychology on child analytic technique, Berta
Bornstein chose to insure Frankie's need for her to relieve his
suffering by advising the school not to permit his mother to
remain in school with him when he became anxious. Although
the aim was to intensity the conflict between the symptom and
reality, the implicit, if not intended, aim was to insure the
basic transference in terms of dependence upon the analyst.

The basic transference, unless it is interfered with by a powerful dynamic factor such as the ambivalence of the parents
toward the analysis, is a major determinant in the child's portraying his discomfort, anxiety, and symptoms in the fantasy
play in the analysis. In Feigelson's eloquent example, a 6-year-
old girl introduced her nuclear neurotic conflict in the first
hour. She told a dream in which she was standing in a lake
and several men like soldiers or guards were poking spears in
her side. When she tood up to go to the bathroom after telling

the dream, there was a pool of water in her chair. In this exchange there is an indication that the child and the analyst interact so that the child turns to the analyst for help as to a parent. The basic interaction has the qualities of a transference in the sense of Loewald's conception of the transference being an interaction between the two centers of psychic activity—the patient and the analyst. Even if the analyst cannot count on the child's active conscious participation in the analytic process or on his ability for reflection and self-observation, the basic transference provides a directional force for the child to present his conflicts and symptoms via play, fantasy, verbal communications, and behavioral interaction with the analyst.

The child's fantasy play in the analytic situation illustrates the effect of the basic transference. Under its influence the ideation connected with wishes and conflicts returns from repression and achieves representation as well as a quality of persistence and continuity in the presence of the analyst, even though the child may have little conscious awareness of the process. One of the major tenets of technique in child analysis is to offer interpretations in the idiom of the play and to choose carefully the time and setting when interpretations are offered directly because the child is so intolerant of them. The child is prone to become anxious, uncomfortable, and uncomprehending in response to a direct interpretation, and to break off the communication by fantasy play. The positive transference is not enough to enable the child to observe himself, nor is the hypercathexis of the integrative function of the ego as a consequence of the interpretation enough to enable the child to overcome the split in the ego in the service of defense which enables him to maintain conflicting beliefs. The inability of the child to do so may not be a resistance as much as it may be an inability of the child to comprehend and carry out the steps of abstraction, conceptualization, and generalization which are implicit in going from the content of a fantasy play, as a symbolic system of representation constructed like the dream, to its structured meaning and function in the psychic life of the child. In the initial phase the adult analysand, too, has to be educated to this feature of the analytic process, but he had the fully matured capacity for abstract thinking and generalization to bring to the task. The analytic process may stimulate precocious development of this capacity in the child, but the usual situation is one of limitation in this regard.

Child analysis takes place during a period of genesis and growth of psychic structure—e.g., the intensification and burgeoning of the instinctual drives in the oedipal period, and the efflorescence of the ego and the organization of the superego in latency. The impact of the analytic process on the genesis and growth of psychic structure is a prime issue for the child analyst. Loewald (1970), in his study of the analytic process, stressed that psychic structure differentiates out of interaction with an external center of psychic activity or the object in the psychoanalytic sense. He emphasizes that the instinctual drives in their psychological aspects, i.e., in terms of wishes and fantasies, also are formed out of the interaction with the object as, for example, in the mother-child interaction. The child analyst is such an external center of psychic activity or object with whom the child interacts at times in his life when new psychic structures are being formed. In the analyst the child interacts with an object who does not respond in the ways characteristic for the particular parents. Presumably the analyst, via his responses to the wishes and fantasies and his verbalization and interpretation of them, offers the ego of the child alternative ways of finding detoured discharge, gratification, or control, which influence the formation of psychic structure or organization. Thereby the child analyst may be instrumental in facilitating the child's fulfilling a developmental need.

A case in illustration is a 10½-year-old enuretic boy living alone with his mother who came to analysis shortly after his divorced father visited him to tell him he would not be seeing him anymore; at the same time his stepfather announced that he was separating from the family. The boy insisted on coming into his mother's bed, and the mother was not very resolute in keeping him out. He was intolerant of the attention his mother received from men and her interest in them. He had never shown any shame or guilt in connection with his wetting. But after he had been in analysis only a month and had begun to bring his oedipal wishes and his fears of retaliation into his fantasy play in the analysis, his mother reported that he began to show signs of shame about his wetting and tried to hide it. This could be understood as a shift in psychic organization under the impact of the transference in the direction of activation of superego functioning. In this way the analytic process makes the analyst available to the child as an object for his age-appropriate or delayed developmental needs. In those situations in which the parents do not permit the child to interact this way with the analyst, the analytic process has much less to offer the child developmentally and therapeutically.

From the economic and dynamic viewpoints the child's ego, particularly the neurotic child's, easily feels helpless and overwhelmed by the instinctual drives and the wishes they generate. The child responds in analysis as though most of the time he can tolerate only the indirect recognition of his wishes, his fears, and his ways of defending himself as they are disguised in his fantasy play. I think this view helps us to understand why child analysis may succeed in enabling a child to resolve conflicts sufficiently so that he can resume his developmental progress, but insufficiently to prevent later outbreak of neurotic illness. The interpretation and analysis of conflict and defense within the fantasy play afford the ego a degree of mastery and relief. However, due to the developmental limitation the full resources of the mature ego cannot be brought to bear on the neurosis. The child is closer to the primary process. His wishes pervade his verbalizations and his actions more readily than in the adult, and the ego has a lesser capacity for delay and detour. The effect is a passivity to the drives which is characteristic of the child's psychic functioning. With the formation of the superego a further step of internalization occurs. The child's wishes are not only opposed by the threat of external sanction, but a further differentiation in the ego develops which opposes the instinctual drives. Eventually the superego is divorced from the parental authority and impersonalized. The subjective experience accompanying the internalization of the superego is one of being in the grip of forces over which the individual has no control, bowing passively again to the instinctual drives, this time in the form of the peremptory quality of the superego demands. The consequence in the neurotic is again a passive submission to the drives or a compensatory active defense against them. In any case, influencing a change through the analytic process in the sense of ego becoming where id was requires a high degree of sustained self-observation and collaboration with the analyst. The child's capacity for this at any particular time is a function of his maturation as well as resistance and defense.

Not only must the instinctual drive wishes be made conscious, but all the inhibitions, restrictions, and distortions of the ego (interferences with judgment, reality testing, and logical thought) must be exposed to the scrutiny of analysand and analyst. The child is capable of this only to a limited degree, depending on his age and precocity. In the idiom of Freud's aphorism, the id can only become an ego of which the child is developmentally capable. This view of the analytic process in childhood provides a rationale for those child analysts who see an advantage in the child's returning for periods of analysis rather than prolonged continuous analysis in childhood.

In summary, I have tried to identify and describe features of the psychoanalytic process in childhood which are determined by the developmental level of the child and the fact that analysis in childhood coincides with the time of the genesis of psychic structure. As a consequence, the child analyst is significant as an object with whom the child interacts in the genesis of psychic structures. The basic transference functions as a motivational and directional force in the child's communication via fantasy, play, and verbalization. The immaturity of the child's capacity for conceptualization, generalization, and abstraction limits his capacity for the self-observation and comprehension of meanings which are an important part of ego becoming where id was. The child is developmentally much more under the sway of the id, which is discernible in his passivity to the instinctual drives.

BIBLIOGRAPHY

BORNSTEIN, B. (1949), The Analysis of a Phobic Child. *This Annual,* 3/4 : 181–226.

FEIGELSON, C. I. (1977), On the Essential Characteristics of Child Analysis. *This Annual,* 32 : 353–362.

FREUD, S. (1933), New Introductory Lectures on Psycho-Analysis. *S.E.,* 22 : 3–182.

GREENACRE, P. (1968), The Psychoanalytic Process, Transference, and Acting Out. *Int. J. Psycho-Anal.,* 49 : 211–218.

KRIS, E. (1956), On Some Vicissitudes of Insight in Psycho-Analysis. *Int. J. Psycho-Anal.,* 37 : 445–455.

LOEWALD, H. W. (1970), Psychoanalytic Theory and the Psychoanalytic Process. *This Annual,* 25 : 45–68.

HARTMANN, H. (1950), Psychoanalysis and Developmental Psychology. *This Annual,* 5 : 7–17.

WEISS, S. (1976), In Panel: "The Essential Components of the Child Analytic Situation." Meeting of the Association for Child Psychoanalysis, Kansas City.

The Nature of Adolescent Pathology
and the Psychoanalytic Process

MOSES LAUFER, Ph.D.

MUCH OF OUR UNDERSTANDING OF ADOLESCENCE AND OF ADO-
lescent pathology has relied on our insights gained from child
development and from adult pathology. Although this is understandable within the context of the history of the development of psychoanalytic thought, there is the danger that we
adapt what we know about child and adult pathology so that it
fits the ill adolescent's behavior. The severe limitations of such
an approach or of such a view of pathology can be seen in the
manifold efforts (to my mind, rather unsuccessful) of various
people who work with the seriously disturbed adolescent by
introducing a variety of therapeutic methods and techniques
and assuming that these innovations or changes will yield the
answer to adolescent pathology and to the cure of the ill adolescent. The danger is that when these do not work, we say
that the adolescent and the adolescent process do not lend
themselves to analytic help, rather than ask ourselves what it is
that we know and where it is that we are working blindly.

My understanding of the analytic process in relation to the

Director, Centre for Research into Adolescent Breakdown/Brent Consultation Centre, London. Part-time member, Hampstead Child-Therapy
Clinic.

Presented at a Panel on "The Psychoanalytic Process in Different Developmental Phases" at the meeting of the Association for Child Psychoanalysis,
Jerusalem, Israel, on August 21, 1977. An abridged version was presented
at a meeting of the British Psychoanalytic Society, October 1977.

adolescent is based on some of my views about the contribution that the period of adolescence makes to the person's whole psychological development as well as on my view about the specific nature of adolescent pathology. I shall first summarize these views, and then link them to the psychoanalytic process in adolescence.

THE DEVELOPMENTAL FUNCTION OF ADOLESCENCE

The references to Freud's writings on puberty and adolescence often emphasize his belief that adolescence is a recapitulation of one's earlier life, but as early as 1905 he also wrote that it is only after puberty that the person shapes (what he there described as) the "final sexual organization" (p. 234). If viewed developmentally, the assumption of the establishment of a final sexual organization by the end of adolescence means that the part played by this period of psychological life in the person's future mental health is much more specific than is often assumed. As regards adolescent pathology, I would say categorically that illness in adolescence *always* contains some abnormality in *sexual development and functioning,* a view which I shall elaborate later. Of course, I do not disregard Freud's view that adolescence is a recapitulation of one's earlier life, especially since this statement also says that the past determines the present and that the past gives emotional meaning and substance to the present. But we blur the importance of differences in development and in the understanding of the meaning of pathology if we apply Freud's insights too automatically and perhaps without too much relation to the clinical material of our adolescent patients.

During the period of adolescence, from puberty to about the age of 21, the individual unconsciously makes a number of choices which represent his means of finding acceptable solutions to the demands from his sexual body, to the identifications with his parents, to the demands and expectations of his conscience. Although the conflicts, indecisions, and anxieties are experienced in a wide range of relationships and within many contexts, each of these is echoed via the adolescent's relationship to his own sexually mature body. Whether the adolescent likes it or not, by the end of adolescence he has an attitude to his body which reflects his total previous life experiences. During this period the adolescent tests his oedipal wishes within the context of his having physically mature genitals, and he attempts to find a compromise solution (between what is wished for and what can be allowed). It is this compromise solution which defines the person's sexual identity. I would then define *the main developmental function of adolescence as being the establishment of a final sexual organization* (Laufer, 1976)—an organization which, from the point of view of the body representation, must now include the physically mature genitals. All the developmental tasks of adolescence—the change in the relationship to the oedipal objects, the change in the relationship to contemporaries, the change in the attitude to one's own body—are part of the main developmental function and should be viewed in relation to each other rather than as separate tasks in their own right.

Nevertheless, it seems to me that in the solution of these tasks the adolescent's relationship to his own body is the central factor. In my own work with ill adolescents, I assume that fantasies, feelings, and conflicts involve in some way the person's body, and that the shame or guilt or elation or pleasure he feels in relation to it lends his experiences affective meaning. As a generalization, it may be correct to say that until adolescence the person feels himself and his body to be the extension of the mother who first cared for him; in adolescence, when the person has a physically mature body, he normally begins to feel himself to be the owner of his own body (Laufer, 1968). As a consequence, the adolescent assumes responsibility for his actions and feelings; normally he will then feel that he has actively made a choice. In other words, the adolescent becomes the guardian of his sexually mature body[1] and establishes a sexual identity by the end of adolescence, a con-

---

1. In this presentation, I am avoiding any detailed discussion of the structural changes which we assume have to take place for such a result because I want instead to concentrate on the analytic process and the undoing of pathology.

solidated picture of himself as a sexual being, which is *irrevers-ible*—irreversible, that is, without therapeutic intervention.

THE NATURE OF ADOLESCENT PATHOLOGY

Having defined the developmental function of adolescence, I will define adolescent pathology in similar terms, namely, by placing adolescent pathology within a developmental model. This means that I do not view the disorders of adolescence as being similar to those of childhood or of adulthood, even though some disorders (e.g., anorexia, obesity, some of the perversions) may share a common fantasy whenever the pathology presents itself. Rather I consider adolescent pathology to be *a breakdown in the process of integrating the physically mature body as part of the representation of oneself. As regards the timing of the breakdown in this developmental process, I believe that it occurs at puberty and has a cumulative effect throughout adolescence,* the consequences of which will be seen in the adolescent's relationship to his sexual body. Whatever may be the contributory ingredients to this breakdown—preoedipal, oedipal, or preadolescent—the essential component of adolescent pathology is that it is a breakdown in the developmental process whose primary or specific function is that of establishing the person's sexual identity. Whatever may be the specific disorder, the primary interference in the developmental process (which can be defined as adolescent pathology) is in the adolescent's distorted view and relationship to his body, something which is expressed via the hatred or shame of, the fury with, the sexual body. Unlike the child or the adult patient, the adolescent patient experiences his body as the constant representative of that which will overwhelm him with painful or frightening fantasies and affects. He experiences his body as constant proof that he has given in or surrendered passively—and unconsciously surrendered it to the mother who first cared for him. The presence of pathology in adolescence always means, therefore, that there is a disturbance in relation to the person's sexual life, and that the understanding of this disturbance is fundamental to the therapeutic task.[2]

The Psychoanalytic Process in Adolescence

In formulating my views, I have relied on my own clinical experiences gained in the analyses of a number of adolescents, as well as on the experience gained at the Centre for Research into Adolescent Breakdown where a number of seriously disturbed adolescents were treated analytically by colleagues as part of a study into mental breakdown in adolescence, and whose treatment I have been able to follow over a period of some years.

When an adolescent agrees to participate in treatment, he conveys to us that he is unconsciously aware of his being out of touch with part of his internal life; that he feels he does not have the choice to do with his life what he may wish. The reality of a physically mature body confronts him with the fact, albeit also unconsciously, that his fantasies now contain a new dimension, namely, that he is a sexual being and that his past solutions to conflict are now hindering his development; the adolescent may express this either in his symtomatology or in the affect he brings to his sessions. When he talks of his internal life, the adolescent patient is constantly telling us that he feels he now has a passive relationship to his body and to a part of his fantasy life which forces itself upon him and, perhaps more importantly, which forces him to behave in ways which are out of his control. When an adolescent patient tells me, for example, that she hates herself because she has to

2. I am avoiding a definition of adolescent pathology in terms which are commonly used by many people—inability to detach from the oedipal parent, narcissistic disturbance, disturbance in the process of individuation, and so on. These descriptions are of use in delineating specific aspects of an adolescent patient's conflicts, or they may help us make sense of the quality of object relationships, or even of the meaning of a core fantasy. But they should not be relied upon to *explain* what it is that is really going wrong in the life of the adolescent patient.

overeat, and that she feels like ripping out her insides so that she can stop masturbating, she may be hinting at the content of a core fantasy, but affectively she feels that there is nothing inside her to help her deal with the repetitive onslaught from her body. For her, her sexual body is not only an enemy but is the representative of her abnormality.

I have used the word "unconsciously" when referring to the adolescent's feeling or awareness about himself because to put the adolescent in touch with what he feels or what he knows may take a good deal of time in analysis, but when it happens the adolescent conveys, very often with relief, that he is familiar with his hopelessness, or with his feeling of being out of control, or with his awareness of something having been seriously wrong for some time. I will not go into detail about this here because I do not want to talk of technique of therapy with adolescents, nor do I want to describe the parameters which temporarily may have to be introduced in the analysis of some very disturbed adolescents. Rather, what is the course or the unfolding of the process of putting the adolescent in touch with his internal life and with his illness? Or more specifically, what is it that enables the ill adolescent to add meaning to the pathological solutions which he has found to his conflicts, and especially to find the meaning of the breakdown which took place at the time of puberty and which continues to impinge without respite on his present life?

CORE FANTASIES

Through the various forms of communication which the adolescent may use during analysis, we are able to piece together his core fantasies. If these core fantasies can be contained within the analysis, then interpretation and working through are the means by which we and the adolescent make sense of their meaning. However, when acting out is the adolescent's main means of dealing with these core fantasies, then it may be necessary to place limits on the acting out as a way of keeping these core fantasies within the analysis, thereby making it possible for these fantasies ultimately to come under the adolescent's control.[3]

It is the core fantasies which, for us, contain the clue to and the meaning of the adolescent's pathology. For the adolescent, these core fantasies represent his failure of coming to terms with his new sexual body; they also represent for him his abnormality or, in terms of the breakdown at the time of puberty, they represent his feeling of madness or of being out of control.

When I refer to a core fantasy, I have in mind the existence of a hierarchy of fantasies, with the implication that there is one core fantasy which has meaning and power beyond other fantasies, and which ultimately must be woven into the pathology of the person. I would say that the core fantasy—the central masturbation fantasy (Laufer, 1976)—is a universal phenomenon and is itself not pathological. Rather, the core fantasy contains the secret to the pathology, and helps to explain the direction of a person's sexual development and gratifications; in other words, it contains the person's whole oedipal constellation. I consider the piecing together and the ultimate understanding of this core fantasy to be of such importance in work with the ill adolescent because it is only in adolescence that this fantasy is confronted by a person who has physically mature genitals. Moreover, it is only during adolescence that the person will finally weave this core fantasy into his final sexual organization. This statement, however, also implies that during adolescence pathological growth is much more reversible than we tend to believe.

I want to avoid the impression either that these core fantasies are readily available to consciousness or that the analyst's main function is to put together the core fantasies while

3. Recently I described a female adolescent patient who had the compelling need to hitchhike and who, in fact, ran the risk of being attacked or killed; when I realized that this behavior contained the living out of her core fantasy—and the meaning of her pathology—I asked her to give up hitchhiking so that we could understand this, both within the transference and as part of her whole sexual life (Laufer, 1974).

disregarding the rest of the person's functioning. Of course this is not so. But in asking myself what is most important to an understanding of the adolescent's pathology, to reconstruction, to working through, and ultimately to insight and to cure, I conclude that it is the core fantasy as reexperienced in the transference. It will undoubtedly take a very long time to construct in one's own mind a patient's core fantasy, but the clues are there in the clinical material, in the whole range of derivatives from the unconscious—repeated daydreams, those object relationships which take on meaning for the patient, the fantasies which accompany the patient's masturbation or other sexual activities, and repetitive forms of behavior which may be understood partially as an undoing of the repression. In my work with the ill adolescent, it is these entries into the unconscious which enable me, over a period of time, to put together the fantasy which then enables us to understand the motivation, the power of certain kinds of gratifications, and ultimately the pathology. These fantasies will themselves not tell us about the history of their development, nor will their piecing together themselves assure anything but an insight into the unconscious and a meaning to the pathology; but to establish what is this core fantasy is a necessary part of the treatment and a necessary part of the undoing of the illness.

ADOLESCENT PATHOLOGY AND ADULT PATIENTS

Something about these core fantasies and their central part in adolescent pathology may also tell us something about the amnesia which so many adult patients have for their adolescence or, as may often also be the case, why it is that so many adult patients find it so difficult to participate in the reconstruction of their adolescence (A. Freud, 1958). It is not uncommon for adult patients to have memories of their adolescence which will bring with them anxieties or reactions which the patient may feel to be overwhelming and which I, within the treatment, felt to be well beyond what I might have expected. Unconsciously, at least some of our adult patients are aware that the clue to their pathology rests in remembering both the affects and the content of their core fantasies, or more specifically, the excessive shame and despair and the hopelessness associated with them.

Conversely, some adolescents may express their feeling that their sexual bodies are their persecutors. One way of coping with this unending onslaught from their sexual bodies is to give up genital sexuality and give back the nonsexual body to the mother who first cared for it. It is then not difficult to understand that the idea of the sexual body as persecutor may also contain a hint, felt by many ill adolescents, of the mother as the persecutor.

TRANSFERENCE AND CORE FANTASIES

It is only within the safety of the transference relationship that the adolescent's pathology and his core fantasies can begin to take on affective meaning, which includes a sense of their historical development. Possibly of greater importance, the transference can make emotionally real the fact that ultimately he can find a new way of integrating his sexual body and his earlier incestuous wishes into a sexual identity *which is of his choice.* By understanding the superego strictures and infantile ideals, and by connecting these with his present sexual wishes and fears, the adolescent patient is enabled to take charge of his sexual body in a way which does not have to contain the repeated giving of the body to the mother who first cared for it, expressed in the transference by the adolescent's demand for the analyst to participate in his sexual pathology. I have met this repeatedly in the analyses of adolescents, through the adolescent's efforts to force the analyst to take charge of the adolescent's actions and fantasies or, more often, expressed via the demand for the analyst actually to seduce the adolescent sexually. This may be understood in oedipal terms, but it also contains the adolescent's wish to destroy his own sexual body and to offer back the nonsexual body to the mother. Only this kind of transference experience enables the adolescent to see that his wishes, which may seem to be genital, are instead regressively organized so as to perpetuate a relationship to the preoedipal parent which, if understood in terms of the adolescent's sexual life, contains the destruction by the adolescent of his sexual body.

A female patient, aged 19, who had originally come for analysis at 17 because of her obesity, felt that she could not make any decisions without knowing what I thought. She felt forced by me to talk and to confess. She said that unless I did something about her need to masturbate and about her shameful fantasies, she would kill herself. In these shameful fantasies, men were raping other women, and she watched people being raped, or she was the innocent-looking bystander whom nobody would suspect of enjoying these actions. She felt totally hopeless when she began to substitute herself for these women, or when she became the attacker and thought of killing and eating the women. She now felt there was no choice but to kill herself, that is, to kill what she felt to be the source of these awful fantasies—her body. Within the transference, she felt that she had disgusted me with her thoughts, and that I now was as worthless as she was because I heard it all and now her thoughts were part of my thoughts.

I shall not discuss in detail the many meanings which the analysis of this fantasy disclosed. Instead I stress that transference enabled the patient to understand the meaning of women being attacked; her own pregnancy wishes; her wish to have her mother sexually available; and the meaning of the regressive pull to give up her sexual body and remain the good, admired child. All of this might have been understood in terms of object relations or the narcissistic void, but unless these aspects are linked to the adolescent patient's present sexual body and present masturbation fantasies, they do not enable the adolescent to see the connection with his present life.

It is through this kind of understanding that the breakdown which occurred at puberty begins to mean something to the adolescent. Then the analytic process can begin to enable the adolescent to seek a different solution from the original oedipal one which is now participating so centrally in his pathology. Via the transference and the analyst's ability to enable the adolescent to understand it both in historical and in present-day terms, the sexual body, instead of being the persecutor and the source of the pathology, begins to become the vehicle for the satisfaction of wishes which are now chosen by the adolescent. The adolescent gradually understands that his breakdown at puberty was due to his being overwhelmed by sexual wishes and oedipal fantasies, that it was the emotional core of the trauma which still continually threatens him, and that it was his only means of coping with his sexual body and what that represented for him. At the same time, however, this kind of understanding now offers the adolescent new hope. It enables him not only to understand the past and to place it within the context of the present, but it offers the adolescent the possibility first to undo the repression (and to come into touch with the meaning of his illness) and then to find a new solution to the oedipal resolution and to re-repress this, but now with the ability to feel actively in charge of his sexuality. In terms of the establishment of a sexual identity by the end of adolescence, the analytic process has thus created the internal possibility for development to proceed again.

John first came for analysis at 16 after he had been asked to leave his school. It was a school with very high standards, and students who did not meet them were asked to leave. Previously, at 13, he had left a note (found by his mother) in which he said he would kill himself because he was not normal and because he was lonely and worthless. In the course of his analysis, which has now been going on for nearly 4 years, he described a fantasy which has been conscious since the age of 7: he would enjoy thinking of girls, or of his mother, who had a pained facial expression. This fantasy stayed with him and, although he felt ashamed at times, he said that he was quite able to live with this secret without feeling threatened or having to invite too much punishment. Suddenly at puberty, however, he found that he began *to have to* organize his activities around observing girls or women with pained facial expressions. He felt driven to visit sports arenas so that he could observe girls straining themselves and tightening their faces. He became especially alarmed when he felt compelled to hit his mother, at times so forcefully that he and his family feared that he might seriously harm her. He quite often masturbated before coming to his session, and very gradually began to acknowledge how much of his pathology was contained in this fantasy. It took many months before he understood that his excitement in the sessions with me revolved around his telling me things and then his imagining that I had a pained facial expression. He became very frightened when he thought that he might lose control and attack me.

When I became ill for a few days and had to cancel some sessions, he could not stop talking of what he had done to me. I had to maintain telephone contact with him because he was frightened that he might have harmed me irreparably. In the sessions following my illness, he said that there were times when he thought that he actually had attacked me, but that he could not quite remember the details. Via the transference he began to recall the specific circumstances of his breakdown at puberty when he felt he had lost touch with reality, that is, when he believed that he had actually killed his mother and had to search the house frantically to find her alive and well. Exploring his breakdown at puberty, he began to understand that his present avoidance of girls and his enforced isolation contained his fear that he might want to kill them because of his envy of them; he also understood his hitting of his mother in terms of his sexual longing for his father. Although he was at first frightened by this confrontation, it created for him the hope that there was a way out of his pathological impasse. He realized that his very crazy behavior, mainly isolated to his analytic sessions and to his own room when he was alone, was related to his homosexual wishes; and that he needed to keep me away because of his sexual longing for me and the anxiety this engendered. For example, he shouted a good deal of the time when he was talking to me, and this helped him feel that he was keeping me away.

The analytic process thus enabled him to understand the meaning of his illness in terms of his present and past life. Beyond this understanding, however, the analytic process also offered him the possibility of finding a different resolution to his oedipal conflict, and thereby a different way of experiencing his own sexual body.

Various Therapies and Aims of Treatment

I have emphasized that the period of adolescence has a specific developmental function and that adolescent pathology has an especial destructive force because I feel that our work with ill adolescents becomes diffuse or intellectual or unconsciously strengthens the resistance to change when we do not see our central function as analysts to be the understanding of the illness in terms of abnormal sexual development. It is for this reason that I have expressed my doubts in the introduction to this paper about the use of a whole range of ideas and techniques which, for me, avoid sexuality and view development and perhaps illness in ways which clinically do not quite add up to what it is that the adolescent patient is experiencing.

I am well aware that many people believe that psychoanalytic treatment is contraindicated for the ill adolescent. Among the reasons cited are: the unsuitability of a treatment which expects the adolescent patient to become dependent at a time when independence is needed and wanted; the developmental process itself in adolescence goes contrary to insight and contrary to "inaction." My own view goes completely in the other direction. Various therapies may contribute something to progressive development by enabling the adolescent to deal better with age-appropriate demands and to maintain contact with the outside reality so that real demands may counter the fantasied demands. But if these therapies claim or expect to undo pathology, that is, to cure the ill adolescent, then I believe they are mistaken. They may be more than mistaken, in that their view of the function of therapy may produce harm in the life of the adolescent. By this I mean that unless the treatment process confronts the adolescent with the abnormality of his relationship to his sexual body, and unless the treatment creates the possibility of a different solution from the original oedipal one (that is, via the understanding of the core fantasies), it confirms the adolescent's feeling that change, especially of his sexual body image, is not possible. Help with age-appropriate conflicts may be useful and necessary, but the adolescent must not be made to feel that this is synonymous with the cure of illness.

CONCLUSION

I will comment only briefly on the differences between the analytic process in adolescence as compared to the process in childhood and adulthood. One way of emphasizing these differences would be by looking at the nature of the transference in each period. With the adolescent patient, the incestuous wishes within the transference are ever present, but intensely defended against, not only because of the superego prohibition, but because the battle which the adolescent is constantly waging with himself revolves around his sexual body and its being experienced as a source of pathology. The child does not yet have a sexually mature body capable of physically carrying out his fantasies. The child does not yet experience pathology as abnormality, whereas in adolescence pathology and abnormality (that is, sexual abnormality) are synonymous insofar as the superego of the adolescent for the first time condemns pathology and thereby condemns his own sexual body. With the adult, the pathological solutions which he adopted in adolescence have created a relation to his sexual body which is more firmly established and less reversible. The incestuous nature of the transference and of the wishes may still be present in the adult patient, but the adult, unless he is psychotic or near-psychotic, has an awareness of the unreality of his wish, and an ability to respond to it as unreal. This is not so with the adolescent.

The adolescent patient demands of the analyst that he accept the adolescent's present sexual body image and thus make his abnormality feel normal. But the analytic process in adolescence must go contrary to this. The adolescent must be able to experience his own condemnation of his abnormality, and he must be able to see the analyst as representing the hope of having a sexual body which does not contain the abnormality. We may say that we want to make the abnormal adolescent sexually normal. Some analysts do not agree with this approach, insofar as they may feel that the adolescent can choose any sexuality he seeks, but I believe that offering the possibility of a different sexuality and a different image of the sexual body is a most crucial task of the analytic process in adolescence.

Some colleagues may not agree with me in other respects. I may give the impression that I am either directly active in my interventions, or that I intrude in the patient's privacy, or that I take away the patient's right to choose the direction of his present and future life. It may be said that the analyst should be passive and allow for the unfolding of the treatment. To my mind, such a role for the analyst is not only fictitious; but even if it were true, it would go contrary to what I believe to be the role of the analyst in the curing process of the ill adolescent. When I say fictitious, I mean that there is no such thing as a passive analyst, inasmuch as every intervention is experienced by the patient as an active intervention, and that every analyst chooses either to intervene or not in direct relation to his understanding of the patient's pathology. If I apply my view of what constitutes the central pathology to the treatment of the ill adolescent, whose sexual identity is still in the process of being defined, then it is the analyst's function to keep the conflict alive in the patient's mind and to represent a mode of functioning and a direction of development which are contrary to the solutions adopted by the ill adolescent. I do not mean by this that the analyst of the adolescent should offer himself as an object for identification and unconsciously demand that the adolescent mold himself in the image of the analyst. This could be catastrophic for the future of the ill adolescent. Instead, by analyzing the transference and by showing the adolescent how his demands inevitably are for the analyst to accept the adolescent's abnormal development and how this contains the adolescent's need to destroy the analyst as well as his own sexual body, the analyst keeps the conflict alive and continues to confront the adolescent with the fact that his solutions are pathological ones. This is the way in which the adolescent can begin to allow for a different outcome, and it is this which can enable the adolescent to risk giving up his pathological solutions. These are some of the things I have in mind when I refer to giving the ill adolescent hope of change.

BIBLIOGRAPHY

FREUD, A. (1958), On Adolescence. *W.*, 5 : 136–166.
FREUD, S. (1905), Three Essays on the Theory of Sexuality. *S.E.*, 7 : 125–243.
LAUFER, M. (1968), The Body Image, the Function of Masturbation, and Adolescence. *This Annual*, 23 : 114–137.
———(1974), The Analysis of an Adolescent at Risk. In: *The Analyst and the Adolescent at Work*, ed. M. Harley. New York: Quadrangle, pp. 269–296.
———(1976), The Central Masturbation Fantasy, the Final Sexual Organization, and Adolescence. *This Annual*, 31 : 297–316.

The Psychoanalytic Process
in Adult Patients

PAUL A. DEWALD, M.D.

THE CONCEPTUAL UNDERSTANDING OF THE PSYCHOANALYTIC process in adult patients has undergone a progressive expansion since the earliest formulations proposed by Breuer and Freud (1893). Each successive elaboration of the curative factors has moved us further away from an emphasis upon a single therapeutic element. The earlier cathartic model of therapeutic action was replaced during the era of the topographic theory by the conceptualization that the analyst's interpretations make the unconscious become conscious. The significance of the transference was recognized, but the analyst was to be a passive mirror, reflecting whatever transference distortions the patient chose to project.

The introduction of the structural theory led to significant expansion of ego and superego analysis, but conceptualizations of the analyst's role still involved interpretation and reconstruction, and in the therapeutic interaction the analyst was to remain "neutral, aloof, a spectator, and . . . never a coactor" (Macalpine, 1950, p. 535). Sterba (1934, 1940) had described the alliance between patient and analyst, a subject

Medical Director, St. Louis Psychoanalytic Institute, and Clinical Professor of Psychiatry, St. Louis University School of Medicine.

Presented at panel on "The Psychoanalytic Process in Different Developmental Phases" at the meeting of the Association for Child Psychoanalysis, Jerusalem, Israel, August 21, 1977.

subsequently elaborated by Greenacre (1954), Zetzel (1956), and Greenson (1965). Loewald (1960) added the formulation that the interaction between analyst and analysand serves as a prototype of an effective interpersonal relationship, the internalization of which mediates changes in the patient as a result of the analytic process. Greenson and Wexler (1969) and Greenson (1971) spoke to the importance of the real relationship between patient and analyst, emphasizing that the analyst must at times respond to the patient at the level of objective reality.

There is general agreement that during the development and elaboration of the regressive transference neurosis the patient experiences a variety of transference-inspired expectations emanating from id, ego, and superego functions, and projects them onto the analyst as part of the transference neurosis. In 1976 I added that by maintaining the classical psychoanalytic posture and interaction in the face of regressive transference expectations and provocations, the analyst provides the patient an opportunity to relive and reexperience infantile and early childhood core psychic conflicts in a new and optimal relationship. This is not a transference repetition; rather it is an opportunity to modify, in an experiential, regressively activated way, the conflicts and the adaptive devices established to cope with them during the patient's early development and maturation. Novey (1968) had called this *The Second Look,* emphasizing the cognitive elements in the process, whereas I stressed the regressive affective and experiential elements.

Langs (1976a) described the "bipolar asymmetrical interactional field" which evolves between patient and analyst, and which provides a safe "framework" for the interactional processes that occur during therapeutic psychoanalysis. He further elaborated these interactional concepts and their implications for the evolving psychoanalytic process in his work on the therapeutic interaction (1976b).

At present the psychoanalytic process in adults can be conceptualized as an evolving and progressive interaction between the two participants, each of whom is acutely sensitive to the input and responses of the other. This interaction evokes intrapsychic elaborations in each of the participants, leading to subsequent interpersonal interactions, all of which occur within the framework of the relatively circumscribed and defined limits of the psychoanalytic situation. The analyst serves as a catalyst, inasmuch as his presence and activity are necessary in order for the process to occur, but he remains *relatively* unchanged, while in successful cases the patient undergoes major psychological reorganization.

Most analysts agree upon the common elements of the adult psychoanalytic situation, technique, and relationship. These include: the use of the couch; the technique of free association; the analyst's active listening; the optimal frustration of the patient's transference wishes; the promotion of regression in the service of the therapeutic task; the analyst's interpretations and reconstructions of defenses and contents of conflict; the unfolding of the therapeutic alliance and the transference neurosis; the use of the regressive transference neurosis for the exploration of infantile and early childhood core psychic conflicts; the gradual achievement of insight by the patient and its application in the working through process; and the ultimate partial resolution of the transference neurosis through voluntary renunciation of transference wishes and objects, particularly during the termination phase.

Instead of elaborating on these, I shall concentrate upon some of the less well-delineated therapeutic elements of the process, as it might be seen in the ideal analytic patient, though I recognize that the individual case may require differing parameters or emphases.

Although patients enter analysis with varying degrees of basic trust and capacities to form a therapeutic alliance, there is a circular relationship between the self-observing alliance and the regressive transference experiences. In their early transference expectations virtually all patients find it necessary to "test" the safety and constancy of the analytic situation. As the analyst "passes" these tests by his consistently therapeutic, empathic, neutral, observing responses, the patient becomes willing to permit deeper regression and more directly conscious awareness of transference fantasies and experiences. When these are continually responded to by the analyst with empathy, appropriate interpretation, and neutral participant observation, the alliance is enhanced, thus again promoting greater tolerance for the further regressive manifestations of the transference neurosis.

With the intensified regressive pull of the analytic process, the derivative levels of psychic conflict and function are progressively replaced by increasingly direct experience and conscious recognition of the infantile and earliest childhood core psychic conflicts and the structures which evolved from them. These regressively activated transference wishes, superego expectations, ego states, adaptive or defensive functions, and self and object images produce in the patient's consciousness a variety of primitive and conflict-induced distortions of the interactional processes and the interpersonal field of the analytic relationship and situation. Simultaneously or in oscillation with these evolving intrapsychic and interpersonal processes, the patient experiences the reality of the analyst-analysand relationship, but his regressive transference expectations are not fulfilled by the analyst.

This situation presents to the patient disparate, internal and external, significantly incompatible sets of images and processes. On the one hand, there are his transference-inspired regressive expectations, fantasies, wishes, and distortions of the analyst, emanating from the patient's memory systems and primary process elaborations and distortions. On the other hand, there are his perceptions, experienced *at the level of psychic regression,* of the actuality of the analyst's behavior vis-à-vis the transference provocations and expectations. This places the patient in a situation of reliving the infantile and childhood core experiences and conflicts, but with an object (the analyst) whose manifest and observable responses are significantly different from the actual or fantasied behavior of the original objects.

These differing and mutually contradictory sets of perceptions of the analyst are simultaneously recognized, explored, and ultimately reconciled by the adult, synthetic, rational, and reality-oriented components of the patient's psychic functions. The repetitive process of working through involves the reconciliation of these disparate images—a reconciliation that ultimately leads to the patient's renunciation of the incompatible infantile and early childhood wishes, objects, and fantasies. It is in this reconciliation and renunciation that the curative process of psychoanalysis occurs.

An important part of this sequence is a progressive desensitization as the previously unconscious and warded-off conflicts, danger situations, and anxiety- or guilt-producing fantasies emerge into the patient's consciousness. One of the essentials in the process is repetition, which facilitates a progressively more direct and complete approach to previously warded-off psychological danger situations and fantasies. Each time these conflicts are approached by the patient in the presence of the safe, holding relationship with the analyst (who by his interventions titrates and helps control the intensity of the unpleasurable experiences), the patient's tolerance for unpleasure and conflict is enhanced, and he becomes increasingly capable of facing the danger situations in fantasy without immediate recourse to the previous, neurotogenic, automatic, and unconscious defense mechanisms. This regressively relived infantile and childhood situation is analogous to the situation of the immature child dealing with conflict in the presence of the "good enough" parental figure. By his manifest tolerance, freedom from anxiety, nonpunitive, nonreactive, generally accepting, and empathic responses, the analyst provides the patient with a new object for identification in regard to ego and superego functions. This process of identification occurs simultaneously at the levels of the regressively reactivated infantile and childhood experiences, and the adult rational self-observing functions that in part constitute the therapeutic alliances.

This same process of desensitization occurs in connection with an increased tolerance for the drives themselves, as well as the affects accompanying them. As the patient's capacity consciously to tolerate these elements of his psychic life is enhanced, he can utilize more conscious and reality-oriented defensive and adaptive functions to cope with them. There occurs a progressive sense of conscious mastery over previously psychologically overwhelming situations of stress and conflict, ultimately leading to dissolution of those organizing, primitive, primary process fantasy systems that had promoted the neurosis.

In other words, the interactions between patient and analyst in the analytic situation serve to promote a progressively expanding insight and awareness. This process occurs simultaneously at several levels. There is the progressively conscious recognition and awareness of the infantile wishes, fantasies, and expectations as they arose during the patient's early sequential maturation and development. At the same time there is a regressive reexperience of these infantile and childhood wishes, fantasies, ego states, and danger situations, but now in the presence of the analyst, a new and uniquely different object. Simultaneously, with the help of his self-observing and reality-oriented capacities, the patient achieves cognitive understanding, integrates and reconciles the other two levels of experience, and checks them against the new options, and potential solutions that his adult status offers him.

In a general sense, the psychoanalytic situation and the psychoanalytic process which emerges and unfolds within it represent an intermediate type of interactional relationship—intermediate, that is, between the self-contained, unconscious, intrapsychic, primitive core conflicts and experiences of the patient's neurosis, and the demanding interpersonal responsibilities and reactions that occur in his external life situations and relationships. In this intermediate form of relationship the patient is free to experience and verbally express the full gamut of his emotional and psychological reactions and distortions without having to assume immediate and direct behavioral responsibility for their consequences.

Loewald (1975) used the analogy of a dramatic play in which the patient is the author and in which both the actors and the audience simultaneously recognize the emotional reality of the experiences being portrayed, and the unrealistic nature of the undertaking. I prefer to think of this situation as a safe "laboratory" in which well-established ground rules prevail. In it old patterns of behavior and experience can be tested and practiced and through trial and error new ones developed, all in a relatively safe stable situation of acceptance by the analyst.

As a result of the cumulative impact of all the various therapeutic factors, the patient progressively *unlearns* the previous primitive distortions of his pathogenic fantasy systems, self and object representations, and the archaic and inappropriate compromise solutions for his intrapsychic conflicts. At the same time he achieves a greater sense of *psychic continuity and cohesiveness* in several areas: his personal life experiences, his object representations, his conscious and unconscious mental processes, his affects and drives, and his various partial self images. He also has the opportunity to *learn* new and more adaptive responses to irreconcilable conflicts. Furthermore, he accepts a partial *renunciation* of archaic, but unfulfillable, wishes in favor of realistic and age-appropriate achievable gratifications.

Turning now to the question of how the analytic process differs in the adult as compared with the adolescent and child, I can see advantages as well as disadvantages. The ideal, analyzable adult patient is presumably better equipped for free association and verbal communication than the child and is under less pressure toward disruptive acting out of conflicts. This capacity for effective free association implies greater conscious access to some of the subjective experiences of intrapsychic phenomena. The classically analyzable adult is better able to tolerate the degree of transference abstinence and frustration necessary for the development of a regressive but stable transference neurosis. The adult is more likely to have the necessary capacity for reality testing to allow recognition and acceptance of the "as if" quality of the transference neurosis and its necessary role in the treatment process. The analyzable adult tends to have more highly developed stability, reality testing, object constancy, sublimation, and other secondary process adaptive and consciously controlling ego organizations. The adult patient has realistic opportunities for independence from his parents, as well as a variety of potential new external objects and activities available for need fulfillment and age-appropriate drive gratifications. The adult patient can usually be treated independently of the important persons in his environment, and the analyst usually has no need for contact with other people in the patient's life, either his parents or other therapists who may see the patient's relatives. The patient can usually assume responsibility for his own treatment; and the treatment is less vulnerable to various forms of sabotage practiced by external objects. And since genital primacy normally occurs as a postadolescent developmental step, this can occur during the analysis of an adult, while it remains only a potential for the child or adolescent.

These advantages are offset, however, by a number of significant disadvantages. The adult must function under the impact of the various life decisions and choices which he made earlier under the influence of his neurotic disturbances. These can have significant effects on his career, marriage, and relationship to his own children; or on decisions not to marry or to have children; they may also add significant complications to the working through and resolution of neurotic disturbances. As a result of such choices the patient may have lost forever a variety of opportunities for developmental experiences which he can never recapture and for which he now must mourn. In contrast, if the child is relieved of his neurotic disturbances, he can still enjoy the normal and pleasurable experiences and satisfactions that latency, adolescence, and young adult life can provide to people who are relatively unhampered by neurotic distortions. Furthermore, the child and the adolescent normally experience thrusts of developmental energies which, if not disrupted by neurotic disturbances, tend to promote healthy maturation. In the adult such developmental thrusts of energies no longer occur, and not infrequently, particularly in older patients, the trend may be in the reverse direction.

Although I have never myself analyzed a child, I am aware that the techniques necessary for achieving access to the child's intrapsychic experiences are significantly different from those used in analysis of adult patients. Anna Freud (1975) has indicated that experience with the analysis of children demonstrates how effective and valid are our techniques for analyzing adult patients.

However, we must keep in mind the significant distinctions between the technique of analysis and the process of analysis. The technique of analysis provides the situation, tools, and method necessary for the actual psychoanalytic process to unfold and evolve. The psychoanalytic process consists of the intrapsychic and interpersonal experiences and their evolutionary elaborations, which occur as a result of the application of psychoanalytic technique. The specific technical tools required will vary in different age groups, and in different types of patients within such groups; and the specific needs of the particular patient will in part dictate the technical procedures to be used. The major elements of the psychoanalytic process, however, are essentially the same, regardless of the age of the patient. In regard to the important elements of the analytic process as I have attempted to delineate them, it is my belief that the qualitative similarities between patients in the various age groups far outweigh the differences. In its essence, the psychoanalytic process is universal for all patients.

BIBLIOGRAPHY

BREUER, J. & FREUD, S. (1893), On the Psychical Mechanism of Hysterical Phenomena. *S.E.*, 2 : 3–17.
DEWALD, P. A. (1976), Transference Regression and Real Experience in the Psychoanalytic Process. *Psychoanal. Quart.*, 45 : 213–230.
FREUD, A. (1975), Remarks made during discussion, Int. Psychoanal. Assn., Precongress Meeting, London.
GREENACRE, P. (1954), The Role of Transference. *J. Amer. Psychoanal. Assn.*, 2 : 671–684.
GREENSON, R. R. (1965), The Working Alliance and the Transference Neurosis. *Psychoanal. Quart.*, 34 : 155–181.
——— (1971), The "Real" Relationship between the Patient and the Psychoanalyst. In: *The Unconscious Today*, ed. M. Kanzer. New York: Int. Univ. Press, pp. 213–232.
——— & WEXLER, M. (1969), The Non-Transference Relationship in the Psychoanalytic Situation. *Int. J. Psycho-Anal.*, 50 : 27–30.

LANGS, R. J. (1976a), *The Bipersonal Field*. New York: Jason Aronson.
——— (1976b), *The Therapeutic Interaction*. New York: Jason Aronson.
LOEWALD, H. W. (1960), On the Therapeutic Action of Psycho-Analysis. *Int. J. Psycho-Anal.*, 41 : 16–33.
——— (1975), Psychoanalysis as an Art and the Fantasy Character of the Psychoanalytic Situation. *J. Amer. Psychoanal. Assn.*, 23 : 277–299.
MACALPINE, I. (1950), The Development of the Transference. *Psychoanal. Quart.*, 19 : 510–539.
NOVEY, S. (1968), *The Second Look*. Baltimore: Johns Hopkins Univ. Press.
STERBA, R. F. (1934), The Fate of the Ego in Analytic Therapy. *Int. J. Psycho-Anal.*, 15 : 117–126.
——— (1940), The Dynamics of the Dissolution of the Transference Resistance. *Psychoanal. Quart.*, 9 : 363–379.
ZETZEL, E. R. (1956), Current Concepts of the Transference. *Int. J. Psycho-Anal.*, 37 : 369–376.

CLINICAL CONTRIBUTIONS

Reconstruction in a Case of
Postpartum Depression

HAROLD P. BLUM, M.D.

THIS PAPER WILL EXPLORE PROBLEMS OF DEPRESSION VIA ANA-lytic reconstruction. The investigation also involves corollary questions concerning the value and validity of preoedipal reconstruction, and the reconciliation and integration of analytic data and the data of direct infant observation. The clinical basis for this paper derives from the psychoanalysis of a woman with postpartum depressions; hence the study has the unique advantages, tempered by an awareness of the uniqueness, of a particular psychoanalytic case.

In view of the rich analytic literature on depression, and the expanding psychoanalytic studies of the psychology of pregnancy and parenthood, it is noteworthy that there have been few psychoanalytic investigations of postpartum depression. Postpartum depression is a significant and not uncommon condition occurring at a crucial point in the life cycle, with repercussions and implications of pathogenic vulnerability for both mother and infant.

Mild postpartum "blues" may be overlooked or rationalized in terms of physical fatigue and lack of sleep. The relative universality of postpartum psychological problems in both parents is often disregarded, except for more dramatic and serious syndromes such as agitated or psychotic depression

Editor of the *Journal of The American Psychoanalytic Association;* Training and Supervising Analyst at the Downstate Psychoanalytic Institute.

Harold P. Blum

(Asch and Rubin, 1974). Psychiatric hospitalization may influence descriptive and diagnostic considerations (Pugh et al., 1963).

There is little agreement about the true incidence and duration of postpartum depression because of wide variation in definition, recognition, and reporting of the syndrome. For some observers, postpartum depression may nonetheless include prepartum depression during pregnancy. Others consider postpartum depression as precipitated by childbirth and a syndrome limited in onset from the third to the tenth days postpartum. Still other surveys consider postpartum depression as appearing in the first three to even six months after parturition (Hamilton, 1962; Melges, 1968). This paper concerns idiopathic postpartum depression and not the depression which may be anticipated with illness in the mother or neonate, or the birth of a defective child (Solnit and Stark, 1961).

Numerous other questions and possible correlations have been noted. No specific relationship has been confirmed between postpartum depression and the age of the mother, the number of her pregnancies and children, the interval between pregnancies, or the duration or difficulty of labor and delivery.

Because of the massive shifts in hormonal activity during pregnancy, and again in the postpartum period, endocrine factors have been implicated. The dramatic changes in body state and image and actual physiological upheaval have also led many observers to postulate an organic etiology or predisposition. The hormonal and other physiological alterations are also thought to contribute to other mood disturbances associated with the menstrual cycle, e.g., premenstrual depression and tension, menstrual and menopausal depression. The physiology of depression is a very important dimension of the problem and, as a facilitating force, has to be distinguished from somatic concomitants and consequences of depression. Such factors, however, have unfortunately remained obscure, and no consistent endocrine or neurophysiological finding or aberration has been established to be specifically linked with or contributing to postpartum depression or other psychological disorders of the female reproductive cycle. It seems likely that endocrine and neurophysiological factors are involved, but may not have a regular or perhaps even predominant role in some cases. The importance of psychogenic factors is further suggested in similar initial psychological reactions observed in adoptive parents (Bental, 1965).

Women who have had one postpartum depression are more likely to have another than might be expected without such an antecedent history, but is such depression specifically postpartum, or does it occur in other situations of life-stress or normative crisis? Are these women depression-prone, and were there depressive episodes or equivalents in childhood? Where the depressive psychopathology has not been mastered, are there masked subclinical depressions which may predispose and persist after the postpartum depression subsides? At least some of these patients are chronically depressed, beginning in early life, even if the condition has not been recognized or consciously identified.

I shall attempt to explicate some of these problems, simultaneously demonstrating the value of reconstruction in analytic work. I refer here to reconstruction of adult disorders about which the patient may be confused, as well as to the classical reconstruction of infantile development and disorder. Analytic reconstruction does not emphasize actual historical events per se, but their meaning and impact, their consequences and sequelae (Greenacre, 1975; Kanzer and Blum, 1967).

Reconstruction has been a significant tool, not only in psychoanalytic treatment, but in the development and validation of psychoanalytic theory. Reconstruction leads to a unique way of understanding individual development and permits the reintegration of dissociated fragments of both the life experience and the inner world. During clinical psychoanalysis, parallel with the mastery of intrapsychic infantile conflict, infantile amnesia is uncovered, memory distortions are corrected, and a unique individual history is reassembled and reconstructed (Kris, 1956; Ekstein and Rangell, 1961). Reconstructions are tested and remodeled by analyst and patient with increasing refinement of the initial hypotheses, and expanding explanatory value. The continuing comparison and integration of clinical reconstruction with developmental studies and other psychoanalytic research are important to the identification and resolution of controversy concerning infantile development and pathogenesis.

Recognizing all the problems inherent in reconstruction of this early phase of life with all its ambiguities and uncertainty, I shall present current clinical material and analytic inferences organized around a reconstruction of the organization and disturbance of mental life between 20 and 28 months of life, essentially within the preoedipal phase that Mahler et al. (1975) have designated as the rapprochement subphase of separation-individuation, overlapping with the anal phase of development. Psychoanalytic knowledge of drive and ego development, of infantile object relations and the process of separation-individuation will be utilized in the testing and interpretation of analytic data and inferences. The preoedipal focus in this case is partially for heuristic descriptive purposes, and is not meant to indicate a diminished significance of oedipal and later development. Similarly, the studies of separation-individuation are most pertinent to a deeper understanding of postpartum depression, and have enriched analytic insights into many related complex clinical phenomena.

The reconstruction here is also pertinent to theories of the origin of depression, enriching understanding, rather than detracting from the importance of the superego, guilt, and self-reproach in adult depression. Personality development can be peculiar and uneven, regressed and retarded in some areas, advanced and precocious in other areas, sometimes with a mosaic appearance rather than the neat layering of development or conflict that was once popular in analytic constructs. However, in adult analytic work with an analyzable patient, genetic reconstruction is based upon clues, derivatives, and patterns emerging in predominantly verbal data filtered through advanced ego structures and a postoedipal organization.

There is no reason to expect that any of the later normal developmental phases of life or pathological states will exactly replicate in any point-to-point correspondence any of the subphases of separation-individuation or psychosexual development. The early phases of development are not literally recapitulated; various consequences are inferred in terms of residue and influences, of forerunners which undergo further developmental vicissitudes. The childhood precursors and roots of adult depression are not identical with adult depression, and careful study of the personality in the psychoanalytic process and the emerging life history are prerequisites for reconstruction of infantile pathogenesis and depressive predisposition. It is important to follow affective states and style, the form as well as the content of the transference, and behavior patterns.

In this case, there was a transference neurosis, albeit with periods of severe regression. Preoedipal determinants and traits were regularly observable along with narcissistic vulnerability. There was no evidence of psychosis, major structural defects, or inability to participate in a coherent psychoanalytic process. What I observed from the inception of treatment was a very complicated picture of a depressive personality with many preoedipal character traits and with an oedipal transference neurosis. (Actually, many cases of depressive neurosis are also oral characters, just as obsessives typically demonstrate anal character.) The transference frequently manifested preoedipal imprints and influences and brief fluctuating periods of dyadic quality. Preoedipal problems and some regressive ego fragility were nevertheless not of the severity usually found in the borderline personality. Susceptibility to severe regression was balanced by latent ego resilience and capacity to reverse regression. Antecedent preoedipal development will influence the formation and form of the infantile neurosis that underlies the later transference neurosis. Preoedipal influences on the oedipus complex and character structure are universal. In a patient without major ego modifica-

tion there is no artificial isolation between character analysis
and transference neurosis or between preoedipal and oedipal
analysis.

CASE REPORT

Mrs. A., a tall, well-groomed, serious, and articulate mother in
her early 30s, had three children. A postpartum depression
followed the birth of each child. Feelings of depression, dejec-
tion, denigration, and lassitude lasted several weeks after each
delivery. She had awakened from the obstetrical anesthesia
crying on each occasion, although she had anticipated happiness and regarded the pregnancies as precious life experiences. A nurse had had to take over the mothering of her first
child during the first two months after the baby was born,
arousing great envy and further self-reproach in the patient.
What Mrs. A. described as the postpartum blues gradually
cleared and each time she resumed her maternal functions
with great energy and single-minded dedication. The acute
depression became a subclinical depression with serious recurrent depressive disturbances. When she was not subject to
depressive episodes, there were "depressive equivalents" particularly in the form of insomnia and an eating disturbance.

At the height of her postpartum depression Mrs. A. could
neither eat nor sleep. The insomnia resulted in drug abuse via
sleeping medication to which the patient felt she almost became addicted. Feeling guilty about what she considered to be
her inadequate maternal care and ashamed of her behavior,
she became secretly alcoholic. She smuggled spirits into the
house to calm her almost constant anxieties and to drown her
sorrows in liquor. She made abortive and half-hearted efforts
at obtaining help, but it was only after her family took note of
her increasing depression and Mrs. A. felt increasingly desperate that she finally was referred to a psychotherapist and
ultimately for psychoanalysis.

Shortly after she had begun her first analysis (in a different
city with a different analyst), she noted that her crying had
enormously increased. There were "buckets of tears" during
the sessions, and the sessions were punctuated by crying be-

fore and after the hour. She was admiring and respectful of her analyst, but at the same time intensely ambivalent, with chronic feelings of irritation and anger. She was committed to her treatment, although she was again constantly guilty that because the analyst lived at some distance from her home she had to leave her children in the charge of baby-sitters or the maid. By this time she had given up her reliance on alcohol, but her mood disturbance, indecision, and inability to maintain consistency and child discipline were productive, she thought, of more guilt. As she rushed off to her analyst, or away from home, she felt even more that she was deserting her maternal responsibilities.

In her brief first analysis her constant crying was associated with pleas and demands for the analyst's love and approval. Her acting out was regarded as a defense against feelings of rejection and rage, as well as a disguised gratification of her erotic attachment to the analyst based upon her unresolved guilt-ridden incestuous longing for her father. Her tears and depression were related to her guilt over her prostitution fantasies, which appeared in her dreams and associations.

Mrs. A. felt she made some therapeutic strides and thought she was beginning to understand herself particularly in the area in which her guilt and inhibition over unacceptable sexual impulses had led to constriction, and strong feelings of disappointment and defeat. On the other hand, her crying and depression had not been relieved. She claimed that in her first analytic treatment there had been little if any discussion of her postpartum depressions or her later depressive and addictive reactions. Depression was regarded as a manifestation of oedipal guilt and defeat, but was not specifically tied to conflicts over her children and motherhood. Her reactive overconcern and difficulty in maintaining maternal attitudes toward her children were not interpreted, and her family life remained isolated from her transference attitudes toward her analyst. She also realized that she may have preferred not to discuss feelings of failure as a mother as part of a general avoidance of painful topics—an attitude for which there was a familial model.

Mrs. A. had invested a great deal of her energy and effort

in motherhood and her children. Despite some feelings of accomplishment as a mother, she also experienced feelings of failure in what she considered to be the most important sphere of her life. What was missing in her understanding of her relationship with her children was paralleled by her bafflement about her own childhood. When she moved to another city and began analysis with me, she was clearly confused, impetuous, demanding, and depressed. She had the history and the characteristics of an oral depressive personality, but with a sufficiently intact ego structure to participate in analysis.

In the analysis with me, at first she appeared to be very compliant and eagerly accepting of interpretations. She stated that she had grown up to be a conformist and had been regarded by her parents and friends as a very obedient, dependable, and serious girl. It developed that she handled my interpretations analogously to her food symptoms. She would have eating binges often followed by self-induced vomiting which she concealed from her family. During these times she would eat scraps of food from the table, sweets, and dairy products to the point of abdominal discomfort. Her reactions to interpretations were in some ways analogous to swallowing followed by spitting, but with more assimilation of interpretation as the analysis progressed. There were always complaints about feeling that she was passive toward life, that the analyst and her family acted upon her, and that she could not be decisive, authoritative, and consistent in her relationships. Her children tended to dominate and control her because she was unable to be firm with respect to such issues as play, study, and bedtime.

Given the history of the postpartum depressions, a great deal of conflict over motherhood could have been anticipated. These conflicts were revived in the transference, had often been repeated in various forms with her children, and could be discerned and elaborated in the developmental picture that slowly emerged in the analytic process. Analytic data were supplemented by developmental data that the patient herself was stimulated to elicit about her childhood. Though such extra-analytic data are often obtained from patients in analysis (Novey, 1968), their use requires careful evaluation to avoid their abuse and distortion of the analytic process.

Mrs. A.'s intense and profound separation reactions, her bouts of bulimia and vomiting were associated with introjective and projective processes and a good deal of denial. While high-level defenses including repression were most important, the preoedipal drive-defense constellations were readily evident. She demanded and struggled against any dependency on the analyst, often denying and isolating dependent and affectionate feelings, as she had previously struggled against dependency on her mother and dependency on food and drugs. The first bout of eating and vomiting occurred during the last trimester of her first pregnancy during a separation from her husband. There had been minimal nausea and vomiting during the first trimester and one thereafter except following eating binges. For the most part she had adhered to the nutritional regime prescribed by her obstetrician, and the eating disorder was, in the main, in abeyance. Her bulimia was also despite and because of food and weight restrictions during pregnancy.

Her symptoms, transference, and dreams also indicated the doing and undoing of her incestuous impregnation and masturbation. But the deeper level concerned her unresolved symbiotic wishes and, in instinctual terms, oral greed and cannibalistic devouring with fears of retaliation as well as wishes to be eaten. Dreams of feasts and famines alternated with dreams of children lost and found. There were feasts of dreams and absence of dreams. A dream in which a female dog ate her puppies led to the patient's associations and dawning realization of her impulses to devour—to incorporate her own children. Her enormous guilt arose from the intense conflict between her maternal ego ideal and her infanticidal impulses (Blum, 1976).

At the same time she began to understand her need to feed herself in order to feed the children. The eating binges were discovered to have occurred mostly before the family dinner. She needed to be fed and comforted first, or she would feel she would be too depleted to be a giving mother. She constantly wanted to see herself as nurturant, yet identified herself with the hungry children who needed food and love. She was also envious of the affectionate care the children received, and again had to vomit back the food she in fantasy took from them since she had literally eaten off their plate. Finally, she ate not only their food, but symbolically the children themselves in an ambivalent mixture of primitive love and destruction. Her sleep disturbances were particularly related to her fears of being devoured, in her struggle against both the cannibalistic and passive wishes of the oral triad (to eat, to be eaten, and to sleep). If she did not vomit after incorporation, she might be devoured from within.

In both her symbolic behavior and fantasy she indicated her ambivalent wish for merger and her fear and rage at separation. She came to understand her longing for the narcissistic bliss of fusion with an idealized good mother. In one dream she reached orgasm eating lox and bagel, representing the feeding mother. In another, she controlled a pulley which moved a loaf of bread in and out of her vagina, offering her a never-ending "alimentary orgasm" (Rado, 1927).

She began to perceive the impossible and insatiable demands she made for therapeutic help and magical relief on her analyst and the nature of her irrational demands on and fantasies about her husband. In her husband she had wanted a mother, a preoedipal mother, who was screened behind the heterosexual oedipal father. She had split the image of her mother into the eternally benevolent and feeding supportive figure, the bread that was life, and the depriving, castrating, and punitive mother whom she associated with her anger and depression. The split between the pure mother and prostitute, faithless mother had been superimposed upon the earlier splitting of the maternal representation which she had failed to integrate completely and cohesively in later development.

The patient had defensively idealized her mother and motherhood, although her maternal ideals had other important determinants. In her conscious thoughts and daydreams there had been no more important ideal than that of becoming a perfect mother of angelic children. Her mother had emphasized the joys of motherhood and had wanted Mrs. A. to think of her as an ideal mother and an ideal daughter to the patient's grandmother. Although the patient in many ways rejected femininity, for example, crying when she developed breasts in adolescence, she also wanted many children. There had been intense and prolonged doll play centered around maternity and child care. The play was generally idealized and she had no conscious thoughts of doll injury or death.

This case is also of interest from the point of view of the knowledge of the early mother-child relationship that can be obtained in the analysis of mothers. A great deal can be learned about a mother's empathy and responsiveness to her children, about her mode of play and recreation, discipline, organization, and direction of the children's growth and development based upon her own resources and the intrusion of her own problems into the mother-child relationship. This woman constantly sought to be an ideal mother, a kind of supermother who struggled against her hostile feelings toward her own mother and her children. No one else was allowed to shop for the food which was carefully selected. Every family menu was deliberately planned and had to be properly executed and served. The bathing, washing, and dressing of the children; the purchase of their clothes; the necessary chauffeuring; the arrangements and plans for lessons; or special appointments—all were made by Mrs. A. The children were the objects and objectives of the specific ministrations of the mother. She lamented her husband's preoccupation with his profession, yet made it clear that the home was her domain. She wanted him to be much more helpful and invested in the children's care, but remained unconsciously controlling and possessive. She liked her husband's somewhat seductive and easygoing play with the children, but at the same time she was envious of his relationship with them. She was pained at the children's frustrations, and took great pleasure in their achievements. This mother was highly ambitious for her children, and they developed their own unusual talents and sensitivities as well as neurotic disturbances.

Each child starting school aroused feelings of loneliness and separation in this mother. Repeating the anxiety and depression of childbirth, every separation from the children, and later from the analyst, could reactivate this syndrome in muted form. Her oral regression and fusion fantasies were partial and reversible, so that in the transference and at the end of the hour or week, upon awakening from anesthesia, sleep, and dreams, ego boundaries and object relatedness were rapidly reinstated.

The patient's depression was associated with feelings of intense disappointment and disillusionment as well as intermittent feelings of failure and helplessness. She could never be the perfect mother she wanted to be, and every unhappy encounter with the children's anxiety, frustration, or anger left her feeling anxious and guilty. Whatever she did for them was never enough, and she was filled with self-reproach. She was not sufficiently attentive as a daughter, feeling selfish and insensitive, despite her daily telephone contact and the frequent visits with her own mother.

Her complaints that her husband's discipline tended to become "overkill" in the form of extended lectures and verbal reprimands projected her own impulses. The overkill really referred to the fear of the breakdown of her compensatory undoing in her "supermomism." Her unconscious hostility to motherhood and the children led to reaction formations of maternal overconcern and overprotection. Her own wishes to destroy or desert the children or to replace them and be mothered by them also led to fear of aggressive encounters with them as well as to close involvement with their activities. The constant preoccupation with the compulsory undoing of wishes to be rid of the children was confirmed repeatedly. When I was away at a research conference, children were lost in research libraries in her fantasies. She had separation dreams and fantasies: mothers search for children, grandmothers search for mothers, children fall off bicycles, die in plane crashes, and so forth. In nightmares, she was pursued because children had been burned on the stove or abused by predators, crushed by cars.

Motherhood was a fulfillment of her ego ideal but also an oedipal crime in which she was guilty of replacing her mother. Childbirth also represented castration for this woman who had serious unresolved bisexual conflicts and castration anxiety (Zilboorg, 1958). She was fearful of injury, experienced intensified anger in connection with the anticipation of sexual intimacy, and had numerous dreams in which one foot was in a man's shoe or ski. At the same time, the castration anxiety was related to a profound separation anxiety, indicating unresolved preoedipal separation conflicts. The loss of food or feces signified castration, but also separation and object loss. The birth of the baby was less significant as castration than as a traumatic rupture of symbiosis; her postpartum crying was an identification with the crying baby, an expression of her depression, loss, and wish for maternal care and comfort on an oral level. In contradistinction to her conscious yearnings to be a mother, following the birth of her children, she felt incomplete and alone and came to understand in the analysis her longing to be the baby united with mother, "one and inseparable, now and forever."

Awakening crying from obstetrical anesthesia was in itself emergence from a state of symbiotic sleep, a fantasy of birth and rebirth which was realized in the actual concurrent childbirth. The loss of the fantasied state of fusion and of the biological fusion of pregnancy was intolerable, and associated with severe ambivalence, aggression, and regression. She had unconscious fantasies of the destruction and desertion of the child (as an external object) associated with wishes to restore the previous narcissistic fusion. Identifying with her child, a narcissistic object, she turned her aggression on herself and felt intensely guilty, self-accusatory, and masochistic.

The ambivalent relationship to her own mother, the ambivalent splitting into idealized "good" and denigrated "bad" maternal representations, was associated with repeated transference configurations concerning birth, feeding, and separation. Initially, the first analyst was the frustrating, rejecting, devalued mother, and I was the feeding, approving, idealized mother. Global identifications with her mother appeared in

repetitive dreams when Mrs. A.'s mother gave birth to the patient's sibling who was born 2 years after the patient. This
could be dated precisely because of the events surrounding
the birth of this sibling, who had a minor congenital anomaly.
Attention was focused upon the new baby, dethroning the patient who had been the prior object of the parents' and grand-
parents' rather exclusive concern. It appeared that the
mother's pregnancy and delivery during the patient's preoedipal (anal and rapprochement) development were not related
to problems of actual physical separation from her mother,
but rather to the mother's problems and withdrawal of interest and perhaps increased maternal pressure upon the little
girl toward mature behavior in anticipation of another infant.
She magically did not allow the new baby to cry, while she was
fretful and a finicky eater. Her guilt was also related to her
unconscious fantasy that she was the cause of her sibling's
birth "injury." The patient had always felt she had to be compliant and "properly behaved" in the analysis—a transference
which she viewed ultimately as her relationship to her mother.
She could be defiant or "disrespectful" toward her mother
only when she was inebriated, and the capacity to be assertive
and to exert considerate self-interest developed slowly during
her analysis. Doubtless the mother's own anxiety and guilt
were intensified and communicated when her son's anomaly
required medical attention and repair.

Mrs. A.'s own feelings of injury and envy, her fears of aggression and attack, were disguised, and her depression and
regression, excessive clinging, crying, and complaining were
rationalized by her parents as a terrible 2-year-old stage which
she would outgrow. Her later depression, postpartum and in
response to other real or fantasied separations or object losses,
seemed to have crystallized as an enduring configuration at
the time of her sibling's birth. The anlage of the adult postpartum depression was related specifically to her mother's
pregnancy and sibling's birth. The configuration and depressive proclivity were latent during her too sober and serious
childhood, but were reactivated when she gave birth to her
own children. Becoming a mother revived not only unresolved
oedipal conflicts, but deeply regressive unresolved preoedipal

problems. Another consequence of feeling that her mother
and mother's love had been lost or devoured by the new baby
was that her deprivation entitled her to compensatory consolation, e.g., via boundless feeding and coercive dependency. In
the postpartum depression she reversed roles with the baby
who was a narcissistic self-object, and became the devouring
infant rather than the nurturant mother. Her baby represented her externalized and disavowed demanding in-
fantilism, and both her devalued self and sibling, while she
was identified with the "frustrator," a depriving and deserting
mother figure. In many disguised dreams she was pregnant
with the food she had gorged, having all the ice-cream cones,
father's penis and baby, but also mother's breasts and love for
herself. Her sibling was devoured and eliminated in fantasy,
and was an object of identification for infantile gratification
and replacement.

Despite the tremendous difficulties in (both genetic and
longitudinal) prediction, many analysts will have anticipated
that this patient had a feeding disturbance in the earliest
period of life. Mrs. A. was allergic to her mother's milk and
was rapidly weaned to a bottle in the first weeks of life. Milk
could not be found that would agree with her, and abdominal
colic persisted for the first 6 months. In addition, her rigid
mother followed the rigid feeding schedule prescribed by the
pediatrician, allowing the patient to scream between the timed
feedings. The colicky infant was relatively inconsolable and
cried protractedly. She was skinny, frail, fretful, and petulant,
and had an overconcerned, anxious mother who hovered over
her nutrition. Mrs. A.'s mother had herself been fixated on
food, and had also been very distressed during both her pregnancies with hypermesis gravidarum. This familial information about Mrs. A.'s first year of life and her mother's hypermesis gravidarum was not based upon analytic reconstruction
or derivative recollection. Strict and careful about the patient's
eating habits, the mother had bribed, cajoled, and demanded
that the patient's food be finished. Though the little girl
usually conformed with her mother's wishes, her sibling
turned the meals into altercations.

After the finicky eating of early childhood, the patient was never satisfied with her weight, always considering herself either too fat or too thin. The great tension at meals would increase as the patient attacked her food slowly and carefully, not permitting herself the pleasure of this basic gratification while unconsciously prolonging it. Early in analysis she was aware of tension in her jaws, and antecedent brauxism had probably led to dental disorder, later requiring "oral reconstruction." Her unconscious rage was related to self-reproach that simultaneously punished her mother. She constantly attempted to draw her mother's attention and interest away from the envied younger sibling, and later mine from her transference rivals. Her fear of boring me concealed her wish for my exclusive affection and love, and competition with my family and other patients. Analytic discussion was associated with feeding, and silence with deprivation.

The anxiety and rigidity that characterized the feeding relationship continued into other areas of the mother-child interaction. Toilet training for bowel and bladder was reputed to have occurred very early, possibly before 18 months. Illness and constipation were both "dangerous" and treated by enemas. Prunes adorned the breakfast table to insure regularity. All the routines of the house were carefully regulated. Early elements of transference in which the patient attempted compliance and conformity to insure my approval apparently repeated important elements of her relationship with her mother. Spanking was rare, but the withdrawal of approval and affection was an ever-present silent threat. Moreover, aggression and hostility were denied, and only loving feelings among members of the family were acknowledged during childhood despite flagrant evidence of the mother's irritation and hostility. While there was undoubtedly genuine parental affection, to some degree parental hostility was disguised as discipline for the benefit of the child. "Eating for mother," demanded of Mrs. A. in childhood, in the analysis came to represent for the patient the confused mother-child dialogue. Recalling maternal threats to have the police take her away if she did not eat, she began to understand that this early mode of communication with her mother was suffused with anxiety and hostility, submission and covert defiance. The mother as aggressor in the feeding situation reinforced the patient's ambivalence, which was symbolized in her ambivalent attitudes toward food as object and object love (A. Freud, 1946). The oral struggle was also a regressive recapitulation of fantasies of symbiosis and independence.

In childhood, her unresolved separation conflicts were associated with difficulty falling asleep. Bedtime rituals (also related to the primal scene) disappeared during a favorable adolescent disengagement from her parents and further personality consolidation. However, severe insomnia appeared when the patient first left home to go to college, marking the beginning of her adult depressive disorder. It should be noted that for the most part the depression was subclinical, the patient being regarded not as a sad, but a sober and serious child and adolescent.

The colicky, comfortless, and crying child of the early years of infancy did not reappear until she had her own infant, beginning with the immediate postpartum depression. The immediate postpartum crying was a harbinger of the depression of the first postpartum months and preceded the massive physiological changes of the first days after delivery. While I do not rule out constitutional and physiological factors,[1] the reconstruction here points to the importance of the psychological disturbance which began in the last trimester of her first pregnancy, as she anticipated motherhood. The first eating binge occurred when her husband was away and when she began to worry that she had not gained sufficient weight during the pregnancy. The thought occurred to her that she could injure the unborn baby, a disguised version of her infanticidal thoughts and her inability to be truly nurturant as

---

1. Genetic and constitutional factors might include the infantile colic and allergy, the low frustration tolerance, abnormal glucose tolerance, and metabolic lability, tendency toward mood disturbance, and other factors. The patient's strengths and inner resources doubtless were constitutionally determined, e.g., her capacity to reverse regression and efforts at reintegration. The complex determinants results in circular and cross-interactions between endowment and environment.

delivery approached. Her fears of starving herself and her infant represented a reversal of her devouring and withholding
attitudes. How could she be the mother of a separate, living,
unique individual when she wanted and dreaded to be fused
with her mother, clinging and separating, and regressively eating, rather than feeding and caring for her own infant?[2] It is
of interest that her adult problems in mothering were not
global, that there were many varied and changing areas of
"good enough" mothering, and that apart from the postpartum depression, her reactions to each of the children were different.

DISCUSSION

In this patient, the yearnings for the good mother of symbiosis
coexisted with more mature object relations, just as many
areas of archaic ego functioning coexisted with advanced and
intact ego functions. The reconstruction of the trauma surrounding her own mother's pregnancy and the birth of her
sibling during the anal phase and the rapprochement subphase of separation-individuation is consistent with the intrapsychic assessment of the patient's deficient ego strength and
other areas of positive ego development.

2. It is of interest that Freud (1892–93) provides an illuminating preanalytic description of a similar patient, successfully treated by hypnosis. It was
a case of a mother who was unable to feed her newborn baby. She had
serious postpartum psychopathology following each of three pregnancies.
The mother attempted to breast-feed, but she lost appetite and also developed insomnia. She vomited all her food and became agitated when the
baby was brought to her bedside. Freud's first intervention was a suggestion
that the patient would be able to feed the baby, and that the baby would
thrive. The patient improved, but soon relapsed. Freud's next hypnotic intervention was in a sense a remarkably intuitive interpretation. "I told the
patient that five minutes after my departure she would break out against her
family with some acrimony: what had happened to her dinner? did they
mean to let her starve? how could she feed the baby if she had nothing to
eat herself? and so on" (p. 120). The patient had been very depressed and
"furious at her inability to feed the baby" (p. 119). Freud's suggestion was an
implied acceptance of her anger and interpretation of her aggression and
wishes to be fed. His uncanny insight preceded his self-analysis.

The specific reconstruction I wish to emphasize here concerned not a shock trauma of her sibling's birth, but rather the extended strain in the mother-child relationship in the months before and after her sibling's birth when she was 2 years old. The first 18 months of life were already indicative of preceding strain in the dyadic relationship: this patient's rigid, controlling mother was intolerant of the child's aggression and regression, while the child was allergic and "hypersensitive."

The oral phase extends into and influences later development, and every developmental advance is also associated with regression. The rapprochement phase is ushered in with oral regression, revived stranger anxiety, and increased separation anxiety (McDevitt, 1975), and the preceding problems accentuated the crisis potential. The fear of loss associated with ano-urethral and early castration conflicts is also confluent. The mother's pregnancy and birth of a sibling compound the child's conflicts, and the predisposition at that time to negative affect and a basic depressive mood (Mahler, 1966). Ambivalence is intensified and clinging to and coercion of the object may be associated with strenuous efforts to protect the relationship from the child's hostility and anal sadism.

This patient's feelings of loss of maternal closeness and support, separation panic, helplessness, and "negative ambivalence" predisposed her to her adult depressive neurosis. The interference with development at this time can be conceptualized in terms of oral regression to previous oral fixations, and to anal ambivalent struggles over the loss and preservation of the fecal (narcissistic) object. The evidence also points to a protracted rapproachement crisis, with pathogenic sequelae as a clinical inference rather than as literally recapitulated in adult life or psychoanalysis.

As stated previously, it is not to be expected that earlier psychosexual phases or the process of separation-individuation will be exactly recapitulated. Structuralization, differential progression and regression, defensive and adaptive alterations occur during development. Since the process of separation-individuation is closely connected to the formation of psychic structure, early forms of object relatedness and ego states nei-

ther persist unaltered nor reappear regressively in a specific
phase organization, as occurs with libidinal drives. Instinctual
regression usually follows more regularly defined patterns
than ego regression. Highly variable regressive alternations
occur among different ego functions. The determination of
levels of regression and of ego development or deficit becomes
a much more complex task than the more limited historical
consideration of libidinal fixation and regression.

In this case, persistent transference and character configurations, the transference and genetic interpretation of dreams
and symptoms were especially valuable guides to reconstruction. At 2 years of age, the patient was in an early verbal development phase, when words were becoming important in
conjunction with gesture and affectomotor communication. It
seems reasonable to assume reciprocal identifications between
a vulnerable child and an anxious guilty mother with hypermesis gravidarum. The reenactment of the infantile trauma of
her sibling's birth may be inferred in the patient's specific
predisposition to postpartum depression. The preoedipal
traumas were also determinants of her adult acting-out tendencies (Greenacre, 1950; A. Freud, 1968; Blum, 1976). Her
preoedipal problems influenced and to some degree coexisted
with later conflicts and advanced development. The importance of preoedipal determinants of depression (e.g., narcissism, orality, aggression, loss of object love, and self-esteem)
outlined originally by Freud (1917) and Abraham (1924) are
corroborated and extended.

The analytic data also are consistent with Mahler's formulations concerning unresolved rapprochement difficulties, leaving behind a depressive basic mood, persistent anger and
overconcern which may become internalized. This is more
likely to occur with protracted, intense rapprochement crises
with persistent negative affects. The depressive proclivity may
become structuralized and, if not later resolved, reactivated in
later life. Differentiated from transient states of earlier infancy that resemble grief and sadness, the depressive affect of
rapprochement and the feeling of loss and helplessness, narcissistic vulnerability, and ambivalent strivings toward symbiosis and separation with heightened separation anxiety

suggests some preoedipal crystallization and specificity for the predisposition to neurotic depression. The outcome would be dependent upon antecedent and subsequent development, with epigenetic remodeling, and developmental transformations. In this respect, the patient's changing relationship with her father was quite significant, although not elaborated in the case report. The narcissistic injury when her sibling was born was a forerunner of her intense oedipal disappointment. She described her father as warm, devoted, and outgoing. Along with her grandmother, he was probably an alternative source of supportive nurturance, but was seductive in his play, and later withdrew from her and became more involved in activities with her sibling. Aggression toward the father was almost tolerable, but her mother was protected and idealized in Mrs. A.'s preanalytic conscious thoughts.

Tendencies toward splitting of the self and parental object representations may remain or regressively recur. In Mrs. A.'s case, excessive unneutralized aggression invested both the self and the object representations. Object constancy was not sufficiently stable to resist regression. Basic trust, confidence, and self-esteem were injured. Magical thinking, omnipotent and idealized fantasies were not sufficiently attenuated and replaced by secondary process, but a secure attachment to reality existed. The patient displayed severe separation anxiety with intense fears of and wishes for fusion, again analogous to the developmental problems of rapprochement. The 2-year-old readily regresses under stress, and is especially vulnerable during this period of psychic structuralization and rapid differentiation of ego functions.

The birth of the sibling in the second year of life heralded the loss of the throne to this princess, the partial loss of (undivided claim to) her parents, her family position, her feces, and fantasied penis. I would hypothesize that the normal danger situations of object loss and loss of love, and the depressive disposition of the rapprochement phase were reinforced by the preceding strain and the psychological stress of her sibling's birth on the patient and her parents. This appears to have led to the later crystallization of the infantile narcissistic depressive configuration.

She apparently felt lost, left, and bereft, and developed more of a negative affective state of depression rather than a defiant negativism with externalized aggression. An ambivalent dependency and exclusive possessiveness tended to persist instead of the more gradual relinquishment of claims upon the mother. Doubtless the picture was complicated by the patient's constitutional vulnerability, sensitivity, and oral fixations as well as by the lack of maternal empathy. Her yearning to re-create symbiotic omnipotence appeared to be associated with an awareness of separateness and a chronic resentment at the love objects she regarded as withholding themselves and narcissistic supplies from her.

Her hidden, repetitive, coercive, and resentful demands for contact and control were screened by characterological conformity and negative oedipal conflicts. That wishes to incorporate the penis, to have exclusive possession of mother or father, and to have babies by them may also defend against preoedipal wishes, e.g., for the breast instead of the penis, is not a revolutionary formulation. Both the oedipal and preoedipal problems require analysis, and it is an important technical issue to decide whether the transference is triadic or dyadic, how and in what form preoedipal material is to be interpreted. The patient was pessimistic with moments of despair, but never appeared to be on the verge of complete depressive collapse. There were always efforts to extract gratifications, supplies, and, on a higher ego level, interpretative understanding from the analyst.

The ambivalence and splitting of the object representation associated with the depressive mood also may have contributed to some of the superego problems observed in her adult depression. Frequent self-reproach and self-effacement were related to magical fears of retaliation, e.g., for her forbidden wishes toward her children, and earlier, her mother. The projection of her aggression contributed to the internalization of a harsh and punitive superego, while the fantastic and untamed idealization of the object led to ego ideals which demanded her impossible efforts and aspirations to be a perfect mother. The perfect and all-giving mother was the ideal omnipotent mother she wanted to have, incorporate, and become. The idealization also defended against the aggressive devaluation and envy of her mother and sibling (Kernberg, 1970). The sibling envy and rivalry contributed to her later inability to be a comforting, confident, and competent mother. She had not wanted her sibling to cry for the maternal attention that she demanded, and had wanted him taken away where he could not be heard or seen. She would be the only "crybaby." The unattenuated infantile ideals and fixation to archaic superego precursors left her with a primitive all-or-none value system which lacked perspective or proportion.

The evidence pointing to the crystallization of difficulty during this (rapprochement) developmental period is cohesive, internally consistent, and articulates with modern developmental theory and the psychoanalytic concept of depression as an affect and as a syndrome. (Consistency does of course not mean confirmation.) I do not see the material and formulations as competitive with the oedipus complex as the nucleus of neurosis or as a denigration of drive theory and the importance of the oral and anal phases of development. The process of separation-individuation does not compete with, but rather enriches and complements, psychosexual and other dimensions of developmental knowledge.

With more focus upon the drives, much more could be said about the patient's oral fixations and the constant anal struggle between retention and expulsion of the fecal narcissistic object. However, the coercive efforts to woo the object, the clinging and darting away, the awareness of helplessness and separateness, the wish to fuse and the fear of reengulfment, the splitting of the self and object representations during rapproachement are different levels of discourse than "anal ambivalence," sadism, and negativism. Autonomous ego development, libidinal phases, and the processes of separation-individuation have overlapping, but also different orientations and timetables.

An integration of rapprochement considerations with ego and drive development is desirable, and my reconstruction is not limited to this developmental period or any one developmental line (A. Freud, 1965) in isolation. This is consistent with the contemporary reconstruction of psychic organization, of ego states and development, rather than simple drive-defense constellations or single traumatic situations. The oral fixations of the patient are apparent, as they are important to the understanding of adult depression. Her basic depressive mood, fears of loss of the object and the object's love, and narcissistic vulnerability at approximately 2 years of age were probably influenced by the preceding infantile colic and feeding disturbance during the first year of life. Does the "inconsolable" crying and helpless infant with oral-phase disruption develop a proclivity toward ego depletion and depression? Mahler (1966) noted:

> We could frequently observe that the "confident expectation" (Benedek, 1938) of those toddlers who were already, whether for extrinsic or intrinsic reasons, carrying over a deficit of emotional supplies from the previous subphases was more readily depleted during the second 18 months of life. They succumbed more easily than others to an increasingly angry mood, which was interpreted by Bowlby (1960) as "continual protest." In some instances, they seemed periodically to fall prey to a desperate feeling of helpless loss (from which, however, a child usually recovers intermittently, and with relative rapidity). The intrapsychic experience of loss is compounded by the affect-laden symbolic significance of toilet training, and by the advent of the castration anxiety of the phallic phase of psychosexual development [p. 162f.].

Convergent with the increasing psychoanalytic understanding of depression (e.g., Freud, 1917; Abraham, 1924; Rado, 1927; Lewin, 1950; Bibring, 1953; Mahler, 1966; Jacobson, 1971), this material also indicates the convergence and synthesis of developmental knowledge and analytic reconstruction. Reconstruction utilizes and reciprocally influences the interpretation of analytic and developmental data.

A longitudinal survey which includes reconstruction of the patient's preoedipal problems permits an overview of the determinants and pathogenesis of adult (postpartum) depression. This patient's postpartum depressions were not discrete or isolated syndromes, but were acute manifestations of a persistent adult depressive disorder. Analysis revealed antecedent symptoms, e.g., during the last trimester of her first pregnancy, and in adolescence. The occurrence of an infantile depressive configuration and proclivity was reconstructed as a cautious approximation at the end of the second year of life, between about 20 and 28 months of age. The assignment of predisposition priority to this period rather than the first year difficulties is based upon analytic and theoretical considerations of structuralization and conflict.

During rapprochement ambivalence first appears, and intrapsychic conflicts may persist. Depression and other affects may also tend to persist in association with the child's newly developed capacity for fantasy, symbolic thought, and increasingly effective language communication. The child's sense of helplessness, separation, and narcissistic vulnerability can be correlated with the basic depressive mood (Mahler, 1966). Aggression directed toward the differentiated and well-defined object may be in conflict with superego precursors, favoring repression, reaction formation, and other defenses. The child's dependence upon the object and object's love, and both external and internal prohibitions, may foster internalization of aggression and/or splitting of aggressive and libidinal, "good and bad" object and self representations.

The presence of persistent ambivalence at this time in conjunction with loss of the now differentiated object helps explain the ego identification with the devalued worthless object and the anlage of the superego identification with the idealized omnipotently punitive object so commonly inferred in depressions (Jacobson, 1971, p. 226). This infantile period of increasing stability, consolidation of mental representations, and enduring structure and conflict significantly influences later development and the possibilities for mastery or pathogenic vulnerability (Mahler et al., 1975).

As previously stated, this patient's sensitivity to separation, object loss, and narcissistic injury was undoubtedly heightened by her earlier oral-phase problems. But the oral fixation per se does not explain her relatively intact ego, and the level of differentiated, albeit still narcissistic, object representation and relatedness she achieved. Her oral character and lifelong oral preoccupation, with hidden oral dependence and rage, imperative and devouring demands, is readily discerned. The understanding of her oral and aggressive conflicts in relation to her level of ego function and recapitulation of loss of a relatively well-defined object requires consideration of ego development and the process of separation-individuation.

The oral phase precedes, but contributes to, character formation. Many adult "oral characters" have different overall personality structures, and much depends on which defenses are later mobilized, and the parallel ego development. These issues involve fixation and regression, and also illustrate the importance of epigenesis, with preceding phase influence, later reorganization, and possible transformation on new developmental levels. In this case depressive tendencies and a basic depressive mood developed (at about 24 months), but many fascinating questions remain concerning earlier and later determinants of depression.

The meaning of loss, separation, and depression undergoes defensive and developmental changes, and is expressed and experienced differently at different phases of life. Given the complexities of development and structuralization, there are probably no simple infantile prototypes of adult depression, and later influences are very important. In analysis, the progressive influence of the working through of reconstructed material on new levels of development and ego synthesis can be observed. The reconstruction of preoedipal precursors of postpartum depression is significant not only for therapy, but for the testing and integration of new theoretical concepts of depression.

Summary

Postpartum depression is a common and very important disorder with implications for the mother-child relationship and maternal adaptation. Postpartum depression is not a discrete and circumscribed entity, but a symptom of an underlying preexistent disturbance. In the case described, the patient was a depressive character with masked depression before and between the acute postpartum depressions, and with related symptoms of appetite and sleep disturbance and addictive tendencies. While constitutional and somatic factors were doubtless involved, the case illustrates the importance of psychogenesis with depressive predisposition.

Reconstruction is a valuable therapeutic tool, but is also valuable in the testing and integration of new data and theory. Analytic reconstruction uncovered the presence of a preoedipal depressive configuration which developed during the period just before and after her sibling's birth when she was 2 years old. The reconstruction highlighted the role of this persistent infantile depressive configuration and predisposition, crystallizing during the anal phase and rapprochement subphase of separation-individuation. An intense negative ambivalence and depressive basic mood developed, associated with oral regression.

Developmental and analytic data also indicated significant oral fixation and oral-phase disorder. These formulations are consistent with classical psychoanalytic contributions to the theory of depression. The data articulate with and are illuminated by contemporary analytic theory, and point to the role of preoedipal influences on the oedipus complex, as well as superego and character formation. As anticipated by Freud and A. Freud, the utilization of both analytic and developmental data obtained from direct infant observation potentiates the investigation of early development and pathogenesis.

BIBLIOGRAPHY

ABRAHAM, K. (1924), A Short Study of the Development of the Libido: Part I. In: *Selected Papers*. London: Hogarth Press, 1949, pp. 418–480.

ASCH, S. & RUBIN, L. (1974), Postpartum Reactions. *Amer. J. Psychiat.*, 131 : 870–874.

BENEDEK, T. F. (1956), Toward the Biology of the Depressive Constellation. *J. Amer. Psychoanal. Assn.*, 4 : 389–427.

BENTAL, V. (1965), Psychic Mechanisms of the Adoptive Mother in Connection with Adoption. *Israel Ann. Psychiat.*, 3 : 24–34.

BIBRING, E. (1953), The Mechanism of Depression. In: *Affective Disorders*, ed. P. Greenacre. New York: Int. Univ. Press, pp. 13–48.

BLUM, H. (1976), Masochism, the Ego Ideal, and the Psychology of Women. *J. Amer. Psychoanal. Assn.*, 24(5) : 157–192.

——— (1977), The Prototype of Preoedipal Reconstruction. *J. Amer. Psychoanal. Assn.*, 25 : 757–786.

EKSTEIN, R. & RANGELL, L. (1961), Reconstruction and Theory Formation. *J. Amer. Psychoanal. Assn.,* 9 : 684–697.

FREUD, A. (1946), The Psychoanalytic Study of Infantile Feeding Disturbances. *This Annual,* 2 : 119–132.

——— (1968), Acting Out. *Int. J. Psycho-Anal.,* 49 : 165–170.

FREUD, S. (1892–93), A Case of Successful Treatment by Hypnotism. *S.E.,* 1 : 115–128.

——— (1917), Mourning and Melancholia. *S.E.,* 14 : 217–258.

GREENACRE, P. (1950), General Problems of Acting Out. *Psychoanal. Quart.,* 19 : 455–467.

——— (1967), The Influence of Infantile Trauma on Genetic Patterns. In: *Psychic Trauma,* ed. S. S. Furst. New York: Basic Books, pp. 108–153.

——— (1968), The Psychoanalytic Process, Transference, and Acting Out. *Int. J. Psycho-Anal.,* 49 : 211–218.

——— (1975), On Reconstruction. *J. Amer. Psychoanal. Assn.,* 23 : 693–712.

HAMILTON, J. (1962), *Postpartum Psychiatric Problems.* St. Louis: Mosby.

JACOBSON, E. (1971), *Depression.* New York: Int. Univ. Press.

KANZER, M. & BLUM, H. (1967), Classical Psychoanalysis since 1939. In: *Psychoanalytic Techniques,* ed. B. B. Wolman. New York: Basic Books, pp. 93–146.

KERNBERG, O. F. (1970), Factors in the Psychoanalytic Treatment of Narcissistic Personalities. *J. Amer. Psychoanal. Assn.,* 18 : 51–85.

KRIS, E. (1956), The Recovery of Childhood Memories in Psychoanalysis. *J. Amer. Psychoanal. Assn.,* 11 : 54–88.

LEWIN, B. D. (1950), *The Psychoanalysis of Elation.* New York: Norton.

MAHLER, M. S. (1966), Notes on the Development of Basic Moods. In: *Psychoanalysis—A General Psychology,* ed. R. M. Loewenstein, L. M. Newman, M. Schur, & A. J. Solnit. New York: Int. Univ. Press, pp. 152–168.

——— PINE, F., & BERGMAN, A. (1975), *The Psychological Birth of the Human Infant.* New York: Basic Books.

MELGES, F. (1968), Postpartum Psychiatric Syndromes. *Psychosom. Med.,* 30 : 95–108.

McDEVITT, J. B. (1975), Separation-Individuation and Object Constancy. *J. Amer. Psychoanal. Assn.,* 23 : 713–742.

NOVEY, S. (1968), *The Second Look.* Baltimore: Johns Hopkins Univ. Press.

PUGH, T. F., JERATH, B. K., REED, R. B., & SCHMIDT, W. M. (1963), Rates of Mental Disease Related to Childbearing. *New Eng. J. Med.,* 268 : 1224–1228.

RADO, S. (1927), The Problem of Melancholia. *Int. J. Psycho-Anal.,* 9 : 420–438, 1928.

SOLNIT, A. J. & STARK, M. (1961), Mourning and the Birth of a Defective Child. *This Annual,* 16 : 523–537.

ZILBOORG, G. (1957), The Clinical Issues of Postpartum Psychopathological Reactions. *Amer. J. Obst. & Gyn.,* 73 : 305–312.

Dream Experience,
Analytic Experience

A Point of View on Psychoanalytic Technique

CHARLES I. FEIGELSON, M.D.

THE THEORY OF PSYCHOANALYTIC TECHNIQUE IS BASED ON THE psychoanalytic theory of neurosis. The latter guides our technical work. We interpret defenses, we interpret what is defended against, we interpret the reasons for the defense. In so doing we underscore for the patient all sides of his mental conflict. This is the classical psychoanalytic approach with which we are all familiar.

The thesis of my paper is consistent with this approach, though I will not discuss issues of impulse, defense, and conflict. What I will discuss has to do with making the issues of impulse, defense, and conflict meaningful to the patient in his experience of the psychoanalytic situation. It involves the analyst's way of working with his patient. Specifically, it involves what might be called "training" the patient to be in psychoanalysis. By "training" I mean the analyst's focusing upon and enlarging the patient's capacity for self-observation and self-reporting. The beginning of this training is in the analyst's attitude toward himself during the analytic work. Freud (1912) writes:

Faculty, New York Psychoanalytic Institute.
This paper was presented to the Freudian Society, New York, in April 1972.

> The technique . . . is a very simple one . . . it rejects the use of any special expedient (even that of taking notes). It consists simply in not directing one's notice to anything in particular and in maintaining the same 'evenly-suspended attention' (as I have called it) in the face of all that one hears. In this way we spare ourselves a strain on our attention which could not in any case be kept up for several hours daily, and we avoid a danger which is inseparable from the exercise of deliberate attention. For as soon as anyone deliberately concentrates his attention to a certain degree, he begins to select from the material before him; one point will be fixed in his mind with particular clearness and some other will be correspondingly disregarded, and in making this selection he will be following his expectations or inclinations. This, however, is precisely what must not be done. In making the selection, if he follows his expectations he is in danger of never finding anything but what he already knows; and if he follows his inclinations he will certainly falsify what he may perceive. It must not be forgotten that the things one hears are for the most part things whose meaning is only recognized later on. . . .
>
> It will be seen that the rule of giving equal notice to everything is the necessary counterpart to the demand made on the patient that he should communicate everything that occurs to him without criticism or selection [p. 111f.].
>
> To put it in a formula: he [the analyst] must turn his own unconscious like a receptive organ towards the transmitting unconscious of the patient. He must adjust himself to the patient as a telephone receiver is adjusted to the transmitting microphone. Just as the receiver converts back into sound waves the electric oscillations in the telephone line which were set up by sound waves, so the doctor's unconscious is able, from the derivatives of the unconscious which are communicated to him, to reconstruct that unconscious, which has determined the patient's free associations [p. 115f.].

Freud's recommendation to the analyst through the principle of evenly suspended attention is that the analyst should allow himself to observe his own mental processes as well as his patients'. In doing this, the analyst begins to train or educate his patient to be in analysis.

Formally, when a patient begins analysis, he is given instructions in the "fundamental rule." For most analysts, this has come to mean that the analyst tells the patient he should say "whatever comes to your mind." Taken literally, this is quite correct. In usage, however, this means to most people that they should tell all their thoughts. Since it is not just the realm of thought and idea that interests us, I believe that we misguide our patients in telling them to say "whatever comes to your mind."

We are interested in getting the patient to observe and report his mental processes as they are happening; to tell us from moment to moment what is happening in his mind; to continue reporting his mental experiences while he is on the couch. This is the analytic experience. It includes ideas and thoughts, but not *only* ideas and thoughts. It includes perceptions of emotions or their absence, daydreams, night dreams, bodily feelings or sensations, visual images, and so forth.

In introducing the patient to the fundamental rule, I believe it is very important that we also introduce the patient to the variety of mental experiences that can be observed. He should be told that he is to tell about all those types of mental experience as he observes or experiences them. This is free association, as I conceive of it.

In the analysis of children, who are not capable of either free association or self-reflective introspection, we try to evoke communication of their intense experiences by offering them opportunities for role playing and for other appropriate playroom activities with toys and games, according to the child's developmental interests and tolerances. In early adolescence, introspection and the free-association processes begin to be available in a dependable way (A. Freud, 1965), but the analyst continues to help his adolescent patients to come closer to a genuine free-association experience as the analytic process unfolds. While these developmental considerations have always been applied to the psychoanalytic treatment of children and adolescents, I believe we have not paid sufficient attention to the ways in which the analyst treating adult patients must throughout an analysis foster the patient's capacities to pursue the details of his experiences in free association.

In analytic work the productions of the patient are seen as derivatives of unconscious processes. Visual images are derivatives that are nearer to the unconscious processes than affectless ideas. The immediate mental experience of the analysand on the couch is nearer to the unconscious processes than a logical rendition of events from the day before yesterday. The closest example of the clinical usefulness of the analysand's immediate experience is in the insight gained from analysis of the transference.

The royal road for his "sound waves" to travel is through a description of his immediate experiences on the couch. This is the seldom-reached, but ideal condition for analytic work to proceed.

Freud (1900) compared self-observation with free association when he wrote:

> I have noticed in my psycho-analytical work that the whole frame of mind of a man *who is reflecting is totally different* from that of a man who is *observing his own psychical processes* [my italics]. In reflection there is one more psychical activity at work than in the most attentive self-observation, and this is shown amongst other things by the tense looks and wrinkled forehead of a person pursuing his reflections compared with the restful expression of a self-observer. In both cases attention must be concentrated, but the man who is reflecting is also exercising his *critical* faculty; this leads him to reject some of the ideas that occur to him after perceiving them, to cut short others without following the trains of thought which they would open up to him, and to behave in such a way towards others that they never become conscious at all and are accordingly suppressed before they are perceived. The self-observer on the other hand need only take the trouble to suppress his critical faculty. If he succeeds in doing that, innumerable ideas come into his consciousness of which he could otherwise never have got hold. The material which is in this way freshly obtained for his self-perception makes it possible to interpret both his pathological ideas and his dream-structures [p. 101f.].

I ask you now to shift your mobile attention from Freud to Camus, to a passage from *The Stranger* (1942) that beautifully illustrates the quality of experience conveyed when a man is attentively observing himself and reporting his perceptions. It is from the scene on the beach just before he murders the Arab.

> There was the same red glare as far as the eye could reach, and small waves were lapping the hot sand in little, flurried gasps. As I slowly walked toward the boulders at the end of the beach I could feel my temples swelling under the impact of the light. It pressed itself on me, trying to check my progress. And each time I felt a hot blast strike my forehead, I gritted my teeth, I clenched my fists in my trouser pockets and keyed up every nerve to fend off the sun and the dark befuddlement it was pouring into me. Whenever a blade of vivid light shot upward from a bit of shell or broken glass lying on the sand, my jaws set hard . . . the heat was beginning to scorch my cheeks; beads of sweat were gathering in my eyebrows. It was just the same sort of heat as at my mother's funeral, and I had the same disagreeable sensations—especially in my forehead, where all the veins seemed to be bursting through the skin . . . at the same moment all the sweat that had accumulated in my eyebrows splashed down on my eyelids, covering them with a warm film of moisture. Beneath a veil of brine and tears my eyes were blinded; I was conscious only of the cymbals of the sun clashing on my skull, and, less distinctly, of the keen blade of light flashing up from the knife, scarring my eyelashes and gouging into my eyeballs [p. 73].

Were this man on the couch reporting as he does his self-observations, we would recognize his behavior as "free associations" of the type that makes him eminently analyzable. The passage I chose from *The Stranger* illustrates a moment-to-moment account of an intense psychic experience. The book actually conveys the life experience of a man who is detached and emotionally uninvolved. When I speak of conveying the analytic experience, I do not necessarily mean feelings. I mean experience, and that experience, as in *The Stranger,* can mean the experience of absence of feeling.

Patients must be helped, trained in self-observation. Were the protagonist of *The Stranger* to report his experience, "It was terribly hot, 90 degrees in the shade, I felt like I was going berserk," it would be reasonable for the analyst to point out to him that such feelings involve intense inner experiences, perhaps he could try to describe what he actually noticed going on in himself. Patients differ greatly in their capacity for self-observation. I believe that those who do it best, either naturally or with the help of their analyst, are the patients who benefit most from analysis.

Dreams are of special importance in fostering self-observation by patients. When a patient reports a dream as if he is telling a story about someone, little will come from it analytically. For dreams to become optimally meaningful the patient and analyst together must attempt to re-create the experience of the dreamer as he dreamed the dream. Few patients will do this spontaneously, and achieving this experience requires the interest of the analyst as well as his awareness of its importance. A dream dryly told without re-creating the dream experience is like a rose under glass. One can see it, but the touch and smell, those qualities that make it alive, are lost.

We are all accustomed to asking about day residues that may have stimulated a dream. We ask for associations to given parts of the dream. These efforts will be more effective when both dreamer and analyst are "into" the patient's dream experience.

Lewin (1946) describes the analytic experience which led him to formulate the dream screen concept:

> The dream screen came to my notice when a young woman patient reported [from the couch] as follows: 'I had a dream all ready for you; but while I was lying here looking at it, it turned over away from me, rolled up, and rolled away from me—over and over like two tumblers.' She repeated the description several times at my request, so that I could substantiate the gist of her experience, namely, that the dream screen with the dream on it bent over backwards away from her, and then like a carpet or canvas rolled up and off into the distance with the rotary motion of machine tumblers [p. 420].

I use this example for it is one of the classics in the analytic literature where the lively contact between patient and her dream experience is illustrated, followed by the analyst's successful efforts to enter this experience with the patient and experience her dream as she did. Lewin emphasized his effort to "substantiate the gist of her [dream] experience."

An adult male patient of mine had begun to talk about masturbatory conflicts. He reported the following dream: "I was climbing a mountain feeling fearful that I might fall off. There was a child in front of me, I was pushing him up the mountain." My own immediate associations had to do with his pushing something in front of him in his masturbation. Yet, the visual picture of the dream was unclear to me and I asked him to visualize the dream image of pushing the boy up the mountain and describe the visual picture. To this he responded by saying that he held his hand snugly on the boy's rear end and was pushing him up like that. Then his associations trailed off into thoughts leading to conflicts over anal masturbation. It was my question asking him to visualize his dream image that helped him first to re-create the dream experience and finally, from this, the anal masturbation.

Re-creation of the dream experience is not synonymous with "getting at the feelings." The experience may involve the feeling, or it may not. The dream experience refers literally to the way the dream was experienced. Usually this is a visual experience; therefore training the patient to revisualize the dream helps him to recapture the experience. That experience may involve an absence of feeling so that the experience would be an absence of feeling; the experience may be auditory, it may involve tactile sensations, and so forth. It is important to differentiate between "the feeling" and "the experience."

Another patient, a man in his early 20s, had been a long-distance runner in middle and late adolescence. Pressures of college and other obligations had forced him to give up the running. During the second year of his analysis he began to "smoke dope" heavily. This posed a rather formidable resistance to the analysis of certain passive trends in his personality. Exploration of the experience he had while smoking—my asking him to describe directly what he experienced—helped to focus his attention on its psychological meaning. He described how, when stoned, "I follow my thoughts, kind of a euphoric feeling, tension free, thoughts roll over one another and next day I don't remember them."

One day he presented the following dream: "I was out running and I was moving in a controlled and powerful way. A couple of guys started to run with me. I was rounding a curve and a guy comes up and says he's going to have trouble beating me. I go by him and win the race."

As the patient told the dream, I recalled the times when he had described his running in the past and felt that something was missing from his dream experience as he told the dream. I asked him if he could go back to the dream and describe his experience of it. He said, "I was out running in a controlled, powerful way. A couple of guys started to run with me. I was rounding a curve and had that good feeling in my body— feeling real g-o-o-d! A guy comes up and says he's going to have trouble beating me. I feel down. Then I feel the 'lift' as I go by him, a kind of good feeling throughout my body, like riding up on an elevator." As he talked about the "experience" of the dream, he became aware of sensations he had experienced in getting "heavily stoned" just before going to sleep. It became clear to him and to me, through this dream experience, that the experience of running and of smoking were very similar. This insight enabled us to see that the smoking had come to serve the same function for him that running had in the past. A rather formidable resistance in the analysis, the smoking, was beginning to give way and, indeed, the weeks of analysis following this bore analytic fruits.

Isakower (1938) quotes a patient as saying:

> When I'm feverish, I get a curious sensation in my palate—I can't describe it. Yesterday I noticed it when I was going to sleep, although I wasn't feverish. At the same time I have a feeling as if I were on a revolving disc. Giddiness and a kind of general discomfort. It's as if I were lying on something crumpled, but this crumpled feeling's in my mouth at the same time; the whole thing begins in the palate—*I can almost feel it now when I think of it* [my italics]. I've had it fairly often,

especially as a child. I feel as if I were lying on a crumpled cloth which is winding itself round; the crumpled object isn't under me, like a crumpled sheet, but round me and it's disagreeable [p. 331f.].

Hearing these descriptions, and finally seeing a patient fall into such a state during her analytic hour where it was reported by the patient as her analytic experience, Isakower was led to the formulation of the concept of a phenomenon which now bears his name.

I now turn to a slice of analysis drawn from the lengthy analysis of a male homosexual patient. It begins following his first heterosexual experience. He was 34 years old and in his third year of analysis. The material presented describes a regressive experience whose analysis was effective—primarily because of the patient's ability to describe both dream and analytic experience so that interpretation and working through resulted in conviction.

The patient described his first heterosexual experience, which was with a prostitute. He felt somewhat removed from the experience, and it was not particularly enjoyable to him. Though he had thought he would be elated at having had a successful heterosexual experience, he was surprised to find himself somewhat depressed. Following the sexual experience he had a dream: "I was in a Spanish-style house; there was a room which had cracked walls like the canvas had been torn away. It was like a room that I canvassed for my mother; it was wet and moist." As he described the wet, moist sensations, he began to experience them. This suddenly reminded him of the feeling of his penis in the woman's vagina, and he commented, somewhat surprised, that though he had felt this during intercourse, he had not actually allowed an awareness of that feeling. Also, in this room, there were feces coming out of the cracked walls. Walking around in this Spanish house was the Pope; he was a benevolent Pope, and the patient used the word "district" in referring to the Pope's areas of jurisdiction, and felt in his dream that he was being somewhat irreverent to the Pope. There was also a tiny bull lodged in some concrete or cement, and it had shiny golden horns, and he talked about the horns representing penises, he thought, and about the damage that they could do. I commented on how it seemed to him that the sexual experience which he had had was like a bullfight, and that his precious golden horns would be dirtied by the woman's dirty crack. He responded to this by wondering who would be the bull and who would be the matador; he felt that the woman had the position of advantage and that it was she who would be the matador and his anxiety must be that he might be killed. It was the experience of wet and moist which came to him as part of his dream experience that helped him to know that his dream had to do with his sexual experience. It lent conviction to the interpretation of the dream.

Several days later the patient had a dream in which he had a cut behind the ear. He was not able to associate to this directly, though he later recalled a memory, which he had already reported in the analysis, about his having a mastoid or some kind of ear operation when he was a very tiny child, and that it was done in the kitchen of his home.

For a few days he expressed feelings of defiance of me, and was somewhat discouraged about the analysis and felt that I was demanding too much of him. He then reported a dream: "I was sitting in a chair like your chair here in the office, only it seemed like it was in a classroom, and I was sitting there in a hat like yours and an overcoat and longjohns." He started talking about the dream and remembered a classroom in which he had been when he was 7 or 8, when he, together with a few other boys, had stolen some cherries. He began talking about one of these boys and about how this boy would step on anybody to get what he wanted. I interpreted to him that it seemed like after he had a heterosexual experience, he felt that he was stealing something and taking my place, as evidenced by his sitting in my chair and wearing my hat. He dealt with this intellectually, but it did not seem to mean a great deal to him.

During the following days he reported that he was in an apprehensive mood, that he felt danger was imminent, but he could not really describe the feeling further. He said that even in the waiting room he had felt very apprehensive—he had some valuable things in his overcoat, and he stewed about whether he should hang them in the closet or bring them into the office and drape them over the patient's chair. This was actually what he had done, and I reminded him of his wearing an overcoat and sitting in my chair in the dream. Here dream experience became analytic experience. He responded to this by saying that he had no angry feelings toward his father, and spoke rather timidly of his love for his father. Most of his associations in this context had to do with his being a little boy. He spoke about how in the waiting room, on the way out from the previous session, he had felt he wanted to be near my things, like a child who wanted to be near his toys and be comforted by them. He spoke about having seen a movie which upset him very much; it was about a little girl who was away from her father and who "was too excited to handle her feelings by herself." Following this he had a homosexual experience. He talked about how he had felt hot and flushed and extremely anxious and even without any sexual desire, but he had felt compelled to go cruising. In the sexual experience he penetrated his partner rectally, and said he felt like his penis made him continuous with his partner, as if they were one. He had had a feeling of relief afterward, and voiced to himself the feeling of enormous impotence he had had before the cruising experience. Prior to that he had felt, he said, "like a soft, amorphous mass of clay covered with fatty tissue without arms or legs," and in the sexual experience somehow he was strengthened. He recalled how often on Saturday afternoon his father would sit listening to the opera, and he would sit with his head against his father's leg. This brought to his mind that he had the other day been in the ten-cent store near my office and had seen some stuffed animals and said he was mad, crazy for them; he felt he just wanted to grab them and hold them, particularly a very large stuffed animal snake. The waiting room experience of wanting to be near my things and be comforted by them, and the feeling of being continuous with his homosexual partner which gave relief from his experiencing himself as "a soft, amorphous mass of clay with fatty tissue without arms or legs," led him to the memory of sitting against his father's leg. He knew from within and with conviction that leaning on his father's leg as a child gave him a feeling of being strengthened and that this was one determinant of his homosexuality.

He accepted his passivity when it related to his feeling like a little boy. It became intolerable to him when he touched on his feminine identification. He told the following dream: "I was seeing you and someone who was your wife in a bedroom, and it seemed to be that I had to walk through the waiting room of your office and by some bathroom—you wanted me to go with you and we went down on the street and I was wearing my cruising clothes. You asked me to go with you and I said 'No' and turned to go and as I turned I tripped. In the second part of the dream I was wearing a business suit and I saw a very masculine-looking man on the street. I tripped him and began to ferociously beat him. The man had a brace on one leg, but as I beat him I no longer noticed the brace." The patient recognized the latter part of the dream as an experience he very often had when he went cruising after leaving the office. From his associations to the first part of the dream I interpreted to him that he felt like a little boy in relation to me, and that he had to ward off his passive wishes toward me by becoming the active one, beating another man. He responded by telling me about being tripped, and how that reminded him of a custom in a small Italian town, where the women, in their confessions to the priest, would refer to having had extramarital affairs as "having tripped." He himself realized the implication of his identification with the woman, and became extremely irritable and hostile toward me.

About this time his law partner went on a trip to Europe. The patient's associations pointed to his feeling that with his partner gone he had "no balls." Earlier in the analysis there had been indications that he tended to regard the partner as the masculine side of the firm. He drifted for several days in a state of extreme irritability and agonizing passivity and repeatedly expressed his hostility toward me and accused me of being inadequate. This reminded him of how in certain situations he saw his father as being so weak vis-à-vis his mother. Then he had a dream where he was in the office, but had rearranged the office and was lying on the couch so that I was sitting on one side of him and another man sitting on the other side. The man on the other side of him was saying to him that he should not have an analysis, that he did not deserve it because of what he did. The patient's associations to this man led him to thoughts about his mother. His associations to what he did led him to a past cruising experience in which he had been very sadistic toward his partner, in thought more than in action. He said that in the dream he turned to me, that I would be the one who would protect him from this overwhelming threat coming from the other person, and he felt quite sure that I was his father (an inadequate one) and the other person was his mother.

A few days later the patient was tempted to do something that was quite uncharacteristic of him. He was on his way to a meeting in connection with his work and stopped at a public bathroom where he was strongly tempted to go down on someone himself. This was uncharacteristic in two respects: he did not usually put himself in such jeopardy and bring his homosexuality so close to his work; and it was only recently that he had become aware of how strongly he wanted to go down on somebody rather than have the other person go down on him. The evening after he had been tempted to seduce somebody in a public bathroom and go down on him there, he had the following dream: he was seated in a chair at his desk in his office, looking at some pornographic pictures, which may have been men or women, and masturbating, and his penis was erect; a man and woman came in and caught him doing it. He felt extremely humiliated in the dream and became overwhelmingly helpless, trying to convince them that he wasn't really doing it when they obviously could see that he was. This dream led him back to the temptation he had felt and eventually to an experience he had had as an adolescent: he was looking at some pictures of nude women when his sister and a girlfriend came into the room, and he became overwhelmingly embarrassed and afraid that he would be humiliated. What emerged here was not only his fear of being humiliated by a woman, but some need to be humiliated which he seemed to be acting out. He talked about the fear that he had always had about going to see a woman—that she would tease him if he was not able to perform well sexually. During the next few days, he continued with this theme, which led to his fear of showing himself to a woman, his fear of exposing himself to a woman because the woman would let the men know that he was either impotent or homosexual. This reminded him of the usual way that his mother would threaten him at home by saying that she was going to tell his father.

On the day that the patient's partner returned from Europe, the patient began talking about his recently having had heterosexual fantasies, but whenever he began to have one it was replaced by a homosexual fantasy. He also said that he felt very reluctant to tell me about these fantasies, feeling that I would belittle him, much as he had been belittled in the dream. He spoke a good deal about thoughts of punishment. Following a session in which he had talked a lot about punishment, I met him in the lobby of my office building, where he was meeting a woman. He seemed somewhat upset about meeting me and about my seeing him meeting this woman. The following day he told me that he had felt enormously guilty that he had not mentioned this; he also had the feeling that he was taking something away from me in meeting that woman there, even though it was not a date but just a mutual friend whom he was taking to someone's home. He talked on about his feeling that he was taking something from me. I interpreted to him that he seemed to feel that there could only be one man who could have a woman; and if he met one, then that meant to him that he was taking something from me. Again, the analytic experience, arranging to meet the woman, and the subsequent guilt in relation to me helped the patient to deep emotional insight. His live experience of guilt in the transference left no doubt in his mind that, to him, having a woman meant to be against me. In technical terms, we call this oedipal guilt.

He became very passive in response to this interpretation until I reminded him of how, following his first heterosexual experience, he had had a dream in which he was sitting in my chair and wearing my hat as if he were replacing me. He started to talk and burst into tears, saying that there was something that he had not told me: that when he was in Italy in the army, when he was 24, he had gone to see a prostitute and attempted to have sexual intercourse; it would have been his first heterosexual experience, but he was impotent with her. Following this experience he went back to his apartment where a few hours later he received a telegram that his father had died. There was an enormous outburst of crying and guilt on the couch. I pointed out to him how, since he had already had the fantasy that his being heterosexual would kill his father, this reality coincidence had strongly reinforced this fantasy, even to the point of his believing that he had killed his father.

He talked about this for several sessions, saying that he had experienced an enormous feeling of relief and that he felt that there had even been some qualitative change in his fantasy life since he had had heterosexual fantasies and had felt sexually excited by them. He made a date to go to see the prostitute again; before going there, his associations had to do with his need not to look at a woman, which was related to his avoidance of looking at her genital. He was able to have intercourse with the prostitute. When he left her, he felt that it was not a very satisfactory experience, that he wanted to have sexual relations with somebody he cared for. He was rather dejected and depressed and felt somewhat reluctant to tell me about the experience. This was interpreted as his difficulty in showing his father that he had any heterosexual feelings because of the enormous guilt he felt toward his father and his fear of punishment. In this context I interpreted to him that it was for this reason that he could not allow himself to be pleased.

Prior to the heterosexual experience but after he had told me about the coincidence of his visiting a prostitute around the time of his father's death, the patient brought up some new material concerning his father. At one time during the war his father had illegally bought meat and then had felt the need to call up the meat house from which the meat had been stolen and complain that his meat order had not been delivered. After talking about this, the patient felt that he had to make up for it by telling some lie on the couch to make his father appear in a good light, but make himself feel bad since he was telling the lie. I interpreted this as his need to make himself feel worse so that he could not be in a position to feel critical of his father. He said, "I had to make myself a bigger crook than he was." The interpretation was almost redundant. He had experienced it and knew it from his analytic experience. He then talked about a memory of his father's having dragged a drunk woman out of the store (the woman had blocked the doorway by lying down in it) and the father had been somewhat rough with her. He was talking about this in a critical tone, about how rough his father had been. I interpreted that he seemed to feel that if he were to be like his father, he would have to be rough in his mind and sadistic and do illegal things; and that we also knew that having heterosexual interests was illegal because it meant replacing his father.

The patient's ability to describe his immediate experience had made me optimistic about the outcome of his analysis. This optimism proved to be warranted. Following the working through of the material presented, he became functionally heterosexual and developed a capacity for a satisfying relationship with a woman. He married and terminated his analysis, which had lasted 6 years.

SUMMARY

Beginning with our goal—that we analyze to make that which is unconscious conscious—I stated that the productions of our patients are to be seen as derivatives of unconscious processes. Certain derivatives, such as accounts of "things that happened yesterday," are important to the analysis, but can be understood as derivatives more distant from the unconscious than a description of that which is happening now "on the couch"; the nearer the derivatives, the more clearly can conflicts be seen and worked with in a way that achieves conviction. With this in mind, I emphasized the importance of educating the patient to a way of free association that includes self-observation of his experiences. This training of the patient, however, is not confined to the beginning phases of an analysis. It is a continuous process in which the analyst helps the patient to describe his dream and analytic experience in detail.

BIBLIOGRAPHY

CAMUS, A. (1942), *The Stranger,* tr. Stuart Gilbert. New York: Alfred A. Knopf, 1962.

FREUD, A. (1965), Normality and Pathology in Childhood. *W.,* 6.

FREUD, S. (1900), The Interpretation of Dreams. *S.E.,* 4 & 5.

——— (1912), Recommendations to Physicians Practising Psycho-Analysis. *S.E.,* 12 : 109–120.

ISAKOWER, O. (1938), A Contribution to the Patho-Psychology of Phenomena Associated with Falling Asleep. *Int. J. Psycho-Anal.,* 19 : 331–345.

LEWIN, B. D. (1946), Sleep, the Mouth and the Dream Screen. *Psychoanal. Quart.,* 15 : 419–434.

The Mother's Eye

For Better and for Worse

ANNELIESE RIESS, Ph.D.

Thou hidest thy face, they are troubled.
PSALM 104, VERSE 29

What overwhelmed me were the terrible blue eyes. . .
by which I was reduced to nothing.
FREUD (1900, p. 422)

THIS PAPER INTENDS TO EXAMINE THE NATURE AND SIGNIFICANCE of eye-to-eye contact in the mother-child dyad and to consider its potential contribution to later pathology, as seen in several adult patients.

Eye-to-eye contact is one of the essential elements in human encounters. It gives nonverbal advance notice, so to speak, of the other, even when he is unknown to us. Its absence in the blind causes us discomfort and feelings of loss of direction. Even in animals, looking at and estimating the other set the stage for what follows in their encounter. Recent studies found that animals use eye-to-eye contact as one means of establishing dominance in the group. The leader of the pack stares his challenger down into submission (Schaller, 1963). Mythology, literature, folklore, and colloquial language have always understood and conveyed the powerful effect of mu-

Formerly Assistant Clinical Professor, Department of Psychiatry, Albert Einstein College of Medicine, New York. At present Adjunct Associate Professor, City College, City University of New York.

tual gazing behavior in its potential positive and negative sense, i.e., in its life-enhancing and life-threatening properties. "Throwing loving glances" at another person or "falling in love at first sight" expresses one extreme of these general human experiences, while the killing face of Medusa and the feared effect of the "evil eye" describe the other extreme. "Seeing eye to eye" on something and "if looks could kill" are additional sayings which stress the impact of reciprocal eye contact in a direct and in a metaphorical sense. All seem to be emotionally charged and speak to the nature of the interpersonal event.

The global and powerful role of eye-to-eye contact in human relations and its expression in the cultural heritage of language and myth suggest origins deeply rooted in common and universal experiences of humanity. In recent decades eye-to-eye contact has become a subject of scientific investigation. One avenue of research has been a developmental approach. These studies focus on the early phases of eye contact between mother and child as one major aspect of their evolving emotional interaction. As a result mutual gazing behavior between infant and mother has been found to elucidate increasingly the important contribution of the visual mode of communication to the forging of preverbal affective ties. In addition, the nature, frequency, and intensity of the mother's wish for eye contact with her child have been shown to be to a large extent a function of her own emotional state, which is in turn influenced by the infant's responsiveness to her (Spitz and Wolf, 1946; Stern, 1971; Robson, 1967). This visual feedback system carries within it the potential of mutual gratification as well as frustration. Since it begins to form within the first hours of life, it can be expected to have a strong bearing on the quality of the growing mother-infant attachment (Klaus and Kennel, 1976). Nor is it unreasonable to expect that it may also leave "visual" traces in the child's personality development—that is, a proneness to pleasures, disturbances, or conflicts experienced and expressed in the visual mode.

Psychoanalysis from its very inception has shown an interest in "looking" behavior and its pathological ramifications. Scoptophilia, voyeurism, and exhibitionism, symptomatic phenomena such as hysterical blindness and compulsive looking, as well as eye-related mythological stories of Oedipus, Medusa, and the Cyclops were explored with the investigative tools of psychoanalysis (Freud, 1910; Abraham, 1913). In the case of patients with eye-related problems, their verbalizations, memories, dreams, and transferences were the raw material from which the events of their childhood, real and imaginary, were reconstructed. The source of their pathology was usually understood to be unconscious, unresolved conflicts originating in the phallic phase. The phallic child is a youngster in full command of language and has a nearly complete psychic structure, necessary preconditions for the formation of neurosis. The case of Little Hans (Freud, 1909) is an illustration of this point. Much less was known at that time about the early formation of psychic structure, hence about the development and the object relations of the preverbal child whose past could not be readily reconstructed. Many of the missing parts are now supplied by direct observation of young children, frequently from birth on. Therefore the potential for reconstruction of preverbal relatedness between mother and child has been enhanced.

Before presenting the clinical data, I will give a brief outline of the development of visual cognition in the young child, with special reference to the face in general and to the mother's or caretaker's face in particular.

It can be assumed that since time immemorial mothers have reflected on their faces their pleasure, indifference, or displeasure at the sight of their children. Quite spontaneously they must have shown smiles of pleasure and approval and frowns or scowls of disapproval or worry, without expecting their children to be or become aware of their feelings, perhaps often without acknowledging these feelings themselves. Yet every mother must become conscious, if only intermittently, of the fact that her child, even the very young child, responds to the affect displayed on her face. In this way the mother's facial expressiveness, a window to her own emotional experiences and stability or pathology, is one of many possible influences

on the forging of affective ties with her child and contributes
to the emotional reciprocity. The originally spontaneous facial
display of affect on the part of the mother in response to her
child can in time become a tool of her conscious or unconscious attempts to influence the child's behavior. The mother
would expect that her show of pleasure or displeasure, approval or disapproval, would be "read" correctly by the child
and could therefore be responded to as desired. This capacity,
however, is known to be a function of the child's chronological
age. The newborn infant does not yet have the perceptual
know-how to recognize the mother's "educational" intent and
has a long time to go before he becomes capable of decipher-
ing such complicated messages as the mother's facial-expres-
sive language.

A large body of research has found eye-to-eye contact between mother and infant to play a central role in the establishment and expression of their mutual emotional attachment.
Mothers of full-term as well as premature infants have been
observed to seek eye contact with their children hours and
even minutes after birth, some of them verbalizing their gratification when the infants seemed to focus on their faces. They
also tended to put themselves and the infants in an "en face"
position to elicit and enjoy the infants' opening their eyes. The
sooner after birth these mothers were allowed contact with
their infants, the more intense and efficient seemed to be their
attachment behavior (Klaus and Kennel, 1976). During the
fourth week observable change takes place in the baby's visual
attention to faces. The earlier vague focusing becomes what
the mothers experience as the first real eye-to-eye contact—and what Wolff (1963) called a precondition to smiling.
Around 2 months of age most infants have learned to smile
consistently in response to a smiling face, thus signifying to
the smiling person the pleasure experienced in the social contact (Spitz and Wolf, 1946). All young parents not burdened
by sobering research findings are happy to see the first smiles
on their infant's face and quite naturally believe that the smile
is a sign of recognition, but the child cannot yet distinguish between different faces. Hence at this early age he will smile just

as brightly at any face, be it smiling, frowning, or grimacing—in fact, even at things that resemble a face such as a mask or dummy. What parents notice soon, however, is the infant's positive response to the presentation of a face in frontal view. They see that the infant becomes animated and activated, moving his limbs and trunk while smiling back in what looks like excited pleasure. Breaking the eye-to-eye contact usually leads quickly to the disappearance of the infant's smile and an expression reminiscent of disappointment and loss. Many infants then indicate that they seek renewed eye contact by cooing, moving arms and legs, and searching glances. When eye-to-eye contact is restored, the infant again comes to life and lights up with a bright smile. One could summarize the assumed subjective experience of eye-to-eye contact for the infant as one of undifferentiated, unmitigated, and vitalizing enjoyment.

Gradually the infant becomes more discriminating until he learns to see the difference between two faces, between that of a familiar person, his mother or father, and that of a stranger. At about 3 months he may look soberly and searchingly at unfamiliar faces, as if he noticed a difference. Then at about 6 to 8 months, when confronted with a stranger's face, most infants are known to respond temporarily with anxiety by crying, withdrawal, or hiding (Spitz and Wolf, 1946; Benjamin, 1963). This wariness, the result of forward development, reflects both visual awareness of the unfamiliar face and the negative affect accompanying this awareness, which represents a new refinement of visual discrimination. In other words, the infant has to pay the price of at least temporary alarm in the presence of a stranger's face—the price of greater social vulnerability—for having mastered a new cognitive-visual-social skill. This so-called stranger anxiety is known to fade away more or less quickly in most infants and to make way for a "wider world" of visual discrimination in which the infant can have social contact with familiar and unfamiliar persons and can respond to their individual ways with his own more individualized, ever-widening repertory of behavior.

When by the middle of the first year of life the infant can

see the difference *between faces,* he still does not recognize differences between facial expressions such as between a smile and a frown. This means that the 6-month-old cannot yet "see" mother's facially displayed affect or moods, even if these are communicated in modes other than visual and probably felt. The necessary visual-cognitive skills to distinguish between smiling approval and frowning or angry disapproval mature at best late in the first year but probably mostly during the first half of the second year of life (Ahrens, 1954). It is a significant and meaningful developmental fact that the infant's new cognitive ability—to "read" mother's face—coincides more or less in time with greatly increased motility. The majority of children begin to locomote at the end of the first and during the first several months of the second year. The child's greater potential responsiveness to his mother's socializing messages can therefore be put in the service of the necessary curbs and restrictions of the roaming toddler who is in constant danger of hurting himself. It must be assumed that mothers resort to many and varied methods of dealing with a newly locomoting "practicing" toddler with a penchant for impulse-ridden independent action. One possible method may be the facial display of approval and disapproval. Some mothers may be more inclined than others to use the visual mode, i.e., facial expressiveness, as an educational or socializing tool. It is also known that some children are endowed with a specifically high sensitivity to visual stimuli in general and hence to facial-visual cues in particular (Freud, 1910; Bergman and Escalona, 1949; Mahler et al., 1975). They may be prematurely sensitized to their mothers' facial cues and may even be predisposed to greater anxiety at the demand for early impulse control. One could speculate that "visual" prohibition signaled to very young children may have a more disturbing effect than "verbal" prohibition since the visual experience precedes the verbal one developmentally, is perhaps the more poignant one, and reaches a less mature and hence more vulnerable organism with fewer means of control of impulse and anxiety (Freud, 1923). There are also mothers who due to their own pathology withdraw at times from eye-to-eye

contact with their children. The children in need of acknowledgment, approval, or disapproval are then left bewildered
and frightened, their world depleted of the life-giving force of
the mother's eye and of her emotional availability.

With increasing verbal comprehension and expression on
the part of the child, the earlier intensity of and emphasis on
the eye-to-eye contact may be superseded by many other,
mostly verbal forms of communication, prohibition, limit setting, or demanding on the part of the mother. Yet mothers
can often be seen sending nonverbal messages to older children by "dirty looks" and all kinds of other looks, whether or
not accompanied by words. Prohibitive glances continue to
coexist with other forms of parental educational interventions;
nor are they limited to parent-child interaction. Adults also
throw "dirty looks" at each other, a heritage of behavior whose
universality and very early origin in life have just been traced.
Many adults talk quite freely of their mothers' and fathers' coercive or punitive glances which frightened them and still do
so in retrospect. One adult patient said to me repeatedly,
"When my mother frowned, all hell broke loose."

The most powerful effect of the eye as compared to the
much less poignant impression left by words even in adults is
vividly described by Freud (1900) in his discussion of his *"Non
vixit"* dream. He recalls a meeting with Professor Brücke who
chided him angrily for coming late to his teaching job at the
laboratory. Freud states, "His words were brief and to the
point. But it was not they that mattered. What overwhelmed
me were the terrible blue eyes with which he looked at me and
by which I was reduced to nothing. . . . No one who can
remember the great man's eyes . . . and who has ever seen
him in anger, will find it difficult to picture the young sinner's
emotion" (p. 422).

The young child who begins to talk is likely to be less helpless than the preverbal one in the face of frightening glances
by the mother. He can "talk back" in some way (Katan, 1961).
A barely 2½-year-old who could say to her mother, "Take that
angry face away Mommy," clearly indicated her understanding that the anger resided visibly in her mother's face. In

daring her mother, she opened a dialogue, expressed verbally her displeasure, and tried to avoid whatever demand may have been made on her, or to soothe or distract her mother's feelings. This was an active approach to a conflict situation with her mother in which she made herself into a partner and did not have to be the passive object or victim.

The infant's maturational advances are closely intertwined with his developing object relations. Progress in one opens up new vistas, a new panorama, in the other. Visual focusing begins at birth. The mother's face, the most regularly present stimulus in the infant's life, becomes one of the first objects of his extended focusing, of his visual attention, and therefore also of his emotional attachment. From about 2 months of age all faces or facelike configurations are responded to indiscriminately by the infant with a smile, that is, with pleasure in the social-emotional interchange. The absence of the face is reacted to with searching glances or negative affect. In the middle of the first year the infant learns to discriminate *between* faces, between those of familiar persons and those of strangers. In turn, this maturational advance allows the infant to single out the mother visually as the preferred object over all other objects and introduces at the same time a new vulnerability in the infant's life, namely, anxiety in response to unfamiliar faces. Late in the first year or in the early months of the second year the child begins to recognize the difference between facial expressions, a new refinement of the maturational process. This allows the "reading" of mother's facial messages of joy and anger, approval and disapproval, and attempts at social adaptation to them, a complex and active social task not under his control earlier in his life. In a locomoting toddler this potential of social "seeing" and learning becomes an integral part of his object relations. If mother and child cannot make an appropriate accommodation to each other at this time, severe conflict may ensue.

While most early face-eye experiences, including threats, between mother and child must be presumed to have been forgotten as conscious memories, there seem to be in some or perhaps in many people unconscious memories like echoes from a dim past of a threatening, often female face or eye which will occasionally surface in their fears, fantasies, or dreams, and possibly also in their symptoms (Freud, 1916–17; Greenacre, 1944). Frank (1969) calls it the "unrememberable" and the "unforgettable" realm of the mind.

In the course of psychotherapy (the treatment of choice due to diagnostic considerations) with two adult patients some of the emerging clinical material led me to assume that starting early in their lives their disturbed object relations were reflected at times in their emotionally frightening eye-to-eye contacts with their mothers. Their hyperalertness and vulnerability to visual contact played a decisive role in their later object relations and in some of their pathology.

Common elements in these patients were inability to carry out their goals, including intellectual goals (both were college dropouts) paired with severe inhibition of pleasure-seeking. The lives of both were devoid of enjoyments and self-created gratifications and spent in boring and disliked routines about which they complained bitterly. Their considerable creative talents had remained undeveloped and their life-styles were strongly masochistic. Initiatives for making changes in their lives were frequently planned, yet never carried out. Discussions of this difficulty in therapy always led to severe states of anxiety and to much expression of diffuse guilt, as if doing something for themselves were not allowed by an internal censor. This unfocused, powerful censoring force remained inaccessible to verbal analysis for years and could not be connected with known or remembered early events or conflicts in the lives of the patients.

It was the elusiveness of the source of the patients' debilitating guilt and self-demeaning lives which eventually suggested reconstructions of its origin in nonremembered preverbal experiences. Similar attempts by Greenacre (1941) and Mahler (1971) are encouraging precedents.

CASE 1

Mr. W., an intellectually gifted, even sophisticated man of 20, sought treatment because he had dropped out of college twice, both times in the first semester at different universities.

He was depressed, unable to concentrate and attend to his studies. His life was joyless, and he drifted aimlessly through his days. He was tall, handsome, and verbally very articulate, but a procrastinator, passive and ruminative, endlessly deliberating over decisions which he then found difficult to carry out. He usually spoke with his eyes averted and glanced at me only occasionally when he seemed to need some kind of reassurance that I was with him. After several years of treatment he reported to me an unusual inhibition which had come fully to his awareness only in connection with a self-created summer job he was about to begin. He had discovered that he was unable to make telephone calls to strangers. The job required telephone solicitation of services. Finding that he could not carry through and experiencing severe anxiety when he attempted to place calls, he gave up the job. My probing into the underlying meaning of the inhibition proved unsuccessful for a long time. Only much later in his treatment, when his relationship to his mother came under closer scrutiny, could we begin to conjecture on the origin and significance of this inhibition.

Mr. W. grew up in a New York suburb in a family with comfortable means. His father was a well-meaning, gruff, self-made man who had not finished college, yet had become a top executive in industry. He wanted his son to complete his college education and offered financial support. The patient's mother seemed to have been seductive, manipulative, and intrusive during his childhood, but emerged only as a hazy figure. The patient avoided talking about her, in contrast to his uninhibited verbal attacks on his father. He engaged the father in angry verbal battles during each visit to his parents' home, and came away bruised but satisfied that he had confronted "the old man." His ambivalence toward both parents was great, and after each visit with them he felt disgusted and enraged. Yet at times he would admit to feeling a certain affinity with his mother's artistic inclinations and interests, which he contrasted with his father's rough and less refined ways.

The patient had a number of successive girlfriends who always dominated him and treated him shabbily while he tried to be kind and giving. When he eventually decided, painfully and slowly, to terminate such a relationship, he was overcome with anxiety that the assertion of his wishes and his breaking up with the girl would destroy her. It often took him months to carry through his intention while the relationship dragged on endlessly and unsatisfactorily. Once the break was made, the patient marveled at the girl's resilience and readiness to let go of him.

Only after several years of treatment and repeated unsuccessful exploration of his inhibition to telephone strangers could the patient uncover the unconscious source of his anxiety. He became aware that he always needed to scrutinize the faces of people with whom he was talking to "read" their expressions and assure himself of their approval of his statements. Once he had "read" their faces, he could make the appropriate adjustment in his own utterances. In other words, he had to take his cues for his own views from the other persons' faces. Then he had partially or totally to submit or yield to the others' plans, wishes, or opinions while neglecting, suppressing, or even abandoning his own, thus allegedly securing their affection or esteem. The need for submission to others readily explained the patient's puzzling inhibition. The absence of facial cues when talking to a stranger on the telephone left the patient stranded and without direction as to his own response. Consequently he was overcome with anxiety.

Childhood memories, slowly recaptured, brought us closer to the possible origin of the "facial dependence" in this patient. They also suggested tentative reconstructions. Mr. W. reported that throughout his childhood, disagreements with his mother used to lead to hysterical outbursts on her part during which she frequently ran out of the room and returned only much later, making the boy feel guilty and of course abandoned. A precursor of such physical leaving behavior might have been long-forgotten psychological leaving in infancy and early childhood. The toddling child learned early that not pleasing his mother threatened punitive "abandonment." We conjectured that this threat led him to scan his mother's face carefully for signs of an approaching emotional storm. By thus "reading" his mother's face he could react with acceptable behavior and avoid rejection by being left. The patient's chronic avoidance of confrontation with his mother in adult years, or even of a discussion with her of issues of an impersonal nature, must also have been the result of expected and feared emotional displays on her part. Her arguments were usually devoid of logic or empathy, quite narcissistically insistent on total agreement with her. Reported fights between the patient's parents were clearly of a similar nature, the father's logic or matter-of-factness contrasting with the mother's illogical emotionality. The disagreements often ended with the mother's running out of the house.

The patient's strikingly averted glance during the treatment hours appeared to be his way, a necessary one, of coping with the basic rule to tell all. By avoiding my glance he spared himself the task of scanning my face for signs of approval or disapproval. In this way he was able to tell me what was on his mind as best he could. Had he looked at me more frequently, this very anxious patient would have suffered even more severe anxiety. "Choosing" to avoid the facial threat he eliminated one source of anxiety and put his verbal facility into the service of the basic rule, this avoidance simultaneously serving as a defense by safely isolating the affect.

The patient's inhibition disappeared gradually as he became more self-assertive and less needy of acceptance at all cost. With this personality change came a greater ease in looking at me more frequently and more directly.

DISCUSSION

The whole life of Mr. W. stood in the shadow of his fear of loss of love, the great potential trauma of the second year of life. All his relationships were colored by it, those with women more so than those with men. His eye-related symptom, his inhibition to telephone strangers, was but an elaboration of the same theme. It must be understood as a result of a continuous and disturbing visual trauma experienced by the patient in relation to his mother. The beginning occurrence of the traumatic constellation can be placed quite safely in the second year of life, in accordance with the above-discussed facts about the state of emotional and maturational development at that age. The patient's joyless life, his stunted pursuit of gratification, interpersonal as well as intellectual, and his helpless, passive resignation to these limitations of daily life may well have been his reaction to a general atmosphere of disapproval. He had indeed come to feel consciously that nothing he did as a child or later ever met with the approval of his parents. Discussing the toddler's dilemma, his being caught between wish fulfillment and parental prohibition, Kris (1950) poignantly said: "the fear of loss of love has added a new dimension to the child's life and with it a new vulnerability" (p. 33). It seems that Mr. W. had indeed become hypersensitive to and needy of the approving gaze of his mother early in his life, probably before language was developed. Or conversely, he had learned quite early to fear and hence to avoid her disapproving glance because of the ominous message it bore, namely, withdrawal of her affection or disappearance from his presence. His "choice" was abandonment of his pleasure goals and passive submission at all cost to the mother's expectations. Apparently he avoided direct confrontation as a toddler. If ever there was open rebellion, it must have been short-lived. As far as he could remember, he never had been an openly rebellious youngster. In terms of Spitz's third organizer (1957, 1965), the child's use of "no" around the age of 15 months, it seems that Mr. W. never clearly and decidedly went through the "no" phase in identification with his mother's stated "no." His failure to take this necessary developmental step toward separation and autonomy was one of the failures in his growth toward self-assertiveness, and this was one of the patient's most outstanding characteristics when he entered therapy. One could speculate about the reasons for the absence of open conflict between this toddler and his mother. She may never have set clear limits and may have left her child with confused notions as to what was permitted and what was not. Her at times indulging and seductive ways with her son alternated with rejecting behavior throughout his remembered childhood. Possibly the toddling child did not know clearly what the limits were since they were inconsistent and changed with the mother's moods. They were unpredictable, subjective, and not necessarily reality-oriented. Consequently the "do's" and "don'ts" were not formed reliably in the child's mind. The anxious haze which always permeated the patient's talk and memories of his mother may well have been a reflection of the early uncertainties and implied threats that he had experienced in relation to her and to her changing or vague expectations of him.

In time, passive submission and masochistic self-denial became the trademark of the patient's childhood and young adult years and also shaped his relationships with his girlfriends. His fearful fantasies that he would destroy the young women if he showed his true colors, his feelings and his intentions to leave them, had the archaic flavor of the fantasies of the toddler who had come to believe that he was hurting and driving away his mother by "being himself." What he had experienced in his relationship with his mother was transferred to his relationships with his girlfriends in a twofold way. He retained his childhood fear that he would lose his partner's love if he asserted himself. Hence he was always a very passive-submissive boyfriend, too "nice" to be treated with respect by his girlfriends. Moreover, he had identified with his mother's message that he was destroying her and hurting her, if he did what he wanted to do—satisfy his own needs and wishes. Hence doing what he wanted to do was equated in his mind with destructive aggression, which had to be curbed lest it destroy the other.

The same conflict over fear of loss of love entered the patient's life in still another disguise, namely, in the form of certain academic difficulties. His painful, drawn-out, and anxiety-laden writing of college papers was a paradigm of the anal conflict between mother and child. The paper had to be perfect for the professor so that he would like it and praise the patient, his student. This is what the patient said. Yet his description of how he wrote his papers evoked the scene of a mother waiting to inspect and judge the child's "anal product." Abraham (1913) states: "an equation of the products of the brain (thoughts) and those of the bowels" (p. 211). The paper had to be completed in his head and was written down only when he deemed it perfect. He stored long passages of it in his head and recited them to me in his treatment hours. He could not ever write a first draft and then rewrite and perfect it. It was in the context of our discussion of this problem that the patient casually mentioned for the first time that he was suffering from constipation. Again it became clear how his need for approval and fear of disapproval had affected not only his original but also his later object relations and general functioning, in this instance, in the intellectual arena, in the form of a writing inhibition. The professor's approval or evaluation of his papers was much more important to the patient than his own. This did not change for a long time, even though his papers were usually highly praised for their stylistic as well as intellectual qualities. His low self-esteem required external support with unending neurotic repetitiveness and prevented a more objective self-appraisal and intellectual independence.

Hartmann, Kris, and Loewenstein in a series of joint papers (1946, 1949, 1962) address themselves to the questions of the formation of early psychic structure. In their discussion of genetic and dynamic issues they suggest that toddlers cannot yet neutralize their libidinal and aggressive energies and have few defenses to resort to when threatened with loss of impulse control and loss of love. The as yet rudimentary defenses of internalization and identification are viewed as prone to pathological solutions since internalization of nonneutralized aggression may lead to a self-punitive, masochistic ego.

Mr. W., finding as a toddler that his pleasure goals and attempts at self-assertion were unacceptable, hence "bad," needed to inhibit them by adopting his mother's view—by identifying with her prohibitions. He turned his drive energies against himself with resulting feelings of guilt and self-defeating and masochistic goals.

Mahler et al. (1975) place the fear of losing the love of the mother and increasing sensitivity to her disapproval, the two assumed major issues of Mr. W.'s toddlerhood, in the third subphase of separation-individuation, the rapprochement phase, roughly at the age of 15 to 24 months. "Fear of loss of the love of the object goes parallel with highly sensitive reactions to approval and disapproval by the parent" (p. 107). Mahler et al. view the subphase of rapprochement as the potential harbinger of severe crises due to the beginnings of internalization of parental demands and conflicts which leads to the concomitant formation of superego precursors. The junior toddler of 15 to 18 months begins to recognize his separateness, smallness, and helplessness and has to abandon his illusion of grandeur and his inflated sense of omnipotence.

This characterization of the rapprochement subphase and its dangers certainly matches this patient's vulnerabilities and problems. As mentioned above, he apparently never struggled for autonomy and never showed the expected temper tantrums or stubborn resistance to parental authority. Passive surrender appeared early, whether he was born with a tendency to passivity or developed it under the pressure of parental prohibitions and threat of abandonment. Mahler's picture of the intrusive mother and the nonavailable father resembles closely the family constellation of Mr. W.'s early life. Under these conditions he had little chance to develop self-esteem.

In summary, Mr. W.'s "facial dependency" must have originated in toddlerhood as the outcome of several interacting forces at that time of his life. Maturational readiness of his visual cognition and the anxieties he suffered in relation to his mother's "facial prohibitions" combined to elicit in him a hyperalertness to his mother's facial expression. This reaction was then generalized to all relationships and eventually produced the patient's symptom, the inhibition to telephone strangers.

According to the attempted reconstruction of Mr. W.'s early object relations, most of his pathology can be derived from his failure to resolve successfully the crucial developmental issues of toddlerhood. This view reinforces the assumption that "eye traumatization" was one of multiple hazards experienced by the patient during this phase.

CASE 2

Ms. A., a bright and attractive-looking woman, came into treatment with me in her 20s in a state of all-engulfing anxiety, agitated restlessness, pressure of speech, feelings of unreality, and a general state of despair and hopelessness. She had just left her five-times-a-week analysis on the couch which she had "endured" for two years. Her analyst had finally told her that she was unanalyzable.

At the time Ms. A. began treatment with me she was teaching a college course in her chosen field of graduate study. She told me that each lecture was an ordeal which heightened her already extreme state of anxiety to the point where her thinking became clouded and she felt panicked. She doubted that she could go on lecturing much longer.

Ms. A.'s external life history was uncomplicated, yet the internal history was highly complex and dramatic. She grew up in a medium-sized university town where she completed her secondary and college education. Then she came to New York City to work for her Ph.D. She did most of her course work and abandoned her graduate studies when she was forced to begin independent research for her dissertation, which threw her into intolerable anxiety. That was about a year before she entered treatment with me. She described vividly how every stirring of curiosity about her dissertation area and every attempt to read were accompanied by the most frightful anxiety attacks which prevented her from doing any work at all. At that time she could not read any book, not even for entertainment, and lived constantly with a feeling of total intellectual paralysis. As evolved during our work, learning had always been accompanied by the same internal, mutually antagonistic pressures: her intense desire for knowledge was interfered with by an internal force, initially not understood, which inhibited her work. Grade school, high school, and college had been no challenge to her outstanding intelligence, and she had done brilliantly throughout in spite of all internal obstacles. She had won many prizes and much praise from her teachers. Even in graduate school she seemed to have been expected to become an outstanding scholar. The disaster finally came with the task of doing her own creative piece of work, her dissertation.

The major source of Ms. A.'s suffering could be easily traced, yet less readily understood. Ms. A.'s mother was an acutely disturbed woman throughout the patient's childhood, often withdrawn and depressed, at times going through psychotic episodes. The patient recalled how on returning home as a child of 6 and 7 she often had to search for her mother in closets where she was hiding in catatonic poses, out of touch with reality. On finding the mother the child had to talk to her and touch her until the mother "came to." The father, an intelligent but passive, helpless, and sick man, never seemed to have stepped in to assist with the mother. The mother's episodes were the most terrifying experiences in the patient's childhood. Her recounting them in her treatment hours almost always brought on tears of despair and the horror of reliving them in memory, and of reexperiencing the unbearable burden of her childhood responsibility.

The mother brought up her only child with the expectation that she would turn out to be a perfect human being, a flawless creature, excelling everywhere and in everything, an improved and idealized representation and an undifferentiated extension of her own imperfect self. The infant must not cry, the child must have no complaints or any feelings or desires of her own, nor could she turn her attention to anything not pleasing to the mother. In short, the mother created a state of symbiotic coexistence between herself and her child, and the child complied to an astonishing degree. The patient was told that she never cried as an infant. Even as a toddler she was strangely compliant except for periods of mad rushing around, as her parents told her later. She remembered her mother taking her hand, and saying: "This is *my* hand." She also recalled her mother telling her how she could not wait for her daughter to begin talking so that she, the mother, could hear what her child's voice sounded like.

Early in treatment the patient said that she felt that all she told me, all her words, were lost to her by telling me. This seemed to have been a repetition of the experience of the child whose mother made everything the child was and said her own, gave the child to understand that she owned her and that there was no differentiation between them. The child's movement toward separation and autonomy was neither supported nor tolerated. On the contrary, if there were minimal steps toward selfhood, they were eliminated quickly.

The atmosphere in the home must have been one of doom. Little was said by anyone, and the expression of feelings or thoughts was not practiced as if by an unwritten law. In sharp and poignant contrast to this horror at home were the patient's frequent visits with her "grandmother," an elderly relative. With this warm and expansive woman she was allowed to do as she pleased, enjoy the pleasures of play, laugh and cry, roam in the backyard, later on grow her own flowers, harvest fruit and vegetables, and often play with an older male cousin who lived in the same house. She remembered her times with this older woman in great detail and with much affection. She also remembered the dread she felt when her mother came to take her back home. She described how one time when she whined and whimpered on the way home, her mother reprimanded her severely. Punishment would consist of not talking to the child for days.

I had observed for several years the patient's habit of occasionally looking briefly over her right shoulder. One day she herself remarked about it spontaneously. She said that she often felt that she was carrying the burden of the world on her shoulder. She could not say more for a long time until she brought an early childhood memory. She was sitting on her mother's lap, wanted to run off, and looked over her shoulder at her mother's face to see whether she could dare take such independent action without incurring her mother's displeasure. She quite easily connected the feeling of burden with her fear of her mother's spoken or unspoken disapproval or her emotional nonavailability, both of which were such large-looming and constant, oppressive experiences of her childhood. During repeated discussion of this material the patient remembered what she thought were even earlier occur-

rences in her life, when she tried desperately and in vain to
"get her mother's eye" for confirmation, so to speak, of her
existence, of her acceptance by the mother, and for permission to pursue some activity. Much of the time the mother
could not respond, was withdrawn, and unaware of her child's
wishes and needs, leaving her with a feeling of being lost,
guilty, and unwanted. This point was brought home dramatically during one of the patient's sessions. A loud sound of
cars crashing under the window of my office made both of us
jump up to look out. When we saw that nobody was hurt, we
sat down again and resumed our work. Yet I turned my gaze
once more toward the site of the crash for a brief moment,
then looked back at the patient. My averted glance, as the patient told me in her next hour, caused her the greatest despair
and feelings of having been abandoned by me. She said she
knew I had taken only a very few seconds, yet the violence and
depth of her reaction were overwhelming and made her feel
hopeless. She spoke about her great need for my looking at
her and my talking to her as confirmation of the reality of her
existence and of the existence of reality around her, both of
which she constantly doubted.

Still later in her treatment Ms. A. began to speak in some
detail of her recent discovery of the role of her mother's facial
expressions throughout her life. She had come to realize how
all her life she had taken her cues for action or inaction from
her mother's face. She described the mother's face looking
"pained" most of the time, angry at other times, with the
anger "directed at herself" for having produced a "nonperfect
child." Worst were the times when the mother was out of
touch, totally withdrawn, and unaware of her daughter. The
mother's acute episodes apparently ceased when the patient
was about 12 years old.

The patient's nearly total submission to her mother's expressed or implied wishes and prohibitions was, as she came to
learn in treatment, a result of her constant fear that any kind
of assertiveness or complaint on her part would bring on one
of the mother's dreadful attacks. She had come to believe unconsciously that her own initiatives, the external expression

and the internal experience of feelings, and the expectation of emotional support from the mother were not only unacceptable but were in fact causing her mother to suffer her "attacks" and to reject her daughter for her "badness." The only road to emotional survival was surrender to the mother at the expense of an existence of her own in a very wide sense. During treatment wishes to be a person and to do something, to exist and to act, occasionally surfaced from deep unconscious repression; these were invariably followed by severe, intolerable guilt, internal "self-flagellation," abandonment of the wishes, and a return to the all-pervasive passivity. The conviction of the unacceptability of any goals, personal, emotional, and intellectual, persisted for years in the treatment. The panic which surrounded each of her lectures forced her eventually to resign from her teaching position and accept a non-challenging job (which she is still holding). Her energies were spent for years in efforts at bare emotional survival against the pressures of constant internal threats and expectations of doom for any desire for selfhood.

DISCUSSION

This patient's eye-related symptomatology was less defensively elaborated and therefore more transparent as to its meaning and origin than that of Mr. W. In addition, the wealth of her early memories, which dovetailed with her parents' spontaneous descriptions of her as a child, allowed a fairly clear view of early and later family interactions and the patient's experience of them. The known nature and time of her mother's severe mental illness practically eliminate the need for speculative reconstruction of early object relations between mother and child. It is as if all the pieces of a mosaic were available and, if put in their proper places, will depict fully the story of the patient's disturbing life history and the resulting pathology of her personality.

Traumatization began in early infancy. One can easily visualize the infant in her crib, bereft of the stimulating presence of her mother, the depressing silence, and the absence of the

mother's life-enhancing and life-confirming eye upon the
child. The mother's depression must have been reflected in an
unmoving, withdrawn gaze. She herself reported that she
avoided contact with the infant. Cognitive and emotional reciprocal exchange must have been minimal. The infant's need
for feedback from the mother through the latter's responsive
mood and gaze must have remained largely unmet (Bennett,
1971). Thus there was a lack of an emotional climate in which
a sense of acceptance, of self and self-worth could grow. The
infant must have come to sense early that her attempts at contact-seeking, her desires for emotional exchange, were not
welcome, and in fact instrumental in driving her mother away.
The patient's characteristic "searching look" on entering the
office and spotting immediately anything new or changed
must have originated in infancy when she was trying to catch
the mother's "absent" eye. Kris (1956) mentions a remark
made to him by Anna Freud about visual contact-seeking on
the part of children of depressed mothers. Ms. A.'s terrified
feeling of abandonment by me in the transference when I
averted my glance from her for a few seconds must have been
a reexperience of her mother's turning away from her when
she was in her crib, needy, as the patient said, of "confirmation of the reality of my existence" and "of the existence of reality" around her. In the second half of the first year, when
differentiation between infant and mother evolves gradually
and the child becomes more active, the patient's mother did
not favor the child's moves in that direction. Her clearly artic-
ulated wish to own her child's body and mind suggests that
she could not let go of the infant who at that age was still "in
her arms," could not locomote, and could be easily prevented
from carrying out "independent" moves in emotional and
physical terms. The child's attempts toward differentiation
must have met with nonparticipation or withdrawal by the
mother, both signifying disapproval to the child. With locomotion achieved at an early 10 to 11 months, the child's dilemma
increased. The characteristically enterprising spirit of this
phase found little support from the mother. From then on,
and for many years to follow, the child was caught between

her strong desire to separate from the mother, to be active and to explore, and the experienced and perceived disapproval or lack of approval by the depressed, withdrawn, symbiotic mother. The patient became "frozen" in the middle, unable to act and unable to renounce all wishfulness. At this age, she could already "read" her mother's face and must have seen there little consent or encouragement for what she wanted. Greenacre's characterization (1957) of the gifted young toddler as having "a love affair with the world" never fit this patient. On the contrary, locomotion brought to a head the struggle between the symbiotic mother and the infant now on her feet and raring to go. Kierkegaard, as quoted by E. James Anthony (1971), offered the most touching and poignant description of the dilemma at this moment of development for the infant of a psychotic mother. Speaking of the ordinary mother who encourages her child's walking, he said: "Her face beckons like a reward, an encouragement. Thus, the child walks alone with his eyes fixed on his mother's face *not* on the difficulties in his way." In contrast, for the child of a psychotic mother, "There is no beckoning encouragement, no blessing at the end of the walk. . . . For now there is fear that envelops the child. It weighs him down so that he cannot move forward. There is the same wish to lead him to the goal, *but the goal becomes suddenly terrifying.*" Anthony comments: "The psychotic mother fills these moments with apprehension so that the child not only has nowhere to go, but he is afraid to get anywhere" (p. 262f.). Again one can easily picture Ms. A. as a toddler not reaping at all the pleasures of the practicing subphase by her newly won freedom of locomotion. Instead she remained tied to her mother and entered the third subphase, rapprochement, without having achieved the major task of the preceding phase, namely, some measure of differentiation and separation from the mother.

The child's strange alternation between quiet compliance and uncontrolled and uncontrollable and aimless running around, as described earlier, was not what the parents believed it to be: cooperative compliance alternating with "fun." It was instead the child's passive surrender to the mother's expectation alternating with severe restless anxiety. Both of these behaviors were brought on by the mother's emotional unavailability, by her "averted eye," so to speak, and both reflected the child's inability to cope with the tasks of this phase, moving toward autonomy and tolerating the pressures of the ambivalent affect toward the mother. Discussing the crisis of the rapprochement phase, Mahler et al. (1975) interpreted the toddler's hyperactivity and restlessness as a defense against sadness and crying, an interpretation convincingly applicable to this patient. We remember that she was never allowed to register complaints or to express negative feelings, be they of sadness or hostility. To this day she displayed much motor restlessness in times of great internal stress, and went on long aimless walks through the city.

One can now place in its developmental context the patient's habit of looking over her right shoulder and feeling as if she were "carrying the burden of the world on my shoulder." Glancing backward at her mother's face while sitting on her lap must have occurred when she could already recognize her mother's facial expression, at the end of the first year or the beginning of the second. At that age she was walking and obviously looked for approval to leave the mother's lap. The approval may not have been forthcoming, and the child found herself burdened with the unsolvable conflict between her wish to move away and her mother's nonverbal, possibly facial prohibition to do so. This was "the burden of the world on my shoulder," and it was eventually internalized as her own life-long dilemma.

Finding herself so grossly impeded by her mother in the pursuit of pleasure and the use of initiative, the patient had only one recourse to emotional survival—empathic identification with the mother's withdrawn rigidity and with her nonverbal eye messages which suggested ambiguously not leaving her while leaving her alone. The patient's constant desperate efforts at pleasing her mother, meaning efforts at impulse control—in fact, at controlling anything that made her feel alive and separate—resulted eventually in the most pathological characteristic of her personality, her total internal immobilization. From childhood on she came to function like a robot by going through the motions of "achieving" to please her mother with minimal emotional and intellectual investment. At the same time, she resorted to extreme masochistic self-denial and to constant internal self-reproach for any stirring of wishfulness. The result was total passivity in relation to pleasure or intellectual goals. Her intense anxiety during teaching was found to be related to her forbidden wish to learn and know more. This wish, as all other wishes, had to be disowned since it betrayed a striving toward differentiation, separation, and autonomy unacceptable to the mother. The patient never left the symbiotic dyad with her mother to become a separate and autonomous person. Her final breakdown came with the inescapable demand on her for the use of her own creative intelligence, for the writing of her dissertation. She became paralyzed with fright, dropped out of her Ph.D. program, and avoided thinking about school.

The attempted analysis on the couch with the analyst out of sight could not but lead to an increase of the patient's feelings of unreality and a growing loss of sense of self, both experiences of disintegration from which she had to flee in panic. She needed to be faced and to see her therapist to develop her selfhood and to walk the painful and lengthy road toward separation and autonomy.

In summary, for Ms. A. the emotional deprivation began in her first year of life, as documented through the known history and nature of her mother's illness. For the infant it was initially the absence of the mother's eye on her or an unresponsive face which from early on impeded growth toward selfhood and self-confirmation. The patient's strikingly searching glance, ever present, may have originated in her first year when she was trying to "get her mother's eye." Somewhat later when the child became more mobile and began to locomote, every step in development was met with obstacles by the mother's symbiotic needs. The implications of differentiation, practicing, and rapprochement were not acceptable to the mother, nor were they handled by her in phase-appropriate ways. Ms. A. began to locomote early and, reading her mother's facial disapproval, submitted to it early. To this day she retains an acute awareness of her mother's facial messages, which are mostly signaling disapproval or anger and which greatly influence her actions and initiatives. Anxiety resulting from conflicts around separation and individuation was the prime moving factor in this patient's life, psychopathology, and psychotherapy. Her "eye" dependency was never truly repressed or transformed and disguised in the form of symptoms, possibly a function of the severity of her pathology and the early phase in which it began.

THEORETICAL CONSIDERATIONS

Discussing the component parts of the superego and their relationship to the categories conscious-unconscious, Freud (1923) states, "it is impossible for the super-ego as for the ego to disclaim its origin from things heard" (p. 52). And: "Verbal residues are derived primarily from auditory perceptions. . . . The visual components of word-presentations are secondary, acquired through reading. . . . In essence a word is after all the mnemic residue of a word that has been heard" (p. 20f.).

Freud thus makes it clear that superego formation takes place at a time when words can be understood and remembered. The superego, considered to be the heir to the oedipal conflict, consolidates at the end of the oedipal period, a time when the ego structure is almost completely developed and the child has full command of language. That is indeed the time when "the inner voice" can be heard.

There are, however, indications of superegolike reactions in the preverbal child, often described in the behavior of toddlers and usually called superego forerunners. The "guilty" behavior of the toddler clinically resembles the guilt-stricken behavior of the older child in many ways, manifesting itself, for example, in an exaggerated search for approval, in inhibitions of impulse, and sometimes also in self-injuring tendencies. What then could be one possible source of this superegolike behavior of the toddler?

In light of the clinical material discussed in this paper I would suggest that visual experiences play a very large, decisive, and hitherto underestimated role in their effect upon the child's development before the advent of language. In particular, eye-to-eye contact, a powerful ingredient of the relationship between mother and infant, may among other socializing functions take on the forbidding and controlling elements in the early mother-child dyad that later on are assumed by the word.

Among the few authors who have addressed themselves specifically to the question of component parts of superego forerunners are Spitz and Peto. Spitz (1958) suggests that "among the primordia which will form the superego" are physical restraining of the child and visual impressions such as facial expression (p. 385). Peto (1969) concurs with Spitz that the visual function is of major importance in the "dialogue between mother and child." In his discussion of a number of dismemberment dreams of adult patients he found "seeing" a very prominent feature of the manifest dreams. It is Peto's hypothesis that the looking, glaring eyes in the dreams are archaic somatic forerunners of the superego and are a remnant of the earliest phases of the child's development.

Both authors agree with my assumption that the mother's angry facial expression in early, preverbal eye-to-eye contact with her child may be a source of severe anxiety to the infant and contribute significantly to the development of superego forerunners by its frightening and forbidding qualities.

SUMMARY

Eye-to-eye contact is one of the universal modes of communication between people in general and between parent and child in particular. Its slowly evolving cognitive and emotional complexity from infancy to later childhood has been traced. Its potential positive and negative contribution toward object relations between mother and child has been described. In particular, an attempt has been made to show the preverbal child's vulnerability to eye-to-eye contact with his mother and its potentially damaging and even devastating effect on the child's personality development. In the two patients discussed in this paper, the damage was in the direction of severe impulse inhibition and massive guilt. Their infantile wishes for emotional and intellectual gratifications seemed "frozen" by the mothers' stern eye or its unavailability. In empathic identification with their mothers' prohibitive attitudes, these patients early in life rejected their strivings for pleasure and autonomy and came to see themselves as unworthy and undeserving of love. In adulthood, their relationships were characterized by conflict and disappointment, and an inability to assert themselves. They abandoned their intellectual pursuits and eventually dropped out of college. Their traumatization early in their lives required long-term psychoanalytic psychotherapy and some speculative reconstruction of the nature of their preverbal relations with their mothers.

The potential contribution of preverbal, visual experiences to the formation of superego precursors has been discussed.

BIBLIOGRAPHY

ABRAHAM, K. (1913), Restrictions and Transformations of Scoptophilia in Psycho-Neurotics. In: *Selected Papers on Psycho-Analysis*. London: Hogarth Press, 1949, pp. 169–234.

AHRENS, R. (1954), Beitrag zur Entwicklung des Physiognomie- und Mimikerkennens. *Z. exp. angew. Psychol.*, 2 : 412–454; 599–633.

ANTHONY, E. J. (1971), Folie à Deux. In: *Separation-Individuation*, ed. J. B. McDevitt & C. F. Settlage. New York: Int. Univ. Press, pp. 253–273.

BENJAMIN, J. D. (1963), Further Comments on Some Developmental Aspects of Anxiety. In: *Counterpoint*, ed. H. S. Gaskill. New York: Int. Univ. Press, pp. 121–153.

BENNETT, S. L. (1971), Infant-Caretaker Interactions. *J. Amer. Acad. Child Psychiat.*, 10 : 321–335.

BERGMAN, P. & ESCALONA, S. K. (1949), Unusual Sensitivities in Very Young Children. *This Annual*, 3/4 : 333–352.

FRANK, A. (1969), The Unrememberable and the Unforgettable. *This Annual*, 24 : 48–77.

FREUD, A. (1965), Normality and Pathology in Childhood. *W.*, 6.

FREUD, S. (1900), The Interpretation of Dreams. *S.E.*, 4 & 5.

———— (1909), Analysis of a Phobia in a Five-Year-Old Boy. *S.E.*, 10 : 5–149.

——— (1910), The Psycho-Analytic View of Psychogenic Disturbance of Vision. *S.E.,* 11 : 209–218.

——— (1913), Totem and Taboo. *S.E.,* 13 : 1–161.

——— (1916–17), Introductory Lectures on Psycho-Analysis. *S.E.,* 15 & 16.

——— (1923), The Ego and the Id. *S.E.,* 19 : 3–66.

GREENACRE, P. (1941), The Predisposition to Anxiety. *Psychoanal. Quart.,* 10 : 66–95; 610–638.

——— (1944), Infants' Reactions to Restraint. *Amer. J. Orthopsychiat.,* 14 : 204–218.

——— (1957), The Childhood of the Artist. *This Annual,* 12 : 47–72.

HARTMANN, H., KRIS, E., & LOEWENSTEIN, R. M. (1946), Comments on the Formation of Psychic Structure. *This Annual,* 2 : 11–38.

——— ——— ——— (1949), Notes on the Theory of Aggression. *This Annual,* 3/4 : 9–39.

——— & LOEWENSTEIN, R. M. (1962), Notes on the Superego. *This Annual,* 17 : 42–81.

KATAN, A. (1961), Some Thoughts about the Role of Verbalization in Early Childhood. *This Annual,* 16 : 184–188.

KLAUS, M. H. & KENNEL, J. H. (1976), *Maternal-Infant Bonding.* St. Louis: Mosby.

KRIS, E. (1950), Notes on the Development and on Some Current Problems of Psychoanalytic Child Psychology. *This Annual,* 5 : 24–46.

——— (1956), The Recovery of Childhood Memories. *This Annual,* 11 : 54–88.

MAHLER, M. S. (1971), A Study of the Separation-Individuation Process. *This Annual,* 26 : 403–424.

——— PINE, F., & BERGMAN, A. (1975), *The Psychological Birth of the Human Infant.* New York: Basic Books.

PETO, A. (1969), Terrifying Eyes. *This Annual,* 24 : 197–212.

ROBSON, K. S. (1967), The Role of Eye-to-Eye Contact in Maternal-Infant Attachment. *J. Child Psychol. Psychiat.,* 8 : 13–24.

SCHALLER, G. B. (1963), *The Mountain Gorilla.* Univ. Chicago Press.

SPITZ, R. A. (1957), *No and Yes.* New York: Int. Univ. Press.

——— (1958), On the Genesis of Superego Components. *This Annual,* 13 : 375–404.

——— (1965), *The First Year of Life.* New York: Int. Univ. Press.

——— & WOLF, K. M. (1946), The Smiling Response. *Genet. Psychol. Monogr.,* 34 : 57–125.

STERN, D. (1971), A Microanalysis of Mother-Infant Interaction. *J. Amer. Acad. Child Psychiat.,* 10 : 501–517.

WOLFF, P. H. (1963), Observations on the Early Development of Smiling. In: *Determinants of Infant Behaviour,* ed. B. Foss. London: Methuen, 2 : 113–134.

A Double Helix

Some Determinants of the
Self-Perpetuation of Naziism

ERICH SIMENAUER, M.D.

THE PSYCHOANALYTIC INVESTIGATION OF THE WORLDWIDE STU-
dent protests and rebellions of the 1960s, which were the topic
of a panel discussion at the 26th Congress of the International
Psycho-Analytical Association (see Francis, 1970), has so far
led to one generally agreed-upon conclusion—that they are
based on unresolved oedipal conflicts. Yet, if one takes into account the great variations in the vicissitudes and resolutions of
these conflicts which are held responsible for the revolutionary attitudes and their symptomatic manifestations, the explanatory value of this statement must be questioned. The
purpose of this essay is to describe further differentiations in
the psychic processes that lead to these explosive social phenomena.

Elsewhere (1970) I have pointed out that the oedipal constellations which the literature regards as the most important
motivation in the choice of the protest appear to be mutually
exclusive. The many variables that are at work are further
multiplied by the predominant conflicts of the preoedipal
phases and the experiences and transformations that occur
during adolescence. In addition, they frequently lead to severe

Dr. Simenauer is a training analyst of the German Psychoanalytic Association and served for many years as an officer of its Council.

ego distortions (Gitelson, 1958). Moreover, many of the more recent papers dealing with the psychopathology of the war generation, at least in the German literature (see Symposium, 1969), report findings which were gained not in classical psychoanalytic therapy but in analytic group therapy or in the course of psychological counseling and similar therapeutic methods. Extreme caution must be exercised in any comparison of assessments obtained by such diverse approaches. For the purpose of this paper it suffices to draw attention to the uncertain and often confusing modes, goals, and directions of transference aspects in a given group coupled with the necessarily inadequate working through of an individual's pathology in the setting of what has been called group personality. We need only think of the diffuse and frequently confusing transference manifestations in groups, which differ considerably from the development of the transference in the analysis of an individual patient; or of the lack of working through of the psychopathology of the total personality (Argelander, 1968) in groups. The partial replacement of the individual's ego by a "group ego" leads to a series of parameters which are not confined to the methodology but decisively change the course and the outcome of the analytic process.

If we seek to understand the psychological mechanisms that have led to the persistence and perpetuation of Naziism, we must study the generation of German youth born shortly before and during World War II. They are our best source material and have been studied by some of the contributors to the symposium mentioned above. These authors believe that the crisis in the lives of the students occurred when their defeated and completely powerless hero fathers returned to the families which until then had been fatherless. The conflicts arising from this situation frequently were solved by a depreciation of the father figure, with the resulting negative identification then blocking the road to sexual and social identity. The decline of the father image thus was assumed to constitute the decisive experience that led to the worldwide student rebellion. The frustrations of the processes of identification were regarded as the mechanism responsible for releasing the protests. By turning against their beaten and impotent fathers, their beliefs and aspirations, the student rebels appear to espouse opposition to tradition, established customs, and institutions.

These children undoubtedly experienced serious frustrations for a prolonged period of time. As their intellectual development progressed, they must have become increasingly aware of the older generation's uncertain and futile attempts to deal with its compromising past. The guilt-ridden parents were incapable of giving their children the information they wished to have; they could not frankly discuss their own Nazi past and involvement, be it active participation or silent condonement. The sons experienced their parents' guarded evasiveness as a severe deprivation. Sensing their fathers' denials, displacements, and feelings of guilt, the sons turned against them. The insecure behavior of the parents and their attempts at concealment in turn cemented the sons' opposition to the world of their fathers and constituted a second phase in their rebellion. In both cases we can conceive of this psychopathology as the result of a primary conflict between ego and superego, a conflict that is especially harmful due to the distortion of the ego ideal by faulty identification processes. An adolescent's helplessness is immeasurably increased when the main pillar of his ideal formation has been destroyed (Lampl-de Groot, 1960).

While this general picture of the psychic determinants accords well enough with the phenomenology of the sociopolitical scene in the early and middle 1960s in Western Germany, it is less applicable to the subsequent social developments in this country, in which a reversal in the attitude to Jews and Jewish affairs occurred. The original bewilderment and confusion gave way to indignation for having submitted to a sense of shame after the 1945 catastrophe. Whatever goodwill had arisen following the dimly comprehended events, it is evidently withering away, though notably not in the official pronouncements and actions of the Government. Friendly feelings are being superseded by critical attitudes, and protests against indemnification of the victims of persecution and against prosecution of Nazi and war criminals abound. It is significant that these protests and criticisms are directed above all to the State of Israel—a displacement which obviously serves as an escape from renewed feelings of guilt. It can be said that anti-Jewish feelings and attitudes enter the political scene by a back door, and that the reemerging anti-Semitism in Germany must, for historical reasons, be of a kind which is tinged by elements of the Nazi stigma and its particular brand of psychopathology.

It is obvious that analytic investigations, such as those referred to above, cannot provide us with an instrument to understand the underlying psychic mechanisms which precisely determine those social attitudes and feelings. As analysts we seek the specific primary psychic experience that shapes the sociocultural phenomena and attempt to evaluate the dialectics of their mutual dependence.

I first encountered, almost accidentally, the effects of this self-perpetuating Nazi-colored anti-Semitism some 15 years ago when I analyzed a recently graduated physician who was born in 1939. His deep anti-Jewish feelings were wholly inconsistent with his conscious convictions and with his sense of identity and self representation. His father, a former member of the Nazi party, was a psychiatrist who had been involved in the official euthanasia schemes. The fantasies of this patient can be characterized as revolving around the thought: if my father lent support to this scheme, then there must have been some moral justification for it at that time, even though it is condemned by the world today. The analysis of this patient's split in personality presented great difficulties, but my understanding of the mechanisms involved was enhanced when in several subsequent cases it was possible to work through similar tendencies. My conclusions are derived from the analytic material of five patients, three male and two female students and graduates who were born between 1937 and 1943. I shall confine my description to those elements of their psychopathology which they had in common and disregard other aspects of their character and neurotic symptom formation. I am aware of the fact that thereby individual differences become blurred and that the development of their reaction patterns will appear less distinct than is desirable, but reasons of discretion leave me no other choice. I should say at the outset that these patients who belonged to the war generation either never knew their fathers (two were killed in the war) or had only dim memories of them from their early childhood.

The two young women had in an early phase of their development experienced the libidinal mother as the sexually frustrating and prohibiting person who was responsible for separating them from the highly idealized love object, the father. This led in both cases by way of identification with the absent father to a homosexual object choice and to hostile and destructive fantasies in relation to all men. It so happened that the fathers of both women were judges, a circumstance that both used for specific rationalizations.

One of the women, a graduate in the arts, was an only child born in 1940. Her analysis disclosed several determinants of her identification with her father. She knew that her parents had wanted a son and had been greatly disappointed by her birth. She was given a name which represented an unusual version of a boy's name. She was determined to live up to her parents' expectations and to become like her father. She never engaged in girls' activities; for example, she never played with dolls. When she was 5 years old, her father was killed, near the end of the war. Her mother assiduously maintained a myth of him as a hero who died for his fatherland. During her adolescence, however, she gradually put together bits of information obtained from members of the family which made it clear that her father had been posted to an occupied Eastern territory where among other things he was concerned with liquidating the assets left by the victims of the extermination camps and where at the end of the war he was killed by "partisans." She would not and could not believe that her father had been a war criminal and to support her denial erected a complex system of defense. One of its components was a general ego regression which resulted in an intellectual inhibition.

For years she attempted to follow a strategy according to which she apparently worked very hard to find out the truth for herself. She evolved a plan in which she was eagerly waiting for her mother to leave the house so she could force open a drawer of her mother's desk that was always kept locked. She fantasized that there she would find letters and documents that would provide proof of the truth. But when the desired opportunity finally arose, she suddenly gave up her long-cherished plans. She knew that in reality there was no need to burglarize the desk, but she was incapable of admitting the obvious. Instead she behaved as though she doubted the occurrence of Nazi crimes and atrocities. Had their deeds really been as bad and as horrible as "propaganda" depicted them? Most of her personality traits bore the imprint of such processes of denial. Yet they also helped her to maintain rather successful repressions because whenever something repressed threatened to break through into consciousness the denial mechanisms succeeded in again warding it off. In this way she could, for example, retain her hatred of all men without being at all disturbed by it.

The second woman, a university graduate born in 1937, attempted to find a more subtle solution of her conflict. Her psychopathology was primarily hysterical, with a mixture of character neurosis and neurotic symptoms. While she too had strong repressions, she also used less primitive defense mechanisms than the first patient. As an undergraduate she had been an active member of a radical left-wing group which rebelled against everything that her Nazi father, a superior court judge, had stood for. He had been the presiding judge in an institution labeled "genetic health court," which was chiefly concerned with the enforced sterilization of all men considered to be undesirable or opposed to the regime. The pursuit of her political activities was apparently facilitated by the fact that she could replace her father as an incestuous love object with her 5-year-older brother with whom she had always had an intimate relationship. Although she had been 4 years old when her father was called up for duty, she had a complete and stubborn amnesia for anything relating to his person. Early in the analysis she claimed that she knew him only from photographs and from what her mother had told her about him. Later on astonishingly precise memories emerged which corresponded exactly to the fantasized idealized image of the father. Near the end of the war her father was made commander of a battalion and placed on active duty on the Eastern front, where he finally was shot by his own men. The patient still shuddered at the thought of what a terrible disgrace it would have been if her father had returned from the war, and would have been arrested and brought to trial as a war criminal, which is what happened to one of her uncles, a brother of her mother. She thought she would feel very guilty and at the same time genuinely pity him. She certainly would have forgiven him and excused whatever he did, for under no circumstances would she "foul my own nest." She had read all the books and reports about high-ranking Nazis, especially about the commander of Auschwitz, and had reached the conclusion that her father could not have been nearly as bad as these people—her father who had had such a lofty sense of honor. As far as she was concerned, he remained a stern but just personage.

In her torturous career as a revolutionary student she finally reached a phase when she denounced Zionism and the state of Israel as imperialistic enemies of the people. At this point the following successive steps could be observed in her analysis: she tried to deny her anti-Jewish attitude by protesting that she had Jewish friends. By adding that these were, of course, Jews who had relinquished their traditions, she indicated that she was a proponent of the distinction between "good" and "bad" Jews. Eventually she overcame her strong resistances and admitted to having anti-Semitic prejudices, but as she did so she boasted that her type of enmity to Jews proved that she was in no way influenced by the Nazi ideology because hers was the traditional rather than a racial anti-Semitism. This example illustrates her way of reasoning in which she persisted almost to the end of her analysis. It is an expression of her main mechanism of defense—intellectualization. It was only after the underlying anxieties had been uncovered and worked through that she was able to gain insight into the displacement which had been operative in her condemnation of Zionism and Israel. This process was in fact initiated by a slip of the tongue in which she referred to her father not as judge (*Richter*) but as executioner (*Scharfrichter*), a parapraxis which became a turning point in her analysis.

The fathers of the three male patients all returned from the war, though two of them only after having spent many years as prisoners of war. Although there were considerable differences in the personal histories, circumstances, and developmental courses of these patients, they showed great similarities in the psychic mechanisms which they used to ward off the emotionally unbearable and intellectually unfathomable that aroused their anxiety.

Without delineating the other psychic processes that occurred at various levels, I shall limit my description to the vicissitudes of their feelings of guilt and the successive roles which these played, as reactions to instinctual demands, in the formation of these patients' attitudes and behavior. These boys certainly experienced rage and aggression when their unknown fathers returned from the war and succeeded in reclaiming the mothers, but these hostile feelings were accompanied by feelings of guilt in relation to the incestuous love object. In later phases of their development these boys became aware of the humiliations to which their fathers as defeated and dejected repatriates were subjected. One of the patients, for example, watched his father for some time after his return in 1945 sweeping the streets. When as adolescents these boys again turned against their fathers, their revolt released new feelings of guilt because during the first years of life these same fathers had been highly idealized fantasy objects.

The phase-specific feelings of guilt that arose in the successive stages of these patients' development can serve as indicators of the vicissitudes of the economically predominant component drives. As Freud (1920) pointed out, it is the relative strength of the etiological factors which tips the scale in its final directions, though this becomes apparent only after the final outcome has been established.

The five patients described here represent a highly selective group insofar as they all had a university education, and came from upper-middle-class families. Their fathers were professionals, who had been extremely successful in their careers; among them were two judges, a high government official, and a well-known university professor. At the same time, however, these patients, while representatives of the war generation, are an unselected group insofar as each sought psychoanalytic treatment for individual reasons in the course of several years. The psychopathology on which I focus here was not discernible in any of the cases until after the analysis had started.

What clearly came into view was the idealization of the father which persisted throughout the various phases of their development and which ultimately reemerged unexpectedly in spite of the various shifts in the vicissitudes of the instinctual drives. The originally positive identifications with the real father or the fantasized image of the father were the economically active forces that determined the dynamic processes in these patients' psychopathology.

Phenomenologically they belonged to those students who, according to Lidz (see Francis, 1970), are just continuing the ideology of their parents, though Lidz did not specify the psychological processes that are involved.

In my cases these factors became apparent only during a relative late phase of their analyses when the transference to the analyst changed. Originally viewed as an all-powerful and demanding attacker, I became the image of a respected love object. At the same time the paranoid anxieties diminished, though there still occurred frequent progressive as well as retrogressive moves. These forward and backward shifts in the transference phenomena seemed to occur with greater frequency in these patients than one usually finds in other cases. With each shift in the transference there was a change in the resistances and the mechanisms of defense that were consistent with the particular position gained at the moment. Whenever the patient became aware of positive transference feelings, these again evoked a hostile attitude, which in turn led once more to feelings of guilt and masochistic surrender. In this way a vicious circle became established and the constant shifts were maintained and perpetuated. It is noteworthy that in these patients the working through of the specific psychic mechanism involved required long and strenuous efforts before they were capable of accepting my interpretations.

In one of my cases a narcissistic character structure prevented the unfolding of genuine transference phenomena. The resulting difficulties in the conduct of his analysis, however, did not extend to the clarification and resolution of the processes discussed here. On the contrary, his omnipotent fantasies and his great reliance on his ego ideal contributed to his actual self living up to his ideal, a factor that facilitated the progress in the analysis of his anti-Semitic attitudes.

It is to be expected that special countertransference problems are bound to arise when the analyst treating such cases is a Jew, especially when he himself suffered painfully from the persecution of the Nazi machinery. Confronted with the re-emergence of Nazi tendencies in his patients, he is forced to deal once more with his internalized objects and to reexamine his defensive formations. The immediate self-analysis which is required is facilitated by the previously achieved self-awareness and analytic insight into his own conflicts and modes of coping with them. Yet he will be aware of having to make a conscious effort whenever an analysand's attack against him begins to unfold. He then not only must reexamine his own reactive aggression and immediately deal with it, but also consider masochistic tendencies and curtail any inclination, be it ever so slight, to an identification with the aggressor. Other important elements of his self-analysis are concerned with paranoid reactions and possible scars resulting from his own experiences of persecution. In addition, more general personality characteristics and modes of thinking may play a certain role, for example, a basically pessimistic attitude or an idiosyncratic outlook on life.

To illustrate the problem, I describe a few concrete situations. After reading Solzhenitsyn's *Gulag Archipelago,* one of my analysands experienced me as Stalin and submissively identified with the aggressor, whereas on other occasions he voiced anti-Semitic feelings of the virulent Nazi kind which led to countertransference difficulties. He called me a dirty Jew, a member of the notorious band of Jewish homosexuals, a greedy Shylock and bloodsucker. After such outbursts, he would feel impelled to prostrate himself and kiss my feet. He understood that this urge was an expression of his feelings of guilt, and in his case it was not difficult to give him insight into the motives of his outbursts by confrontation and interpretation. For example, in one of his fantasies he saw himself as an S.S. man in the Warsaw ghetto inflicting humiliations on and beating his prisoners; he reveled in the idea of singeing the long beard of an old Jew who was none other than his analyst. At this moment the story of Freud's patient who fantasied smelling Freud's after-shave lotion came to my mind and I asked the patient to turn and look at me. When he saw my shaved face, he was genuinely astonished and bewildered by his hallucinatory distortion. He was a young intelligent psychiatrist who said that he himself had never before experienced such an intense regression and omnipotence of thought. On other occasions interpretations had an immediate therapeutic effect since at that point in the analysis he had gained insight into his chief mechanism of defense—projection. Thus he was able to realize that his accusation of my being one of "the notorious band of Jewish homosexuals" was based on a projection of his own infantile homosexual longings for his father and memories of subsequent homosexual relations. His insight into his conflicts was especially enhanced when in the throes of hostile attacks on me he abruptly became aware of his wish to take my penis into his mouth, a wish that was also connected with exhibitionistic impulses. In the same way, the destructive and persecutory tendencies which he projected onto me were rooted in his own destructive wishes. He had repetitive dreams in which he took great pleasure in ripping open the genitals of women and cutting them up. Characteristically, he simultaneously manifested a sentimental sympathy for animals and all signs of a "protection of animal" mentality, which was of course linked to memories of mutilating animals as a child—in fact, he occasionally still indulged in such activities as an adult (for example, he would throw live beetles and other insects on an anthill).

Preoccupations with soiling and smearing formed a prominent part of his personality structure due to an anal fixation,
and these persisted in his life and his habits. Overt anal fantasies were numerous and largely determined his toilet habits;
he was frequently concerned about memories of bad odors
and feared he was suffering from halitosis. With great satisfaction he pictured himself smearing the analyst's couch with
feces. It is consistent with this and other aspects of his analysis
that there were frequent oral-sadistic regressions coupled with
fixations to anal aggression. Evidently, the latter were used to
ward off the former. Having a narcissistic character structure,
he used multiple defenses. During certain phases of his analysis obsessive-compulsive mechanisms of defense in the wake of
anal fixations were particularly prominent. Thus, the "Jewish
spirit of a profit-seeking monger" had its counterpart in some
questionable activities engaged in by the patient. Feeling taken
advantage of by what he regarded as too high an analytic fee,
he laboriously began to find out from my other patients how
much they were paying me. At the same time, however, he
was ashamed of this indiscretion.

It appears to me that the analytic findings described above
are directly related to the German sociopolitical scene and
especially to the social changes in recent years. In the face of
total defeat and the complete breakdown of their ideology and
convictions, the older generation initially reacted with stunned
helplessness and largely hypocritical adaptations to the new
conditions. While new guidelines to social and political attitudes developed quickly, they frequently were no more than
the old basic attitudes in new disguises, aided by displacements
and especially by identifications with the political forces that
now were in power—a process described by Freud (1921) in
his study of group psychology. These sociopolitical developments coincided with the war generation's taking over the
management of public affairs—and here one must include the
35- to 45-year-olds who as children had been subjected to intense Nazi indoctrination. This particular generation is politically very active, especially in shaping public opinion, and its
influence on the mass media is steadily rising.

Conducting a sociological study Medzini (1972) interviewed journalists, publishers, editors, and other press, radio, and television people, as well as scientists in the field of the mass media in the Republic of West Germany. He concluded that since 1968 the "goodwill" for Israel has been steadily on the decline in the German mass media and been replaced by an increasingly unfriendly and critical attitude. He notes, for example, that people have become tired of the various restitution payments and of hearing about the much-advertised "special relationship" to Israel. This change, he believes, is based on a general attitude: many of the young journalists, even though they are critical of their parents' past crimes, nevertheless do not want to or cannot believe that this past really had been that horrible and that their own parents had been active or passive participants in it. It is especially relevant to what I have tried to show that Medzini confirms that the youths rebelling against their parents have in fact taken over the old prejudices in a new guise. He believes that the anti-Israel attitude among the young journalists represents only one means by which they rebel against and revenge themselves on their parents. In view of the case material presented, I would also regard this attitude as a revenge for their parents' fate.

DISCUSSION

The phenomena observed on the social scene appear to correspond closely to the psychopathology revealed in the individual case histories of the representatives of the war generation. Having said this, however, we are once more made aware of the uncertain explanatory value of sociological and sociopsychological concepts and theories, and turn to psychoanalytic metapsychology for insight into the motivations of these social phenomena.

In these students' development with its energy transformations due to external circumstances and intrapsychic experiences, the identification with the internalized father clearly has been undone, but these changes take place only in those identifications which are localized in the ego. In contrast, the original ideal formation in the superego is not affected by the vicissitudes of the libidinal and aggressive drives and their derivatives. It has never been relinquished. If this difference in the localization of the identificatory processes is not taken into account, the attitudes and thought processes of these student rebels cannot be fully understood. Above all, their "just continuing the ideology of their parents" (Lidz) in spite of their hostile protests against them must appear to be wholly incomprehensible.

One might speculate whether the same fixations and transformations take place in the entire sociological field. The aims of diverse radical groups seem to support this assumption. In essence, these ideologies represent an extreme disavowal of the traditional values of the world of the fathers. In this context, one could conceive of the revolutionary sociopolitical models as reaction formations against the vicissitudes of the identification processes in a (hypothetical) social ego, in the course of which the original identifications are given up. Yet, the aims striven for by these ideologies with their messianic overtones, such as the improvement of everyone's life, individual happiness, and greater freedom, also reveal themselves as heirs to the oedipus complex: in the persistent impact of the ego ideal on the superego. With regard to the individual characteristics of these analysands, I would say that their egos bore the economically effective imprint of early fixations which unequivocally influenced their behavior. Their ideal formation derived in part from the preverbal phase and in part from an oedipal phase that was not yet clearly defined.

It seems to me that current discussions of the causal factors of social phenomena and of the roles which society and the individual play in them would benefit greatly if social psychology would draw on the findings of psychoanalysis. As Freud (1921) has demonstrated, many sociocultural pursuits and institutions represent projections of the individual's unconscious strivings. Conversely, these institutions in their specific historical contexts influence the individual's psychopathology because they provide the individual with well-defined avenues for expressing his unconscious wishes with less guilt.

BIBLIOGRAPHY

ARGELANDER, H. (1968), Gruppenanalyse unter Anwendung des Struktur-modells. *Psyche,* 22 : 913–933.

FRANCIS, J. J. (1970), Panel Report: Protest and Revolution. *Int. J. Psycho-Anal.,* 51 : 211–218.

FREUD, S. (1920), The Psychogenesis of a Case of Homosexuality in a Woman. *S.E.,* 18 : 145–172.

———— (1921), Group Psychology and the Analysis of the Ego. *S.E.,* 18 : 67–143.

GITELSON, M. (1958), On Ego Distortion. *Int. J. Psycho-Anal.,* 39 : 247–257.

LAMPL-DE GROOT, J. (1960), On Adolescence. *This Annual,* 15 : 95–103.

MEDZINI, M. (1972), [The Mass Media in Germany and Israel]. *State and Government* (Jerusalem), 2 : 110–122.

SIMENAUER, E. (1970), Der behandlungsbedürftige Proteststudent als "Tiqueur." *Psyche,* 24 : 526–530.

SYMPOSIUM (1969), Die Unruhe der Studenten [contributions by C. P. Kuiper, E. Mahler, M. L. Moeller, M. Pohlen, H. Roskamp, H. U. Ziolko]. *Psyche,* 23 : 721–802.

Notes on the Analysis of a
Prelatency Boy with a Dog Phobia

ROBERT L. TYSON, M.D.

THE AIM OF THIS PAPER IS TO DEMONSTRATE HOW IN THE COURSE of childhood development a phobia can serve in the solution of various conflicts involving different drive derivatives and wishes, and how it can also mitigate changing anxieties while the outward form of the symptom remains unchanged. This view is consonant with Freud's comment (1917): "The content of a phobia has just about as much importance in relation to it as the manifest façade of a dream has in relation to the dream" (p. 411). Lewin (1952) expanded on this point when he discussed the fact that the function of the "claustrum" symbol in claustrophobia varied in different contexts, "much as one and the same dream symbol may be used in the expression of different latent thoughts" (p. 303). I believe that this idea can be applied to the understanding of fears and phobias in children.

The traditional framework within which psychoanalysts

This paper was written when Dr. Tyson was in psychoanalytic practice in London, where he was also Research and Training Analyst at the Hampstead Child-Therapy Course and Clinic, Consultant Psychiatrist at the Paddington Centre for Psychotherapy. Dr. Tyson is now on the Faculty, San Diego Psychoanalytic Institute, La Jolla, California.

A shortened version of this paper was presented at the Meeting of the Association for Child Psychoanalysis, London, July 1976.

I wish to express my appreciation to Dr. Susannah Davidson and Mrs. Hansi Kennedy with whom I have discussed this case.

have understood phobic mechanisms was established by Freud
in two well-known studies of childhood animal phobias (1909,
1918). Later (1926) Freud showed that the two patients as
children had to deal with different drive-related wishes, but
that both of them feared castration as an anticipated punishment for their various forbidden wishes, an anxiety which for
each child "was therefore a realistic fear, a fear of a danger
which was actually impending or was judged to be a real one"
(p. 108). Thus Freud set phobias in the context of the oedipus
complex. Not neglecting preoedipal factors, Freud went on to
say, "I am well aware that a number of cases exhibit a more
complicated structure and that many other repressed instinctual impulses can enter into a phobia. But they are only tribu-
tary streams which have for the most part joined the main current of the neurosis at a later stage" (p. 127).

Much of the extensive psychoanalytic literature on phobias,
which I will not review here, can be understood as attempts to
corroborate Freud's views, or to demonstrate some of the
"many other repressed instinctual impulses" which can be involved in phobia formation, or to establish that anxieties other
than castration anxiety may be the motive for the appearance
of the phobic symptom, i.e., that phobias may occur outside
the oedipus complex. I shall describe material which emerged
in the analysis of a 5-year-old boy, Larry, to show that the developing psychological organization underlying his fear of
dogs and the manifest fear itself were complicated and composite evolving structures which reflected the course of events
in his life. Larry's fear of dogs was well established before the
age of 3; in contrast to Little Hans, there was little to suggest
its earlier origins. Perhaps it first appeared as an "archaic
fear" (e.g., as described by A. Freud, 1966, p. 161) based on
the frailty of an immature ego and without any basis in conflict. Once established, his fear of dogs can be understood as
expressing developmental interferences or developmental
conflicts (Nagera, 1966) which were subsequently superseded
by neurotic conflicts, while the earlier mechanisms of externalization and projection were supplemented by regression,
displacement, and more sophisticated forms of projection. It is

only in the last stage of this structural development that there is a firm metapsychological justification for calling such a fear a phobia, and the earlier preneurotic fears deserve to be distinguished from the later ones. The typical descriptive criteria for the diagnosis of phobia (an involuntary and uncontrollable reaction of fear out of proportion to the situation, which cannot be reasoned away and which leads to the avoidance of the feared situation) fails to make this distinction.[1] In Larry's case, the original fear persisted in its outward appearance while structurally it developed into a phobia, the symptom thereby undergoing a change of function and perhaps achieving some degree of secondary autonomy (Hartmann, 1939, 1950).

The analytic material is selected to highlight the evolution of the manifest appearance and the structure of Larry's fear of dogs as I came to know about it. It will become evident that this fear was expressed in a variety of ways at different times and that it included: fear of the sight of a dog; fear of large but not small dogs; fear of being bitten by a dog; fear of a dog's bark, a dog's tail, and a dog's messing. Inevitably the material also indicates how the emergence of aspects of Larry's fear affected the course of treatment, and how the vicissitudes of his dog fear and phobia provided important clues to the understanding of his developmental difficulties and conflicts as well as to his problems in object relationships.

CASE PRESENTATION

I first saw Larry L. when he was 5½ years old. Both parents were actively involved in seeking treatment for their son,

1. The importance of making this distinction applies not only to the assessment of childhood disturbances, for example, in decisions of what form of treatment is suitable for the patient; it also applies to adult symptoms such as the relatively sudden onset of a monosymptomatic phobia, an event known often to have ominous significance as heralding the failure of the patient's defensive system. The descriptive definition of phobia, moreover, fails to take into account the fact that the appearance of the symptom, when it is the product of a neurotic or preneurotic struggle, is the consequence of attempts at inner adaptation, as contrasted with outer adaptation, which may not be so well served by the phobia.

being concerned that his development seemed arrested and that everything about him appeared infantile. They first noticed signs of his backwardness shortly after Larry's brother Melvin was born, when Larry was 2¾ years old. Mrs. L. noticed that Larry's speech development progressively lagged behind that of his peers; he made peculiar grimaces and screaming noises at home and in public; he had frequent incomprehensible temper tantrums, cried long and often, had difficulty in sleeping, and occasionally wet his bed. He did not mix or play with other children of his age and preferred to play alone with toy cars. Larry's mother thought he had improved in this area since he had begun to attend nursery school at age 5. However, no mention was made of his dog phobia until after treatment began. The parents were particularly anxious that Larry enter analysis because they had already taken him to "play therapy" three times weekly when he was about 4½, but they felt nothing had been done in this treatment and they were more than ever concerned that his development had stopped.

FAMILY HISTORY

Mrs. L. was the older of two girls. Her unmarried sister lived with her widowed mother and an invalid aunt in another city a few hours' train journey away. Mrs. L. took her children for frequent visits without their father, and Larry always shared a bed with his mother there. This household placed great emphasis on cooking, eating, and cleanliness. During the visits, Mrs. L. relinquished the care of her children to her mother and sister, who did not tolerate Larry's noisiness and messiness. A point of dissension between Mrs. L. and her mother was Larry's increasingly obvious disturbance which the grandmother persistently minimized, maintaining that Larry would "grow out of it," and opposing any form of treatment.

Mr. L. was the younger of two sons in an emotionally distant and unsympathetic family. He was reluctant to say much about them, but once when discussing Larry's difficulty with separations he referred to his own experiences of being repeatedly left in childhood. He simply had decided there was no point in getting upset and he did not see why Larry should not come to the same conclusion. Another time he remarked that he had given Larry more attention in 5 years than his own father ever gave him in his lifetime. Mr. L. clearly yearned for a close relationship with his son, but felt rebuffed by Larry's inability to respond; finding Melvin more responsive, he gave Larry progressively less of his attention. Also, Larry's father was often away from home for a week or more on business trips.

Both parents had relatively little schooling owing to their families' financial difficulties, and they realized that their ambitions for their son might be thwarted by Larry's disturbance. They had high expectations of treatment and hoped that Larry would be quickly transformed into the bright little boy they wished him to be. Larry's need for treatment was about the only thing his parents agreed on. While initially the parents had presented their marriage as quite good, it gradually emerged that they had a long history of marital discord, with Larry witnessing their arguments and battles. Several times in the course of Larry's treatment Mr. L. seriously considered leaving the family, though he never acted on this threat.

DEVELOPMENTAL HISTORY

Larry and his brother were both planned children. The pregnancy was uneventful and labor and delivery were normal. Breast-feeding was attempted but given up after the first week because "there was not enough milk." Mrs. L. was inconsistent in giving a history of feeding but most often said that there had never been any feeding problems. Larry sucked his thumb from infancy and the mother seemed not to have interfered with this habit. Motor and speech milestones appear to have been within normal limits.

It gradually emerged that Mrs. L. ran an au pair agency from her home, spending hours on the telephone and at her desk. Larry's care was left to a succession of au pair girls who had quite varying attitudes to the care of a baby and varying competence in speaking English. I could understand that part of Mrs. L.'s excessive vagueness about Larry's development was due to the fact that she was not taking care of him much of the time, in addition to whatever emotional factors kept her relatively uninvolved with him in his first few years.

A consistent element in Mrs. L.'s relationship with Larry was her often unrealistically high expectation of his performance. For example, toilet training began at 9 months when Larry was put on a potty after meals by au pair girls. Mrs. L. was quite disappointed that he achieved bladder and bowel control only at the age of 2½ years. The occasional episodes of bed-wetting apparently were handled matter-of-factly by the mother or by the current au pair girl. Mrs. L. described Larry as "very neat and clean," and said his play was also "neat." He sat quietly for hours and repeatedly lined up his toy cars in straight lines. The family doctor noted that the house was so tidy it did not seem that a child lived there.

From early in life Larry had great difficulty in separating from his mother. He would get so upset if she left in the evening that she often tried to fool him by telling him she was staying, then leaving after he fell asleep.

When Larry was 2¾ years old his brother was born. One month before Melvin's birth, Larry was told that a new baby was coming and that his mother would go to the hospital for it. Labor began in the middle of the night and Larry woke in the morning to find his mother gone. He cried bitterly, but his father and grandmother told him he should smile and be glad because he had a new baby brother. The mother returned after 10 days. Larry soon showed jealousy toward his brother, and when treatment began the mother still had to protect Melvin from Larry's occasional physical attacks. Some months after Melvin was born, Larry fell off a windowsill, striking his upper front teeth and forcing them into his gums so they seemed to have disappeared in a bloody pulp. Larry and his mother were both frightened and upset, but the doctor reassured them and the teeth eventually grew out normally.

Throughout all these stresses there was no reported disruption of Larry's increasing sphincter control, nor of his feeding behavior.

It is unclear precisely when in relation to these events Larry's difficulties began, or which of them appeared first. Certainly by the time he was 3 years old, all the symptoms listed at the time of referral were established: apparent lack of further social and intellectual development, difficulties in speech and language, peculiar screaming noises and grimaces, frequent temper tantrums, sleeping difficulties, lack of ability to play with other children including difficulties in coordination as in playing ball, and stereotyped solitary play with toy cars. Almost as an afterthought, after treatment began Larry's mother added that he was terrified by dogs. He was also fearful of the sound of the wind, especially at night, and thunder and lightning. Mrs. L. believed that all these fears had been present long before the age of 3. There was no obtainable history of an early frightening experience with a dog. Only months after treatment had begun I learned that Mrs. L. had a phobia for cats, and that Larry and his mother would cooperate with each other in avoiding one or the other of these animals.

Larry's sleep was disturbed frequently and he would wake crying, sometimes screaming. On occasion he would be taken to the toilet, other times just comforted by one of his parents. He often wanted to crawl into bed with his mother, who found it easy to accede to Larry's wish especially when the father was away, and this always seemed to quiet him. He did not have so much trouble sleeping at the grandmother's house where he regularly slept with his mother.

Mrs. L. held herself responsible for all of Larry's troubles, which she thought stemmed from her being a "bad mother." She believed that she had neglected him too long, and it seemed that her guilt was pushing her to be the "perfect mother," which meant getting treatment for Larry, and providing him with all kinds of stimulating experiences. She felt that recently he had responded to her increased attention, but she was convinced he had somehow been damaged and this necessitated treatment, because, as she herself said, her love was not enough.

REPORTS FROM NURSERY SCHOOL AND PSYCHOLOGIST

Larry began school at age 5; his teacher was very concerned that he was so quiet in class and acted like a 3-year-old. He was unable to use a pen or crayon; he often simply withdrew, sucked his thumb while holding on to his ear with his other hand, and appeared to "switch off." He was able to participate in some of the group activities, for example, singing. He sought contact with the teacher and frequently solicited her approval, by saying clearly, "You are proud of me, aren't you?" He seemed to have periods of anxiety and agitation, asking many questions, "Is it time for Mummy? Is it lunchtime? Is it assembly? Is it hometime?" She thought he had difficulty retaining the elements of a time schedule.

A psychologist found it impossible to make a reliable assessment of Larry's intellectual abilities because his behavior was negativistic, he was easily distracted, and his concentration span was very brief. However, his language could be understood and on the basis of the tests performed, Larry was judged to be of normal intelligence.

ASSESSMENT INTERVIEWS

From the information available I was concerned that Larry might be suffering from a symbiotic infantile psychosis (Mahler, 1952), or from some form of borderline disturbance or ego deviation and that analysis would not be the most suitable treatment. However, two assessment interviews gave me a different impression. I will summarize them to show that he appeared to have a readiness to use the analytic setting and how he responded to trial interpretations.

Larry was a small, handsome, dark-haired, and neatly dressed boy who greeted me politely after prompting from his mother. He separated from her without difficulty and went straight to a box of toys which he began to explore. Larry talked on and off, more than I had expected, although there were long silent periods in which I felt pointedly excluded. His facial expression was vacant or slightly sad, occasionally interrupted by a broad, forced smile. There were some neologisms, much of his speech was quite indistinct, and I could not always understand him. I did understand simple declarative sentences such as: "This is paper; this is a cow." He tentatively made some random marks on paper and told me it was a drawing. On discovering a toy toilet, he asked, "Can I make wee-wee please?" He used the real toilet efficiently, washed his hands thoroughly, explored the waiting room a little, and returned to me. He did not respond to what I said, but I felt he was listening sometimes. After a while he said, "I want to go home now, please," and left. It made no difference when I said we had more time, and perhaps he was worried about where his mother was. In the waiting room I explained that his mother would stay there until we were through and we could go back to the toys and talk some more. Nothing happened until I said I knew he had seen lots of people already though not more than once, but that he was going to see me again in a few days' time. At this, Larry returned with me. He played the rest of that session with plasticine, molding various figures and naming them. First were snails, then snails with wings, which turned into snakes. Using dolls he had a little boy urinate and asked, "Where's his dicky?" He played taking the doll's clothes off and putting them on and made additional clothes out of plasticine. At the end of the session he spontaneously started to clean up carefully and said next time he wanted a pencil to draw with. I repeated that I would be seeing him again in a few days. On the way out Larry commented to his mother, "He's not the kind of doctor who gives injections."

Before the next meeting, Larry's mother phoned, anxiously saying her son told her that I was going on holiday by plane to America. She was surprised to learn that I had not told him that and she realized it must have been Larry's fantasy. She had been unaware of how much he must pick up by listening to his parents' talking to one another, and how much she was reading things into what he said. Larry had asked his mother when he was going to see me again.

The second session began by Larry smiling more warmly in greeting. He promptly began to play with a boat. I took up the holiday theme by saying I knew his daddy traveled a lot and that Larry must miss him then. He said nothing and turned to play monotonously with toy cars, again seeming purposefully to avoid me, but later he asked if he could take the boat home with him. I said I thought he wanted to remember me until he came back again in a week, but after that he would be coming almost every day. After this he made several exits to the waiting room and asked if it was time to go. I said maybe he wanted to be the one to leave instead of my leaving him, whereupon he went to the toilet, shut the door and urinated. His mother commented that it was very unusual for him to shut the door. When he came out, he seemed quite excited and distractible, spoke less, and at the end of the session said, "You clean up," and dashed out.

Larry's mode of behavior in these sessions seemed that of a 3-year-old, but it had more the quality of a regression used defensively rather than that of an arrest in development. Although there were indications of ego restrictions and limitations, Larry's instinctual development appeared to have reached the phallic-narcissistic level (Edgcumbe and Burgner, 1975) with lingering anal conflicts. While his language was definitely limited and his speech not always comprehensible, at times he could use words sufficiently well to get across his thoughts. He conveyed his feelings of sadness and low self-esteem and showed difficulties with separations. His chief defenses seemed to be a regressive withdrawal, reaction formations, and attempts at denial. There were also some signs of an ability to identify with the aggressor. It was difficult to assess how much of Larry's apparent immaturity was due to the deprivation about which his mother felt so much guilt, and how much was due to regressive factors affecting primarily his ego functioning. When I learned about his fears and phobias a little later, I could only guess that they might be signs of ongoing developmental conflicts (Nagera, 1966).

The question remained whether a prelatency child with apparent ego defects or distortions was ready for analysis, or whether a prior "ego strengthening" was indicated (Weil, 1973). Fortunately, Larry had just begun with an exceptionally sensitive teacher who agreed to tutor him privately several times a week. In view of this external support, Larry's parents and I agreed that he should begin analysis as soon as possible, five times weekly, and Mrs. L. and I made arrangements to meet on the sixth day each week.

THE ANALYSIS

First Phase (the first 3 months)

I saw my task in the first phase of treatment to be watchfully and unintrusively available to Larry for those moments that he could manage to emerge from behind the barrier where he spent much of his time silently playing with his toy cars. He very gradually began to use me in some of his play, for example, by having me assist him in repetitively washing his cars, without specific reference to dirt. Areas of conflict began to emerge. At the ends of sessions he sometimes did and sometimes did not want to clean up, occasionally wanting to leave early and other times wanting to stay longer. For some weeks he played with plasticine, and then was concerned about washing his hands thoroughly because they were "filthy." His stereotyped and automatic smile seemed to be employed in the denial of anxiety and sadness, and I noticed how similar it was to his mother's smile. The smile appeared especially when he played with snakes, and with water, and when he repetitively flushed the toilet. From some of this material I could interpret his fear of disappearing down the toilet, in response to which Larry said, "I like staying here with you," and he tried to prolong the treatment session. Next, for a number of sessions he played in an increasingly excited way around the toilet, which was noticed by his mother in the waiting room. Later she described that her going to the toilet at home was an exciting experience for both of her sons. Since they screamed if she closed the door when she took a bath or was on the toilet, she found it more convenient to leave the door open.

As the mother began to use the toilet less openly at home as a consequence of our discussions, Larry became more provocatively excited in playing with water in the sessions and in his own use of the toilet. This eventually subsided when I repeatedly interpreted his testing me to see if I would be like his mother who might not close the door to help control his excitement. I began to understand that home for Larry was not a peaceful place, but rather was a source of erotic overstimulation and excitement which he found threatening and difficult to control. Another source of excitement for Larry became evident when his mother described how the parents' bedroom door was kept open at night on her insistence, even though she and her husband would sometimes argue loudly. She made no connection at the time between this and Larry's insistence on keeping his own bedroom door open. In the sessions Larry was sad more often and more overtly than previously, curling up in a chair, looking very pathetic, and sucking his thumb; there seemed to be a connection between his sadness and the anxiety aroused by hearing terrifying noises from the parental bedroom. I began talking with Larry about these feelings and I mentioned how his crying at night might make him feel safer when one of his parents appeared, because then he could see they were all right and also have one of them to himself.

Larry now began to enact what I understood and interpreted as primal scene material by closing himself in the cupboard, having me turn off the light, and then screaming. He took to drawing and to having me draw a big fish and a myriad of tiny baby fish. Once he said the big one would eat up all the little ones, and for the first time he told me he was frightened of dogs biting him and also fearful of the wind at night. He appeared to feel helpless in his efforts to control himself and his threatening and overstimulating environment; moreover, he could never live up to the expectations his parents had of him, which in fact were quite unrealistic for any child his age. We began to work on his fears of his projected oral-aggressive impulses and his fears of being devoured by a mother who in many ways was all-engulfing and encompassing. The theme of babies appearing and disappearing was clearly contained in these sessions as well. One day Larry wet his trousers, took them off and whimpered like a baby, then gave them to me and told me to put them on. He agreed gleefully when I interpreted his wish to be the big one and sit with Mummy, and that I be the little dirty one. Following this he began to cut his hair off with a pair of scissors and tried to cut off mine as well. Then he held his penis and said that it hurt, whereupon he took pieces of his cut hair and put them back on his head.

This material was dealt with at a strictly phallic and oedipal level over a period of several weeks. I interpreted Larry's incestuous wishes for his mother and his murderous wishes toward his father and consequent fears of retaliation. I included Larry's concerns about ensuring the intactness of his body and his penis, which were often expressed in terms of his fears of noises at night and of being bitten by a dog.

By the second month of treatment, the mother reported that Larry's behavior at home had improved, his nighttime crying now occurring only once or twice each week instead of every night. As counterpoint to the material that Larry brought around his instinctual conflicts and regressive defenses, there was a progressively more prominent theme based on his deprecated self image. His habitual mode of relating to adults was to be ingratiating in search of praise while showing himself unable to do simple things and being easily discouraged. He was quite sensitive to any sign of what was expected of him, he felt threatened by the rapid developmental and intellectual progress made by his little brother, and he became increasingly unhappy with his own performance in school as he grew more aware of the differences between himself and his classmates. He developed a poignantly sad and evocative demeanor which stirred up countertransference wishes of my own to be a "better mother." As Larry grew more attached to me, he showed his sadness and uncertainty as the weekend separations approached and often expressed the wish to take something home with him on Fridays, as a concrete reassurance that I wanted to keep him. Then Larry discovered a roll of sealing tape, the first of many which he consumed by running tape back and forth between opposite walls of the room, keeping me at one end, and connecting me, himself, and the opposite walls by yards and yards of sticky stuff. Larry developed some inventive elaborations in the ensuing jungle of tape, which he re-created each session. It gave us an opportunity to understand and to work through his wish to be connected, to be part of me in the transference, and to do some further work on his feelings around separations.

Second Phase of Treatment (4th to 14th month)

The second phase of treatment can be seen as being based on the established use of words and speech for communication, and on Larry's growing ability to make sense of, and connections between, feelings and words. Larry now was also able to include role play among his modes of expression, and at home his mother became important to the therapeutic work by giving him appropriate explanations. For example, one night the parents had a fight in the bedroom, with the door open as usual. This led to "lovemaking" with loud noises, interrupted by Larry screaming that he had wet his bed, followed by the usually inconsolable crying. Mrs. L. left her husband and went to Larry's room, recalling our conversations about what he might hear at night and what it might mean to him. She explained to Larry that he must have been frightened because of their noises and told him that they had had a fight, and made a lot of noise when they made up and loved each other. He calmed down with this explanation and thereafter had no further episodes of bed-wetting. For Larry, any explanation might have been better than none, or at least better than the products of his own fantasies.

Larry began to bring up more material about his fear of dogs, which emerged in the form of role play. One day he asked me to pretend to be a dog. But at my first tentative barks, he became immediately both frightened and excited, objected at once, and told me to be a pussycat instead. This episode heralded a regression in his play, which then took on an anal character; for example, he mushed up plasticine with water, and his speech became less understandable. He volunteered that he did not like dogs, and I linked his regressed anal play and soiling with his dislike of dogs because they messed in the garden and represented his own impulses to mess, those impulses he so wanted to disown. We then went on to work on his fears of his mother's anger at his own dirtiness, messing impulses, and failure to live up to her rather strict standards, and I could interpret that the scary, barking dog represented his angry mother.

One day on the way to his session, Larry's mother bought him a toy watch, which he lost in the park without being aware of it until he entered my office. He had wanted very much to show me this new prize and he cried stricken with grief. His mother volunteered to look for it in the park while he stayed with me. Throughout this session Larry was painfully distraught. He looked out the window and wailed that a dog took the watch from him. He began to draw a watch, interrupted by outbursts of crying. The crying was renewed when his mother returned without the watch, though she promised to get him another. Larry thoroughly ignored my interpretations about the dog taking away his valued possession and would not talk about the loss when he returned next day with a replacement watch. He said how pleased he was to have one just like me and just like his daddy. I was then able to take up with more certainty aspects of his identification with his father and with me in the transference. We worked quite some time on his castration anxiety, which was now manifest in his fear that dogs could take away something valuable of his.

As this work progressed, so did Larry's social and academic behavior, slowly and painfully, but noticably to parents, teachers, and other children. He was now able to engage in play with other children, although for the most part the boys would not have much to do with him. He had not been able to make any regular friends in class, but he was tolerated much better by the others and sometimes even invited to participate.

Up to this point the analytic material had not seemed to offer much opportunity to work on Larry's feelings around his mother's departing for the hospital in the middle of the night when his brother was born. We had done some work on his murderous rivalry with Melvin, but perhaps he first had to renew his trust in me after his return from the summer break before he could very gradually bring something more of this early experience that I could use. Larry asked me to draw a man, but before I could draw the mouth on the face he insisted that I should make it a "smiling face" and showed me by gouging in a heavy mouth, which in fact was not smiling. Then he showed me on his own face, making a grimace, dragging up the corners of his mouth, and showing his teeth. While recognizing the oral-aggressive content, I decided to take up the defensive elements first. I said he was showing me a fake smile, showing how he had to keep his smile over all his feelings underneath, especially when he got furious at Melvin. He suddenly got very angry at me and hit out, cried inconsolably for his mother, and would not listen anymore. He snuggled up on his mother's lap, but could not be comforted. Finally she said, "Don't cry and get upset, Larry, because when you're upset it gets me upset." This gave me the opportunity to say that Larry was learning that it really was all right to be upset and angry. After this Larry came back with me, but for the rest of the session he worried if Melvin would be home for lunch when he got home, and told me how he wanted to kill a classmate at school. In the next session, Larry played with trains and pretended that they departed from various stations, alternately carrying sad people and angry people. Putting together his smiling grimace and the departures with sad and angry people, I said I knew that he had been sad and angry when his mother had left to go to the hospital and he did not know she was leaving, and that he also had been angry when his grandmother and daddy told him not to cry but to smile instead because his baby brother was born. From time to time during this session, Larry made visits to the waiting room to check that his mother was still there, still smiled at him, and still loved him, although he was expressing such hostile and angry thoughts about his parents with me. He asked me to repeat what I said several times. A little later I added that he felt abandoned and that he felt he had lost his mother when she went to the hospital and was afraid she no longer loved him. While quietly listening to this, Larry began to draw a house which for the first time contained a family within, and which I took to indicate that he accepted these interpretations.

It was during this particular week that Mrs. L. commented to me that Larry seemed no longer afraid of dogs, although I learned that this fear could come and go. Sometimes the changes seemed to be in relation to the ongoing analytic work, and at other times had no apparent connection with it. But his fears of wind and thunder gradually began to disappear as he became less anxious about his parents' fighting. His increased ability to verbalize his feelings was seen in his attempts to moderate his parents' behavior. For example, the mother described the beginning of an argument one evening, when the father raised his voice in anger at the mother. Larry then said to him calmly, "Don't shout at Mummy." This intervention was sufficient to restore some degree of calm to them all. At another point, when out of her guilty feelings she was talking with Larry about how he must feel that she did not love him, he asked her to go downstairs and to get him an apple, and finally, "Will you stop talking about it?" It seemed that Mrs. L. had caught on to the idea that Larry and I were working on the difficulties in their relationship and I had the impression that she was trying to be the analyst at home.

In the tenth month of treatment Larry and his family went abroad for a week. On his return, Larry enacted his departure and return repeatedly, the departures occurring more frequently than the returns. He became attentively interested in my facial expression and what it meant, and I took this together with some indications of anxiety about the play departures to signify that, in the transference, he was fearful that I was angry at him for going away and leaving me. On one occasion at about this time he was looking out the window to see if he could find his father who was to pick him up after the session. Seeing his father approach, Larry commented that his father looked "serious." This was a new addition to his vocabulary with which he was quite pleased, and eventually we were able to learn what an important addition it was. In this family it was forbidden to be sad—one either smiled or was furious. Therefore, to know that his father was serious meant that Larry was coming to realize that other emotions were also possible; if his father *looked* "serious," it meant that he was not *furious* with Larry and would not retaliate, that is, he would not hurt or punish him. I saw this as one of several signs that Larry progressively employed his thought processes on the secondary process level.

One day Larry began a session by saying he was pretending he had a little doggie. This kind of pretending now seemed tolerable to Larry as long as nothing was actually physically present, since he was still frightened of a dog puppet, of a toy dog, and even of the image of a dog on television. When I said I could pretend having a little doggie too, he became quite upset and ran crying to his mother. He did not want me to have a doggie, and this incident helped us to understand that the feared dog had now come to represent a baby, a focus for a considerable amount of Larry's hostility and for his consequent fears of retaliation. With his anxiety somewhat lessened in this area, he began to experiment with angry feelings toward his father; slowly he came to appreciate that his father could survive the overt expression of Larry's anger, and that he could survive his father's retaliation as well.

By the beginning of the second year of treatment, the analytic work centered on the problem of making babies: whether Larry could make one by himself; whether he wanted to make one with his mother; or whether he wanted to be a baby again and return to his mother's womb and start all over again, because then there would be no fighting, no rivals, no changes, and he would be close to his mother. Among the multiple functions served by Larry's wish to reunite with his mother was the defensive protection it offered against his archaic destructive rage which we learned was involved in his reactions to separations. It had been easier for him to cope with anger at his father, and now we understood that Larry's difficulty in permitting himself any angry feelings at his mother had a connection with the events around her disappearance when Melvin was born. He felt that his rage had made her disappear or destroyed her, perhaps forever, and that her returning with a baby meant that she no longer loved him. As we worked through this material, Larry's mood seemed to lighten, but Mrs. L. told me that now he seemed to be afraid of cats. This was the point at which I was surprised to learn that Mrs. L. herself had a cat phobia, and I took it up with Larry along the lines of his identification with his mother, an area in which we had already done some work.

Unfortunately this work was interrupted by a holiday. On his return, Larry brought a new theme regarding dogs expressed in role play. I was a big dog who had to chase Larry, the little dog. Then he approached me, saying, "I love you, big dog," and put his arms around me. In succeeding sessions he became increasingly silly and excited, and he often clutched at his penis. I learned that Larry's dog phobia had returned, and on one occasion when he screamed on seeing a dog, he admitted he was afraid of the dog's erect tail. From attempts at doll play, often disrupted by his excitement, I gathered that the entire family had stayed in one room over the vacation and that Larry most likely had again been exposed to his parents' sexual activity, probably including his father's erect penis. Very gradually Larry was able to regain some useful distance from his anxiety-arousing passive excitement and frightening impulses and to put them into words.

Third Phase of Treatment (15th month to termination)

I will end my description of Larry's analysis by giving some clinical vignettes from the last year of treatment in order to illustrate how some of the previously mentioned themes came together, and how the termination evolved.

Larry's difficulties over separations were worked through in many ways. To Larry, separation meant abandonment, loss of love, and the arousal of his hostile and destructive impulses as a consequence of which he feared terrible retaliation. In reality his father was going away regularly and his mother was frequently leaving him in the house without saying good-bye, and without explanation. The experience in which his mother disappeared and returned with a baby collected meanings from many previous and subsequent separations. On one of the many occasions when we were discussing his mother's hospitalization, Larry said, "And I hurt myself." He recalled the episode at the age of 3 when he fell off the windowsill and struck his teeth. He remembered his terror, and the pain and the blood, and how frightened his mother had been. He had experienced this as a punishment for his rivalrous feelings toward his brother and for his forbidden aggressive wishes toward his mother. We learned that he protected his mother and brother from these impulses by appearing infantile and helpless. In the sessions with me he depicted the frightening aspects of his mother in a doll he named "Mrs. Angrish." She rapidly developed into a large and terrifying monster who let out peculiar nocturnal screams, frightening a baby who feared that he would be bitten. Indeed, she proceeded to bite the baby on the mouth, at which point Larry became quite anxious for several sessions. The analytic work enabled us to understand Larry's early wish to bite and chew up his brother, then to spit him out and flush him away. In the play with Mrs. Angrish, Larry demonstrated his fear that his mother would seek revenge and retaliation for his destructive wishes. Larry's speech became noticeably and consistently more clear and articulate in the course of this work.

Outside the sessions Larry seemed to be trying out a counterphobic attitude toward dogs. His mother reported that on several occasions he would deliberately run up to a strange dog and pet it, then feel very pleased with himself. Larry did not mention these episodes to me, but at that point the analytic work was focused on the oedipal level. For example, Larry attempted to get me to control his behavior as he became more excited and ran in and out. This coincided with his father's going on another trip and telling Larry, "Now you're a big boy, look after Mummy when I am away." When I took this up in terms of his need to have some help controlling his excited feelings when his daddy was away, he brought his mother into the treatment room and had us go through everything again with her as audience. The difficulty Mrs. L. had in getting the point and her continuing wish to be the "analyst at home" were demonstrated later when she told me what happened prior to another trip by Mr. L. She said to Larry, "You're glad Daddy is going away because then you'll have your Mummy to yourself." Larry looked at her and said, "I'm not so glad." Only very gradually did she gain some degree of awareness that her need for her son was expressed in a way which interfered with his development.

Larry's increasing verbal skills led to a decrease in physical attacks on his brother and to intensified verbal hostility. He composed a song entitled "Kick him in the dustbin, kill, kill, kill!" which he sang at first primarily to his brother, but then progressively more to his father as he resented his frequent departures. Suddenly Mrs. L. decided to take her sons and visit her mother, canceling a treatment session with no warning for Larry and no perception of his being upset by it. I learned that the parents were fighting yet again, with Larry's father threatening to depart. Larry brought in his feeling of being unsafe by telling me a story of falling into the water on holiday. He could not swim, he could not breathe, and somebody had to pull him out, and he did not know where his mother was. There were other stories of being left alone at home, not knowing when anybody would come back or who would feed him. Just at this moment Larry's most beloved teacher announced that she was leaving the school. He broke into tears in class and the headmistress telephoned me. He reexperienced all the fears of being abandoned and attacked as a consequence of his hostility which made him feel so unloved and unworthwhile. But as we worked through his concerns (the parents reconciling as usual, the school introducing Larry to a nice new teacher), Larry, now 7½ years old, showed increasing signs of identifying with the active father and of looking for his admiration rather than the mother's. Larry said he did not want to see me anymore because he loved Mummy and Daddy more. I became the aggressive one: if he had to see somebody, he wanted to see a nicer doctor. He experienced interpretations as aggressive attacks. He told me he was no longer afraid of dogs, and I pointed out he was now afraid of me.

Over a period of time I took up some of the various roles I had represented for Larry in the transference. For example, I was the frightening, threatening father who left because he did not love the family or Larry, or who preferred Melvin. Or I was the engulfing mother whose retaliatory rage was one of several projected manifestations of his own aggression. Gradually I wondered if I might also represent knowledge of his wishes and fantasies that Larry was making an effort to repress. I tried suspending my interpretive work in this area, and Larry then came to look for my admiration in much the same way he sought his father's. He brought in work he did at school for my approval, he showed me how well he could read and write, sometimes doing his homework in the sessions. He told me about how well he could now ride a bicycle and brought in a football for us to play with together. I learned that Larry was much more involved in play activities with boys his own age rather than with girls as before, and he no longer sought direct comfort, approval, and reassurance from his teacher.

Larry began to make remarks which hinted at termination, and his mother more openly wondered if he might be big enough to handle his own problems now, especially since he was so much better. Larry said that he could talk with his mother about any problems, which suggested to me that Mrs. L.'s ambition to be the "perfect mother" might entail her replacing me if she could perform my functions as well. The accuracy with which he reflected his mother's sentiments about termination indicated that the tie between them was still a close and intimate one. We were able to discuss his fears of losing his mother's love if he should want to continue treatment, in effect choosing me over his mother. But the threat of the loss of his mother's love was still too real for Larry, and while it was clear that more analysis would be very helpful, I felt that the ensuing loyalty conflict would put at risk many of the gains Larry had made. In addition, it seemed to me that definite signs of latency had appeared, that in many areas he had regained lost ground along the pathways of forward development, and that although areas of conflict remained, his further development might best be served by bringing his analysis to a close.

We agreed to a gradual termination which ended 2 years and 4 months of work. Larry went through a brief recapitulation of some of his symptoms within the sessions but not outside. I interpreted this development in terms of Larry's fears about separating from me, that he might never see me again and that I would no longer love him, repeating with me the fears that he had permanently alienated or killed his mother when his brother was born. Therefore, I agreed with his wish that he might see me again sometime after treatment had stopped. Although throughout this period his defenses seemed chiefly age-appropriate, there was a persistent tinge of slightly euphoric denial, which I had noticed in his parents as well.

Mrs. L. contacted me several times in the 4 years since treatment ended. Larry has been able to keep up with his class at school and seems to have become reconciled to being outdistanced intellectually by his younger brother. He has developed friendships and appears quite average to his teachers, though some social awkwardnesses remain. His dog phobia is hardly noticeable to his mother, who told me that Larry does seem able to avoid dogs, but she has seen no overt anxiety in him about dogs since treatment ended.

DISCUSSION

I have presented aspects of Larry's analysis to demonstrate how a persisting symptom in childhood can maintain its outward form while the underlying psychic structure evolves and the conflicts, drive derivatives, and related anxieties change in the course of development. Among the many possible issues that arise, I have chosen to focus on a selected few.[2]

2. I thereby leave out many issues central to this topic. Though these issues are not discussed here, they are necessary to any thoroughgoing study of phobias, which of course would go beyond the limits of a single case report. Some of these issues are: the distinctions between fear and anxiety, and between anxiety and signal anxiety; the relationship of anxiety to other affects and the applicability of the signal function to other affects; the changes in the course of development and with progressive internalizations.

1. A recurrent question is whether a particular phobic manifestation is "truly" a phobia or whether it is an archaic fear, one of the frequent "transient fears of childhood," or a phobic manifestation in a complicated disturbance. The mechanisms in a classical phobia have been summarized by Anna Freud (1977) as follows:

> At one point of the process, presumably when fantasy activity has failed to protect against massive unpleasure, a different mechanism comes into operation, namely, condensation, which precedes externalization. This means that fears and anxieties do not remain diffuse but are compressed by the child into one encompassing symbol which represents the dangers left over from preoedipal phases as well as the dominant ones due to phallic-oedipal conflicts. It is, then, this symbol . . . which, as a supposed part of the outside world, is dealt with by avoidance. According to this view, the missing piece in the cases of diffuse anxiety would be the mechanism of condensation [p. 88].

Clearly, the degree to which these mechanisms can be employed by a child in his efforts to avoid unpleasure and anxiety will be related to the extent to which his mental apparatus has developed and structuralized. Unless a sufficient degree of structure exists, avoidance phenomena as such would not quality as phobias in the classical sense.

In Larry's case, his defensive structure repeatedly failed to protect him from panic, and his development seemed to have been arrested in some areas and to have regressed in others. In fact, it might be said that Larry could hardly afford to give up any defense or symptom he had managed to construct along the way. Whether the original fear of dogs was based on an early frightening experience, or was among Larry's archaic fears, or even began in direct relation to his mother's cat phobia (Burlingham et al., 1955), or was due to fear of loss of his mother (Freud, 1926, p. 137), by the time treatment began Larry was subject to repeated panic states which can be viewed as evidence of failure of his defensive system. This failure to develop or perhaps to use signal anxiety can be understood as a consequence of the mother's earlier inability to respond well enough to her child's "rescue signals" (Tolpin, 1971, p. 335). Thus Larry's fear of dogs need not have had the underlying structure of a classical phobia at the time he began treatment, and one is led to examine the developmental line of anxiety in Larry's life (A. Freud, 1963). There is a likelihood that Larry underwent a backward movement along this line, which has been described as beginning with the diffuse somatic excitation of birth, and as progressing to pervasive psychic anxiety and then to signal anxiety (Yorke and Wiseberg, 1976).[3] With his progress in treatment Larry was gradually able to reinstitute the signal anxiety function. At the same time the internal dangers with which he had to deal became progressively more age-appropriate. They next expressed certain aspects of his experience of developmental interferences and developmental conflicts, for example, at the anal level, where we have seen evidence that Larry was frightened of his impulses to mess. In the analysis the work then centered on his phallic-oedipal conflicts. At some point before termination of treatment, Larry's anxiety seemed thoroughly contained in his fear of dogs, which then appeared to have all the attributes of a classical phobia, though mild and not particularly disruptive; moreover, overt anxiety remained confined to this one area.

2. The remarkable persistence of Larry's fear of dogs requires explanation. A number of authors have enlarged our understanding of the durability and persistence of certain aspects of mental structure and function (e.g., Rapaport, 1957; Gill, 1963; Holt, 1965; Sandler and Joffe, 1966, 1967), but it was Hartmann (1939) who first pointed out that an "attitude which arose originally in the service of defense against an instinctual drive may, in the course of time, become an independent structure . . . [and] come to serve other functions" (p. 26). So it may have been through a change of function that Larry's early fear of dogs came to serve later as a dog phobia, while the associated successive conflicts became progressively more internalized ones. However, the implied "secondary au-

---

3. The developmental view of affects has also been discussed by Brenner (1974, 1975).

tonomy" I describe here does not necessarily remove the structure in question from the area of conflict into the "non-conflictual sphere" (Hartmann, 1950, p. 81). Instead it may come to be utilized by a number of conflicts other than the one which originally gave rise to the defense, or which took an available mechanism and put it to work in the service of defense.

Thus the dog as a symbol representing many preoedipal dangers comes to encompass phallic-oedipal conflicts as well, and one might view the succeeding anxieties reflected in the various changes in the particularly feared aspects of the dog figure as steps along the way to a change of function. The persistence of the framework of a dog figure in Larry's mind is the persistence of a mental structure which is altered in certain limited aspects of its appearance as it is used in his attempts to solve a series of problems. This differs from a suggestion by Sandler and Joffe (1967) which emphasizes the persistence of normally inhibited primitive modes of functioning. Larry used the relatively unchanging mental representation of the dog while with advancing development he evolved progressively more sophisticated modes of functioning. It could be said that widely differing ego organizations in the same person at different times utilized the same symptom (in a descriptive sense) in the attempt to solve differing conflicts, much as Eissler (1953) asserted that "fairly similar symptoms may be combined with two entirely different ego organizations—one barely, the other severely, modified" (p. 118).

Certain aspects of Larry's mental representation of the feared dog did change, however, in the course of treatment. In working with Little Hans, Freud (1909) described how the child had an opportunity to "unfold his phobia" (p. 43). Freud emphasized what he called the "diffuse" aspect of a phobia, in which various elements are utilized for the external expression and representation of corresponding internal constituents of the conflict. With Little Hans, horses, heavily loaded carts, falling and biting, and particular kinds of horses, all found their places in the currently expressed anxiety about horses as this anxiety changed and evolved in the course of his treatment

(p. 124). Perhaps because he felt that the psychoanalytic treatment itself would be blamed for many of Little Hans's symptoms, Freud stated categorically that the apparent further development of the phobia really represented the emergence of material already in existence, "not of fresh productions for which the treatment might be held responsible" (p. 138).

Some of this kind of "unfolding" undoubtedly also took place in Larry's treatment. However, his forward development proceeded during the course of the analysis in such a manner that the fear of dogs took up elements which it did not contain in its initial form, and which came about partly as a consequence of the analytic work, and partly because of the characteristic problems appropriate to the particular concomitant stage of development. It is the reverse of Tolpin's statement (1970) that "in some cases, symptomatology and even the structure of symptoms may change while the basic pathology remains the same" (1970, p. 275n.). With Larry, his symptom—fear of dogs—remained the same, though the underlying conflicts and the structure of the symptom—the mechanisms employed in its manufacture—were progressively more elaborated and sophisticated as his ego functions matured and enlarged their area of successful control. If we understand the "basic pathology" underlying the symptom to be the series of anxieties in Larry which gave rise to the need for defensive activities of the ego, then these anxieties and the associated conflicts changed as Larry developed, though the symptom in a descriptive sense remained grossly the same. Tolpin (1970) warns of the necessity "to distinguish symptomatology and the structure of a particular symptom from the underlying structure of the ego organization in which the symptom occurs" (p. 276). I would agree and add that it is also important to make a distinction between particular conflicts (which may be expressed in identical or in various symptoms) and the matrix of the ego organization in which the conflicts occur. As an example from Larry's treatment, his cognitive development as well as the developmental lines of his anxiety and object relationships all played some part in the concurrent picture of his fear of dogs. However, certain qualities and limitations in Larry's ego, perhaps to some extent constitutional, circumscribed his ability to cope successfully with the difficulties he encountered from early on in life. Though beyond the scope of this paper, further investigation of this factor would undoubtedly be in the frame of reference developed by Mahler et al. (1975).

3. An understanding of how Larry's delayed speech development was related to his fear of dogs may shed some light on the question of his underlying ego organization. It also helps in linking his disturbances in drive development to his deficiencies in the ordinarily conflict-free sphere of the acquisition of speech. I have recorded the first initial comprehensible remarks Larry made, but clinically his early vocalizations in treatment more often served to distance himself from me, much as he seemed pointedly to avoid any contact with me (Rubinfine, 1962; Ritvo and Provence, 1953). From the beginning of the analysis it was clearly important to Larry that he was learning to use words, both in terms of an inner language and in terms of speech (Balkányi, 1964), and that he was using words to identify feelings, to permit the resumption of normal development, thus demonstrating the role of verbalization as A. Katan (1961) described it. Kolansky (1967) and Sirota (1969) have written about the role of primitive language and primary process thinking in the genesis of psychopathology in children, including the appearance of phobias, while de Hirsch (1975) has focused on the important reciprocal relationship between language and developing ego functions. In Larry's case, both his early language and speech development were hindered at the time by a combination of circumstances which included his mother's relative unavailability and lack of interest in him, and the many non-English speaking caretakers in his first two years of life. The simultaneous early development of intense oral-aggressive wishes combined with the impact of the bloody damage to his mouth probably posed insuperable difficulties for him. All of this undoubtedly contributed to the establishment of the threatening external symbol of the dog, which combined the expression of the various constituents of Larry's conflicts.

4. The qualities of and limitations in Larry's ego development already referred to contain an aspect of personality functioning which might be called the problem of maintaining narcissistic equilibrium, and to which I will refer only briefly. There was abundant evidence that Larry had difficulties in this area, such as his repeatedly asking his teacher, "You are proud of me, aren't you?" his fear of the omnipotent power of his rageful reaction to his mother's disappearance, his feelings of worthlessness stemming from this and other sources, and his utter helplessness in the face of everyday events. Spruiell (1975) has made the helpful distinction between self-love, the regulation of self-esteem, and omnipotence. He has discussed the early development and interrelationship of these narcissistic "strands" in the first years of life and described their connections with the evolution of early object relationships. In terms of Larry's need to regulate his tenuous narcissistic equilibrium, his fear and phobia of dogs functioned as an adjunct in his efforts to maintain his painfully low self-esteem, when aspects of the dreaded animal from time to time served as a despicable external representation of anal and oral impulses which it was important for him to disown in himself. Treatment was helpful to Larry particularly in this area, because the remaining dog phobia no longer seemed to carry the burden of maintaining narcissistic equilibrium which it had in his earlier fear of dogs.

5. It may be only an academic exercise to ask whether consideration of Larry's dog fear and phobia can assist in making a prognosis. He was certainly able to use analysis to his advantage in many areas; just as clearly, many areas of disturbance remained. There are very few authors who consider this issue. For example, Anthony (1962) and Lebovici (1970) compare Little Hans and the Wolf-Man and adduce reasons why the outcome was so much less satisfactory in the latter case. Lebovici seems to find the explanation in terms of the libidinal level achieved, while Anthony includes a number of features: (1) the phobia is circumscribed, (2) and related to phase-specific problems, (3) which are predominantly intrapsychic, (4) without significant constitutional elements, (5) and it is set in an af-

fectionate family environment. In view of the fact that Larry was treated in childhood, and that at termination further development was accessible to him, his prognosis might be better than supposed from the literature.

Summary and Conclusions

Aspects of the analysis of a 5-year-old boy with a fear of dogs were presented to demonstrate the development of a pre-neurotic fear into a classical phobia. I discussed some ways of distinguishing between fears and phobias and argued that while the external appearance of a symptom may remain essentially the same, the underlying structure of it may change. The persistence of the plastic figure of a dog as an object of fear was seen as a formal kind of structural persistence, while development of ego functioning proceeded. Many possible origins to the patient's fear of dogs were considered, though delayed language development made a significant contribution. The fear and possibly the phobia also figured in Larry's efforts to maintain a narcissistic equilibrium made precarious by the peculiarities of his early relationship to his mother. In Larry's case, an otherwise poor prognosis was tempered by the fact that he had analysis in childhood and that he was largely restored to the path of further development.

BIBLIOGRAPHY

ANTHONY, E. J. (1962), In Panel on: Classical Forms of Neurosis in Infancy and Early Childhood, E. B. Kaplan. *J. Amer. Psychoanal. Assn.*, 10 : 571–578.
BALKÁNYI, C. (1964), On Verbalization. *Int. J. Psycho-Anal.*, 45 : 64–74.
BRENNER, C. (1974), On the Nature and Development of Affects. *Psychoanal. Quart.*, 43 : 532–556.
——— (1975), Affects and Psychic Conflict. *Psychoanal. Quart.*, 44 : 5–28.
BURLINGHAM, D., GOLDBERGER, A., & LUSSIER, A. (1955), Simultaneous Analysis of Mother and Child. *This Annual*, 10 : 165–186.
DE HIRSCH, K. (1975), Language Deficits in Children with Developmental Lags. *This Annual*, 30 : 95–126.
EDGCUMBE, R. & BURGNER, M. (1975), The Phallic-Narcissistic Phase. *This Annual*, 30 : 161–180.

EISSLER, K. R. (1953), The Effect of the Structure of the Ego on Psychoanalytic Technique. *J. Amer. Psychoanal. Assn.*, 1 : 104–143.

FREUD, A. (1963), The Concept of Developmental Lines. *This Annual,* 18 : 245–265.

——— (1966), Normality and Pathology in Childhood. *W.,* 6.

——— (1977), Fears, Anxieties and Phobic Phenomena. *This Annual,* 32 : 85–90.

FREUD, S. (1909), Analysis of a Phobia in a Five-Year-Old Boy. *S.E.,* 10 : 3–149.

——— (1917), Introductory Lectures on Psycho-Analysis: Part III. *S.E..,* 16 : 243–463.

——— (1918), From the History of an Infantile Neurosis. *S.E.,* 17 : 3–123.

——— (1926), Inhibitions, Symptoms and Anxiety. *S.E.,* 20 : 77–175.

GILL, M. M. (1963), *Topography and Systems in Psychoanalytic Theory* [*Psychol. Issues,* Monogr. 10]. New York: Int. Univ. Press.

HARTMANN, H. (1939), *Ego Psychology and the Problem of Adaptation.* New York: Int. Univ. Press, 1958.

——— (1950), Comments on the Psychoanalytic Theory of the Ego. *This Annual,* 5 : 74–96.

HOLT, R. R. (1965), Ego Autonomy Re-Evaluated. *Int. J. Psycho-Anal.,* 46 : 151–167.

KATAN, A. (1961), Some Thoughts about the Role of Verbalization in Early Childhood. *This Annual,* 16 : 184–188.

KOLANSKY, H. (1967), Some Psychoanalytic Considerations on Speech in Normal Development and Psychopathology. *This Annual,* 22 : 274–295.

LEBOVICI, S. (1970), Clinical and Technical Notes Concerning Psychoanalysis with regard to Phobias Affecting Men. *Int. J. Psycho-Anal.,* 51 : 23–32.

LEWIN, B. D. (1952), Phobic Symptoms and Dream Interpretation. *Psychoanal. Quart.,* 31 : 295–322.

MAHLER, M. S. (1952), On Child Psychosis and Schizophrenia. *This Annual,* 7 : 286–305.

——— PINE, F., & BERGMAN, A. (1975), *The Psychological Birth of the Human Infant.* New York: Basic Books.

NAGERA, H. (1966), *Early Childhood Disturbances, the Infantile Neurosis, and the Adulthood Disturbances.* New York: Int. Univ. Press.

RAPAPORT, D. (1957), Cognitive Structures. In: *The Collected Papers of David Rapaport,* ed. M. M. Gill. New York: Basic Books, 1967, pp. 631–664.

RITVO, S., & PROVENCE, S. (1953), Form Perception and Imitation in Some Autistic Children. *This Annual,* 8 : 155–161.

RUBINFINE, D. L. (1962). Maternal Stimulation, Psychic Structure, and Early Object Relations. *This Annual,* 17 : 265–282.

SANDLER, J. & JOFFE, W. G. (1966), On Skill and Sublimation. *J. Amer. Psychoanal. Assn.,* 14 : 335–355.

——— ——— (1967), The Tendency to Persistence in Psychological Function and Development. *Bull. Menninger Clin.,* 31 : 257–271.

SIROTA, M. (1969), Urine or You're In. *This Annual,* 24 : 252–270.

SPRUIELL, V. (1975), Three Strands of Narcissism. *Psychoanal. Quart.,* 44 : 577–595.

TOLPIN, M. (1970), The Infantile Neurosis. *This Annual,* 25 : 273–305.

—— (1971), On the Beginnings of a Cohesive Self. *This Annual,* 26 : 316–352.

WEIL, A. P. (1973), Ego Strengthening Prior to Analysis. *This Annual,* 28 : 287–301.

YORKE, C. & WISEBERG, S. (1976), A Developmental View of Anxiety. *This Annual,* 31 : 107–135.

APPLICATIONS
OF PSYCHOANALYSIS

Creativity and Adolescence

The Effect of Trauma in Freud's Adolescence

K. R. EISSLER, M.D.

THE PSYCHOLOGY OF MALE ADOLESCENCE, DESPITE ALL THE progress that has been made in its investigation, remains a puzzle. One youngster enters adolescence most promisingly, alert and spontaneous in his originality, but leaves it with constraints and inhibitions and lacking in interests. Yet in another youngster just the reverse takes place. I do not know of any explanation of this seeming paradox.

In speaking of creativity, I am not thinking of the sense in which every human being is creative. Perception per se, after all, can be regarded as a creative act. Here I speak of creativity in the narrower sense, the ability to give existence to unusual, original values. In this respect our species shows remarkable contrasts. The lives of some individuals are rich with creation of original values, and creativity can be said to be their existential center. The lives of others, however, are totally bare of this kind of creativity. I shall not contribute to a clarification of this problem. Indeed, the main inference I shall have to draw will be trivial, but the path I shall take to reach it may offer something of interest.

The problem of male adolescence and creativity has two aspects: hypercreative adolescence per se, and the adolescence

Faculty, New York Psychoanalytic Institute.

An extended version of a paper read to the plenary session of the American Psychoanalytic Association, New York, on December 16, 1977.

of the man who will be hypercreative in later years. Blaise Pascal (1623–62) and Everiste Galois (1811–32) are outstanding examples of the first type of adolescence. Before he was 16 Pascal wrote a work on conic sections in which he laid down a series of propositions of such importance that they are still the foundation of the modern treatment of the subject. Galois was killed in a duel at the age of 20. "His complete works fill only sixty-one small pages. They prove indubitably that he was one of the greatest mathematicians of all times, whose fundamental ideas have influenced the whole of mathematical philosophy. It is likely that when mathematicians of the future contemplate his personality at the distance of a few centuries, it will appear to them to be surrounded by the same halo of wonder as those of Euclid, Archimedes, Descartes and Newton" (Sarton, 1948, p. 83f.).

But hypercreative adolescence is probably the exception in the development of the genius. Clark (1939) pointed out that Leonardo's greatness became visible comparatively late, and one may observe that the adolescence of talented persons is often more promising than that of those who later develop into geniuses. Freud's adolescence, which will be the subject matter of this essay, belongs to the latter type, even though he succeeded in some noteworthy achievements during middle adolescence and late adolescence. I shall try to reconstruct some processes that occurred during his adolescence, and to identify their effects on the unfolding of his later creativity.

FREUD'S ADOLESCENCE

EARLY LITERARY PRODUCTIONS

The earliest record of Freud's writing, a childhood letter, gives no hint of future creativity. His aphorisms (Freud, 1974), written when he was 15 years old for a school magazine, give a different picture. Of course, no one could have predicted that they were produced by the mind of a man destined to become the foremost psychologist of his time—no more than one could, on the basis of *Titus Andronicus,* predict

Hamlet. Yet the aphorism is rarely chosen as the vehicle for the literary productions of an adolescent (Bernfeld, 1924). It is a literary form that is particularly difficult to handle. Thus the very form of the writing suggests that the author is a talented individual, a belief which is confirmed by its content.

All five aphorisms are devoted to psychological peculiarities of man. The first, in translation, reads, "Gold inflates man like air a hog's bladder."[1] This sounds like the pert remark of a precocious 15-year-old about one of man's many narcissistic weaknesses.[2]

The second aphorism is more complex. In free translation: "The most egotistical of all is the man who never considered the possibility that he may be an egotist." Again an arrow is shot at man's narcissism, but this time self-observation and self-judgment are called in as moral agencies that may reduce the gravity of a vice.

The beginning of the third aphorism declares that "Some people are like a rich, never completely explored mine." I may project too much into this sentence, but it strikes me as an anticipation of a basic psychoanalytic theme: man's inexhaustible unconscious, which is not directly accessible to view.

Four aphorisms are critical of man, and only in the last does Freud praise man: "Any larger animal outdoes man in something, but he outdoes them in everything." The young pessimist apparently needed some hope, just as later, when he was an aged man, he clung to the hope that the voice of intellect wins out in the long run, although someone so well versed in the history of mankind must have known that this hope was an illusion.

1. Pigs' bladders were used as air reservoirs or bellows because of their great distensibility.

2. The youth's cynicism might be—aside from personal factors—referable to the mood of the time, that is, 1871. This was the middle of the so-called *Gründerzeit,* when an unscrupulous crowd precipitously industrialized Central Europe. Wealth was accumulated rapidly: the weak were mercilessly economically exploited; and a reprehensible materialism was rampant. Freud's father was a typical example of a weak man crushed by a ruthless and inexorable economic process.

Each single aphorism succeeds and only one falls flat because of its awkward imagery.

Two years later, in the well-known *Matura* letter, it becomes evident that Freud had made immense progress in the development of his gifts. It is remarkable that a 17-year-old wrote a letter in an incomparable German whose beauty went beyond anything one could expect. The letter sparkles with wit and contains an analogy so striking that involuntarily one may wonder whether Freud had read it somewhere, even though his later writings abound in equally striking imagery. In the International Exposition of 1873, he wrote, he was unable to find the great panorama of human activity, as newspapers had declared one could, "any more than I can find the features of a landscape in a herbarium" (Freud, 1960, p. 5). This is perfect in content as well as in form.

Thus we find Freud at 17 a master of language exceptional for his age. His writing had a style that attracted his teachers' attention. His knowledge of the ancient authors was profound; he had read them in Greek and Latin. His wit, alertness, quickness of observation, originality of judgment—all are well documented by the early letters. A youth who had been given such rare and rich talents could easily have become a renowned professor of German literature; he would also have had the opportunity of rapidly acquiring distinction as a well-known essayist, sought after by leading newspapers. In brief, a promising literary career awaited him.[3]

CHOICE OF PROFESSION

Before pursuing the vicissitudes of Freud's literary talents, I must mention that Freud's earliest choice of profession was to

3. The origin of Freud's remarkable gift of language is unknown. There is no indication of familial endowment except in the report of one of Freud's distant relatives (of which Prof. Ernst Simon informed me) that Freud's father wrote a particularly sophisticated and elegant Hebrew. Freud's linguistic ability is all the more surprising inasmuch as his earliest speech patterns were acquired in a small provincial town and his parents, who had grown up in small Jewish communities, very probably did not speak a pure German.

be a lawyer. The idea of becoming a politician and of being active in changing the sociopolitical environment of his society may have been connected with this choice. Such a connection would have been in agreement with the behavior of historical figures like Hannibal and Marshal Masséna who had served earlier as ego ideals (Freud, 1900, p. 196f.) as well as with the revolutionary spirit that was directly expressed in early years and later in dreams.[4] It is, however, likely, as Freud intimated (1960, p. 378f.), that the idea of becoming a lawyer was not spontaneous but resulted from identification with, or more probably imitation of, Heinrich Braun (1854–1927) (Freud, 1925a, p. 8), who was Freud's classmate for six years in secondary school. Braun, who later became an outstanding political figure (Vogelstein-Braun, 1932, 1966), was a charismatic personality. As the scion of a wealthy family, he had a large library at his disposal and gave Freud access to books that had a decisive influence on the enlargement of his views of the world.

A calling card has been preserved on which was printed *Sigismund Freud: Student der Rechte* [student of law] (Stanescu, 1965, p. 127).[5] Since Freud never studied law at the university, this indicates juvenile acting out and probably a lack of serious intent.

One of the central events in Freud's adolescence that requires psychoanalytic investigation—not only because it is quite puzzling but also because it was the principal adventitious event on his way to later psychological discoveries—is his decision to study medicine. I wish I could be as certain about my explanation of it as I am of its oddity, even outlandishness.

What really happened here was that an adolescent threw his treasure of innate talents to the winds by choosing the study of medicine, which provided for the expression neither of his literary talents nor of his burgeoning imagination. The explanation Freud gave decades later of the puzzling turn of his inter-

4. See Schorske (1973). When Freud was a boy of 11, a fortune teller predicted he would become a cabinet minister.

5. Stanescu wrongly assumed that the calling card referred to a namesake of Freud's.

ests is incorrect and is reminiscent of the legends mighty nations form about their low beginnings (1910, p. 83f.; 1918, p. 20).

In his autobiographical essay, Freud wrote: "it was hearing Goethe's beautiful essay on Nature read aloud at a popular lecture by Professor Carl Brühl just before I left school that decided me to become a medical student" (1925a, p. 8). In his book on dreams, that is, 27 years after the decision, Freud had given a similar if not identical explanation (1900, p. 441), for there he had written that the recital caused him "to take up the study of natural science." "Natural science," of course, would not necessarily have meant medicine. Indeed, those of Freud's letters which have been preserved also do not make it quite clear whether the initial decision was to study medicine or to study science. It is, however, probable that Freud equated medicine and the natural sciences.

Be that as it may, there is documentary evidence that Freud's decision to study medicine was not a sudden and last-minute one, as he later described it, but rather a choice made much earlier and only after a period of hesitation and doubt. Thus in the middle of March of 1873, that is, about three months before he passed his finals at secondary school, Freud wrote to his friend Fluss about his plan: "I can report what is perhaps the most important bit of news in my miserable life" (1969, p. 423). He calls the matter "undecided," "half-baked," and does not want to reveal what it really is and "then have to take it back later." On May 1, however, he seemed to have felt more assured and announced to his friend, "I have decided to be a Natural Scientist." He seemed pessimistic, because he added that any plan "can turn into a Tower of Babel."[6]

I infer from these passages that the young Freud had to surmount inner doubts for quite some time before reaching a firm decision. Since it is probable that he wrote his friend after he had started to consider the possibility of studying natural science or medicine, we must go back to an even earlier date

6. The German, literally translated, reads: "turn into the building of a tower of Babel." The translator made a confusing mistake by writing "any being can turn into a tower of Babel" (p. 424).

than is documented in the letter to discover the moment when this idea arose in his mind.

One receives the impression that Freud somehow had a bad conscience about his choice of study. This may have been the reason for his hesitation in communicating it to his friend and for his subsequently adding the embellishment that it was after all Goethe who persuaded him to study medicine—as if belatedly he wanted to make sure that he had not betrayed in his youth the great men who had served from early on as his ideals and by whose works he was entranced, not only in his youth but for the rest of his life. There is certainly nothing in Goethe's panegyric essay that could induce anyone to study medicine.[7]

THE GISELA EPISODE

If we go back, searching for an event with which this puzzling turning point in Freud's life could be sensibly connected, I feel compelled to agree with Jones (1 : 32), who attributes relevant effects to the Gisela experience, which had taken place barely six months before Freud mentioned his decision to Fluss (who as it happened was the young girl's brother).

As Bernfeld (1947) discovered and as is now agreed upon, the patient whom Freud let present a screen memory and the many associations attached to it in his paper of 1899 was Freud himself. There he described what evidently was the first passionate experience of the adolescent and, as I may already add here, the last one for the next decade. The episode took place in 1872, when the 16-year-old Freud spent a summer in his birthplace. The event was behaviorally unruffled. As Freud stated, "It was my first calf-love and sufficiently intense, but I kept it completely secret. After a few days the girl went off to her school . . . and it was this separation after such a

7. It has been claimed that there is a connection between Goethe's essay and later theories of Freud. But even if this should be correct, it would not obviate the inadequacy of Freud's later report on how he happened to come to the study of medicine.

short acquaintance that brought my longings to a really high pitch" (1899, p. 313).

Freud referred to his love for the girl as "passionate" but added, "A strange thing. For when I see her now . . . she is quite exceptionally indifferent to me." Nevertheless, Freud said that such screen memories as he preserved illustrate the most momentous turning points in life (p. 316). The 1899 paper is remarkable, since it is one of only two instances in Freud's writings in which a childhood memory is used to screen a memory of adult or preadult years. He called such memories "retroactive" or "retrogressive." The other instance concerns the memory of his nurse who, like Gisela, disappeared abruptly after she had gained the child's affection. The nurse, as Freud described it, insisted on the child's handing over to her the small coins he had received as gifts—"a detail which can itself claim to have the value of a screen memory for later experiences" (1901, p. 50). It is noteworthy that Freud did not report retrogressive screen memories in any of his patients. Since the two such reports in Freud's work referred to himself, one may feel tempted to surmise a meaningful association between them. If this is accepted, Gisela would be an offspring of the old nurse.[8] The common elements would be that both had disappeared abruptly after having caused a strong affective response and that both had deprived Freud of something valuable: the nurse of the coins and Gisela of his peace of mind, perhaps of his emotional innocence.

Not only the possible subterranean interrelationship between Gisela and the nurse of early childhood but also several other factors suggest with great probability that Freud's first experience of love was traumatic. He evidently felt utterly helpless against the sudden onslaught of passion. Helplessness vis-à-vis a sudden, unaccustomed, and threatening stimulation is a well-known breeding ground of traumatic experiences.

Moreover, Freud had a number of strange, quite unusual

8. It should be noted, however, that the nurse herself was an element of one retroactive screen memory, whereas the Gisela experience was only represented in the other—that is, Gisela herself was not one of its elements.

reactions in relation to Gisela which suggest that this experience had an almost unique position in his memory. This can already be observed in Freud's attitude toward the paper on screen memories. It has no parallel in his attitudes toward other publications. He tried to keep it from republication in volumes of his selected papers or in the *Psychopathology of Everyday Life,* into which it would have fitted well (Jones, 1 : 24). He could no longer avoid its republication in 1925, when the edition of the *Gesammelte Schriften* was prepared. Yet on this occasion he erased from *The Interpretation of Dreams* a passage that would have betrayed the true identity of the patient in the 1899 paper (Jones, 1 : 24f.). One does not encounter here that freedom in reporting about the self which makes *The Interpretation of Dreams* a book of great nobility. It is, indeed, most impressive to contrast the intimacy of details regarding his own and his family's personal lives as in the book on dreams with his reluctance to see in print the seemingly trivial details of the Gisela affair, whose recollection obviously aroused great uneasiness in him.[9]

There is other evidence that Freud felt haunted by Gisela's memory. Sixteen months after his engagement to Martha Bernays, he felt prompted to make a confession. He asked her whether he had ever told her that Gisela was his first love. He referred to his age at the time of this first love in a noteworthy way: he numbered 16 *Lenze,* which is a poetical term for springtime and here used in a self-ridiculing way. He asked Martha to have a good laugh at him because of his poor taste, and because he never spoke even a neutral, let alone amiable, word to the "child." Looking back, he believed that he had become soft because of his return to his hometown (E. Freud, 1969).

This letter shifts the center of the experience away from a severe adolescent crisis to the incidental sojourn at his birthplace. Freud succeeded in hushing the virtually tragical impact

9. Bernfeld (1951, p. 208) pointed out that the aspect of self that Freud presented in the book on dreams is one-sided and that "he censored with great consequence any reference to love."

of the event by calling Gisela a child and by describing himself
as nothing but a naïve young boy at that time. Any indication
that the event was a turning point in his life, as was brought
out by Freud in the paper written 16 years after the letter to
Martha, is missing. But when a patient mentioned the name of
Gisela Fluss 35 years later, Freud set three exclamation marks
after it in the written record (Freud, 1955, p. 280).

The preserved letters to Gisela's brother,[10] written shortly
after the separation from her, also permit an approximate
reconstruction of what followed upon his return to Vienna. As
Freud wrote his friend, he "lost almost all recollection of the
past"; he felt as though "dazed," submitted to everything without protest, and did not open his mouth (1969, p. 419), that is,
there was apparently danger of betraying a secret. Vienna
aroused in him only feelings of disgust. It looks as if he had to
fight off a depression.

The sexual excitement during the railroad trip home is evident from Freud's reaction to a 12-year-old girl whom he described as having the head of an angel and a face so neutral
that it possibly might turn into that of a boy (1969, p. 420).
But most important, we learn Gisela's nickname, "Ichthyosaura,"[11] meaning an aquatic reptile of dinosaurian
proportions, that is, in man's imagination a fear-arousing

10. Emil Fluss was a few months younger than Freud. The letters sound as
if they were addressed to a person older and more experienced than he, a
constellation repeated years later in the correspondence with Wilhelm Fliess,
who was one year Freud's junior. This is undoubtedly a clue to an important
aspect of Freud's personality, but its meaning is not readily unraveled.

11. In an earlier paper (1974), I erroneously traced the history of the
nickname to Daniel Spitzer (1855–93), whose satirical essays made him
famous all over Europe and whose wit Freud greatly cherished. I owe
thanks to Dr. Gerhard Fichtner, who called my attention to *Gaudeamus,* a
collection of student songs published in 1867 and containing a poem entitled "The Last Ichthyosaurus." Its author was Josef Victor Scheffel
(1826–86), who in his time was Germany's "most read author" (Meyer, 1900,
p. 507). Therefore, one can be reasonably certain that Freud was familiar
with it. Scheffel's poem made fun of the undoing of the ichthyosauri. An old
ichthyosaurus laments moral decline. In the stanza in question he complains
that a lout of an ichthyosaurus who becomes more and more impudent as
time goes on has kissed the ichthyosaura in open daylight. Whether an in-

beast. Since in another letter of that period (September 28, 1872) it becomes clear that Freud had already met Gisela two years before that fateful summer, it cannot be decided at what time the derogatory nickname was coined. Whatever the exact time may have been, its choice leaves hardly any doubt as to what the adolescent's unconscious or preconscious fantasy about women was at that time. It says: women are dangerous monsters, a fear-arousing species whose phallic nature seems obvious.[12] How ready the unconscious association was that women are of a different species—and this is after all the strongest barrier against physical contact—can be learned from a remark ostensibly made in the spirit of self-mockery which Freud included in a letter to another friend. He spent the Easter holiday of 1876 in Trieste, a southern seaport of the Austro-Hungarian monarchy. From there he wrote that he was "only able to appreciate from afar the beauty of Italian women" (Stanescu, 1971, p. 203). "Physiologically," he continued, "I only know that they like walking." A propos anatomical investigations, he added that "it is unfortunately forbidden to dissect humans." But what he was dissecting in reality were eels, descendants of ichthyosauri. The episode is illustrative of the extent and intensity of defense. Freud was

---

cident of that kind prompted Freud's choice of nickname for Gisela is not known. The German text reads as follows:

> Der Iguanodon, der Lümmel,
> Wird frecher zu jeder Frist:
> Schon hat er am hellen Tage
> Die Ichthyosaura geküsst!

It is improbable that the girl's last name, Fluss (river), inspired the choice of epithet.

12. Gedo and Wolf (1970, p. 76) write, "A swain who can call his beloved 'Ichthyosaura' hardly appears to require further drastic defenses against his love of women." If this should mean that the young Freud was not exposed to conflicts, one would have to correct this by adding that the choice of appellative was only one of the defenses, even though a strong one, since the epithet not only denied any attraction the beloved sweetheart could exert, but even converted the attraction into disgust and horror.

under the sway of the Italian springtime, which he experienced for the first time, away from his family, under the impact of Italian sensuality and voluptuousness, the traditional attraction and source of temptation and seduction to men coming from the North to which Freud's ideal, Goethe, had also succumbed exactly 90 years earlier.

The conjoining of all these tantalizingly alluring circumstances did not succeed in distracting the young man from carrying out one of the dreariest jobs an imaginative youth ever had to face. The 20-year-old student in his fifth term of medical studies had been assigned the task of dissecting 400 eels. The difficulty of the undertaking cannot be fully appreciated by the histologist of our times, since he is unfamiliar with the primitive equipment used when histology was in its infancy. How many young men would have been able to accomplish Freud's task under such circumstances? A problem had to be solved that had puzzled biologists since Aristotle's time. It concerned the propagation of eels. That it was not just mechanical travail which the student felt duty bound to carry out can be inferred from the fact that he was the first one to propose the possibility that the eel may be intersex at birth, that is, that the gonads differentiate only later into male and female under the influence of external factors (Gicklhorn, 1953, p. 13f.).[13] It would be highly interesting to know to what extent he was helped in considering this possibility by the unconscious fantasy of the "intersex" phallic woman.

At any rate, derogation remained Freud's attitude toward the girl who had aroused the first passionate storm in him. In the letter of September 28, 1872 he already assured his friend that the whole affair was nothing but dalliance without any serious implications. He even went so far as to say that the episode was motivated by sarcasm and scorn, and he reported, apparently in order to dispel any possible doubt, that in his

13. Gicklhorn was the first one to attribute theoretical importance to Freud's eel paper. Freud himself felt disappointed in it, and Jones (1 : 38f.) even suggested that Freud's feeling of frustration with this paper may have caused him to leave Claus's Institute. See Bernfeld (1949, p. 166) for a rather negative evaluation of this paper.

meetings with his friend Silberstein in Vienna "the poor [girl] was torn to shreds" (1969, p. 421).

This contradicts what Freud wrote to Silberstein from Freiberg on September 4, 1872, shortly after Gisela's departure:

> She left Wednesday,[14] not without some slight deceit, which for quite some time annoyed me. I took leave sadly and went to Hochwald, my little paradise, where I spent a very pleasant hour.[15] I quieted all my turbulent thoughts and am only slightly startled when at table Mother[16] mentions the name of Gisela. This sentiment for Gisela appeared like a nice day in spring but my nonsensical "Hamlethood," my shyness, prevented me from indulging in refreshing conversation with the partly naïve, partly educated, young lady. One day I shall explain to you fully the difference between this sentiment and another passion. For the moment, I merely wish to say that it was in conflict between ideal and reality and that I am unable to ridicule Gisela [Stanescu, 1971, p. 202f.].

The Gisela experience evidently precipitated intensive and extensive defenses. The tragic implications are vigorously denied, and where, after a short outbreak of passionate love, despondence and grief had reigned, there now reigned sarcasm and scorn, at least on the surface.

Gisela reappears three years later in a letter to Silberstein (October 2, 1875), written on the occasion of Gisela's marriage. Freud added to the letter an epithalamium (1967, p. 203) and a postscript (Stanescu, 1967, p. 16). That both refer to Gisela is made clear by the first hexameter of the poem, burlesquing the beginning of the *Odyssey:* "Sing for me, oh Muse, the glory of the ichthyosauri communes." The glory, however, becomes an accumulation of the most acid invectives.

> Not all too tall was her figure, she did not look like the poplar
> Which by faultless growth aspires straight to the sky,

14. September 4, 1872 was a Wednesday. Therefore it is difficult to determine how many days after Gisela's departure the letter was written.

15. Cf. Freud (1899, p. 313): "I passed many hours [after Gisela's departure] in solitary walks through the lovely woods."

16. This does not refer to his own mother, but to Mrs. Fluss, in whose house Freud spent the vacation.

Nor like the spruce and the fir, the jewels of Nordic forests,
Nor Lebanon's cedar, the classic tree of the Jews,
But like the highest of all forms, the ideal of figures,
Her appearance was that of the globe and wonderfully fully
    rotund,
Rotund the face with spirited, sparkling eyes,
Rotund the body's enclosure.

The intuitive poet does not doubt that that which is not the
privilege of others to see but which the blissful evening of the
wedding night will reveal to the happy husband will also follow the principle of rotundness.[17] This is a specimen of the
downpour of invective and sarcasm directed at Gisela. Neither
was the girl's future husband spared sarcasm.

An outbreak of this sort is most unusual for Freud. He
always behaved with exemplary chivalry toward women and
no instance is known of any woman complaining about his
comportment. His letters testify to a primary tenderness and
gentleness, but these qualities are glaringly absent, not only in
this poem but almost always when he referred explicitly to
Gisela. The girl herself was really innocent, and no one knows
whether she might not have responded with a passion equal to
Freud's, had he but confessed his feelings to her. As is well
known, intense reproaches against another person, particularly when unfounded, substitute for equally intense self-
reproaches.

The meaning that the Gisela episode had for Freud comes
into the open with surprising distinctness in the postscript to
the epithalamium. There he says that a rare occasion such as
the marriage of a principle[18] deserves a special effort. He
could swear on his oath that he would make a similar poem on
like occasions, provided that he did not have to do so more
often than once a year. "Herewith this period ends, here I

17. Freud was well aware that his excessive shyness was due to a conflict
caused by aggressiveness, and he referred specifically to fantasies about the
wedding night (1899, p. 316).

18. According to Stanescu (1971, pp. 202, 206, n. 15), "principle" was a
secret term in the correspondence with Silberstein for "female," "love affair," or "flirtation," as the context required.

submerge the magic wand that has contributed to its organization: a new time may commence without secretly active forces, a time that does not need poesy and fantasy. Nobody may search for a principle in the alluvium and diluvium or elsewhere but in the present, nowhere but among the children of human beings but not in the grisly primordial past" (Stanescu, 1967, p. 16). Even though this statement evidently contains ironic elements, it is a formidable one. At one point Freud speaks with the voice of Prospero, who said: "I'll break my staff, Bury it certain fathoms in the earth, And deeper than did ever plummet sound I'll drown my book."

That is what the young Freud says he is doing after learning that Gisela is to marry. But Prospero is the playwright who renounces his magic art after he had exhausted himself by putting a new, never-dreamed-of world on the stage. Now the aged man had to resign from the arena and withdraw into oblivion, but here was a young man who would one day create a new, never-dreamed-of world and was in the process of preparing himself for his role on the stage of the world. What a perplexing world in which the young man at the start of his career as a genius gives utterance to the same sentiments as the retiring genius.

But what should have compelled Freud to bury Prospero's staff and drown the book? He renounces all secretly active forces and all poesy and fantasy, which he had loved with all his heart. A ban was proclaimed against all derivatives of the unconscious, and all concern with his own past was forbidden. Only the *hic et nunc* of the external world were acceptable matters for his attention. The *hic et nunc* were well defined and bare of the world of the id, which might throw the self into perplexity and helplessness. Of such magnitude was the trauma that the pubescent had suffered that summer when the ambiance of his birthplace had made him "soft."

For the time being the hostility and the defense against any erotic manifestation progressed to an alarming degree. When Silberstein, studying law in Leipzig, reported to Vienna on his love life, Freud resorted to the strongest admonitions, finally even warning against kisses.

> The indifference [he wrote on March 7, 1875] with which you
> mention the first kiss of your 'principle' appears to me a bad
> omen, first because you so easily get kisses and second be-
> cause you take a kiss so easily. I consider it my duty to draw
> your attention to a calculation by the famous statistician,
> Malthus, who proved that kisses tend to multiply in an ever-
> increasing proportion so that within a short time from the
> start of the series, the small area of the face does not suffice
> and they are then forced to migrate. Because of this, Malthus
> is a definite opponent of kisses and a young rational econo-
> mist should take his authority into consideration [Stanescu,
> 1971, p. 202].

The admonitions and warnings sent to Leipzig were serious,
but here again humor and irony give coloring. It is, indeed,
the pronounced sense of humor that comes to attention in
Freud's early letters. Without the paper on screen memories
there would exist no primary evidence of the tragic quality
that pervaded the Gisela experience. It was this sense of
humor that provided the youth with a kind of mastery of dire
experiences. Even in the disappointments he had to tolerate in
daily life, it was readily at hand. As an example, one can well
imagine how eagerly Freud, while working in Trieste, was
looking forward to the only day he was apparently free from
work, a Sunday. When after a week of gorgeous sunshine
there was bad weather, and he was prevented from swimming,
he remarked to his friend that he could explain this only in
the following way: "The Adriatic Sea . . . perhaps like a true
Italian, hates the Pope, those in black coats,[19] and the Sundays" (Stanescu, 1971, p. 204).

Here an annoying incident that would cause rage or depression in a weaker person is used to channel aggression against
the traditional enemy of liberalism and liberty in a way most
pleasing to the person who was disappointed. The incident
that was destined to annoy the subject is converted into a successful attack against an archenemy. Indeed, an apposite sense
of humor leads to narcissistic triumphs (Freud, 1927b) that

---

19. In the German original (Stanescu, 1965, p. 126) it says *Pfaffen,* which
is a derogatory vernacular term for priests.

may afford exquisite delight. In one sphere it undoes reality and in another it acknowledges it with particular incisiveness. In negation (Freud, 1925b) the reality principle is deceived. Only the unconscious existence of truth is acknowledged, but the conscious ego is exposed to hurt by a reality that is denied. Humor, however, undoes the unpleasantness and tragedy of life without denying it. The self is well protected against being hurt by unbending reality. And thus one observes Freud working his way out of adolescence without a catastrophe.

An outsider well trained in depth psychology ought to have been greatly alarmed on observing that an exceedingly gifted youth turned away from the field of his talents, stayed aloof from girls, objecting even to a kiss, and filled his whole life with academic studies, and all this as a reaction to falling acutely in love for the first time with a girl for a few days.

That the adolescent's passions were intense is evident, nor can there be doubt about the intensity of the defenses. How long would the psychic apparatus be able to withstand the excess of stress and strain such hostility to the drives must create? How would he settle down and prosper in medical studies, having chosen them under the domination of hostility against literature and beauty that had been so close to his heart?

STUDENT YEARS

Initially, Freud thought he would be able to make a compromise, which by the way would have been of a kind Goethe had arrived at in an equivalent situation. Freud and Goethe were in many respects akin. When the 16-year-old Goethe was sent by his father to study law, which he detested, he made his father believe that he carried out the latter's wishes while actually studying the subjects of his personal preference.

In Freud's instance, his father gave him full freedom of choice in his studies. However, the internalized father did not permit the young Freud to abandon himself to the enjoyable subjects of his primary interest. Thus he decided on the following compromise in his studies, which he confided to friend Silberstein on July 11, 1873:

> About the first year at the university, I can tell you that I shall spend it entirely in studying humanistic subjects, which have nothing at all to do with my future profession, but which will not be useless to me. [If his friend should want to become a physician later, it would be easy for him to catch up.] If, however, you are going to be a diplomat, nobody will ever catch up with you, not even history. To this end, I am joining in the first year the faculty of philosophy. Accordingly, if anybody asks me (or asks you about me) what I intend to do, refrain from giving a definite reply and say merely—Oh, a scientist, a professor, something like that [Stanescu, 1971, p. 198].

Evidently even after the decision to study medicine Freud looked at it only as an avocation. Nevertheless he registered in his first semester for 23 hours of premedical courses a week (Bernfeld, 1951, p. 204). To be sure, from the third to the sixth semester (Bernfeld, 1951, p. 216) Freud participated in the courses of Franz Brentano,[20] whose lectures had the effect of fascinating him (Stanescu, 1971, p. 199), and from whom he may have received cues that appeared later in psychoanalytic theory. It sounds almost like psychoanalytic metapsychology when Brentano says that only the psychic has direct, absolute reality. Furthermore, he taught that psychology is the foundation of philosophy and logic.

In his first semester with Brentano, Freud wrote Silberstein:

> I should be very sorry if you, the student of law, would entirely neglect philosophy, while I, the godless, the empirically-minded man of medicine, am attending two philosophy courses and . . . am reading Feuerbach. One of the courses . . . deals with the existence of God, and Professor Brentano, who lectures on it, is a marvelous person. Scientist and philos-

20. Franz Brentano (1838–1917) decided to study theology after his Ph.D. at the age of 24. He was ordained as a Catholic priest but led the fight against the Pope's dogma of infallibility. He defrocked himself, resigned his professorship at Würzburg, and, in 1874, at the insistence of Viennese liberal scholars, was appointed professor of philosophy at the University of Vienna (Bernfeld, 1949, p. 141f.). Some of his publications are: *Die Psychologie des Aristoteles* (1867), *Psychologie vom empirischen Standpunkt* (1874), *Vom Ursprung sittlicher Erkenntnis* (1889), *Das Genie* (1892), *Über die Zukunft der Philosophie* (1893).

opher though he is, he deems it necessary to support with his expositions this . . . [ethereal] existence of divinity [Stanescu, 1971, p. 199f.].

In 1875 Freud's enthusiasm seems to have reached its peak. He and a fellow student sent two letters to the philosopher in which they stated their objections to his views. They were invited twice to his house. Brentano's influence stimulated Freud so extensively that he arrived at the decision, as he wrote Silberstein, "to take my Ph.D. in philosophy and zoology" (Stanescu, 1971, p. 220).[21]

Although Brentano as well as the university administration favored that decision, the plan was dropped. At times one is inclined to compare the young student with a wild but firmly harnessed colt that tries to break out to the right or the left and is kept on a straight path only with difficulty. Despite all temptations and the constant lure of the humanistic subjects, Freud remained loyal to his intention to study medicine.

The first teacher to play a major role in Freud's medical studies was Carl Claus (1835–91), his teacher in biology, who had been called to Vienna in 1873 from Göttingen. Claus must have been quite impressed by the young student, since he supported Freud's two stays in Trieste and submitted the results of his research for publication in the *Bulletin of the Academy of Sciences.* As will presently be seen, Freud's chances of advancement were evidently more propitious there than at Brücke's Institute, which he joined later.

One of the two other students who were with Freud in Trieste [22] was Karl Grobben (1854–1945), who was born in

21. Stanescu (1951, p. 205) reconstructed from Freud's choice of courses his intention of shifting in his third year of medical studies from medicine to zoology. Freud may have referred indirectly to the hidden ambiguity in his studying medicine when he wrote to Fliess on August 29, 1888: "There was a rent in my medical development which was later laboriously knotted together"—a sentence which has reached the English-speaking reader in a terribly mutilated form.

22. The third one, Roscher, born in 1853, studied in Vienna from 1873 to 1877. He never graduated and it is not known what became of him. I owe Prof. Franz Gall thanks for this information.

Brno, not far from Freud's place of birth. He became Claus's assistant in 1876, graduated in 1877, and became Dozent in 1879, and associate professor in 1884; in 1893 he was a full professor, Claus's successor. That or a similar career might easily have been Freud's.

Freud's motives for leaving Claus in favor of Brücke's Institute have puzzled biographers, particularly since Freud's professional interest in evolution would have been far better served by staying with Claus than with Brücke (Ritvo, 1972b). In seeking an understanding of why a particular personality was suitable to function as an ideal in the development of a person, one cannot always rely on surface traits, even though the fact that certain surface traits have been taken over is sometimes the only manifestation of the ideal's influence on the subject. More frequently than not, I surmise, there is a subterranean mental parentage between the younger one and the person prominent by accomplishments to whom the younger one turns. The subterranean current between subject and ideal model may consist of a variety of factors; it may be a community of elements in their past histories; it may be the mastery of shared conflicts. Oddly enough, the personality of the revered awe-inspiring ideal model may also convey a warning signal of what solutions to beware of.

There is a series of personalities—Brühl, Claus, Brücke, Fleischl, Meynert, Breuer, Charcot—who in the course of Freud's development as a scientist served as ideals, though to varying degrees[23] and with varying effects. Did these representatives of ego ideals have something in common? Who of them had a lasting effect and how deep did the effect go? Of Carl Brühl, for example, it is reported that he never used a manuscript when lecturing. It is known that Freud stuck to this rule, breaking it only once. Brühl lectured on Sundays, an odd time. Freud, in turn, lectured on Saturday afternoon, which was also an odd time.[24] His histological interests may well have been aroused by Brühl, and though it was not the

23. I would not include Fliess in this series.
24. Lectures on Sunday were later not customary.

recital of Goethe's essay that prompted Freud to choose medicine as the object of his study, it may well have been Brühl's lectures that aroused his desire to make science his academic subject matter.

I shall briefly outline Claus's and Brücke's biographies.[25] Carl Claus, born in 1835 in Kassel, Germany, graduated in biology in 1857 in Marburg. After having held the professorship in several German universities, he came from Göttingen to Vienna in 1873, with the task of reorganizing the department of zoology and of starting the administration of the planned zoologic station in Trieste. He was well known by his many articles, a very popular textbook, and his advocacy of Darwin's theory (Ritvo, 1972b). He died in 1899 in Vienna. Despite his successes as a scientist and as a teacher, he seems to have been an unhappy man. During his early university career in Germany, he already felt dissatisfied because his ambition to have all medical students examined in zoology was not achieved. He was at first reluctant to accept the call to a chair in Vienna because of the catastrophic experience of his predecessor Karsten (1872), who had to examine medical students in botany. The students felt so unfairly treated by him that riots broke out and Karsten was assaulted. He was retired against his will. Claus went "with uneasiness" (*beklommenen Herzens*) (Claus, 1899, p. 21) to Vienna, but he did not suffer Karsten's dire fate, even though it was his duty to examine 400 medical students yearly in zoology. In the end, however, he felt heartbroken because his ambition to unite all zoological institutes into one comprehensive organization was not heeded by the faculty. A second parallel institute in zoology was founded against his protest and his former student, the aforementioned Grobben, was put in charge. Claus felt so upset that he asked prematurely for retirement, which was granted in 1896.

Claus's private life was most unhappy. His first wife died in 1869, and his second in 1872; the third marriage ended in divorce in 1883. His favored daughter died in 1897 of leuke-

25. For Claus's biography see Claus (1899) and Ritvo (1972a, 1972b).

mia. His son-in-law described him as physically weak by nature and tending toward a pessimistic outlook on life (Claus, 1899, p. 24).

Ernst Wilhelm Brücke,[26] born in 1819 in Berlin, was the first-born of his father's first wife. When Brücke was 3, shortly before his mother died, the family moved to Stralsund, whence it hailed. His father, an artist, moved to Rome. The child grew up with a maternal aunt and her husband who were childless. The uncle had a high position in the Protestant Church, but was greatly interested in the natural sciences, and gave Brücke a good foundation in science. He attended a humanistic gymnasium and spoke French, English, and Italian fluently. When he was 18, his uncle died, a few years after the aunt. Brücke wrote a funeral hymn on that occasion.

In the following year he passed the *Matura* with honors. Brücke was in doubt as to what profession to choose. His means did not permit him to become an agriculturalist. He had some artistic talent, and he would have liked to follow the family tradition (father and uncle were painters), but he was not gifted enough. Thus he decided to study medicine, which he was able to do since the mother's inheritance was sufficient for that purpose.

The study of medicine did not make him abandon his humanistic interests, and in the first three semesters he attended courses in philosophy, logic, the German classics, and Greek tragedy. In 1840 he visited Italy for the first time. In the same year Johannes Müller, Germany's most eminent physiologist, chose him as co-worker. By 1842, when he obtained his medical degree, he had published three papers.

Since his mother's inheritance had been used up Brücke decided to become a surgeon, but Johannes Müller made his academic career possible. From that moment on his career was one-dimensional, free of interruptions and crises. In 1847 he became professor of physiology and general pathology at the University of Königsberg, with an adequate salary of 800 Tha-

26. The following is mainly based on Brücke's biography by his grandson (E. T. Brücke, 1928).

ler. In 1849 he was called to the University of Vienna, where he stayed until his retirement in 1890. Two years later he died of pneumonia.

In 1848, shortly before moving to Königsberg, Brücke married a girl a few months his junior. Apparently it was a love of long standing. The marriage was particularly happy and seemed conflict-free. She preserved her personal character and "wanted to know of physiology absolutely nothing" (E. T. Brücke, 1928, p. 48). Two sons were born (1849, 1853). In 1873 Brücke suffered the greatest loss of his adult years, the death of his older son. Two grandchildren died at an early age. In 1878 the younger son married the sister of Carl Wittgenstein. A shadow cast over Brücke's later years was his wife's sickness. She became ill with Bechterew's disease and severe bladder trouble. She died one year after Brücke's death.

Brücke received all the honors an academic career could provide: he rose to the top of the university's hierarchy, and he was ennobled by the Emperor and made a permanent member of the Upper House of the Parliament.

His bibliography comprises 140 references, among them several books. There was hardly any topic of contemporary physiology to which he did not make a contribution. In order to keep abreast of contemporary methods, he did not shy away from any sacrifices. Thus, after his call to Vienna, he took classes in chemistry like a student. But he did not follow his investigations to the last details, preferring rather to take up a new subject. The consequent richness of his investigations, though stimulating to others, contributed indirectly to his missing discoveries, such as the famous *Augenspiegel* (E. T. Brücke, 1928, p. 72). A characteristic feature of his scientific procedure was the use of observations made in everyday life which became the source of experiments (E. T. Brücke, 1928, p. 111). Brücke was not a night worker as Freud was. He had an extraordinary memory and the ability to bring the contents of widely separated fields into associative connection.

The grandson in his analysis of Brücke's personality and development stressed that his grandfather had gone through an intense *Sturm und Drang* period, that the rationality and calmness for which he was admired later were a wall behind which there may have been a rich emotional life (p. 123). Brücke was a universalist inasmuch as he did not specialize. Problems of art and of language were as close to him and aroused his interest as much as digestion and respiration. His biographer rightly refers the great assets of his character to the attitudes of sons to their fathers that prevailed in the nineteenth century. There was distance and a strong sense of duty and cultural obligation. "Kant's imperative stood before the optative" (p. 136).

These outlines, brief as they are, show that Bernfeld (1949) was possibly wrong when he tried to explain Freud's preference by correlating Claus's age with that of Freud's half-brother, a rival for mother in childhood, and Brücke's age with that of Freud's father, omniscient and beloved.

Claus was pessimistic, conflict-torn, and narrow in his research. He seemed generous and liberal, a personality type not suitable as Freud's ego ideal at that time. In contrast, the social image Brücke presented was that of a man who was free of conflict, steadfastly, unwaveringly, and resolutely devoted to his duty, endowed by nature with the gifts necessary to reach his scientific goals. No crisis in his scientific pursuits ever came to light.

Anyone familiar with Freud's personality will easily acknowledge parallels and differences in Brücke's and Freud's development and personality, and recognize the elements by which Freud was so strongly attracted and those which might have been a warning.

Brücke was a monolithic personality, the ideal substitute for a weak father. Thus Brücke was the ideal superego figure the young Freud needed at that time. These probably were the main reasons why Freud (1927a, p. 253) wrote later that Brücke "carried more weight with me than anyone else in my whole life." Characteristically enough, he still dreamed in his mature years of Brücke's "terrible blue eyes by which I was reduced to nothing" (1900, p. 422). Freud's misdemeanor had been trivial. Because he lived far away from the Institute and had worked late at night, his arrival had been delayed.[27]

Freud's finding "rest and full satisfaction" (1925a, p. 9) in neurohistological work and with an almost martinetlike superego figure such as Brücke must be viewed together. This conjunction seems to confirm my proposition regarding the repressive pressure that dominated the decade between Gisela and Martha. Although Freud recalled memories of aggression against and anxiety about his father from his early childhood, his relationship to his father was on the conscious level almost unambivalent. To be sure, in puberty, when the growing youth had to turn from his parents, he found fault with his father and criticized him silently for not having been a hero. But the father was amazingly undemanding and indulgent, even though he was occasionally critical of his son, as when the latter's debts in the bookstore accumulated beyond his means (Freud, 1900, p. 172). Evidently Freud needed an adoptive father who was stricter than the natural one.

Yet it was probably not only his father's leniency but also the father's relative inactivity and failure in the practical affairs of the world that might have made the young Freud look out for a more satisfactory ideal.

Brücke's strictness as well as his great success were features which Freud sorely missed in his father. It seems to me that at a time when, as we may be almost certain, the self was constantly exposed to the lure of regression and the pleasure principle, the young student needed such external support in addition to the inner defenses he had built up. An equivalent conclusion may be drawn from Freud's predilection for neurohistological microscopy.

Of all the various activities that were going on at Brücke's Institute, I can hardly imagine a more boring one than staring

27. From a passage in a letter of the aged Freud written to Arnold Zweig in 1936, one can ascertain the extent of his identification with Brücke as well as the integration of surface details into the ego ideal. He wrote: "When my Master Ernst Brücke received the Award [of Honor for Art and Science], I became aware of the wish that I myself might sometime attain it" (Jones, 3 : 208f.).

for hours without end into a microscope. It seems to be a static activity, so to speak, strictly bound to a frozen, unmoving picture, far removed from that nature which Goethe had presented in his essay and which allegedly cast a spell of fascination upon Freud. The adolescent who had found delight in Virgil, Sophocles, and Goethe narrowed his principal interest to the choking confines of a static visual field that imposed maximal constraint on fantasy and power of imagination.

One has to revise, however, this primary impression since, according to Brücke himself, there were two different kinds of histologies: "the pure unsullied microscopy," which is boring, since it limits itself to description, and the microscopy which he pursued, which was sullied by physiological problems (Lesky, 1965, p. 266). The young Freud's microscopy was of the sullied kind, and the neurohistological papers he published in Brücke's Institute show that looking at the slide was for him not a "static" activity. The dead image was converted into something dynamic. Not only did he observe morphological details that had escaped the attention of others, but scattered cells were recognized as indicating "the path taken by the spinal ganglion cells in the course of evolution" (Freud, 1897, p. 229). Bernfeld (1949, p. 178) rightly calls this solution "a triumph of precise observation and genetic interpretation." Furthermore, Freud recognized in those cells transitional forms from a lower to a higher stage and thus closed a gap in the reconstruction of evolution.

Evidently the strong repressive forces at work in this period of Freud's career did not constrain fantasy and imagination entirely. Certain limited freedoms were granted, but these did not include the freedom of the artistic mind when it converts daydreams into artistic products that abide by loose rules of aesthetics, but rather that of the scientist to interpret visual structures in conformity with the cold rules of reason and rationality that provided sufficient protection against derivatives of repressed drives.[28]

28. In a later lecture, Freud (1884) presented the foundation of the neuron theory (Brun, 1936; Jelliffe, 1937). Study of morphology led to insight into genesis and function, seeing led beyond observation to the apper-

Freud's remark (1927a, p. 253) of many decades later that "physiology . . . in those days was too narrowly restricted to histology" was interpreted as a belated apology for his fixation to the microscope, which remained his preferred tool for the rest of his neurological period. Thus Bernfeld (1949, p. 187) pointed out that the physiological and experimental research were lively goings on at Brücke's Institute, and he concluded that "the ability for physiological work was missing and therefore he[Freud] was forced into microscopy."[29]

I felt the same way until I discovered in an article on the history of physiology in Vienna by Exner (1910) the following report: "When in later years I once asked Brücke why histological research was done almost exclusively, he pointed to the impossibility to come closer to experimental-physiological problems in the limited space and with the limited means [at the disposal of the Institute]." The large number of those who sought instruction and wanted to do research had to be located in a relatively small lecture room which made the use of the smallest possible equipment necessary. Thus microscopy was forced on the young student if he wanted to stay with Brücke. It nevertheless is true that whenever Freud tried to do physiological research that required the use of other methods, he failed. There was, no doubt, an affinity between him and the microscope.[30]

Yet I cannot leave this subject without pointing to another problem. Was it Brücke or the young student who proposed

---

ception of living forces that had taken the form of the frozen, immovable structure in the slide. Here the young scholar demonstrated that which he would later admire so much in Charcot, of whom he wrote (1893, p. 12): "He used to look again and again at the things he did not understand, to deepen his impression of them day by day, till suddenly an understanding of them dawned on him." Even in his student days Freud already experienced that "greatest satisfaction a man could have [which, according to Charcot,] was to see something new . . . recognizing it as new" (p. 12).

29. This view is supported by the fact that among Brücke's publications there are only 25 of a microscopic, anatomical nature (Lesky, 1965, p. 266).

30. The correspondence between microscopy and psychoanalysis with regard to goals and function needs only passing mention in this context.

the microscopic study of the central nervous system? What would have been the direction of Freud's later interests if the task of studying any other organ system had been assigned to him? Research in the field of neurohistology, after all, was what enabled Freud to enter medical practice as a neurologist or neuropathologist, as his specialty was called at that time. This, in turn, brought him into contact with neurotic patients, and this was the first requisite step on his fateful course toward psychoanalysis in the far future. What would have been his further development if he had started with research in the histology of the digestive tract, which was of great interest to Brücke?

It is most unfortunate, with regard to the problem of understanding the development of a genius, that we do not possess any record of Freud's initial meeting with Brücke, when they discussed what the student's first assignment would be. It would be most relevant with regard to the problem of choice versus accident to know whether it was the student's request or the teacher's accidental needs that got the former on the path of neurohistology. A profound knowledge of the brain was one of the prerequisites for Freud's tenacious adherence to the fundamental concept of a psychic apparatus.

The main part of my thesis regarding the reasons why Freud at last found all he wished for in Brücke's Institute seems to be substantiated by a sentence in his dream book: "the Institute in which I spent the happiest hours of my student life, free from all other desires" (1900, p. 206). The original uses a far stronger term: *sonst ganz bedürfnislos,* "otherwise totally without wants." The wants of which Freud was thinking become evident from the next association, which refers to "clinging at the breasts of Wisdom," a direct sexual reference. The latent meaning of the dream was that "one should . . . always take what one can even when it involves doing a small wrong," a lesson which "had among other meanings a sexual one" (p. 207). Here it is openly stated that the work at Brücke's Institute kept the student free of forbidden drives and rendered his defenses impenetrable, an effect which never could have been attained at Claus's Institute with its hustle and bustle of reorganization under the leadership of a man who himself was pessimistic.

Ten years after the Gisela trauma a turning point occurred in Freud's life. It became clear that the plan of becoming a great physiologist devoted to the unraveling of the secrets of brain structure was a dream. Ananke interceded and forced the young scholar to think of social survival by earning a livelihood, a task he had not considered worthy of attention. His medical license would have permitted him to start a practice, but because of his past absorption in research, he evidently did not feel adequately prepared to meet the demands of clinical practice, and he enrolled at the General Hospital for what we would call a rotating internship. Although only two years of working and living at the hospital were necessary, he would spend three years there.

MARTHA BERNAYS

With Freud's turn toward the matter-of-fact side of reality in order to become a skilled and accomplished practitioner of medicine, preferably of neurology, another event took place, probably the most consequential in his life: he fell in love. It apparently was the matter of a moment that the *coup de foudre* of a great passion hit him. As it turned out, it would not relent for the next four years until marriage brought fulfillment and peace.

The choice of love object in a genius's life is precarious: it may spell disaster, as happened to Dostoevsky in his first marriage, or be a blessing, as happened in his second (A. Dostoevsky, 1975). In Freud's case it was the latter. The young woman, charming, a paradigm of virtues and control, was ideally suited for the role destiny had determined for her. And here we confront a problem: how did this young man, who had passed a decade decisive for psychosexual development and maturation in isolation from the other sex and who therefore was inexperienced in dealing with women, automatically make the right choice?[31] How did he come to have the stamina to endure the next four stormy and frustrating years of courtship, which caused him to feel without hope that his impecuniousness would never permit him to attain his passionate desire?

It is most remarkable that after such an extensive period of strong repression Freud's personality had preserved the freedom and flexibility of opening the floodgates of his passions and letting them flow toward a love object. The four years of courtship were Freud's *Wertherzeit,* filled with incredible stresses and frustrations that would have threatened the intactness of personality of many another man. The letters to Martha Bernays are so remarkable because they demonstrate Freud's freedom in expressing intense emotions which one would not have suspected in the shy, inhibited youngster who was impelled to break off any ties to the other sex after the trauma he had experienced at 16. The sublimation that was initiated by the trauma evidently had not irretrievably diverted libido from its natural goals.

One may think of constitutional factors operating in Freud that in 1882 made a comparatively rapid change possible from the repressed scholar to the man who actively and successfully grappled with all dimensions of social reality.

What clinically appeared to be a period of repression was in reality evidently a period of silent maturation that made of the youngster who had been tongue-tied at 16 the man more persuasive than Cyrano in the protestations of love, and more successful in attainment, at that. The farewell to an academic career and the falling in love must be interconnected, as Bak (1973) has sensitively pointed out.

There is a question that is of decisive importance but cannot be answered: what would the consequences have been if Freud had not been forced by external conditions to leave the Institute of Physiology? Would he have fallen in love with

31. Of course, it must be considered that the home environment of the young Freud was dominated by the distaff side. The mother and five sisters had a clear majority over the male element. Here may be the source of Freud's exquisite manners toward women and the know-how of courtship.

Martha Bernays and voluntarily have sacrificed an academic career? Marriage to Martha and the long-lasting impecuniousness to which the aspirant to an academic career in a theoretical subject was condemned could not have been combined. Was Freud's personality really endowed with such unusual autonomy that it was within his choice either to continue the style of the decade that followed the Gisela experience or to turn with full force toward the practical tasks of reality? This is not probable. The early development of Freud depended on the changes and intrusions of external reality that necessitated action, as in the lives of other mortals. It is remarkable, however, that Freud held his own magnificently, whatever turn reality took.

From Freud's letters to Martha Bernays ample evidence can be culled that discloses the true state of his mind during the decade of medical study and physiological research. In terms of observable behavior, the student and scholar passed a decade of tranquillity and devotion to his professional purposes. But then we hear, "In my youth I was never young"; "I have always oppressed[32] myself" (Freud, 1960, p. 202f.); "I would just have strayed miserably about and gone into a decline [if I had not met you]" (p. 57); "Before I met you I felt totally indifferent toward life" (p. 43).[33] Yet Freud's alienation from life did not prevent him from living up to the requirements of the situation and splendidly fulfilling the function of a research worker.

A remarkable change occurred in the four years of courtship, even though they were even unhappier than the previous decade as a result of the massive frustrations he had to withstand: Freud at last attained the feeling that his life had been worthwhile. He wrote to Martha, "if today were to be my last on earth and someone asked me how I had fared, he would be told by me that in spite of everything—poverty, long

32. *Ich habe mich unterdrückt* has been translated "I have constrained myself." "Constrain" is far too weak an expression in this context.

33. The original *Ich war ganz lebensunlustig* was translated "I did not know the joy of living." But "listless," "dejected" may come closer to the term Freud used without fully reaching its intensity.

struggle for success, little favor among men, oversensitiveness, nervousness, and worries—I have nevertheless been happy simply because of the anticipation of one day having you to myself and of the certainty that you love me" (p. 201). This confession was likely made under the influence of cocaine, and yet it probably expressed the truth. It shows that in those years a structural change had taken place in Freud's personality. It is most remarkable that this man who is the symbol of an insatiable Faustian crusader after truth found before his passionate love was consummated the fulfillment of his life in the state of loving and being loved. The Gisela trauma seemed overcome, and indeed it was, for the capacity of loving fully was attained.

RESPONSE TO BREUER'S CATHARTIC TECHNIQUE

Yet even at the risk of overstraining Freud's early traumatogenic theory, I believe one may recognize consequences of the Gisela trauma in another area. In a genius's life the realization of his mission to create extraordinary incomparable values is even more important than object relations. I emphasize this because just in 1882, when Freud left or had to leave Brücke's Institute, an unexpected event took place that should have resulted in a turning point in his creative life. Breuer, to whom he was bound not only in intimate friendship but also by mutual exchange in professional and scientific matters, conveyed to him his surprising experiences and observations made in the course of the treatment of Bertha Pappenheim. One knows that Breuer was so preoccupied with the new world he had discovered and spoke so incessantly about this patient that it resulted in a marital crisis, since his wife felt unable to listen to his reports any longer (Jones, 1 : 224).

It is important to reconstruct Freud's response to Breuer's communication. Freud's hesitation and procrastination regarding the adoption of the cathartic technique are intimated in his own writings. A reader of his autobiographical study may get the impression that it was not so long before Freud's departure to Paris (1885) that Breuer introduced him to Anna O.'s case, since he fixes the time of first acquaintance

as: "Even before I went to Paris."[34] The subsequent "He repeatedly read me pieces of the case history" (Freud, 1925a, p.
19), however, suggests an earlier date. As a matter of fact, in a
letter of July 13, 1883, Freud let Martha Bernays know that
Breuer had spoken with him "again"[35] about Bertha Pappenheim. The "again" permits the consideration of the possibility that Breuer started to tell Freud of his surprising observations shortly after having terminated the treatment. This is
confirmed by Jones (1 : 226), who reports that Freud heard of
Breuer's case at the latest on November 18, 1882, that is, four
months after termination. Freud (1925a, p. 20) continued to
report his intention of informing Charcot of Breuer's discoveries. When Charcot showed no interest, "I allowed it to pass
from my mind" (*bei mir fallen liess*). To be sure, Freud was
overawed by his great new teacher, but it was very unusual for
him to let an authority influence his judgment to such an extent. I would suggest that the quickness with which Freud
changed his mind about a subject which had, or ought to have,
occupied his mind for two if not three years indicates an inner
readiness to withdraw from it.

"When I was back in Vienna," Freud continued (1925a, p.
20), "I turned once more to Breuer's observation and made
him tell me more about it." Be that as it may, for a few years
there is no indication that Freud was seriously interested in
the cathartic method.

As he reported, in clinical practice he used electrotherapy,
the contemporary method of choice.[36] He felt indignant about
its lack of efficacy, forgetting that after having listened to
Breuer he had no right to expect anything but failure. Then
he chose Bernheim's method of suggestions given in the state
of hypnosis. He seemed quite proud of the successes obtained
(Jones, 1 : 235).

As late as 1889, Freud spent several weeks in Nancy, in

34. In German, *ehe ich nach Paris ging,* this impression is even stronger.

35. "Again" was left out in the English edition. Furthermore, it says that
the subject "cropped up," whereas the original does not imply anything
unexpected or unintentional.

36. Jones (1 : 235) reports that Freud limited himself to electrotherapy
for 20 months.

order to "perfect" his hypnotic technique. He even persuaded
a highly gifted hysterical patient to follow him to Nancy
(1925a, p. 18f.) in order to be treated by Bernheim. Thus one
can hardly escape the impression that Freud may almost have
forgotten what Breuer had told him seven years earlier, for
one would have expected that in such a clinical situation he either would have asked Breuer to repeat his tour de force or
would have applied the method himself. The few words Freud
spent in describing the patient's personality may call to mind a
comparison with Anna O., and it baffles the reader that after
being apprised of Breuer's discovery Freud could have ever
thought that a patient of that sort could be cured by hypnotic
suggestions. Freud later stated stated that from the very
beginning he had employed hypnotism not only for the purpose of giving suggestions but also for "questioning the patient upon the origin of his symptom" (1925a, p. 19); Jones's
commentary (1 : 240f.) that "Some doubt on the accuracy of
his [Freud's] memory is perhaps permissible here" is very
probably correct.

As far as one can rely on documentation, Freud's "first attempt at handling that [Breuer's] therapeutic method"
(Breuer and Freud, 1893–95, p. 48; see also p. 105n.) came in
the year 1889 (or 1888).[37] Although it is quite correct that
"handling a method" would not exclude a previous "questioning a patient upon the origin of his symptom," Freud's report
on the first patient he treated with Breuer's method strongly
indicates that he was not familiar with the practical handling
of Breuer's technique (Jones, 1 : 240).

Inaccuracies and minor contradictions regarding a far-off
period of the past can easily be explained by the passage of
time, and nevertheless one may be able to use them for the
reconstruction of an unconscious process that took place at the
very time to which inaccuracies and contradictions refer.
Thus, even though Freud was impressed by Breuer's communications, he was far less so than would have been expected

37. For a detailed discussion of the correct year when Freud used the
cathartic method for the first time, see Strachey (1955).

of an ambitious young man who was intensely driven by eagerness to discover something new and by curiosity to understand the world. Even a far less talented, ambitious, and curious person than Freud would have been easily awed by Breuer's excited reports.

Freud's comparative equanimity in the face of Breuer's reports is all the more surprising since Freud knew that one day he would have to deal with patients suffering from the disease that got Breuer in touch with Anna O.

In summary, Freud acted for many years as would a contemporary psychiatrist who, after reading the *Studies on Hysteria,* had decided to treat neuroses by dispensing bromides. We should not hesitate to suspect such a psychiatrist of being dominated by particularly intense defenses. And this inference we have to draw in Freud's case as well. When one puts oneself into Freud's position of 1882, one cannot marvel enough about this virtual indifference toward Breuer's great discovery. After all, Freud was at that time a witness of an event whose consequences not only would have the deepest effect on the course of his later creative output but—one can safely say—would set a chain reaction into motion the aftereffects of which are still felt at present.

Therefore, it is hardly understandable that Freud was so deeply impressed by Charcot's demonstration that traumas cause hysteria, as if he had not known this from Breuer's reports. One has to draw the inference that the cathartic method, filled with close id derivatives, was unacceptable to Freud at that time and aroused such strong defenses as to make him blind to its true meaning, whereas Charcot's and Bernheim's more or less mechanical models of the human mind that circumvented the human factor could be integrated without touching upon the weak spots of Freud's defenses. The cocaine episode, after all, can also be evaluated under the aspect of Freud's attempts to find a drug that would cure neurotic symptoms. As a matter of fact, he thought for quite a while that by the intake of cocaine he would overcome his own psychosomatic symptoms, shyness, and occasional depressions. Even after his return from Paris, where his attention had been so strongly drawn toward the psychogenic factor, he wrote Martha that he had "another therapeutic idea," which evidently referred to a new drug comparable to coca, that is, another physical means of treatment (1960, p. 216). The preoccupation with cocaine must therefore be judged as the manifestation of a colossal resistance to Breuer's method.[38]

Over and over one can observe during that period Freud's effort to evade in his creative work the confrontation with the human factor, although it is clear from the *Matura* letter that he had been most interested in understanding man's psyche.

In short, the Gisela trauma had been overcome with regard to the love of a woman but apparently still impeded Freud's creative work, preventing him from picking up the riches Breuer had spread before him. It is even noticeable that the quality of his scientific output temporarily declined during the four years of courtship. I see in that a process equivalent to that which can be observed in the severe reduction of Goethe's creative output during his courtship of Frau von Stein, which also was a period during which a relevant change in personality structure took place. It seems to be difficult to serve two masters at the same time.

ANANKE AND THE CREATION OF PSYCHOANALYSIS

Finally, it was Ananke again that compelled Freud to take up his mission. His medical career forced him to treat neurotic patients. Only after it turned out that none of the contemporary techniques had any therapeutic effect did he throw himself with full force and without inhibition into the great adventure of conquering man's mind for science. The necessity of finding a causal therapy of the neuroses enforced by an un-

---

38. Later Freud may have been vaguely aware of the defensive function of the cocaine episode; see the sentence in a letter to Wittels: "The study of coca was an allotrion," a term which, as Bernfeld (1953) explains, "Gymnasium teachers used with a punitive connotation for everything that detracted from the serious fulfillment of duty, in favor of a hobby or of mischief" (p. 334f.).

bending professional reality was the proximate factor that led to the creation of the science we call psychoanalysis.[39]

What would have happened had there been a vacancy at Brücke's Institute remains, however, an open question. Freud was so much taken by neurohistology and the lure of a university professorship was so intense that one can hardly imagine that he would have renounced either of them voluntarily.[40] It is not inviting to think that the birth of psychoanalysis demanded such an accidental factor, but one has to admit the possibility that Freud would have become one of the greatest physiologists of our time, possibly distinguished by becoming a Nobel laureate, an honor he gave up when he chose to disturb the sleep of the world.

When at the celebration of his eightieth birthday he would have answered the many dinner speeches by declaring that his accomplishments in neurohistology were as nothing compared with what would have been his, had he followed up the interest of his early years and devoted his talents to the exploration of man's psyche, all present would have smiled and thought that the old man was telling a fantasy.

Against the view that an accidental circumstance of external reality, such as the lack of a vacancy in an institute, should have been one of the decisive factors that led to psychoanalysis, one may refer to the end of Freud's *Matura* letter. There he wrote: "I do not want to bid you, should you find yourself in any state of doubt, mercilessly to dissect your emotions, yet if you do so, you will perceive how little certainty you have in yourself. The world's magnificence after all is based upon this manifoldness of possibilities, yet unfortunately it is no solid

39. This emphasis on reality factors that helped to bring about the birth of psychoanalysis does not diminish Freud's personal merit in throwing off the rationalizations that kept others from using methods whose inefficiency they knew or should have known.

40. See Freud (1925a, p. 10): ". . . It was generally thought that I was marked out to fill the next post of Assistant that might fall vacant there [at the Institute of Physiology]"; and "I myself had nourished a still livelier wish [than Joseph Paneth's wish to have his superior out of the way] to fill a vacancy" (1900, p. 484).

foundation for any self-recognition" (my tr.). Adolescents are sometimes uncannily intuitive. When Freud died sixty-six years later, the world knew that the merciless dissection of emotions is the only solid foundation for self-recognition.

Did it ever happen before that an adolescent who later became a genius foretold his life's mission in the negative, as the 17-year-old Freud did? We know that negation contains a truth that is repressed (Freud, 1925b); and one is compelled to assume that when the adolescent wrote that negative statement, somewhere in his unconscious it must have dawned on him that he was destined to become a great psychologist. From this point of view, one would postulate that whatever may have happened in external reality, nothing could ever have stood in the way of Freud's becoming the founder of analysis.

However, I am inclined toward the view that attributes more weight to Ananke and believe that the Gisela trauma might have pushed Freud away from the interest in man's inner world and might have kept him bound to the study of the conflict-free subject of neurohistology for the rest of his life. This would not have disproved the fact that he was one of mankind's great psychologists. It is the same question (sometimes raised in the past) as that of whether Raphael would have been one of the world's greatest painters if he had been born without hands.

The keenness of Freud's psychological interest and insight is already visible in the early aphorisms. The letters to Martha Bernays, written at a time when he was not explicitly interested in the exploration of the mind, abound with psychological observations. One finds there, to cite just one of the many instances, comments which later became a part of the psychoanalytic theory of dreams. Thus prior to the psychological period one can already observe Freud constantly at work in exploring the human mind, but all this would not have led to psychoanalysis.

Yet there is another clue worthy of being taken up. "I became a physician," wrote Freud (1927a), "through being compelled to deviate from my original purpose; and the triumph of my life lies in having, after a long and roundabout journey, found my way back to my earliest path" (p. 253). Freud does not state explicitly what his "original purpose" was, but it can hardly be doubted that it was exploration and understanding of man's psychological and cultural world. The deviation from this original purpose, however, was not enforced by external forces. There is no indication that Freud was "compelled" to give up the early interests of his youth. So why did the return to the original purpose produce a feeling of triumph? Under what conditions does man experience a triumph of the sort Freud recorded? Certainly not when an external enemy lies conquered at the victor's feet, as Michelangelo limned it in his statue *Victory,* a young, vigorous male imposing himself on a crouching old man.

In *Moses and Monotheism* (1939) Freud discussed the narcissistic pleasure a person may derive from a renunciation of instinctual gratification that has been accomplished for internal reasons. A person then feels elevated, proud, and liberated. This elevation of self-regard arises also when an advance in intellectuality is achieved (pp. 111–122).

According to Freud, an advance in intellectuality is attained when a new abstraction can be wrested from that which our senses convey. Perceptions exert pressure on the sensory part of the psychic apparatus. Therefore, it needs a definite effort to free oneself of that pressure, to step behind the perceptual content in order to find an abstraction that appears to be in contradiction to what the senses convey. (This, approximately, is equivalent to Kuhn's concept [1962] of the discovery of a paradigm.) Yet in Freud's instance the advance in intellectuality took a form that probably will be rarely observed in the history of science. When Freud withdrew from Gisela and finally took flight into Brücke's Institute, he renounced the gratification of a drive. But evidently the renunciation did not liberate him and did not result in anything that could have been compared with a triumph, even though that renunciation made it possible for him to enter a new realm of knowledge and to achieve some noteworthy successes.

In the subsequent years of passionate courtship of Martha

Bernays there was also no advance in intellectuality. Only when he turned his back on neurology and embraced the study of man did he initiate an advance which led to *Totem and Taboo,* an achievement that must have given him a feeling of triumph, since his own work made true an expectation he probably had entertained silently as a student, when "the theories of Darwin, which were then of topical interest, strongly attracted me, for they held out hopes of an extraordinary advance in our understanding of the world" (1925a, p. 8). When Freud turned toward Martha, he gave up an inhibition, but when he resorted to the exploration of the unconscious, he had to occupy his mind with all the contents that first parental authority and then his superego, supported by tradition and society, had declared to be taboo and forbade as a subject of discourse. Defenses had to be broken down all around, but without yielding to regression or permitting the drive to obtain forbidden gratification in any other way. Here indeed was an unusual advance of intellectuality that went beyond the replacement of sensory perceptions by abstract ideas. In fact, it was just the opposite, for it extended sensory perception to most dangerous areas, and thus it will be understandable why Freud retrospectively spoke of a triumph: it was a double triumph, the personal one of having maximally overcome his own defenses against id derivatives and that of having at last returned to his early "curiosity, which was . . . directed more towards human concerns than towards natural objects" (1925a, p. 8). At this point one may add that not only the renunciation of drives provides a feeling of pride but also the giving up of a defense.

The cultural advancement of intellectuality was one that had been thought to be impossible. All or almost all of the technological and scientific advances mankind has made had been preformed in folklore, fairy tales, and, often, in the fantasies of gifted science fiction writers, but here a step forward in intellectuality was taken that no one had sensed in advance or anticipated.[41]

41. This may be doubted in view of the many precedents and predecessors of Freud which have been recorded. I should dare the following comparison: Galileo had many predecessors and a historian even claimed that

Looking back, we can now understand the constructive value of that 15-year period during which Freud withdrew from following up his primary interest in "human concerns." He had not "grasped the importance of observation as one of the best means" of gratifying that primary curiosity (1925a, p. 8), as he added almost as an explanation for the detour he had taken before he achieved his final triumph. The adolescent, indeed, was in danger of taking the vivid and elaborate imagery he had formed about man and the world at its face value and not subjecting it to the strict and tedious scrutiny of the secondary, that is, scientific process.

I have always taken the following sentence of Freud's as autobiographical: "An abstinent artist is hardly conceivable; but an abstinent young savant is certainly no rarity. The latter can, by his self-restraint, liberate forces for his studies; while the former probably finds his artistic achievement powerfully stimulated by his sexual experience" (1908, p. 197).

Thus the artist not only may, but must surrender to id derivatives. They are the incentives and main carriers of his achievements, for his efforts are directed toward giving external form to inner experiences, whereas the scientist in the service of exploring outer objects can only be disturbed when these derivatives taint the instrument of observation. Thus, the 15 years of medical and neurohistological pursuits served the integration of scientific methodology. Scientific observation became deeply rooted and so much an integral part of the psychic apparatus that it did not give way when the observer turned toward his own unconscious and that of others.

What inferences can be drawn from the foregoing? One that is trivial, as I mentioned initially, namely, that the outcome of the creative individual's adolescence depends on imponderabilia and the accidental. Here, however, differentiation is necessary. Something like the Gisela episode had to come to pass in Freud's life. The 16-year-old was bound to meet one

most of what is in his writings "may be found in the writings . . . of some predecessor" (Gillispie, 1960, p. 7), but prior to Galileo, I believe, no one suspected the possibility that the laws of all visible movements that occur in the universe could be represented by a few more or less simple mathematical equations.

day a girl who would set his drives aflame. The external circumstances were propitious for Freud's later career, since the
girl soon vanished from sight, facilitating the ensuing period
of grave repression and suppression. It would not have been
auspicious for the adolescent's future as a scientist if he had
become involved in a drawn-out love affair at that time of his
career, but this might easily have happened if he had been exposed to Gisela's attraction for a prolonged time. Yet the
inhibiting effect which the Gisela episode had on his early interests in "human concerns" was serious and easily might have
been permanent.

The lack of a vacancy at Brücke's Institute was fortuitous,
and a promising career as a physiologist might have deprived
the world of the works of a great psychologist. That Freud
came to create a new psychology, I must conclude, was fortuitous.[42]

CLINICAL INTERVENTIONS WITH TALENTED ADOLESCENTS

When one pursues the history of an abundantly creative person retrospectively from the end result backward to its beginning, it looks as if all relevant factors had conjoined to lead to
the admirable result. Yet if one reverses the direction of the
inquiry and starts out at the beginning, then one perceives
how perilous the future genius's development has been, how
easily even a very promising beginning may have led to failure
or relative failure. We just do not know how much potential
creativity is constantly and relentlessly destroyed and never
comes to the point of blossoming as a result of unfortunate co-
incidences.

DIFFERENTIAL RATE OF MATURATION

There is one perilous situation that cannot be spared the hypertalented adolescent and is a crucial test of his stamina and

42. The reader may be surprised that in this essay no mention is made of
Freud's mother, even though it is after all more than just sentimentality or
fancy to say that the mother is the *fons et origo* of male creativity. The failure

solidity. It is a general rule that very talented males mature physically late (H. Meng, personal communication).[43] Now as a result of the premature development of their intellectual ego functions, talented boys skip classes and are also otherwise associated with older boys. This association with adolescents older than themselves further accentuates the delay in physical maturation. Thus for many years talented boys are usually exposed to a serious experience of defeatism with regard to the maturational prospect. The effect of this struggle may be quite variable, depending on personality structure and circumstance, but the unfavorable rate of maturation in the talented adolescent is a potent force that determines the outcome of puberty. The three following instances concern highly talented young men who had matured late around 15 or 16 and were associated in their schools with considerably older boys.

In one instance, an analytic patient flatly refused for many years, because of a deep distrust in his erectile power, to expose himself to any situation that eventually might lead to intercourse. Despite an unusual intelligence and evident endowment for research, he stubbornly limited his activity to practical pursuits and refused to set goals worthy of his high creative potential.

The second patient of my series suffered for years from the fear that he would die before having had intercourse. After the first and successful intercourse, he developed an adequate and replete sexual life, but in his career, despite his undeniable originality and richness of ideas, he lacked the determination to give his creative ideas an objective form, and most of his attempts remained in a form unsuitable for publication.

The third instance was most remarkable. Despite intellectual superiority, the degree of sublimation remained frightfully low. Art, nature, music were ridiculed. This man's skills in the

to mention Freud's mother in this essay is necessitated by the unavailability of documentation. This situation may change after Freud's letters to Silberstein have been published.

43. Whether this is also true of highly gifted girls, I do not know, but it is probably also valid for them.

practical aspect of his profession were considerable, but he looked with disdain and contempt on anyone who did more than earn money.

I do not want to say that differential rates of maturation create such outcomes. They are ultimately determined by childhood experiences. But puberty is, as Erikson (1968) says, a moratorium; the pubescent is given a chance of choice, as it were, among possibilities that evolved in childhood and latency. The differential rate seems to be an additional weight that often turns the scales in disfavor of the creative potential.

In other instances the differential rate is a challenge. It makes the pubescent particularly alert and he mobilizes all his assets in the service of defeating rivals on the cultural-mental plane, compensating for the defeatism nature had decreed upon him. Obviously, the differential rate did not defeat Freud but stimulated his talents. Nevertheless, one wonders if Freud was concerned about the rate of his own maturation. He complained almost all his life about the insufficiency of his intellect (which may reflect the boy's feelings of being retarded in maturation); he suffered for years from anxiety about being late for the departure of a train (which may reflect the boy's anxiety that he will never mature); and he was initially driven by excessive ambition (which may reflect the intensity of impatience with which he had to wait as a boy for maturation).

ACCIDENTAL FACTORS

I have stressed the accidental factors in puberty with regard to the course creativity may take and shall now briefly further illustrate them.

On a few occasions I saw an adolescent who was heavily engaged in drug use. He was a college dropout, and I was certain his prognosis was a poor one when it turned out that he was unable, despite superior intelligence, to start any promising professional career, preferring instead to peddle drugs. He took offense at the designation of drug peddler, and we compromised on his being a gentleman pusher. I saw him perhaps three times a year. The interviews had not the slightest effect. There were no signs of a positive or negative transference. His appearances in my office were like social calls. He was very fond of my dog, as he was passionately interested in pets. One day, when he was playing with my dog, I said casually and without any therapeutic intent, just to make conversation, "Why don't you become a vet?" When he replied, "Yes, why don't I become a vet?" his voice sounded as though from one moment to the next a sudden revelation had struck him. Soon thereafter he enrolled in college and graduated with high marks. When it turned out that it was impossible to become a veterinarian, he decided to study medicine. Because of his talents he was accepted for a special program. Soon he started to do research. His record as a student was exemplary.

It is most disheartening that in some instances despite the greatest therapeutic efforts it seems impossible to help an adolescent in setting free his creativity, whereas in an instance like that just reported a chance remark that might just as well have been made by an untrained person and is nothing but a trivial commonsense comment causes a turning point in his development. Of course, one may say that I overrate the effect of my remark: that in reality the patient was ready for a change; that he was bound eventually to outgrow his sociopathy; and that only by a fortunate coincidence did I happen to accelerate the beginning of a phase that inevitably would have set in. I should not know how to counter this suggestion. It may be correct, but the fact remains that a chance remark, made to a talented adolescent who found himself in a highly perilous and precarious situation, brought about a profound change, even though not a change in his personality structure.

A quite different outcome must be attributed to another chance remark. A 17-year-old high school student sought advice because he always had had great difficulty in his academic studies and barely made the grade despite his efforts. He felt quite discouraged. Yet he not only had a great talent for the piano but also played it with unusual passion and enthusiasm. I saw him a few times and suggested to him that I would try to persuade his father to let him discontinue his studies and devote himself entirely to practicing his favorite instrument. He would have to spend a minimum of time with a tutor to prepare for graduation from high school. The father gave permission, to the son's greatest surprise and delight. At the end of the final interview, he asked me what he owed me. I told him, nothing, but that I should like to have "two tickets, third row center" for his first concert at Carnegie Hall. Later, I heard that he had given up the instrument, not least because he had had the feeling he would not be able to live up to the expectations I had expressed at our farewell. When I had seen him, he had been certain that his talent was sufficiently distinguished to make him into a concert pianist. So many adults complain that when they were young, they were not given encouragement and shown trust in their talents and therefore were impeded in the full flourishing of their creativity. When I met the young man, he struck me as particularly talented; I had already heard this from another source, and my remark at our farewell was made in all sincerity. Here the chance expression of full confidence burdened the adolescent and contributed to his final discouragement. Again one may object that this young man was probably destined eventually to drop his avocation, whatever my concluding remark may have been. I doubt, however, that I can free myself completely from guilt for his abandoning a promising career. It is quite possible that my words burdened him with a great responsibility and he was crushed by an expectation he felt to be too great for him.

I should draw the conclusion that adolescence is such a precarious situation that we cannot predict the full effect of therapeutic measures upon the adolescent's creative potential. Therefore, such measures have to be looked at as imponderables in such instances.

An even more complex situation was encountered in the instance of a patient whom I had in full analytic treatment for several years. He sought relief at the age of 17 for inability to ejaculate when masturbating. He had the personality makeup of a most promising youth. At the age of 14 he had performed successfully as a violinist, and he was passionately devoted to music. His enthusiasm extended to all cultural fields.

He could become profoundly stirred by problems of philosophy, and his interest in people, the profundity of his experience of nature—all these promised unusual creativity (Greenacre, 1957). After two years of analysis, he was able to ejaculate, and after two more years he entertained heterosexual relations. But concurrently with this progress in sexual ability and maturation, the lustre of his creativity declined. He gave up practicing the instrument which he had played so promisingly and his creative output lagged far behind his potential. The level of his interests did not decline, and the passion for mental matters persisted, but he was not able to become entirely absorbed in a particular problem. He even considered the possibility of changing his profession and going into business. The sense of a true commitment to the creation of an original value was weak.

I must seriously question whether the clinical success served the patient's creativity well. One may assume without further question that the inability to ejaculate at the peak of puberty must be a very troublesome problem. When at a time of maximal hormonal levels the total output of sexual discharge is reduced to infrequent nocturnal emissions, one would take it as a foregone conclusion that the mind must be torn by sexual preoccupations and almost untamable desires. Yet this was not the case with this patient. When I remarked that the paucity of sexual gratification must keep him in great tension and cause an almost constant restlessness, the patient was surprised and reported that he never felt anything of that sort. I first thought that this was the result of denial, but I think this patient represented one of those rare instances in which a total displacement of libido to collective alternates (Greenacre, 1957) takes place. But looking back, I am struck that the patient did not ask for the therapy of his sexual inability because he desired sexual gratification or was driven by sexual dissatisfaction. The motive for wanting to be cured of his inability was narcissistic. He could not tolerate that others were able to display and enjoy their masculinity, whereas he was unable to do so. The proper technique would have been to limit the treatment to the question of why the patient demanded so urgently the fulfillment of a wish that was not genuine but the upshot of envy and pride. One hundred years ago or more his inability to ejaculate would have nourished his pride and amounted to a narcissistic triumph that probably would have been most favorable to an unfolding of his unusually great gifts. Treatment, inasmuch as it brought back libido to serving its natural goals, deducted these energies from cultural pursuits. The creative function per se was not harmed by that process, but the intensity with which it operated was diminished. The creation of original values remained a possibility he viewed favorably, but it was no longer an inner necessity for him. He could take it or leave it, a background that is not propitious for the coming about of great achievements.

A SPECULATION CONCERNING FREUD

We grope our way in utter darkness in clinical dealings with a hypertalented adolescent. One might imagine what might have happened if Freud after the Gisela incident had been sent for psychotherapy or psychoanalysis and the excess of defense, the hostility against the drives, had been abated and subdued. In Freud's instance the clinical situation was particularly precarious, for a deficit in that observational power which he was able to acquire only during an extensive repressive period would never have been able to balance his ravishing imagination, which so effectively filled the elaborate linguistic canvasses with which his restless mind was filled. My point will become clear when I extend the problem to Kafka and speculate what would have happened if Kafka had been freed in adolescence from his devastating oedipus complex by psychoanalysis. He would hardly have written a line worthy of reaching us. Freud's literary ability permitted immediate discharge as can be seen from those freely flowing masterful letters which the adolescent was able to produce. Science requires patience, postponement of discharge, a difficult task for a person with an impetuous temperament such as Freud shared with his ancestor, the Egyptian Moses. Language in such eminent form as Freud possessed is a danger to scientific pursuits. An iron will had to develop to tame language. And the 10 years that followed the Gisela episode served the purpose.

The longing, however, to be permitted unshackled indulgence in the free expression of enchanting linguistic structures remained in Freud to the end of his life, as his letters to authors like Schnitzler and Romain Rolland testify (Kanzer, 1977).[44]

Thus a therapeutic interference with the sharp repression that set in after the Gisela episode would have upset a most delicate process that no one at that time would have been able to recognize as foreshadowing the formation of a uniquely scientific mind.

Geneticists may one day be able to organize genes in such a way as to form the biological foundation of extreme creativity. But it is a long way from the gene to the perfect works of the

44. However, I disagree with Kanzer on a point of principle. He gives a genetic explanation of Freud's unmistakable envy of literary men by reference to the child's envy of the younger brother. Would Freud not have envied poets and authors if he had not had a younger brother? I doubt that Freud's envy was neurotic, that is, caused by a displacement of infantile envy. Freud had successfully warded off his inner temptations to succumb to his artistic talents and propensities. Yet the gratification derived from aesthetic creativity is usually greater than that which the scientist can derive from his work. The scientist's creations are ephemeral, the next or immediately following generation replaces them by more accurate ones. And Freud was fully aware of the transiency of what he left to posterity. I could cite many another factor that would strongly suggest that artistic creativity is closer to the pleasure principle than scientific creativity. Freud's envy of the *littérateurs* was based on a harsh reality whatever its genetic history might have been. Oddly enough, a possibly intuitive though utterly untrustworthy writer (Papini, 1934) published a report of an interview in which Freud allegedly said: "Everybody thinks that I stand by the scientific character of my work. . . . This is a terrible error that has prevailed for years. . . . I am really by nature an artist. . . . I would have liked to have become a poet, and my whole life long I've wanted to write novels, etc." Proofs abound that Freud could never have told Papini what the latter reported, but the possibility remains that quite independently of whether or not he had ever met Freud, he may have intuitively estimated correctly significant elements in Freud's unconscious; see also Wittels (1924, p. 13) who mentions Stekel's communication to him that Freud allegedly had told him that he later wanted to become a novelist.

genius, adolescence being one of the most important stations on this path.

How it happens that in the development of a genius all the necessary important (and less important) elements conjoin, harmonize, and seem to unite for the realization of one exclusive goal remains a secret to this day. Freud's times were restless, and the forthcoming of a new psychology was in the air. But what was it that made it possible for the 17-year-old youth to write such extraordinary German? An unfriendly critic called me a hagiographer because of my rhapsodic words with regard to young Freud's literary abilities. A dunce who does not marvel when reading the *Matura* letter. A great psychologist, a contemporary of Freud, had a brother who was a great writer. In Freud, a William and a Henry James were united. Had these abilities been split again, as in the James brothers, Freud would never have moved to the top of the psychological pyramid.

CONCLUSION

The following generalizations may be tentatively proposed. Among the many features differentiating the human species from subhuman primates, adolescence is prominent. The oedipus complex, the latency period, language, symbol formation, the evolvement of superego, knowledge of death, culture with religion and art and philosophy and science, all these evolutionary and acquired formations constitute with puberty and adolescence a conglomerate of factors that belong together. Knowledge of their interrelations is still lacking, but I am inclined to attribute a major role to puberty and adolescence. One day it may be possible to make a reasonable estimate of how far mankind would have developed without that delay in maturation. Since—surprisingly—some of the subhuman primates are able to use tools, I would speculate that if mankind matured fully directly after childhood, as subhuman primates do, instead of going into latency, it would have evolved tools but hardly anything that would have gone beyond facilitating physical biological survival.

I seriously doubt, however, that culture in the narrower sense as it has flowered in art, religion, science, philosophy, and mathematics could have evolved if delay in maturation had not been granted the species. It seems to me that all cultural achievements by great minds are in a direct genetic connection with their adolescence. Indeed, it may be questioned whether true original values can be formed after adolescence.

This may appear wrong, at first glance, in view of the great achievements of which some are capable even in old age. Yet the following considerations seem directly relevant. In a creative puberty and adolescence the youth's entire past with all its judgments, beliefs, and values is scrambled. One can approximately describe in what directions this scrambling process goes: there is commingling and intermingling, a disarranging in the form of disjointing and discomposing, that is, a general disorganization. As in many other instances, a process in the opposite direction also takes place and new assemblages of images are formed. This involves recombination: merging, amalgamating, and consolidating, that is, a process of reorganization. In addition, the adolescent is stirred up by the huge number of experiences to which the quality of newness is attached (comparable to the many experiences of newness which he had had when he initially came into touch with the world during infancy and childhood).

Thus, apart from the new formations created out of the old ones, new contents are channeled into the unconscious. It is my impression that during adolescence a huge stock of highly cathected imagery accumulates that serves as a store for the rest of life. Creative minds, I imagine, have only to reach back into that store in order to obtain new imagery, new problems, new tasks. The richness of that store will depend on the extent and intensity of disorganization and reorganization that take place during adolescence.[45] These processes contribute a great deal to the storminess, upheaval, and anguish of that period.

45. This proposition should not imply a devaluation of the preoedipal and oedipal phases, for the richness of adolescence also depends on the quality and extent of the material submitted to the scrambling process.

A quiet adolescence in a person of later high creativity is hardly imaginable.

Therefore, I must object most strongly to those who like Jones (1 : 24), and Gedo and Wolf (1970), believe that Freud's adolescence was a relatively quiet one. This can be disproved if only by Freud's later remarks in his letters to Martha Bernays about the way he felt prior to falling in love with her. The error of these authors is referable to their relative underrating of Freud's capacity to internalize conflicts and escape acting out. Furthermore, we possess only those letters of the adolescent Freud that he wrote to peers. The biographer of Goethe is in a more advantageous position in that respect. In his instance some of the letters are preserved which he wrote not only to peers but also to an older person, Behrisch,[46] who served as transitory authority and counselor. There one observes that Goethe concealed from peers the tragic aspect of grave adolescent conflicts which he described in detail to Behrisch. The equivalent of such letters is not available with regard to Freud's adolescence. But the foregoing should make it amply clear that Freud's adolescence was stormy and rich in conflicts, as befits a truly creative personage.

Necessary as a stormy adolescence of high intensity seems to be for great future accomplishments, it is dangerous. Galois, whom I mentioned as an example of hypercreative adolescence, perhaps exemplifies the danger. The creativity of his adolescence was almost beyond belief, but it ended in a catastrophe. He became involved in a love affair that led to the fatal duel. I surmise, furthermore, that he was not destined to live long even if optimal conditions had been granted him. Such early hypercreativity is prone to burst the vessel asunder, the adolescent not yet being sufficiently solidified to bear unusually intensive excitations and strains.

In my estimation, this is in general terms the meaning of the tragedy of Romeo and Juliet. Poetical license called their love ill-starred, as if the tragic outcome was destined by ineluctable

46. Ernst Wolfgang Behrisch (1738–1809), a tutor in aristocratic families, served as a kind of father confessor to the young Goethe when he went through his first passionate love experience at Leipzig.

forces hostile to their permanent reunion. In truth, however, it seems that love of such intensity, seriousness, and determination cannot be borne at that tender age. It is different with what is called infatuation, which has a better chance of evaporating and granting a temporary respite. Creativity put Galois's psychic apparatus under a strain and stress comparable to that under which the famous lovers in vain contended for survival.

A man, a psychologist of note who knew Freud in his most productive years, averred that Freud never struck him as a genius. Asked who did, he named Weininger,[47] whose personality was of a type comparable to Galois's in certain respects. Weininger committed suicide at the age of 23, after having written *Sex and Character,* a book which proves him to have been one of those hypercreative minds. The book was a sensation and it went through twenty-eight editions and was translated into many languages. There will be few who would read it nowadays and agree with its content. Nevertheless, it is written with an intensity, richness of thought, right or wrong, and originality that will hardly be found in any mind at that early age.

Galois and Weininger were personalities that may be compared with comets or fireworks. Their energetic output during adolescence was so consuming that they had to collapse exhausted after a short period. One may think here also of Mozart's early death. Was Freud in danger of following a similar path? It is not probable that his talents, as one learns from his early letters, were large enough to permit retrospectively the fear that if he had gone on at the same pace as he started, some unfortunate complexities may have resulted. Nevertheless, the Gisela experience may have put a wholesome brake on the speed of his development and thus protected him. Therefore one must be grateful to her for her sudden appearance and disappearance in Freud's life.

But there is still another factor to be considered. The Gisela

47. Otto Weininger (1880–1903), philosopher, main subjects: psychology and metaphysics of the sexes, psychology of genius, represented forcefully the theory of psychobiological bisexuality.

experience contributed much to the strengthening of the defensive, repressive apparatus in the youth. Freud never discarded this apparatus. One has the impression that he made his discoveries against an inner resistance, that the richness of his accomplishments came to pass against a background of hard labor, the expression of a counterforce which Freud himself intimated when he wrote to Lou Andreas-Salomé about a recent discovery: "It is a discovery of which one ought almost to be ashamed, for one should have divined these connections from the beginning and not after thirty years" (1960, p. 361).

The danger may have been that if Freud's defense had not been sufficient, he might have traveled a path like that of Stekel and Wilhelm Reich, who though highly talented lacked self-discipline and therefore went astray because of exaggerations and one-sidedness in so many of their endeavors. In contrast, one finds in Freud something like a harmonious balance between biological and environmental forces, ego and id, drive and society, the constitutional and the accidental, and so forth. This balance between force and counterforce, the ability to perceive the complexity of problems with all their inherent contradictions and ramifications, might have been made possible, among other factors, by the equilibrium between drive and defense, which was achieved after a brake had been put upon the onslaught of pubertal drives.

The main point I have in mind—that adolescence is the fountainhead of all later creativity—I cannot prove. To do so would probably be possible if we knew all the fantasies, daydreams, and night dreams of an adolescent who later became hypercreative. One may anticipate that one would then recognize the unformed material out of which the genius in the course of his maturation forms his creations. Even though I cannot prove this, I wish to support it by two quotations. Alfred de Vigny surprisingly said, "What is a great life? It is a thought of youth wrought out in ripening years."

Sarton (1948, p. 98) adds:

> The fundamental conception dawns at an early age—that is,
> it appears at the surface of one's consciousness as early as this

is materially possible—but it is often so great that a long life of toil and abnegation is but too short to work it out. Of course, at the beginning it may be very vague, so vague indeed that its host can hardly distinguish it himself from a passing fancy, and later may be unable to explain how it gradually took control of his activities and dominated his whole being.

This was said in connection with two very special instances, those of Niels Henrik Abel (1803–29) and Galois. Yet I think, if generalized, these words express my point full well.

BIBLIOGRAPHY

BAK, R. (1973), Being in Love and Object Loss. *Int. J. Psycho-Anal.,* 54 : 1–8.
BERNFELD, S. (1924), *Vom dichterischen Schaffen der Jugend.* Leipzig: Internationaler psychoanalytischer Verlag.
———— (1947), An Unknown Autobiographical Fragment by Freud. *Amer. Imago,* 4 : 3–19.
———— (1949), Freud's Scientific Beginnings. *Amer. Imago,* 6 : 163–196.
———— (1951), Sigmund Freud, M.D., 1882–1885. *Int. J. Psycho-Anal.,* 32 : 204–217.
———— (1953), Freud's Studies on Cocaine, In: *Cocaine Papers Sigmund Freud,* ed. R. Byck. New York: Stonehill, pp. 323–352.
BREUER, J. & FREUD, S. (1893–95), Studies on Hysteria. *S.E.,* 2.
BRÜCKE, E. T. (1928), *Ernst Brücke.* Wien: Springer.
BRUN, R. (1936), Sigmund Freuds Leistungen auf dem Gebiet der organischen Neurologie. *Schweiz. Arch. Neurol. Psychiat.,* 37 : 200–207.
CLARK, K. (1939), *Leonardo da Vinci.* Cambridge Univ. Press.
CLAUS, C. (1899), *Autobiographie.* Marburg: Elwert [continued by his son-in-law Guido von Alth].
DOSTOEVSKY, A. (1975), *Dostoevsky Reminiscences.* New York: Liveright.
EISSLER, K. R. (1974), Über Freuds Freundschaft mit Wilhelm Fliess nebst einem Anhang über Freuds Adoleszenz und einer historischen Bemerkung über Freuds Jugendstil. *Jb. Psychoanal.,* 10 : 39–100.
ERIKSON, E. H. (1968), *Identity, Youth and Crisis.* New York: Norton.
EXNER, S. (1910), Ein Rückblick auf die Physiologie in Wien. *Wien. klin. Wschr.,* 23 : 1335–1337.
FREUD, E. L. (1969), Introduction [to:] Some Early Unpublished Letters of Freud. *Int. J. Psycho-Anal.,* 50 : 419.
FREUD, S. (1884), Die Struktur der Elemente des Nervensystems. *Jb. Psychiat. Neurol.,* 5 : 221–229.

5I6   K. R. Eissler

——— (1893), Charcot. *S.E.*, 3 : 11–23.

——— (1897), Abstracts of the Scientific Writings of Dr. Sigm. Freud, 1871–1897. *S.E.*, 3 : 227–257.

——— (1899), Screen Memories. *S.E.*, 3 : 301–322.

——— (1900), The Interpretation of Dreams. *S.E.*, 4 & 5.

——— (1901), The Psychopathology of Everyday Life. *S.E.*, 6.

——— (1908), 'Civilized' Sexual Morality and Modern Nervous Illness, *S.E.*, 9 : 181–204.

——— (1910), Leonardo da Vinci and a Memory of His Childhood. *S.E.*, 11 : 63–137.

——— (1918), From the History of an Infantile Neurosis. *S.E.*, 17 : 3–123.

——— (1925a), An Autobiographical Study. *S.E.*, 20 : 3–74.

——— (1925b), Negation. *S.E.*, 19 : 235–239.

——— (1926), The Question of Lay Analysis. *S.E.*, 20 : 179–258.

——— (1927a), Postscript to the Question of Lay Analysis. *S.E.*, 20 : 251–258.

——— (1927b), Humour. *S.E.*, 21 : 161–166.

——— (1939), Moses and Monotheism. *S.E.*, 23 : 3–137.

——— (1955), Addendum [to a Case of Obsessional Neurosis]. Original Record of the Case. *S.E.*, 10 : 259–318.

——— (1960), *Letters of Sigmund Freud,* ed. E. L. Freud. New York: Basic Books.

——— (1967), Hochzeitscarmen. *Deutsch für Ausländer: Informationen für den Lehrer,* Königswinter: Verlag für Sprachmethodik, January issue.

——— (1969), Some Early Unpublished Letters of Freud. *Int. J. Psycho-Anal.,* 50 : 419–427.

——— (1974), Zerstreute Gedanken. *Jb. Psychoanal.,* 10 : 101.

GEDO, J. E. & WOLF, E. S. (1970), The "Ich" Letters. In: *Freud: The Fusion of Science and Humanism,* ed. J. E. Gedo & G. H. Pollock [*Psychol. Issues,* Monogr. 34/35]. New York: Int. Univ. Press, pp. 71–86.

GICKLHORN, J. (1955), Wissenschaftsgeschichtliche Notizen zu den Studien von S. Syrski (1874) und S. Freud (1877) über männliche Flussaale. *Sitzungsber. der Österr. Akademie der Wissenschaften,* Mathem.-naturw. Kl., Abt I, 164. Bd, 1 & 2. Wien: Springer.

GILLISPIE, C. C. (1960), *The Edge of Objectivity.* Princeton Univ. Press.

GREENACRE, P. (1957), The Childhood of the Artist. *This Annual,* 12 : 47–72.

JELLIFFE, S. E. (1937), Sigmund Freud as Neurologist. *J. Nerv. Ment. Dis.,* 85 : 696–711.

JONES, E. (1953–57), *The Life and Work of Sigmund Freud,* 3 vols. New York: Basic Books.

KANZER, M. (1976), Freud and His Literary Doubles. *Amer. Imago,* 33 : 231–243.

KARSTEN, H. (1872), *Die Fäulnis und Ansteckung: Im Anhange der Darstellung meiner Erlebnisse an der Wiener Universität in den Jahren 1869–1871.* Schaffhausen: Carl Bäder.

KUHN, T. S. (1962), The Structure of Scientific Revolutions. *Int. Encyclopedia of Unified Science,* vol. 2, no. 2. Univ. Chicago Press.

LESKY, E. (1965), *Die Wiener medizinische Schule im 19. Jahrhundert.* Graz/Köln: Hermann Böhlaus Nachf.

MEYER, R. M. (1900), *Die deutsche Literatur des neunzehnten Jahrhunderts.* Berlin: Bondi.

PAPINI, G. (1934), A Visit to Freud (May 8, 1934). In: *Freud as We Knew Him,* ed. H. M. Ruytenbeck. Detroit: Wayne State Univ. Press, 1973, pp. 98–102.

RITVO, L. B. (1965), Darwin as the Source of Freud's Neo-Lamarkianism. *Amer. J. Psychol.,* 13 : 499–515.

———— (1972a), Carl Claus as Freud's Professor of the New Darwinian Biology. *Int. J. Psycho-Anal.,* 53 : 277–283.

———— (1972b), *Darwin's Influence on Freud.* Dissertation, Yale Univ. Ann Arbor: Univ. Microfilms.

SARTON, G. (1948), *The Life of Science.* New York: Schuman.

SCHORSKE, C. E. (1973), Politics and Patricide in Freud's "Interpretation of Dreams." *Amer. Hist. Rev.,* 78 : 328–347.

STANESCU, H. (1965), Unbekannte Briefe des jungen Freud an einen rumänischen Freund. *Neue Literatur,* 16 : 123–129.

———— (1967), Ein "Gelegenheitsgedicht" des jungen Sigmund Freud. *Deutsch für Ausländer: Informationen für den Lehrer.* Königswinter: Verlag für Sprachmethodik, January issue, pp. 13–16.

———— (1971), Young Freud's Letters to His Rumanian Friend, Silberstein. *Israel Ann. Psychiatr. & Rel. Discipl.,* 9 : 195–209.

STRACHEY, J. (1955), Editor's Introduction and Appendix A. In: *S.E.,* 2 : ix–xxviii and 307–309.

VOGELSTEIN-BRAUN, J. (1932), *Heinrich Braun: Ein Leben für den Sozialismus.* Stuttgart: Deutsche Verlagsanstalt, 1967.

———— (1966), *Was Niemals Stirbt.* Stuttgart: Deutsche Verlagsanstalt.

WITTELS, F. (1924), *Sigmund Freud.* Leipzig/Wien/Zurich: E. P. Tal.

———— (1930), Goethe und Freud. *Psychoanal. Beweg.,* 2 : 431–466.

The Art Work as a Force in the Artist's Life

Thomas Mann's Exile and *Joseph and His Brothers*

GEORGE C. ROSENWALD, Ph.D.

> The work proceeds as it can and often presents itself to the author as something independent or even alien.
>
> FREUD (1939, p. 104)

WITHIN TRADITIONAL PSYCHOLOGICAL FRAMEWORKS, MANIFESTA-tions of creativity are viewed predominantly as products of human activity, bearing the stamp of the artist and expressing his or her character in the widest sense. Creative activity is seen as mainly expressive, but the reflexive effect of the work on the artist is proportionately neglected. This approach, though in consonance with psychological interest in talent, genius, and the process of creation as well as with ancient sources in the philosophy of art, does not do full justice to the insights of contemporary psychoanalytic scholarship. In tracing the effect of the work on the artist, psychological theory is more fully mobilized, and a more rounded picture of both creativity and art results. The present paper seeks to demonstrate this broadening by reference to a study of Thomas Mann.

Professor of Psychology, University of Michigan, Ann Arbor, Mich.

I

Psychoanalytic investigations of creativity usually proceed
from the general working hypothesis that a literary text
presents us with a partial, coded reflection of the author's—
and, by extension, our own—inner life. We look for corre-
spondences between the writer's own biographical experience
and his fiction. Such correspondence can pertain to the material of fiction (Beres, 1959; Kanzer, 1959) or to the choice of
art as expressive medium (Deutsch, 1959; Greenacre, 1957).
In its general form, this hypothesis states that the author reproduces and stabilizes himself in the medium of his craft.
The creation of aesthetic novelty equilibrates him. The psychoanalytic interpreter may emphasize—this varies from case
to case—the literary precipitates of lifelong unresolved conflicts, repetitive patterns of object relations, traumatic experiences and the modes of their mastery, problematic ego states,
morally significant struggles and resolutions. Sometimes he
demonstrates that the author depicts a private state or tension
in the work and sometimes that the author corrects or nullifies
such a state by means of artistic transformation. In either case,
the writer is assumed to be the source of the literary objectivation, revealing himself, though indirectly, as he is or strives to
be.

   This psychoanalytic approach to life-and-letters, as I shall
call it, has met with far less acceptance in literary circles than
another psychoanalytic contribution—that of symbolic interpretation—which has been easily absorbed into the traditional apparatus with which critics undertake the clarification
of literary symbols, themes, and images.[1] A common objection
by writers and readers to the life-and-letters approach is that it
introduces extraneous and reductive categories into the field
of aesthetics. In this paper I shall, however, explore a different sort of objection, namely, that this approach also over-

   1. These two approaches coincide roughly with Eissler's concepts (1968)
of exopoietic and endopoietic interpretation. He regards the former as beset
with grave methodological difficulties, as does Beres (1959).

simplifies the psychology of the author—and, by extension, that of the reader.

Does artistry produce novelty only for the reader? Is it one sublimation among many, encountered in those with a specific endowment? Is the impact of the art work on the artist's own life completely under his (unconscious) control? I shall argue that the literary work can be, and perhaps always is, more than the author's product; that its status as cultural object, accessible to a multitude of readers, endows it with values which have psychological *force,* even though they are not wholly derivable from the author's psychology; and that, by virtue of this greater value which it acquires as an objective symbol, it can have a formative effect on the author himself. That is, the author becomes one of the beneficiaries of his own creation. The implications for our view of human development are significant: Whereas the traditional life-and-letters hypothesis guides us toward an appreciation of how the author corrects an imbalance in himself and achieves an archaic equilibrium consonant with the pleasure principle, my intent is to show that art may, in addition, develop the author and bring him to new syntheses.

The argument shall rest on the evidence of material from a single case rather than on the collation of multifarious research studies. Drawing selected themes from the life and work of Thomas Mann, I shall suggest that a political and familial crisis which he underwent in his early 40s was partially healed through his subsequent literary productions. My point will be that his art proved formative and reintegrative, rather than merely cathartic or curative. Most of the paper will set forth the terms of his crisis and its resolution in detail. I shall supply relevant biographical material as well. In conclusion, the implications for the psychoanalytic theory of creativity will be discussed.

POLITICS AND ART

Twice in his life, Thomas Mann cut himself off from a major current of his nation's life—each time in deep, painful conscientiousness. Toward the end of World War I, he published a passionate political pamphlet of 600 pages, the *Reflections of an Apolitical Man* (1918), in which he expressed his horror at the rise and spread of political democracy in Europe. He declared his support of the German national destiny and of the freedom of mind and art which could flourish only in a monarchy.

Not long afterward, Mann saw these ideals being sullied by the fascists and, in effect, repudiated his stand. After the rise of the Weimar Republic, he began to accept the principles of democracy, finally taking a firm stand against National Socialism. In essays and on lecture tours he attacked Nazi policy and even expressed sympathy with Socialist thought insofar as it upheld humanism and freedom as its goals.

When Hitler became chancellor in 1933, Mann, then on vacation in Switzerland, was warned by his son and daughter not to return to Germany. Mann eventually settled in America and became the acknowledged spokesman for German refugees the world over. During the Second World War, he made many anti-Nazi broadcasts into Germany. Having abjured all participation in politics in his 40s, he devoted himself unstintingly to political tasks in his 60s, actively espousing the principles he had previously denounced. On his eightieth birthday he was hailed as a "free spirit . . . [who] during a time of enslavement . . . preserved the honor of Germany" (Mauriac, 1955, p. 21). After World War II, he was approached with an offer of the presidency of the new German republic. But Mann never returned to live in Germany, choosing to remain an exile for the rest of his life.

In the years intervening between his first and second dissents, Mann was occupied with his largest and perhaps grandest work, the tetralogy *Joseph and His Brothers.* I shall explore in the following pages the role this work may have played in mediating a personal change in the author.

THE CRISIS

The *Reflections of an Apolitical Man,* three years in the writing, were the result of a long and painful personal struggle precipitated by the political events of World War I. On the horizon Mann saw the inevitable defeat of Germany not only in the military sense, but in the national and moral sense as well. With Germany's defeat, he forecast, Europe would collapse spiritually. All of life would soon be seized and politically organized by the merchants of democracy. So frightening was this prospect that his own work on *The Magic Mountain* was stalled; his life as a German artist seemed menaced by the tide of Western politization. In the *Reflections* he championed the Germanic tradition of freedom and individualism against the leveling effect of political organization, which would surely snuff out the ethical humane passion of the German *Bürger*. He praised the authoritarian state as the form of government best suited to the German people. His political struggle was potentiated by a bitter quarrel with his older brother. For the novelist Heinrich Mann was an ardent advocate of republican egalitarianism on the French model.

What Thomas Mann stood for, considering his later clarifications, was sufficiently ambiguous that reactionary elements gaining strength after Germany's defeat felt confident that they could count on Mann as one of them. With the appearance of the *Reflections,* Mann cut himself off from many liberal-minded people who had been his readers for two decades. On the other side, it has been argued that the *Reflections* were more democratic than Mann himself indicated when he later spoke of them apologetically (Flinker, 1959). It is clear, then, that some controversy surrounds the depth and nature of Mann's change in conviction. While some critics at the time of his second dissent looked askance at his abrupt shift from right to left, Mann himself played down the difference, declaring that his own commitment to humaneness was steady— that he had been just as opposed to terror and obscurantism in 1918 as he was now to the politization of art and inwardness.

This ambiguity is characteristic not only of Mann, but of all personal change, as we know from the psychoanalytic study of life histories. It is not surprising that even a man of unusual resources does not turn over an entirely new, unmarked leaf.

To expect such disruptive psychological effects from a work of art would be to mock the self-formative effect of creativity which is under discussion in this paper. This much seems clear: throughout his life, Mann's ethical relationship to his society was and remained that of exile; this theme recurs in his fiction no less than in his essays, letters, and public acts. But his exile underwent a transformation in the course of the years, and the present discussion focuses on the contribution made by literary creativity to this transformation.

Thomas Mann had felt all his life that, as a child of the nineteenth century and as an artist, he was a stranger in his time and in his society. This sense of strangeness gathered momentum from the time when he made his dramatic entrance on the world stage of literature with his first novel, *Buddenbrooks,* until the crisis recorded in the *Reflections* some 20 years later. Even in *Buddenbrooks* he charted the decline of *Bürgerlichkeit,* the patrician order of the past century. The Buddenbrook family whose fall he chronicled was closely patterned on his own family. In spacious, wistful, dignified chapters he related the advancing decadence. His ironic tone revived the moribund era once more. *Tonio Kröger,* a novella written shortly thereafter, dealt with the artist as outcast. He yearns for the simple, strong, and mindless life of the blue-eyed burgher, but he is suspect in society, marked by the sympathy for morbidity and wickedness which he must cultivate if he is to be a true artist and to fathom true morality. The theme of an exile identity was already discernible in these early works.

It extended into the political realm when he wrote an essay on Frederick the Great during the second year of World War I. In this he glorified the misunderstood military hero, the great sufferer. A weakling and dandy in his youth, Frederick became a self-denying, intrepid leader and an ambitious, relentless conqueror. All Europe, wrote Mann (1915), stood united against him, challenging his right to invade neutral Saxony in a preventive war that had been forced on him. But his right, Mann asserted, "was the right of a rising power. As a right it was still problematic, still illegitimate, still unrecognized; it was a right which had yet to be fought for, yet to be created" (p. 55).[2] But he was chosen by God and scourged by Him, "a sacrifice to and instrument of a higher will" (p. 63). The essay was offered as a contribution to the "order of the day" and was widely understood as a justification of Germany's invasion of Belgium under the pretext of defending Prussia's invasion of Saxony 150 years earlier. Mann was less moved by the turmoil of a nation or a people than by the struggle of a hero, the redemption of a splendid sufferer by Fate. Not the soldiers who died in the Seven Years' War were celebrated, but the great man who expired after years of loneliness and illness, silently and stubbornly endured. Later on, Mann looked back on this essay as a tribute to Nietzschean psychology and ethics; but at the time, its impact was prosaically political.

Within a few months, Heinrich Mann published an *essai-à-clef* about Emile Zola, intended as a contribution to the contemporary political debate. He recounted Zola's merits as social critic, visionary, meliorist, and political activist on behalf of the common man. To praise Zola meant praising the republican form of government as the remedy for Germany's mounting catastrophe. Only a republic could create happiness for the people, wrote Heinrich Mann (1915) speaking for Zola, for happiness has to be created by an inner impulse, not by great men who let it soak down: "Democracy strives not for great men, but for man's greatness!" (p. 1350). The artist and the man of letters had their obligations: "The novel should not merely describe; it should ameliorate" (p. 1315). Also: "[The writer] knows that his work becomes more human insofar as it becomes more political. Literature and politics, both of which have man as their object, cannot be separated" (p. 1324). The essay began with a description of young Zola's early groping and intellectual uncertainties. The second sentence read: "Those whose fate it is to dry up in young years have a way of stepping before the world complacently and self-righteously even in their early 20s." Not for a moment did

2. All quotations from the German editions are my own translations.

Thomas Mann doubt that he himself was the sole intended
target of this reproach. Together with other ambiguous references, he referred to it as an unforgivable, an "inhuman excess" (Mann, 1956, p. 113). Heinrich rejected the imputation,
but Thomas remained unappeased for years. The *Reflections*
were his ardent reply.

Although Thomas Mann was reluctant to descend to political discourse, political consternation had paralyzed his creativity. He felt he owed his audience an explanation of his per-
turbed artistic silence. He sensed the interplay of general
European problems with his personal upheaval: "It is destiny
to be placed into time in such a way that the turning point in
one's personal life coincides with a catastrophic turning point
in one's era" (1918, p. 207). The exile identity became enunciated by the exile himself as a psychosocial constellation.

Mann had reached the age of 40 when, as he put it, one's
future is no longer the general future, but merely one's own
particular future. At this stage his values no longer mediated
adequately between himself and his society. An artist for
whom "art is, above all, a means of fulfilling my life ethically"
was particularly vulnerable to the revolution in contemporary
values: "I am, therefore, concerned about my *life*, not my
work" (1918, p. 97). If politics were allowed to dominate art
and all the rest of life, ethics would no longer take precedence
over aesthetics. Ethics was the deep concern of the *Reflections:*
"This work grew out of scrupulosity, a moral and aesthetic
quality to which I owe any success I may ever have had, which
[is] now playing a trick on me . . . it borders on pedantry, and
one might aptly call this entire book an immense childlike hy-
pochondriac pedantry" (1918, p. 7).

The *Reflections* began with a rigorous distinction between
German *Bürgerlichkeit* and the inimical spirits which jeopar-
dized it from every quarter. The patrician ideals had been at
their peak in the nineteenth century, in the culture of Schopenhauer, Wagner, and Nietzsche. Mann longed for their
irony, their cynicism, and their refusal simply to please. But in
our own days, he lamented, nineteenth-century romanticism,
music, nationalism, humor, and pessimism had given way to

the politization of all public life. Reason and the Heart were trumps once again, as they had been in the eighteenth century. Our air, he wrote, is polluted with activism, meliorism, and voluntarism—nothing but ornate sentimentalities covering up the opportunism of power motives. Wherever one looked, mind had been put in the service of what is desirable. Although Wagner had once boasted that the ardor of music could melt politics as the sun melts the fog, now, in the twentieth century, that seemed an empty boast—politics would surely freeze out music!

The notion that Germany might soon "grow up to democracy" revolted the author deeply, for the German soul could not be reconciled with the political mentality: "We are not a social people, and we are no mine for vagrant psychologists!" (p. 27). The Germans' staunch, mute, crass Lutheran protest had been the chief historic irritant to the "masonic, republican bourgeois-rhetoricians of 1789" (p. 28). Germany stood for mind, not for politics; culture, not civilization; soul, not society; freedom, not voting rights; art, not "literature"; cosmopolitanism, not internationalism. More than a military victory was at stake in its survival. Its recalcitrance was directed, above all, against Latin garrulity, flattery, meddling, and exploitation, and against the oily insinuating elegance of the French. French manners, French asceticism, French political morality, and French history had forged their own propaganda instrument in the midst of Germany—the *Zivilisationsliterat,* the writer-of-civilization, kin to the boulevard-journalist. His was the business of cheapening all values, catering to the mob, and hoodwinking the individual in the name of Progress. What these writers offered, declared Mann, did not honor humanity, but the rabble.

His brother was such a culprit. Mann's despair over the cultural heritage was deepened by that over the personal. As the familiar (and familial) landmarks and symbols of his identity betrayed him, his suspicion and detestation spread from society and brother to himself and his own artistry. Nietzsche had described the Germans as an antiradical people, a people of life, not of letters. An awful contradiction dawned on Mann as

528 George C. Rosenwald

he extolled the German essence: He himself was one of the most voluble and literate Germans of all time. More than anyone else in his day, he had appropriated the French genre of the novel, had developed it, and contributed heavily to the internationalization and democratization of art. He was himself tainted with the abomination: "One does not care about something in this degree, if one does not *need* to care, if it does not concern one, if one does not know about it, if one does not find it in himself, *if one does not have it in his own blood*" (p. 32). Nietzsche, too, had contributed an international style, and Wagner had a universal appeal.

Mann discovered that the German artist was, if not a contradiction in terms, an unstable qualification. His life seemed at an end: "What after all is this long soliloquy and scrawl, but a review of what I was—what I was for a time, justly and honorably—and what I apparently cannot remain any longer, though I do not even feel old yet!" (p. 208). Moving between the artist's and society's viewpoint, he wrote with only a glimmer of irony:

> Those who have perused my writings will recall that I have always reacted with utter distrust to the artist's or the writer's form of life. My astonishment at the honors which society bestows on this species will never cease. I know what the writer is since I am avowedly a writer myself. To put it briefly, the writer is a chap who is absolutely useless in any field of earnest endeavor, always bent on mischief, and not merely useless to his country, but downright offensive. Further, he need not be endowed with unusual intellectual gifts, but may well be as slow-witted and obtuse as I have always been myself. Further, he is childish in his inner life, inclined to extravagance, and in every respect a disreputable charlatan. From his society he should not, and in fact does not, expect anything but silent contempt. However, the fact is that society grants this breed the opportunity to attain the highest honors [p. 565f.].

The writer-of-civilization, who dedicates his talents to the creation of *bellezza,* that is, who prostitutes art by creating a slovenly sort of beauty for the satisfaction of the masses, escapes the artist's predicament. But the true artist cannot be satisfied with being virtuous; his morality must be broad and uncompromising. This requires him to confront sin, man's primal urges, suffering, and death: "Sin is doubt, the attraction to taboo, to adventure; sin is to lose oneself, to surrender, to experience, to search, to know!" (p. 391).

An artist in tune with sober German *Bürgertum* was unthinkable. Mann chose, in all his fiction, to reconcile the contradiction between art and life by his ironic style, by what he referred to as his sublimated mindlessness, the artist's skeptical, modest self-reflection. This was morally preferable to, and in better taste than, the unabashed lordly proclamations of those progressive writers who always stood on soapboxes, one hand upon the heart, the other on the *Social Contract,* spouting universal love of mankind—a love which was humbug, a peripheral erotism substituting for a defective one at the center.

Freedom, Mann declared, was a matter of the individual mind, not of society: "The basic law of German life had always been the unfolding, development, differentiation, multifariousness, and wealth of individuality" (p. 271). Democracy as a political force should yield to democracy as the cultivation of individual personality. As a form of government it rendered people "crude, vulgar, and stupid; envy, arrogance, ambitiousness is all it teaches" (p. 251).

Mann's dissent came to an end, as we have seen, with the perversion of his ideals by the fascists, who claimed the very same spiritual forebears whom he had honored in his book. In 1922, he announced his support for the Weimar Republic. When questioned about his change, he replied that, like Goethe and Nietzsche, he was and remained antiliberal, but without any concessions to human reason and dignity. Humanity was now his overarching concern; he quoted Whitman at length. His pen was no longer directed against politics, but against terror, vulgarity, and fanaticism. In *The Magic Mountain,* which he shortly resumed, "the critique of liberalism is freely confronted with the critique of that critique, and an opening is sought for the transcending of the dialectical deadlock" (Heller, 1955, p. 1015). "Western liberalism, the *bête noire* of the [*Reflections*] is accepted . . . as at the worst a lesser evil" (Hatfield, 1956, p. 210). Nonetheless, this change in political viewpoint did not put an end to Mann's scruples about the artist's morality, which continued to appear in his fiction in sublimated ironic form until the end of his life—in *Doktor Faustus* and in *Felix Krull*.

BIOGRAPHICAL BACKGROUND

Thomas Mann was born in the North German city of Lübeck in 1875. He had an older and a younger brother and two younger sisters. His mother had come to Germany as a child. She herself had been born on a plantation in Brazil of German and Creole parents. She was of southern temperament, bohemian in her tastes, "talented as a female," inclined to the arts, and in most ways remained an alien in Hanseatic society (Mann, 1963, p. 101). It is reported that she liked to reminisce about the jungle with its colorful plants and parrots and about her black nurse. According to Mann, her leanings toward the south remained latent until after her husband's death, at which time she promptly moved to Munich with its gayer, more casual atmosphere. We are told that Thomas was closer to his mother than were the other four children. The ethnic origins of his fictional heroines is often a significant factor in the corruption of a man's morals, for example, in the case of Clavdia Chauchat in *The Magic Mountain* or of Mutemenet in *Joseph in Egypt*. Yet, despite his lavish autobiographical borrowings, he never directly depicted her in any of his works. All the more, his inclination toward dissent and exile may have been derived, at least in part, from her model.

The father, by contrast, was the descendant of a line of successful grain merchants. He became, in addition, an outstanding public figure, senator of Lübeck, a great elegant orator, and a revered statesman of many offices and honors. He has been described as a person of great savoir-faire and appears to have been somewhat vain and self-indulgent. The paternal house was a meeting place for high society. Hanseatic officers, searching the patrician houses of Lübeck for wives with substantial dowries, enjoyed the Manns' hospitality, but the family also received musicians and artists of the stage. While mother sang and played the piano, father's literary and artistic interests were more genteel and circumspect, easily yielding to the demands of business. It is said that he read Zola's revolutionizing novels, but only when he thought himself unobserved!

In the *Reflections* Mann made only brief mention of foreign influence, hinting that it disqualified him from taking up the cause of Germany. Even when he spoke of such contaminations, he emphasized his artistic estrangement from the German tradition more than ethnic impurity. The struggle for purity in the austere terms of his definition took the form of an ideological nostalgia, a wish to return to the generation of his grandfathers. The figures of Goethe, Schopenhauer, Wagner, and Nietzsche represent ancestral idealizations designed to erase the blemishes of his parents' and his own generations. The crisis he sensed was that his identity would expire along with the ambient cultural and moral decline. The atavistic yearning for the giants of the nineteenth century is understandable in part as a family romance canceling his inherited corruption—the Latin influence coursing in his blood, aggravated by his closeness to the exotic mother. His longing for the nineteenth century complements his longing for a purer blood, and his tribulation about the society of his day complements the struggle with his brother.

What does it mean that two brothers became renowned novelists and engaged in such a bitter dispute over their common patrimony? Not enough is known to speak confidently about the *interplay* between Thomas Mann's virulent denunciation of democratic equality and the troubled relationship with his brother. That he sensed the vileness of modernity in himself, but concentrated his fight against it on the person of his brother, is evidence for the deepening mutality of historical and life-historical issues. The themes of troubled fraternity, of creeping degeneracy and moral jeopardy, which reached their rhetorical and sociopolitical climax in the middle of Mann's life, were already unmistakably present in *Buddenbrooks,* his

first great work, and resounded still in *Doktor Faustus* at the
end of his creative career.

EXILE AS WORKSHOP

In the model of his mother, Mann experienced the coincidence of physical (national) and cultural (ethical) displacement. Closeness and affection for one who was herself a
stranger in the midst of proud Northern families may have
supported the youth's artistic sensibilities at the risk of
estranging him from the immediate setting. The idea of distance from one's native context became linked with the ideas
of a return to an authenticating personal artistry and of exposure to moral dubiety. His life bears witness to the fondness
for alien and forbidden zones. They offered him an opportunity to be away from home and yet all the more loyal at a distance. Mann grew up peaceably, without sympathy for rebellious movements. As a child, he played shop rather than
soldiers or Indians. Apart from a penchant for impersonation
and dramatic displays, he was a patient, if not phlegmatic,
youth. When, as an adult, he was asked about his childhood,
he appeared bored by the questions. Though he may not have
known what turns his life would take, he regarded (or later
recalled that he regarded) his youth as an unimportant pre-
lude. After his father's death, Thomas had sufficient funds to
quit his job as office clerk and to join Heinrich, who was then
living in Rome. There, living in a two-room apartment, surrounded by the sensuous countryside and wild sunsets, he
dedicated himself to a trunkful of German, Scandinavian, English, and Russian paperback novels and tried to resist adventure. His days were filled not only with Tolstoy and Turgen-
yev, but also with the growing manuscript of *Buddenbrooks*. It
was typical for this author to linger skeptically in the heartland
of *bellezza* while charting the decline of German *Bürgerlichkeit:*
Ethics before aesthetics!

Subsequently he moved to Munich. Surrounded by Bavar-
ian peasantry, Catholicism, and exuberance, he lived sedately

and without artistic extravagance. *Fiorenza* and *Gladius Dei* continued the dialectic of ethics and aesthetics. Later he recalled his attitude toward Munich:

> The entry of a Neo-German spirit and the Americanization of the German style of life [in Munich] were manifest in a certain gross corruption, in a shysterdom and commercialism of a peculiarly naïve sort. That I remained and did not move, say, to Berlin, was, however, more than mere inertia. It would be pointless to ask me what I would have become, had I spent these years in the keen air of the Prussian-American cosmopolis. In any case, *there is challenge and value in living under protest and in irony against one's surroundings—it heightens one's vitality to live more individually and more self-consciously under these conditions* [1918, p. 133; my italics].

As early as May 1937, Mann wrote to a friend that he planned to spend a part of every year in the United States, in the hope that such removal from Europe would increase his composure and spiritual freedom. After his permanent move to America, his work on the *Joseph* novels and on his novel about Goethe eased his discomfort about Germany: "Everything will be all right once my books arrive; the desk is set up, and the help, a Negro couple, is learning how we like our food. That an ocean lies between me and the liberation of the Sudeten Germans, will, I suppose, facilitate the completion of *The Beloved Returns*. . . . Visit us one day soon, there in the robust realm of the dead!" (1975, p. 82).

This last phrase was meant as a humorous parallel between Mann-in-America and Joseph-in-Egypt. Yet how painful was this humor, how unhappy this adaptation! A year later, he wrote to a friend: "What do you suppose, when will Germany be able to read me once again? This is, after all, the question with which I lie down at night and rise in the morning!" (1963, p. 117).

In his American exile, Mann occupied a position intermediate between refugee and citizen-of-the-world. Throughout the war, his mind was on those left behind. He prepared weekly radio programs, beamed into Germany by the BBC, calling for the defeat of the Nazi leadership. Mann's exile created in him not only solicitude for his compatriots, but a heightened need to keep his work and his personal sense of tradition integrated. It was in this spirit, rather than one of immodesty, that he proclaimed: "Where I am, there is Germany!" (Flanner, 1941, p. 38). At the same time, Mann served as a representative of Germany and the German people to the West. This was a remarkable realization of a position he had enunciated as early as 1918: "I stand between two worlds and am not at home in either; that makes things somewhat difficult for me" (p. 103). In America, he was intent on rescuing the imperiled past into the new and safer realm. At the same time, however, he wanted to be the exponent and protector of culture in a land on which he smiled dubiously. This was indeed "somewhat difficult." He expressed his anxiety about this precarious position, and his fear of losing touch with his native country, in a letter written in 1941 to an émigré friend in Switzerland: "Let us hope that the connection with Europe does not break off completely! The very possibility that this might happen reinforces my wish that you might join the transatlantic European community here in this country, which will, after all, willy-nilly surely assume the leadership of the world. . . . Exile has become something wholly different from the past; it is no longer a condition of waiting, oriented to a homecoming, but a foretaste of a dissolution of nations and a unification of the world" (1975, p. 101). And: "I fear that the longing for Europe will have almost been put to sleep by the time your desperate part of the world becomes accessible again" (p. 103). In fact, Mann remained wide awake on behalf of Germany.

The main difference, seen outwardly, between Mann's first and second dissents was that this time execration was mixed with loyalty and sorrow. He respected the elements he had joined in condemning his own country but remained skeptical about them nonetheless. In contrast, his proclamation of 1918 had been totalistic and remorseless.

II

The story of Joseph concerns a youth who failed to find tolerance in his community, was expelled by his brothers, became one of the most illustrious exiles in the history of Western mythology, and eventually bestowed great benefits on the family he had left behind. In the next two sections I shall explore how the literary creation of the *Joseph* novels may have contributed to the increasingly productive and loyal exertions of their author on behalf of his native land.

THE FORMATIVE EFFECTS OF ART

Several difficulties attend the demonstration of art's formative effect, that is, of its reflexive action upon the creative artist: (a) It is always problematic to establish that a thought or complex of thoughts has indeed influenced the conduct of the thinker unless the connections are supplied by him, as happens in the psychoanalytic situation. One is bound to suspect that the thoughts merely echoed changes which were prepared "on another level" and are themselves inefficacious. In the present case, one might suppose that if Mann's exile in the 1940s differed from his dissent during World War I and if he wrote novels dealing with exiles at the same time, then perhaps the novels were only an expression of life changes already under way and these changes owed nothing to the novels. (b) More specific to creativity, there is a presumption that literary works derive their vital qualities from the author's experience of life, rather than the reverse. That is, the traditional theory which is under discussion in this paper is in principle opposed to the assumptions favoring any formative effect. (c) When drafts, diaries, or discarded versions are available, one may be able to trace an author's intentions and their consequences. But Mann indulged his gift of ironic humor in pretending that he reported, rather than created, details of the Biblical legend. Thus, the role of the creative artist was itself artistically

mystified by him. Rather than granting us any view of the effect which the work might have had on him, he took care to
present himself as authoritative historian.

Other considerations favor the hypothesis of a formative effect: (a) For this work, Mann chose existing material, the well-
known Biblical tale with which every reader can be assumed to
have an acquaintance. Although he chose it freely, that is, in
consonance with his artistic and personal requirements, the
antecedence and objectivity of the material weaken the presumptions of a strict expression theory of creativity such as
underlies the traditional life-and-letters strategy, and allow for
the possibility that the material had the power to attract
Mann's artistic interest. (b) The *Joseph* material occupied the
author from about 1926 until 1943. Its beginnings lay in Munich and its completion in California. It deals artistically with
the struggle between loyalty and adaptation, and this struggle
was also the author's—from the time of his crisis in World
War I to the period when he wrote these novels and beyond
that time as well. It is therefore equally difficult to establish
that the works merely echoed life changes which had been independently wrought as it is to prove that their author drew
edification exclusively from them. The best assumption is
rather that the work accompanied the author during his tra-
vails as German artist and that they were the medium through
which he integrated the earlier contradictions. (Children's play
is commonly said to be the paradigm and matrix of artistic
creativity. If so, then the interplay between actor and medium,
which is recognized in the psychology of play, should be just
as seriously explored in the psychology of creativity.) (c)
Whether the artist *intends* his work to form him is not a critical
point. Mann did occasionally hint at parallels between Joseph's
times and the contemporary world situation, for instance,
when he likened Joseph's economic administration of Egypt to
Roosevelt's New Deal. A better test of the formative effect, but
one which cannot be undertaken in these pages, would be to
evaluate the differences between Mann's essayistic treatment
of the German artist prior to *Joseph* and his subsequent novelistic treatment of the artist in *Doktor Faustus* (1947). (d) Fi-

nally, Mann did want the *Joseph* novels to have an impact on the moral chaos of the times. They were received by the world as the last legacy of German culture (and denounced by the Nazis as decadent and traitorous). An extraordinary assumption of dispensation would be called for if the author himself were to be declared immune to the hortative and healing effect of his theme.[3]

FORMATIVE THEMES

A central symbol in the legend of *Joseph and His Brothers* is God's blessing of Abraham. But the major spring of action is the careless preservation of this blessing throughout the generations of patriarchs. After receiving the blessing from God, Abraham passed it on to Isaac, the son he was once ready to kill in sacrifice and who barely escaped his father's knife. Isaac, in turn, meant to bequeath it to Esau, whose merit was that he could prepare a spicy lamb stew. But a less prudent choice of heir is hard to imagine; Esau had once upon a time demonstrated his heedlessness in matters of heritage when he lightly bartered away his birthright. Only by a deception was Jacob able to wrest it from the intended heir. Jacob, in turn, was careless and self-indulgent in administering the blessing. Instead of passing it to the lawful heir, his eldest son, Reuben, he planned to shunt it to Joseph, the eleventh-born and favorite son. Jacob was crazily infatuated with Joseph because he resembled Rachel, the mother of Joseph and Benjamin and

3. Eissler (1968) has argued that Freud's early attempts to find psychological meaning in *Hamlet* were neither a polemic for the validity of the oedipus complex nor a useful contribution to literary criticism. Rather, they contributed to Freud's own initial formulation of the theory of infantile sexuality at the time when his seduction theory had collapsed. Freud's literary experience is said to have had a formative effect on his theoretical work (which, especially at that time, was most intimately interwoven with his "life"). That Freud did not write *Hamlet* and that Mann did not formulate a psychology of identity and exile does not significantly diminish the convergence of my argument with Eissler's. I postpone for later my discussion of the methodological questions raised by the traditional distinctions between author and reader and between work and life.

Jacob's favorite wife, who had recently died in childbirth. The coat of many colors which Jacob bestowed on Joseph was, in Mann's version, Rachel's retailored wedding gown. With this gift, a symbol of womanly vanity, Jacob, who once deceived and enraged his own brother over the stolen blessing, provoked his sons to murderous hatred of Joseph and initiated his expulsion to Egypt. "Inconsiderate love" is Mann's designation of this preferment.

Given the background of carelessness in the administration of the Hebrew blessing by the patriarchs, the novel narrates a reversal in the relations between generations. From a beginning in which Jacob, through inconsiderate paternal infatuation, instigates an adolescent crisis in his favorite son, we are gradually brought to an ending in which the adult son, in mature filial devotion, arranges the fulfillment of the father's most secret longings. This journey, as I shall try to show, is not only Joseph's; it is also his author's.

As the story unfolds, we meet Jacob, aged 67, under a moonlit sky in his Canaanite tent-city at the very moment when he apprehends the 17-year-old Joseph, nude to the waist and engrossed in a somewhat hysterical worship of the moon and stars, rolling his eyes back in his head and murmuring fervent incantations. Intensely and searchingly Jacob questions him, remonstrates with him about these pagan attitudes, warns him against idolatry and shamelessness before God, and extracts from him a promise of fidelity to the religion of the patriarchs. He warns him especially against the abominable morals of the Egyptian land to the south, where incest, necrophilia, and bestial customs rule. He does not know yet that this is the land in which Joseph will attain highest esteem through his service to mankind nor that Jacob himself will, at the end of the novel, follow him there with all his tribe and that he will die in that godforsaken land.

The remarkable personal transformation which Joseph underwent in his exile can be approached through an understanding of the dynamics of Jacob's conflict and their effect on the son's relationship to his father. Certain interpersonal patterns familiar from the study of pathological as well as normal development are helpful in this connection. Joseph cultivated a life that Jacob had declared abhorrent. He succeeded in a political career in the midst of a forbidden culture despite his father's remonstrations. The key to his success was his father's ambivalence. We have already seen how Jacob's ruinous love for Joseph represented a lapse from the pious wisdom and tact to which he admonished his people. The patriarchal blessing itself—a reification of the identificatory link between one generation and the next—was at risk in the contest between Jacob's piety and vanity. Mann relates Jacob's self-indulgence and stubbornness, his appetite for dynastic glory, his erotic excesses, his vindictiveness and pride, his hoodwinking of his father, brother, father-in-law, and his slyness even toward his grandsons. Not infrequently, vanity outweighed piety. Jacob appears to the reader as a man of great political ambition and possessing a keen eye for opportunity and advantage. To him the covenant with God was at least as much a warrant of Israel's future as a pledge of divine service.

Despite the execrable setting of his exile, Joseph excelled in the very virtues in which his father had shown himself lacking. Not "despite his exile"! Joseph's morality was *supported* by his exile. A high point in these 1,800 pages is the episode between Joseph and Potiphar's wife, the Egyptian temptress to whom Joseph almost succumbed, but whom he eventually resisted—not out of prudery, but out of deep loyalty to the fine Hebrew conception of the divine. Seven reasons are cited for his abstention, but the conclusive deterrent at the moment of highest temptation was the vision of Jacob's admonishing countenance appearing in Joseph's mind—the same Jacob who in his own erotic life knew no restraint and indulged the most comic and histrionic sensuousness.

The Egyptian exile proved salutary for Joseph because it removed him from the heat of Jacob's seductiveness which stimulated regression, promoted narcissistic aims and modes, and cast him into a feminized role. By dint of removal Joseph could preserve those moral features which his father meant to present as a model. So long as Joseph remained in Canaan, his father demanded total emulation of himself. This is a well-

known feature of parents whose own identification is tainted
with ambivalence and guilt. Only a guilty father needs to be
totally vindicated by his son. In the novel, and in the Bible,
Jacob's fastidiousness in bestowing the patriarchal blessing is
properly understood against the background of his own illicit
accession to it. But Joseph escapes this vicious cycle. Having
acquired the secular blessing of the Egyptians' love on his own
merit, he was free of Jacob's demands for vindication. He
could obtain moral guidance uncorrupted by the father's own
needs for absolution. Filial autonomy, as opposed to enforced
emulation, could only evolve in exile. Joseph's social talents,
which he had used to best his brothers as an adolescent, became object-directed in a different way in Egypt. His youthful
presumption that others loved him more than they loved
themselves, which had been utterly false in Canaan, became
eminently true in Egypt. This can be reckoned as a consequence of the emancipation of exile.

A second aspect integrated the experience of exile into the
larger allegiance to his background. Jacob's political ambitions
had won the upper hand over pious resignation when he
tricked Isaac and Esau out of the blessing. After that, guilt
stopped him from acknowledging his ambitions. He became
unctuous and severe in godly matters. But his son, sensing the
extent of the father's ambivalence and its suppressed components, could implement what the father could not. Removed
from his father's censorious sight, he could pursue a career
which he sensed his father yearned for himself behind his de-
nunciations. Even at the time when Joseph was sold by his
brothers to a caravan and laid eyes upon the land of Goshen,
that is, still under the unmitigated impression of his trouncing
and expulsion, he conceived the seemingly farfetched thought
that these would be fertile fields for his father's herds. He
forged his career in Egypt with an eye to Jacob under the
motto: Removal, Elevation, Drawing-After. It was the belief in
an ultimate reunion with Jacob *in Egypt* which supported Joseph's loyalty to the Hebrew heritage. It is this belief in reunion which transformed the outcast from a narcissist into a
circumspect leader. But the reverse seems also true: because

Joseph realized his father's forbidden dream, he could resist the temptations of the alien environment. In Jacob's view, Joseph's secular success was equivalent to the divine blessing. At the time of their reunion, Jacob withholds the blessing from Joseph because he now regards him as disqualified. Instead Jacob adopts Joseph's two sons, Ephraim and Manasse, once again giving unlawful preference to the younger.

A silent pact seems to have been observed by the two men. Joseph did for Jacob what Jacob could not, in good conscience, do for himself. Whereas the father made impressive displays of devoutness, with only occasional eruptions of a greedy appetite for worldly success, the son gave the deceptive appearance of suave, political elegance and opportunism while guiding his life in accordance with the highest self-discipline and culture. The exiled person is perhaps never a mere outcast, but the repository of truths which those who are left behind cannot afford to uphold.

What textual indication is there that these psychological developments healed not merely Joseph's crisis, transforming him from a gossip and egotist to a celebrated benefactor, but radiated beyond him, to the author as well? One recalls that Thomas Mann himself was once rebuked by his older brother on account of insufficient social feeling, of exploiting the mob's chauvinist passions, and of giving himself grand airs. If the hypothesis is correct that the *Joseph* novels mediated a personal and political transformation of the author, then one should look to the text itself for pertinent evidence and not mistake a merely possible connection for a plausible or probable one. To raise the question more explicitly, did Mann use the genre of the novel in such a way that it served not only as a *screen* for the projection of personal fantasies, but as a *source* of reflexive action on himself? The argument for the self-formative effect of literary creativity will be more cogent if, instead of maintaining that such effects are common to all writing, selected features of particular stories, plays, novels, and poems are shown to be consistent with such an effect.

Mann supplies us with a mythological psychology of his own, that is, with a "topographic" framework in which the

events of the story are experienced by the characters themselves. The categories—or types—of his psychology are the
ethics and aesthetics of men who model themselves after the
moon, in contrast with those who labor under the sun. The
heroes of this story are men of the moon in ancient struggle
with the followers of the sun. The moon is an identity symbol
for Jacob, even though he repudiates it as an object of religious veneration. The moon is transformed in unhurried
cycles but retains its original identity. It stands for patience
and for sameness in change. Abraham founded his allegiance
to a supreme Being when he left his father's heathen house
and began to wander with the moon. His adaptation to various
host lands did not impair his fidelity to the covenant. Abel,
Shem, Abraham, Isaac, and Jacob, men with the moon's cool
mildness, had wandered with their sheep, curious and hopeful, seeking greener pastures and more fruitful grounds for
their relationship to God. Their solar counterparts were Cain,
Ham, Ishmael, and Esau, their violent and faithless brothers.
Laban, too, Jacob's father-in-law, was one of these: working
the soil, himself red, rough, and furrowed like the sunburnt
clod of earth. No blessing was upon them; they were not free.
Their minds and bodies were heavy, crude, and fierce from
laboring and sweating behind the stolid oxen. They lacked the
grace and ironic adaptability of the moon-men. The Egyptians
to the south, it goes without saying, worshiped the sun.

The moon was also a filter for reality: history took on a
mythic iridescence in its beguiling light. The names of the patriarchs referred to shifting, timeless, idealized figures as well
as to the familiar, husky shapes of Joseph's kinsmen. Time
had a way of contracting, and circumstance melted away as
Isaac, Joseph's bodily grandfather, dreamily mistook himself
for that son long ago who was nearly sacrificed by his father.
The moon stripped reality of its divisive facts. Thomas Mann
once remarked on this point:

> I do not conceal from myself the difficulty of writing about
> people who do not precisely know who they are, that is, peo-
> ple whose self-awareness rests much less on a clear discern-
> ment of their point of existence between past and future than

on their identity with their mythic types. . . . With this acknowledgment I touch upon a psychological nerve of this entire extraordinary project, the source from which . . . emanates the greatest incentive to my artistic venturesomeness
. . . the ideas of recurrence, incarnation, and celebration, a
dreamy psychology of the ego which stands ajar as it were to
the rear [1928, p. 768f.].

We know that Mann is mocking us with the "difficulty" because these slightly moon-struck characters are his own canny
creation and because the mythic-atavistic form of discourse
had been his refuge even during his crisis, in the *Reflections,*
when the irony of fiction had slipped from his hand.

Another stylistic feature is in line with a formative effect.
Joseph, that is, Thomas Mann's Joseph, has the knack of
regarding himself with detachment. He treats the vicissitudes
of his life with ironic resignation because he knows himself to
be the well-known Biblical Joseph. Setbacks are tolerable for
him because he knows the outcome of his own story. He is
both inside his own story as a character and living out that story
in Mann's novel. Joseph's forbearance in defeat and injustice
was made easier for him by this device. Falsely accused of im-
proprieties toward Potiphar's wife, he spoke not a word in his
defense; willingly he went to jail, his "second pit," expecting to
be elevated to a higher position than ever. I note for later discussion that the novelist's mythic-ironic treatment of Joseph's
attitudes toward his expulsion, his temporary reverses, and his
elevations—that is, the novelistic treatment of Joseph's attitudes toward himself *as hero in a story*—requires a determinate
collaboration of the reader. What the reader knows before he
reads Mann's novel and what use Mann makes of this knowledge, presupposing and yet overlaying it, constitutes the novelist's subject matter and is indispensable to his craft.

Mann's toying with the consciousness of the hero as possibly
knowing his own story is a toying also with the role of the narrator in regard to the story:

The narrator . . . should be in the tale, one with it, and not
outside it, reckoning and calculating. But how is it with God,
whom Abram thought into being and recognized? He is in

the fire but He is not the fire. Thus He is at once in it and outside it. Indeed, it is one thing to be a thing, quite another to observe it. And yet there are planes and spheres where both happen at once: the narrator is in the story, yet is not the story; he is its scene but it is not his, since he is also outside it and by a turn of his nature puts himself in the position of dealing with it. I have never tried to produce the illusion that I am the source of the history of Joseph. Before it could be told, it happened, it sprang from the source from which all history springs, and tells itself as it goes. Since that time it exists in the world, everybody knows it or thinks he does—for often enough the knowledge is unreal, casual, or disjointed. . . . And now it is passing through another [medium], wherein as it were it becomes conscious of itself and re-members how things actually were with it in the long-ago, so that it now both pours forth and speaks of itself as it pours [1938, p. 180f.].

Subtly and ingeniously Mann confuses the reader as to the narrator's position with respect to the events and thereby, at one further remove, as to the relationship between author and audience. The narrator himself alternates between self-efface-ment before the grandeur of universal history and claims to historiographic omniscience. The ironic, playful use of a mythic self-consciousness is the literary device whereby the au-thor lulls not only the heroes of the story, but the audience and himself, into a moon-psychology, a susceptibility to imita-tion and substitution, borrowing of identities and reenact-ment.

In his earlier comment Mann declared that this "psychology ajar to the rear" or, as one might say, the opportunity to re-work old material in new versions, exerted the greatest incen-tive in this artistic enterprise. The abounding ambiguities of narration and the coy treatment of the novel's solemn themes suggest that the author was camouflaging private concerns of long standing with thematic material of utmost objectivity. Under cover of retelling an old story, he seems to have rein-terpreted his own life story as well. The dreamlike mentality of the lunar heroes in this story allows such reworkings. Of course, great self-conscious mastery is required to produce such an effect; the author is in no dream state as he composes the work. But we are entitled to suppose that he struggles with such states and with the possibilities they furnish for putting "ethics before aesthetics"!

The material so far presented suggests that the author's struggle to resolve the earlier political-fraternal crisis would have had to deal with the full meaning of that crisis, including the infantile sources and contributions. The adult author's shifting political and moral profession probably had its antecedents in the ambivalent bond to the mother's un-German artistic influence, and, as we shall see, in a conflict of wills and values with his father. Therefore, if we attribute a self-formative effect to Thomas Mann's writing of the *Joseph* novels, we should be alert to its possible connections with early dynamic conflicts.

Thomas Mann was conscious of writing about a "Jewish" theme at precisely the time when his godforsaken countrymen were exterminating this people. The four *Joseph* novels appeared as clarion calls of human protest against the gathering violence and inhumanity in the Third Reich. "It is essential that myth be taken away from intellectual fascism and transmuted for humane ends. I have for a long time done nothing else," he wrote to Karl Kerényi in a letter about *Joseph* (1975, p. 103). He was no longer concerned with the future of the German race, as in the *Reflections,* but with the human race. Thanks to his gift for irony, he wrote about the ancient Hebrews with affection and yet without mawkishness or glorification; they became flesh-and-blood and yet stood for transposable universal ideals of virtue and failure. These novels, too, were a contribution to the "order of the day."

I have suggested that Joseph, by his success, unmasked Jacob's saintly pretensions and brought out, indeed lived out, a truth which Jacob could not muster. The parallel between the truth around which Joseph's exile revolves and the contemporary truth for which Mann himself went into exile is deepened for us by a childhood memory he recounted in 1942, when addressing an audience in the Library of Congress at the age of 67. The fourth novel had not yet appeared. Speaking about the impetus behind the tetralogy, he began by reminding his listeners that Goethe, too, had been tempted by the same project in his youth. Mann then explained that he had reached a stage of life, when one feels attracted to perennial themes of humanity and therefore to myth. Third, he mentioned the dehumanized forces collecting in Germany in the 1920s which he meant to oppose, and then, rather abruptly, he offered, as though in confidence, an incident of his private life.

> The narrative enters into the highly developed and sophisticated cultural sphere of the Nile Empire, which through sympathy and reading had been familiar to me since the time of my boyhood, so that I knew more about it than even the teacher who during Religion Class had questioned us twelve-year-old boys as to the name of the holy steer of the ancient Egyptians. I showed that I was eager to answer, and was called upon. "Chapi," I said. That was wrong in the opinion of the teacher. He reproached me for having raised my hand when I knew only nonsense. "Apis" was the right name, he corrected me angrily. But "Apis" is only the Latinization or Hellenization of the authentic Egyptian name which I had given. The people of Keme said "Chapi." I knew better than the good man, but discipline did not allow me to enlighten him about it. I kept silent—and all my life I have not forgiven myself for this silence before false authority. An American boy would certainly have spoken up.
>
> Occasionally I thought of this early incident while I was writing *Joseph in Egypt*. A work must have long roots in my life, secret connections must lead from it to earliest childhood dreams, if I am to consider myself entitled to it, if I am to believe in the legitimacy of what I am doing. The arbitrary reaching for a subject to which one does not have traditional claims of sympathy and knowledge seems senseless and amateurish [1943, p. 95].

Within two sentences, Mann affirms the link between exile and the defense of truth: false authority can only be opposed in the shoes of the alien. This is what he has been thinking, as he writes about Joseph, in America. One readily suspects that the incident involving the religion teacher at the age of 12 would have left a less enduring impression on Mann, had he not already been sensitized to misapprehensions by "false authority" and mortified by his own acquiescence. The "secret connections" to "earliest childhood dreams" are a matter for speculation. Yearnings, identifications, and conflicts in his earliest years are the likely "deep roots" to which he alluded. Mann, more than most writers, tapped his childhood experience with little disguise and elaborated it in his fiction.

In his own autobiographical statements he displayed a two-fold and ambivalent connection between his early love of make-believe and the divergent attitudes of his parents toward art. There is, on the one hand, a romantic, oceanic self-surrender to the epic element, its flowing rhythm, its fascinating monotony, the perennial narrative. "Making music and telling stories, marvellously united in the mother, were deeply and essentially related to each other and remained one and the same thing for him" (Mendelssohn, 1975, p. 81). Mann had his first impressive encounters with the art of storytelling when his mother reminisced about her Brazilian childhood or told fairy tales to him and her other children. She was also an accomplished pianist and had a "lovely voice." He listened to her devoutly by the hour, and as an adult still felt indebted to her for the most precious musical experience of his life. During his adolescence they played duets together.

On the other hand, Mann cultivated a roguish and playful vein which was encouraged and applauded by his father. In his childhood he indulged a gift for mocking impersonation, taking teachers, relatives, townspeople, and schoolmates as involuntary targets. In adulthood this penchant reappears as the merciless precision with which he described figures in his novels and stories—figures frequently copied from life. He made numerous enemies of people who were startled to find themselves caricatured in his books. Occasionally, Mann donned the thin mantle of the trickster or confidence man whose success depends on the disdainful imitation of righteousness.

One may assume that Senator Mann treated his wife's artistic leanings with tolerance if not slight irony. His eldest son's literary ambitions he opposed with blunt uncompromising hostility: Heinrich read too much and wrote too much instead of concerning himself with business and civic matters!

Although the brothers did not always get along in their adolescence, they were united in their dislike of school. Heinrich dropped out just before the final exams; Thomas had to repeat several grades and never finished school either. When Heinrich started school and Thomas was still a toddler, the Senator decided that Heinrich was to study law and eventually become a senator and mayor of Lübeck, and Tommy was to become a merchant and succeed the father in the business. Neither son showed the slightest willingness to follow the career which his father had planned for him. The Senator regarded Heinrich's artistic career plans as dishonorable. Only on his deathbed, he astonished him by offering to help him become a writer. Thomas, 4 years younger, did not experience such an overt confrontation with his father; the Senator died when Thomas was 15. And yet, Thomas Mann felt that he was a disappointment to his father: "I may say that his image has always stood in the background of everything I have done, and I have always regretted that I gave him so little hope during his lifetime of ever making something respectable out of myself in this world. . . . I was a frivolous boy when I lost my father, and though I was impressionable I could not experience death spiritually. I do not know what it is like to be separated in one's maturity from a father-friend whom one is used to having beside or rather behind oneself in the shaded background of life" (quoted in Mendelssohn, 1975, p. 134). Judging by the senator's attitudes toward Heinrich's development, which was similar to Thomas's in the relevant respects, he might have become a friend in later years, once the brothers made something respectable of themselves, but he surely cannot have been experienced as a young artist's friend at the time he died.

The choice between two attitudes toward art, the indulgent and the arch, is rooted in the establishment of parental identifications. "I sat in a corner contemplating my father and mother as though I were choosing between them and considering whether life was better spent in dreamy meditation or in deeds and power" (quoted from a story by Mendelssohn, 1975, p. 77). Problems of character development and identity formation are aggravated if the opposing attitudes compete for dominance in one parent instead of being neatly distributed between both. Joseph, we have seen, was victimized in his youth by Jacob's contradictory values and motives. The intolerance with which the senator treated Heinrich only to make a turnabout in the end suggests that this father also struggled against forbidden exotic yearnings, of which his wife was the most visible symbol and exponent in the house.

It is sometimes said that the "Thomas Mann problem" resulted from the clash between his father's urbane, mercantile practicality and his mother's aesthetic, romantic temperament. This formulation is not precise, however, and does not explain Mann's preference for exile as a way of life and as an artistic theme. Rather, the conflict appears to occur between a father who was infected with languor and introspectiveness, but masked these yearnings behind sobriety and elegance, and a mother who was frankly artistic and exotic. She personified one side of the father's own conflict.

Perhaps the most direct evidence pertaining to the father's conflict comes from his last will and testament, written during his final illness.

> God has always been merciful toward me, and I have prayed to Him. A joyous faith has been a heritage in our family. God will also know how to lead my survivors to Himself—I hope not through much suffering!
>
> I pledge my children's guardians to effect their *practical* education. As far as possible, they shall oppose my eldest son's [Heinrich] inclinations toward a so-called literary occupation. In my opinion, he lacks the qualifications for well-grounded, successful activity in this direction, namely, sufficient study and comprehensive knowledge. The basis of his inclinations is a dreamy letting-himself-go and inconsiderateness toward others—perhaps from a lack of *thought*. My second son

[Thomas] is susceptible to calm deliberations; he is good-
natured and will find his way to a practical occupation. I feel I
can expect him to be a support to his mother.

Julia, my eldest daughter, will have to be observed more
closely. Her vivacious temperament must be kept under control.

Carla is not problematic, in my opinion. Together with
Thomas, she will represent an element of calm. Our little
Vicco—may God protect him. Late-born children often develop especially well intellectually. The child has such tender
eyes.

Would that my wife prove herself to be firm with all the
children; all are to be kept steadily in a state of dependency.
If she ever becomes unsure, may she read King Lear
[Mendelssohn, 1975, p. 132].

These evaluations of his children were as false as those of
Lear himself. The "unproblematic" daughter Carla committed
suicide at age 29, and Julia took her life as well. Victor became
a bank official. The senator was a man of contrasts: he had a
sense of irony, even prankishness, and perhaps a yearning for
the exotic. In his official self-presentation, however, he was
the decorous, even self-conscious patrician, down to the clichés in his will. He qualifies as false authority especially in eyes
as observant as his second son's. His blindness to his children's
qualities cannot have been the result of social and moral prejudice only; it reflects a more generalized ambivalence and
curtailment of human interest. Although nothing is recorded
about altercations between Thomas and his father, we can
guess that the son felt misjudged, but declined to protest. His
aggression took more indirect forms such as school failure and
the secret cultivation of a disapproved identity. (When the
preadolescent Hanno Buddenbrook observed how his father
pressed his tired, slack face into the mask of resilient sociabi-
lity a moment before making a business call, he closed his eyes
in pain; he could not contemplate such a life for himself. This
frankly autobiographical portrait is a guide to Mann's exile
identity.) He turned to aloofness and ambiguity because the
parental figures seemed mutually as well as—in the father's

case—internally contradictory. Clear-cut loyalties were hard for him to build and sustain. The pattern and solution are well known.

In magnificent style Mann proved the early authorities wrong. He became himself an authoritative Egyptologist, acquiring greater mastery than one would expect even from the American schoolboy. Indeed, he took authoritativeness so far that it became a new mockery of the reader whom he confronted as the omniscient, and not merely authoritative, storyteller from whom no fact is hidden. That the senator would have been astonished to read his son's life needs no further documentation.

THEORETICAL IMPLICATIONS

ART AS ADAPTATION AND COMMUNICATION

Viewed objectively as the production of novel, self-expressive, and aesthetically satisfying artifacts, creativity is perhaps the most clear-cut example of what Hartmann (1939), following Freud, called alloplastic adaptation. The person molds or remolds a part of the external world in accordance with his needs. The resulting artifact is considered artistically successful if its subsequent reception fulfills the needs of the audience as well. In the early years of psychoanalysis, the universal matrix of libidinal desires and of their elaboration into daydreams served as the link in this transaction. Artist and audience were thought to be in analogous and complementary relationships to the art work (production, consumption). Their relationship to each other was of secondary importance. Each effected an independent adaptation by means of the text. This monadic conception, which treats writer and reader as separate and analogous, generates and maintains what I earlier designated the life-and-letters strategy: "The literary work is taken as an embodiment of the creative mind . . . [research] aims at the reconstruction . . . of the author" (Eissler, 1968, p. 142). A second consequence of this conception is that, having settled on character as the major source of art's contents, scientific interest shifted to the question of process. Most psychoanalytic writing on creativity deals with it in terms which are formal with respect to the thematic material and treat artistry as a series of transformations, worked on whatever subject matter and guided by motives which are common to all artists (Freud, 1908; Greenacre, 1957; Kris, 1952; Kubie, 1958; Levy, 1940; Lee, 1947; Rank, 1932). The difficulties which such investigations encounter, as a matter of definition and scientific logic, are recounted by Rothenberg and Hausman (1974). What I am concerned about here is that they limit our appreciation of the meaning which the work has for author and reader.

Viewed as a species of interaction between artist and audience, as I propose to view it, creativity is neither allo- nor autoplastic; it is most nearly adaptiogenic (Hartmann, 1939). Therein lies the parallel to the psychology of exile. Parr (1926), from whom Hartmann borrowed the term, cited as an example of "adaptiogenic adaptation" the case of a primitive horse which migrated from a region with sandy soil to a firmer tundra where it obtained better support for its hooves, making neither an auto- nor an alloplastic change. The exile, too, migrates to a social-psychological region where he obtains better support for his ontogenetically rooted needs—but with the difference that the migration may be symbolic, rather than physical, and that he may therefore preserve a symbolic, and more than symbolic, relationship to his region of origin. This is a phenomenon familiar to the clinical observer under the rubrics of struggle against identification and negative identity; indeed it is a central assumption which permits us to account for the persistence of infantile influences in later life. Artistic creativity is adaptiogenic, too: the creative artist molds himself as he molds the world. To put it negatively, neither artist nor art world remains unchanged at the expense of the other. The entire field in which artistic creation takes place, including the audience, constitutes the creative act.

I have tried to show that "social relations" did not enter Mann's crisis and epicrisis secondarily, but were integral to them. The psychology of exile and the psychology of creativity do not coincide accidentally in this case. Exile, objectively a severance, appears to the psychological observer as the disguised affirmation and preservation of a bond; creativity, so long as it is viewed superficially, is utterance and externalization, but turns out on closer inspection to be a step in the formation of self. Two cycles of interaction, which are often neglected, are emphasized in this view and require discussion—the interaction of author and work and that of author and audience. Together, these cycles may help to determine how Mann's art functioned to transform one kind of exile into another.

During the "heroic" age of psychoanalysis, it was valuable to vindicate theoretical propositions about psychosexual development by demonstrating the coded presence of libidinally relevant themes in literary texts (Kris, 1952, p. 17). With the rise of ego psychology the emphasis of psychoanalytic literary criticism shifted from wish fulfillment and catharsis to the restoration of ego controls and the pleasure of cathectic displacements themselves. But throughout, the formulations revolved around the psychology of expression, namely, how the artist transforms a highly personal, largely unacceptable fantasy into an acceptable object the expression of which is accompanied by a pleasurable saving of energy for all concerned—to begin with, for the artist himself, then for the audience. Although Kris conceived of art as a communication or "message" (p. 39), this was difficult to reconcile with the fundamental concepts of an expression theory. On the one hand, art was "an invitation to common experience in the mind" (p. 39) and "whenever the unconscious aspect of artistic creation is studied, a public of some kind emerges" (p. 60). On the other hand, that public was not considered to be integral to the creation itself. Author and reader were regarded as distinct authorities dealing with the art work by turns. A psychological process, akin to that of the writer, would unfold in the reader—only in reverse order, from the conscious perception of the art work to the id. In this way, the audience came to share the author's experience and, if the work was successful, to respond with approval which in turn "encourages [the artist's] self-approval" (p. 38). Although

Kris disclaimed two consecutive phases in creation, he described two distinct types of psychological activity: "While the
artist creates, in the state of inspiration, he and his work are
one; when he looks upon the product of his creative urge, he
sees it from the outside, and as his own first audience he par-
ticipates in 'what the voice has done.' Art, we said, always, consciously or unconsciously, serves the purpose of communication. We now distinguish two stages: one in which the
artist's id communicates to the ego, and one in which the same
intrapsychic processes are submitted to others" (p. 61). The
raw artistic conception was thus considered to be presocial,
and the audience entered as corrective or respondent. The
readers compensated the author for the narcissistic losses he
sustained in moving from daydream to fiction; they blocked
his retreat into an egocentric, regressive inner world; they relieved his guilt in sharing the experience he bestowed on
them; they imposed demands for intelligibility and norma-
tivity of form. But they did not figure as primary in the act of
creation itself. By recounting the various interdependencies of
author and reader, they were fixed in their separateness.

CREATIVITY WITHIN INTERACTION

The study of Thomas Mann and the *Joseph* novels provides us
with new hypotheses. Because these novels retell an old story,
the purely expressive aspect of their theme recedes in importance, and attention is drawn to the psychological force of features which are otherwise overlooked. As Kris pointed out, the
historical development and problems of an artistic medium as
well as the social forces impinging on the creation determine
"the frame of reference in which creation is enacted" (p. 21).
In the case of these novels, however, and even more explicitly
in *Doktor Faustus,* the medium and the times are themselves an
integral part of the message. One might say that the personal
position of Thomas Mann—the formerly apolitical Mann—
and the historical setting in which he wrote (and was read)
served to italicize the entire text of the tetralogy and to emphasize the difference between the ancient legend and the

pointed modern retelling. With his charming irony and with his ambiguous narrative attitude, Mann let the revered Biblical figures appear to us alternately as flesh-and-blood, larger than life, and again as ciphers in an allegory. This device not only is pleasurable, but has the effect of recasting the fundamental stock of our cultural ideas in a new form and of changing our outlook on ourselves and each other in the midst of our historical world. With these books Mann clarified the order of the day, adjured against resignation in the face of evil, and appealed to the infinite ethical resources of human culture. That the stories were a retelling did not weaken this effect, but strengthened it. How central irony is to the aesthetic effect is shown by the grim officious rebukes of irreverence with which book reviewers chastised Mann in the Nazi-dominated newspapers of the 1930s. They sensed that the "how" of the retelling was a cunning, an inspired blow against them. What Foucault (1972) said about variants and commentaries applies: "The novelty lies no longer in what is said, but in its reappearance" (p. 221).

The creative work is a general-cultural object and has psychological value beyond the expressive function it serves for author and reader. This psychological value arises from the fact that the work transforms the culture and us who are grounded in it, as we are grounded in our nature. I am not arguing for an opposition between aesthetic pleasure and other aesthetic effects; they can occur in various combinations. But it is important not to restrict psychological analysis of art to those effects which can be accounted for by an expression theory. We have seen that an expression theory, whether of the id- or ego-psychological orientation, is consonant with an adaptational viewpoint. Yet, to the extent that psychoanalysis deals with the process of correcting the (pathological and pathogenic) interpretation of experience and communication, an extended theory of art may be more in line with our heuristic interests. I shall return shortly to the concept of adaptation.

I have earlier shown that Mann aims his irony at the reader's recollection of the Biblical legend. He depends on our naïveté and piety and then challenges them. Thus, the relationships of author and reader to content are unequal. Irony is one term we apply to such inequalities. It not a feature which is added to the "basic" story; the *Joseph* novels are unthinkable without it. Their aesthetic effect depends on it. There is no inspired material which is *then* "submitted to others." The others are part of the irony which is part of the inspiration. To put it differently, it is misleading to think of novels as being written and then distributed to the reading public. Only outwardly is this true; psychologically speaking, there are no stages and no types of activity; the novel is written and read at once.

As long as we think of authors drawing on their inspiration during a first stage, the emphasis remains psychic-structural. The element of risk in innovation is conceptualized as the product of regression in the service of the ego. But when the audience is acknowledged as psychologically integral and indispensable to inspiration, then the element of risk is also an interactive one. Irony is only one instance of a general relation of inequality or asymmetry between authors' and audiences' relationships to the form and content of art works. To the temporary alteration of psychic-structural relations, there corresponds a temporary alteration of social-experiential relations.[4] By and large, it seems true that the artist is more candid about his experience than are the members of the audience. The risklessness in which they benefit from his work aggravates his risk.

Every author, every artist adheres to traditional norms and beliefs and yet surmounts them. Conservative and progressive tendencies constitute the authorial attitude, but that attitude is inconceivable outside a readership. It will not do to allocate

4. An analogy occurs when a joke is told. The discrepancy between the teller's and the listener's relationships to the joke material does not merely add to the enjoyment of the material, but makes the joke possible to begin with and often is essential to its success; we call it delivery. Whether the humor of the joke survives the first telling, which terminates the asymmetry, often depends on whether the listener manages to "surprise himself" with the punch line he already knows!

the innovative inspiration to the author and the normative restraint to the (internalized) audience. It is equally true that the artist innovates on behalf of the audience ("truths it cannot afford") and restrains himself for his own sake. Insofar as the author enables the audience to share in his experience, he is like them. But when we stress that he *invites* them to share it, then we recognize that he is in a more exposed, in a different position, perhaps like a host sharing a meal with his guests. The artist's sense of his own exposure is probably universal (Sachs, 1929). If only in the limited sense that authors have a headstart before their readers and invite them to share an experience, their situation resembles that of the analyst. Despite serious differences, which need not be discussed here, the analytic dialogue may serve as a better model for a psychology of literature than dreams, play, or daydreams. In these latter models the complicity of the audience is not systematically recognized. Of course, both sets of models are compatible since dreams and fantasies are also frequently constituted in a context of potential dialogue. Just as metapsychological concepts become enriched by interactional analyses, the psychoanalytic study of creativity may begin to emphasize the social-interactive and historical aspects of artistry in addition to the traditional preoccupation with the endowment and development of genius. Loewald (1975) has discussed the connections between art and psychoanalysis in a way which is highly compatible with the present discussion.

It may be objected that only in unusual cases, perhaps when authors suffer dramatic disturbances of creativity itself, as was true of Mann at one time, will such complexities of interaction appear, and that the formative effect of art is a rare phenomenon. This is indeed possible; in the case of many artists, the work is not only a less onerous activity, but it may also touch less deeply on their lives. By the same token, these artists will perhaps also express the regnant themes of their lives less clearly in their works! That is, the life-and-letters strategy sometimes also yields meager results. A transparent instance, like that of Mann, is needed to demonstrate the methodological constraints which the life-and-letters approach has been placing on our investigations. Traditional psychoanalytic studies of artistic creativity and its products can be supplemented by further studies which evaluate the art work as a force in the artist's life. Wherever the influence of life history has been illuminated in the work, the circle may be closed by studying the creation as itself a life-historical event. The closing of this circle is characteristically psychoanalytic in that interpretation moves at times from the past to the present and at other times in the reverse direction—in alternating steps (Schafer, 1978). Similarly, biography, which has always been invoked as the explanation of the creative work, is itself more thoroughly understood by reference to the later creation.

TEXT AND CONTEXT

To say that novels are written to be read, or, more precisely, are written and read at once is to say that the author derives benefits which depend on the benefits he brings to the audience. It serves to emphasize that the art work is more than a product, that it continues to influence the author as a value after—and because—it has achieved public status independent of his artistry. The *Joseph* novels represented a high value at the nadir of German culture. The racist mythology of the Nazis was unmasked and ridiculed. If one considers Mann's own political history, the novels also represented a conversion or rectification. The motif of unmasking and rectification occurs on three levels: (1) The work unmasked the fascist corruption of the author's and the readers' shared cultural tradition and reflexively rectified Mann's own earlier political aberration. (2) Within its text, it unmasked the pieties of Jacob and the patriarchs and rectified Joseph's youthful narcissistic excesses. (3) Within the realm of Mann's own recollection, it proved the "false authorities" false and it rectified Mann's old acquiescence in the face of misapprehensions which he had "never forgiven himself." The integrity of the art work—personally expressive and culturally objective at the same time—requires that we consider these three levels of analysis together. The discovery of formative effects would seem to rest on this methodological guideline.

If the task were to outline a general theory of the formative effect of literary works on authors (and on readers), account would have to be taken of the fact that the third-mentioned thematization of the motif was private, that is, tied to Mann's particular life history and that the first thematization was historically specific to readers who became acquainted with the novels when they were published, rather than 30 years later, and who had one kind of relationship to the historical personage of the author rather than another. But the task is not a comprehensive theory; it is to sketch and support an example that extends existing theory further. Only a brief discussion of the work's effect on the author is therefore offered.

It would be absurd to imply that Mann had committed himself to a tetralogy of 1,800 pages so as to prove his father wrong or to rehabilitate himself as a humanist before a partially skeptical readership. It seems reasonable, however, that the creation of these novels was psychologically sustained by their role in reinterpreting, for Mann himself, the meaning and relevance which his childhood experience had for his current engagements in the object world. The novels could help in this reinterpretation because they were anchored in material which is antecedent and independent of the author; they had, as I have tried to show, an innovative, formative effect on the author to the extent that they were more than self-expressive. Mann was attracted to myths not only because they are perennial, we may suppose, but because writing about them meant to invoke them and to be developed by them as though celebrating a ritual.

When self-expression is taken to be the chief operative factor in artistic-creative efforts, we usually think of the discharge or masking of tension. By contrast, the experiential transformation of the object world on which the present analysis focuses concerns the categories of meaning. The transformation, in Mann's case, can be traced in his biography. The *Reflections* of 1918 had been an earlier, but unsuccessful attempt at resolving the conflict with false authority. The difference between the two attempts is that the later solution freed Mann for communication and action in the contemporary world, whereas the former had paralyzed and disqualified him. The writing of these novels, I suggest, was helpful to him in converting the exile identity from the political expropriation of his midlife into the moral arrival of his later years.

It would be an error to suppose that he overcame an infantile rebelliousness against false authority. Rather, he intensified his protests against a new and timely target. The threefold vindication of the exile identity by unmasking-and-rectification—in the literary text, in private recollection, and in social relations—probably strengthened Mann's sense of fraternal loyalty, freed him from conflicts about his own creative talents, and energized him for the struggle against tyranny. The former grumbler was installed as herald in all three domains. The severe antinomies of the *Reflections* were abandoned, supplanted by the gentle dreamy mythopsychology of the ancients. The hero was no longer menaced by the encircling enemy. Rather, he sheltered himself in the midst of distractions, safe from a greater distant threat. The shift which occurred in Mann's own ethics can also be interpreted as a displacement of emphasis in identifications. From the exclusionary and inflexible values of his father, he turned to the comprehensive, tolerant authority of his mother. Paradoxically, he preserved himself as symbol and exponent of German culture by integrating his exotic and indulgent vein.

HISTORY AND ADAPTATION

Was he now better adapted? I have dwelt on the exile identity and its transformation by art to show how little is signified by speaking of artistry as adaptive. Mann's art sustained his symbolic relocation in his world. This relocation was nothing so gross or simple as a reconciliation after an altercation, the development of a skill or relationship, the muting of a style, or a "getting along." He was still an exile, still unhappy, still aloof. Exile, the protection of the self as a carrier of culture and humanity, does not correspond to adaptation in the usual sense and may even be opposed to it. By achieving a transformation of his self, Mann made history—both for himself and for us all. He arose as a moral challenge and offered moral solace. Art formed him to become what we needed, but it formed him through us. Just as exile was not an adaptation, so artistry was not adaptive. If we wish to speak of the benefits provided by the art work, we must analyze it through life history, which lies within general history. Only if artistry, talent, or genius are treated as merely processual terms or formal types, may one say that they are potentially adaptation-producing per se. But this will tell us little about the place and meaning—the benefit—of particular works. The significance of an adaptation concept within psychoanalytic hermeneutics requires a separate investigation.

BIBLIOGRAPHY

BERES, D. (1959), The Contribution of Psycho-Analysis to the Biography of the Artist. *Int. J. Psycho-Anal.,* 40 : 26–37.

DEUTSCH, F. (1959), Creative Passion of the Artist and Its Synesthetic Aspects. *Int. J. Psycho-Anal.,* 40 : 38–51.

EISSLER, K. R. (1968), The Relation of Explaining and Understanding in Psychoanalysis. *This Annual,* 23 : 141–177.

FLANNER, J. (1941), Goethe in Hollywood. *New Yorker,* 17 : 31–42 (December 20).

FLINKER, M. (1959), *Thomas Manns politische Betrachtungen im Lichte der heutigen Zeit.* s'Gravenhage: Mouton.

FOUCAULT, M. (1972), A Discourse on Language. In: *The Archaeology of Knowledge.* New York: Harper & Row, 1972, pp. 215–237.

FREUD, S. (1908), Creative Writers and Day-Dreaming. *S.E.,* 9 : 141–153.

———— (1939), Moses and Monotheism. *S.E.,* 23 : 1–137.

GREENACRE, P. (1957), The Childhood of the Artist. *This Annual,* 12 : 47–72.

HARTMANN, H. (1939), *Ego Psychology and the Problem of Adaptation.* New York: Int. Univ. Press, 1958.

HATFIELD, H. (1956), The Achievement of Thomas Mann. *Germanic Rev.,* 31 : 206–214.

HELLER, E. (1955), Thomas Mann's Place in German Literature. *The Listener,* 53 : 1014–1016.

KANZER, M. (1959), Autobiographical Aspects of the Writer's Imagery. *Int. J. Psycho-Anal.,* 40 : 52–58.

KRIS, E. (1952), *Psychoanalytic Explorations in Art.* New York: Int. Univ. Press.

KUBIE, L. S. (1958), *Neurotic Distortion of the Creative Process.* Lawrence, Kansas: Univ. Kansas Press.

LEE, H. B. (1947), On the Esthetic States of the Mind. *Psychiatry,* 10 : 281–306.

LEVEY [LEE], H. B. (1940), A Theory Concerning Free Creation in the Inventive Arts. *Psychiatry,* 3 : 229–293.

LOEWALD, H. W. (1975), Psychoanalysis as an Art and the Fantasy Character of the Psychoanalytic Situation. *J. Amer. Psychoanal. Assn.,* 23 : 272–299.

MANN, H. (1915), Zola. In: *Die weissen Blätter,* 2 : 1312–1382. Leipzig: Verlag der weissen Bücher.

MANN, T. (1915), Friedrich und die grosse Koalition. In: *Das essayistische Werk: Politische Schriften und Reden,* 2 : 20–65. Frankfurt a.M.: Fischer, 1968.

——— (1918), *Betrachtungen eines Unpolitischen [Reflections of an Apolitical Man].* Frankfurt a.M.: Fischer, 1956.

——— (1928), Ein Wort zuvor: Mein *Joseph und seine Brüder. Stockholmer Gesamtausgabe der Werke von Thomas Mann: Reden und Aufsätze,* 1 : 767–770. Frankfurt a.M.: Fischer, 1965.

——— (1938), *Joseph in Egypt,* Vol. 1. New York: Knopf.

——— (1943), The Joseph Novels. *Atlantic Monthly,* 171 : 92–100.

——— (1956), Letter to Heinrich Mann of January 3, 1918. In: *Heinrich und Thomas Mann,* ed. A. Kantorowicz. Berlin: Aufbau Verlag, pp. 110–114.

——— (1963), *Briefe 1937–1947,* ed. E. Mann. Frankfurt a.M.: Fischer Verlag.

——— (1975), *Mythology and Humanism: The Correspondence between Thomas Mann and Karl Kerényi.* Ithaca, N.Y.: Cornell Univ. Press.

MAURIAC, F. (1955), Letter reprinted in: *Hommage de la France à Thomas Mann.* Paris: Editions Flinker, p. 21.

MENDELSSOHN, P. DE (1975), *Der Zauberer: Das Leben des deutschen Schriftstellers Thomas Mann.* Frankfurt a.M.: Fischer Verlag.

PARR, A. E. (1926), Adaptiogenese und Phylogenese. In: *Abhandlungen zur Theorie der organischen Entwicklung.* Berlin: Springer, pp. 1–60.

RANK, O. (1932), *Art and Artist.* New York: Agathon, 1968.

ROTHENBERG, A. & HAUSMAN, C. R. (1974), Creativity. In: *Psychoanalysis and Contemporary Science,* ed. L. Goldberger & V. H. Rosen. New York: Int. Univ. Press, 3 : 70–97.

SACHS, H. (1929), Kunst und Persönlichkeit. *Imago,* 15 : 1–14.

SCHAFER, R. (1978), *Language and Insight.* New Haven: Yale Univ. Press.

Michelangelo's *Pietàs*

JEROME D. OREMLAND, M.D.

> Two hearts led by one spirit
>   and one wish,
> And if two bodies have one soul,
>   grown deathless,
> That with like wings, lifts both
>   of them to Heaven.
>   MICHELANGELO (1532)

AMONG THE WIDE VARIETIES OF APPLICATIONS OF PSYCHOANAL-
ysis, one of the most fruitful, interesting, and yet controversial
has been the study of talented and creative people. In his classical study of Leonardo da Vinci, Freud (1910) took the autobiographical account of a childhood fantasy and developed it
into a theme unifying a number of apparently diverse qualities
of Leonardo's life, and suggested a possible relationship between the fantasy and the compelling, enigmatic smile in his
painting of the *Mona Lisa del Gioconda,* of St. Anne and the
Virgin Mary in the so-called *St. Anne with Two Others* in the
Louvre, and of Saint John. In a somewhat different vein,
Freud (1914) attempted to reconstruct Michelangelo's artistic
intention by meticulously studying a number of apparent inconsistencies in the postural attitudes of Michelangelo's *Moses*

Chief of Psychiatry, San Francisco Children's Hospital and Adult Medical
Center; Faculty, San Francisco Psychoanalytic Institute; Director of Continu-
ing Education, Department of Psychiatry, University of California, San
Francisco.

I wish to express my appreciation to Professor Erik H. Erikson for helpful
suggestions and much-needed encouragement.

statue. He formulated that the power of and the unwaning interest in the *Moses* stemmed from its capacity to generate within the viewer the experience of rage inhibited in order to preserve ideals.

In general, psychoanalytic investigations of creativity have been modeled after the Leonardo monograph, resulting in a large body of work on talented and creative people, particularly writers, and their products. These studies usually involve finding recurrent themes in a masterpiece or in a number of works by a creative person and relating them to known biographical data about the artist from as large a variety of sources as possible. Less frequently, as in the *Moses* paper, the masterpiece itself is studied not primarily in reference to knowledge about the artist or his situation but in its own right. The psychoanalytic understanding of the work itself helps to reveal its relationship to universal themes as a partial explanation of its enduring appeal.

Such studies, either following the model of the Leonardo monograph or the *Moses* paper, are of course fraught with difficulties because they rest ultimately on interpretation of data, usually far removed from direct inquiry or psychoanalytic verification (Eissler, 1961; Schapiro, 1956). The allegation of lack of validity is greater when the psychological interpretation is of a painting or a sculpture than of literature, for in literature themes develop and characters speak and interact over a period of time. In a sense, hypotheses can be verified within the context of the work. However, painting and sculpture generally represent a moment that induces a feeling, and the psychological inferences are almost entirely subjective and individual. Freud skillfully obviated this pitfall in the *Moses* paper by methodically presenting several scholars' interpretations of Michelangelo's artistic intentions, comparing them, and eventually evolving a new one which most economically interrelated and explained what previously were felt to be the artistic inconsistencies in the statue.

My study, somewhat closer to the *Moses* paper than the Leonardo monograph, offers a psychoanalytic exploration of a peculiarity readily observed, and, in fact, criticized at the time of the original presentation of Michelangelo's first *Pietà,* the *Pietà* in St. Peter's, in which the Holy Mother is of the same age as the young dead Son. I suggest that in this statue and the subsequent *Pietàs,* Michelangelo portrayed a continuing evolution of the themes *return to, reunion,* and *union* with the mother of infancy. Although the primary emphasis is on interpreting the artistic portrayal, it is pivotal to my discussion that Michelangelo had two mothers, an ill mother from whom he was separated shortly after his birth and who died during his childhood, and a nursing mother who cared for him in his infancy.

CREATIVITY AND EARLY DEVELOPMENTAL PHASES

Originally, the psychoanalytic understanding of talent and creativity closely paralleled the understanding of symptoms and pathological character traits. With more biographical and direct clinical study, there has been a trend toward understanding exceptional abilities as having origins separate from, though at times inextricably involved with, pathological structures. Kris (1952) led the way by emphasizing the relationship between exceptional ability and flexibility rather than pathology in psychic organization. Erikson (1954, 1972), Greenacre (1957, 1958), Jacobson (1964), and Weissman (1971), each from different perspectives, cautioned against emphasizing the narcissistic aspects of creativity and indicated the greater varieties and manifestations of creative people's object relationships.

Greenacre (1957), in her remarkable speculations about the childhood of the artist, stresses the importance of innate sensorimotor, conceptual endowment with its potential toward development of a different order of object relatedness, the "collective alternates." As she points out in a subsequent discussion (1962), "the reality of the artist is different from that of the less gifted person . . . in the markedly creative person experiences are multi-dimensional, with a resonance of imagery . . . personal relationships are also invested with interest in many alternative figures and forms" (p. 131).

Many psychoanalytic investigators have discussed the importance of topographical regression in the creative process, emphasizing access to the unconscious as a source of ideas and
experiences and forms of expression (Freud, 1900, 1908; Kris,
1952). Others, using a different emphasis, stressed the closely
related role of structural regression and the capacity for dedifferentiation of self and object, which many believe to be
derived from early developmental phases and to be akin to inspiration and to mystical experiences (Freud, 1930; Horton,
1974; Kris, 1952; Lubin, 1976).

The role of self-object dedifferentiation in creative moments is also related to Winnicott's (1953, 1967) conceptualization of a metaphoric space in the mind, "the transitional
space," an heir to the transitional object, as the psychic "location" of cultural and artistic creative experiences. These investigations provide a strong direct link between creativity and
exploration and utilization of aspects and parts of the mother
as they differentiate from aspects and parts of the self. Hamilton (1974), McDonald (1970), Modell (1970), Oremland
(1975), and Weissman (1971) have expanded on the importance of the relationship between creativity and the transitional object and transitional states. This work places increased
emphasis on the early developmental phases, suggesting that
the creative person maintains an ongoing access to the transitional period, the time of first explorations, initial discoveries,
and concurrent experimentation with newly developing symbols and novel forms of communication as differentiation progresses (Oremland, 1975).

The emphasis on access to transitional phenomena links artistic creativity to another creative activity in which even the
most ordinary people nightly create the most extraordinary
new symbols and intriguing communications, the dream. Lewin's (1953) inference regarding the importance of the maternal object for the "location" and purpose of dreaming adds
further evidence in support of a relationship between the
early transitional phases of development and creativity, placing the earliest concept of the mother central to the creative
process (Erikson, 1972).

MICHELANGELO'S PIETÀS

The *Pietà* of St. Peter's was sculpted when Michelangelo was scarcely 25. The statue is of awesome beauty, remarkable in its concept and execution, often referred to as the most "finished" of his sculptures (fig. 1). The expression on the face of the Holy Virgin as she holds the crucified Christ, as an exquisite portrayal of love, acceptance, and resignation, has held countless thousands transfixed for nearly five centuries. Part of its magic includes a striking curiosity. Mary and the adult Jesus are about the same age (fig. 2). What the genius of Michelangelo was trying to express through this artistic device has been pondered since its initial unveiling (Symonds, 1892).

The Pietà was a major theme of Michelangelo's sculptural work. Of particular interest is the relationship of the first *Pietà* to the two subsequent *Pietàs* done shortly before his death.[1] Vasari (1568), his first biographer, noted that the later *Pietàs*, the one in the Cathedral of Florence and the Rondanini, were begun by Michelangelo in his mid-70s for his tomb.

The *Pietà* in the Cathedral of Florence is a complex, triangular composite of four bodies (fig. 3). The Virgin, as in the first *Pietà*, is tenderly holding the dead Jesus, but the positioning and the style of execution are markedly different. Their two bodies are closely placed and the faces, suggestively executed, are partially fused (fig. 4). Above them, yet part of the unit, is the protective aged onlooker, Joseph of Arimathea, called Nicodemus by Vasari and Condivi, a self-portrait of Michelangelo as an old man (Vasari, 1568). To his right, clearly sculpted, separate from them and done to a different scale, is the Mary Magdalene. It is known that when the statue was nearly completed, Michelangelo broke it into pieces and gave it to his devoted servant. His young student and friend,

1. A fourth, the Palestrina *Pietà*, is undocumented, though frequently attributed to Michelangelo or at least to an immediate student (Pope-Hennessy, 1968). Unfortunately, the time of this work is not known; however, in that it is closely related in theme and execution to the *Pietà* in the Cathedral in Florence, it does not contribute to this study.

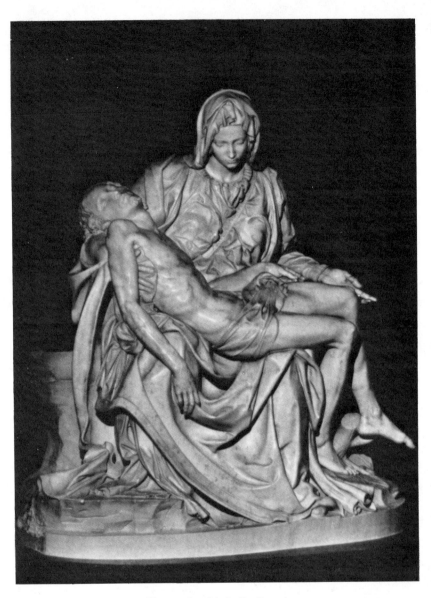

Figure 1. *Pietà*, St. Peter's

St. Peter's, Rome (reproduced with the kind permission of R.F.S.P. Vaticano)

568

Figure 2. *Pietà,* St. Peter's (details)

St. Peter's, Rome (reproduced with the kind permission of R.F.S.P. Vaticano)

Tiberio Calcagni, restored it and probably "finished" the Mary Magdalene, increasing the quality of her being separate from the bulk of the work.

The distinguished art historian and major interpreter of Michelangelo, Tolnay (1975), documents that it was Michelangelo's next to last artistic effort. He notes that following its mutilation and abandonment, Michelangelo near death returned to work on a different conceptualization, a third *Pietà,* now known as the Rondanini *Pietà.* Michelangelo's magnificent drawing (ca. 1540) of a *Pietà* for Vittoria Colonna some 20 years earlier (fig. 5) is of importance for understanding the last two sculptures. In this drawing the body of the dead Son is vertical, pressed between the legs and up against the lower abdomen of the Mother; two supporting angels maintain the arms in an attitude of crucifixion. The positioning of the dead Son is strikingly reminiscent of the baby Jesus between the legs of the *Madonna of Bruges* (ca. 1501; fig. 6). This new positioning of the dead Jesus, which

Figure 3.   Florentine *Pietà*

Cathedral of Florence (reproduced with the permission of Alinari)

Figure 4.   Florentine *Pietà* (detail)

Cathedral of Florence (reproduced with the permission of Alinari)

Figure 5. *Pietà*

Figure 6. *Madonna of Bruges*

Church of the Notre Dame, Bruges (reproduced with the kind permission of Canon V. Laridon,
Church of the Notre Dame)

becomes the central axis of the second *Pietà*, is enhanced and intensified in the third, the Rondanini *Pietà*.

The third *Pietà* was begun in 1552. Michelangelo worked on it intermittently until his final years when it fully absorbed him. It is recorded that as late as six days prior to his death, though terminally ill, he could be found working on it through the night with a candle attached to his cap. In the Rondanini *Pietà*, the naked body of Jesus is almost completely integrated into the body of Mary. Fortunately there are beautiful cartoon sketches (ca. 1550) of several versions of what was to become this *Pietà*, giving us clear evidence of its evolution (fig. 7).[2] In the drawings, with each successive revision, Jesus becomes less a weight supported by, and more a part of, the Mother. In the final stone version, His muscular maleness has been decrementally attenuated until His definiteness becomes indistinct from Hers. Their tender faces, suggestively sculpted, transfigured, are nearly fused into one another. Rather than Mary's needing assistance from Nicodemus and the Magdalene to support the weight of the body, the two are alone and He seems to be carrying them both upward (fig. 8).

In the final Rondanini *Pietà* as we now know it, we can see evidence of earlier versions, for to its right the well-sculpted, muscular arm of an earlier Jesus, an entirely different Jesus from the ethereal one entwined with the Mother, hangs limply

2. Tolnay (1953) presents a remarkable discussion of the influence of Vittoria Colonna on Michelangelo's art. He emphasizes her awakening and refining his religious beliefs, specifically the importance of salvation through faith epitomized by the Crucifixion. It would be equally rewarding to study her influence on Michelangelo's depictions of women and man's relationship to woman for it is clear from the letters and poems that no other woman touched him emotionally as this remarkable, talented, and spiritual woman.

Though there is no direct evidence, it does seem that the conceptualization of the Rondanini *Pietà* (ca. 1550) and the beginning execution of the late *Pietàs* (ca. 1552) were a response to her death in 1547. While there is considerable uncertainty about the dating of the Oxford sketches, it is tempting to conjecture that Michelangelo's abandonment of the all-male Entombment theme, which Tolnay places earlier in the sketches, in favor of the man and woman Lamentation theme for his own tomb, reflects a reawakened desire for maternal woman in response to the Marquise's death (fig. 7).

Last*   First*   Earlier sketches for an   Second*
Entombment depiction

*Order of sketches according to Tolnay (1934)

Figure 7.   Oxford Sketches for *Pietà* and Entombment

Ashmolean Museum, Oxford (reproduced with the permission of the Ashmolean Museum)

Figure 8.   Rondanini *Pietà*

Castello Sforzesco, Milan (reproduced with the permission of Archi
vio Fotografico, Castello Sforzesco)

and weightily. It is mute testimony to how much of the substance of Jesus Michelangelo progressively removed until His naked entirety is sculpted from a solitary column with but outlines of the two figures (Tolnay, 1934).

Some Biographical Data about Michelangelo

For a Renaissance figure who was not of high nobility, there exists a remarkable amount of documented biographical data about Michelangelo through the efforts of two early biographers, Vasari and Condivi, younger fellow artists and close friends. We are also fortunate to have many of Michelangelo's letters, contracts, and his poetry (Linscott, 1963).

As is typical of biographies, the earliest years are obscure; however, Stone and Stone (1962) note that Michelangelo's mother fell from a horse while she was pregnant with him. Vasari (1568) reported that she was ill at the time of his birth. In any case, authorities agree that he was born in Caprese, and shortly thereafter was given to nurse to the daughter and wife of stonecutters in Settignano, a village near Florence where the father owned property. Vasari refers to her as a stepmother, implying that Michelangelo was placed in the home of this woman. It is known that about a month later, the family, probably including the older brother, Lionardo, 2 years old at the time, moved to Florence; however, it is uncertain when Michelangelo returned to his family. Tolnay (1967), acknowledging that no proof can be adduced, speculates that Michelangelo returned to live with his family at age 10, about the time of his father's remarriage.

Tolnay's conjecture suggests that of the five sons only Michelangelo was reared in what amounted to a foster home until the father's remarriage late in Michelangelo's childhood. Although absence of information is weak evidence, it does seem unlikely that such an unusual circumstance, namely, that he was the only child placed in a foster home, would not have been alluded to.

In the absence of confirming data, it seems more likely that Michelangelo was taken to the home of the wet nurse because his mother's illness or injury prevented her from caring for him and that he remained there until he was weaned. By this time his mother probably was sufficiently recovered to receive him, for she was well enough shortly thereafter to become pregnant with Buonorroto. She died when Michelangelo was 6, after having given birth to three more sons.[3] The father remarried when Michelangelo was 10, and there is a vague reference to a possible stepbrother, Matteo.

There is evidence of the importance of the early wet nurse to Michelangelo and even a clearly stated linkage between her and his exceptional ability. He wrote Vasari, "if I possess anything of good in my mental constitution, it comes from my having been born in your clear climate of Arezzo; . . . I drew the chisel and the mallet with which I carve statues in together with my nurse's milk" (Symonds, 1892, p. 6).

It is important for the interpretation which I want to develop with regard to the artistic representation in the *Pietàs* that even in these sparse biographical data there is evidence that Michelangelo had two mothers, an early nursing mother from whom he was taken at the time of his being weaned and a real, sickly, often pregnant mother who was taken from him

3. Sterba and Sterba (1956), using the late-return hypothesis, developed a detailed speculation regarding Michelangelo's tempers, irascibility, and impulsivity. They emphasize the importance of his being the son of a minor nobleman reared as a peasant in a village, in addition to abandonment, as a factor contributing to his hostility. This theme is also utilized by Liebert (1977a, 1977b) in this study of the mutilation of the Florentine *Pietà* and his interpretation of the *Dying Slave,* and by Frank (1966) in her sensitive study of the Rondanini *Pietà.* All of these conjectures, to my mind, including the often-referred-to "distant gaze" of Michelangelo's Madonnas, clinically fit better with the assumption that he experienced an early loss of the nursing mother and that he was returned to an often pregnant, probably chronically ill mother, who died in his early childhood (two early losses), than with the hypothesis that he was reared uninterruptedly by the same nursing mother in a foster family until he returned to his family at age 10 to attend school (psychodynamically speaking, a rather late loss).

by death during childhood (Erikson, 1972). In essence, neither of Michelangelo's mothers ever aged.

It is uncanny that Michelangelo's contemporary, the genius par excellence, Leonardo, had early life experiences which in this regard somewhat paralleled those of Michelangelo. According to Freud's (1910) account, Leonardo was the illegitimate son of Ser Piero da Vinci and a peasant girl, Caterina. He was taken from his mother at about age 4 to the home of his heirless father and his second wife. It was not until some 20 years later that his father married a woman who could have children and gave Leonardo stepsiblings. The point of the similarity is that, like Michelangelo, Leonardo also had two mothers.

In the 1910 monograph, Freud noted that in the so-called *St. Anne with Two Others* in the Louvre, the grandmother, St. Anne, and the Mother Mary are about the same age. The positioning of the bodies is curious for Mary is sitting on Anne's lap holding her arms extended to the infant Jesus. In effect, Mary and Anne are of one body. As Freud wrote:

> Another striking feature of the picture assumes even greater significance. St. Anne, Mary's mother and the boy's grandmother, who must have been a matron . . . still [is] a young woman of unfaded beauty. In point of fact Leonardo has given the boy two mothers, one who stretches her arms out to him, and another in the background; and both are endowed with the blissful smile of the joy of motherhood. This peculiarity of the picture has not failed to surprise those who have written about it: . . . Muther's attempt at an explanation is surely enough to prove that the impression that St. Anne has been made more youthful derives from the picture and is not an invention for an ulterior purpose.
>
> Leonardo's childhood was remarkable in precisely the same way as this picture. He has had two mothers: first, his true mother Caterina, from whom he was torn away when he was between three and five, and then a young and tender stepmother, his father's wife Donna Albiera. By his combining this fact . . . and by his condensing them into a composite unity, the design of 'St. Anne with Two Others' took shape

for him. The maternal figure that is further away from the boy—the grandmother—corresponds to the earlier and true mother, Caterina, in its appearance and in its spatial[4] relation to the boy [p. 113].[5]

MICHELANGELO'S PIETÀS AND HIS TWO MOTHERS

I return to the readily observable peculiarity of the *Pietà* of St. Peter's: the young adult Jesus and the Holy Mother are the same age. It seems to me that the sculpture is intensely autobiographical—a depiction of Michelangelo's never-aging[6] first (perhaps condensed with the second) mother.[7] This artistic device, possibly enabled by the circumstance of Michelangelo's infancy, allows us to reexperience the intimate infant-maternal relationship. As in a dream condensation, the statue pictorializes for us *allegorical man at the end of the torture of life returned to the mother of his infancy.*

Michelangelo, in a way, confirmed this hypothesis, for Condivi (1553) reports that at the time of its unveiling Michelangelo, criticized for this very feature, explained: "this un-

4. In the *Standard Edition,* this word (*raümlich*) is mistranslated as "special" (translation corrected with the help of Hans von Valentini Veith).

5. See Eissler (1961) for a detailed presentation of the difficulty in ascertaining when Leonardo was taken from his mother to live with his father, a difficulty which somewhat parallels the problem of accurately determining when Michelangelo was taken from his wet nurse to live with his family. Of special relevance is his discussion of Schapiro's (1956) criticisms of psychological conjecturing and the problem of historical data which change as new evidence is uncovered.

6. The term never-aging seems to capture more accurately a personal quality than the term ageless. In the context of images and memories, never-aging is used to convey the feeling that something is as it was initially experienced, whereas ageless has the connotation of both indefinite age and unchanging through the ages.

7. This hypothesis, which parallels Freud's speculation about the age-sameness of St. Anne and Mary, is given some support by the fact that Leonardo's painting apparently had special significance to Michelangelo. His drawing (ca. 1501) closely follows Leonardo, with the same condensation of the two mothers by the device of having Mary sitting on St. Anne's lap, their bodies nearly indistinguishable.

sullied bloom of youth may have been miraculously wrought to convince the world of the virginity and perpetual purity of the Mother. This was not necessary for the Son. . . . He did take a human body and become subject to all that an ordinary man is subject to . . . so that His person revealed the exact age to which He had attained. You need not, therefore, marvel if, having regard to this consideration, I have made the most Holy Virgin, Mother of God, much younger relatively to her Son than women of her years usually appear, and left the Son such as His time of life demanded" (Symonds, 1892, p. 46). In short, he describes in religious, mystical terms that he maintained a concept of a never-aging, pure, unsullied mother, the mother(s) of his infancy whom he never knew as older women because he lost both when they (and he) were young.

Michelangelo's phrase, "may have been miraculously wrought," is of particular interest. His description captures the quality of the creative moment, an inspiration, a something which occurs. In the religious lexicon in which Michelangelo fervently and concretely believed, he describes this intrapsychic contact with the image of the never-aging mother as something having come to him from God, from out there yet from within himself, the transitional "location."[8]

THE MADONNA AND THE PIETÀ

Michelangelo's work contains much additional evidence indicating that he depicted the mother-infant relationship in special ways. Tolnay (1975) suggests that the Michelangelo Madonnas are distinguished by his placing the infant Christ

---

8. In his correspondence, little can be found that is descriptive of his creativity. However, in one letter written in his early 80s when asked for a design for the stairs of the Laurentian Library, a structure he had not seen for many years, he gives us a glimpse into this same sense of the process occurring somewhere out there yet within. He wrote, "Concerning the staircase . . . a certain staircase comes to my mind *just like a dream*," and then presented a detailed structural description of what was to become the graceful stairs we now know (Stone and Stone, 1962, p. 201; my italics).

centrally on the body of the mother, a remarkable modification of the womb representation, the mandorla of certain Byzantine characterizations of the Virgin. In commenting on the *Bruges Madonna,* he says, "because of this exceptional positioning, the Child still seems to be contained within the protective womb" (p. 16). This characteristic placement can be seen clearly in one of his earliest marble works, the *Virgin of the Stairs,* which he made as an apprentice in the Medici garden when he was 15 (fig. 9). It is striking to see the muscular, independent, almost Herculean infant struggling to reenter the mother's body, depicted by His powerfully searching in the folds of her garment, which appears again in the *Medici Madonna* (ca. 1531).

This theme of reunion with the mother of Michelangelo's earliest artistic days becomes in his young adult years the *return* of the dead adult Son to the arms of the still young Mother, the *Pietà* of St. Peter's. The "lone Virgin, like a seated Madonna, with her Son on her lap . . . holds the body of Christ with her right arm under His shoulder, as a child is held" (Tolnay, 1967, p. 91). The Son, executed with the grace, softness, and tenderness not found in any previous or subsequent work, appears about the age Michelangelo was when he sculpted Him, perhaps further suggesting an autobiographical theme.

THE PIETÀ AND THE RESURRECTION

It is of relevance that the *Pietàs* are not depictions of an event from the Gospel. According to John (19 : 38–39), Luke (23 : 53), and Mark (15 : 46), when the dead Jesus was removed from the Cross, He was carried by Joseph of Arimathea and Nicodemus to a tomb in the garden of Joseph of Arimathea. This sequence, referred to as the Deposition and Entombment, is of special interest to this study because the Oxford sketches indicate that Michelangelo was at the same time considering, and indeed experimenting with, depictions of the Entombment as he was evolving the conceptualization of the Rondanini *Pietà* (see footnote 2 and fig. 7).

Figure 9. *The Virgin of the Stairs*

Casa Buonarroti, Florence (reproduced with the permission of Alinari)

583

Pietà, best translated as "sorrow," is a moment which has been interposed between the Deposition, the removal from the Cross, and the Entombment, the carrying to the tomb. The addition of the Lamentation, the event of the dead body of Jesus being mourned by His close followers including Mary, began to appear in religious art in the early Middle Ages. In the later Middle Ages as increasing importance was ascribed to the Holy Mother, the Lamentation was intensified, and artistically depicted as the moment of return to the Mother.

The teachings in the late Middle Ages of mystics like Suso and San Bernardino da Siena are especially relevant to the study of Michelangelo's *Pietàs,* because they describe the Virgin taking her dead Son on her lap and imagining Him as a child again, a return to the Madonna configuration. In fact, some artists of this period depicted this as a corpse with the proportions of a child (Tolnay, 1960). This becomes a remarkable condensation of the beginning and the end, birth and death—the Madonna and the Pietà.

Returning the body to the earth with the incantation of "dust to dust" as symbolic return to the mother implies *rebirth* reflecting variations of atavistic experiences given formal expression in the ancient Eleusinian rites that were closely associated with the importance of spring in the history of man. These were to reappear as the most significant of Christian dogma, Resurrection. As no one before and no one since, Michelangelo coupled the lifelong continuing desire to return to the mother of our infancy with death in the *Pietà* of St. Peter's as an exquisite portrayal of this cycle.

This unity of the Madonna and the Pietà is vividly pictorialized in a fascinating drawing Michelangelo made probably for Vittoria Colonna (ca. 1540), the *Madonna de' Silenzio* (fig. 10). In this drawing, the overly large child in what is almost a sleep of death lies half on the Mother's lap. In the background are two mysterious figures, one apparently an old man and the other a masked woman. Reminiscent of the *Madonna of the Stairs* and strikingly suggestive of the subsequent Florentine *Pietà,* His arm hangs limply with the hand curled. This interesting drawing with these four figures is in many

Figure 10. *Madonna de' Silenzio*

National Gallery, London (reproduced with the kind permission of The Lady Anne Bentinck, daughter of The Duke of Portland)

ways the transition from the "Madonna-*Pietà*" in St. Peter's to the *Pietà* in Florence. In the final *Pietà,* his last artistic expression, the reunion theme intensifies, culminating in explicit union with the mother.

THE FINAL PIETÀS

The *Pietà* in the Cathedral of Florence sculpted in Michelangelo's final decade shows a remarkable positional change from the first *Pietà*. Poetically autobiographical, there are the two young mothers: the Virgin grasping Jesus' dead body to hers to support it, her eyes closed, their heads touching, and their faces partially fused, and off at the side, the second mother, the second Mary, distinct and distant. Above them, watching with us, is Michelangelo "holding the right arm of the Body [seeming] to move Him from the side of the Mary Magdalene to that of the Virgin, on whose back he rests his left arm in an ineffably tender gesture of protection. He unites the Mother and Son" (Tolnay, 1960, p. 87).

As previously noted, in his final days, Michelangelo mutilated the statue and returned to work on his final sculpture, the Rondanini *Pietà*. The conventional explanation for the destruction is that the marble, formerly a capitol of a giant pillar of the Temple of Peace, betrayed flaws and that he gouged too deeply on the Virgin's arm. This seems an inadequate explanation of an unusual circumstance because more commonly Michelangelo abandoned rather than destroyed a piece when the marble was found unsuitable or when there was a sculpting error.

I propose that as death approached, Michelangelo found the depiction of the four figures unsatisfyingly distant—a pictorialization of a stage in process, a phase passed—and so destroyed the statue.[9] With this Michelangelo returned to the

9. The question of the mutilation of the *Pietà* in the Cathedral of Florence has been subjected to some psychological investigation. Steinberg (1968) advanced the "slung leg" thesis, inferring that Christ's leg across the lap of the Mother was an unacceptably overt depiction of erotic intimacy and thus led to Michelangelo's removing the leg and breaking up the statue.

two figure theme of the Madonnas and the first *Pietà* now intensified.[10] The sketches and the remnants of the Rondanini *Pietà* indicate that successively he removed more and more of the material solidity of Jesus. Naked as with the Madonna, He was being made of the body of the Mother, the faces roughly hewn, nearly indistinct from each other, with "flat, simplified forms suggesting with great intensity the fusion of the Mother and Son. She seems to rest on Him and yet Christ appears to seek support from her body with both of His arms" (Tolnay, 1960, p. 91). Rather than her supporting His naked weight, as a graceful arc swinging upward, they rise in union (fig. 11).

Summary

It is my thesis that in the *Pietàs* Michelangelo's artistic genius allows us to experience intimate contact with the never-aging mother. In the *Pietà* of St. Peter's, as a portrayal of his contact with the never-aging, "first" nursing (perhaps condensed with his "second" true) mother, Michelangelo allows us to experience return to the young mother of our infancy. As his life was drawing to a close, in the two later *Pietàs,* probably the only works which he made solely for himself, he allows us to

---

Liebert (1977a, 1977b), following the Sterbas (1956), emphasized the hostility toward the mother who abandoned Michelangelo at birth and linked the mutilation to the impending death of the loved and cherished, almost maternal, servant, Urbino.

10. Frank (1966) presents an interesting corollary to this thesis. She rightly questions the striking obscurity of the Rondanini *Pietà* and refers to it as an enigma. Emphasizing the role of early mother loss, she attributes the general disregard of this statue to the potential threat inherent in acknowledgment of loss of and wished-for fusion with the mother.

While her thesis parallels that of this paper, it differs in an important respect. Though Frank senses in the statue, as I do, the "deepest longing; the return to his beginnings, to the womb" (p. 314), she interprets this as Michelangelo's acceptance of the finality of death without hope or immortality or resurrection. In contrast to her view, I see in this the wish for a new beginning, rebirth, the very essence of the Resurrection of Christian dogma. To me, it is poetical that his depiction of his wish for immortality is a major contribution to his deserved immortality.

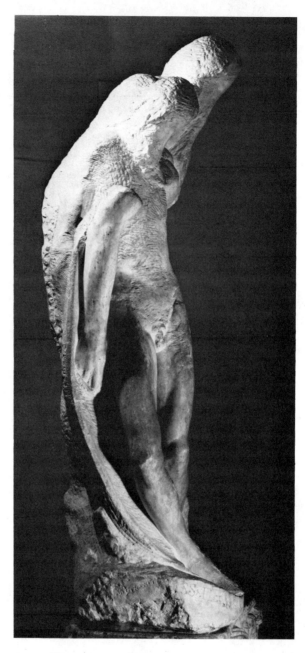

Figure 11.   Rondanini *Pietà* (side view)

Castello Sforzesco, Milan (reproduced with the permission of Archivio Fotografico, Castello Sforzesco)

experience *union* with the body of the mother. This union, evolved from his early Madonna conceptualization, has an awesome intensification for it is an adult with the mother. It is an artistic depiction of early self-object fusion—ecstatic and mystical. The *Pietà* in the Cathedral of Florence is an almost literal autobiographical portrayal as Michelangelo watches and assists his return to the first mother, while acknowledging the distant presence of the second. With death rapidly approaching and with increasing regressive reexperiencing, that work became meaningless to Michelangelo and he returned to the dyadic Rondanini *Pietà,* progressively making the Son and Mother one.[11]

Tolnay, using the metaphor of Catholicism, describes the final statue as depicting Michelangelo's transcendence of death as the Christ and His Mother ascend united. To the psychoanalyst, the *Pietàs* are dreamlike pictorializations of the adult in contact with the primal phases of development. Through them, Michelangelo portrays for us the curiosity of his early experience and at the same time, possibly enabled by it, allows us contact with a continuing desire as we reexperience a progression now lost to our consciousness. The evocation is intense for it is not simply child with mother—the Madonna. For by coupling the Madonna with death in the first *Pietà* and more explicitly by returning the adult dead Son to the body of the Mother in the final work, Michelangelo gives us the promise of rebirth. In this way, the feelings evoked are timeless, universal, and compelling.

---

11. There is some support for this inference of terminal regressive reexperiencing in Michelangelo's letter (dated June 27, 1562, two years before his death) to his nephew Lionardo. Discussing the nephew's wife's pregnancy, Michelangelo suggested that if it were a girl, perhaps she could be named Francesca. In the prior correspondence, there was much discussion of naming Lionardo's children, Michelangelo's only heirs. However, whenever previously he discussed girls' names, Michelangelo always deferred to the nephew's wife, while making definite suggestions for boys, usually names of his brothers. His mother's name, not so acknowledged, appears in this letter, which he wrote when he was close to death, suggesting that at some level, perhaps, she was on his mind.

BIBLIOGRAPHY

CONDIVI, A. (1553), Vita di Michelangelo Buonarroti. In: *Michel Angelo Buonarroti,* tr. C. Holyrod. London: Duckworth, 1911, pp. 1–91.
EISSLER, K. R. (1961), *Leonardo da Vinci.* New York: Int. Univ. Press.
ERIKSON, E. H. (1954), The Dream Specimen of Psychoanalysis. *J. Amer. Psychoanal. Assn.,* 2 : 5–56.
——— (1972), Play and Actuality. In: *Play and Development,* ed. M. W. Piers. New York: Norton, pp. 127–167.
FRANK, G. (1966). The Enigma of Michelangelo's Pietà Rondanini. *Amer. Imago,* 23 : 287–315.
FREUD, S. (1900), The Interpretation of Dreams. *S.E.,* 4 & 5.
——— (1908), Creative Writers and Day-Dreaming. *S.E.,* 9 : 141–153.
——— (1910), Leonardo da Vinci and a Memory of His Childhood. *S.E.,* 11 : 59–137.
——— (1914), The Moses of Michelangelo. *S.E.,* 13 : 211–238.
——— (1930), Civilization and Its Discontents. *S.E.,* 21 : 59–145.
GREENACRE, P. (1957), The Childhood of the Artist. *This Annual,* 12 : 47–72.
——— (1958), The Family Romance of the Artist. *This Annual,* 13 : 9–36.
——— (1962), Discussion and Comments on the Psychology of Creativity. *J. Amer. Acad. Child Psychiat.,* 1 : 129–137.
HAMILTON, J. W. (1974), Transitional Fantasies and the Creative Process. In: *The Psychoanalytic Study of Society,* 6 : 53–70. New York: Int. Univ. Press.
HORTON, P. C. (1974), The Mystical Experience. *J. Amer. Psychoanal. Assn.,* 22 : 364–380.
JACOBSON, E. (1964), *The Self and the Object World.* New York: Int. Univ. Press.
KRIS, E. (1952), *Psychoanalytic Explorations in Art.* New York: Int. Univ. Press.
LEWIN, B. D. (1953), Reconsideration of the Dream Screen. *Psychoanal. Quart.,* 22 : 174–199.
LIEBERT, R. S. (1977a), Michelangelo's Mutilation of the Florence Pietà. *Art Bull.,* 59 : 47–54.
——— (1977b), Michelangelo's *Dying Slave. This Annual,* 32 : 505–544.
LINSCOTT, R. N., ed. (1963), *Complete Poems and Selected Letters of Michelangelo,* tr. C. Gilbert. New York: Random House.
LUBIN, A. (1976), Mysticism and Creativity. In: *Mysticism: Spiritual Quest or Psychic Disorder?* Group for the Advancement of Psychiatry, Report 9.
McDONALD, M. A. (1970), Transitional Tunes and Musical Development. *This Annual,* 25 : 503–520.
MODELL, A. H. (1970), The Transitional Object and the Creative Act. *Psychoanal. Quart.,* 39 : 240–250.
OREMLAND, J. (1975), An Unexpected Result of the Analysis of a Talented Musician. *This Annual,* 30 : 375–407.

POPE-HENNESSY, J. (1968), The Palestrina Pietà. In: *Essays in Italian Sculptures*. London & New York: Phaidon, pp. 121–131.

SCHAPIRO, M. (1956), Leonardo and Freud. *J. Hist. Ideas,* 17 : 147–178.

SCHOTT, R. (1963), *Michelangelo*. New York: Tudor Publishing Co.

STEINBERG, L. (1968), Michelangelo's Florentine *Pietà:* The Missing Leg. *Art Bull.,* 50 : 343–59.

STERBA, R. & STERBA, E. (1956), The Anxieties of Michelangelo Buonarroti. *Int. J. Psycho-Anal.,* 37 : 325–330.

STONE, I. & STONE, J., eds. (1962), *I, Michelangelo, Sculptor: An Autobiography Through Letters*. New York: Doubleday.

SYMONDS, J. A. (1892), *The Life of Michelangelo Buonarroti*. New York: Modern Library.

TOLNAY, C. DE (1934), The Rondanini Pietà. *Burlington Mag.,* 65 : 146–157.

——— (1953), Michelangelo's Pietà Composition for Vittoria Colonna. *Record of the Art Museum*. Princeton Univ., pp. 45–62.

——— (1960), *The Final Period*. Princeton Univ. Press.

——— (1967), *The Youth of Michelangelo*. Princeton Univ. Press.

——— (1975), *Michelangelo, Sculptor, Painter, Architect*. Princeton Univ. Press.

VASARI, G. (1568), *Lives of the Most Eminent Painters, Sculptors, and Architects*, ed. R. N. Linscott. New York: Modern Library, 1959.

WEISSMAN, P. (1971), The Artist and His Objects. *Int. J. Psycho-Anal.,* 52 : 401–406.

WINNICOTT, D. W. (1953), Transitional Objects and Transitional Phenomena. *Int. J. Psycho-Anal.,* 34 : 89–97.

——— (1967), The Location of Cultural Experience. *Int. J. Psycho-Anal.,* 48 : 368–372.

Children and Death

As Seen through Art and Autobiographies

EMMA N. PLANK, M.A. AND
ROBERT PLANK, J.D.

WITH SO MANY SCIENTIFIC INVESTIGATIONS OR SPECULATIONS about the meaning of death to children, it may be strange that this article deals with the expression of direct experiences with death and with recorded sayings of children about death as we find them in autobiographies or in art, in stories written by children, or sayings of young children noted by observers. They shed light on children's reactions to death and their fantasies in different developmental phases.

We have deliberately excluded reports from the professional literature based on the individual treatment or observations on psychopathological situations, where the reaction to a death was the core of a developmental problem and often expressed in acting out or dramatic play. Because of the uniqueness of the times and the observers we have included a few examples of children's sayings from the Hampstead War Nurseries.

The selections from literature, art, observations, and children's work are not intended to be a representative sample. The material is much too rich and varied for that. They are

Emma Plank is Professor Emeritus, Department of Pediatrics, School of Medicine, Case Western Reserve University. Robert Plank is Adjunct Associate Professor, Department of Psychology, Case Western Reserve University, Cleveland, Ohio.

chosen because they speak directly from emotional experience to emotional experience. Rather than being average, they are especially meaningful because they show with special clarity different ways of coping with the problem.

Our interest in this area is easily explained. One of us worked for many years as a member of the pediatric team in a hospital where death—at times expected and hoped for, at other times striking suddenly and viciously—forced us to focus our attention on life and in some ways to come to grips with our very personal reactions to the death of a child. For us, the beauty of some of the writings we have assembled in this article brought insight and relief.

The psychoanalytic literature has from Freud and Hug-Hellmuth before World War I, followed by Anna Freud's and Dorothy Burlingham's observations during World War II, led in the 1960s to many papers detailing the bereavement reactions of individual young children as well as children's reactions to the fear of dying (Solnit and Green, 1959, 1963). These were followed by Nagera's (1970) study of developmental interference through death of a close person, and Erna Furman's (1974) and her colleagues' extensive and decisive study describing the insights gained through analysis of bereaved children or counseling with the surviving parent.

DEALING WITH THE RAW REALITIES OF DEATH

James Agee (1957) poetically described how the reaction to the death of a parent is formed by the child's early attachment to them. Here is part of the passage he wrote, on the pattern of the Psalms:

> I hear my father; I need never fear.
> I hear my mother; I shall never be lonely, or want for love.
> When I am hungry it is they who provide for me; when I am in dismay, it is they who fill me with comfort.
> When I am astonished or bewildered, it is they who make the weak ground firm beneath my soul: it is in them that I put my trust. . . .

I need never fear: nor ever shall I lack for loving kindness [p. 82f.].

But the peace of the family in this autobiographical novel is broken. Having driven to the Tennessee hills to visit the seriously ill grandfather, the father suffers a fatal accident on the way home when the steering wheel of his car malfunctioned. The very sensitive, shattered mother has to tell her two children, ages 6 and 3, of their father's death.

"Come close"; and she touched each of them. "I want to tell you about Daddy." But upon his name her voice shook and her whole dry-looking mouth trembled like the ash of burned paper in a draft. "Can you hear me, Catherine?" she asked, when she had recovered her voice. Catherine peered at her earnestly as if through a thick fog. "Are you waked up enough yet, my darling?" And because of her voice, in sympathy and for her protection, they both came now much nearer, and she put her arms around both of them, and they could smell her breath, a little like sauerkraut but more like a dried-up mouse. And now even more small lines like cracked china branched all over her face. "Daddy," she said, "your father, children": and this time she caught control of her mouth more quickly, and a single tear spilled out of her left eye and slid jaggedly down all the jagged lines: "Daddy didn't come home. He isn't going to come home ever any more. He's— gone away to heaven and he isn't ever coming home again. Do you hear me, Catherine? Are you awake?" Catherine stared at her mother. "Do *you* understand, Rufus?"

He stared at his mother. "Why not?" he asked.

She looked at him with extraordinary closeness and despair, and said, "Because God wanted him." They continued to stare at her severely and she went on: "Daddy was on his way home last night—and he was—he—got hurt and—so God let him go to sleep and took him straight away with Him to heaven." She sank her fingers in Catherine's springy hair and looked intently from one to the other. "Do you see, children? Do you understand?" They stared at her, and now Catherine was sharply awake.

"Is Daddy *dead?*" Rufus asked. Her glance at him was as startled as if he had slapped her, and again her mouth and then her whole face began to work, uncontrollably this time, and she did not speak, but only nodded her head once, and then again, and then several times rapidly, while one small, squeaky "yes" came out of her as if it had been sneezed out [p. 251f.].

[The children are then sent to breakfast with a greataunt.]

All through breakfast, Rufus had wanted to ask questions, but now he felt so shy and uneasy that he could hardly speak. "Who hurt him?" he finally asked.

"Why nobody hurt him, Rufus," she said, and she looked shocked. "What on earth made you think so?"

Mama said so, Catherine thought.

"Mama said he got hurt so bad God put him to sleep," Rufus said.

Like the kitties, Catherine thought; she saw a dim, gigantic old man in white take her tiny father by the skin of the neck and put him in a huge slop jar full of water and sit on the lid, and she heard the tiny scratching and the stifled mewing.

"That's true he was hurt, but nobody hurt him," her aunt Hannah was saying. How could that be, Catherine wondered. "He was driving home by himself. That's all, all by himself, in the auto last night, and he had an accident."

Rufus felt his face get warm and he looked warningly at his sister. He knew it could not be that, not with his father, a grown man, besides, God wouldn't put you to sleep for *that,* and it didn't hurt, anyhow. But Catherine might think so. Sure enough, she was looking at her aunt with astonishment and disbelief that she could say such a thing about her father. Not in his *pants,* you dern fool, Rufus wanted to tell her, but his Aunt Hannah continued: "A *fatal* accident"; and by her voice, as she spoke the strange word, "fatal," they knew she meant something very bad. "That means that, just as your mother told you, that he was hurt so badly that God put him to sleep right away" [p. 258].

Agee certainly was not trying to write a "psychoanalytic novel," but one can hardly imagine it written before Freud. What may seem bizarre, even gross humor is actually authenticity. Toilet training does loom that large on that developmental level, but earlier writers would not have seen it that way.

Very different, but equally eloquent is Sean O'Casey's description (1939) of the last time the 6-year-old saw his father alive:

> Once again, when the parlour door had been left open, Johnny, passing by, had ventured to peep into the room. . . . There was his poor da, or, his father, as Johnny's mother spoke of him to his brothers and sister, sitting facing the fire. . . . He must have sensed the boy peering in at him, for the head in the cricket-cap suddenly turned, and the boy caught a frightening glimpse of a white, wasted agony-lined face, jewelled with deep-set eyes now gleaming with appealing anger at the boy who was looking at him. Johnny saw the blue veins swell in the delicate hand that rested on the chair, and his ears were shocked by the sound of the low weak voice trying to shout at him, Go away, go away, you, and shut the door at once—this is no place for little boys.
>
> Johnny had closed the door quick, had run for his life through the hall out into the street, full of the fear of something strange, leaving his da, his poor da, shrinking from something that everyone thought of, but nobody ever mentioned [p. 42f.].

Soon thereafter the father died. On the day of the funeral Johnny was playing outdoors when a neighbor urged him into the house to kiss his father before they closed the coffin:

> —I couldn't, I couldn't, he sobbed. Don't ask me, mother, don't ask me to kiss him, I'm frightened to kiss a dead man.
>
> He felt a gentle, sympathetic pressure of an arm around him, and softened his sobbing.
>
> —No one'll ask you to do it, she said. I'll kiss him goodbye for you myself. Just touch the side of the coffin with the tip of your finger.
>
> She gently drew out his arm, and he shuddered deeply when he felt the tip of his finger touching the shiny cold side of the coffin.
>
> —That's the brave little son, she murmured; and now I'll give your father a last kiss from his little boy [p. 57].

In both these autobiographies the response of the sensitive mother has helped to lessen the immediate fear, though Agee lived his rather short life under the shadow of this loss. O'Casey became a fighter for causes and did not submit to the pain and restrictions of his ophthalmologic difficulties.

Very different was the reaction of Anton Wildgans (1928) who lost his mother when he was 3½ years old. She died of tuberculosis, shortly after she had given birth to another boy. It seems from his memories that nobody took any notice of the boy or talked to him about the death. On the day of the funeral he was left alone in the dining room of a typical small middle-class apartment in Vienna before the turn of the century:

> My memory reemerges with the dusk of the day. I see myself in the dining room, and I was alone. A little pitcher half filled with milk was standing on the edge of the table where I had so often got to feel the rod because I refused to eat the soup; a roll was next to the pitcher. The moment came when I appropriated these good things, dipped the roll into the milk and ate it. So I could still my hunger, and I had no fear either: nobody had given me much care lately. . . .
>
> Today, though, the father was not here, and all was silent in the apartment. There—and to this day I feel it, bodily!—something strange and new got hold of me: an excitement out of myself, a stirring in the darkness around me! I can no longer fathom how long this lasted. But when at last there was sound again in the apartment and the father entered through the kitchen door, he found his boy sitting on the floor in the dark room. The empty glass and a little leftover of the milk-softened roll were lying beside him. He had taken off his shoes and socks and he talked—as he had sometimes done in earlier days before falling asleep in the evening—to his own feet, feverishly whispering. So I have often heard it told later, and that was the afternoon when my mother was buried [p. 5f.].

We strongly sense the withdrawal from the outside world, the use of his own body as consolation in his isolation and in the darkness. Since the father was involved in his own grief, there was nobody to turn to.

Another young boy who fits into this group is Maxim Gorky (1913) who was present at his father's death during a cholera epidemic. His unique recollection combines the father's death and the birth of a brother:

> On the floor, under the window, in a small, shuttered room, lay my father, dressed in a long white garment I had never seen him in before. His feet were bare and the toes were strangely distended, while the fingers of his hands, resting on his breast, were curled in. The blackened disks of two copper coins covered his eyes, shutting out their accustomed, cheerful gleam. All the light had gone out of his still face. But what scared me most was the snarl his open mouth showed with the bared teeth.
>
> Beside him, on her knees, was my mother, in an undergarment. She was combing his long, fine hair back from his forehead to the nape of his neck. The comb she was using was the one with which I scraped edible shreds from watermelon rinds. As she combed away, she talked to him without stopping, through tears that fell without stopping, until it seemed that they must finally flood her eyes out of their sockets.
>
> I saw all this holding on to the hand of my grandmother, whose dark head and eyes and nose looked enormous—the nose shapeless and pitted like a sponge—but a gentle, yet vividly interesting, woman. She, too, wept with sobs that were like cadences to my mother's. Shuddering herself, she pushed me toward my father, but I was too terrified to let go and clung to her.
>
> This was the first time I had ever seen grownups cry, and I could not understand her repeated bidding, "Say good-by to your father. You'll never see him again. He's dead before his time" [p. 3].
>
> Then a policeman and some grave-diggers appeared at the door. "Get a move on!" bellowed the policeman. . . .
>
> All at once my mother dropped to the floor and immediately turned over, her hair in the dirt. Her mouth came open on her now-livid face so that her teeth were bared like my father's. In a terrifying voice she ordered me out, and the door to be shut.
>
> Pushing me aside, grandma rushed to the door crying out, "Friends, there's nothing to be alarmed about; it's not the cholera; she's giving birth. For the love of God, leave us! Good people, go away!" . . .

> I shook with fright. . . .
>
> Suddenly there was the whimper of a child. "Thank God!" grandma called out, "it's a boy!" and got up to light a candle.
>
> And at that point, I must have fallen asleep in the darkness . . . because that was all I remembered.
>
> My next memory is a solitary spot in a cemetery, in the rain [p. 4f.].

Though the primitivity of the Russian environment differs from the settings of the other memories, the message is the same. Gorky could become a self-made man and forceful writer through the support of a mother figure in a crucial situation, here his grandmother. This soothing influence was missed in Wildgans's experience. He not only lost his mother at the beginning of the oedipal period, his only comfort was his own body, his toes. In one of his poems he movingly described the warping of a character by being orphaned. Nevertheless, the traumas these four writers underwent in their childhood did not destroy them; they may in fact have contributed to the great sensitivity to others in their work.

Anton Chekhov, himself a physician, relates running from death in "The Runaway" (1887). Seven-year-old Pashka, hospitalized for surgery on his elbow, has been tricked into staying in the hospital by the doctor's promise to take him to a fair, show him a live fox, help him catch thrushes. He shares a room with a very sick old man and sees other frightening fellow patients, but trusting the doctor and looking forward to his mother's promised visit the next day, he falls asleep in peace.

> Later he was awakened by a noise. Men walked in the adjoining ward and spoke in whispers. The dim gleam of night-lights . . . showed three figures moving near Mikhailo's bed.
>
> "Shall we take him on the mattress, or as he is?" asked one.
>
> "As he is. There's no room for the mattress. Akh, he is dead at a bad hour, heaven rest his soul!"
>
> Then—one of the figures taking Mikhailo's shoulders, another his feet—they lifted him. . . . The third . . . crossed himself; and all shuffling their feet, tripping in the folds of his dressing gown, went out of the ward. . . . Pashka . . .

looked in fright at the black windows, and jumped out of bed in panic. "Mother!" he screamed.

And, without awaiting an answer, he rushed into the adjoining ward. . . . The patients, agitated by Mikhailo's death, were sitting up in their beds. Grim, dishevelled, haunted by shades, they looked like giants; they seemed to increase in size. . . . Pashka tore through the small-pox ward into the corridor, . . . recognized the banister and rushed downstairs . . . stumbling sped into the yard, in his head a single thought: to flee, to flee! He dashed around a shed into the shrubbery, stood a second in doubt, then rushed back to the hospital and ran around it. But there he stopped in indecision, for suddenly before his eyes rose the white crosses of a graveyard.

"Mother!" he screamed, and turned back again [p. 312f.].

This gruesome example may not seem pertinent today—except that children still occasionally are housed on adult divisions; their number will be increased if plans succeed to cut hospital expenses by closing some pediatric units.

We experience a very different loss in the memoir (1966), characteristically entitled *Under Gemini,* by Isabel Bolton, an identical twin. At the age of 83, she writes: "When I evoke those hours of childhood to live in them once more, it is not myself I see before me—it is she, the living image of myself" (p. vii). On the last day of their summer vacation on the New England shore, the twins, just 13 years old, took a boat into the inland waters:

. . . we swam around the boat, and then a little puff of wind—the boat was carried off and away and headed for the outlet and the sea. Suddenly filled with panic we did our best to overtake it, swimming as swiftly as was possible; but this we saw was hopeless, a futile thing to do—to waste strength necessary to swim ashore. We were lost and terrified—Grace's strength already spent. Was she clinging to me? No, she was not, she was still beside me in the water, swimming still. What was it she was saying? Clearly I heard her voice; as though I myself were speaking the words, she said, "My darling Mary, how I love you. . . ."

Then there was silence and I saw she was not there beside me. Where was she? Where was I?

I called to her, "Float, Grace, get over on your back, float, keep on floating."

And where was I? What was I doing? Where was I going?

"Float, Grace," I called, and with all the strength that still remained I swam, I kept on swimming towards the shore and always calling, "Float, Grace, keep floating" [p. 126f.].

In an Afterword, Bolton closes her memoir: "I am an old woman now and full of many memories, but those which I have here evoked have for me still the strange and wonderful completeness of having lived another's life that was at the same time my own" (p. 128).

PERSONIFICATION OF DEATH

The skeleton has been used to represent death since ancient times, but in two different ways: as the skeleton of an individually deceased, or as personification. The distinction has been familiar to iconography at least since Lessing (1769) established it in his pioneering work. The skeleton personifying death became very popular in late Gothic art—Hans Holbein's slightly later *Dance of Death* is best known (fig. 1)—and again in baroque art. The now familiar symbols—the scythe (the "grim reaper!"), the hourglass—became fixed emblems of death.

This vogue has subsided, though Gottlieb (1959) goes too far when she says that the "modern artists do not represent death by personification because the spirit of allegory is alien to them" (p. 185). Käthe Kollwitz, who lost a young son in World War I, depicted death as a skeleton in her graphic work, sometimes as a relieving friend, but mostly as an attacker. Alfred Kubin, whom Gottlieb rightly lists among the modern artists, presented death as skeleton in his *Blätter mit dem Tod* in 1918 (fig. 2). Death so appears in Bergman's film *The Seventh Seal,* but characteristically in a medieval context.

On the whole, the spirit of personification is indeed alien to modern feeling, though children may not have followed the trend. Nagy (1948), whose paper, an early and thorough

Figure 1. Hans Holbein the Younger: "The Child"

Woodcut. From *The Dance of Death*
From the original in the Lessing J. Rosenwald
Collection, Rare Book and Special Collections
Division, Library of Congress, Washington, D.C.

study, has come to be considered a classic in American thana-
tology, found personification of death prominent among the
reactions of the children she studied: from ages 5 to 9, "death
is most often personified and thought of as a contingency"
(p. 80f.)—the child's idea is that you die if Death graps you
(fig. 1)—although she is here referring to both possibilities:
"Personification of death takes place in two ways: death is
imagined as a separate person, or else death is identified with
the dead" (p. 88). We quote one example:

Figure 2.   Alfred Kubin: "The Mask of Death"

Pen drawing (1918). From Kubin's *Dance of Death and Other Drawings.*
New York: Dover Publications, 1972

B.G. (4,9): "Death does wrong."
"How does it do wrong?"
"Stabs you to death with a knife."
"What is death?"
"A man."
"What sort of a man?"
"Death-man."
"How do you know?"
"I saw him."
"Where?"
"In the grass. I was gathering flowers."

"How did you recognize him?"
"I knew him."
"But how?"
"I was afraid of him" [p. 90].

As Murphy (1959) pointed out, Nagy's results may well have sprung from "historical, sociocultural or specific local conditions" (p. 321f.). Her material was collected in and around Budapest, apparently in the 1930s. At that time Hungary was still a semifeudal country and medieval traditions may well have been relatively vigorous. Current observations do not seem to bear out Nagy's findings about the personification of death; it seems very doubtful whether a repetition of her study with American children of today would bring similar results.

Where personification is found in the recent literature, it does, however, touch a very responsive chord, for example, in the autobiography of Jean-Paul Sartre (1964), who lost his father as an infant. Before we quote from it a brief remark on the translation is in order. In French, as in all Romance languages, the word for "death" is feminine—*la mort*. This gives the personification of death a certain flavor and direction. We therefore refer to death as "she."

> I saw death. I was 5 years old. She lay in wait for me. In the evening she loitered on the balcony, pressed her snout against the window, I saw her but did not dare say anything. One time we encountered her on Quai Voltaire, an old lady, tall and crazy, dressed in black, she mumbled as I passed, "This child, I'll put him in my pocket." Another time she took the shape of an excavation. That was in Arcachon. . . . I was fearful because I had been told that Gabriel [our host] was sick and would die. I played horse, listlessly hopping around the house. Suddenly I noticed a dark hole: the cellar, it had been opened. Somehow that signified to me terror and solitude. I turned, and singing at the top of my voice I fled [p. 76].

The "singing at the top of his voice" clearly served as a defense against overwhelming anxiety, against the child's ego's fear of annihilation. Sartre continues:

At that time I had a date with death every night in my bed. It was a ritual: I had to lie on my left side, with the back to the wall. Trembling I waited, and she appeared, in the conventional shape of the skeleton with the scythe. With that I had permission to turn on my right side, and I could sleep in peace [p. 76f.].

What was death? A person and a threat. The person was crazy, and the threat was this: Shadowy jaws could open up anywhere, in broad daylight, and snap at me. There was a horrible reverse side of things, you saw it if you lost your mind, and to die was to drive insanity to its extreme and be engulfed by it [p. 78].

William H. Hudson (1918), best known as the author of *Green Mansions,* relates his feelings after recovering from typhoid at age 15:

I had lived till now in a paradise of vivid sense-impressions in which all thoughts came to me saturated with emotion, and in that mental state reflection is well-nigh impossible. Even the idea of death, which had come as a surprise, had not made me reflect. Death was a person, a monstrous being who had sprung upon me in my flowery paradise and had inflicted a wound with a poisoned dagger in my flesh [p. 292].

BUILDING UP DEFENSES: REJECTION OF DEATH

Children who grow up in a religious family receive some consolation from the thoughts of heaven. Those who live in the Here and Now of a hostile world have to dissociate themselves in fantasy or in acting out from the thoughts of their not living forever or of accepting the death of a loved one.

In role playing, the child can become the aggressor rather than the victim and can build up good defenses to ward off anxieties. The American Halloween customs, where young children may dress as witches, ghosts, goblins, or skeletons, lessen the anxiety of the imagined danger of being attacked.

Working with preschool children in Vienna shortly after World War II, I (E. N. P.) saw a dramatic change in a young girl's behavior following St. Nicholas Day, which is December

6. The "Niccolo" comes during the night, accompanied by the "Krampus," a representation of the devil, who threatens to put children in his hopper. The Niccolo brings gifts (apples, oranges, nuts) for the "good" children's stockings, while the "bad" ones get only coal and potatoes from the Krampus. Adolescents love to dress up as Niccolo and Krampus and haunt their neighborhoods on the eve of December 6, terrifying many young children.

To counteract these fears, we suggested to the children that on December 5 they could dress up in any way they wanted, and we talked about who they wanted to be. Five-year-old Ann, whose home had been bombed, lived with her mother in a cellar apartment, never spoke to any adult, and only whispered to some girls in her group. Asked about who she wanted to be, she said barely audibly, "A Krampus." She looked like an angelic Krampus, in her black leotards with red tail and cap and with her sweet smile. She also wanted apples and nuts to give to the others. From that day on she talked. We had neither the time nor the skill to look into her background or to work with her elderly, very unfriendly mother; but at least this acting out—her being the devil rather than the one caught by him and taken to hell—had freed her.

Anna Freud and Dorothy Burlingham (1943) relate how children who lost their fathers in air raids did not mention their experience for many months. Speech did not serve as an outlet until the feelings about the father's death had been dealt with in some other way. "The outlet into conscious thought and speech with consequent relief in their behaviour is unluckily denied to some of our children who would be most in need of it" (p. 139). In Vienna we did not have the opportunity to find the roots of the child's worries, as they are told so well in *War and Children* in Bertie's story (pp. 124–128), but at least Ann could safely begin public school a few months later.

When death has to be rejected by a child to be tolerated, the painting *The Dead Mother and Her Child* (1899) by Edvard Munch the Norwegian may serve as a moving example of how to protect the ego (fig. 3). The girl not only turns away from

Figure 3.   Edvard Munch: *The Dead Mother and the Child*

Oil on cardboard. Bremen, Kunsthalle

the mother but also has to hold her ears—she does not want to see or hear of the tragedy. Munch was 5 years old when he lost his mother, and subsequently a number of his siblings, who all died from tuberculosis. Illness, isolation, pain, and death became his frequent subjects in painting. He once said: "Death is pitch dark, but colors are light. . . . To die is as if one's eyes had been put out and one cannot see anything any more. . . . One is abandoned by all. They have slammed the door and are gone" (Hodin, 1972, p. 93). Another of his paintings, *Life and Death* (1897), conveys a message of biological immortality. Buried in the earth is a woman from whom plants and flowerlike shapes arise.

A 3-year-old as quoted by the Russian writer Chukovsky (1963) expresses a similar idea of restitution: "They bury old people, that is, they plant them in the ground and from them grow little children like flowers" (p. 48).

Another child, 3½ years old, quoted by Anthony (1971) from his mother's diary, asked how plants come up in spring, not having shown above ground in winter. After an explanation he said: "When shall we all be dead and gone and then come back again?" (p. 26).

A possible connection with castration anxiety is indicated by the interrelated questions of a 6-year-old and Piaget's (1959) comment on them:

> "Caterpillars turn into butterflies, then shall I turn into a little girl?"—No—"Why?"—"Why has it [a dead caterpillar] grown quite small? When I die shall I also grow quite small?"
>
> [Piaget adds in a footnote:] These last two questions correspond to two spontaneous ideas of childhood which are well known to psycho-analysts: that it is possible to change one's sex, and that after death one becomes a child again [p. 177; italics omitted].

He does not specify which psychoanalysts he has in mind, but he could have referred, e.g., to Hug-Hellmuth (1912).

DENIAL OF DEATH

Denial of the finality of death in poetry, familiar from such poems as Wordsworth's "We Are Seven," is also used by writers who cannot bear the loss of a child. The German poet Friedrich Rückert (1872) wrote a whole series (420 poems), *Kindertotenlieder,* to manage his grief when two of his daughters died of scarlet fever. Some became widely known since Gustav Mahler set them to music. Poem 36 shows that not only the siblings, but Rückert himself needed to deny the finality of death to bear his loss:

The servant comes to tell the children
Their sister has died. They hear it said,
And yet with one voice say the brothers:
  It is not true, she is not dead.
They see her white, they see her lying,
Her lip so pale that was so red,
And whisper softly as replying:
  It is not true, she is not dead.
They see the mother weeping, waning,
The father's tears his heart has bled,
And yet their chorus is remaining:
  It is not true, she is not dead.
And when the day came and the hours
To lay her in her final bed,
To lower her beneath the flowers:
  It is not true, she is not dead.
May she remain your sister longer,
May every year her beauty spread
And may your love grow ever stronger—
  It is not true, she is not dead.

Hermann Hesse (1960) ends his poem "Kleiner Knabe" ("Little Boy") thus:

Grownup people die:
Uncle, grandpapa.
But I, I shall remain
Ever, ever here.

A similar feeling of omnipotence was expressed by a 4½-year-old boy who "looked out of the bus window at a funeral procession and said, with serenity: 'Everyone will die, but I'll remain' " (Chukovsky, 1963, p. 46f.).

Three great writers of our century present themselves as adult witnesses to a child's death. The agony of a boy dying from plague is the more passionate because of Camus's (1947) clinical tone. Aldous Huxley (1928) and Thomas Mann (1948) each have a haunting chapter in their novels describing the death of a young boy from meningitis. We heard it said that Mann alarmed his family by depicting little Nepomuk, the extraordinarily charming child who dies, as looking and acting like one of his grandsons. Did Mann try to deny the possibility of losing this child by describing (thus magically averting) this most terrible death?

In children the denial can be observed more directly. Few 5-year-olds will be as certain as a boy Chukovsky quotes: "To die—that's very bad. That's for ever." And another child: "She tried to persuade us and her grandmother not to die until she was grown up and would find medicine against old age and death. 'Because there must not be any death'" (p. 58). The same feeling of omnipotence is still operating here.

The finality of death is clearly doubted by children in the Hampstead Nursery reports (A. Freud and Burlingham, 1944).

> Susan, four and one-half, who lost her father in the raids [said]: "My father is deaded, he has gone far away to Scotland; he will come back, much later when I am quite big." . . .
>
> [Same child:] "My daddy is coming next Sunday. Yes, yes, he is coming Sunday. You will see, he will bring me the biggest piece of chocolate you have ever seen."
>
> Bertie, five and one-half, whose father was killed in the raids: . . . "Why can't all killed daddies come back and be little babies and come to the mummies again?"
>
> Peter, four, whose father was killed in the raids: . . . "My Daddy is taking me to the Zoo to-day. He told me last night; he comes every night and sits on my bed and talks to me" [p. 107f.].

The irreversibility of death is questioned constantly by these children. For these boys in the oedipal period the magnification of the father's virtues and powers may aid the process of identification, but it may also camouflage their hidden death wishes.

We also find fantasies about death wishes, this time against siblings, in spontaneously written stories of children. The reversibility of death, a final denial or use of magic power, mitigates the guilt feelings of the writer. Nancy, a child I (E.N.P.) taught many years ago, wrote the following story at age 7:

> There was once a little girl who did not have any father and mother. And she had a little brother who was very good. Once sister said to brother: "Go and get breakfast" and brother says: "if nothing will happen to me I'll go." Brother went and a car passed and ran him over. And little sister cried and cried. A fairy came and said: "Why do you cry so hard?" "Oh my!" said sister, "my little brother died." "Don't worry, I'll make him come to life again," said the fairy.

When Nancy was 8, no good fairy came to the rescue any longer. She had to carry the guilt of her death wishes all by herself.

How a Mother Lost 4 Children

A 6-year-old girl wanted to cross the street with a 3-year-old. The little child wanted to break loose from her sister's hand, the 6-year-old saw her friend and let go of the little one and ran over to her friend. Just then the little girl sat down right in the middle of the streetcar tracks and started to play with sand. All of a sudden a streetcar came along, the big girl did not look at all and the little one was run over and was dead immediately. Now the older child finally wanted to go home, and called the little one, but she did not come. Then she saw many people stand around and as she could not find the little one she started to cry. A policeman came and asked her why she cried. And she says: "My sister got lost, she had a blue coat on." "Yes, said the policeman, she got run over; she is dead." First she did not want to believe it, but when she saw it she sure did. She cried loud with fear and fainted and after she came to she took the little sister but did not dare to go home. Since she wandered around she got lost and did not find the way home anymore.

As the oldest of three children, Nancy had often felt resentful and burdened by having to watch the little ones. The fourth child in the story's title referred to a stillbirth the mother had suffered at that time. When I saw Nancy 40 years later as a well-established adult, she had many memories of her school days, but none of these stories.

A recurrence of the oedipal feelings is strongly expressed in a poem by an 11-year-old French boy who was living alone with his mother who suffered from heart disease. The mother's denial to the boy of the father's death played into this:

> I'd like to know, Mummy,
> Why you always cry
> When I talk of dear Daddy.
> Yet you have told me
> That he is getting better.
> Come, Mummy,
> Stop these lies.
> They don't become you.
> I know quite well
> That Daddy has left us for ever.
> So why isolate us
> In our great pain?
> Lean on
> Your little boy
> Who will love you for two [Heuyer et al., 1955, p. 228].

REACTIONS TO CATASTROPHES

In *War and Children* Anna Freud and Dorothy Burlingham (1943) describe that many months elapsed after bombings before the children began to draw pictures of, or to dictate letters about, what had happened. One child dictated: "my pussy-cat was hurt by a bomb and was hanging on the guard" (p. 66); another said, "my pussy-cat was thrown away" (p. 67).

> The children who lost their fathers in air raids never mentioned anything of their experience for many months. . . . Then after a year, two of them at least told the complete story with no details left out. In all these instances speech does not serve as an outlet for the emotion which is attached to the happening. It is rather the other way round. The child begins to talk about the incident when the feelings which were aroused by it have been dealt with in some other manner [p. 67].

It is interesting to compare these young children who had loving care after the catastrophe with the 9-year-old girl in

Boyer's *Jeux interdits* ("Forbidden Games"), both a book and a film. We witness her tragedy in a crowd of refugees machine-gunned by a German plane. When the parents are killed, she leaves them behind but takes her dead dog with her on the flight South. She finds refuge in a peasants' home where she and the young son become close friends. They secretly bury the dog and then take to collecting dead animals, also killing small ones, and establish a hidden cemetery for which they steal crosses. This morbid game becomes their whole life, as if having and tending the graveyard were soothing the guilt and terror of having left the dead parents and being left by them. Since there was nobody who helped this child to talk about her loss and helped establish her mourning, she reacted in this macabre way.

Wolfgang Borchert, in a short and gripping story (1949), describes a 9-year-old boy who sits day and night in the shambles of his bombed home to protect the body of his 4-year-old brother buried under the debris from rats that he fears would eat the corpse.

What makes it so chilling to read these reports on children coping with death in wartime, be they scientific observations as in the case of the Hampstead Nurseries, be they fiction as with Boyer and Borchert, is the children's familiarity with catastrophic death, so inappropriate for their age. It is difficult to decide whether children under conditions of modern war come to understand death earlier, or whether on the contrary they become so familiar with death because they are not yet able to understand its awesomeness and finality and yet are pushed into it and have to come to terms with it.

Some Theoretical Questions

It would be easier to understand the apparent precocity of children in war if we knew at which age or developmental stage a realistic notion of death emerges under normal conditions; but this we do not exactly know. Nagera (1970) rather understates the case when he says that "there is some disagreement" on this point, for he goes on to cite one psychoanalytic study that ascribes the formation of a reasonably realistic concept of death to children of 3½ to 4, and another to children of 10 to 11 (p. 361).

Much empirical research will be needed to narrow this gap. Bluebond-Langner (1977) reviewed a variety of studies in this area and reported on some new work. Our material furnishes but a modest contribution. It suggests that the truth, as so often, may lie somewhere in the middle. It is reasonable to hypothesize that comprehension of death may depend on the solution of the oedipus complex. As the need to grapple with his death wishes is lessened, the child can use the cooler climate of the latency years to look at death more objectively.

"Neo-Freudians" have reproached psychoanalysis with neglecting social and historical factors. Freud, however, has actually pointed out how war affects attitudes toward death (1915, especially p. 291f.). He knew this decades before his apprehensions materialized in the atrocities of our more recent wars.

Freud (1917) brought out how fate and chance determine a child's acquaintance with death, and so may set the course of his development when he stressed the importance which the deaths of his younger siblings had for the boy Goethe. In those days, more than 200 years ago, it was not war that did it, but infant mortality (Mitchell, 1966, p. 35). It almost seems as though a malignant power saw to it that there was always one or the other scourge to keep children acquainted with death. Pestilence handed the reins to War. Now the silhouette of the third apocalyptic horseman, Famine, presently raging in distant parts of the world, begins to loom on our horizon.

The question at which stage a clear concept of death develops leads to the more generally significant question whether fear of death evolves out of life experience or is inborn; for it is difficult to imagine how a fear could exist before its object can be grasped. Of course, as the history of concept development in the physical sciences has abundantly shown, our inability to imagine a phenomenon does not keep it from occurring. That many generations ago people could not visualize the surface of the earth as anything but flat does not prevent it from being curved.

The view that the fear of death is inborn in man and beast

and that it acts as a most powerful force in the mental development of the human individual has been propounded by philosophers (Schopenhauer, 1818, especially Book IV). It has again been placed much more in the foreground of public consciousness through Becker's influential book (1973). The question is part of the larger one whether—and if so, by what mechanism—mental contents or dispositions can be inherited. While Jung based his system on an unequivocal answer, Freud refrained from rushing in where angels fear to tread; though in some more or less *obiter dicta* (see 1919, p. 241f.) he seems to lean toward inheritance.

On the whole, though, it seems more natural to psychoanalytic thinking to believe that interest in how life ends would emerge as a corollary to the interest in how it begins. Piaget (1923, pp. 178, 206ff.) takes the opposite view: "the idea of death sets the child's curiosity in action, precisely because, if every cause is coupled with a motive, then death calls for a special explanation. The child will therefore look for the distinguishing criteria of life and of death, and this will lead him in a certain measure to replace precausal explanation" (p. 206).

While these theoretical considerations focus on the individual's attitude toward death as a general phenomenon which the child may hear about or observe but which does not necessarily have a direct personal impact, this study is more concerned with that impact when it strikes. How do children handle their grief?

The first personal encounter with death is often the loss of a loved pet. While young children seem heartbroken at the death of a pet (fig. 4), such clearly visible reactions are rarely reported at the death of a family member; their absence is often misinterpreted as "not caring." Children have to be encouraged and helped to grieve and should not be excluded from the family's mourning. Anna Freud and Dorothy Burlingham (1943) explain the difficulties that arise when the surviving parent's wish precludes the staff from letting a child know of the death of the other parent. As we found out in our hospital experience, one has to allow thoughts or reactions to

Figure 4. Roger Wrenn: Child and Dead Dog

Photo "Hit and Run." From Hanns Reich, *Children of Many Lands*. Hill & Wang, 1958

death to come into the open and be talked about to retain the children's trust and to support them in showing their grief, and to clarify their threatening fantasies about their own danger.

Ritual is very important in the child's working through the experience of death. It can help or hamper the child's building of his defenses. We have seen rituals in two different roles, though both are essentially obsessive-compulsive defenses. Rituals developed by adults, and sometimes rigidified by long tradition, may be valuable. They may serve as vessels for the child to pour his anxiety into so that it may be contained. They can also be frightening and damaging. For O'Casey, as his story shows, the ritual was traumatic. Reports of similar reactions were collected by Mitchell (1966, pp. 51–54). Rituals on the other hand that a child invents (Sartre, 1964; Boyer, 1968) may limit and structuralize his neurotic needs.

Historic change intrudes in all these matters, as it did in the matter of infant mortality and war forcing death on the child's attention. We are referring to a phenomenon that is by now well known. In fact, the very attention that has been paid to it may have helped to reverse it. The trend has been particularly well formulated by Ariès (1974):

> Geoffrey Gorer . . . has shown clearly how death has become a taboo and how in the twentieth century it has replaced sex as the principal forbidden subject. Formerly children were told that they were brought by the stork, but they were admitted to the great farewell scene about the bed of the dying person. Today they are initiated in their early years to the physiology of love; but when they no longer see their grandfather and express astonishment, they are told that he is resting in a beautiful garden among the flowers. Such is "The Pornography of Death" . . . and the more society was liberated from the Victorian constraints concerning sex, the more it rejected things having to do with death [p. 92f.].

Thus, what Freud (1930) predicted has come to pass: "And now it is to be expected that the other of the two 'Heavenly Powers', eternal Eros, will make an effort to assert himself in the struggle with his equally immortal adversary" (p. 145). A year later, he added a last sentence to this paragraph: "But who can foresee with what success and with what results?"

One may wonder indeed whether the reemergence of Eros from the dark closet where societal forces of Freud's day confined it, followed by a similar banishment of Thanatos from which he is now again emerging, has taken quite the forms that Freud anticipated. Be this as it may, we have to maintain our effort to humanize both heavenly powers: as scientists and scholars, we must keep trying to penetrate into the thoughts and feelings of children; as practitioners, to help them carry the burdens that press on them. This remains our professional calling.

BIBLIOGRAPHY

AGEE, J. (1957), *A Death in the Family.* New York: Grosset & Dunlap; London: Peter Owen.

ANTHONY, S. (1971), *The Discovery of Death in Childhood and After.* New York: Basic Books, 1972.

ARIES, P. (1974), *Western Attitudes toward Death.* Baltimore: Johns Hopkins Univ. Press.

BECKER, E. (1973), *The Denial of Death.* New York: Free Press.

BLUEBOND-LANGNER, M. (1977), Meanings of Death to Children. In: *New Meanings of Death,* ed. H. Feifel. New York: McGraw-Hill, pp. 47–66.

BOLTON, I. (1966), *Under Gemini: A Memoir.* New York: Harcourt Brace & World.

BORCHERT, W. (1949), Nachts schlafen die Ratten doch. In: *Das Gesamtwerk.* Hamburg: Rowohlt, pp. 236–239.

BOYER, F. (1968), *Jeux interdits.* Paris: Denoël; Le livre de poche, 1969.

CAMUS, A. (1946), *The Plague.* New York: Modern Library.

CHEKHOV, A. (1887), The Runaway. In: *The Stories of Anton Tchekov,* ed. R. N. Linscott. New York: Modern Library, 1932, pp. 306–313.

CHUKOVSKY, K. (1963), *From Two to Five.* Berkeley: Univ. Calif. Press.

FEIFEL, H., ed. (1959), *The Meaning of Death.* New York: McGraw-Hill.

FREUD, A. & BURLINGHAM, D. (1943), *War and Children.* New York: Medical Warbooks.

———— ———— (1944), *Infants Without Families.* New York: Int. Univ. Press.

FREUD, S. (1915), Thoughts for the Times on War and Death. *S.E.,* 14 : 273–302.

———— (1917), A Childhood Recollection from *Dichtung und Wahrheit. S.E.,* 17 : 145–156.

———— (1919), The Uncanny. *S.E.,* 17 : 217–256.

———— (1930), Civilization and Its Discontents. *S.E.,* 21 : 59–145.

FURMAN, E. (1974), *A Child's Parent Dies.* New Haven: Yale Univ. Press.

GORKY, M. (1913), My Childhood. *Autobiography of Maxim Gorky,* vol. 1. New York: Citadel Press.

GOTTLIEB, C. (1959), Modern Art and Death. In: Feifel (1959), pp. 157–188.

HESSE, H. (1960), Kleiner Knabe. In: *Gesammelte Werke,* 1. Frankfurt: Suhrkamp, 1970, pp. 146–147.*

HEUYER, G., LEBOVICI, S., & GIABICANI, A. (1955), Le sens de la mort chez l'enfant. *Rev. Neuro-Psychiat. Hyg. Ment. l'Enfance,* 3 : 219–251.*

*The passages quoted in the text were translated into English by Robert Plank.

HODIN, J. P. (1972), *Edvard Munch* (1863–1943). New York: Prager.

HUDSON, W. H. (1918), *Far Away and Long Ago.* New York: Dutton.

HUG-HELLMUTH, H. VON (1912), The Child's Concept of Death. *Psychoanal. Quart.,* 34 : 499–516, 1965.

HUXLEY, A. (1928), *Point Counterpoint.* New York: Random House.

LESSING, G. E. (1769), Wie die Alten den Tod gebildet. In: *Gotthold Ephraim Lessings Werke,* 6 : 405–462. Munich: Carl Hanser, 1974.

MANN, T. (1948), *Doktor Faustus.* Vienna: Bermann-Fischer.

MITCHELL, M. E. (1966), *The Child's Attitude to Death.* New York: Schocken, 1967.

MURPHY, G. (1959), Discussion. In: Feifel (1959), pp. 317–340.

NAGERA, H. (1970), Children's Reactions to the Death of Important Objects. *This Annual,* 25 : 360–400.

NAGY, M. H. (1948), The Child's Theories concerning Death. In: Feifel (1959), pp. 79–98.

O'CASEY, S. (1939), *I Knock at the Door.* New York: Macmillan.

PIAGET, J. (1923), *The Language and Thought of the Child.* London: Routledge & Kegan Paul, 1959.

RÜCKERT, F. (1872), *Kindertotenlieder.* Frankfurt: Sauerländer.*

SARTRE, J.-P. (1964), *Les Mots.* Paris: Gallimard.*

SCHOPENHAUER, A. (1818), *The World as Will and Idea.* London: Routledge & Kegan Paul, 1883.

SOLNIT, A. J. & GREEN, M. (1959), Psychologic Considerations in the Management of Deaths on Pediatric Hospital Services: I. *Pediatrics,* 24 : 106–112.

—————— (1963), The Pediatric Management of the Dying Child: II. In: *Modern Perspectives in Child Development,* ed. A. J. Solnit & S. A. Provence. New York: Int. Univ. Press, pp. 217–228.

WILDGANS, A. (1928), *Musik der Kindheit.* Leipzig: Staakmann.*

YUDKIN, S. (1968), Death and the Young. In: *Concern with Death,* ed. A. Toynbee. New York: McGraw-Hill, pp. 46–55.

Acknowledgments. The authors wish to thank the following publishers for their permission to quote copyrighted material:

Grosset & Dunlap, New York, and Peter Owen, Ltd., London (James Agee, *A Death in the Family*);

Citadel Press, Secaucus, N.J. (Maxim Gorky, *My Childhood*);

Macmillan Publishing Co., Inc., New York, and Macmillan Press Ltd., Houndmills, England (*I Knock at the Door* by Sean O'Casey; copyrighted 1939 by Macmillan Publishing Co., Inc., renewed 1967 by Eileen O'Casey, Breon O'Casey and Shivaun Kenig).

*The passages quoted in the text were translated into English by Robert Plank.

On the Other Side of Oz

Psychoanalytic Aspects of Fairy Tales

STANLEY H. CATH, M.D. AND CLAIRE CATH, M.Ed.

FAIRY TALES, CHILDREN'S STORIES, AND BEDTIME RITUALS ARE serious business. In part, at least, they provide relief from tension when the need for sleep is countered by unconscious wishes to rework the residues of the day's problems and to hold on to loved ones. Bedtime stories may be thought of as way stations into the world of fantasy and dreams, as the ego's functioning and the hold on reality are progressively relaxed. Anticipation of sleep may bring not only fears of separation, but also changes in body and self images. These threats to cohesiveness are often associated with the transition from waking to sleeping states and enhance the possibilities for splitting, dissociation, and fragmentation of the self.

While fairy tales serve many masters (Waelder, 1960), we can select only a few for discussion. We will touch on the child's obvious and not so obvious attempts to deal with eruptions of instinctual anxiety and on the hierarchy of defenses mustered against these eruptions: the creative subliminatory functions of the ego ideal and superego of the child who listens and the parent who reads.

Claire Cath is the Program Coordinator and an outreach worker on the Family Support Program at Tufts New England Medical Center, Boston, Mass. Stanley Cath is an Associate Clinical Professor at Tufts New England Medical Center, and a member of the Boston Psychoanalytic Society.

It is generally accepted that parents, during the maturation of their offspring, have another opportunity to rework some of their own childhood conflicts related to age-specific tasks at hand. This process of identification by the adult with the child may be clearly in evidence when he reads to or plays with his children. In such intimate personal interactions, the reader and listener may be unconsciously working through similar issues, but find that they are syntonically or dystonically excited, fascinated, absorbed, or repelled by the creative contribution of the author. This is in part due to the fact that, almost invariably, these shared themes have to do with disguised parent-child relationships, even though thinly layered with tragicomic or seemingly far-fetched ludicrous veneers. This disguise reaches its acme most covertly and cleverly in fairy tales and nursery rhymes. Conflicts between generations can be subtly revealed and at times openly discussed quite safely through the author's usually innovative and creative versions of interpersonal and intrapsychic realities. His mechanisms include symbolization, displacement, distancing, and distortion. So it is that most fairy tales begin, "Once upon a time . . ." and often take us to a strange or fantastic land with highly improbable combinations of animal and human forms. Each of these mechanisms—animism, displacement, distancing, and distortion—enhances the effect of the other, making it safe to accomplish the purpose at hand—the consolidation of the love-hate bond by means of controlling the fear of the consequences of separation from others and from the waking self at bedtime. The process of such ambivalent deathlike separation may be counterpointed by the adaptive binding and affirmation of good winning over evil in the transition to the inner dream world. This transition may be facilitated if closeness, goodness, and lifegiving forces are affirmed, while the powers of the about-to-be-encountered primary process are, as it were, for the moment at least denied. When it works, this interaction euphemistically might be called "fairytale bedtime prophylactic therapy."

In this presentation, we look at some of the themes in *The Wizard of Oz,* and try to understand why this particular, relatively modern, fairy tale has had such enormous appeal to readers, listeners, and movie goers for over three quarters of a century.

SUMMARY OF STORY

The Wizard of Oz, written in 1900, is about a latency-age orphan, Dorothy, seen through the eyes of the author, L. Frank Baum. Having had four sons, Baum longed for a daughter, whom he would have named Dorothy.[1]

As the story opens, the heroine is living in a "barren, colorless, empty, dead and infertile" environ. (The author accentuates this depressive chord as he reiteratively describes each scene as "gray, gray, gray.") There seems to be an absence of warmth in Dorothy's relations with her affectless Aunt Em and Uncle Henry, who find her noisy spontaneity painful. This is in contrast to the warm closeness she enjoys with the farm hands and the little dog, Toto.

From the psychoanalytic point of view, it is significant that the threat of losing this transitional object triggers the nightmare which follows. Toto has been angrily barking at the woman next door. This "mean" neighbor, seemingly devoid of empathy or love,[2] arrives with the sheriff and actually takes Toto away in a basket on her bicycle. The aunt and uncle seem helpless, and Dorothy goes to her bedroom agitated and afraid (to be sure, Toto escapes). The ensuing cyclone depicts Dorothy's intrapsychic conflict, her rage and frustration over her loss, and her fear of fragmentation of the self.

But the cyclone also is Dorothy's vehicle to enter Baum's many lands. The little girl, her dog, her house are spun away by the wind to land in Oz. When she opens the door, to her wonderment, she finds herself among friendly, happy, dancing, little people. Yet, here, too, sudden violence seeps in. In landing, the house from Kansas fell on a witch; now only her magic silver shoes emerge from under a corner of the build-

1. Dorothea, gift of the gods.
2. In the film she plays the part of one of the cruel witches.

ing. Dorothy, although innocently responsible for the death of the wicked Witch of the East, finds to her surprise that she is warmly greeted as a heroine by the tiny people who are protected by the good Witch of the North. This lady not only miraculously knows Dorothy's name, but matter-of-factly calls her a "noble sorceress" because by *accidently* killing the wicked Witch, Dorothy has freed from bondage these little people, called by the suggestive name, "Munchkins."[3] (This feat seemed beyond the capacities of the Witch of the North.)

This good Witch explains the strange, but seemingly natural, juxtaposition of good and evil in such a happy place: there were two bad Witches, one of the West and one of the East, but the latter now is happily deceased.

There are also two good Witches of the North and South. Dorothy professes to be astonished by such goings-on for her Aunt Em had taught her that there were no witches left in the world. As in all children's stories, Dorothy obediently listens and naïvely follows the advice, rules, customs, and social practices as reverently outlined by the seemingly powerful, although at times strangely limited, Witch. Dorothy soon learns there is a great Wizard, who dwells in the City of the Emeralds. He is represented as more powerful than all of the witches together, but he remains an idealized, inaccessible object.

Then, for the first time a most important theme which runs like a red thread through the story is introduced: although she is in this land of great beauty and magical power, Dorothy expresses a great need to get home (p. 197). But the Munchkins seem unable to help her find the way. Then the good Witch of the North balances her tall pointed cap on her nose, whereupon it changes into a slate on which is written: "Let Dorothy go to the City of Emeralds." The Witch suddenly seems very sure that the Wizard will be able to fulfill Dorothy's wish if she will only undertake the "perilous journey."[4] The

3. William Niederland suggests this is a condensed form of *Menschenkinder* (kindly children).

4. A common literary dream symbol for a transition into or out of a depression, for example, Dante's *Inferno* (a mid-life crisis) or psychoanalysis.

Emerald City just happens to be in the center of Oz and Dorothy must walk there on a yellow brick road which passes through a "sometimes pleasant and sometimes rough and terrible" country (p. 34).[5]

The kind Witch, with no explanation for her actions, presents Dorothy with the magic silver shoes of the dead witch and kisses her gently on her forehead, clearly leaving a round shiny mark. This mark later not only magically protects Dorothy from harm, but becomes a badge of admission to forbidden places including the inner sanctum of the Wizard. With such a double gift from a protective parent, Dorothy, *apparently* innocent of all evil, sets out.

Then follows the part of the story which is best remembered, probably because of the interplay between the animate and the inanimate, the distinctions between them being completely abandoned and "tossed in the wind"; and the free-flowing love between people, animals, and seemingly lifeless things. In gathering a little surrogate family band together, Dorothy first rescues the Scarecrow from a pole. Then they are joined by a Tin Woodsman, who feels the need to be like other people: to have a heart. She gives life and motility to him by oiling his rusted joints. Lastly they are joined by a Lion who longs to have the courage befitting the king of the jungle.

It is fascinating to reflect upon the composition and evolution of character traits of this little band of travelers. It is soon apparent that the Tin Woodsman in search of a heart acts as if he has the most heart of all; the straw Scarecrow in search of brains becomes the leader who has the most spontaneous and cleverest of ideas; and the Lion in the face of danger is the most courageous. Dorothy in search of home is the source of warmth and unification as she assumes the role of caring for all the others. Thus, we have a rescue story par excellence: by mothering all characters, Dorothy secures a nourishing family who in turn protects her on her journey away from home.

5. Yellow bricks are often synonymous with gold bars. It is of interest that Baum once operated a store for miners on their "gold rush" to the West. He was often found on the curb, telling his stories to children rather than minding the store.

One aspect of Baum's version of the Tin Woodsman's history is relatively unknown. Once a man of flesh and blood, he was in love and betrothed to a beautiful Munchkin girl, who had promised to marry him as soon as he could build her "a better house" (p. 56). However, his beloved, like Cinderella, lived with an old woman who, not wanting to lose her services as a house maid, opposed her marrying anyone. This old woman hired a witch to cause the Tin Woodsman, while chopping trees[6] for the house of his bride-to-be, to cut off his leg. After replacing his lost leg with a new one of tin, he returned to his task, but through the terrible enchantment the affectless tragedies continued. Soon he had lost the other leg, both arms, and his head. Finally, he split himself into halves and lost his heart. The evil woman seemed to have won because, without a heart, he no longer loved his betrothed or cared whether they married or not.

After a series of incredible obstacles and miraculous escapes from death, this intrepid band finally reaches the Emerald City. The guard, so impressed by the mark on Dorothy's forehead and her silver shoes, immediately informs the Wizard of their arrival. After an appropriate delay, the Wizard bids them enter for an audience.[7]

Most readers apparently overlook the revelation of "the Wizard's" impotence in dealing with powerful evil women. He will grant the requests of the travelers, who seem so young, naïve, and helpless, only if they take on the terrible task of killing the wicked Witch of the West who still rules in the land of the Winkies.

Thus begins the second odyssey in which Dorothy again accomplishes another miraculous feat, "innocently." At the denouement, the Witch has kidnapped Dorothy and her friends with the aid of flying monkeys. Completely under her power, they are imprisoned in her remote castle. Then she makes the fatal mistake of personally attempting to take away Dorothy's

6. The word for tree in German is *Baum*.

7. One must always wait at such moments (Delphic oracle, doctor's offices) to set the proper mood of expectation of the miracle.

magic shoes. Failing because Dorothy refuses to give them up, the Witch in her fury sets the straw man ablaze. Dorothy, so innocently provoked, throws a handily available bucket of water to douse the flames, but accidentally also douses the Witch, causing her to dissolve into "an ugly brown mess." Then she blithely sweeps the "ugly brown mess" out the door.

The return to the Emerald City becomes a third odyssey. There, much to the shock, relief, and disappointment of the little band of travelers, the Wizard is confirmed to be not an imposing, omnipotent and terrifying magician, but a gentle, somewhat sniveling and conniving little old humbug.[8] Yet he does have the redeeming features of a ventriloquist, a manipulator of illusions. Like some fathers, he seems kindly, but a little addled and preoccupied. He attempts to wheedle out of his promise by telling them that they really possess in themselves the very characteristics they are searching for in the external world. But they proceed to talk him into providing what they feel they need to complete themselves, and he does it most reluctantly, with tongue in cheek. Brains for the Scarecrow are made out of a mixture of brain, pins, and needles; a heart is cut out of silk, and filled with sawdust for the Tin Woodsman; and a greenish liquid, which only works inside the body, is provided to give courage to the Lion. Ultimately he devises a plan for Dorothy's still perilous "over the desert" voyage home (p. 233).

They learn that the Wizard is a former circus performer from Omaha, who, like Dorothy herself, had been inadvertently carried to Oz in a balloon by the seemingly ever-present "winds" (furies, fates). He has been living in constant fear that the people in Oz will discover that he is really a fraud, a foreigner, who inwardly longs to give up his throne and return to his home. Tired of being a "lonely humbug," he finally drifts away, still alone, in the balloon that he and Dorothy had secretly built together for their planned escape. Again, capri-

8. We are grateful to Dr. Niederland (1976), who notes that in German *Humbug machen* is to make fun, to act, to pretend.

cious air currents and Toto's unpredictable running away converge to prevent her from getting aboard the balloon in time for their secret romantic "abdication."

Then the good Witch of the South decides to reveal to Dorothy the secret of those magic shoes which Dorothy had "innocently" defended with her life. They have had the power to grant her wish all along. After an appropriately tearful good-bye to her friends, Dorothy claps the heels of her silver shoes together three times, saying, "Take me home to Aunt Em." She whirls through space with the wind whistling past her ears, rolls over and over on the grass, and finds herself sitting on the broad Kansas prairie in front of her aunt and uncle's house, "so glad to be home again" (p. 237).

Some Intrapsychic Themes

THE QUEST FOR ALL-LOVING PARENTS

In the Oz series, we repeatedly encounter the theme of the innocent, or abandoned child, who has set out on an odyssey in search of lost or idealized parents. The hero or heroine is likely to be found in constant threat of destruction by supernatural forces which act as substitutes for intrapsychic regression and the danger of fragmentation. One way for the helpless separated child in danger of such ruptured relationships or fantasied annihilation to survive is through the consistent reappearance and restoration of benevolent parents often in the guise of wise and omnipotent good witches.

But evil witches, their enslaved human or animal creatures, or frightening forces of nature (thick woods, trees that come alive, sleep-producing poppies or darkness) often block the way toward this restitution. Yet even idealized parents or magical new wonders are limited in the inevitable struggle between good and evil, and disillusion and disappoint the child in the attainment of his cherished utopian goal. The chosen mechanisms for building moral structures and containing omnipotent wishes, aggression, and other powerful drives are renunciation and reconciliation. At the same time, however, in all such stories, the impossible always seems possible, love triumphs over hate, and violence is controlled and rejected.

ATTACHMENT TO PAINFUL RELATIONSHIPS

Running away to Utopia is frequently followed by a renunciation of the idealized symbiotic fantasy. This is expressed as: "It's so good to be home." This issue was well stated by the Scarecrow: "I can't understand why you should wish to leave this beautiful country and go back to the dry gray [9] place you call Kansas." Dorothy: "It's because you have no brains. No matter how dreary and gray our homes are, we people of flesh and blood would rather live there than any other country, be it ever so beautiful; there's no place like home" (p. 17). This story suggests there are those who *can* renounce fantasy worlds, in spite of the difficulties in breaking primary attachments to parental witchlike objects. This separation-individuation aspect represents a sensed incompleteness, a threatening weakness of the ego, which motivates the search for the idealized infallible objects (the idealized transference in psychoanalysis).

A striking example of this attachment to painful relationships may be found in battered, failure-to-thrive, or neglected children. Having invested in a painful relationship, such children paradoxically "prefer" an abusive parent to a kindly stranger or to nonsibling peers. Furthermore, a battered child may later identify with this aggressive aspect of his parent. When the affect is repressed and disassociated from the experience, he may himself become a batterer. Giving up such an introject, however negative, would be like giving up an integral, "protective part" of the self because the negative introject has become a part of the cohesive self (ego and superego.) This identification with a negative object is needed to hold in check overwhelming aggression, some of which may be justified by the projection of "badness" onto the child. This

---

9. Baum uses the word "gray" nine times in one paragraph to describe Dorothy's affective surround.

attachment of the abused child to his early, abusing love object
as well as to his painful experience is effectively expressed in
Anne Sexton's (1976) poem, *Red Roses:* [10]

> Tommy is three and when he's bad
> His mother dances with him.
> She puts on the record,
> Red Roses for a Blue Lady
> and throws him across the room.
> Mind you she never laid a hand on him
> only the wall laid a hand on him.
> He gets red roses in different places,
> the head, that time he was as sleepy as
> a river,
> the back, that time he was a broken scarecrow
> the arms, like a diamond had bitten them,
> the leg, twisted like a licorice stick,
> all the dance they did together,
> Blue Lady and Tommy.
>
> You fell, she said, just remember you fell.
> I fell, is all he told the doctors
> in the big hospital. A nice lady came
> and asked him questions but because
> he didn't want to be sent away, he said, I fell.
> He never said anything else although he could talk fine.
> He never told about the music
> or how she'd sing and shout
> holding him up and throwing him.
>
> He pretends he is her ball.
> He tried to fold up and bounce
> but he squashed like fruit.
> For he loves Blue Lady and the spots
> of red roses he gives her.

10. From *45 Mercy Street* by Anne Sexton. Copyright (c) 1976 by Linda
Gray Sexton and Loring Conant, Jr. Reprinted by permission of Houghton
Mifflin Co.

INTRAPSYCHIC REPAIR

Dorothy's dream story might be considered a creative attempt at an intrapsychic repair of a threatened separation created by a wished-for "rupture." This affective anxiety state created a sensation of "cyclonic" fragmentation, precipitated by her "innocent" wish for destruction of her hated, helpless, and depressed parent substitutes. After all, they had seemed unempathic to her physical and emotional well-being.

Dorothy is a latency-age child, struggling intrapsychically to hold on to her object ties, reality sense, and a feeling of belonging. Her tremendous appeal to all children is probably due to her surprising and naïve self-confidence in the face of all kinds of overwhelming symbols of core problem areas. Most child readers are able to identify with such courage and faith in the continuity of self—with the idea that somehow, no matter what the risk, things will work out.

From direct observations of children, we have learned something about the ontogenesis of self and self-confidence as well as of factors in parent-infant interaction that enhance or diminish these attributes (Piaget, 1936; Mahler et al., 1975; Wolff, 1961; Sander, 1975; Samaraweera and Cath, 1977).

The smiling response (4 to 6 months) sets the stage for a sequential "mutual reciprocity" in the 7- to 9-month period. Initiative is gradually linked with an awareness of the capacity to manipulate the environment, an important precursor of awareness of self and self-confidence. By 10 to 15 months this initiative becomes charged with intended motor and aggressive activities which may lead the child away from or toward his mother. Now he actually experiences his own intended rupturing and restoring of their interchanges as her responses to his decisions. This requires a new synthesizing of tolerances for self-generated ambivalent feeling states which are related to continuity of self and continuity of relationships with others. When the child is left alone or going to sleep, this continuity is challenged: the degree of anxiety experienced may relate to the availability of acceptable substitutes both in the animate and inanimate surround (the transitional world) or the capacity to create these substitutes in imagination.

COHESIVENESS AND SPLITTING

When repression replaces splitting as a dominant mode, there are no longer two separate bad (degraded) and good (idealized) objects, but one object that may elicit a multitude of emotional responses and still remain the same (person) from moment to moment (Hartocollis, 1974). As this shift (which in all probability is never completed) occurs, superego development progresses because of minute internalization of these images (Kohut, 1971). With further maturity there is an acceptance of the limitations of self, of others, and even of the idea of death with its ultimate loss of relationships and one's own being. It is generally thought that the interplay with omnipotent idealized objects is essential for development of faith in the self and in one's self-initiated actions. The move from life-nourishing activities to playfulness and from parents to peers requires a background of safety, which is based upon the child's having been the center of affirming attention by someone he regards as omnipotent. By incorporating and internalizing this self-object, the child achieves a sense of separateness and freedom from the source of the object's power, and his need to keep good and evil objects separate is lessened. This is an essential part of the shift to secondary process thinking, which contributes to the capacity to achieve and maintain a cohesive and confident self. If this process, which continues through latency and adolescence, is slowed or halted, and especially if one's body ego is sensed to be defective or actually deformed, for example, if it contains a weakened heart, as was true in Baum's case, the integrative synthesis may not be complete and "the search for a wizard" goes on. Mother or father may then remain split into good and evil, and such split objects are always powerful, inaccessible, and frighteningly awesome. They are especially to be revered if they contain that mixture of magic, sorcery, wit, and charm that is so much a part of the fairy tale world.

These same mothers and fathers, like Dorothy's aunt and uncle, will at times emphatically fail their children. They may either wittingly or unwittingly, sometimes even willingly, expose them to danger or disease. In many fairy tales, these themes or secrets about parental weaknesses are detected and punished, often innocently, or they may be compensated for, defended against, or corrected by concealed innate powers or by loving attempts to protect still another helpless creature, as Dorothy defends the straw man.

CONTINUITY AND A SENSE OF TIME

We have already noted that when initiative and aggression are directed as hostility at an ambivalently regarded parent, a discordance is experienced as an intense fear of self and/or object loss. This loss is often colored by the nature of defective body or self images (narcissistic insults). This regressive discordance may include not only anxiety or other defensive-affective positions, but also alterations in the basic sense of time, self-regulation, and levels of consciousness—phenomena frequently experienced when going to sleep. The stage at which a sense of time and a personal sense of timeless growing develop is therefore relevant to our thesis that the repeated fairy tale is a waystation into the world of sleep. The sense of time is thought to emerge early out of the awareness of one's own heartbeat. Madow and Schaefer (1977) note that the sense of time and timelessness serve, along with other psychic structures with which they are complexly interwoven, several defensive functions. The heartbeat, by its very repetitive, rhythmic nature, assists in controlling panic and aggression. It provides one familiar form of affirmation of continuity and contributes to intrapsychic stability. Thus, as in Oz, the child can be reassured against this panic by the search for a new heart or the reconstruction of a tin man, or of a tick-tock man, or the use of time mechanisms, or many other beating mechanical wonders, all to be found repeatedly in fairy stories, especially those cloaked in the veneer of our mechanical age.

THE REWORKING OF DIFFICULTIES

Fairy tales are capable of fueling not only the child but also adult readers, as they take the opportunity to "while away a pleasant hour before bedtime" (Baum, 1900) with their child. In the magical world of Oz, the overwhelming affect of many mid-life traumas may be projected into the story characters and reworked in the same way as the latency-age child attempts to cope with his problems. Latency-age children have difficulty in synthesizing male and female splits, passive and aggressive strivings, and nurturing and depriving forces in the self and love objects. Therefore, it is not surprising that fairy tale characters often exhibit a shallowness of relationships and affects. These traits reflect the latency child's fluctuations in fidelity and empathy, a fluidity which is further evident in the ease with which characters come together and separate, even as the ego strives for, but fears, deeper personal relatedness. It is reasonable, then, to consider the Scarecrow, the Lion, and Tin Woodsman as representing feared and split-off positive and negative introjects or fragments of the self, along with a sensed lack of heart, brain, and courage.

HELPLESSNESS AND THE MAGICAL STRUGGLE AGAINST IT

The Witch of the West's childlike (bedtime?) fear of the dark seems to represent the child's projection of helplessness and fear of the unknown upon an adultlike figure. The subsequent "innocent" destruction of a witch by water may also be an appropriate identification with the aggressor at bedtime, when children often feel like put-upon and helpless victims of mother's washing. We know that in religion, water has been used as protection against the devil (the unconscious) who shrinks from it, as in exorcism rituals. For Dorothy to dissolve the wicked Witch into an ugly brown mess and virtuously sweep her out of the door may have represented a fitting fantasy revenge. It is consistent with a common urethral fantasy of little boys (and little girls) whose streams of urine possess great magic power.

The revelation of the Wizard as a humbug may be understood on one level as a self-revelation of impotence and, on another, as the process by which an idealized parent is made more realistic (much as the child passes through an idealization phase in order to reach a better level of reality testing). In fairy tales, people and animals are portrayed as desiring or moving toward greater self-control, mature growth, and mastery of the external world. Yet, the child listening to the tales is left free to return to his family and the dependence he originally had desired to leave.

We know that all adolescents and many young adults retain idealized parental imagoes. When reality does not provide the basis for such imagoes, people may construct them in their imagination. Dorothy and her friends insist on idealizing the Wizard, who protests, "How can I help being a humbug when all these people make me do things that everybody knows can't be done?" (p. 188).

One could speculate that Dorothy's friends represent the universal longing for heart, brains, and courage without which the child is helpless. Confronted with this dilemma, the Wizard first tried to reassure, much as a parent does a child, or as we might do with some of our patients, that there were more resources within the self than had been realized. This reassurance was premature and rejected. Additional internalizations of symbolic substitutes, powerful grandiose figures, were needed. This was reworked through another odyssey, another fantasy trip through Oz. So the Wizard remained a potentially grandiose contributor to new strengths, even though he felt unequal to the task. Later, Dorothy forgave him for his limitations and bungling "promises"; for after all, like many parents, he was a good man, albeit a wizard, and he had done his best. At this point she could deny the perils to which he had exposed her and her friends and even the revelation of adult impotence in protecting her from evil women. This represents the maturational task for the child who gradually accepts his parents on more realistic terms. It is also a maturational task for the parents who, having accumulated their own quota of mistakes in raising children, come to forgive their own aged parents for not having been perfect. After all, no one is omnipotent enough to protect one from life's vicissitudes in childhood or adulthood. Thus, on her return home, Dorothy seems to be reconciled to the inevitable and to the "good enough" realities she had left.

CONCLUSION

We have discussed only selected themes of fairy tales and their functions for child listeners and adult readers. In general, within the family's "psychic" interactional system, a discharge of tension between generations is likely. Research, however, is lacking as to how many children lie spellbound and excitedly awake, how many go peacefully to sleep, or how many are fragmented and emotionally overwhelmed.

In all probability, most children do rework age-appropriate themes, relating to unfulfilled cravings in a creative or imaginative synthesis of their fantasy. These attempts are marked by splitting, grandiosity, body-image distortion, and magic. Yet we have also encountered some precocious and compulsive children who very early cannot abide fairy tales and find them "silly." In clinical work we have observed that certain fairy tales or favorite repetitive pieces of literature become symbolic representatives of core problem areas. One patient, intensely envious of a younger, more attractive, and favored sister, saw the film, *Wizard of Oz,* when she was an adolescent. She immediately identified herself as the evil Witch of the West. Later in conflict about her envy of the mothering she was giving her own children, she felt that she deserved the Witch's fate—to be destroyed and discarded.

Like recurrent dreams, favorite fairy tales screen unresolved psychic issues to which it is obligatory to return. In psychoanalysis and psychotherapy such stories and their derivatives may also function as screen memories and be utilized as resistances in neurotic transferences (Schreiber, 1974). A not unfamiliar resistance is a transference to the therapist as a wizard capable either of maintaining illusions or alleviating frightening realities. Such transferences may become an essential phase of the healing relationship evident in early "curative fantasies" (Ornstein, 1977).

From the epigenetic point of view, fairy tales become a preferred context or vehicle in which child and parent can vicariously review and practice the mastery of certain developmental tasks, especially those having to do with the reconciliation of narcissistic discrepancies between the ego ideal and the realities of day-to-day actualizations and frustrations. This occurs in both reader and listener, because intrapsychic issues are similar in childhood and parenthood.

In both parent-reader and child-listener, a regression from the constant strain of reality testing and aspirations associated with necessary limitations of gratifications is facilitated by the special camaraderie of a shared bedtime fantastic voyage. A deep emotional experience may be safely undertaken and shared.

We have stressed that fairy tales are usually read at bedtime when the ego is in the process of relinquishing its grasp on reality and diurnal variations of separation anxiety are, in all probability, at their peak.[11] Marjorie McDonald (1976) stressed the silent and unconscious nature of the process, but we would also point to the prolongation of contact between adult and child who frequently continue to discuss the tale after it has been read. We agree with Bettelheim (1976) and McDonald that at their best, fairy tales foster mastery and are *shared* communicative creative excursions.

When the excursion is successful, it leads to a consolidation of the grandiose self, an affirmation of innocence, and a more realistic appreciation of the "humbug" qualities of adults. For the adult coping with the developmental task of parenthood, it provides a safe distance in a light vein to rework his or her own narcissistic disappointments. This working through is supported and mirrored not only by the empathic parent who guided the perilous journey, but also by the good forces in the

---

11. When rage at "the mother of separation" must be neutralized (Mahler et al., 1975).

fairy tale. These reflect in part the artist's contribution across the ages, and in part the reader's and listener's positive introjects from past internalized relationships. It is the latter which make the meaning of the tale different for each.

The very things that terrify us in fantasy and in our dreams usually become more familiar and less threatening with repetition. The intense affective experience associated with reading fairy tales leads some children to select only particular adults with whom to share this experience, as McDonald (1976) has noted. In addition, this may well have to do with how the fairy tale is read, that is, with the associated affects.

Fairy tales seem a desirable accompaniment of the period of life in which a child is progressing to secondary process thinking, which involves concepts of logic, time, animism, space, and causality. As in good therapy or analysis, in creating or sharing fairy tales, the meaning or experience of meaning must be conveyed in a language based on the available conceptual framework and sensitive to the needs for mirroring grandiosity, magic, and dependency.

Therefore, playing and playfulness with thought and language in a permissive surround are essential precursors for mature meaningful adaptation, which in turn lead to the freedom not to make sense before it is necessary to make sense. To insist upon reality before its time may result in premature closure, too early a consolidation of the subjective sense of self and reality, and work inhibitions.

In this paper we have traveled the path which resonates with the experience and fantasies designed by another mind. Like all myths, dreams, and fables, *The Wizard of Oz* provides an age-appropriate mirror lighted by a distant and indirect source, filled with double messages and ambiguities. The final resolution is the protagonist's "return home," a little wiser, a little more tolerant, and a little more mature (one hopes).

BIBLIOGRAPHY

BANCROFT, L. (1907), *Policeman Blue Jay*. Chicago: Reilly & Britton.
BAUM, F. L. (1900), *The Wizard of Oz*. Chicago: Rand McNally, 1956.

BAUM, J. B. (1961), *To Please a Child.* Chicago: Reilly & Lee.

BETTELHEIM, B. (1976), *The Uses of Enchantment.* New York: Knopf.

FREUD, S. (1916–17), Introductory Lectures on Psycho-Analysis. *S.E.,* 15 & 16.

HEARN, M. (1973), *The Annotated Wizard of Oz.* New York: Clarkson N. Potter.

HARTOCOLLIS, P. (1974), Origins of Time. *Psychoanal. Quart.,* 43 : 243–361.

KOHUT, H. (1971), *The Analysis of the Self.* New York: Int. Univ. Press.

MCDONALD, M. A. (1974), Little Black Sambo. *This Annual,* 29 : 511–528.

———— (1976), Fantasy, Fairy Tales and Children's Fiction. Read at Tufts New England Medical Center.

MADOW, L. & SCHAEFER, C. (1977), The Ways of the Heart. Read at Amer. Psychoanal. Assn., Quebec.

MAHLER, M. S., PINE, F., & BERGMAN, A. (1975), *The Psychological Birth of the Human Infant.* New York: Basic Books.

NIEDERLAND, W. G. (1976), Personal communication.

ORNSTEIN, P. & ORNSTEIN, A. (1977), The Curative Fantasy and the Transference. Read at joint meeting of the Amer. Psychiat. Assn. and the Amer. Psychoanal. Assn., Toronto.

PIAGET, J. (1936), *The Construction of Reality in the Child.* New York: Basic Books, 1954.

SANDER, L. W. (1975), Infant and Caretaking Environment. In: *Explorations in Child Psychiatry,* ed. E. J. Anthony. New York: Plenum Press, pp. 129–166.

SAMARAWEERA, S. & CATH, C. (1977), The Tufts Family Support Program (in press).

SCHREIBER, S. (1974), A Filmed Fairy Tale as a Screen Memory. *This Annual,* 29 : 389–410.

SEXTON, A. (1976), *45 Mercy Street,* ed. L. G. Sexton & L. Conant, Jr. Boston: Houghton Mifflin.

WAELDER, R. (1960), *Basic Theory of Psychoanalysis.* New York: Int. Univ. Press, p. 56.

The Wizard of Oz (1939), M.G.M. 90 Min. Sound, Technicolor, 16mm. Motion Picture. Credit: V. Fleming.

WOLFF, P. H. (1961), Observations on the Early Development of Smiling. In: *Determinants of Infant Behaviour,* ed. J. Bowlby. London: Methuen, 2 : 113–138.

The School Consultant as an Object for Externalization

KATHRYN KRIS, M.D.

IN FORMULATIONS OF THE FUNCTIONS OF THE PSYCHIATRIC
school consultant, the psychoanalytic concept of transference
reactions has played an important part (Berlin, 1966; Hitchcock and Mooney, 1969). When applied to the consultation
process in the original sense of a revived object relationship
from the past, transferred to the therapist, who becomes the
object of the patient's drives, it is misleading. On the one
hand, in the practice of psychiatric school consultation, interpretations of such transferences, with their focus on individual past histories of consultees, rarely need be made, if ever
(Babcock, 1949; Caplan, 1970; Coleman, 1947; Hitchcock,
1977; Maddux, 1950). On the other hand, as noted by Berlin
(1966), management of transference along lines appropriate
for the purposes of individual psychotherapy and psychoanalysis would promote unwelcome regression in the consultation
process.

The psychoanalytic concept of externalization, however, as a
"subspecies of transference" (A. Freud, 1965, p. 43) does justice to the projective distortions that are regularly encoun-

Associate Attending Psychiatrist, McLean Hospital, Belmont, Mass.; Clinical Instructor in Psychiatry, Harvard Medical School.

This paper is an expanded version of a contribution to the Skills in Consultation to Human Service Agencies Course, at the 130th meeting of the
American Psychiatric Association, May 5, 1977, in Toronto.

tered in the consultee's attitudes to the consultant and does
not imply dynamics that call for technical management at odds
with established experience in the practice of consultation.
Further, the concept of externalization contributes a useful
dimension to the formulation of the supportive functions of
the consultant.

The purpose of this paper is to apply the psychoanalytic
concept of externalization to an understanding of the process
of psychiatric consultation in schools. The paper will review
the psychoanalytic concept of externalization. It will illustrate
the use of externalization in several clinical examples and relate it to some published descriptions of school consultation.

EXTERNALIZATION

Anna Freud has distinguished externalization as a "subspecies" of transference from transference proper—the regressive displacement of an old object relationship onto the therapist. She writes:

> Not all the relations established or transferred by a child in
> analysis are object relations in the sense that the analyst be-
> comes cathected with libido or aggression. Many are due to
> externalizations, i.e., to processes in which the person of the
> analyst is used to represent one or the other part of the pa-
> tient's personality structure.
>
> So far as the analyst "seduces" the child by tolerating free-
> dom of thought, fantasy, and action (the latter within limits),
> he becomes the representative of the patient's *id,* with all the
> positive and negative implications this has for the rela-
> tionship. So far as he verbalizes and helps in the fight against
> anxiety, he becomes an *auxiliary ego* to whom the child clings
> for protection. Due to his being an adult, the analyst is seen
> and treated by the child also as an *external superego.* . . .
>
> The child thus re-stages his internal (intersystemic) conflicts
> as external battles with the analyst, a process which provides
> useful material. To interpret such externalizations in terms of
> object relationship within the transference would be a mis-
> take, even though originally all conflicts within the structure
> have their source in earliest relationships [p. 41f.].

Externalization of one side of an inner conflict may also occur in instances where the conflict is principally intrasystemic, as between opposing drives or between two attitudes in conflict. Externalization provides a temporary solution to a variety of problems of indecision. Properly interpreted, it can lead to inner solutions.

The term externalization, to be useful, must be reserved for readily clarifiable psychological events, not fully unconscious but closer to preconscious processes. Novick and Kelly (1970) distinguish it from the projection of an unconscious drive derivative onto an object. Externalization is of course related to, and in fact relies on, displacement, but is a more specific term in that it indicates the new location of internal content. Furthermore, externalization has some overlap with the concept of projective identification (for example, see Brodey, 1965; Giovacchini, 1967), but it is considerably broader in scope. On the other hand, as used here, the term externalization is not as broad as to refer "in general to the tendency to project into the external world one's instinctual wishes, conflicts, mood, and ways of thinking (cognitive styles)" (Moore and Fine, 1968, p. 45). Externalization, as I use it, occurs within the context of an object relationship and consists of the attribution of a part of the mental structures or their contents to the object.

EXAMPLES OF EXTERNALIZATION IN SCHOOL CONSULTATION

The examples that follow are taken from the experience of the first four years of consultation in a large middle-class suburban school system. The McLean School Consultation Program[1] (M.S.C.P.) was hired by the School System's Director of Pupil Personnel. As a member of the M.S.C.P., I was assigned as the original and continuing consultant.

The main tenets of the M.S.C.P. are:

1. Environment influences a child's emotional stability and development.

1. I wish to thank Dr. Maurice Vanderpol, Director of the Program, for his support and wise counsel throughout the consultation.

2. The consultant's influence on the child's school environment may provide an important measure of preventive psychiatry.

3. There is a consultative process and a progressive continuum in the uses made of the consultant, ranging from direct service to promotion of institutional change.

4. In-school consultation differs from office psychiatry in focusing on development rather than on pathology and in using consultation techniques rather than treatment techniques (Vanderpol, 1976; Vanderpol and Waxman, 1974).

I was introduced to each of several schools within the system by the school's psychologist or social worker. The flexibility of approach, individual consultations around problems with children or with the institution, informal small group discussions with teachers, continuous seminars of eight to twelve sessions with psychologists and social workers and with high school counselors proved to be a particularly felicitous arrangement. The group process which developed in the continuous seminars heightened and led to verbalization of many of the silent prejudices or externalizations which accompanied involvement with each school or group.

"Here comes the sex maniac." "Here comes the mind reader." These are two common initial greetings. Psychiatrists and psychoanalysts are likely to encounter them in many settings. Stereotyped and impersonal, they reflect a fearful anticipation, an anxiety engendered by the consultation. Characteristically they are experienced by the consultant as powerful and disruptive, impeding discussion and understanding. If one recognizes them as neither attributes of the consultant nor as expressions of deep regressive transference, they become manageable. They can best be seen as externalizations of one aspect of the consultee's personality; externalization of libidinal wishes in the first greeting, with the consultant as the seducer; externalization of superego aspects in the second greeting, with the consultant as critic.

Do we always clarify these externalizations explicitly? Rarely. In fact, open verbalization of such externalizations does not occur in most instances of consultation with an *indi-*

vidual. Usually it is sufficient for the consultee to meet us and to clarify the problem for consultation. It is my impression that the initial introductory phase in consultation, with collegial manner and explanations of purpose, offers a more or less silent confrontation with the consultee's prejudices or negative externalizations, as withholding mind reader, authoritarian critic, or irresponsible promoter of license (Berkowitz, 1975; Berlin, 1966; Bloch, 1972; Caplan, 1970; Hitchcock and Mooney, 1969). However, if the consultees are in a *small group* where irrational elements may be heightened, such externalizations are commonly verbalized. As a consultation progresses, one may be able to clarify the externalizations, thereby increasing the group's awareness of the specific conflict of which one side or the other, or both alternately, are externalized onto the consultant.

A group of high school counselors was meeting with me for the second year, on a twice monthly basis. In the first meeting they established their agenda to be the sexual problems of the teen-ager. For their second meeting they requested a lecture by me. In the third meeting they became increasingly dissatisfied, unable to focus on any of their case material, misunderstanding one another and me. Jokingly they attributed the sexual behavior of their students to the students' sensing the psychiatrist was coming. At the same time they complained that I expected from them constant supervision, even 100 percent control of their students! Their group behavior oscillated between "can you top this" sexual exploits and silent withdrawal. The specific jokes and complaints might have been missed, but certainly no one could miss the feeling of discontent and frustration at that meeting. But the jokes and complaints about the consultant, recognized as externalizations, were helpful in showing the group their conflict over license and control. Clarification of the group's attribution to me of *their own fears* of inciting their students' sexuality and *their demand of themselves* for its total control helped them recognize their concerns. They could appreciate my suggestion that the students might be approaching sexuality in a similar manner. In subsequent sessions, perhaps in part because they felt supported by the commonness of conflict, the group discussions included the still more delicate topics of their students' incestuous and suicidal fears, and finally recommendations to their principal for the management of a school tragedy. Such a sequence illustrates that when externalizations are clarified, understanding can be extended and problem solving can proceed.

It should be noted that to recognize and clarify such externalizations of conflict between libidinal wishes and superego attitudes did not require my focusing on individual pathology or development. This is in keeping with the cautions of many authors in regard to consultation (Babcock, 1949; Berlin, 1966; Caplan, 1970; Coleman, 1947; and Maddux, 1950). Perhaps because it was a group of high school counselors one could clarify such externalizations within the group. With another group one might elect to clarify the externalizations in a displaced fashion, as recommended by Caplan (1970), Parker (1958), and Bindman (1959).

A group of mature women professionals were complaining about the unresponsiveness of their male superior. They felt excluded by him and resented their own helplessness in regard to a piece of school policy. With them it was sufficient to question their attitudes and not necessary to spell out the externalization onto their superior of their own wish to exclude *him* from *their* intimate women's group or their wish to hold more power and be free of the uncertainties and anxieties produced by the need to negotiate. They decided to approach him, and they were surprised both by his immediate agreement to their administrative request and by his wish to attend their next meeting. No longer able to view themselves as helpless, they felt proud of their problem-solving ability. To have viewed this episode primarily in terms of a group transference, as a feeling of rejection by the father, as the castrated impotence of women, or the regressive homosexuality of oedipal failure would have been utterly without foundation in the data of the group consultation setting, and futile technically.

As a consultant one often has the surprising experience of finding out that someone who seemed irredeemable is in fact approachable. The consultant must be particularly alert to instances where such externalizations are focused on important administrators, fostering avoidance rather than contact and possible problem resolution. Where the personal contact is the least, the externalizations are likely to exert their greatest influence. In general we promote contact rather than avoidance, adhering to the precept that reality can be handled but irrational externalizations are self-fulfilling.

Such externalizations are likely to occur at times of heightened anxiety, at the beginning or ending of a consultation, or with a new task, or when an opportunity arises for contact with a member from another group, for example, teachers with parents or consultees with their superior in the school system.

Sometimes a state of helplessness and demoralization may be externalized onto the consultant. I have seen this when the consultation was coming to the end, both at the end of a school year, despite the possibility of continued contact in the future, and, in another school system, when the consultation services were being terminated because of a change in the chief administrator responsible for hiring. The danger here is that the consultant may feel helpless and demoralized rather than help the consultees to recognize their sense of helplessness and demoralization in the face of change. If the consultees can recognize their helplessness, they may begin to be able to master it. Berlin (1966), in particular, has delineated some of the consultant's difficulties in seeing a consultation to its end.

Up to this point I have given examples of externalizations that interfere with the consultative or administrative relationship. I want to turn now to the way externalization enhances the relationship between consultant and consultee. As indicated by Anna Freud, the "auxiliary ego" functions depend upon externalization. The consultant in this sense becomes the representative of the consultee's ego.

Several writers have referred explicitly or implicitly to externalization in the consultation process. Caplan (1970) speaks of the consultant functioning as a role model for the consultee, as a superego and ego ideal (p. 92). Hitchcock and Mooney (1969, p. 355), in particular, have singled out the consultee's work difficulties leading to a temporary superego regression to a "preautonomous superego schema" with an externalization of superego functions onto the analyst as described by Sandler (1960).

In what ways may the consultant be thought to function as an auxiliary ego? He may help the consultees verbalize their psychological observations or offer a conceptual framework for their observations, be it the psychology of character, principles of child development, or systems theory. In addition, he supports the consultees in the face of their anxiety. This may be done verbally, as when a consultant suggests an action or points to an aspect of avoidance on the consultee's part or indicates the basis for feelings of helplessness. Support may also be given by example, as when a consultant offers to present the first case to be discussed in a counselors' group where there is overt anxiety about being criticized in their first attempt at case discussions (Sarason et al., 1966; Parker, 1958). In another aspect of auxiliary ego functioning, the consultant offers himself to his consultees for identification with certain traits, in his problem solving and reality orientation, in withstanding tendencies toward helplessness, rebellion against authority, withdrawal from power, and intolerance of human limitation (Berlin, 1962, 1966).

As consultants we also perform the function of valuing our consultee's work (Coleman, 1947; Sarason et al., 1966). This seems best conceptualized as supporting the function of the ego ideal, contrasted with the critical function of the superego (Lampl-de Groot, 1962). Often the consultee lacks not only a conceptual framework for what he does psychologically but also a recognition and esteem for his work. This may be the most immediately satisfying part of a consultant's job—to help the consultee recognize that he did something, that it made a difference, and that it may be conceptualized and thereby made applicable to other situations. This is not the same as fostering the consultee's dependence, compliance, or denial. It is support for his valuing of his psychological skills.

Conclusion

Viewing the consultant as an object for externalization enables one to understand many of the principles of consultation. Several generalizations about our tasks as consultants, what we should and should not do, are widely agreed upon. First, it is vital to approach our consultees as colleagues who share a common interest but have a different training (Berlin, 1966; Caplan, 1970). The danger of trying to be an expert on teaching or one who knows all the answers is all too familiar for those psychiatric and psychoanalytic consultants who have experienced the power of consultees in various settings to prove one's ineffectiveness. Second, our job is to act only as consultants. We do not replace our consultees at their jobs even when tempted by them to do so or criticized by them for not doing so. Consultees readily try to turn over their clients to us, promoting their own helplessness and externalizing onto us unrealistic expectations of omniscience. This does not mean, however, that we would not interview a child; we simply would not take over primary responsibility for teaching him. Third, we attempt to clarify explicitly the task with which the consultees want help and to formulate explicitly with them how we and they are to achieve the solution to the task. If the task cannot be defined or implemented, this alerts us to a problem, very frequently the result of externalizations interfering with the consultative working alliance. Each of these three general rules of procedure for consultants can be seen to protect the consultant from inadvertently accepting an omnipotent ego and superego role, defined by the consultee's externalizations, thereby deviating from the ego attitude of collaboration.

It would be an error to suppose, however, that all transference reactions encountered in the consultation process are externalizations. For example, the externalizations of feelings of helplessness at termination are often accompanied by transference reactions based upon reactivation of past object losses. Nor will it then suffice to respond only to the externalizations. It has been my purpose here, however, to demonstrate the

wide applicability and usefulness of the concept of externalization in the functions of the psychiatric or psychoanalytic
school consultant.

BIBLIOGRAPHY

BABCOCK, C. (1949), Some Observations in Consultative Experience. *Soc. Serv. Rev.*, 23 : 347–357.
BERKOWITZ, M. I. (1975), *A Primer on School Mental Health Consultation.* Springfield, Ill.: Charles C Thomas.
BERLIN, I. N. (1962), Mental Health Consultation in Schools as a Means of Communicating Mental Health Principles. *J. Amer. Acad. Child Psychiat.*, 1 : 671–679.
——— (1966), Transference and Countertransference in Community Psychiatry. *Arch. Gen. Psychiat.*, 15 : 165–172.
BINDMAN, A. (1959), Mental Health Consultation. *J. Consult. Psychol.*, 23 : 473–482.
BLOCH, H. S. (1972), Experiences in Establishing School Consultation. *Amer. J. Psychiat.*, 129 : 63–68.
BRODEY, W. M. (1965), On the Dynamics of Narcissism: I. *This Annual*, 20 : 165–193.
CAPLAN, G. (1970), *The Theory and Practice of Mental Health Consultation.* New York: Basic Books.
COLEMAN, J. (1947), Psychiatric Consultation in Casework Agencies. *Amer. J. Orthopsychiat.*, 17 : 533–539.
FREUD, A. (1965), Normality and Pathology in Childhood. *W.*, 6.
GIOVACCHINI, P. (1967), Frustration and Externalization. *Psychoanal. Quart.*, 36 : 571–583.
HITCHCOCK, J. (1977), Interventions by the Psychoanalyst in the Consultant Role. *J. Philadelphia Assn. Psychoanal.*, 4 : 45–49.
——— & MOONEY, W. E. (1969), Mental Health Consultation. *Arch. Gen. Psychiat.*, 21 : 353–358.
LAMPL-DE GROOT, J. (1962), Ego Ideal and Superego. *This Annual*, 17 : 94–106.
MADDUX, J. F. (1950), Psychiatric Consultation in a Public Welfare Agency. *Amer. J. Orthopsychiat.*, 20 : 754–764.
MOORE, B. E. & FINE, B. D. (1968), *A Glossary of Psychoanalytic Terms and Concepts.* New York: Amer. Psychoanaly. Assn.
NOVICK, J. & KELLY, K. (1970), Projection and Externalization. *This Annual*, 25 : 69–98.
PARKER, B. (1958), *Psychiatric Consultation to Nonpsychiatric Professional Workers* [*Public Health Monograph*, 53]. Washington, D.C.: U.S. Public Health Service.

SANDLER, J. (1960), On the Concept of Superego. *This Annual,* 15 : 128–162.

SARASON, S., LEVINE, M., GOLDENBERG, I. I., CHERLIN, D. L., & BENNETT, E. M. (1966), *Psychology in Community Settings.* New York: Wiley.

VANDERPOL, M. (1976), Mental Health Consultation in Schools. In: *The Changing Mental Health Scene,* ed. R. G. Hirschowitz & B. Levy. New York: Spectrum Publications.

—— & WAXMAN, H. (1974), Beyond Pathology. *Psychiat. Opinion,* 11 : 18–24.

Bibliographical Note

S.E.   *The Standard Edition of the Complete Psychological Works of Sigmund Freud,* 24 Volumes, translated and edited by James Strachey. London: Hogarth Press and the Institute of Psycho-Analysis, 1953–1974.

W.   *The Writings of Anna Freud,* 7 Volumes. New York: International Universities Press, 1968–1974.

G.W.   Sigm. Freud, *Gesammelte Werke,* 17 Volumes. London: Imago Publishing Co., 1941–1952.

Index

Father (*continued*)
  seductive, 355
  see also Parents
Fear
  of abandonment, 110–11, 218–32, 445–47
  of affect, 92, 107
  of aggression, 346, 348, 356
  archaic, 176
  of death, *see* Death
  of loss of love, 219, 223, 225, 227, 392–96, 447
  of monsters, 176, 217
  of object loss, 218–32, 353, 355–58, 450–51, 633
  preneurotic, 429
  of reengulfment, 357
  of retaliation, 248, 343, 356, 439, 444–48
  of sexuality, 644–45
  of starvation, 352
  symbolic expression, 176
  transient vs. phobia, 450–51, 456
  of women, 376
  see also Anxiety, Danger situation, Panic, Phobia
Federn, P., 156, 160
Feeling
  need to keep private, 205
  of unreality, 397, 405; *see also* Depersonalization
  see also Affect
Feifel, H., 116, 619–20
Feigelson, C. I., 297–300, 305, 363–79
Feigenbaum, D., 133–35, 156, 159–60
Fenichel, O., 4, 158–60
Ferenczi, S., 128, 130, 133, 147, 156, 158–59, 161, 232, 235
Fetish and transitional object, 54
Fichtner, G., 470
Fine, B. D., 239–40, 257–59, 643, 650
Fintzy, R. T., 54, 77
Fisher, C., 237
Fixation
  anal, 422
  of drives, 173–74
  oral, 353–54, 357–61
  see also Regression
Fixation points, 32, 230
Flanner, J., 534, 561
Flavell, J. H., 244–45, 249, 258
Fleischl, E., 480
Fliess, W., 83, 207, 470, 479–80
Flinker, M., 523, 561
Fluss, E., 466–67, 470

Fluss, G., 467 77, 485, 489, 491–92, 496, 498–502, 509, 513–14
Food binges, 256
Forgetting, 241; *see also* Memory, Repression
Foss, B., 409
Foucault, M., 555, 561
Fragmentation, 102, 107–08, 174–76, 178, 181, 284, 621, 628, 631, 634
Fraiberg, S., 20–22, 45, 215, 235, 242, 258, 279, 291
Francis, J. J., 411, 419, 425
Frank, A., 389, 408
Frank, G., 578, 587, 590
Free association, 325, 329, 364–79
Freud, A., 12, 15, 66, 146, 156–57, 159, 167–68, 170–74, 178, 207, 214–15, 231, 262, 279, 314, 351, 354, 357, 361, 402
  bibliographical references to, 45, 77, 114, 161, 183, 211, 235, 258, 276, 291, 322, 331, 362, 379, 408, 457, 619
  cited on:
  adolescence 19–22, 266
  child analysis, 242, 249, 331, 365
  childhood fears, 428
  defense, 152
  deficiency illness, 169, 171
  externalization, 641–42, 647
  genetic series of anxieties, 176
  infantile neurosis, 229–30
  mechanism of phobia, 450
  object loss in childhood, 594, 607, 611, 613, 616
  projection, 152, 160
  psychoanalytic technique, 172–73
  regression, 171–72
  trauma, 86
  treatment of adolescents, 19–22
Freud, E. L., 469, 515
Freud, S., 5–6, 12, 40, 72, 167–68, 175–76, 178, 285, 323, 354, 361, 386, 418, 421–22, 424, 537, 551–52, 594, 596, 615–16
  bibliographical references to, 45, 77, 113–14, 161–63, 183, 211, 235, 276, 291, 305, 322, 331, 362, 379, 408–09, 425, 457, 515–16, 561, 590, 619, 639
  biography
  adolescence of, 462–503, 508–15
  choice of medicine, 464–67, 477–89, 498–99
  creation of psychoanalysis, 496–502
  dreams of, 119

Space, 263–65, 267, 272
Speech, 189
  acquisition: 30; and experience of communicative, 193
  in child analysis, 440–48
  delayed, 430, 454
  precocious, 218, 228, 230
  problem, 191–94
  role in psychoanalysis, 8–9
  see also Language, Verbalization
Sperling, M., 54, 79
Spitz, R. A., 67, 72, 79, 105, 116, 382, 384–85, 393, 407, 409
Spitzer, D., 470
Splitting, 180, 221, 255–59
  and cohesiveness, 632–34, 636
Sports, 70, 160
Spruiell, V., 224, 231–32, 236, 287, 292, 455, 458
Stammering, 226–28, 232
Stanescu, H., 465, 471, 473–79, 517
Stark, M., 336, 362
Stealing, 54, 255, 372
Steinberg, L., 586, 591
Steingart, I., 245, 255, 259
Stekel, W., 509, 514
Sterba, E., 578, 587, 591
Sterba, R. F., 223, 332, 578, 587, 591
Stern, D., 382, 409
Stern, M. M., 92, 97–98, 116
Stevenson, H., 78
Stevenson, O., 47, 49–51, 53, 62–63, 65, 68, 79
Stimuli, affects and excitations, 87
Stimulus barrier, 81, 85, 98, 111
Stone, I., 577, 581, 591
Stone, J., 577, 581, 591
Stone, L., 180, 184
Strachey, J., 83, 116, 124, 156, 158–59, 166, 494, 517
Strain trauma, 87, 89
Stranger anxiety, 72, 353, 385
Structuralism, 152, 158
Structuralization, 147, 215, 229–31, 353–61
Structural viewpoint, 144, 158
Structure, *see* Mental organization, Psychic structure
Student protest, 411–24
Sublimation, 176, 490, 503, 521
Submissiveness, 256, 394–96, 400–06
Substitute object, 48, 56, 59–61, 72–73
Suggestion, 352, 493
Suicide, 104–05
  in adolescence, 261–76

  attempted, 263
  notes, 269–76, 317
Sullivan, H. S., 262, 277
Suomi, S. J., 55, 58, 78
Superego, 286, 621, 629
  and child analysis, 303–04
  and depression, 338, 356, 358
  development: 180, 406–08, 632; precocious, 230, 247
  and externalization, 642, 644, 646, 648
  fear of, 140; *see also* Guilt
  identification, 359
  modification, 251
  precursors, 188, 396, 406–08
  primitive, 356
  and projection, 136
  and psychoanalytic therapy, 323–24, 326
  punitive, 270
  and student protest, 412, 424
  and transference neurosis, 215
Superstition, 131, 158
Surgery
  in childhood, 372
  preparation for, 196–200
Surrender, 92–95, 104–13
Sutherland, J. D., 159, 166
Symbiosis, 347, 351, 398, 403–05
  see also Merger, Wish
Symbiotic phase, 247, 275
Symbol
  formation, 26–27, 38, 51, 67, 494
  and phobic object, 450–54
Symbolic function, 81, 95, 241
Symbolism, 67, 76, 270, 542, 622, 624–25
Symonds, J. A., 567, 578, 581, 591
Symptom
  aggressive, 217–18
  change of function, 429, 451–54
  formation, 26, 108, 112–13, 123, 125, 127, 150, 173
  neurotic vs. neuroticlike, 173–75
Synthetic (integrative) function, 257, 301
  impaired, 176

Taboo, 131, 150, 158
Tactile experience and transitional object, 48, 50, 59, 67
Taste, 160
Tausk, V., 133–34, 156–57, 159, 166
Temper tantrum, 396, 430–33
Terror, mortal, 97, 103
Thanatos, 6, 618